The Palgrave Handbook of European Banking

Thorsten Beck • Barbara Casu
Editors

The Palgrave Handbook of European Banking

palgrave
macmillan

Editors
Thorsten Beck
Cass Business School
City, University of London
London, UK

Barbara Casu
Cass Business School
City, University of London
London, UK

ISBN 978-1-137-52143-9 ISBN 978-1-137-52144-6 (eBook)
DOI 10.1057/978-1-137-52144-6

Library of Congress Control Number: 2016959995

Cover image Deco Images II / Alamy Stock Photo

Printed on acid-free paper

This Palgrave Macmillan imprint is published by Springer Nature
The registered company is Macmillan Publishers Ltd.
The registered company address is: The Campus, 4 Crinan Street, London, N1 9XW, United Kingdom

Preface

The European banking landscape has profoundly changed as a result of the regulatory response to the 2007–8 global financial crisis and ensuing sovereign debt crisis in the Eurozone. Moreover, the extensive changes in the economic and regulatory environment have highlighted a number of unresolved issues in European banking. This Handbook offers a comprehensive overview of these key issues, taking stock after the recent crises and looking forward.

Although the new regulatory architecture is now mostly in place, its successful implementation depends crucially on how the Eurozone deals with the legacy of the financial crises. Even after substantial regulatory reforms, debates on further reforms needed to strengthen the EU regulatory framework to limit future risks arising from the banking system are ongoing. The persistent weakness of some Eurozone banking systems puts the implementation of the newly agreed rules to a test.

It is against this background that this Handbook aims to provide an understanding of the key issues facing European banks. The Handbook is composed of five main parts. Part 1, *European Banking: Through the Crisis and Beyond*, offers an overview of the European banking sector in terms of financial structure, ownership and business models and corporate governance, as well as the payment system. Part 2, *Performance and Innovation in European Banking*, discusses the key themes of bank competition, efficiency and performance. In addition, it looks at the impact of technological development on the banking sectors and how banks are embracing the opportunities it offers. Finally, it explores the issues of bank diversification and the relevance of small business lending.

Part 3, *Financial Stability and Regulation*, addresses the key issues of financial reforms and the increasing complexity of financial regulation. It also looks at the impact of state aid and the impact of monetary policy. Finally, it considers the increasing interactions between banks and markets. Part 4, *Cross-border Banking*, looks at recent trends in cross-border banking in Europe and evaluates the establishment of the Banking Union. Finally, Part 5, *European Banking Systems*, offers a detailed analysis of the main issues facing national banking system in key European banking markets.

The chapters of this Handbook document major trends across European banking systems and the implications of a changed regulatory and monetary environment. Building upon a close interaction between researchers, practitioners and policy makers, this Handbook aims to provide the necessary tools to understand the current practical and policy challenges.

London, July 2016

Thorsten Beck
Barbara Casu

Acknowledgements

This text could have never been completed without the help and support of a number of individuals. First and foremost, we wish to thank the contributors to this Handbook. We are delighted to have brought together an outstanding group of experts, ranging from senior policy makers to academics, each with a wealth of expertise in their field. Their expert contributions, together with their commitment to the project, have helped us deliver a text that offers an in-depth analysis of the key issues facing European banking.

We are indebted to Aimee Dibbens, Senior Commissioning Editor Economics & Finance, whose enthusiasm was crucial in convincing us to undertake the project. We also wish to thank the editorial team at Palgrave Macmillan, in particular Alexandra Morton, Editorial Assistant Finance, who has worked closely with us during the entire project ensuring a timely delivery and high-quality content.

We would like to acknowledge the support of our home institution, Cass Business School, City, University of London.

Finally, we wish to thank our families and friends for encouragement and support. Thorsten Beck thanks his wife and sons for their patience with his skewed work–life balance. Barbara Casu thanks her husband and her children for their enthusiasm, their patience and support.

Contents

List of Abbreviations

ACHs	Automated Clearing Houses
ACM	Authority Consumer and Market (The Netherlands)
ACPR	Autorité de contrôle prudentiel et de résolution
AE	Allocative Efficiency
AFECE	Association Française des Etablissements de Crédit et des Entreprises d'investissement
AGP	Asset Guarantee Program
AISPs	Account Information Service Providers
AMA	Advanced Measurement Approach
AMAFI	Association Française des marchés financiers
AMEX	American Stock Exchange
AMF	Autorité des marché financiers
ASF	Association Française des Sociétés Financières
AT1	Additional Tier 1
ATM	Automated Teller Machine
ATMs	Automated Teller Machines
B2B	Business-to-Business
BBAs	Basic Bank Accounts
BCBS	Basel Committee on Banking Supervision
BEEPS	Business Environment and Enterprise Performance Survey
BHCs	Bank Holding Companies
BIC	Business Identifier Code
BIS	Bank for International Settlements
BLS	Bank Lending Survey
BRRD	Bank Recovery and Resolution Directive
BTS	Binding Technical Standards

BU	Banking Union
BUA	Banking Union Area
CAP	Capital Assistance Program
CAR	Cumulative Abnormal Returns
CASS	Current Account Switch Service
CCAR	Comprehensive Capital Analysis and Review
CDCI	Community Development Capital Initiative
CDS	Credit Default Swaps
CE	Cost Efficiency
CEBS	Committee of European Banking Supervisors
CEEC	Central and Eastern European Countries
CEO	Chief Executive Officer
CET	1 Common Equity Tier 1
CFO	Chief Financial Officer
CGGs	Codes of Good Governance
CMA	Competition and Markets Authority (UK)
CMU	Capital Markets Union
COREP	Common Supervisory Reporting Framework
CPMI	Committee on Payment and Market Infrastructures
CPP	Capital Purchase Program
CR	Concentration Ratio
CRD	Capital Requirements Directive
D-SIIs	Domestic Systemically Important Institutions
DFAST	Dodd-Frank Act Stress Test
DSGE	Dynamic Stochastic General Equilibrium Model
DTAs	Deferred Tax Assets
EACB	European Association of Cooperative Banks
EAPB	European Association of Public Banks
EBA	European Banking Authority
EBRD	European Bank for Reconstruction and Development
EC	European Commission
ECB	European Central Bank
ECOFIN	EU Council of Finance
ECSC	European Coal and Steel Community
EDIS	European Deposit Insurance Scheme
EEA	European Economic Area
EEC	European Economic Community
EESA	Economy Emergency Stabilization Act
EIOPA	European Insurance and Occupational Pensions Authority
EMIs	Electronic Money Institutions

EMU	Economic and Monetary Union
EPC	European Payment Council
ESFS	European System of Financial Supervisors
ESM	European Stability Mechanism
ESMA	European Securities and Markets Authority
ESRB	European Systemic Risk Board
EU	European Union
FAAF	Financial Assets Acquisition Fund (Spain)
FBF	Fédération Bancaire Française
FCA	Financial Conduct Authority
FDI	Foreign Direct Investment
FDIC	Federal Deposit Insurance Corporation
FGDR	Fonds de Garantie des Dépôts et de Résolution
FI	Financial Institutions
FPC	Financial Policy Committee
FROB	Fund for Orderly Restructuring of the Banking Sector (Spain)
FSA	Financial Services Authority (UK)
FSAP	Financial Services Action Plan
FSB	Financial Stability Board
FSF	Financial Stability Forum
FSMA	Financial Services Modernization Act
FX	Foreign Exchange
G-SIBs	Global Systemically Important Banks
G-SIIs	Global Systemically Important Institutions
GAAP	Generally Accepted Accounting Principles
GDP	Gross Domestic Product
GIIPS	Greece, Ireland, Italy, Portugal and Spain
GMM	Generalised Method of Moments
GVA	Gross Value Added
HHI	Herfindahl–Hirschman Index
IAS	International Accounting Standards
IBAN	International Bank Account Number
IFR	Regulation on Interchange Fees (for Card-Based Payment Transactions)
IFRS	International Financial Reporting Standards
IGA	Intergovernmental Agreement
IICADD	International Institute of Cooperatives Alphonse and Dorimène-Desjardins
IMF	International Monetary Fund
IPOs	Initial Public Offerings

ISFS	International Initiative for Sustainable Financial Systems
JSTs	Joint Supervisory Teams
LCFIs	Large Complex Financial Institutions
LCR	Liquidity Coverage Ratio
LIBOR	London Interbank Offered Rate
LTI	Loan-to-Income
LTV	Loan-to-Value
M&As	Merger and Acquisitions
MaRS	Macroprudential research network
MES	Marginal Expected Shortfall
MFIs	Monetary Financial Institutions
MIFs	Multilateral Interchange Fees
MLE	Maximum Likelihood Estimation
NASDAQ	National Association of Securities Dealers Automated Quotations
NCA	National Competent Authorities
NCBs	National Central Banks
NEIO	New Empirical Industrial Organization
NPLs	Non-Performing Loans
NSFR	Net Stable Funding Ratio
NYSE	New York Stock Exchange
OECD	Organisation for Economic Co-operation and Development
OLS	Ordinary Least Squares
OTC	Over the Counter
P&L	Profit and Loss
P2P	Peer-to-Peer
PBT	Profits Before Tax
PE	Profit Efficiency
PIIGS	Portugal, Ireland, Italy Greece and Spain
PISPs	Payment Initiation Service Providers
PPI	Payment Protection Insurance
PRA	Prudential Regulatory Authority
PSD	Directive on Payment Services
QFIs	Qualifying Financial Institutions
R&D	Research and Development
ROA	Return on Assets
ROE	Return on Equity
RWA	Risk-Weighted Assets
SAFE	Survey of Access to Finance of Enterprises

SAREB	Company for the Management of Assets proceeding from the Restructuring of the Banking System (Spain)
SBA	Small Business Act (European Commission)
SCAP	Supervisory Capital Assessment Program
SCM	Synthetic Counterfactuals Method
SCP	Structure-Conduct-Performance
SDIRB	Single Deposit Insurance and Resolution Board
SDM	Single Deposit Guarantee Mechanism
SEPA	Single Euro Payments Area
SFA	Stochastic Frontier Analysis
SHV	Shareholder-value
SIFI	Systemically Important Financial Institutions
SMEs	Small and Medium Enterprises
SMR	Senior Managers Regime (UK)
SRB	Single Resolution Board
SREP	Supervisory Review and Evaluation Process
SRF	Single Resolution Fund
SRM	Single Resolution Mechanism
SSEs	Significant Supervised Entities
SSM	Single Supervisory Mechanism
STV	Stakeholder-value
TARP	Troubled Asset Relief Program
TBTF	Too Big To Fail
TE	Technical Efficiency
TFEU	Treaty on the Functioning of the EU
TFP	Total Factor Productivity
TIP	Targeted Investment Program
TLAC	Total Loss-Absorption Capacity
TOC	Total Operating Costs
VaR	Value-at-Risk
VLTROs	Very Long Term Refinancing Operations

Notes on contributors

Rym Ayadi is Professor of International Finance and International Business at HEC Montreal International Business School in, Montreal, Canada. She is Director of the Alphonse and Dorimène Desjardins International Institute for Cooperatives and Founding Director of the International Research Centre on Cooperative Finance (IRCCF) at HEC Montreal. She is also Associate Senior Fellow at the Euro-Mediterranean University of Slovenia, Founding President of the Euro-Mediterranean Economists Association in Barcelona and Scientific Director of the Euro-Mediterranean Network for Economic Studies. She has published widely on banking and finance, financial regulation, financial development. She is senior member of several high-level groups and scientific committees.

Elena Beccalli is full Professor of Banking at the Faculty of Banking, Finance and Insurance (Università Cattolica del Sacro Cuore), where she is the Dean of the Faculty. She is Visiting Professor at the Department of Accounting and research associate at the Centre for Analysis of Risk and Regulation (both London School of Economics), and academic fellow at the Centre for Responsible Banking and Finance (University of St Andrews). She is department editor (financial institutions) of the *Journal of Financial Management, Markets and Institutions*. She is the author of numerous academic articles and books in the field of banking.

Patrick Behr is Associate Professor of Finance at the Brazilian School of Public and Business Administration at the Getulio Vargas Foundation, Rio de Janeiro, Brazil. His areas of research are banking, corporate finance and microfinance. He has published two books and several articles in journals such as the *Review of Finance* and *Management Science*. He has done referee work for *American Economic Review*, *Review of Finance*, *Review of Financial Studies*, and *World Development*. He is currently a director of the Brazilian Finance Association and co-founder and co-director of the Center for Banking and Finance Research in Rio.

Wilko Bolt is a Senior Economist in the Economics and Research department at De Nederlandsche Bank in Amsterdam. His current research focuses on the economics of payments, the theory of two-sided markets and antitrust implications. He has published in journals such as *American Economic Review*, *European Economic Review*, *Economic Theory*, *International Journal of Industrial Organization*, and *International Journal of Central Banking*. His book *Credible Threats in Negotiations: A Game-theoretic Approach*, written jointly with Harold Houba, was published in 2002. Bolt was awarded the Hennipman Prize by the Dutch Royal Economic Association in 2007 for his research.

Santiago Carbo-Valverde is Professor of Economics and Finance at the Bangor Business School, UK. Head of Financial Studies of Funcas Foundation, he is a member of the Group of Economic Advisers (GEA) of ESMA. He has been consultant, among others, for the European Central Bank, the European Commission, and the Federal Reserve Bank of Chicago. He has published articles in peer-reviewed journals such as Review of Economics and Statistics, European Economic Review, Review of Finance, *Journal of Money, Credit and Banking*, *Journal of Financial Stability*, and *Journal of Banking and Finance*.

Elena Carletti is Professor of Finance at Bocconi University, Milan, Italy. She is also the Scientific Director of the Florence School of Banking and Finance at the European University Institute, a member of the Advisory Scientific Committee of the European Systemic Risk Board and of the Bank of Italy Scientific Committee for the Paolo Baffi Lectures. She is Research Fellow at Centre for Economic Policy Research (CEPR), Fellow of the Finance Theory Group, Extramural fellow at TILEC, Fellow at the Center for Financial Studies, at CESifo, at IGIER and at the Wharton Financial Institutions Center. Her main research areas are financial intermediation, financial crises and regulation, competition policy and sovereign debt.

Olivier De Jonghe is an associate professor at the Finance department of Tilburg University (the Netherlands). He is also affiliated to the European Banking Center. Olivier is also a (long-term) visiting researcher at the National Bank of Belgium. Prior to joining Tilburg University, he was a postdoctoral researcher at Ghent University (Belgium). His research focuses on various topics in financial intermediation, regulation and stability. Olivier publishes regularly in academic journals in the field of financial intermediation.

Maaike Diepstraten is a PhD candidate at Tilburg University (the Netherlands) and a visiting researcher at the Dutch Central Bank. Prior to joining the PhD programme, she worked as a research assistant for the European Banking Center. Maaike's research interests include empirical banking and household finance.

Panagiotis Dontis-Charitos is Assistant Professor of Finance at ESCP Europe Business School. His main research interests are in the areas of bank diversification and regulation, and financial markets and institutions. His research has been published in US and European peer-reviewed journals, and has been presented at various international conferences. Panagiotis is a member of the advisory board of the BAFA Financial Markets and Institutions Special Interest Group. In the past, he has worked as a stock analyst and sales analyst in the financial services sector.

Mintra Dwarkasing is an Assistant Professor of Finance at Erasmus University, the Netherlands. She pursued her PhD studies in finance at Tilburg University, the Netherlands. Her research focuses on corporate finance, financial intermediaries, inequality and social capital.

Narly Dwarkasing is an Assistant Professor of Finance at the University of Bonn, Germany. She holds a PhD in finance from Tilburg University, the Netherlands. Her research focuses on corporate finance, financial history, and financial intermediaries.

Rients Galema is an Assistant Professor of Finance and Financial Markets at Utrecht University School of Economics. He has worked in a postdoctoral capacity on the project "Markups and trade in international financial services", for which he spent half a year at the Deutsche Bundesbank to do research in international banking. His research interests are empirical banking, socially responsible investment and microfinance.

Claudia Girardone is Professor of Banking and Finance and Director of the Essex Finance Centre at the University of Essex, UK. Her current research focus is on banking sector performance and efficiency, the industrial structure of banking, SME finance and integration in banking and financial markets. She has published widely in the banking area and has recently co-authored the 2nd edition of the textbook *Introduction to Banking* (2015). She is currently on the editorial board of several journals including the *Journal of Banking and Finance* and the *European Journal of Finance*.

John Goddard is Professor of Financial Economics at Bangor Business School, Bangor University, Wales, UK. Before joining Bangor University in 2005, he was Professor of Economics at Swansea University. His research interests are in industrial organization, the economics of financial markets and financial institutions, and the economics of professional sports.

Willem Pieter de Groen is a Research Fellow at the Financial Institutions and Prudential Policy Unit at the Centre for European Policy Studies (CEPS) in Brussels (Belgium) and an associate researcher at the International Research Centre on Cooperative Finance (IRCCF) of HEC Montréal, Canada. He has (co)-authored many studies on EU and Near East banking regulation, as well as diversity in bank ownership and business models, small and medium-sized enterprises, obstacles to growth and access to finance.

Reint E. Gropp is the President of the Institute for Economic Research Halle (IWH) and Professor of Economics at the Otto von Guericke University Magdeburg, Germany. Prior to his appointment at the IWH, he was a Professor of Sustainable Banking and Finance at the Goethe-University Frankfurt am Main and worked for the International Monetary Fund (IMF) as well as the European Central Bank (ECB), where he was Deputy Head of the Financial Research Division. He is Fellow of the Center for Financial Studies, Frankfurt, and Associate Editor of the *Review of Finance*. And has published widely in the areas of financial economics, banking and corporate finance, including in the *Quarterly Journal of Economics*, the *Review of Financial Studies* and the *Review of Finance*.

Ralph De Haas is the Director of Research at the European Bank for Reconstruction and Development. He is also a part-time Associate Professor of Finance at Tilburg University and a Fellow at the European Banking Center. Ralph is the recipient of the 2014 Willem F. Duisenberg Fellowship Prize. He has published work in the *Review of Financial Studies*; *American Economic Journal: Applied Economics*; *American Economic Review Papers and Proceedings*; *Journal of Money, Credit, and Banking*; and the *Journal of Financial Intermediation*, among others. Ralph's research interests include global banking, development economics and small-business finance.

Jens Hagendorff is Professor of Finance at Cardiff University, UK. His research focuses on the drivers behind bank risk-taking and systemic risk as well as the corporate governance and risk-return profile of banks. He was recently a visiting fellow at the Federal Reserve Bank of Atlanta and the Bank of Spain in Madrid. Jens' work has been published in leading international journals such as *Review of Finance*, *Journal of Corporate Finance* and *Journal of Banking & Finance*.

Andrew G. Haldane is the Chief Economist at the Bank of England. He is also Executive Director, Monetary Analysis, Research and Statistics. He is a member of the Bank's Monetary Policy Committee. He also has responsibility for research and statistics across the Bank. Andrew has an Honorary Doctorate from the Open University, is Honorary Professor at University of Nottingham, a Visiting Fellow at Nuffield College, Oxford, a member of Economic Council of Royal Economic Society, a Fellow of the Academy of Social Sciences, Trustee of National Numeracy and Member of Research and Policy Committee at NESTA. Andrew is Chairman and co-founder of 'Pro Bono Economics', a charity which brokers economists into charitable projects. Andrew has written extensively on domestic and international monetary and financial policy issues and has published over 150 articles and four books. In 2014, TIME magazine named him one of the 100 most influential people in the world.

Reinhard Harry Schmidt is Professor Emeritus of International Banking and Finance at Goethe-University in Frankfurt, Germany, where he has worked since 1991. He has authored, co-authored and edited 25 scholarly books, some 150 academic articles in journals and books. The focus of his research in recent years has been on comparative banking and finance in industrial or advanced countries and finance in developing countries, especially microfinance. Schmidt has been actively involved in development finance as a consultant and researcher for numerous international organizations and as the chairman of the supervisory board of a large development finance institution; his most recent book in this area, *From Microfinance to Inclusive Finance* (with H.D. Seibel and P. Thomes; 2016). Moreover, he is a frequent commentator on current financial topics in German and international media.

Rainer Haselmann is Professor of Finance, Accounting and Taxation at Goethe University and Director of the research area "Financial Institutions" at Sustainable Architecture for Finance in Europe (SAFE). Previously, he was Professor of Finance at Bonn University, where he started as an Assistant Professor of Corporate Finance in 2011. Since 2015 he has also been a Research Professor at the Deutsche Bundesbank. His areas of research interests include the real effects of financial frictions, financial sector regulation as well as law and finance.

Neeltje van Horen is a Research Advisor at the Bank of England and a Research Fellow of the CEPR. Prior to joining the Bank of England she worked as a Senior Economist at De Nederlandsche Bank and as a Financial Economist at the World Bank. She has visited and worked at the International Monetary Fund, the Federal Reserve Bank of Chicago and the European Bank for Reconstruction and Development. Her research focuses on macro-financial linkages, international finance and global banking. She has published articles on foreign banks, financial crises, international shock transmission, small business lending, sovereign debt and trade.

Nicole Jonker started working in the Research Department of the Netherlands' Bank in 2001. In 2004 she joined the Cash and Payment Systems division. Nicole has been involved in various studies, including the impact of survey design on measuring cash usage, the impact of budget control on consumers' choice for cash or cards and the pricing of card payments. She has also been involved in policy work related to the payment cards market and SEPA. Nicole graduated with honours in Econometrics at the University of Amsterdam in 1996, and she obtained a PhD in Economics in 2001.

Michael Koetter is Professor of Financial Economics at Otto von Guericke University in Magdeburg and head of the Financial Markets Group at the Leibniz Institute for Economic Research in Halle (IWH). His current research interests concern the consequences of unorthodox monetary policy, (inter)national policy transmission, and crowdfunding. Michael's research received funding from the Netherlands Organization of Scientific Research (NWO), the Leibniz Association, and others. His work appeared in general interest and field journals, such as the *Review of Economics and Statistics*, the *Review of Financial Studies*, and others.

Sam Langfield is Principal Economist at the European Systemic Risk Board, based in the European Central Bank, where he has worked since 2011. He was a visiting researcher at Princeton University's Economics Department and Bendheim Center for Finance, 2015–16. Previously, he was an economist at the Bank of England and the UK Financial Services Authority. He holds an MA degree in Philosophy, Politics and Economics from Oxford University.

Agnese Leonello is an economist in the Financial Research Division at the European Central Bank. She holds a PhD in Economics from the European University Institute. Prior to joining the ECB, she was a postdoctoral research fellow at the Wharton Financial Institutions Centre. She conducts her research in the areas of financial intermediation, financial crises, financial regulation and competition policy.

Laetitia Lepetit is Professor of Economics at the University of Limoges, France, and has authored/co-authored numerous academic articles on financial institutions, bank risk and prudential regulation. She contributed to several European Commission funded research projects, is Associate Editor of the *Journal of International Financial Markets, Institutions & Money*, and has held recurrent visiting positions at the University of Birmingham since 2002. She is also currently the Director of Doctoral Studies at the University of Limoges, and has previously served as its Vice-President in charge of Human Resources.

Joaquin Maudos is Professor of Economic Analysis at the University of Valencia, Spain, Research Deputy Director at the Ivie and collaborator with Colegio Universitario de Estudios Financieros (CUNEF). He was been visiting researcher at the Florida State University, at the College of Business of the Bangor University and at the School of Business of the University of Glasgow. He has worked as a consultant for the European Commission, the European Investment Bank and the United Nations. He has jointly published 13 books and nearly 90 articles in specialized journals.

Donal McKillop is Professor of Financial Services at Queen's University Belfast, UK. His subject specialisms are financial theory, financial regulation and risk management. He is Head of the Finance and Actuarial Group at Queen's. Currently he is working on two major funded projects: the integration of residential property and private pensions in the EU and the development of web-based tools to enhance the financial capability of those in debt. Outside his academic position at Queen's Donal has recently been appointed by the Minister of Finance (Ireland) to advise the Minister and the Central Bank on matters relating to credit unions. He has also advised the Office of the First Minister and Deputy First Minister (Northern Ireland) on intervention measures to help mitigate financial hardship due to the introduction of welfare reform.

Céline Meslier is Associate Professor at the University of Limoges, France. Her research interests are in the areas of financial institutions, bank risk and the link between financial development and economic development. She serves as a Vice-Dean for International Relations of the Faculty of Law and Economics and is currently in charge of the promotion of international Master's degree programme at the University of Limoges.

Philip Molyneux is the Dean of the College of Business, Law, Education and Social Sciences and Professor of Banking and Finance at Bangor University, UK. His main areas of research are on empirical banking issues and he has published widely in this area including recent publications in the *Journal of Money, Credit Banking, Review of Finance* and *Journal of Banking and Finance*. He has co-authored various texts including: *Introduction to Banking* (2015, Pearson), *Introduction to Global Financial Markets* (2015, Palgrave Macmillan) and the *Oxford Handbook of Banking* (2014, Oxford University Press).

Tobias Neumann is a Senior Economist at the Bank of England, working in its Prudential Policy Directorate. Tobias has represented the Bank of England at the Basel Committee's Trading Book Group working on the Fundamental Review of the Trading Book. His research interests include banking regulation, in particular how regulations should be designed in the context of complexity, and how prudential regulation interacts with monetary policy.

Steven Ongena is Professor in Banking at the University of Zurich and the Swiss Finance Institute in Switzerland. He is also a research fellow of CEPR and a research professor at KU Leuven. He has published more than 55 papers in refereed academic journals, including in the *American Economic Review*, *Econometrica*, *Journal of Finance*, *Journal of Financial Economics*, *Journal of International Economics*, *Journal of Political Economy*, *Management Science and Review of Finance*, among other journals, and he has published more than 50 papers in books and other collections. In 2012 he received a NYU-Fordham-RPI Rising Star in Finance Award.

Marco Pagano is Professor of Finance at University of Naples Federico II, Italy, where he also directs the Centre for Studies in Economics and Finance (CSEF). He is also president of the Einaudi Institute for Economics and Finance, Rome. From 2004 to 2011 he was managing editor of the *Review of Finance*. Currently he chairs the Advisory Scientific Committee of the European Systemic Risk Board. His research focuses on banking, corporate finance and market microstructure, and in 2011 he received an ERC Advanced Grant.

Giovanni Petrella is Professor of Banking at Università Cattolica in Milan, Italy, where he teaches derivatives and market microstructure, and serves as academic coordinator for the graduate programme in banking and finance. He is currently a member of the Banking Stakeholder Group at the European Banking Authority in London and the Securities and Markets Stakeholder Group at the European Securities and Markets Authority in Paris.

Mirjam Plooij started working as a policy advisor at De Nederlandsche Bank in 2011, after completing master's degrees in sociology at Utrecht University and Euroculture (European studies) at the universities of Göttingen and Uppsala. From 2011 until early 2014 she was a member of the SEPA Programme Agency of the Dutch National Forum on SEPA Migration. After that, her focus areas shifted to innovation in retail payments and European regulatory developments related to payment services. She has also been involved in research on topics such as payment behaviour by consumers and interchange fees for card payments.

Andrea Resti is Professor of Banking and Finance at Bocconi University, Milan, Italy, and the author of numerous books and academic articles on financial risk management and regulation. Andrea has served as the vice-chairman of the Banking Stakeholder Group at EBA, and currently advises the European Parliament on banking supervision matters. Formerly he was the managing director of CAREFIN,

Bocconi's Centre for Applied Research in Finance, and acted as a consultant for the European Investment Bank, the Bank of Italy and other large financial institutions, as well as for the Italian magistrates investigating financial scandals.

Francisco Rodriguez-Fernandez is Professor of Economics at the University of Granada, Spain. A senior economist at Funcas, he has been visiting researcher at the Universities of Modena and Bologna, the ECB, and the Federal Reserve Bank of Chicago. He has been a member in several national and international research projects. He has published articles in peer-reviewed journals such as *Review of Economics and Statistics*, *Journal of Money, Credit and Banking*, *European Economic Review*, *Review of Finance*, and *Journal of Financial Stability*.

Glenn Schepens is an economist at the Financial Research Division (DG Research) of the ECB. His primary research interests include Financial Intermediation, Empirical Banking and Financial Regulation and Supervision. Before joining the European Central Bank, he worked as an economist at the National Bank of Belgium (2013–15). He obtained his PhD in 2013 from Ghent University. His contributions to this Handbook are his personal views and do not necessarily reflect the views of the European Central Bank or the Eurosystem.

Dirk Schoenmaker is Professor of Banking and Finance at the Rotterdam School of Management, Erasmus University, and a Senior Fellow at the Brussels-based think-tank Bruegel. He is also a Research Fellow at the CEPR and a member of the Advisory Scientific Committee of the European Systemic Risk Board at the ECB. Dirk is author of *Governance of International Banking: The Financial Trilemma* (2013, Oxford University Press) and co-author of the textbook *Financial Markets and Institutions: A European Perspective* (2015, Cambridge University Press).

Armin Schwienbacher is a professor of finance at SKEMA Business School (France). He previously worked at the Lille 2 University (France), Louvain School of Management (Belgium), Universiteit van Amsterdam (the Netherlands) and Duisenberg School of Finance (the Netherlands). He has presented his research on crowdfunding (including regulation of equity crowdfunding), venture capital, and various other topics in corporate finance at many universities, financial institutions and international conferences, including the European Commission, the European Central Bank and the OECD, and his work has been published in several international academic journals.

Jonas Sobott is a PhD student at the Bonn Graduate School of Economics and the Max Planck Institute for Research on Collective Goods.

Abhishek Srivastav is a Lecturer in Banking and Finance at the University of Leeds, UK. His research focuses on bank governance and risk-taking. Abhishek has a track record of publishing at leading finance journals, including *Journal of Corporate Finance*, *Journal of Banking & Finance*, and *Corporate Governance: An International Review*.

Sotiris K. Staikouras is Associate Professor of Banking & Finance at Cass Business School, City University, London. His research interests are risk analysis and management of financial institutions, asset pricing and financial modelling. He has worked as a research advisor at London Clearing House and has delivered training courses for other institutions. He is the Director of the Undergraduate programmes, and he also served as Director of various Masters' programmes. He has published widely in peer reviewed academic journals and his research has been covered by the media.

Amine Tarazi is a Professor of Economics and Director of LAPE research centre at the University of Limoges, France. He served as a research consultant for ACPR (French Prudential Supervisory Authority) and is currently a member of its Scientific Committee. He is associate editor of the *Journal of Banking and Finance* and the *European Journal of Finance*, among other journals. He has coordinated European Commission projects and visited universities in many countries. His work on bank risk and prudential regulation has appeared in the *Journal of Financial Economics*, *Review of Finance*, *Journal of Banking and Finance*, *Journal of Comparative Economics* and others.

Lena Tonzer has been a postdoctoral researcher in the financial markets department of the Halle Institute for Economic Research (IWH), Germany, since May 2014. She coordinates the research group "Regulation of International Financial Markets and International Banking". She studied International Economics at the University of Tübingen before joining the doctoral programme in Economics at the European University Institute (EUI) in Florence in 2010. Her research focuses on banking and sovereign debt crises, integration of financial markets, and banking regulation.

Xavier Vives is Professor of Economics and Finance at IESE Business School, Spain. He has been a Fellow of the Econometric Society since 1992, of the European Economic Association since 2004, and member of the Academia Europaea since 2012. He has taught at INSEAD, Harvard, UAB, UPF, UC Berkeley, Pennsylvania, and New York University. He is editor of the *Journal of Economic Theory* and President-elect of EARIE. He has published in the main international journals and is the author of *Competition and Stability in Banking* (2016).

Paul Wachtel is a Professor of Economics at New York University Stern School of Business and the academic director for the BS in Business and Political Economy. He is the co-editor of *Comparative Economic Studies* and chair of the International Faculty Committee of the International School for Economics in Tbilisi. His areas of research include the finance growth nexus, central banking in the post-crisis world, and financial sector reform in economies in transition.

Jonathan Williams is Professor of Banking and Finance at Bangor Business School and Joint Director of the Institute of European Finance. He holds an Honorary Fellowship for Teaching from Bangor University. Jonathan's current research interests focus on executive compensation in banking and the economic performance and development of national banking sectors. His earlier research focused on European savings banks with published works on management behaviour; bank efficiency; regional banking; technical change and productivity; and economies of scale. His more recent work centres on financial liberalization in banking sectors in the emerging markets, and includes studies of bank restructuring; market power and competition; bank privatization; foreign bank entry; governance; and mergers and acquisitions. His most recent works cover education and bank performance, performance and risk at family firms, and the risk effects of diversification.

John Wilson is Professor of Banking & Finance and Director for the Centre for Responsible Banking & Finance at the University of St Andrews, Scotland. He has published over 50 refereed journal articles and authored numerous books, including: *European Banking: Efficiency, Technology and Growth*; and *Banking: A Very Short Introduction* (2016). John edited a five-volume *Routledge Major Works in Banking*, and co-edited the first and second editions of the *Oxford Handbook of Banking*. In the period June 2011 to April 2012, John served as a full member of a Commission on Credit Unions established by the Irish Government.

List of Figures

List of Tables

Part I

European Banking: Through the Crisis and Beyond

1

European Banking: An Overview

T. Beck and B. Casu

Introduction

This Handbook aims to offer a broad overview of key issues in European banking, taking stock of its performance after the recent crises and looking forward to challenges ahead. The European banking landscape has profoundly changed since the mid-2000s, partly driven by the regulatory response to the 2007–8 global financial crisis and subsequent sovereign debt crisis in the eurozone. Even after substantial regulatory reforms, debates on further steps needed to strengthen the EU regulatory framework to limit future risks arising from the banking system are ongoing. A distinct political debate on the benefits of increased integration has moved to the forefront of the political agenda in light of the results of the Brexit referendum, which might end the "passporting rights" of UK based financial institutions. This historic choice is already having a profound impact on financial markets. For many economists and policy makers the key aim is now to ensure that the eurozone is resilient to potential negative shocks, possibly encouraging further reform and increasing integration.

To this end, the European Commission (EC) pursued a number of initiatives, including stronger prudential requirements for banks, improved depositor protection and common rules for managing bank failures. An important step in the direction of increased integration was the creation of a

T. Beck • B. Casu (✉)
Cass Business School, City, University of London, London, UK
e-mail: Tbeck@city.ac.uk; b.casu@city.ac.uk

T. Beck, B. Casu (eds.), *The Palgrave Handbook of European Banking*,
DOI 10.1057/978-1-137-52144-6_1

Single Rulebook, applicable to all financial institutions in the EU and foundation for the Banking Union (BU), which is currently made up of the Single Supervisory Mechanism (SSM) and the Single Resolution Mechanism (SRM) and applies to countries in the eurozone, though with the option of other countries opting into it.

Although the new regulatory architecture is now in place, its successful implementation depends crucially on how the eurozone deals with the legacy of the financial crises and it is here that the USA and the eurozone seem to have taken divergent paths after 2008 (Hoshi and Kashyap 2015). The eurozone's banking industries appear increasingly segmented, with an overexposure to domestic risks. The persistent weakness of some eurozone banking systems puts the implementation of the newly agreed rules to the test, as the discussions in 2016 on the recapitalization of Italian banks through the bail-in of retail investors holding junior debt instruments show.

Beyond the banking system, regulatory reforms have covered an array of other segments of Europe's financial system, ranging from insurers to equity funds. The Banking Union initiative has recently been complemented with a Capital Market Union (CMU) initiative. Unlike the Banking Union, this initiative relates to the whole European Union and not only the eurozone. Unlike the Banking Union initiative, the CMU contains a series of different initiatives in the regulatory, legal and infrastructure frameworks of financial markets. The Banking Union and CMU initiatives also complement each other, however, in that they constitute efforts to move away from a bank-bias in most European financial system towards more market- and equity-based systems.

It is against this background that this Handbook aims to provide an understanding of the key issues facing European banks. The Handbook is composed of five main parts. Part I, *European Banking: Through the Crisis and Beyond*, offers an overview of the European banking sector in terms of financial structure, ownership and business models and corporate governance, as well as the payment system. Part II, *Performance and Innovation in European Banking* discusses the key themes of bank competition, efficiency and performance. In addition, it looks at the impact of technological development on the banking sectors and how banks are embracing the opportunities it offers. Finally, it explores the issues of bank diversification and the relevance of small business lending.

Part III, *Financial Stability and Regulation*, addresses the key issues of financial reforms and the increasing complexity of financial regulation. It also looks at the impact of state aid and the impact of monetary policy. Finally, it considers the increasing interactions between banks and markets. Part IV, *Cross-Border Banking*, looks at recent trends in cross-border banking in

Europe and evaluates the establishment of the Banking Union. Finally, Part V, *European Banking Systems*, offers a detailed analysis of the main issues facing national banking system in key European banking markets.

The reminder of this chapter offers a summary of the key issues discussed in the Handbook as well as an overview of European banking.

The EU Single Market for Financial Services

The European Union (EU) was formally established in 1993 by the Maastricht Treaty; although its history dates back to the post-war period.[1] The signing of the Maastricht Treaty also marks the official start of the EU single market project, leading to the establishment of the single currency, the euro, and of the European Central Bank (ECB) in 1999. The current constitutional basis of the EU is the Lisbon Treaty, which came into force in 2009. Membership of the EU has grown through a number of enlargements.[2] Today, the EU is the largest integrated economic area in the world, accounting for more than 20 % of the world's gross domestic product (GDP). Campos et al. (2014) and Campos et al. (2016) show that the economic benefits from EU membership are large and substantially outweigh the costs. Using a methodology known as SCM (synthetic counterfactuals method) to provide an estimate of per capita GDP if a given country had not become a member of the EU, the authors suggest substantial and permanent benefits, concluding that there are positive pay-offs of EU membership, clearly above the direct costs.

Since the introduction of the First Banking Co-ordination Directive in 1977 (77/780/EEC), the deregulation of financial services, the establishment of the Economic and Monetary Union (EMU) and the introduction of the euro have helped create the Single Market for financial services. European authorities consider financial integration one of the key issues for making Europe more efficient and competitive and, ultimately, for contributing to sustainable economic growth.

Until the 1980s the EU financial and banking sectors were mainly domestically oriented. National governments regularly acted as protectors of their banks

[1] In 1951, Belgium, France, Germany, Italy, Luxemburg and the Netherland formed the European Coal and Steel Community (ECSC) and in 1957 the Treaty of Rome established the European Economic Community (EEC).

[2] Denmark, Ireland, United Kingdom joined in 1973. Greece joined in 1981. Portugal and Spain joined in 1986 whereas Austria, Finland and Sweden joined in 1995. Cyprus, the Czech Republic, Estonia, Hungary, Latvia, Lithuania, Malta, Poland, Slovenia and the Slovak Republic joined in 2004; Bulgaria and Romania in 2007 and Croatia in 2013.

and state ownership was still prevalent in some EU countries. Interest rate restrictions and capital controls were common, and branching restrictions existed. The First Banking Co-ordination Directive in 1977 started a legislative process directed towards creating an integrated and competitive European banking system. These objectives reflected wider changes in the domains of economic policy, internationalization, technological advances and globalization. Possibly the most far reaching legislation in the harmonization of EU banking, the 1989 Second Banking Co-ordination Directive (89/646/EEC), sought to enhance competition by establishing EU-wide recognition of single banking 'passports' issued in any member state as well as the principle of home-country supervision with minimum standards (including capital) at EU level. The EU passport meant that a financial services provider authorized in a EU member state was able to offer the same services throughout the EU, competing on an equal basis and within a regulatory framework that is consistent across the Union.

In addition, the Second Banking Co-ordination Directive allowed banks to operate as universal banks: that is to engage directly in other financial activities, such as financial instruments, factoring, leasing and investment banking. The single market for financial services also implied the liberalization of non-bank financial intermediaries: insurance companies and investment firms were granted a single EU 'passport' with mutual recognition as a result of directives enacted in the early 1990s.

As part of the EU's single market programme, the introduction of the euro in 1999 was viewed as a central element in the harmonization process. The euro first replaced national currencies in 1999, while the eurozone now comprises 19 member states.[3]

A milestone towards the realization of the single market was the launch of the EU's Financial Services Action Plan (FSAP) in 1999: the fundamental aim of the FSAP was to promote a more competitive and dynamic financial services industry. In 2005, the FSAP was replaced by the White Paper on Financial Services which set out the Commission's objectives from 2005 to 2010. One of the White Paper's key objectives was to ensure the coherence of the regulatory framework and the development of consistent legislation. Co-ordination and harmonization of financial supervision in the EU was pursued through the so-called Lamfalussy procedure which was launched in 2001 and aimed to simplify and speed up the complex and lengthy EU legislative process.

[3] The euro area (also known as and referred to in this book as the Eurozone) includes the following countries: Austria, Belgium, Cyprus, Estonia, Finland, France, Germany, Greece, Ireland, Italy, Latvia, Lithuania, Luxembourg, Malta, the Netherlands, Portugal, Spain, Slovenia and Slovakia.

From this very brief overview, it is apparent that since the mid-1990s, a large body of EU regulation has been put in place to improve cooperation, convergence, harmonization and standardization of financial regulation and supervision. These initiatives, however, created a rather complex framework of sometimes overlapping committees. Critically, this EU-level framework was not adequate to address the 2008 global financial crisis, as became clear during the financial turmoil and government interventions. Many governments first took national measures before gradually coordinating EU-wide responses. This led to widespread criticism and a major public debate about changes in EU institutional arrangements, particularly with respect to the resolution of cross-border bank groups.

In 2009, a High-Level Group on financial supervision published a report outlining the proposals for reform of the EU regulatory framework (High-Level Expert Group on financial supervision in the EU 2009). The report, known as the de Larosière Report, outlined recommendations on regulation and supervision of EU financial markets. A key issue highlighted by the report related to the lack of a common rulebook across EU member states, which led to inconsistencies in crisis management and financial stability oversight. Therefore, the report proposed a two-level approach to reforming the EU financial architecture centred around the creation of a new systemic risk board for the oversight of financial markets and high level co-ordination among national supervisors. The report recommended the creation of a European Systemic Risk Council (ESRC), chaired by the President of the European Central Bank.

The European Commission followed most of the report's recommendations and the new structure for European financial supervision started to take shape in November 2010 when the EU Council of Finance (ECOFIN) agreed upon the creation of a new European Systemic Risk Board (ESRB) and a European System of Financial Supervisors (ESFS), comprising three functional authorities: the European Banking Authority (EBA), the European Insurance and Occupational Pensions Authority (EIOPA) and the European Securities and Markets Authority (ESMA).

The establishment of the European System of Financial Supervision has contributed to improving cooperation between national supervisors in EU member states. It has also contributed to the development of a single rulebook for financial services. To further strengthen cooperation and improve supervision with the aim of restoring confidence in banking markets and in the euro, in 2012 the European Commission put forward a longer-term plan (known as the Van Rompuy plan). This plan included the Banking Union, which aims to deliver an integrated financial safety net for the Eurozone, consisting of (i) a single European banking supervision (Single Supervisory Mechanism—SSM); (ii) a common deposit insurance (Single Deposit Guarantee Mechanism, or SDM); (iii) a common resolution framework (Single Resolution Mechanism, or SRM) and (iv) a single rulebook (common legal framework, EBA single rulebook). We will discuss this in more detail in the "Cross-Border Banking" section of this introductory chapter.

When discussing cross-border banking services, it is important to distinguish between retail and wholesale activities. Wholesale banking services are often supplied in an international competitive market. On the other hand, retail banking services are essentially national in nature and traditionally provided on a domestic basis. It has long been recognized that it may be difficult to achieve a single market for retail financial products. Since the earliest assessments of conditions in European financial services, there has been the recognition that retail financial services markets are segmented by national boundaries. Cross-border trade in retail financial services is limited and markets are far from integrated. Various studies have identified that there remain substantial price differences in retail financial services across the EU. These price differences reflect a broad array of factors, not least the different institutional, legal and risk features in the various national markets relating to labour, taxation, health and safety, consumer protection and contract law.

In general, most integration obstacles seem to be a result of natural or policy-induced elements. Such obstacles to further integration are apparent in a wide range of areas; some of these barriers are natural and therefore can only be partially influenced by policymakers, others require further regulation.

Regulations governing the retail financial services sector are also country-specific and it remains problematic to undertake cross-border activity without physical establishment of branches or subsidiaries. The existing fragmentation in retail financial services has also been in some cases intensified by the response of some national supervisors to potential stability concerns triggered by the eurozone crisis, including prudential measures with "ring-fencing" effects, such as measures aimed at retaining liquidity, dividends and other bank assets within national borders. EU regulators have reacted to concerns of decreased integration by promoting EU the development of a Single Rulebook, to ensure common rules, supervision and resolution across the EU.

The global financial crisis and the eurozone crisis clearly have had a profound impact on the EU banking landscape. The regulatory framework has changed in the direction of a more integrated Banking Union. In the next section we will review the main structural features of EU banking markets.

European Banking Through the Crisis and Beyond

National banking systems within the EU vary considerably in terms of bank size, types of banks and ownership structure. The size of the banking and financial sectors varies considerably across EU area countries, ranging from Luxemburg (over 100 times GDP) to Lithuania (below 100 % of GDP), as illustrated in Fig. 1.1. While size decreased slightly between 2008 and 2014, the broader financial sector remained unchanged in more recent years, thus reversing the trend initiated by the outbreak of the financial crisis. Cross-country differences are also evident in relation to the presence of foreign banks (either branches or subsidiaries) and their relative weight in the domestic banking system.

The process of consolidation of the banking sectors in eurozone countries has continued, due to increased pressure on cost-cutting and restructuring. With a few exceptions, most countries experienced a marked decrease in the number of banks between 2008 and 2014 (ECB 2015). Austrian, French, German and Italian credit institutions accounted for around 69 % of eurozone credit institutions at the end of 2014, a slight increase compared with 67 % in 2008. At the end of 2014, France and Germany still had the largest banking sectors in the eurozone, with total asset values of €7.2 trillion and €7.1 trillion, respectively (ECB 2015). The decrease in the number of banks was also reflected by the increase in banking sector capacity indicators: population per branch and assets per bank employee increased between 2008 and 2014. Market concentration, proxied both by the Herfindahl Index and

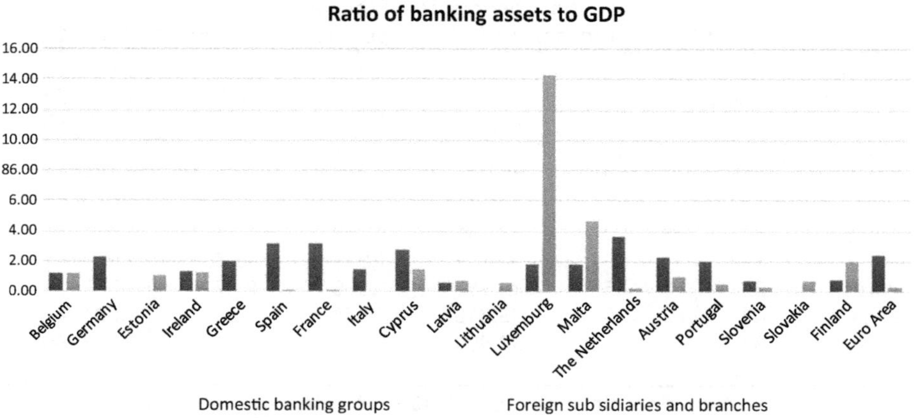

Fig. 1.1 Ratio of banking assets to GDP (*Source*: EBC structural financial indicators (2015) and authors' elaborations)

by the concentration ratio, has increased since the financial crisis. Table 1.1 illustrates the key banking sector statistics for the eurozone countries in 2014.

Despite the aforementioned reduction in the number of banks across the eurozone, a recent report by the European Systemic Risk Board (ESRB 2014) asks whether Europe is overbanked. Recent statistics seem to indicate that the European banking sectors are large relative to the size of the economy following an exponential growth which accelerated in the 1990s. They are also large compared with other sources of financial intermediation, such as bonds and equity markets. European banks are among the largest in the world and European financial systems have failed to become more market-based, bucking international trends (ESRB 2014).

Langfield and Pagano address these issues (Chap. 2, *Financial Structure*) and ask whether the structure of financial markets matters in terms of the efficiency of financial intermediation. Financial structure should optimally reflect the comparative advantages of banks and capital markets in mitigating financial frictions (Allen and Gale 2000). Langfield and Pagano argue that bank-based financial structure can either help mitigate market frictions or exacerbate them. As a result, the relative importance of banks and markets can substantially affect the quantity and the quality of credit allocation among firms and households, the stability of the financial system, and ultimately productivity and economic growth. However, a country's financial structure not only reflects the comparative advantages of banks and capital markets in

Table 1.1 Eurozone banking sector statistics (2014)

	N. of credit institutions	N. of foreign branches	Population per credit institution	Population per branch	Assets per bank employee	HHI	CR(5)
Belgium	43	65	108,320	3,093	19,466	982	66
Germany	1,698	105	45,552	2,334	12,054	301	32
Estonia	30	7	35,562	10,785	4,415	2,445	90
Ireland	414	33	10,347	4,643	37,400	677	48
Greece	21	20	274,820	4,090	8,713	2,195	94
Spain	144	84	205,593	1,452	14,744	839	58
France	413	90	133,405	1,759	19,895	584	48
Italy	592	79	90,739	1,979	13,424	424	41
Cyprus	32	25	14,956	1,386	8,320	1,303	63
Latvia	49	10	33,816	6,254	3,292	1,001	64
Lithuania	82	7	32,909	4,801	2,847	1,818	86
Luxemburg	110	40	3,772	2,573	37,297	329	32

Source: **EBC structural financial indicators (2015). HHI refers to the Herfindahl Index, calculated as the square of the market share of all the credit institutions in the respective banking sector. The HHI index ranges between 0 and 10,000. CR(5) refers to the share of the five largest credit institution in percentage. Assets per employee are in € thousands.**

mitigating financial frictions; it is also influenced by public policy and political structures. In the EU, the expansion of the banking sector occurred against the background of financial integration following monetary unification. This possibly reflected an attitude of "banking nationalism" (Véron 2013), aimed at fostering the growth of large universal banks as national champions in an attempt to prevent a wave of cross-border mergers and acquisitions (M&As). Bank supervisors helped to promote national champions by treating banks leniently. The authors suggest that by overprotecting domestic banks, governments encourage moral hazard and excessive risk-taking. In addition, inadequate regulation and lax supervision further distort banks' incentives. They conclude that moral hazard is mitigated by improved bank regulation and supervision frameworks and by removing barriers to the developments of capital markets.

In terms of banking models, the EU banking landscape is dominated by large universal banking groups. EU deregulation fostered the growth of a "market-based banking" model, whose effect was to create wide-ranging interconnectedness between banks and markets. The prevailing argument is that universal banking offers diversification benefits. However, the reality during the crisis demonstrated the dangers of the way in which the universal banking model operates and a number of major structural reforms to contain banks' "financialization" (that is a substantial growth not only in size but also in the scope and volume of financial markets activities carried out by banks.) This trend is reflected by the growth and composition of bank's balance sheets, with a shift from traditional lending activities to dealing and market making activities. This shift occurred in parallel with the growth of the *shadow banking sector*, defined as a system of credit intermediation involving entities and activities outside of the regular banking system (FSB 2012). This alternative financing system has been in place since the early 1980s and can be potentially beneficial to the economy by complementing traditional banking in support of economic activity or by supporting market liquidity, maturity transformation and risk sharing. However, the system can also become a source of systemic risk, as evidenced during the global financial crisis. Both the increase in shadow banking activities and their interconnections with banks have spurred an academic and policy debate on their role in the financial system, and renewed the need to understand their operations.

A consensus narrative seems to argue that the excessive diversification of EU banks, as well as the presence of large and complex financial conglomerates, has led banks into risky non-bank activities and acted as a catalyst for the global financial crisis. This claim is analysed by Dontis-Charitos, Staikouras and Williams (Chap. 3, *Bank Diversification and Financial Conglomerates in*

Europe). The authors present a comprehensive review of the literature and conclude that despite the voluminous work on bank diversification, the evidence still yields conflicting conclusions and fails to provide a clear answer as to whether bank diversification increases systemic risk.

This inconsistency may also be derived by the fact that not all types of banks faced the same challenges and/or responded in the same way to crises because of their diverse business models. Ayadi and de Groen (Chap. 4, *Banks' Business Models in Europe*) propose a definition of bank business models based primarily on a distinction between the key banking activities (i.e. retail versus market or mixed) and the funding strategies (i.e. retail versus market or mixed), which broadly builds on an asset-liability approach. The authors identify four main business models: investment banking, wholesale banking, focused retail banking and diversified retail banking. After identifying the business models in European banks, the authors examine the interaction with the ownership structure.

EU banking markets are also characterized by the existence of different types of bank: commercial banks, saving banks, cooperative banks and, in some countries, state-owned banks. Goddard, McKilliop and Wilson (Chap. 5, *Ownership in European Banking*) provide an overview of the key features of the different ownership forms. One key distinction is between shareholder-based and stakeholder-based institutions. Commercial banks are primarily shareholder-based institutions whereas cooperatives, savings and mutual financial institutions are also known as stakeholder-based. In most European countries they are the main providers of credit to the household and corporate sector and of retail payments services. It is often argued that the key difference between stakeholders-based financial institutions and shareholder-oriented commercial banks lies in the objectives pursued by managers. While the key objective for commercial banks is shareholders' wealth maximization, managers of stakeholder based financial institutions have to fulfil a range of different targets, from providing banking services to specific geographical areas, professions or individuals with specific characteristics. However, this does not imply that managers of stakeholder based financial institutions do not have in their remit profit generation, insofar that profit is related to the institution's solvency and growth prospects. This is also known as a "double bottom line", i.e. where profit maximization has to be combined with social and other objectives (Anguren Martín and Marqués Sevillano 2011).

The global financial crisis highlighted significant differences among EU banking sectors, both in terms of the overall losses and the speed of the subsequent recovery. Another key aspect emphasized by the crisis relates to flaws in corporate governance, which are thought to have played a key role in promoting and rewarding excessive risk-taking (Mehran et al. 2011; Adams and Mehran 2012; Beltratti and Stulz 2012). At the EU level, the crisis prompted a revision of the comprehensive corporate governance rules already in place, either in the form of directives or outright in the form of a European regulation. At the same time, a number of EU regulators are considering quotas for publicly listed companies′ board as a requirement of their Codes of Good Governance (CGGs).

Working on the notion that corporate governance is influenced by cultural values, the standard classification of a market-based Anglo-Saxon system versus a bank-based continental European system seems to be still prevalent in shaping corporate governance arrangements. Hagendorff and Srivastav (Chap. 6, *Pay Structures in European Banks*) discuss executive compensation and its implication for the banking industry and assesses recent proposals to reform pay in the banking industry. They highlight the need to understand better how to structure managerial compensation in a way that it can mitigate risk-taking behaviour and align the interests of managers and shareholders while also ensuring financial stability. European pay reforms have largely adopted a prescriptive format to address the risk-taking incentives embedded in compensation contracts. For instance, the Capital Requirements Directive—IV (CRD-IV) proposes an upper limit on the proportion of performance-based compensation and that a substantial proportion of variable pay should consist of long-term instruments (e.g. equity) that should be deferred over a period of at least three years.

The shift in regulatory attitudes towards performance-based pay in European banks is also evident in the fraction of bonuses in terms of managerial pay: bonus payments have fallen since 2008, although the proportion of equity-based compensation has increased over the same period, this shift has largely been towards long-term deferred equity awards. As a result, the wealth of European bank executives should have become more aligned with long-term bank stability.

Performance and Innovation in European Banking

The profound changes in the economic and regulatory environment in which European banks work have important repercussions for their efficiency and performance. However, banks also face renewed competition from non-bank providers using technological advances for financial innovation in the form of new products, new delivery channels and new institutions and markets. At the same time, the crisis has negatively affected SME lending, resulting in multiple regulatory and policy responses. The ultimate question, however, is whether the increased competition and the new regulatory frameworks make European banks more efficient and stable at the same time. The chapters in this section of the handbook touch on these different areas.

One often overlooked key component of a well-functioning markets is the payment system, defined as any organized arrangement for transferring value between its participants. The payment system is a by-product of financial intermediation, as it facilitates the transfer of claims in the financial sector. Bolt, Jonker and Plooij (Chap. 7, *European Retail Payments Systems: Cost, Pricing, Innovation and Regulation*) provide an overview of recent developments in European retail payments, including changes in instrument composition, payment costs, innovations, new players and regulatory framework. In recent years, the EU adopted regulation aimed at lowering several entry barriers for new providers of payment services and to provide the market with the regulatory stimulus to further the development of an efficient, competitive and innovative EU-wide retail payments market. Without doubt, one of the key developments is retail payment innovations: contactless payments, mobile payments and digital wallets, which will affect pricing and competition in the retail payment market. Key drivers for payment innovation are technological change, end-user preferences, the increasing number of non-banks offering payment services and regulatory framework.

The recent crises and the regulatory responses have also had profound repercussions for market structure and competition in European banking. De Jonghe, Diepstraten and Schepens (Chap. 8, *Competition in EU Banking*) provide an overview of different measures of bank concentration and competition and their development across Europe over time. They also discuss the vast theoretical and empirical literature on the relationship between market structure, competition and bank stability, whose conclusions are still ambiguous. One important recent finding, however, has been the critical interaction between regulatory frameworks and competition in their effect on bank stability (Beck et al. 2013).

The theme of innovation is also explored by Schwienbacher (Chap. 9, *The Internet, Crowdfunding and the Banking Industry*). He discusses network effects and the horizontalization of financial institutions that arise from the Internet and the data possibilities offered by social media. He also discusses crowdfunding and peer-to-peer lending and the extent to which this will affect banking business models. This area is clearly still very under-researched and as data will become available over the next years, we can expect substantial new research here.

The crisis has turned the focus of policy makers to small and medium-sized enterprises (SME) lending, as this segment of the corporate population has been more than other segments negatively affected by the financial crises and the consequent lending retrenchment. Given that two-thirds of employees work in SMEs, multiple policy initiatives have tried to address this challenge, using guarantee and special funding schemes. Carbo-Valverde and Rodríguez-Fernández (Chap. 10, *Small Business Lending*) analyse small business lending in Europe, both from the theoretical and empirical perspectives. They document SMEs' challenges in accessing external funding and show substantial variation both across countries and over time. The authors also offer an extensive survey of different lending techniques to reach out to SMEs, including relationship lending and different forms of transaction-based lending, such as asset-based lending or credit scoring.

The recent changes in the regulatory framework and institutional structure raise questions on their effects on bank efficiency. Galema and Koetter (Chap. 11, *European Bank Efficiency and Performance*) provide an overview of the key estimation methods for efficiency and discuss selected applications to the European banking sector. They then go on and apply stochastic frontier analysis to investigate the extent to which the reallocation of supervisory powers is associated with efficiency differences between European banks. Their evidence suggests that supranational supervision by the SSM coincides with larger inefficiencies. This result may indicate the additional administrative burden, at least during the run-up towards a more homogenous approach banking supervision in the EMU. It is important to stress, however, that these findings do not necessarily imply causality. In the context of the debate on the perceived benefits of increased integration of eurozone banking markets following the global financial and sovereign debt crises, a recent study by Casu et al. (2016) evaluates the long-term impact of regulatory reform on bank productivity, starting from the inception of the Single Market in 1992. The authors also assess the cross-border benefits of integration in terms of technological spillovers. Their findings suggest that productivity growth has occurred for eurozone countries, driven by technological progress, both at the country and the eurozone level, although the latter slows or in some cases reverses since the onset of the crisis. They also find some evidence of technological spillovers, which have led to progression toward the best technology. However, they also note significant long run differences in productivity and conclude that technological improvements are increasingly concentrated in fewer banking industries.

Financial Stability and Regulation

The global financial crisis has led to an array of regulatory reform initiatives, while the European sovereign debt crisis has led to the introduction of the Banking Union, which we have already discussed and will return to below. The post-2008 regulatory reforms can be understood in the context of regulatory super-cycles, as identified by several observers (Aizenman 2009; McDonnell 2013), bringing to an end a long period of regulatory easing and financial liberalization that started across the developed world in the 1980s. These regulatory reforms, mostly agreed on by global fora such as the G20, have been implemented across the EU in the form of the CRD IV, as already discussed above.

Carletti and Leonello (Chap. 12, *Regulatory Reforms in the European Banking Sector*) discuss not only these recent regulatory reforms, including capital and liquidity requirements and activity restrictions, but also assess them on the basis of theoretical models of bank fragility and how to address such fragility. Specifically, they point to three market failures that call for regulatory responses: the vulnerability of banks to retail and wholesale runs, moral hazard problems within the banking system resulting in the tendency towards excessive risk-taking and different sources of systemic risk. They also point to the tendency of financial system actors of evading new regulations by shifting certain transactions and products into the non-regulated, shadow banking system. This more general challenge for regulators concerning the regulatory perimeter requires a dynamic regulatory approach looking beyond existing rules (Beck et al. 2015). It is important to remember that regulating one type of institution will lead to the emergence of others and point to the need to design regulation in a forward-looking way. This would imply that the regulatory perimeter has to be adjusted over time and that the focus of prudential regulation (both micro- and macro-prudential) might have to shift over time as new sources of systemic risks arise.

One important challenge for regulators is the increasing complexity of financial intermediaries, which regulators typically address with increasingly complex regulations. Haldane and Neumann (Chap. 13, *Complexity in Regulation*) question this approach. They first describe the historical path towards increasing complexity in regulation across European countries; while the Basel I Accord ran to 30 pages, the Basel II Accord ran already to 347 pages, more than a tenfold increase. Importantly, these figures understate the trends towards complexity due to the use of internal risk models under Basel II. More complex regulation also increased the use of resources in supervision. Haldane and Neumann make a strong case that this increased regulatory complexity ultimately failed during the crisis, both due to mis-assessments and regulatory arbitrage induced by the complexity of the regulations. Steps toward using simpler tools, such as the leverage ratios under the Basel III Accord, are certainly a welcome development in this context.

One important feature of crisis resolution in Europe since 2008 has been the use of state aid and guarantees of both assets and liabilities. Specifically, while any state aid has to be approved by the EC under EU rules, the EC issued a blanket permission to apply such state aid to failing banks in 2008, with the caveat that remedial measures would be taken at a later stage. This quid pro quo has been subject to intense debate (Beck et al. 2010), as several large European banks were forced to divest themselves of some of their subsidiaries in return for having received state aid during the crisis. Gropp and Tonzer (Chap. 14, *State Aid and Guarantees in Europe*) offer a systematic overview of the different forms of state aid and guarantees applied during the crisis across Europe and provide a theoretical and empirical assessment of their effects on financial stability. Critical for such assessment, they gauge whether the application of such aid and guarantees can be explained by political factors. Theory predicts opposing effects of state aid and guarantees, on the one hand strengthening franchise value and sound lending by banks, on the other hand providing incentives for excessive risk-taking. The authors' reading of the empirical literature lets them conclude that the ultimate outcome depends on the institutional and political setting in which such guarantees are applied.

One important factor explaining excessive risk-taking and fuelling real estate booms in several peripheral eurozone countries has been the very low interest rates environment, especially after the entry into the eurozone by countries with previously much higher interest rates. This loose monetary policy resulted in higher risk-taking by banks, both in intensive (higher volume of lending) and extensive (lending to riskier borrowers) margins. Dwarkasing, Dwarkasing and Ongena (Chap. 15, *The Bank Lending Channel of Monetary Policy: A Review of the Literature and an Agenda for Future Research*) provide a comprehensive literature review of the recent empirical literature on the risk-taking channel of monetary policy, focusing on both local and international channels. Critical in identifying the impact of monetary policy on risk-taking by financial institutions is being able to distinguish between demand and supply factors and controlling for endogeneity. The use of loan-level as well as application data as provided by credit registries and their combination with bank-level and borrower-level information allows disentangling of demand and supply, while the fact that eurozone interest rates are set in Frankfurt for the average of the eurozone rather than (possibly diverging) individual economies allows addressing the identification challenge. The authors document evidence for the risk-taking channel of monetary policy; this finding has been critical in challenging the pre-2007 inflation targeting paradigm, which saw monetary policy as exclusively targeting monetary stability and micro-prudential regulation targeting financial stability. The break-down of this separation of instruments has also given rise to an extensive discussion and increasing research on macro-prudential regulation.

One important supervisory tool applied both during the crisis resolution phase, but also institutionalized in the aftermath of the crisis, are supervisory stress tests, as discussed by Petrella and Resti (Chap. 16, *Supervisory Stress Test Results and Investor Reactions*). These tests were successfully used by the US authorities in 2008 as an entry point to the recapitalization of banks. In the EU, on the other hand, several rounds of such tests have lacked credibility, partly due to divergent national standards and political interference in the process. It was not until late 2014 and in the context of establishing the SSM, that the Comprehensive Assessment, consisting of the Asset Quality Review and the stress tests, of the largest 125 banks in the Eurozone, provided some comfort on the actual state of eurozone banking. The Asset Quality Review had the objective of making asset evaluations consistent across the eurozone, resulting in quite aggressive adjustments in some cases, while the stress test had the objective to gauge the resilience of banks' capital position to a severe recession. Comparing the implementation of stress tests and market reactions to them between the USA and Europe allows the authors some critical conclusions, including that (i) the definition of the macroeconomic scenarios is particularly significant, (ii) the results of the stress test depend crucially on the assumption used to simulate the evolution of the banks' balance sheets over time, (iii) the market reaction to the publication of results in times of turmoil is strongly affected by the availability of a strong, credible, unconditional public backstop (existing in the USA, non-existing until recently in the Eurozone) and (iv) that the information provided by the supervisors after the stress-tests might have different impacts on market reactions.

Cross-Border Banking

Several chapters in this Handbook touch on the construction of the Banking Union within the eurozone. The Banking Union was designed with the primary purpose of cutting the deadly embrace between sovereigns and banks that could and can be observed (at the time of writing) across several peripheral eurozone countries. Discussions on creating a supra-national financial safety net started soon after the onset of the crisis, although it was the sovereign debt crisis that ultimately provided the necessary impetus for governments to proceed.

The sovereign-bank loop works in two ways. First, banks carry large amounts of bonds of their own government on their balance sheets (Battistini et al. 2014). As a consequence, a deterioration of a government's credit standing would automatically worsen the solvency of that country's banks. Second, a worsening of a country's banking system could worsen the government's budget because of a potential government financed bank bailout. Another important reason for a supra-national financial safety net is the sustainability and stability of a Single Market in banking across the eurozone. The financial trilemma states that the three objectives of financial stability, cross-border banking and national financial policies cannot be achieved at the same time; one has to give (Schoenmaker 2011).

The Banking Union consists of several pillars, as documented by Schoenmaker (Chap. 17, *The Banking Union: An Overview and Open Issues*); most importantly, the SSM, hosted by the ECB since November 2014 and the SRM that came into effect in January 2016, together with new bail-in rules under the Banking Recovery and Resolution Directive (BRRD). Mainly for political reasons (and more specifically related to the fact that legacy problems from the recent crises have not been addressed), a European Deposit Insurance Scheme has not been implemented yet. Schoenmaker concludes that that bank risk-sharing is only partly achieved in the current set-up of the Banking Union and some work remains to be done, notably in the field of deposit insurance. Moreover, the mix of national agencies (for deposit insurance) and European agencies (for supervision and resolution) makes the Banking Union arrangement potentially instable.

Re-establishing a Single Market in banking has been one important objective of the Banking Union. What have been the pre- and post-crisis trends in cross-border banking across Europe? De Haas and van Horen address this question in their chapter (Chap. 18, *Recent Trends in Cross-Border Banking in Europe*), considering both the physical presence of multinational banks and direct cross-border bank flows. They document a strong reliance in Central and Eastern Europe on multinational, especially West European, banks, while there were increasing cross-border bank flows across all regions of Europe before the crisis. Several countries in Eastern Europe, most notably Ukraine, experienced a reduction in foreign bank presence after 2008. However, in spite of the trends towards retrenchment, especially by Western European banks that needed to comply with stricter capital requirements in the wake of the crisis, the successful implementation of the Vienna Initiative also helped ensure that foreign banks continued their operations in many of these countries. The downward adjustment in cross-border bank flows, on the other hand, has been much more severe and has led to an increasing fragmentation of the European banking market. The decline in cross-border bank lending has partially been replaced by bank lending from other source countries—in particular the USA—and by an increase in corporate bond issuance and the funding of the European corporate sector has slowly shifted towards more bond-based and less bank-based funding. As it stands right now, it might be too early to say whether the funding and asset structure of Europe's banking systems has reached a new equilibrium, given that new regulations and the outstanding resolution of the Eurozone crisis still have to play out.

European Banking Systems

This Handbook includes five chapters that discuss the major EU banking systems and document their diversity. Molyneux (Chap. 19, *Banking in the UK*) discusses the development of the British banking sector, especially post-2008. The turmoil of the global financial crisis, the euro sovereign debt crisis, the mis-selling of payment protection insurance (PPI), Libor, FX and other rate fixing scandals have been a litany of disasters, resulting in the failure of several banks, the nationalization of two major banks, but also by significant regulatory reforms, partly driven by global initiatives, discussed above, and partly by the findings and recommendations of the Vickers Commission, which proposed sweeping changes to the structure of banks, including ring-fencing core bank business for stability purposes. In addition, the regulatory structure was changed, combining prudential regulation and monetary policy responsibilities under the roof of the Bank of England. Molyneux provides an extensive overview of these different developments and their effect on banks, including also the emergence of challenger banks, fostered by policy makers to address the lack of competition in the UK banking market. He concludes that, overall, the capacity for the UK banking system to withstand major shocks has improved. It remains to be seen what further challenges and adjustments are in stock for the UK banks and regulators following the vote for Brexit (Britain exit from the European Union as a result of a referendum vote in June 2016).

An analysis of the Italian banking system—as undertaken by Becalli and Girardone (Chap. 20: *Banking in Italy*)—has to start with the 1936 Banking Act, which was in force for over 50 years. The process of liberalization started in Italy in the mid-1980s and was substantially influenced by the wide deregulation and harmonization efforts at the EU level. It culminated with the enactment of a new banking law in 1993. The long crisis, which since 2007 has affected both financial systems and the real economy and has resulted in, among other things, a large amount of non-performing loans (NPLs) in the balance sheets of European, and particularly of Italian banks, a problem that has not been addressed for many years. At the time of writing, the crisis of the Italian banking system has come yet again to the fore after the Brexit vote in the UK.

Germany's banking system is rather special for an advanced country, in that less than half of banking assets are privately owned, with the remainder made up by locally owned savings banks and stakeholder-based cooperative banks. Behr and Schmidt discuss the structure and challenges of Germany's banking system (Chap. 21, *Banking in Germany*), pointing out that, in contrast to other countries, the three-pillar structure in Germany has proven surprisingly stable, partly for political reasons. They discuss how the financial crisis of 2007–8 affected the German banking system and threatened the existence of some large private-sector banks as well as banks with government involvement, most prominently the Landesbanken. The role of government ownership in the German banking system has been subject to intensive debates, as documented in this chapter. The authors conclude that "whether the German banking system would be better off with or without a strong role of the state, remains an open question".

Maudos and Vives discuss the structure and development of the Spanish banking system (Chap. 22, *Banking in Spain*). Pre-2007, the Spanish banking sector was comprised of three types of deposit institutions: commercial banks, saving banks (*cajas de ahorros*) and cooperative banks. Following the financial crisis, savings banks were restructured and most of them have become banking foundations that own a commercial bank, with the result of a more concentrated banking system. Apart from the direct impact of the outbreak of the Great Recession in mid-2007, the Spanish banking sector has suffered the consequences of the bursting of the property-market bubble resulting from the imbalances that built up in the preceding years of expansion. The Fund for Orderly Restructuring of the Banking Sector (FROB), created in June 2009, has been the first important crisis resolution tool, followed by changes in the regulatory framework for savings banks and the creation of a bad bank following a bail-out by European authorities in 2012. The authors provide an extensive discussion of the different policy actions and lessons learned from the Spanish crisis.

Lepetit, Meslier and Tarazi document the structure of the French banking system (Chap. 23, *Banking in France*) and the major developments since the mid-1980s with the deregulation process triggered by the Banking Act of 1984 and the broader reform of capital markets in 1985. Following these reforms, the French banking system has undergone a consolidation wave, resulting in a system dominated by six banking groups that also include insurance and wealth management subsidiaries, with three of them among the largest 20 European financial institutions. The 2007–8 global financial crisis and the subsequent sovereign debt crisis have led to significant changes in the level and the distribution of foreign exposures. Since 2010, French banks have reduced their involvement in eurozone countries and they have increased their expansion in other Organisation for Economic Cooperation and Development (OECD) countries (United States and Japan).

The final chapter in this section offers a comprehensive discussion of banking sector development in Central and Eastern Europe (Chap. 24, *Credit Institutions, Ownership and Bank Lending in Transition Economies*). Specifically, Haselmann, Wachtel and Sobott document the remarkable development of banking in the former transition economies and note that by the early years of the twenty-first century, the transition of banking sectors in Central and Eastern Europe (though not in many countries of the former Soviet Union) was largely complete. An important dimension of this transformation were foreign banks, mostly from Western Europe. However, while foreign banks were at the core of the transformation of banking systems in the region, they were also at the core of the credit boom that created financial fragilities, which amplified the crisis shock in 2008. As much as a story of foreign ownership, however, the story of banking in transition countries is also a story of substantial institution building, as documented by the authors. Having passed through the first post-transition boom-and-bust cycle, banking systems in the region face new challenges related to regulatory developments in the EU, the continuous weaknesses of some of the large multinational banks in the regions and political developments.

Looking Forward

The chapters of this Handbook document major trends across Europe's banking systems. They also show the uncertainty of future trends. Europe's banking systems still have to come to grips with a changed regulatory environment, a monetary environment of zero or negative interest rates undermining their profitability and increased competition from non-bank financial institutions. The British vote to exit the EU will provide another shock to the system, with possibly important changes in the financial landscape playing out in the next few years.

Banking research has received another boost with the recent crisis; access to bank-level and micro data has proven critical in pushing forward the research agenda. A close interaction between researchers, practitioners and policy makers is important to provide researchers with the necessary access to data and questions and provide practitioners and policy makers with rigorous analysis of practical and policy challenges.

References

Adams, R. B., & Mehran, H. (2012). Bank board structure, and performance: Evidence for large bank holding companies. *Journal of Financial Intermediation, 21*, 243–267.

Aizenman, J. (2009). *Financial crisis and the paradox of under- and over-regulation* (NBER working paper 15018).

Allen, F., & Gale, D. (2000). *Comparing financial systems*. Cambridge, MA: MIT Press.

Anguren Martín, R. & Marqués Sevillano, J. M. (2011). Cooperative and savings banks in Europe: Nature, challenges and perspectives. Available at SSRN: http://ssrn.com/abstract=1856966.

Battistini, N., Pagano, M., & Simonelli, S. (2014). Systemic risk and home bias in the euro area. *Economic Policy, 29*, 203–251.

Beck, T., Coyle, D., Dewatripont, M., Freixas, X., & Seabright, P. (2010). Bailing out the banks: Reconciling stability and competition (CEPR). Available at http://dev3.cepr.org/pubs/other/Bailing_out_the_banks.pdf

Beck, T., De Jonghe, O., & Schepens, G. (2013). Bank competition and stability: Cross-country heterogeneity. *Journal of Financial Intermediation, 22*(2), 218–244.

Beck, T., Carletti, E., & Goldstein, I., (2015). Financial institutions, markets and regulation: A survey. Mimeo.

Beltratti, A., & Stulz, R. M. (2012). The credit crisis around the globe: Why did some banks perform better? *Journal of Financial Economics, 105*(1), 1–17.

Campos, N., Coricelli, F., & Moretti, L. (2014). Economic growth and political integration: Synthetic counterfactuals evidence from Europe. Mimeo.

Campos, N., Coricelli, F., & Moretti, L. (2016). Economic growth and political integration: Estimating the benefits from membership in the European Union using synthetic counterfactuals. Mimeo.

Casu, B., Ferrari, A., Girardone, C., & Wilson, J. O. S. (2016). Integration, productivity and technological spillovers: Evidence for eurozone banking industries. *European Journal of Operational Research, 255*(3), 971–983.

European Central Bank. (2015). Report on financial structures. Available at https://www.ecb.europa.eu/pub/pdf/other/reportonfinancialstructures201510.en.pdf

European Systemic Risk Board. (2014). Is Europe overbanked? Reports of the Advisory Scientific Committee No. 4/June 2014. Available at https://www.esrb.europa.eu/pub/pdf/asc/Reports_ASC_4_1406.pdf

Financial Stability Board. (2012). Global shadow banking monitoring report. Available at http://www.fsb.org/wp-content/uploads/r_121118c.pdf

High-Level Expert Group on financial supervision in the EU. (2009). Report, (de Larosiére Report). Available at ec.europa.eu/internal_market/finances/docs/de_larosiere_report_en.pdf

Hoshi, T., & Kashyap, A. (2015). Will the U.S. and Europe avoid a lost decade? Lessons from Japan's postcrisis experience. *IMF Economic Review, 63*, 110–163.

McDonnell, B. (2013). Dampening financial regulatory cycles. *Florida Law Review, 65*, 1602–1608.

Mehran, H., Morrison, A., & Shapiro, J. (2011). Corporate Governance and banks: What have we learned from the financial crisis? Federal Reserve Bank of New York, Staff Report 502, June.

Schoenmaker, D. (2011, April). The financial trilemma. *Economics Letters, Elsevier, 111*(1), 57–59.

Véron, Nicolas. (2013). Banking nationalism and the European crisis. Bruegel. Available at https://piie.com/sites/default/files/publications/papers/veron20130627.pdf

2

Financial Structure

Sam Langfield and Marco Pagano

The financial structure of an economy is the set of institutions that channel resources from its savers to its investors, allocate them across alternative uses and enable investors to share risks and diversify their portfolios. These functions can be performed by capital markets (such as bond and stock markets) or by financial intermediaries (such as banks) that match savers and borrowers independently of markets.

Economists have long debated whether financial structure matters for the efficiency with which these functions are performed and therefore for real outcomes. In the absence of frictions, intermediaries have no comparative advantage. However, the real world is characterized by transactions costs owing to asymmetric information between users and providers of funds and to limited enforcement of contracts. In the presence of these frictions, comparative advantages can emerge: compared with markets, a financial structure dominated by banks performing direct intermediation can mitigate frictions—but

Useful comments were kindly provided by Franklin Allen, Thorsten Beck, Barbara Casu Lukac, Ashoka Mody, Andrei Sarychev and Nicolas Véron.

S. Langfield (✉)
European Systemic Risk Board, Frankfurt, Germany
e-mail: samlangfield@gmail.com

M. Pagano (✉)
Department of Economics and Statistics, University of Naples Federico II, Naples, Italy
e-mail: pagano56@gmail.com

T. Beck, B. Casu (eds.), *The Palgrave Handbook of European Banking*,
DOI 10.1057/978-1-137-52144-6_2

in some cases also exacerbate them. As such, the relative importance of banks and markets can substantially affect the quantity and the quality of the allocation of funding among firms and households, the stability of the financial system and, ultimately, productivity and economic growth. In view of vast differences in financial structure across countries, these effects are potentially sizeable: as we shall see, Europe features bank-based structures, while the USA, Canada and Australia are more market-based.

Europe's Financial Structure in Perspective

Empirical measures of financial structure capture the relative importance of different institutions in providing funding. To a first-order approximation, financial structure can be captured by the size of the banking sector relative to the size of equity and bond markets, where the former is measured by the total assets of domestic banks,[1] and the latter by the total market value of all listed shares on domestic stock exchanges and of outstanding domestic private debt securities.[2] Figure 2.1 plots this benchmark measure of financial structure from 1900 to 2011. Until around 1960, the financial structures of Germany and of the UK were similar to that of the USA. Since then, Germany and the UK have become more bank-based—a trend that accelerated in the late 1990s. By contrast, the USA's bank–market ratio has remained flat since 1995.

Figure 2.2 shows the same ratio for a cross-section of countries in 2011. According to this measure, European countries' financial structures are bank-based not only in comparison with the USA, but also with other developed economies such as Canada and Australia. Even Japan, which historically has been a paragon of bank-based intermediation, is less bank-based than Europe as of 2011. Similarly, developing economies such as Brazil and India are less bank-based than most European countries.

Underlying these trends is a sharp increase in the size of European banks, which began in earnest in the late 1990s. This increase was in turn driven by growth in the size of the largest banks. If the total assets of the largest 20 European banks had grown in line with nominal gross domestic product (GDP) from 1997, the European banking system as a whole would not have grown relative to nominal GDP, as shown in Fig. 2.3. In this counterfactual scenario, Europe's financial

[1] An alternative measure of banking sector size is total domestic private sector credit held by domestic banks (which excludes claims on non-residents, claims on the public sector and non-funding activities such as derivatives trading).

[2] Alternatively, capital markets can be measured by the volume of markets' liquidity services (such as the total value of transactions).

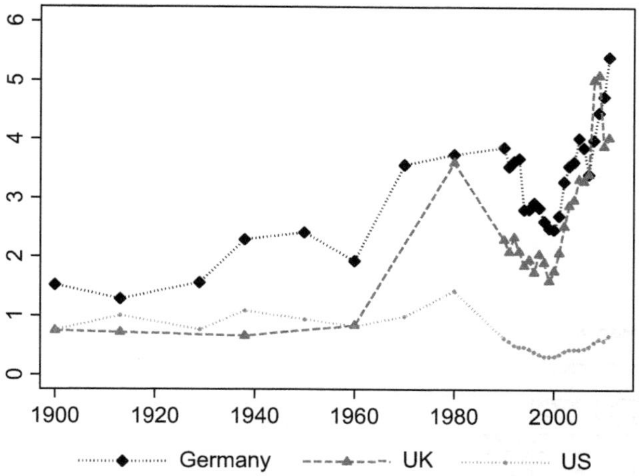

Fig. 2.1 Financial structure in Germany, the UK and the USA, 1900–2011
Note: The bank-market ratio is defined as the ratio of total bank assets to stock and private bond market capitalization, as in Langfield and Pagano (2016)
Sources: Rajan and Zingales (2003) and World Bank for stock and private bond market capitalization data (Čihák et al. 2012). German bank assets data are sourced from the Deutsche Bundesbank. UK bank assets data are sourced from Sheppard (1971) for 1880–1966 and from the Bank of England for 1977–2011. US bank assets data are sourced from the 'Statistical Abstract of the United States' for 1880, 1885 and 1890; from 'All-bank Statistics, United States, 1896–1955', published by the Board of Governors of the Federal Reserve System, for 1896–1939; from the 'Statistical Abstract of the United States' for 1940–1949; from the 'Statistical Abstract of the United States' and FDIC for 1950–1983; and from FDIC for 1984–2011

structure would have become more market-based. The fact that it did not is therefore entirely due to the largest 20 European banks. This insight implies that Europe's banking system also became more concentrated as it expanded.

The growth of the largest banks—particularly, but not exclusively, in Europe—not only reflects increased lending to domestic businesses, but also the expansion of other services (Pagano et al. 2014). This expansion occurred primarily in five areas. First, banks lent more to households, especially secured against residential property, as Jordà et al. (2016) document. Second, European banks expanded both sides of their balance sheet outside of their home region, particularly in America, as shown by Lane and Milesi-Ferretti (2007) and Shin (2012). Third, trading with other banks, especially derivatives and interbank loans, inflated the aggregate bank balance sheet in gross terms. Fourth, banks acquired non-banking financial businesses such as insurance and asset management. Fifth, after the onset of the financial crisis, banks located in stressed euro-area countries increased their holdings of government securities, especially those issued by their domestic sovereigns (European Systemic Risk Board 2015).

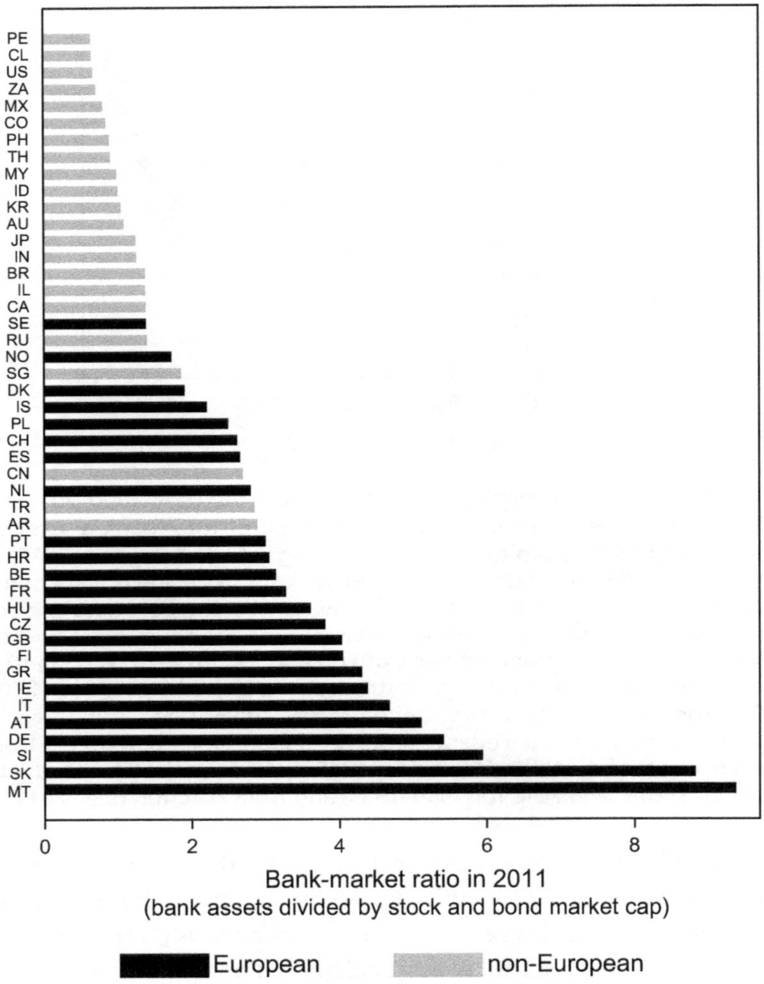

Fig. 2.2 Financial structure in 2011 in European and non-European countries
Note: The bank–market ratio is defined as the ratio of total bank assets to stock and private bond market capitalization, as in Langfield and Pagano (2016)
Source: World Bank (Čihák et al. 2012); see footnote to Fig. 2.1 for sources of bank assets data

It is important to include these additional activities in a thorough analysis of financial structure, as they determine how banks interact with each other and with financial markets, non-financial firms and policy makers—and ultimately the amount of systemic risk that bank distress may generate. Nevertheless, as a complementary measure of financial structure, one can zoom in on domestic non-financial firms' sources of external funding in order to gauge their reliance on banks. Financial accounts (or "flow-of-funds") data—shown in Table 2.1—provide a breakdown of firms' liabilities into publicly listed shares, other equity,

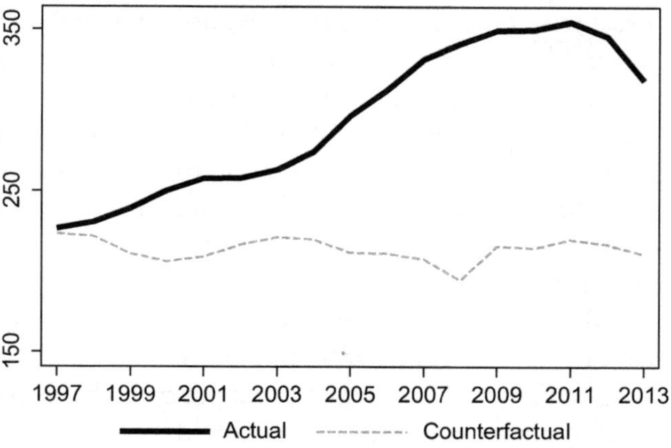

Fig. 2.3 Actual and "counterfactual" total EU banking system assets as a percentage of GDP
Notes: "Actual" plots actual observations on the ratio of total EU banking system assets to GDP. "Counterfactual" is the same, except that the assets of the largest 20 EU banks are assumed to grow in line with nominal GDP from 1997. The largest 20 EU banks are BNPP, BBVA, Santander, Barclays, Commerzbank, Danske, Deutsche, Dexia, HSBC, I`NG, Intesa, KBC, LBG, Natixis, RBS, SEB, Société Générale, Standard Chartered, Svenska Handelsbanken and UniCredit. The denominator is the sum of the nominal GDPs of the nine EU countries home to at least one top 20 bank (i.e. BE, DK, DE, ES, FR, IT, NL, SE and the UK). The nominal GDPs of the non-EA countries (DK, SE and the UK) are converted into euros using end-year exchange rates
Sources: Bloomberg for bank-level total assets data; ECB for exchange rate data. See Langfield and Pagano (2016) for further detail)

Table 2.1 Liabilities of non-financial corporations in 2013 (€tn)

	USA	Japan	Eurozone	UK	Sweden
Listed shares	12.6	3.1	4.3	1.7	0.4
Other equity	11.1	1.9	9.6	1.1	1.0
Debt securities	3.5	0.5	1.1	0.5	0.1
Loans	4.7	2.4	9.2	1.2	0.6

Sources: Financial accounts of the Federal Reserve Board; Bank of Japan; ECB; Bank of England; Riksbank

debt securities and loans. Like Figs. 2.1 and 2.2, Table 2.1 sheds light on the US's market-based financial structure: only 20 % of US firms' external funding comes from loans; the bulk is instead made up of marketable securities (i.e. listed shares and debt securities).[3] By contrast, nearly two-thirds of Eurozone firms' external funding comes from loans.

[3] Other equity, which includes inside ("closely held") equity, is excluded for the purposes of this cross-country comparison of external funding sources.

Our first measure of financial structure—banks' assets divided by the market value of tradeable stocks and private debt securities—suggests that the financial structures of many European countries became more bank-based between the late 1990s and the early 2010s. The same insight can be inferred from our second measure of financial structure, based on flow of funds data. Figure 2.4 shows that Eurozone firms' reliance on loans for funding increased from just over 50 % in 1999 to nearly two-thirds in 2013. The share of loans in UK firms' liabilities also increased after the late 1990s, albeit from a lower base. This upward drift in Europe contrasts with the downward trend in the USA and Japan between the mid-1980s and 2013.

Loans are used in Table 2.1 and Fig. 2.4 as a proxy for bank-based intermediation because they are mostly originated and held by banks, whereas marketable securities are widely held by other financial institutions and households. Who-to-whom financial account matrices for the end of 2013 published by the ECB reveal that banks supply €4.3tn of firms' loan liabilities; other non-bank financial institutions supply €1.3tn. Similarly, 13 % of UK firms' loans are held by non-bank financial institutions.

Globally, non-bank institutions comprise an increasing share of the financial system, particularly in the aftermath of the 2008–09 banking crisis.

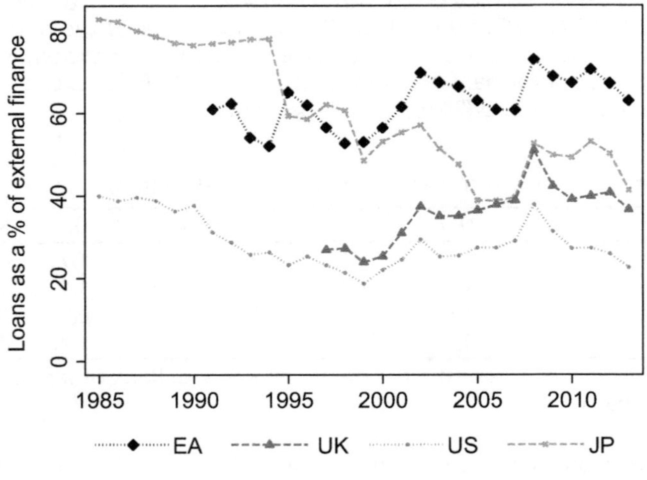

Fig. 2.4 Loans as a percentage of external finance
Notes: "External finance" is defined as the sum of listed shares, debt securities and loans. It excludes "other equity", as this category includes inside (closely held) equity. The Eurozone series refers to 19 Eurozone countries, except 1991–98 where the Eurozone series is proxied by German data from the Deutsche Bundesbank
Sources: Financial accounts of the Federal Reserve Board; Bank of Japan; ECB; Deutsche Bundesbank; Bank of England

The "non-bank financial institutions" category is a motley one, comprising mutual funds, pension funds, hedge funds, insurance companies, special-purpose vehicles, and private equity and venture capital firms. Most of these institutions can either be considered "bank-like", and therefore effectively a component of the banking system, or instead an integral part of the capital markets ecosystem. As such, the prevalence of non-bank financial institutions in developed economies does not pose a challenge for the banks–markets typology of financial structure.

The challenge is rather one of proper attribution of nominal "non-banks" to the banks–markets typology, which depends on the nature of the economic function carried out by such entities. For example, pension funds mostly invest in marketable securities traded on exchanges; private equity and venture capital firms are funded by illiquid long-term liabilities and depend on the availability of initial public offerings in deep equity markets (Black and Gilson 1998). By contrast, other non-bank financial institutions, such as special-purpose vehicles and bank loan mutual funds, form part of the so-called "shadow banking" system: they engage in maturity transformation (by funding long-term illiquid assets with short-term liquid liabilities) and, sometimes, feature high leverage (by funding assets with minimal equity)—two quintessential features of banking. For the purposes of the banks–markets typology of financial structure, such "shadow banks" should be assigned to the banking sector, broadly defined. Owing to the heterogeneity of the "non-bank financial institutions" category in the financial accounts, micro data on these institutions' economic functions would help researchers to refine measures of financial structure. Meanwhile, in the absence of better data, the measures presented in Figs. 2.1, 2.2 and 2.4 are useful first-order approximations of financial structure.

Determinants of Financial Structure

Between the late 1990s and the early 2010s, Europe's already bank-based financial structure became even more dependent on banks, while the USA became slightly more market-based. What explains this divergence? To put this question in context, it is necessary to consider the determinants of financial structure more generally.

The Role of Comparative Advantage in Determining Financial Structure

Financial structure should optimally reflect the comparative advantages of banks and capital markets in mitigating financial frictions (Allen and Gale 2000). According to this view, financial structures develop endogenously as the most efficient institutional arrangements to supply external funding in the presence of incomplete markets.

Banks are likely to have a comparative advantage in mitigating the financial frictions arising from certain types of informational and contract enforceability problems. On the informational front, banks specialize in gathering data and processing information ("screening") before originating loans, and in subsequently servicing loans ("monitoring"). This specialization in information processing is shared by some institutions in the capital markets ecosystem: venture capital firms, for example, exploit privately acquired information. Banks' information-processing specialization can be distinguished from that of market-oriented institutions such as venture capital firms in two ways. First, many banks act as relationship lenders: over time, relationship banks accumulate soft information about borrower types, mitigating information asymmetries (Boot 2000) that would otherwise lead to adverse selection and credit rationing (Stiglitz and Weiss 1981). By contrast, venture capital is typically a one-shot process of acquisition and liquidation of an equity stake. Second, banks are more suited than venture capital firms to cater to many small and medium sized firms because the issuance of tradeable stocks and debt securities entails a prohibitive fixed cost owing to listing and underwriting fees and disclosure and compliance costs. Small firms may also find it impossible to develop a liquid market for their securities, owing to economies of scale in market liquidity.

Banks can overcome the difficulty of contract enforcement in countries where property and creditor rights are weak and bankruptcy procedures ill-defined and inefficient. Contract enforcement is typically most problematic in civil law countries, particularly those with French legal origin, owing to weaker investor protection (La Porta et al. 1998). As a result, civil law countries tend to be characterized by more concentrated ownership of firms and thinner capital markets (La Porta et al. 1997). Banks have a comparative advantage in these environments because they are able to demand collateral, which mitigates losses in the event of default. Seizing and liquidating collateral would entail high coordination costs for bondholders; as such, most market-based finance is unsecured. This reasoning implies that financial structure is endogenous to the industrial structure of the real economy (Carlin and Mayer 2003; Allen et al. 2007). An industrial structure with many capital-intensive firms may be more efficiently served by a bank-based financial structure, as these firms tend to have more tangible collateral. By contrast, an economy intensive in firms that use human and other intangible capital in production may be better served by a market-based financial structure.

Conversely, markets may be more efficient than banks when enforcement problems are less severe. They are also more efficient in situations where transparency is more important for financing, as tradeable securities aggregate investors' decentralized information in a price signal; by contrast, in the absence of price signals, bank managers condition their lending decisions on the information acquired from screening and monitoring. Markets are also at an advantage when firms have established a solid track record (Diamond 1991): mature firms are typically more transparent, obviating the need for specialist screeners and monitors such as relationship banks.

Capital markets can to some extent overcome information asymmetries by virtue of their symbiotic relationship with specialized financial institutions such as venture capital firms, investment banks and financial analysts. Like relationship banks, these institutions perform the function of delegated screeners and monitors, allowing markets to be efficient even in the presence of information asymmetry. Venture capital firms, for example, specialize in screening and monitoring young firms with high growth potential. More generally, markets tend to be better financiers of innovation where there is a wide diversity of prior beliefs about the expected value of new projects, since decentralized market-based financial structures permit optimistic investors to finance projects and pessimistic investors to "agree to disagree" (Allen and Gale 1999). Disagreement is most likely for potentially transformational (but uncertain) general purpose technological innovations, which typify many recent innovations (Brynjolfsson and McAfee 2014). Perhaps because of this, most innovations occur in countries with market-based financial structures (Allen 1993). Among capital markets, stock markets are best suited to provide external financing to firms engaging in high-risk research and development: equity contracts are typically optimal to fund such firms, since the payoff to the equity-holder is strictly increasing in the value of the firm (Casamatta 2003). Moreover, these firms typically do not have access to pledgeable collateral preferred by debt-holders (Williamson 1988). Therefore, stock market development should be expected to proceed in synchronization with the expansion of innovative sectors in the real economy (Hsu et al. 2014).

The Role of Public Policy in Determining Financial Structure

These insights regarding the comparative advantages of markets versus banks shed light on long-term changes in financial structures, but they cannot explain Europe's shift towards a more bank-based financial structure between the late 1990s and the early 2010s. The shift has taken place in tandem with improvements in the strength of political institutions and the quality of legal enforcement; with a relative decline in tangible capital-intensive industries such as heavy manufacturing; and with an increase in research and development. These structural changes would lead one to expect Europe to have become less, not more, bank-based. What explains this apparent tension between theory and reality?

Financial structure not only reflects the comparative advantages of banks and capital markets in mitigating financial frictions; it is also influenced by public policy and the politics that govern its formulation (Calomiris and Haber 2014). Policy is particularly active in the regulation and supervision of banks, owing to the peculiar severity of moral hazard problems in banking. Banks borrow from a large pool of unsophisticated and dispersed depositors, creating risk-shifting incentives for banks' shareholders and managers. These moral hazard problems, coupled with banks' intrinsic fragility stemming from their maturity transformation, explain why public policy typically protects depositors with insurance schemes.

Deposit insurance schemes create their own moral hazard by shifting insolvency risk onto taxpayers. This justifies the prudential regulation and supervision of banks, curbing their risk-shifting by requiring minimum levels of equity and funding liquidity. Bank regulation and supervision might be inadequate, however, given the strength of bank managers' and shareholders' risk-shifting incentives, and managers' ability to game regulations and hoodwink or capture supervisors. Capital requirements, for example, are often softened by banks, especially the largest ones, by manipulating the internal models used to calculate risk weights (Mariathasan and Merrouche 2014; Behn et al. 2014).

Moral hazard is a challenge for policymakers and bank supervisors worldwide. However, the response of Europe's policymakers and bank supervisors to moral hazard problems was particularly weak in the early years of the twenty-first century, and in some cases even exacerbated the moral hazard inherent in banking. This is witnessed by the fact that Eurozone banks, and to a lesser extent UK banks, benefited from a greater reduction in funding costs owing to government support than US banks, as shown by Lambert et al. (2014). What explains this enhanced preferential treatment bestowed on EU banks?

First, the expansion of banking in the Eurozone occurred against the background of financial integration following monetary unification. In this context, European governments nurtured the growth of large universal banks as national champions—an attitude that Véron (2013) labels "banking nationalism". Encouraged by politicians, large universal banks attempted to outgrow each other in expectation of a wave of cross-border acquisitions that never materialized. It never materialized precisely because governments protected national champions against hostile takeover attempts by foreign banks. Governments also practiced banking nationalism by sheltering domestic banks against competition from foreign ones, maintaining entry barriers with respect to non-bank financial institutions and capital markets, and acquiescing in the build-up of leverage and risk before 2008. Perhaps most strikingly, politicians cajoled banks to inflate their balance sheets by purchasing central and regional government debt. As a result, Eurozone banks' government bond portfolios exhibited pronounced home bias: in 2008, the fraction of banks' own-country sovereign bond holdings to total sovereign bond holdings stood at 80 % (European Systemic Risk Board 2015). This fraction actually increased during the crisis, to a peak of 95 % in 2013, as governments in vulnerable countries desperately sought buyers for their debt (Altavilla et al. 2015; Battistini et al. 2014; Becker and Ivashina 2014a; De Marco and Machiavelli 2014; Ongena et al. 2016).

Second, bank supervisors helped to promote national champions by treating banks leniently. Before the advent in 2014 of the Single Supervisory Mechanism (SSM) in the Eurozone, bank supervision was exclusively a national purview, thereby subjecting supervisors to greater domestic political influence. For example, a broad audit conducted by the Central Bank of Ireland concluded that the Irish Financial Services Regulatory Authority had been reluctant to exercise its supervisory powers, with an attitude to enforcement that favoured "voluntary compliance" characterized by "deference and diffidence to the regulated entities" (Honohan 2010). Diffidence to banks was not exclusive to Eurozone supervisors, however. In a speech in 2006, John Tiner, then head of the UK Financial Services Authority (FSA), argued that "firms' managements—not their regulators—are responsible for identifying and controlling risks" (Tiner 2006). Unsurprisingly, following the failure of Northern Rock—a bank that had built up excessive maturity mismatch—a review by the internal audit division of the FSA concluded that the authority had failed in its responsibility to identify and control risks (FSA 2008).

Third, governments' policy of banking nationalism was facilitated and exacerbated by inadequate regulation, both in terms of prudential rules and resolution frameworks. In 2006, the recast Capital Requirements Directive of the European Union (EU) allowed "advanced" banks to use approved internal models to calculate their own risk weights. The advent of internal models permitted supervisors to exercise "light-touch" or "principles-based" supervision (Caprio 2013): after swift approval, the subsequent use of models was barely monitored, allowing banks to manipulate the risk weights associated with advanced internal ratings based portfolios (Mariathasan and Merrouche 2014; Behn et al. 2014). At the same time, European authorities exhibited no willingness to create a credible resolution framework. Only in the aftermath of the crisis did policy makers establish the Bank Recovery and Resolution Directive (BRRD) in the EU and the Single Resolution Mechanism (SRM) in the Eurozone. Before these policy initiatives, supervisors had limited legal powers to wind-down distressed banks: between 2008 and 2012, fewer than 100 EU banks failed, compared with nearly 500 resolutions of US banks by the FDIC.[4] A low rate of bank failures during a systemic banking crisis hints at forbearance by supervisors of undercapitalized banks. Rather than resolving insolvent banks, European governments rescued them by bailing out bondholders or by facilitating mergers with (or acquisitions by) other banks,[5] despite concerns regarding excessive concentration and lack of competition.[6] Moreover, by exacerbating banks' moral hazard, supervisory forbearance is likely to have contributed to excess risk-taking (Marques et al. 2013).

Fourth, local politicians in some European countries had a direct interest in supporting publicly owned or controlled "regional champions". In Germany, this applies to the savings banks (*Sparkassen*), owned by their respective municipalities or counties, and regional banks (*Landesbanken*), many of which are major universal banks with nationwide operations (Hau and Thum 2009). In Spain, the management of savings banks (*cajas*) is closely connected with local politicians, which Garicano (2012) sees as a factor in Spanish supervisors' protracted forbearance towards banks with bad loans to households and real estate developers. In Italy, political influence on banks is also pervasive, albeit more indirect: politicians, especially local ones, affect the governance of "banking foundations" (*fondazioni bancarie*), which in turn have important stakes in the ownership of many banks.

[4] Sources: Open Economics' Failed Bank Tracker (http://openeconomics.net/failed-bank-tracker/) and FDIC. Although the FDIC mostly resolves small banks with assets under $100m, it occasionally resolves medium and large banks. The largest bank resolved by the FDIC is Washington Mutual Bank, which held $307bn of assets at the time of its closure in September 2008. Only about 20 banks in the EU are larger than Washington Mutual; over 7,000 EU banks are smaller, and could feasibly be resolved by a European transplant of the FDIC.

[5] For example, Banco di Napoli, a distressed publicly owned bank, was sold by the Italian government in 1997 for a nominal sum to Banca Nazionale del Lavoro and the Istituto Nazionale delle Assicurazioni, and resold in 2002 by these banks to the Sanpaolo IMI (which later merged with Banca Intesa). Similarly, the UK Treasury facilitated the merger of Lloyds with the ailing HBOS in September 2008, overruling the competition concerns raised by the Office of Fair Trading by not referring the case to the Competition Commission. In 2008–09, the Irish government brushed aside the Irish Competition Authority to promote mergers among distressed Irish banks. Once Spain's property bubble burst in 2008, many of the *cajas* that had funded the housing boom were distressed or insolvent. The Banco de España's rescue strategy was to merge them with other banks. Seven *cajas* merged into a single entity—Bankia—in December 2010. Bankia was subsequently recapitalized by the Spanish government in May 2012.

[6] Between August 2008 and February 2014, the EU Commission received 440 requests from EU member states to provide state aid to financial institutions. The EU Commission did not object to most (413) of these requests, although state aid approvals often entail bank restructuring requirements.

The Real Effects of Financial Structure

We have argued that financial structure is determined both by the comparative advantages of banks and markets and by public policies. The trend toward greater bank-based intermediation in Europe was supported by policies such as a weak resolution framework, supervisory forbearance with respect to distressed banks, artificial barriers to the entry of non-banks, and public ownership and control of banks. But does the resulting difference in financial structure have any bearing on the real economy in terms of its growth or stability?

To answer this question, researchers must identify changes and cross-country differences in the determinants of financial structure, and trace the causal impact of financial structure upon real economic outcomes. The difficulty of this second step lies in the potential reverse causality running from the real economy to financial structure. For example, an economy well-positioned to generate technological innovation (for instance, with advanced research institutions) may give rise to a market-based financial structure. Depending on the needs of the real economy, a bank-based or market-based financial structure may be more effective in promoting the efficient allocation of funding; thus financial structure may optimally adapt to the characteristics of the real economy, rather than simply responding to changes or differences in legal institutions, rules or enforcement.

The Effects of Financial Structure on Long-Run Growth

In view of this potential endogeneity, it might not seem surprising that Levine (2002) finds no relationship between financial structure and long-run growth in output per capita in World Bank data spanning 1980–1995. After carrying out many robustness checks, Levine concludes that "the results are overwhelming. There is no cross-country empirical support for either the market-based or the bank-based views. Neither bank-based nor market-based financial systems are particularly effective at promoting growth."

Recent evidence suggests that these conclusions do not hold when Levine's regressions are estimated on more recent vintages of the World Bank's global financial development dataset (described in Čihák et al. 2012). Pagano et al. (2014) re-estimate the cross-sectional growth regressions in Levine (2002), and find that economies with bank-based financial structures experience lower economic growth over 1989–2011—precisely the period over which Europe's financial structure became more bank-based. Similarly, Claessens (2016) reports descriptive statistics suggesting that the sensitivity of economic growth to banking sector development declined and perhaps even reversed around the turn of the century. Langfield and Pagano (2016) find corroborating evidence in panel regressions with 45 countries and non-overlapping five-year periods. They also control for a wider set of variables, including measures of regulatory reform to instrument for the potential endogeneity of financial structure to economic growth. Their result is robust to the exclusion of observations over 2008–11, and to alternative measures of financial structure.

In investigating the effect of financial structure on real economic growth, these papers do not distinguish between growth in productivity and growth of the capital input in production: as highlighted by Pagano (1993), financial development can contribute to economic growth both by improving the allocation of resources, raising the pace of technical progress and hence total factor productivity (TFP); and by channeling more capital from savers to investors, thereby boosting firms' investment.

Several studies suggest that financial structure affects economic growth especially through the first of these two channels—by improving TFP. In this vein, Demirgüç-Kunt et al. (2013) find that capital markets become increasingly important as economies approach the technological frontier. Brown et al. (2013) study a broad sample of firms in 32 countries and find that strong shareholder protection and better access to stock market financing lead to substantially higher long-run rates of investment in research and development (R&D), particularly in small firms, but are unimportant for fixed capital investment. Credit market development, by contrast, has a modest positive impact on fixed investment but no impact on R&D. One explanation for this finding is that market-based financial structures facilitate venture capital firms (Black and Gilson 1998; Jeng and Wells 2000), which boost real innovation by reducing entrepreneurs' external finance premium (Kortum and Lerner 2000; Popov and Roosenboom 2013) and by harnessing venture capitalists' expertise (Hellmann and Puri 2000; Kerr et al. 2014). These findings square with the notion that legal rules promoting market-based financial structures, improving access to external equity funding and supporting innovative firms tend to facilitate risky, intangible investments that are not easily financed with debt.

These findings do not preclude that deeper capital markets boost firms' real investment also by relaxing their external finance constraint. The relaxation of restrictions on foreign investors' share purchases correlates with increases in private investment. In a sample of 11 developing countries that liberalized their stock markets, Henry (2000) finds that the growth rate of private investment rose above the median pre-liberalization investment rate one year later in nine countries, two years later in ten, and three years later in eight. The average growth rate of private investment in the three years following liberalization exceeds the mean of Henry's sample by 22 percentage points.

A related reason as to why bank-based financial structures may be less conducive to productivity-enhancing investments is that banks have increasingly financed households' and firms' real estate purchases and related construction activity, rather than productivity-enhancing innovation. In a sample of 17 advanced economies, Jordà et al. (2016) document that the share of real estate lending in total bank lending rose from 40 % in 1970 to 55 % in 2011—at a time when bank balance sheets as a whole were also expanding. Certain EU countries experienced a particularly large increase: the share in Spain went from 12 % to 58 %; Italy from 29 % to 48 %; and France from 33 % to 47 %. Lane (2013) and Lane and McQuade (2014) document that, before the crisis, international capital flows in the Eurozone were associated with abnormal expansions of credit in the Eurozone periphery, fuelling property market bubbles. Benigno and Fornaro (2014) and Benigno et al. (2015) characterize this mechanism as a "financial resource curse": sustained current account deficits induce a shift of resources towards non-tradable sectors such as property construction, hampering productivity.

The rising importance of property finance in banks' balance sheets is particularly impressive considering that over the same time interval the composition of large banks' balance sheets was also shifting towards new financial instruments such as derivatives.[7] What explains the rising importance of property finance on banks' balance sheets? Residential mortgages in particular are relatively standardized and generally well collateralized. As such, they are easily scalable. Bank managers who pursue size as an objective per se—either to extract rent from TBTF subsidies for the benefit of the bank's shareholders (O'Hara and Shaw 1990), to extract outsized compensation from shareholders (Bliss and Rosen 2001), or to loot from both society and shareholders à la Akerlof and Romer (1993)—may turn to their bank's residential mortgage book. By relying on real estate collateral, banks can economise on the screening costs necessary to evaluate firms' business plans. The availability of such collateral encourages competing banks to engage in "lazy" behaviour, in which they do not exert the socially efficient level of screening (Manove et al. 2001). Since the 1990s, such behaviour has been amplified by securitization, as real estate loans, being highly standardized, are particularly well suited to being funded by asset-backed securities.

[7] Derivatives were a negligible part of banks' activities in the early 1990s, but by 2011 comprised 35–40 % of the balance sheets of institutions such as Deutsche Bank and Barclays. (Like other European banks, Deutsche Bank and Barclays report under IFRS accounting standards. Hoenig (2013) discusses the differences between IFRS and GAAP accounting standards, particularly with respect to the treatment of derivatives.)

Banks' proclivity for real estate financing was encouraged by preferential regulatory treatment. The first EU Capital Requirements Directive (CRD), which entered into force in 2000 to consolidate seven pre-existing banking directives implementing the Basel I accord, stipulated a risk weight of 50 % for mortgages secured on residential property.[8] Loans to corporates, by contrast, were assigned a risk weight of 100 %. Subsequently, Europe pioneered the implementation of the Basel II accord: a recast CRD, adopted in 2006, provided for a lower risk weight of 35 % for residential mortgages under the standardized approach,[9] with the option for "advanced" banks to instead use approved internal models to calculate their own risk weights, allowing them to game prudential requirements.[10]

The Effects of Financial Structure on the Volatility of Economic Output

Besides affecting long-run economic growth, financial structure can also affect the volatility of output and its sensitivity to financial crises. Regressions estimated by Langfield and Pagano (2016) show that an increase in a country's bank-dependence is associated with lower real GDP per capita growth during housing market crises than in countries with market-based structures. No such amplification effect is present during stock market crises, highlighting the key role that house prices play in determining the value of the collateral attached to bank loans: when house prices drop, banks are constrained in their ability to provide new funding to profitable projects. This amplification mechanism is more powerful in bank-based financial structures than in market-based ones, owing to banks' higher leverage and the elevated importance of housing-related assets on banks' balance sheets (Jordà et al. 2016).

Langfield and Pagano (2016) document that this amplification effect is asymmetric: bank-based financial structures amplify the recessionary effect of housing crises, but not the expansionary effect of booms. Real economic activity responds asymmetrically to the tightening and relaxation of the borrowing

---

[8] See Article 43 of CRD I (2000). In that directive, mortgage-backed securities carried the same risk weight as unsecuritized mortgages. However, in the USA, mortgage-backed securities issued or guaranteed by government-sponsored agencies (such as Fannie Mae or Freddie Mac) were assigned a preferential risk weight, incentivizing the development of the MBS market (Acharya et al. 2011).

[9] See Articles 78-83 and Annex XI of CRD II (2006) regarding the standardized approach. Note that the provision of a 35 % risk weight for residential mortgages remains in place in CRR IV (see Article 125), which entered into force in 2013. Exposures to corporates, by contrast, are assigned higher risk weights, except for corporates in the highest credit quality step, which receive a risk weight of 20 %.

[10] See Articles 84-89 and Annex XII of CRD II (2006) regarding the advanced internal ratings approach.

constraints arising from changes in the price of real estate. To see this, suppose that good projects, if financed, boost productivity and therefore output growth. When the typical firm is not credit-constrained, it is able to fund all of its good projects, so that its marginal project has low productivity in expectation. Instead, when banks and firms are up against a leverage constraint, many good projects go unfunded—such that the marginal project has high productivity in expectation. This implies asymmetry: one euro less of lending has a greater impact on average productivity in bad times than good times. Hence, a drop in the value of collateral has a larger impact on real output than an increase of the same magnitude. Collateral fire sales are an additional reason for the asymmetry: when housing prices drop, banks simultaneously deleverage by selling collateral, and prompt borrowers to do the same. These fire sales in turn feed the house price collapse, and induce banks to deleverage even further (Shleifer and Vishny 2011; Greenwood et al. 2015)—a vicious cycle with strong recessionary effects.

These insights are consistent with the "spare tire" view of capital markets, namely the idea that security market financing acts as a stabilizing factor when the supply of bank credit contracts. Because of this substitution effect, financial structures with well-developed capital markets tend to be associated with less severe fluctuations in the provision of external finance and therefore in aggregate output. Evidence that firms turn to the bond market to substitute for scarce bank loans is provided by Kashyap et al. (1993), who show that following a monetary tightening non-financial corporations tend to issue relatively more commercial paper. More recently, Becker and Ivashina (2014b) examine new debt issuances across the business cycle, and find evidence of substitution from loans to bonds during times of tight monetary policy, tight lending standards, high levels of non-performing loans, and low bank equity prices. Gambacorta et al. (2014) and Claessens (2016) show that in recessions accompanied by financial crises the impact on GDP is on average approximately three times more severe in bank-based economies than in market-based ones—although they also find evidence that healthy banks are able to mitigate adverse shocks during mild recessions. Levine et al. (2016) provide microeconomic evidence that during banking crises stock markets provide an alternative corporate financing channel capable of mitigating the severity of crises: using firm-level data from 36 countries for the period 1990–2011, they find that banking crises have smaller adverse effects on measures of firm performance in countries with stronger shareholder protection laws. However, even in market-based financial structures, most small and medium firms have no access to the bond and stock markets, due to the fixed costs typically associated with security issuance (such as underwriting fees, disclosure costs and listing fees), as well as to their limited track record and greater opacity: as a result, firms that issue bonds tend to be larger and of higher credit quality (Denis and Mihov 2003). This implies that, even though capital market financing may act as a "spare tire" for larger firms, their mitigating role tends to be more limited for smaller ones.

Conclusion

This chapter has discussed the nature of financial structure, its determinants, and its interactions with the real economy. The starting point was a set of stylized facts about the evolution of financial structure in advanced economies over recent decades. Since financial structure is defined as the set of institutions that channel resources from savers to investors, it can be measured in two ways: from the perspective of savers (by quantifying the relative size of banks and capital markets), or from the perspective of investors (by observing the source of firms' external funding). On both measures, European countries are more bank-based than most advanced economies. Moreover, the extent of Europe's bank-dependence increased between the 1990s and 2011.

Financial structure is influenced by legal institutions and by industrial structure. Banks thrive when contract enforcement is weak—often in civil law countries with inefficient judiciaries. To overcome enforcement problems, banks demand collateral from borrowers. Economies with an abundance of tangible, pledgeable collateral are therefore amenable to banking. Banks also have a comparative advantage when economies consist of small, opaque firms, as banks are able to acquire information about borrower type from a sustained borrower–lender relationship.

Trends in Europe since the 1990s—with stronger political institutions, a declining manufacturing sector, and growth among research-intensive and large firms—are at odds with the coincident shift towards bank-based intermediation. This apparent tension can be explained by the role of public policy in influencing financial structure. In the early 2000s, European governments' implicit guarantees of bank creditors were particularly pronounced, reflecting an inadequate supervisory, regulatory and resolution architecture, and a tendency by politicians to see domestic banks as regional and national champions in need of protection from capital markets and foreign competitors.

Financial structure that is shaped by public policy choices, rather than just banks' and capital markets' comparative advantages, can affect the performance of the real economy. Early empirical results on the impact of financial structure on economic growth found no such effect, but including data since

1995—when pertinent policy choices were made—generates a statistically significant negative relationship between financial structure and economic growth. This result is robust to instrumenting for the endogeneity of financial structure to economic growth. Moreover, recent empirical work suggests that bank-based financial structures are associated with greater macroeconomic volatility owing to their more extensive use of leverage and concentrated exposure to house prices. Firms' external financing constraints are more likely to bind as capital markets are too thin to adequately substitute for contracting bank credit supply, unlike in market-based structures.

Two important policy prescriptions follow from this analysis. First, do no harm. By mollycoddling domestic banks, governments and supervisors distorted banks' incentives, setting the stage for moral hazard and excessive risk-taking. Second, remove barriers to the development of capital markets. Capital markets smooth aggregate fluctuations by providing a "spare tire" for firms' access to external finance. Equity markets in particular are well suited to fund innovative, research-intensive firms with high growth potential.

Reassuringly, policy is now heading in the right direction. Moral hazard in banking is mitigated by improved bank regulation and resolution frameworks; in the Eurozone, supervision and resolution powers now reside with supranational authorities. In parallel, the EU Commission has committed to delivering a European "capital markets union" (CMU), with the intention of developing pan-EU securities markets to reduce Europe's dependence on bank funding. The evidence presented in this chapter suggests that these recent policy initiatives can help to rebalance Europe's bank-based financial structure.

References

Acharya, V., Richardson, M., Van Nieuwerburgh, S., & White, L. (2011). *Guaranteed to fail: Fannie Mae, Freddie Mac, and the debacle of mortgage finance*. Princeton: Princeton University Press.

Akerlof, G., & Romer, P. (1993). Looting: The economic underworld of bankruptcy for profit. *Brookings Papers on Economic Activity, 24*(2), 1–74.

Allen, F. (1993). Stock markets and resource allocation. In C. Mayer & X. Vives (Eds.), *Capital markets and financial intermediation*. Cambridge: Cambridge University Press.

Allen, F., & Gale, D. (1999). Diversity of opinion and the financing of new technologies. *Journal of Financial Intermediation, 8*, 68–89.

Allen, F., & Gale, D. (2000). *Comparing financial systems*. Cambridge, MA: MIT Press.

Allen, F., Bartiloro, L., & Kowalewski, O. (2007). *Does economic structure determine financial structure?* AFA 2007 Chicago meetings paper.
Altavilla, C., Pagano, M., & Simonelli, S. (2016). Bank exposures and sovereign stress transmission. European Systemic Risk Board working paper no. 11.
Battistini, N., Pagano, M., & Simonelli, S. (2014). Systemic risk, sovereign yields and bank exposures in the euro crisis. *Economic Policy, 29*(78), 203–251.
Becker, B., & Ivashina, V. (2014a). *Financial repression in the European sovereign debt crisis*. Swedish House of Finance Research paper no. 14–13.
Becker, B., & Ivashina, V. (2014b). Cyclicality of credit supply: Firm level evidence. *Journal of Monetary Economics, 62*, 76–93.
Behn, M., Haselmann, R. F. H., & Vig, V. (2014). *The limits of model-based regulation*. SAFE working paper no. 75.
Benigno, G., & Fornaro, L. (2014). The financial resource curse. *Scandinavian Journal of Economics, 116*(1), 58–86.
Benigno, G., Converse, N., & Fornaro, L. (2015). Large capital inflows, sectoral allocation, and economic performance. *Journal of International Money and Finance, 55*, 60–87.
Black, B., & Gilson, R. (1998). Venture capital and the structure of capital markets: Banks versus stock markets. *Journal of Financial Economics, 47*(3), 243–277.
Bliss, R., & Rosen, R. (2001). CEO compensation and bank mergers. *Journal of Financial Economics, 61*(1), 107–138.
Boot, A. (2000). Relationship banking: What do we know? *Journal of Financial Intermediation, 9*(1), 7–25.
Brown, J., Martinsson, G., & Petersen, B. (2013). Law, stock markets and innovation. *Journal of Finance, 68*(4), 1517–1549.
Brynjolfsson, E., & McAfee, A. (2014). *The second machine age: Work, progress, and prosperity in a time of brilliant technologies*. New York: W. W. Norton & Company.
Calomiris, C. W., & Haber, S. H. (2014). *Fragile by design: The political origins of banking crises and scarce credit*. Princeton: Princeton University Press.
Caprio, G. (2013). *Financial regulation after the crisis: How did we get here, and how do we get out?* LSE Financial Markets Group special paper no. 226).
Carlin, W., & Mayer, C. (2003). Finance, investment, and growth. *Journal of Financial Economics, 69*(1), 191–226.
Casamatta, C. (2003). Financing and advising: Optimal financial contracts with venture capitalists. *Journal of Finance, 58*(5), 2059–2086.
Claessens, S. (2016). Regulation and structural change in financial systems. In: The future of the international monetary and financial architecture. Conference proceedings from the European Central Bank forum on central banking in Sintra, Portugal.
Čihák, M., Demirgüç-Kunt, A., Feyen, E., & Levine, R. (2012). *Benchmarking financial systems around the world* World Bank Policy Research working paper no. 6175.
De Marco, F., & Macchiavelli, M. (2014). *The political origin of home bias: The case of Europe*. Mimeo.

Demirgüç-Kunt, A., Feyen, E., & Levine, R. (2013). The evolving importance of banks and securities markets. *World Bank Economic Review, 27*(3), 476–490.

Denis, D. J., & Mihov, V. T. (2003). The choice among bank debt, non-bank private debt, and public debt: Evidence from new corporate borrowings. *Journal of Financial Economics, 70*(1), 3–28.

Diamond, D. (1991). Monitoring and reputation: The choice between bank loans and directly placed debt. *Journal of Political Economy, 99*(4), 689–721.

European Systemic Risk Board. (2015). Report on the regulatory treatment of sovereign exposures.

Financial Services Authority. (2008). The supervision of Northern Rock: A lessons learned review.

Gambacorta, L., Yang, J., & Tsatsaronis, K. (2014). Financial structure and growth. *BIS Quarterly Review*, March, 21–35.

Garicano, L. (2012). Five lessons from the Spanish cajas debacle for a new euro-wide supervisor. In T. Beck (Ed.), *Banking Union for Europe*. VoxEU.

Greenwood, R., Landier, A., & Thesmar, D. (2015). Vulnerable banks. *Journal of Financial Economics, 115*(3), 471–485.

Hau, H., & Thum, M. P. (2009). Subprime crisis and board (in-)competence: Private vs. public banks in Germany. *Economic Policy, 24*(60), 701–751.

Hellmann, T., & Puri, M. (2000). The interaction between product market and financing strategy: The role of venture capital. *Review of Financial Studies, 13*(4), 959–984.

Henry, P. B. (2000). Do stock market liberalizations cause investment booms? *Journal of Financial Economics, 58*, 301–334.

Hoenig, T. M. (2013). *Basel III capital: A well-intended illusion*. Speech to the International Association of Deposit Insurers 2013 Research Conference in Basel, Switzerland.

Honohan, P. (2010). *The Irish banking crisis: Regulatory and financial stability policy, 2003–2008*. A report to the Irish Minister of Finance by the Governor of the Central Bank.

Hsu, P.-H., Tian, X., & Xu, Y. (2014). Financial development and innovation: Cross-country evidence. *Journal of Financial Economics, 112*(1), 116–135.

Jeng, L., & Wells, P. (2000). The determinants of venture capital funding: Evidence across countries. *Journal of Corporate Finance, 6*, 241–289.

Jordà, Ò., Schularick, M., & Taylor, A. M. (2016). The great mortgaging: Housing finance, crises, and business cycles. *Economic Policy, 31*(85), 107–152.

Kashyap, A. K., Stein, J. C., & Wilcox, D. W. (1993). Monetary policy and credit conditions: Evidence from the composition of external finance. *American Economic Review, 83*(1), 78–98.

Kerr, W. R., Lerner, J., & Schoar, A. (2014). The consequences of entrepreneurial finance: Evidence from angel financings. *Review of Financial Studies, 27*(1), 20–55.

Kortum, S., & Lerner, J. (2000). Assessing the contribution of venture capital to innovation. *RAND Journal of Economics, 31*(4), 674–692.

La Porta, R., Lopez-de-Silanes, F., Shleifer, A., & Vishny, R. (1997). Legal determinants of external finance. *Journal of Finance, 52*(3), 1131–1150.

La Porta, R., Lopez-de-Silanes, F., Shleifer, A., & Vishny, R. (1998). Law and finance. *Journal of Political Economy, 106*(6), 1113–1155.

Lambert, F. J., Ueda, K., Deb, P., Gray, D. F., & Grippa, P. (2014). How big is the implicit subsidy for banks considered too important to fail? Chapter 3 in Global Financial Stability Report, International Monetary Fund, April.

Lane, P. R. (2013). *Capital flows in the euro area.* EU Commission Economic papers no. 497.

Lane, P. R., & McQuade, P. (2014). Domestic credit growth and international capital flows. *Scandinavian Journal of Economics, 116*(1), 218–252.

Lane, P. R., & Milesi-Ferretti, G. M. (2007). Europe and global imbalances. *Economic Policy, 22*(51), 519–573.

Langfield, S., & Pagano, M. (2016). Bank bias in Europe: Effects on systemic risk and growth. *Economic Policy, 31*(85), 51–106.

Levine, R. (2002). Bank-based or market-based financial systems: Which is better? *Journal of Financial Intermediation, 11*(4), 398–428.

Levine, R., Lin, C., & Xie, W. (2016). Spare tire? Stock markets, banking crises, and economic recoveries. *Journal of Financial Economics, 120*(1), 81–101.

Manove, M., Jorge Padilla, A., & Pagano, M. (2001). Collateral vs. project screening: A model of lazy banks. *RAND Journal of Economics, 32*(4), 726–744.

Mariathasan, M., & Merrouche, O. (2014). The manipulation of Basel risk-weights. *Journal of Financial Intermediation, 12*(3), 300–321.

Marques, L. B., Correa, R., & Sapriza, H. (2013). *International evidence on government support and risk taking in the banking sector.* Federal Reserve Board International Finance discussion paper no.1086.

O'Hara, M., & Shaw, W. (1990). Deposit insurance and wealth effects: The value of being 'too big to fail'. *Journal of Finance, 45*(5), 1587–1600.

Ongena, S., Popov, A., & van Horen, N. (2016). *The invisible hand of the government: Moral suasion during the European sovereign debt crisis.* CEPR Discussion Paper no. 11153.

Pagano, M. (1993). Financial markets and growth: An overview. *European Economic Review, 37*(2/3), 613–622.

Pagano, M., Langfield, S., Acharya, V., Boot, A., Brunnermeier, M., Buch, C., Hellwig, M., Sapir, A., & van den Burg, I. (2014). Is Europe overbanked? Report no.4 of the European Systemic Risk Board's Advisory Scientific Committee.

Popov, A., & Roosenboom, P. (2013). Venture capital and new business creation. *Journal of Banking & Finance, 37*(12), 4695–4710.

Rajan, R.G. and L. Zingales (2003). The great reversals: the politics of financial development in the twentieth century. *Journal of Financial Economics, 69*(1), 5–50.

Sheppard, D.K. (1971). The growth and role of U.K. financial institutions, 1880–1962. Methuen, London.

Shin, H.S. (2012). Global Banking Glut and Loan Risk Premium. Mundell-Fleming Lecture, *IMF Economic Review, 60*(2), 155–192.
Shleifer, A., & Vishny, R. (2011). Fire sales in finance and macroeconomics. *Journal of Economic Perspectives, 25*(1), 29–48.
Stiglitz, J. E., & Weiss, A. (1981). Credit rationing in markets with imperfect information. *American Economic Review, 71*(3), 393–410.
Tiner, J. (2006). Principles-based regulation: The EU context. Speech at the APCIMS Annual Conference.
Véron, N. (2013). Banking nationalism and the European crisis. Bruegel.
Williamson, O. (1988). Corporate finance and corporate governance. *Journal of Finance, 43*(3), 567–591.

3

Bank Diversification and Financial Conglomerates in Europe

Panagiotis Dontis-Charitos, Sotiris Staikouras, and Jonathan Williams

Introduction

Does the presence of large financial conglomerates benefit the financial system or should the new financial architecture be based on a process functional separation that aims to reduce the risks associated with large financial conglomerates by breaking them up?[1] This question has been at the heart of an intense debate since the 2007–09 financial crisis sent shockwaves through

[1] We adopt the definition of financial conglomerates/universal banks of Vander Vennet (2002). The Basel Committee on Banking Supervision and the Joint Forum on Financial Conglomerates offer similar definitions. The latter defines financial conglomerates as "any group of companies under common control whose exclusive or predominant activities consist of providing significant services in at least two different financial sectors (banking, securities, insurance)".

The authors are grateful to Thorsten Beck and Barbara Casu for their constructive feedback. Special thanks to Tuna Alkan for dedicated research assistance at the early stages of this study. The usual disclaimer applies.

P. Dontis-Charitos
ESCP Europe Business School, ESCP Europe, London, UK

Labex ReFi, 79 Avenue de la Republique, 75011 Paris, France
e-mail: pdontischaritos@escpeurope.eu

S. Staikouras
Cass Business School, City University of London, London, UK
e-mail: sks@city.ac.uk

J. Williams (✉)
Bangor Business School, Bangor University, Bangor, UK
e-mail: jon.williams@bangor.ac.uk

T. Beck, B. Casu (eds.), *The Palgrave Handbook of European Banking*,
DOI 10.1057/978-1-137-52144-6_3

global financial markets and institutions. The reform process that seeks to prevent such an episode from reoccurring continues to transform the industry, in particular, the ways in which large and complex financial institutions (FIs) operate (Stiroh 2015).

Although the exact causes of the financial crisis are still being debated, a widespread consensus exists among market participants that the excessive bank diversification into risky non-banking activities, coupled with the rise of large, complex, and interconnected financial conglomerates, acted as the catalyst of the systemic collapse.[2] Hence, the issue of effective regulation and supervision of systemically important FIs (SIFIs) is centre stage in the ensuing regulatory debate (Elyasiani et al. 2016), with discussions focusing on the optimal size and the range of permissible activities of these institutions.[3] The overarching aim of these policies is to create a safer, sounder, more transparent, and responsible financial system.[4]

While it is too early to draw any conclusions about the exact causes of the financial crisis and to assess the effectiveness of new regulations, it is useful to review what is known about bank diversification into non-banking and financial conglomerates. An increasing number of contributions have emerged following the financial crisis. Nevertheless, and despite the increasing importance of European FIs, the majority of studies focus on the US market. Furthermore, extant review studies cover broader topics, such as FI mergers and acquisitions (Pilloff and Santomero1998; Santos 1998; Berger et al. 1999; Kwan and Laderman 1999; Amel et al. 2004). These reviews were written prior to the recent crisis and, thus, do not cover recent contributions on the systemic risk implications of bank diversification into non-banking. The aim of this chapter, therefore, is twofold: (1) To overview bank diversification into non-banking activities with focus on European conglomerates; and (2) to offer an update of studies on bank diversification.

[2] During the 2007 financial crisis, co-movement among financial intermediaries' assets and liabilities distorted the supply of capital and significantly disrupted the economic system. Such systemic failure is usually attributable to (a) common asset shock (for example, mortgages, equities and so on), (b) contagion (for example, investors' psychology, panic and so on) and/or (c) interconnected financial intermediaries and to their funding maturity (Allen et al. 2012).

[3] The US response came through the Dodd-Frank Act in 2010 with the UK following with the Financial Services (Banking Reform) Act in 2013. The EU, a long-established hub for universal banks and financial conglomerates, is currently engaged in a decisive overhaul of bank regulation and supervision.

[4] Michel Barnier, Commissioner for internal market and services, set up a High-level Expert Group and appointed Erkki Liikanen, Governor of the Bank of Finland and a former member of the European Commission, as Chairman. The group's mandate was to assess the need for structural reform of the EU banking sector. Commissioner Barnier added among others: "The proposed measures will further strengthen financial stability and ensure taxpayers do not end up paying for the mistakes of banks…The proposals are carefully calibrated to ensure a delicate balance between financial stability and creating the right conditions for lending to the real economy, particularly important for competitiveness and growth". See European Commission's pages on Structural Reform of the EU Banking Sector.

We identify two phases of conglomeration involving European banks. From the early 1980s, banks and insurance companies had begun to form alliances and joint ventures in a process known as *Allfinanz* or *bancassurance*. Banks were motivated to rebuild their customer bases and improve retention rates, whereas insurance companies sought to build direct relationships with their customers.[5] The combination of banking and insurance yielded one of the most important benefits of diversification, namely, the opportunity to cross-sell financial products and services to a larger customer base.[6]

The second phase includes developments from the late 1990s, which ended abruptly in 2007, and is characterized by increasing and inextricably linked relationships between banks and capital markets (Adrian and Shin 2010). The intensification of financial deregulation and financial innovation allowed banks to combine traditional activities with capital market products. As a result, financial conglomerates increased both in size and in complexity. Ultimately, the growing interconnectedness between financial conglomerates proved to be a channel for contagion effects and the transmission of systemic risk.

The chapter is organized as follows. The section "The Business Structure of Financial Conglomerates" provides an overarching discussion on the corporate structure of financial conglomerates along with some data on these institutions. The section "The Drivers of Financial Conglomerates" presents the driving forces behind the evolution of these heterogeneous institutions. The section "Financial Conglomerates and Theoretical Arguments" reviews the theoretical arguments behind the creation of financial conglomerates. The section "Empirical Work on Financial Conglomerates" complements the review by presenting the empirical findings on the effects of bank diversification on financial intermediaries. The section "The European Conglomerates Landscape" reviews the evolution of bank diversification into non-banking activities, by offering key statistics on European banks and financial conglomerates and a summary of key regulatory developments. "Concluding Remarks" brings the chapter to a close and presents some aspects of modern financial markets that require further thought.

---

[5] The overlap in the two sectors is even more apparent in modern capital markets, where products extensively used by banks, such as credit-default swaps, closely resemble a casualty insurance policy; albeit without either an insurable-interest requirement or any role for an insurance adjuster.

[6] Different types of combinations took place. (1) Bank acquisitions of life insurers (for example, Lloyds Bank and Abbey Life, UK; Rabobank and Interpolis, Netherlands). (2) Mergers of banks and insurers (for example, Nationale-Nederlanden and NMB Postbank, Netherlands). (3) Joint ventures (for example, Generale Bank and AC Group, Belgium; RBS and Scottish Equitable, UK). (4) Banks establishing life insurance subsidiaries (for example, Deutsche Bank, Germany; Crédit Agricole, France). (5) Insurers acquiring banks (for example, GAN and CIC in France). (6) Insurers establishing banks (for example, Mapfre, Spain; Baltica, Denmark). (7) Distribution agreements often supported by cross-shareholdings (for example, Generali and Mediobanca, Italy; Allianz and Dresdner Bank, Germany).

The Business Structure of Financial Conglomerates

The gradual relaxation of structural regulation had allowed banks to diversify their product mix and geographical focus.[7] Motivated by expectations of economies of scale and scope, and arguably the benefits of too-big-to-fail status, many large financial conglomerates had reoriented their business models. Certainly, the number of diversifying deals involving European banks and other financial services firms was accelerating up until the financial crisis in 2007.[8] For instance, German banking giants Deutsche and Dresdner acquired UK merchant banks (SG Warburg and Morgan Grenfell) to gain access into investment banking. Other banks, such as Barclays in the UK, substantially increased their investment banking capabilities. Such moves resulted in varying degrees of success and failure; for instance, in the UK, Northern Rock fell because overreliance on short-term funding created maturity mismatches leading to a bank run as investor confidence withered. As at 2015, several European banks including Barclays, HSBC and RBS in the UK, UBS in Switzerland, and Deutsche Bank in Germany, amongst others, are in a process of partial retreat from investment banking activities as the leading US investment banks increase their market shares.

Prior to 2007, many banks had revised their business models by either acquiring subsidiaries to enter specific activities, or revising strategic priorities to target particular lines of business.[9] Analysing bank asset and funding structures, Hryckiewicz and Kozlowski (2015) identify two banking models within a traditional group (more diversified; specialized model), and two models for non-traditional activities (trader model; investment model). Their analysis offers some stylized results: pre-crisis, banks' asset structure was the main driver of systemic risk due to high correlation of securities; in crisis, banks' funding structure was the main source of systemic risk notably for banks following the investment model. Nevertheless, the authors argue that bank regulators should encourage

[7] In the EU, the Second Banking Directive of 1989 legally endorsed universal banking; whilst the 1999 Financial Services Modernization Act (FSMA) ended over 50 years the functional separation of commercial banking and investment banking in the US. Less than a decade later, the sub-prime crisis ignited and the global economy headed into the worst recession since the 1930s, which ironically was when the USA and others implemented functional separation as a means to ensure financial stability.

[8] Shoots of recovery started to emerge in 2013. See "Financial conglomerates and theoretical arguments" for more details.

[9] Merck Martel et al. (2012) classify large internationally active banks into two specialized business models (commercial banks; investment banks) and two universal business models (investment banking oriented universal banks; commercial banking oriented universal banks) based mainly on bank asset and funding structures.

diversification because of a beneficial impact on stability. Gambacorta and van Rixtel (2013) show that (income) diversification leads to stronger bank profitability (RoE) but the relationship is non-linear. This result infers that scope economies do exist but dissipate once banks attain a certain degree of diversification. The optimal level of diversification has fallen post-crisis, with non-interest income accounting for a smaller share of total income.

Taking advantage of hindsight, the changes banks made to their business models, which reflected their strategic decision-making, identified practices that proved to be unsustainable. Adrian and Shin (2010) cite problems associated with securitization; the complexity of financial intermediation when operating via capital markets; the inseparability of banking and capital market developments; declining lending standards; the use of short-term liabilities to fund long-dated assets; and the role of leverage and the use of innovative products. Certainly, bank regulators had been aware of potential problems associated with financial conglomerates for a long time.[10] The Financial Stability Forum (FSF) coined the term "large complex financial institutions" (LCFIs) to exemplify the size, diversity and complexity of 16 of the world's most important financial services firms.[11]

The severity of the crisis promoted a change in financial architecture. In April 2009, the G20 established the Financial Stability Board (FSB) (the successor to the FSF) with mandate to identify Global Systemically Important Banks (G-SIBs) and to ensure that each institution filed a credible resolution and recovery plan. A methodology has been set out for identifying G-SIBs based on (equal) weighting of size; interconnectedness; substitutability; complexity; and cross-jurisdictional activity. Based on the score for this indicator of systemic importance, G-SIBs will be allocated into four buckets, which require different levels of additional loss absorbency requirements, that is, Common Equity Tier 1, ranging from 1 % of risk-weighted assets (bucket 1) to 2.5 % (bucket 4). Whilst the Basel Committee on Banking Supervision has set the requirements, national regulatory authorities can demand higher requirements. A gradual phasing-in of the requirements will occur alongside the capital conservation and countercyclical buffers between January 2016 and year-end 2018 with full effect from 1 January 2019 (see BCBS 2011 for details).

---

[10] In 1999, the G7 created the Financial Stability Forum (FSF) to consider likely problems arising from the wind-up of a large, financial conglomerate. A Group of Ten Report (2001) later considered the potential problems associated with the growth of financial conglomerates.

[11] Of the 16 LCFIs, 13 remain. Lehman Brothers is the most notable casualty. Merrill Lynch is now part of Bank of America. Just before the crisis, a consortium of banks bought ABN AMRO including RBS, which the UK government later had to nationalize. Morgan Stanley converted from securities firm to a bank. Other LCFIs had to be supported by their governments in both the US and Europe.

The FSB increased the number of G-SIBs to 28 in comparison with the 16 LCFIs. The most recent list (November 2015) shows 30 G-SIBs. Table 3.1 ranks the G-SIBs by total assets. The average G-SIB has 90 shareholders and operates 2,084 subsidiaries. Data for 2015 show that on average, the balance sheet total equals €1,392,060 million, Tier 1 and Total Capital ratios are 13.36 % and 16.18 %, whilst profitability (return on average equity) has fallen from 10.33 % to 7.99 % between 2010 and 2015. In terms of five-year asset growth, 11 European G-SIBs are below the median (of 11.37 %) with only four above. For 7 of the 11 banks, the balance sheet total has fallen over time. Table 3.1 shows HSBC and JPMorgan Chase require the highest amount of additional loss absorbing capital (bucket 4), with BNP Paribas, Barclays and Deutsche Bank the other European banks in bucket 3 alongside Citigroup. We note the emergence of Chinese banks and their spectacular rates of (nominal) asset growth (in excess of 70 %) over a five-year period.

The regulatory response has centred on structural regulation. Whilst one could argue that the new initiatives invoke the spirit of a Glass-Steagall type of functional separation, the reforms do not go far enough in that direction and instead, in the context of this chapter, implicitly acknowledge that the potential benefits of financial conglomeration outweigh the costs. Nevertheless, expectations are that the new approaches will reduce the size of financial conglomerates and lessen the opportunities to realize economies of scope. The reforms target the universal banking model by denying banks the right to carry out certain activities mostly relating to proprietary trading, and isolating safer activities from riskier ones within a holding company framework. The new processes are institutional separation (US), subsidiarization (EU), and ring fencing (UK) (see Chow and Surti 2011; Gambacorta and van Rixtel 2013).

This type of reform is neither new nor unknown to FIs and policy makers. Over the last century the financial services industry underwent cycles of regulation, regulatory avoidance and re-regulation, or deregulation, as depicted in Kane (1981).[12] Thus, history is there to remind all stakeholders that re-regulation might not represent an optimal solution to the problem. Some, for example, question the feasibility and the costs of ongoing re-regulation (Chow and Surti 2011). Re-regulation will most certainly introduce costs to FIs and other stakeholders, while its effectiveness is unknown. Aside from direct costs, and consistent with the theory of contestable markets (Baumol 1982), regulation can shift economic rents across sectors, thus altering the industry's com-

[12] Kane (1988) uses the term 'regulatory dialectic' to describe the cyclical interactions between regulation, regulatory avoidance and re-regulation, or de-regulation. It is also worth noting that these reforms are usually based on a *de jure* implementation. There is evidence, however, of a de facto structure in some European markets that existed for decades (Kalotychou and Staikouras 2007).

Table 3.1 Global systemically important financial institutions, November 2015 (2015 data (2014[a]; 2013[b]); € million)

Bank Name	Country	Total Assets	5 year growth, %	Tier 1 capital	Tier 1 ratio, %	Capital ratio, %	ROAE, 2015, %	ROAE, 2010, %	NPL/TA %	GSIFI bucket	Shareholders, #	Subs. #
ICBC	China	2,774,378	82.42	204,779	12.19	14.53	19.62	22.13	1.25	1	33	76
CCB	China	2,253,986	84.51	166,486	12.12	14.87	19.62	21.44	1.50	1	36	56
HSBC Holdings	UK	2,169,740	18.11	125,811	12.50	15.60	7.60	9.77	0.47	4	175	2,274
Agricultural Bank of China	China	2,150,337	84.08	138,134	9.46	12.82	19.13	21.44	2.24	1	19	25
Mitsubishi UFJ	Japan	2,140,830	27.55	109,351	12.62	15.68	7.08	4.20	0.36	2	68	2,598
Bank of China	China	2,053,042	73.69	151,751	11.35	13.87	16.52	17.96	1.24	1	37	55
JPMorgan Chase	USA	2,090,202[a]	21.51[a]	134,571[b]	11.60[b]	13.10[b]	9.82[a]	10.36	0.55[a]	4	120	6,122
BNP Paribas	France	1,994,193	−0.20	70,378[a]	11.50[a]	12.60[a]	7.27	11.04	1.31	3	77	2,834
Bank of America	USA	1,969,554	16.19	166,045	12.90	15.70	6.36	-0.97	0.57	2	122	3,908
Crédit Agricole	France	1,762,763	1.84	73,150	14.80	18.40	6.09	5.38	1.26	1		
Barclays	UK	1,745,758	0.03	66,932	13.00	16.50	1.30	7.54	0.40	3	147	1,629
Deutsche Bank	Germany	1,708,703	−10.33	63,898	16.10	17.20	2.64	5.27	0.31	3	49	6,051
Wells Fargo & Co	USA	1,641,940	74.38	125,666[a]	12.45[a]	15.53[a]	12.34	10.46	0.65	1	127	4,743
Citigroup	USA	1,590,116	11.01	135,644[a]	13.10[a]	14.53[a]	7.97	6.79	0.73	3	123	1,168
RBS	UK	1,350,887	−20.67	60,575	13.20	17.10	−4.54	−1.94	1.66	1	61	959

(continued)

Table 3.1 (continued)

Bank Name	Country	Total Assets	5 year growth, %	Tier 1 capital	Tier 1 ratio, %	Capital ratio, %	ROAE, 2015, %	ROAE, 2010, %	NPL/TA %	GSIFI bucket	Shareholders, #	Subs. #
Mizuho Financial	Japan	1,426,094	7.18	58,043	11.50	14.58	7.57	7.98	0.29	1	47	1,286
Sumitomo Mitsui	Japan	1,386,639	20.00	66,001	12.89	16.58	7.08	7.56	0.44	1	80	119
Banco Santander	Spain	1,340,260	10.08	73,478	12.55	14.40	7.78	11.76	1.98	1	288	1,613
Société Générale	France	1,334,391	17.87	44,650[a]	13.50	16.30	7.24	8.80	1.15	1	69	1,114
BPCE Group	France	1,166,535	11.26	52,200	13.30	16.80	5.94	8.13	1.06	1		
UBS	Switz.	884,682	−15.68	36,717	19.00	25.60	7.01	15.60	0.07	1	6	699
ING Bank	Neth.	828,602	−11.20	37,100	12.52	15.53	7.79	13.80	0.72	1	1	125
UniCredit	Italy	860,433	−7.43	45,499[a]	11.64	14.36	4.21	2.52	5.48[a]	1	136	1,715
Goldman Sachs	USA	705,285	3.41	64,605	13.80	16.00	10.47	11.12	0.03	2	104	4,156
Credit Suisse	Switz.	759,913	−7.55	49,126	18.00	21.30	−6.54	12.96	0.001	2	82	3,610
BBVA (exit list Nov. 2015)	Spain	750,078	35.70	48,539	12.10	15.00	6.22	14.64	2.49[a]	1	221	715
Morgan Stanley	USA	660,204	9.22	52,867	14.10	16.40	5.20	9.65	0.02	2	83	5,427
Nordea Bank	Sweden	646,868	11.37	26,516	18.50	21.60	12.03	11.34	0.41	1	90	1,163
Standard Chartered	UK	488,993	26.49	30,697	13.10	18.00	9.04	13.22	0.51	1	110	402
Bank of New York Mellon	US	293,238	115.46	15,445	13.34	13.74	8.65	10.59	0.04	1	1	71
State Street	USA	225,209	87.48	14,020	15.30	17.40	9.29	9.64	0.02	1	101	5,714

Source: BankScope; bank annual reports

petitive landscape and, leading to regulatory arbitrage. The latter can severely impair tax revenues, lead to job reductions and ultimately lead to a reduction in the economic activity of countries with heavily regulated financial systems (Andriosopoulos et al. 2016). Herring and Carmassi (2015) emphasize how complex the corporate structures of financial conglomerates are, which they suggest is a source of systemic risk. They also point out the difficulties associated with mapping a conglomerate's business activities into its legal entities, which are subject to different national regulatory and bankruptcy procedures. It's worth remembering that any reforms aim to limit the occurrence of crises, their severity, as well as the impact on the taxpayer. Carletti and Leonello (2016) review the recent regulatory reforms and for each one they highlight the rationale behind it, the institutional details, as well as identifying the possible challenges and open issues related to design and implementation.

The Drivers of Financial Conglomerates

Over the last two decades the financial services industry has been consolidating at a torrid pace, often via mergers and acquisitions. Actually, the process had started much earlier in the 1980s with the creation of the first multinational financial supermarkets. Examples include Prudential-Bache Securities (Prudential Financial acquiring Bache Halsey Stuart Shields in 1981); Shearson/American Express (American Express acquiring Shearson Loeb Rhoades in 1981); Sears (Sear acquiring Dean Witter Reynolds Organization and Coldwell Banker & Co. in 1981); Bank of America (Bank of America acquiring Schwab in 1983); and Shearson Lehman Brothers (Shearson/American Express buying Lehman Brothers Kuhn Loeb in 1984). The recent wave of consolidation has been broadly attributed to technological and financial innovations, globalization, as well as to substantial financial deregulation (Amel et al. 2004; Berger et al. 1999, 2010; DeYoung et al. 2009; Goddard et al. 2007). Specifically, technological progress has drastically improved banks' back-office, front office and payments systems (Berger 2003), and facilitated financial innovation, particularly the development of new capital market securities with similar functionality to traditional intermediary services. This has resulted in an international disintermediation process, with capital flows being reallocated from traditional intermediaries to non-banks and/or to capital markets (Allen and Santomero 2001; Walter 2009).[13] In

[13] Allen and Santomero (2001) find that banks located in countries with highly developed financial markets, such as the USA and UK, are losing market share to finance companies, mutual funds and securities

addition, increased competition due to globalization and deregulation has radically changed the strategic and competitive position of banks. In particular, globalization has resulted in the lowering of implicit and explicit barriers to the integration of markets (Buch and DeLong 2009), while cross-border regulatory imbalances have intensified foreign competition (Herring and Santomero 1990).

The profound impact of these changes on the financial services industry has been paralleled to a "Darwinian shakeout" (Taylor 1999), whereby financial institutions had to evolve to survive. Indeed, traditional intermediaries responded by increasing their scale and scope via mergers and acquisitions (M&A), thus leading to the subsequent eruption of financial conglomerates. Staikouras (2006) argues that there are three key factors for financial conglomerates to evolve and succeed, namely: market-based, strategic and operational. The former is exogenous and deals with issues not controlled by the firm (economic growth, demographic features, regulatory framework, tax environment); while the other two are considered endogenous and refer to the firm's idiosyncratic aspects (strategic factors: business culture, corporate closeness, management initiative, corporate governance; and operational factors: branch environment, customer relations, range of services, financial management, corporate brand), which are elements that a firm could introduce, influence and/or change. He also introduces two further drivers, namely technology and reputation, which can be influenced by both endogenous and exogenous drivers. Finally, he argues that these same drivers of success can potentially backfire and/or exert a negative impact, if the firm does not exploit them at the right time and in the right way.

This notwithstanding, the existence of such institutions would not have been possible without key regulatory reforms that removed structural restrictions on the activities of bank holding companies (BHCs).[14] Key legislation includes the US Financial Services Modernization Act (FSMA) in 1999 and the EU Second Banking Directive (89/646/EEC) in 1989.[15] All EU member states implemented the Second Banking Directive between 1991 and 1994 (see Chen 2007). Molyneux (2016) documents that non-interest income as

---

markets, which contrasts to the experience of banks in Germany, France and Japan. Walter (2009) documents a more prominent decline in commercial banks' share of financial flows in the US than in the EU.

[14] The US Department of Labor defines BHCs as "establishments primarily engaged in holding or owning the securities of banks for the sole purpose of exercising some degree of control over the activities of bank companies whose securities they hold."

[15] Goddard et al. (2007) provide an extensive list of key European legislative changes that have facilitated the integration of European banking and financial markets. Goddard et al. (2010) and Andriosopoulos et al. (2015) discuss legislative and regulatory developments in the EU (15 member states) and US banking industries, respectively.

a proportion of total income was 26 % in 1989 and shot up to 46 % in 1998 and remained at this level up to 2012. Moreover, it is worth noting that harmonization among financial intermediaries was in some countries implemented earlier than 1989. For instance, the French 1984 Bank Law removed the distinction among credit, commercial and saving banks; while the 1990 Bank Act in Switzerland put underwriters along with banking and non-banking institutions under the same regulatory umbrella. The existence of the bank–insurance interface made Norway to launch the first integrated supervisory agency (1986), which was followed by Denmark (1988), Sweden (1991), and the Financial Services Authority in the UK (1997) becoming the single regulator for banking, securities and insurance. Interestingly, looking at financial intermediation from a cross-continent angle what is strictly considered as bank in Europe (institutions granting credit) is not a banking firm in the USA (institutions accepting insured deposits), for example, General Electric Credit Union or Ally Financial Inc. previously known as GMAC Inc. Since these regulatory reforms were introduced, a plethora of theoretical and empirical research has been conducted putting financial conglomerates under the microscope.

Financial Conglomerates and Theoretical Arguments

At the firm level, advocates of bank diversification offer several arguments to support financial conglomerates. First, financial conglomerates are more efficient due to scale- and scope-related cost, revenue, and operational synergies (Saunders and Walter 1994; Vander Vennet 2002). For example, large conglomerates can benefit from scale-related reductions in operating costs due to a superior utilization of existing resources, such as, branch networks, electronic distribution systems, infrastructure software and personnel (Santomero and Eckles 2000). Furthermore, financial conglomerates could benefit from cost- and revenue-based scope economies (Berger et al. 1993). Cost scope economies can accrue by (a) spreading the fixed expenses of managing client relationships, (b) using established distribution channels to deliver additional products at lower marginal cost, and (c) realizing synergies in the use and application of knowledge in the production of services (Herring and Santomero 1990). Alternatively, conglomerates could achieve revenue scope economies through an efficient cross selling of an array of products from the same outlet, albeit limited to the extent to which consumers are willing to pay a premium for the joint consumption of services (Berger et al. 1996).

Second, the extensive functional diversification at financial conglomerates lessens the variability in their profit streams (Boot and Schmeits 2000). In turn, this can lower default risk (Benston 1994; Saunders 1994), improve creditworthiness, reduce both the cost of capital and corporate tax, realise more stable dividends and, ultimately, is conducive to better long-term financial planning. Diversity also allows conglomerates to adapt more readily to changing economic conditions (Herring and Santomero 1990). Finally, conglomerates may exhibit superior resource allocation if they can create effective internal markets (Stein 1997).

Despite the above benefits, the literature offers several counter-arguments. First, financial conglomerates could experience supply side diseconomies. Specifically, their sheer size may lead to inertia, making them (a) unable to adapt to changing customer needs, (b) prone to turf battles and profit attribution conflicts, and (c) susceptible to problems arising from cross-divisional cultural differences among employees (Walter 1997). In addition, the broadness of products and services on offer can raise the likelihood of conflicts of interest; the six most common conflicts are the salesman's stake, stuffing fiduciary accounts, bankruptcy risk transference, third-party loans, product tie-ins and information transfer (Saunders and Cornett 2008).

Second, some dismiss the risk reducing benefits of diversification and instead argue that investors can diversify firm-specific or idiosyncratic risk by forming efficient portfolios. In this respect, Levy and Sarnat (1970) demonstrate that in the absence of synergistic gains and capital cost economies, conglomerate mergers cannot produce economic gains in perfect capital markets. Whereas diversification might reduce idiosyncratic risk, some argue that it exacerbates systematic risk, which could increase the propensity for systemic risk, simply because financial institutions have become increasingly similar (Acharya 2009; Ibragimov et al. 2011; Wagner 2010). It is possible that this negative effect could become more severe should diversification increase the risk appetite of financial conglomerates (Wagner 2008). Whereas these studies highlight the importance of enhanced regulation and supervision of large financial conglomerates, Zhou (2013) provides a model where although bank capital requirements may reduce individual bank risks, they enhance the systemic linkages within the financial system.

Apart from systemic risk, the literature raises a number of public policy concerns. For example, some argue that financial conglomerates are vulnerable to affiliation risk, whereby distress or failure of one or more component firm(s) can extend to the holding company and/or other subsidiaries. This could lead to the subsidization of non-bank affiliates via the bank safety net through bailouts (Flannery 1999; Herring and Santomero 1990; Santomero and Eckles 2000). The presence of implicit guarantees to non-banks may also intensify moral hazard at conglomerates and result in excessive risk-taking.

Finally, the combination of the market power, political influence and safety net access of large financial conglomerates may confer an unfair advantage (Kane 2000) over their specialised, or non-bank peers (Barth et al. 2000), and reduce consumer choices (Black et al. 1978). Herring and Santomero (1990) highlight the importance of the potential market impact of the failure of large and complex conglomerates, the greater cost of their supervision, and the moral hazard issues associated with the access of non-banks to the safety net. Similarly, Kwan (2004) calls for attention to the ever-growing scale and concentration of FIs, and reiterates that "too-big-to-fail" institutions may gradually become a burden to the taxpayer.

Empirical Work on Financial Conglomerates

Research on bank diversification and financial conglomerates houses a number of different avenues to provide an empirical basis to the arguments raised in the theoretical literature. We review the evidence in two strands: (a) performance-related studies that examine the effects of diversification and conglomeration on accounting profit and/or cost–revenue ratios, and (b) risk-return studies that consider changes in the risk-return profiles of financial conglomerates, and/or measure the systemic risk contribution of financial conglomerates. Consistent with the inconclusiveness of the theoretical debate on the relative merits of bank diversification and financial conglomerates, the empirical evidence does not offer a clear result, which leads to the absence of a conclusive answer to the debate.

Operating Performance

Much of what we know about the effects of diversification and conglomeration on bank efficiency draws on the early research on cost scope efficiency. These studies tended to examine the extent of scope economies by comparing the costs of multi-product institutions vis-à-vis specialized firms. In general, multi-output institutions achieve minimal cost savings. For example, and in a study of large US banks, Hunter et al. (1990) examine the subadditivity of costs and fail to uncover evidence of cost complementarities related to multi-product manufacturing. Whereas multi-product cost economies may exist at bank level, there may be dis-economies of scope at the product level (see Chang and Lynge (1994) on US savings banks). In contrast, the evidence from the EU is more positive. For instance, Lang and Welzel (1996) measure economies of scale and scope, cost efficiency and the rate of technical progress for German co-operative banks and find some evidence of economies of scope in small banks, which they attribute to technical progress.

Later studies tend to focus on the effects of bank diversification on the revenue/profit scope efficiency of FIs. For instance, Vander Vennet (2002) compares the cost and profit efficiency of specialised institutions with financial conglomerates and universal banks in Europe. He finds that financial conglomerates are more cost and revenue efficient than their specialized peers and argues that further de-specialization could lead to a more efficient banking system. In the case of Italian banks, Casu and Girardone (2004) report persistent increases in profit efficiency at financial conglomerates. In the USA, Wheelock and Wilson (2001) find that banks could achieve potential economies by expanding the size of their output and adjusting their output mix toward the figures of banks with at least \$300–\$500 million of assets. Furthermore, Berger et al. (1996) find no revenue economies of scope in banking and argue that competitive pressures may prevent banks from charging higher premiums for one-stop-shopping and/or consumers may not value the joint consumption of multiple services. Recent international evidence offers some intriguing insights. Laeven and Levine (2007) unveil that economies of scope are outweighed by agency problems derived from product diversification. Berger et al. (2010) examine Chinese banks and report lower profits and reduced costs associated with bank diversification across loans, deposits, assets, and geography. Nonetheless, they find that banks affiliated with conglomerates exhibit fewer diseconomies of diversification.

Academic survey evidence reaffirms the inconclusiveness of the empirical results. Whereas Berger et al. (1999) find that consolidation in FIs improves their profit efficiency and risk profile, it does not confer cost efficiency benefits. In a review of the European evidence, Berger et al. (2001) suggest that, whilst consolidation may yield efficiency gains accruing from risk diversification, barriers to consolidation may offset much of the potential gain. Survey evidence from international (Amel et al. 2004) and European (Goddard et al. 2007) cross-industry consolidation is also inconclusive. Whilst the international evidence acknowledges potential benefits from diversification, it notes the presence of organizational diseconomies in conglomerate integration. The mixed results reflect a lack of empirical contributions and/or the fact that the basis for the results in early studies was merger simulation techniques.

Risk, Returns and Systemic Implications

Another important question is whether financial conglomerates are superior to specialized institutions in terms of their risk-return profiles. The empirical work on this subject can be broken down into (a) early studies that used merger simulations, (b) later risk-return studies that used actual bank mergers with non-banks and (c) more recent studies that examine the impact of bank diversification on systemic risk. Overall, this strand of studies also offers largely inconclusive results.

The early empirical contributions tend to favour bank diversification into non-banking. For example, Heggestad (1975) finds certain non-bank activities to be safer than banking and advocates the potential diversification benefits of some non-banking operations. Yet Boyd and Graham (1986) could not find any meaningful relationship between diversification and either profitability or risk. Similarly, Brewer (1989) does not establish a link between diversification and BHC risk, although diversification lowers the risk of high-risk BHCs, which Brewer et al. (1988) confirm. The early studies suffer from two shortcomings. First, the non-banking activities are limited to those permitted at the time. Second, they examine aggregate non-banking activities; hence, the risk of any particular activity cannot be isolated.

To overcome these shortcomings, later studies employed merger simulation techniques. Boyd and Graham (1988) find that combinations between BHCs and non-banks increase the return variability and default risk; the only exception is life insurance, which reduces both return volatility and default risk. In contrast, Laderman (1999) finds that insurance underwriting and securities reduce the probability of bankruptcy of BHCs. Using a sample of UK banks, Genetay and Molyneux (1998) report mixed evidence on risk, with significantly lower probabilities of failure but insignificant changes in return on assets volatility for bank combinations with insurance. Despite the advantages of simulation studies over early contributions, some problems remained. In particular, the random pairing of companies may yield hypothetical pairs of large non-banks and small BHCs, which represent unrealistic combinations in terms of risk and return. Boyd et al. (1993) and Lown et al. (2000) account for this problem. Boyd et al. (1993) report risk reducing effects associated with the optimal size combinations of BHCs and insurance companies but combinations of BHCs and securities firms are risk increasing. Although Lown et al. (2000) conclude that BHC combinations with life insurance companies are risk reducing, their study shows that BHC combinations with either securities or property and casualty insurance raises risk for BHCs. Nevertheless, these studies fail to (a) consider the potential diversification benefits from BHC combinations with more than one non-banking firm, (b) control for the fact that BHCs might self-select target companies based on their organizational and financial characteristics, and (c) account for merger and acquisition (M&A) costs and acquisitions premia. Allen and Jagtiani (2000) employ a portfolio approach to overcome the first issue and find that non-bank activities reduce total risk but increase systematic risk. Similarly, Estrella (2001) finds that convergence among banks and insurers can generate diversification benefits.

More recently, studies use actual M&A data between banks and non-banks to overcome any anomalies. Results show positive abnormal returns and no changes in risk when banks acquire insurance companies (Dontis-Charitos et al. 2011; Fields et al. 2007), with risk falling for bank acquirers and their peers (Elyasiani et al. 2016). In contrast, Vallascas and Hagendorff (2011) report a marked increase in default risk when low-risk European banks diversify into non-banking activities. Casu et al. (2016) find that bank combinations with securities firms yield higher risks than combinations with insurance companies, yet provide evidence that size may be responsible, as opposed to diversification per se. Similarly, Weiß et al. (2014a) find an increase in systemic risk following M&A that is not associated with income diversification, but related to managerial hubris and the existence of deposit insurance guarantees. Molyneux et al. (2014) corroborate this result and show that safety net subsidies derived from M&A are positively associated with rescue probability. These results concur with evidence in Hoque et al. (2015) that the presence of deposit insurance schemes increases moral hazard at the largest international banks and leads to greater risk-taking.

Like the empirical evidence, the available reviews on the risk-return effects of bank diversification and financial conglomerates offer no solid conclusions. For example, in an early survey of 18 studies, Saunders and Walter (1994) report a lack of consensus as to whether non-banking activities reduce bank risk (nine studies answer yes, six answer no, while three are inconclusive). However, Kwan and Laderman (1999) review the risk-return effects of the fusion of banking and non-banking activities and conclude that although securities and insurance are riskier than banking, they are more profitable, whilst providing the potential for diversification. In a more recent survey, DeYoung et al. (2009) conclude that the early studies failed to provide conclusive results on efficiency and diversification due to problems in defining the banks' cost and profit functions and/or the inability of simulation studies to capture the cash flow synergies expected in actual mergers. Their review of post-2000 bank M&A evidence suggests that banks have consumed diversification benefits by taking on more risk. Finally, Carow and Kane (2002) review event-study evidence on the relaxation of regulatory restrictions on bank consolidation, and conclude that deregulation may have redistributed, rather than created, value in the financial services industry.

The European Conglomerates Landscape

Bank Mergers and Acquisitions

This section presents and discusses key statistics on European banking M&A and bank diversification into non-bank activities.[16] For this purpose, we compile a sample of deals based on the following selection criteria. First, the deals take place between January 2000 and May 2015. Second, we focus on European deals where banks acquire (or, are acquired by) other banks, asset management companies, brokerage firms, and insurance companies. As such, we define seven subsets of deals: namely, bank–bank contains banks that acquire other banks; bank–asset management contains banks that acquire asset management companies; bank–securities contains banks that acquire securities firms; bank–insurance contains banks that acquire insurance companies; asset management–bank contains asset management companies that acquire banks; securities–bank contains securities firms that acquire banks. Lastly, insurance–bank contains insurance companies that acquire banks. Table 3.2 provides descriptive statistics on the number and value of deals by year and deal type, while Figs. 3.1 and 3.2 provide a graphical representation of the data.

Table 3.2 shows that between 2000 and 2015 the European financial services industry has witnessed a total number of 3,071 deals involving banks, reaching USD 895 billion in value. In terms of M&A distribution based on deal type, 64.0 % (68.4 % based on value) of deals were activity focusing (bank–bank), whereas 36.0 % (31.6 % based on value) were activity diversifying. From an examination of the evolution of the number of deals and their value, we make some interesting observations. In particular, after fluctuating between 2000 and 2003, European deal making activity peaked

[16] Statistics are provided for the EU (28 member states), 5 candidate countries for EU membership (Albania, Montenegro, Serbia, the former Yugoslav Republic of Macedonia, and Turkey), 1 potential candidate country for accession in the EU (Bosnia and Herzegovina) and 17 other European and/or transcontinental countries/states (Andorra, Belarus, Faroe Islands, Georgia, Greenland, Guernsey, Iceland, Isle of Man, Jersey, Liechtenstein, Moldova, Monaco, Norway, the Russian Federation, San Marino, Switzerland, and Ukraine). Note, only countries/states that hosted bidder and/or target banks involved in M&A during the sample period are included. We source data from Thomson Financial.

in 2007, with 263 deals valued at USD 131 billion. A somewhat similar pattern emerges if we segregate the deals as activity focusing or activity diversifying. Second, in the two years leading to crisis event in 2007, we observe a marked increase in the relative percentage of diversifying deals—both in value and numbers. It is important to note that the increase in deal value in 2007 reflects the sharp increase in the value of bank–securities deals.[17] Following the crisis, and although the relative number of diversifying deals remained somewhat constant, their relative value plummeted, before picking up again in 2013 because of a small number of large acquisitions of banks by asset management companies.

On the one hand, one could argue that excessive diversification into non-banking by European banks may have exacerbated their default risk and/or interconnectedness and, thus, intensified any spill over effects emanating from the US banking sector. Indeed, research on European banks documents a marked increase in the default risk of small banks, which had diversified across business lines (Vallascas and Hagendorff 2011). The reduction in the number of diversifying deals after 2007 supports this result and suggests that banks were shying away from diversification. Nevertheless, the reduction of these deals could simply reflect the then uncertainty among bank management regarding impending changes in European FI regulations. Alternatively, others could argue that the marked increase in focusing deals during the same period—and the creation of too-big-to-fail (TBTF) institutions—is equally responsible for the adverse impact of the crisis on the European banking sector. Casu et al. (2016) lend support to this argument; they find bank size to be an important and consistent determinant of risk as opposed to diversification, following M&A deals.

The Diversification of Bank Activities

Apart from engaging in M&A and prior to the crisis episode, banks had been increasing their proportion of profits from non-interest income activities (Brunnermeier et al. 2012).[18] Non-interest income represents all other operating revenues of a bank besides interest income, and includes income from investments in securities, trust and fiduciary, commissions and fees, trading accounts, and foreign exchange income. Activities that produce non-

[17] In 2007, the value of bank–securities deals stood at USD 31.3 billion, that is, a ninefold increase on 2006.

[18] Brunnermeier et al. (2012) report that the average (value-weighted) ratio of non-interest income-to-net interest income for US banks had increased approximately from 0.5 in 2000 to 1.5 in 2007.

Table 3.2 Mergers and acquisitions in the European Financial Services Industry, 2000–2015

Deal type	2000	2001	2002	2003	2004	2005	2006	2007	2008	2009	2010	2011	2012	2013	2014	2015	Total	Mean
Bank-Asset Management																		
Number	18	10	12	29	19	27	26	42	31	29	27	25	29	12	8	2	346	21.6
Value	262.0	255.0	2,700.2	3,172.8	887.2	545.9	260.3	1,861.8	1,584.8	1,241.9	260.6	3,736.5	873.6	1,167.5	452.9	379.1	19,642.0	1,227.6
Bank-Bank																		
Number	190	173	137	123	90	148	127	143	176	119	152	126	101	68	74	19	1,966	122.9
Value	97,157.1	33,501.3	28,920.2	32,724.3	33,388.6	49,765.1	41,369.0	86,427.7	52,752.6	49,300.8	24,638.3	27,004.9	18,476.6	23,803.9	10,896.7	1,719.9	611,847.2	38,240.4
Bank-Securities																		
Number	21	17	13	5	9	10	15	21	10	10	10	5	6	2	4	4	162	10.1
Value	1,236.1	2,446.6	538.0	149.2	3,999.2	2,421.6	3,132.6	31,350.7	681.0	77.1	9.6	0.0	1,400.0	0.0	369.0	94.7	47,905.4	2,994.1
Bank-Insurance																		
Number	25	19	14	13	11	15	9	27	10	14	5	17	6	6	10	3	204	12.8
Value	17,766.4	3,879.5	1,067.9	2,115.1	1,258.1	2,959.2	375.3	6,657.4	937.1	3,369.4	172.7	711.6	8,254.4	1,870.4	511.5	554.5	52,460.5	3,278.8
Asset Management-Bank																		
Number	8	7	8	3	8	12	30	16	16	12	14	16	10	13	7	1	181	11.3
Value	179.7	216.4	274.8	44.2	464.1	23,790.1	2,656.6	2,363.1	929.5	0.0	1,082.3	8,420.9	400.8	36,268.2	589.1	58.7	77,738.6	4,858.7
Securities-Bank																		
Number	6	11	10	13	6	6	7	9	4	13	7	4	7	6	7	1	117	7.3
Value	1,375.1	1,456.7	3,139.4	335.9	382.2	1,872.0	25,154.3	225.7	70.2	12,816.3	84.3	0.0	531.6	4,390.6	1,818.5	0.0	53,652.9	3,353.3
Insurance-Bank																		
Number	21	9	15	4	9	6	3	5	6	6	4	3	1	3	0	0	95	5.9
Value	3,472.8	20,392.6	412.0	340.3	540.6	2,817.9	486.9	2,781.6	0.0	273.4	153.1	35.3	89.6	0.0	0.0	0.0	31,796.1	1,987.3
Total number	289	246	209	190	152	224	217	263	253	203	219	196	160	110	110	30	3,071	191.9
Total value	121,449.3	62,148.2	37,052.6	38,881.7	40,920.1	84,171.9	73,435.0	131,668.0	56,955.2	67,078.9	26,401.0	39,909.1	30,026.5	67,500.6	14,637.8	2,806.8	895,043	55,940.2
Total value bank focus	97,157.1	33,501.3	28,920.2	32,724.3	33,388.6	49,765.1	41,369.0	86,427.7	52,752.6	49,300.8	24,638.3	27,004.9	18,476.6	23,803.9	10,896.7	1,719.9	611,847.2	38,240.4
Pct (%) Total value	80.0 %	53.9 %	78.1 %	84.2 %	81.6 %	59.1 %	56.3 %	65.6 %	92.6 %	73.5 %	93.3 %	67.7 %	61.5 %	35.3 %	74.4 %	61.3 %	68.4 %	69.9 %
Total value bank div.	24,292.2	28,646.9	8,132.4	6,157.4	7,531.4	34,406.8	32,066.0	45,240.3	4,202.6	17,778.1	1,762.6	12,904.3	11,549.9	43,696.7	3,741.1	1,086.9	283,195.6	17,699.7
Pct (%) Total value	20.0 %	46.1 %	21.9 %	15.8 %	18.4 %	40.9 %	43.7 %	34.4 %	7.4 %	26.5 %	6.7 %	32.3 %	38.5 %	64.7 %	25.6 %	38.7 %	31.6 %	30.1 %

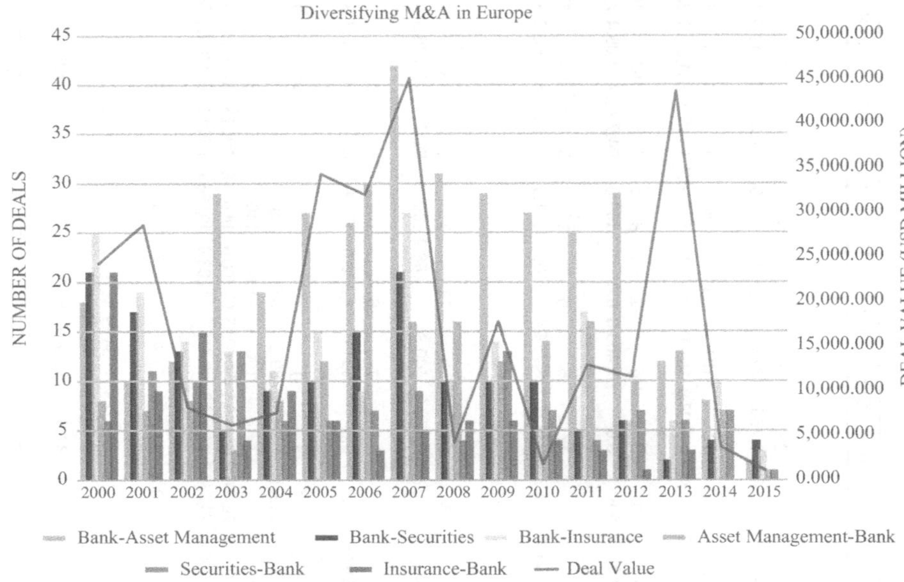

Fig. 3.1 Distribution of diversifying deals by year and deal type
Note: This figure presents the distribution of diversifying deals by year and deal type. The sample consists of completed European M&A deals where banks acquire (or, are acquired by) other banks, asset management companies, brokerage firms, and insurance companies, between 2000 and 2015. We source data from Thomson Financial. The sample of bank–insure consists of deals where the bidder is a bank and the target an insurance company. bank–asset management contains banks that acquire asset management companies; bank–securities contain banks that acquire securities firms; bank–insurance contains banks that acquire insurance companies; asset management–bank contains asset management companies that acquire banks; securities–bank contains securities firms that acquire banks. lastly, insurance–bank contains insurance companies that acquire banks. the deal value represents the total dollar value (USD millions) of deals

interest income include, but are not limited to, trading and securitization, investment banking and advisory, brokerage, insurance and venture capital. Next, we consider the evolution of non-interest income for European banks.

Figure 3.3 presents a proxy indicator of diversification, namely, the average of the ratio of non-interest income-to-net-interest income (DIV) for a sample of 360 publicly traded European banks over 2000–15. On average and over time, DIV has remained relatively stable, fluctuating between 0.81 and 1.27. In fact, there is very little evidence of an excessive increase in bank diversification in the years leading to 2007, despite the rise in the total number of diversifying deals. Nonetheless, a completely different picture emerges when we consider a sub-sample of SIFIs. First, their average DIV ratio is much higher than the whole sample and a sub-sample of non-SIFIs. Second,

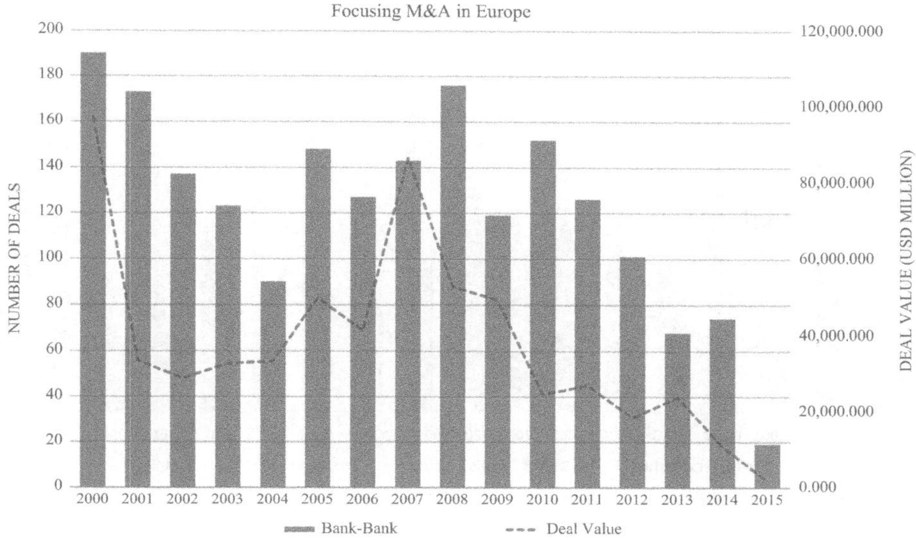

Fig. 3.2 Distribution of focusing deals by year
Note: This figure presents the distribution of focusing deals by year. The sample consists of completed European M&A deals where banks acquire (or, are acquired by) other banks, between 2000 and 2015. We source data from Thomson Financial. The sample of bank–bank consists of deals where both the bidder and the target institution are banks. Deal value represents the total dollar value (USD millions) of deals

the SIFIs' DIV ratio increases sharply in the years leading up to the crisis from 1.58 in 2003 to 2.57 in 2006. This increase mirrors the rise in the number of diversifying deals, and reinforces the view that the growth in consolidation among the largest banks has resulted in the creation of ever larger and more diversified financial institutions.

The diversification of banks into non-banking activities appears more significant if we use a value-weighted mean to proxy for DIV. Figure 3.4 shows that for the largest banks (whole sample) the level of DIV grew from 2.05 in 2000 to 2.22 in 2006. The trend to diversification is greater for SIFIs, with DIV growing from 1.95 in 2000 to 2.7 in 2006. In contrast, Fig. 3.4 shows a sharp decline in diversification levels for non-SIFIs from 2000–04, albeit followed by a small rise until 2006. In response to the crisis, large institutions chose to refocus on core interest activities causing DIV to fall below 1.00 in 2008. Since then, the largest banks have maintained an average DIV ratio of 1.32 and the SIFIs at 1.49. Interestingly, on average the non-SIFIs maintained a balance between non-interest income and interest income until 2012. By 2014, this group had reduced its level of diversification to 0.55.

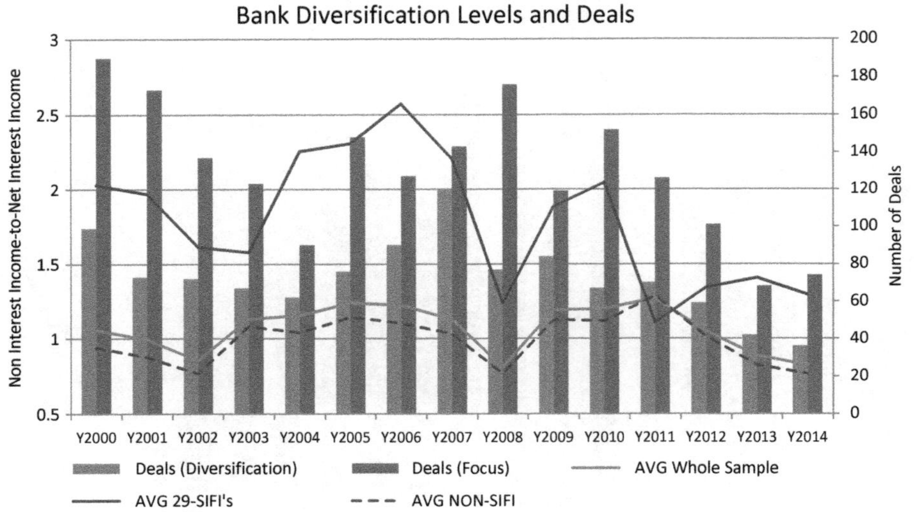

Fig. 3.3 Equally weighted non-interest income-to-total interest income ratio and number of deals
Note: This figure presents the average (equally weighted) non-interest income-to-net interest income ratio for a sample of 360 publicly traded European banks between 2000 and 2014. The number of M&A is also plotted on the figure. We source data from Thomson Financial. Deals (Diversification) represents the number of deals where banks acquire (or, are acquired by), asset management companies, brokerage firms, and insurance companies. Deals (Focus) represents the number of deals where banks acquire other banks. AVG Whole Sample represents the average non-interest income-to-net interest income ratio for the whole sample. AVG 29-SIFIs and AVG NON-SIFI represent the average non-interest income-to-net interest income ratio for the subset of SIFIs (as identified by the European Commission—2010 report—see http://ec.europa.eu/internal_market/financial-conglomerates/docs/201007_conglomerates_en.pdf) and non-SIFIs, respectively

The data on the diversification of EU banks are supportive of arguments in the previous section. In particular, a sharp increase in M&A activity in the European financial services industry until 2007 has helped to create larger and more diversified financial institutions. The extent to which these large and diversified institutions are responsible for the crisis and what did follow remains an open question. To this end, Ayadi and De Groen (2016) argue that not all types of banks are facing the same challenges or responding in the same way to crises. They propose a Business Models Monitor that attempts to address this diversity in banks and hence the response function of each category in a crisis situation. Defining and identifying business models in banking is not a trivial task because of its multi-faceted, ever changing nature and heavy reliance on granular data about banks' activities and risks.

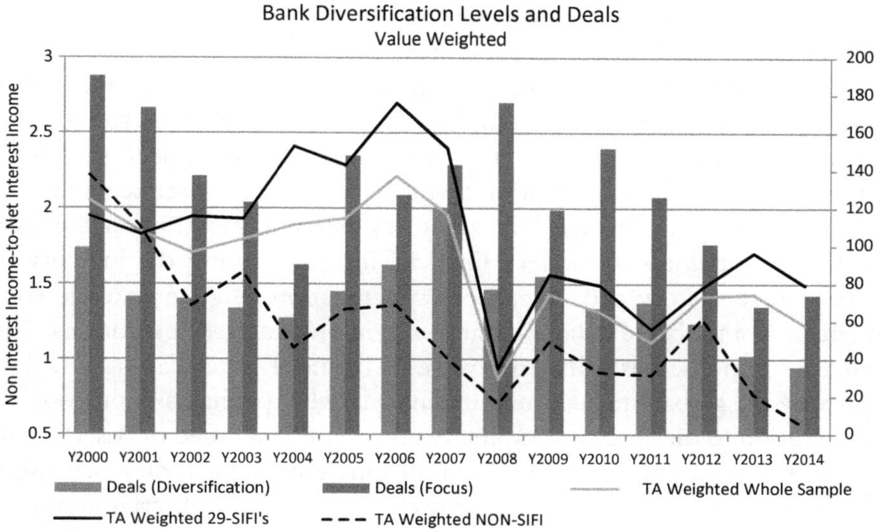

Fig. 3.4 Value-weighted non-interest income-to-total interest income ratio and number of deals

Note: This figure presents the average (value-weighted) non-interest income-to-net interest income ratio for a sample of 360 publicly traded European banks between 2000 and 2014. The number of M&A is also plotted on the figure. We source data from Thomson Financial. Deals (Diversification) represents the number of deals where banks acquire (or, are acquired by), asset management companies, brokerage firms, and insurance companies. Deals (Focus) represents the number of deals where banks acquire other banks. AVG Whole Sample represents the average non-interest income-to-net interest income ratio for the whole sample. AVG 29-SIFIs and AVG NON-SIFI represent the average non-interest income-to-net interest income ratio for the subset of SIFIs (as identified by the European Commission—2010 report—see http://ec.europa.eu/internal_market/financial-conglomerates/docs/201007_conglomerates_en.pdf) and non-SIFIs, respectively

Concluding Remarks

In recent years, financial innovation coupled with the increasing popularity of capital markets has resulted in a disintermediation process, where traditional intermediaries have faced declines in market shares and revenues. These forces have pushed towards a structural evolution in the financial services industry. After years of deregulation and consolidation among FIs, structures such as very large multi-product conglomerates with global reach and power currently represent the norm rather than the exception.

The European financial services industry is responsible for a large part of this consolidation activity. Our review identifies that increased M&A activity in the years leading up to the financial crisis has led to a significant increase in bank diversification into non-interest income sources.

This trend has triggered a long-lasting debate among scholars and policy makers. The literature extends from theoretical contributions on the benefits and costs of conglomeration, to empirical studies that attempt to shed light on the effects of bank diversification on the broader financial services industry and the economy as a whole. The crisis has renewed attention on the level of interconnectedness of modern financial institutions and the inability of the current regulatory and supervisory system to prevent the systemic consequences of a probable default of large and interconnected institutions. The regulatory response has initiated a wave of financial re-regulation aimed at improving the global financial architecture and which remains in process.

In addition to the enhanced capital requirements contained in Basel 3, policy makers have addressed the question of functional separation albeit using different approaches. The principle, however, is similar with each approach identifying a set of impermissible activities and requiring some form of firewall between safe and risky activities. Although these moves nod in the direction of the Glass-Steagall Act of 1933, the fact that they do not demand complete functional separation possibly signals that the benefits of conglomeration outweigh the costs.

At the same time, public policy responses should not just focus on financial conglomerates, but on other "partners" such as the state, regulators and government agencies that ought to share responsibility. It is difficult to bypass the public sentiment that state intervention used taxpayer's money to support the wealth of numerous institutions endorsing poor financial management, which in turn gives rise to the moral hazard problem. Extreme measures by governments and the consequent large exposure of sovereigns to their own banking sectors can be enumerated among the causes of the recent sovereign debt crisis in Europe (Carletti and Leonello 2016). The regulatory framework should act as deterrent to these institutions; while putting in place capital requirements especially for newly created structural products especially when promoted by government-sponsored entities enjoying implicit government guarantee. Finally, credit rating agencies should swift from their ex post reaction to financial distress to a more proactive attitude of issuing warnings before distress takes place, as well as addressing the serious issue of conflict of interest.

Looking forward, the European Commission has recognised the intricacies of modern financial markets and the institutions operating within. The European Commission states that: "the Financial Conglomerates Directive will enhance the prudential soundness and effective supervision of financial conglomerates; will promote convergence in national supervisory approaches, and between sectors; will enhance financial stability and is a significant improvement in the protection of depositors, insurance policy holders and investors."[19] It is the first comprehensive implementation in the world of internationally agreed recommendations on supervision of financial conglomerates. Appropriate supervision of financial conglomerates—large financial groups active in different financial sectors, often across borders—is important because these firms are often systemically important, either in one member state of the European Union or for the European Union as a whole.

Despite the voluminous work on bank diversification, the evidence still yields conflicting conclusions. The impact of diversification on the risk and return of financial institutions is ambiguous. What's more, the literature fails to provide a clear answer as to whether bank diversification increases systemic risk. A common and persistent problem across the literature is the inability of studies to capture the endogenous nature of bank risk-taking, that is, the fact that bank diversification may lead to higher risk-taking. Another problem arises from the lack of a common measure of risk-return and the use of different samples across contributions.

The current regulatory response, therefore, has had to contend with inconclusive evidence. As Casu et al. (2016, pp. 272) point out, "these reforms will not only introduce costs to financial institutions, the taxpayer and the consumer, but will produce renewed imbalances among financial institutions". Given the lack of a substantial basis to these reforms, their effectiveness remains to be known.

References

Acharya, V. V. (2009). A theory of systemic risk and design of prudential bank regulation. *Journal of Financial Stability, 5*, 224–255.

Adrian, T., & Shin, H. S. (2010). The changing nature of financial intermediation and the financial crisis of 2007–2009. *Annual Review of Economics, 2*, 603–618.

Allen, L., & Jagtiani, J. (2000). The risk effects of combining banking, securities, and insurance activities. *Journal of Economics and Business, 52*, 485–497.

Allen, F., & Santomero, A. M. (2001). What do financial intermediaries do? *Journal of Banking and Finance, 25*, 271–294.

Allen, L., Babus, A., & Carletti, E. (2012). Asset commonality, debt maturity and systemic risk. *Journal of Financial Economics, 104*, 519–534.

Amel, D., Barnes, C., Panetta, F., & Salleo, C. (2004). Consolidation and efficiency in the financial sector: A review of the international evidence. *Journal of Banking and Finance, 28*, 2493–2519.

[19] http://ec.europa.eu/finance/financial-conglomerates/index_en.htm

Andriosopoulos, K., Chan, K. K., Dontis-Charitos, P., & Staikouras, S. K. (2016). *Wealth and risk implications of the Dodd-Frank Act on the U.S. financial intermediaries. Journal of Financial Stability, forthcoming,* available at: http://dx.doi.org/10.1016/j.jfs.2016.09.006

Ayadi, R., & De Groen, W. P. (2016). Banking business models in Europe. In T. Beck & B. Casu (Eds.), *Handbook of European Banking*. New York: Palgrave Macmillan.

Baele, L., De Jonghe, O., & Vander Vennet, R. (2007). Does the stock market value bank diversification? *Journal of Banking and Finance, 31*, 1999–2023.

Barth, J. R., Brumbaugh, R. D., & Wilcox, J. A. (2000). Policy watch: The repeal of Glass-Steagall and the advent of broad banking. *Journal of Economic Perspectives, 14*, 191–204.

Baumol, W. J. (1982). Contestable markets: An uprising in the theory of industry structure. *The American Economic Review, 72*, 1–15.

BCBS (2011) Global systemically important banks: Assessment methodology and the additional loss absorbency requirement—Rules text. BIS, November.

Benston, G. J. (1994). Universal banking. *Journal of Economic Perspectives, 8*, 121–143.

Berger, A. N. (2003). The economic effects of technological progress: Evidence from the banking industry. *Journal of Money, Credit and Banking, 35*, 141–176.

Berger, A. N., Hunter, W. C., & Timme, S. G. (1993). The efficiency of financial institutions: A review and preview of research past, present and future. *Journal of Banking and Finance, 17*, 221–249.

Berger, A. N., Humphrey, D. B., & Pulley, L. B. (1996). Do consumers pay for one-stop banking? Evidence from an alternative revenue function. *Journal of Banking and Finance, 20*, 1601–1621.

Berger, A. N., Demsetz, R. S., & Strahan, P. E. (1999). The consolidation of the financial services industry: Causes, consequences, and implications for the future. *Journal of Banking and Finance, 23*, 135–194.

Berger, A. N., DeYoung, R., & Udell, G. (2001). Efficiency barriers to the consolidation of the European financial services industry. *European Financial Management, 7*, 117–130.

Berger, A. N., Hasan, I., & Zhou, M. (2010). The effects of focus versus diversification on bank performance: Evidence from Chinese banks. *Journal of Banking and Finance, 34*, 1417–1435.

Black, F., Miller, M. H., & Posner, R. A. (1978). An approach to the regulation of bank holding companies. *Journal of Business, 51*, 379–412.

Boot, A. W. A., & Schmeits, A. (2000). Market discipline and incentive problems in conglomerate firms with applications to banking. *Journal of Financial Intermediation, 9*, 240–273.

Boyd, J. H., & Graham, S. L. (1986). Risk, regulation, and bank holding company expansion into nonbanking. Federal Reserve Bank of Minneapolis. *Quarterly Review, 10*(2), 2–17.

Boyd, J. H., & Graham, S. L. (1988). The profitability and risk effects of allowing bank holding companies to merge with other financial firms: A simulation study. Federal Reserve Bank of Minneapolis. *Quarterly Review, 12*(2), 3–17.

Boyd, J. H., Graham, S. L., & Hewitt, R. S. (1993). Bank holding company mergers with nonbank financial firms: Effects on the risk of failure. *Journal of Banking and Finance, 17*, 43–64.

Brewer, E. (1989). Relationship between bank holding company risk and non-bank activity. *Journal of Economics and Business, 41*, 337–353.

Brewer, E., Fortier, D., & Pavel, C. (1988). Bank risk from nonbank activities. *Economic Perspectives, 12*, 14–26.

Brunnermeier, M.K., Dong, G.N., & Palia, D. (2012). *Banks' non-interest income and systemic risk*. AFA 2012 Chicago meetings paper. Available at: http://ssrn.com/abstract=1786738.

Buch, C. M., & DeLong, G. L. (2009). Banking globalization: International consolidation and mergers in banking. In A. N. Berger, P. Molyneux, & J. O. S. Wilson (Eds.), *The Oxford handbook of banking* (pp. 508–530). New York: Oxford University Press.

Carletti, E., & Leonello, A. (2016). Regulatory reforms in the European banking sector. In T. Beck & B. Casu (Eds.), *Handbook of European banking*. New York: Palgrave Macmillan.

Carow, K. A., & Kane, E. J. (2002). Event-study evidence of the value of relaxing longstanding regulatory restraints on banks, 1970–2000. *Quarterly Review of Economics and Finance, 42*, 439–463.

Casu, B., & Girardone, C. (2004). Financial conglomeration: Efficiency, productivity and strategic drive. *Applied Financial Economics, 14*, 687–696.

Casu, B., Dontis-Charitos, P., Staikouras, S. K., & Williams, J. (2016). Diversification, size and risk: The case of bank acquisitions of nonbank financial firms. *European Financial Management, 22*, 235–275.

Chang, C. E., & Lynge, M. J. (1994). An empirical examination of scale and scope economics of U.S. savings banks. *American Business Review, 12*, 100–109.

Chen, X. (2007). Banking deregulation and credit risk: Evidence from the EU. *Journal of Financial Stability, 2*, 356–390.

Chow, J. T. S., & Surti, J.. (2011). Making banks safer: Can Volcker and Vickers do it? IMF WP/11/236.

De Jonghe, O. (2010). Back to the basics in banking? A micro-analysis of banking system stability. *Journal of Financial Intermediation, 19*, 387–417.

De Jonghe, O., Diepstraten, M., & Schepens, G. (2015). Banks' size, scope and systemic risk: What role for conflicts of interest? *Journal of Banking and Finance, 61*, S3–S13.

DeYoung, R., Evanoff, D., & Molyneux, P. (2009). Mergers and acquisitions of financial institutions: A review of the post-2000 literature. *Journal of Financial Services Research, 36*, 87–110.

Dontis-Charitos, P., Molyneux, P., & Staikouras, S. K. (2011). Does the stock market compensate banks for diversifying into the insurance business? *Financial Markets, Institutions and Instruments, 20*, 1–28.

Elyasiani, E., Staikouras, S.K., & Dontis-Charitos, P. (2016). Cross-industry product diversification and contagion in risk and return: The case of bank-insurance and insurance-bank takeovers. *Journal of Risk and Insurance, 83*, 681–718.

Estrella, A. (2001). Mixing and matching: Prospective financial sector mergers and market valuation. *Journal of Banking and Finance, 25*, 2367–2392.

Fields, L. P., Fraser, D. R., & Kolari, J. W. (2007). Is bancassurance a viable model for financial firms? *Journal of Risk and Insurance, 74*, 777–794.

Flannery, M. J. (1999). Modernizing financial regulation: The relation between interbank transactions and supervisory reform. *Journal of Financial Services Research, 16*, 101.

Gambacorta, L., & van Rixtel, A. (2013). *Structural bank regulation initiatives: Approaches and implications*. BIS working papers no. 412.

Genetay, N., & Molyneux, P. (1998). *Bancassurance*. London: Macmillan Press Ltd.

Goddard, J., Molyneux, P., Wilson, J. O. S., & Tavakoli, M. (2007). European banking: An overview. *Journal of Banking and Finance, 31*, 1911–1935.

Goddard, J., Molyneux, P., & Wilson, J. O. S. (2010). Banking in the European Union. In A. N. Berger, P. Molyneux, & J. O. S. Wilson (Eds.), *The Oxford handbook of banking* (pp. 807–843). New York: Oxford University Press.

Heggestad, A. (1975). Riskiness of investments in non-bank activities by bank holding companies. *Journal of Economics and Business, 27*, 219–223.

Herring, R. J., & Carmassi, J. (2015). Complexity and systemic risk: What's changed since the crisis? In A. N. Berger, P. Molyneux, & J. O. S. Wilson (Eds.), *The Oxford handbook of banking* (2 ed., pp. 77–112). New York: Oxford University Press.

Herring, R. J., & Santomero, A. M. (1990). The corporate structure of financial conglomerates. *Journal of Financial Services Research, 4*, 471–497.

Hoque, H., Andriosopoulos, D., Andriosopoulos, K., & Douady, R. (2015). Bank regulation, risk and return: Evidence from the credit and sovereign debt crises. *Journal of Banking and Finance, 50*, 455–474.

Hryckiewicz, A., & L. Kozlowski (2015). Banking business models and the nature of financial crisis. Available at SSRN: http://ssrn.com/abstract=2557097

Hunter, W. C., Timme, S. G., & Yang, W. K. (1990). An examination of cost subaddivity and multiproduct production in large U.S. banks. *Journal of Money Credit and Banking, 22*, 504–525.

Ibragimov, R., Jaffee, D., & Walden, J. (2011). Diversification disasters. *Journal of Financial Economics, 99*, 333–348.

Kalotychou, E., & Staikouras, S. K. (2007). De facto versus de jure bank-insurance ventures in the Greek market. *Geneva Papers on Risk and Insurance, 32*, 246–263.

Kane, E. J. (1981). Accelerating inflation, technological innovation, and the decreasing effectiveness of banking regulation. *Journal of Finance, 36*, 355–367.

Kane, E. J. (1988). Interaction of financial and regulatory innovation. *American Economic Review, 78*, 328–334.

Kane, E. J. (2000). Incentives for banking megamergers: What motives might regulators infer from event-study evidence? *Journal of Money, Credit and Banking, 32*, 671–701.

Kwan, S.H. (2004) Banking consolidation. Federal Reserve Bank of San Francisco, *FRBSF Economic Letter*, 15.

Kwan, S. H., & E. S. Laderman (1999) On the portfolio effects of financial convergence—A review of the literature. Federal Reserve Bank of San Francisco, *FRSBS Economic Review*, 2.

Laderman, E. S. (1999). *The potential diversification and failure reduction benefits of bank expansion into nonbanking activities*. Federal Reserve Bank of San Francisco working paper, No 2000-01.

Laeven, L., & Levine, R. (2007). Is there a diversification discount in financial conglomerates? *Journal of Financial Economics, 85*, 331–367.

Lang, G., & Welzel, P. (1996). Efficiency and technical progress in banking empirical results for a panel of German cooperative banks. *Journal of Banking and Finance, 20*, 1003–1023.

Levy, H., & Sarnat, M. (1970). Diversification, portfolio analysis and the uneasy case for conglomerate mergers. *Journal of Finance, 25*, 795–802.

Lown, C.S., Osler, C.L., Strahan, P.E., & Sufi, A. (2000). The changing landscape of the financial services industry: What lies ahead? Federal Reserve Bank of New York,. *Economic Policy Review*, 39–55.

Mercieca, S., Schaeck, K., & Wolfe, S. (2007). Small European banks: Benefits from diversification? *Journal of Banking and Finance, 31*, 1975–1998.

Merck Martel, M., van Rixtel, A., & Mota, E. González. (2012). Business models of international banks in the wake of the 2007–09 global financial crisis. *Estabilidad Financiera* No. 22 (Bank of Spain).

Molyneux, P. (2016). Structural reform, too-big-to fail and banks as public utilities in Europe. In S. P. S. Rossi & R. Malavasi (Eds.), *Financial crisis, bank behaviour and credit crunch* (pp. 67–80). NewYork: Springer.

Molyneux, P., Schaeck, K., & Zhou, T. M. (2014). 'Too systemically important to fail' in banking—Evidence from bank mergers and acquisitions. *Journal of International Money and Finance, 49*, 258–282.

Pais, A., & Stork, P. A. (2013). Bank size and systemic risk. *European Financial Management, 19*, 429–451.

Pilloff, S. J., & Santomero, A. M. (1998). The value effects of bank mergers and acquisitions. In Y. Amihud & G. Miller (Eds.), *Bank mergers and acquisitions* (Vol. 3, pp. 59–78). Boston/Dordrecht: The New York University Salomon Center Series on Financial Markets and Institutions.

Santomero, A. M., & Eckles, D. L. (2000). The determinants of success in the new financial services environment: Now that firms can do everything, what should they do and why should regulators care? Federal Reserve Bank of New York, *Economic Policy Review*, 11–23.

Santos, J. A. C. (1998). Commercial banks in the securities business: A review. *Journal of Financial Services Research, 14*, 35–59.
Saunders, A., & Cornett, M. (2008). *Financial institutions management: A risk management approach*. NewYork: McGraw Hill.
Saunders, A., & Walter, I. (1994). *Universal banking in the United States: What could we gain? What could we lose?* New York: Oxford University Press.
Saunders, A. (1994) Banking and Commerce: An overview of the public policy issues. *Journal of Banking and Finance, 18*, 231–254.
Staikouras, S. K. (2006). Business opportunities and market realities in financial conglomerates. *Geneva Papers on Risk and Insurance, 31*, 124–148.
Stein, J. C. (1997). Internal capital markets and the competition for corporate resources. *Journal of Finance, 52*, 111–133.
Stiroh, K. J. (2004). Diversification in banking: Is noninterest income the answer? *Journal of Money, Credit and Banking, 36*, 853–882.
Stiroh, K. J. (2006). A portfolio view of banking with interest and noninterest activities. *Journal of Money, Credit and Banking, 38*, 1351–1361.
Stiroh, K. J. (2015). Diversification in banking. In A. N. Berger, P. Molyneux, & J. O. S. Wilson (Eds.), *The Oxford handbook of banking* (2 ed., pp. 219–243). Oxford University Press, Oxford, UK.
Stiroh, K. J., & Rumble, A. (2006). The dark side of diversification: The case of U.S. financial holding companies. *Journal of Banking and Finance, 30*, 2131–2161.
Taylor, B. (1999). The Darwinian shakeout in financial services. *Long Range Planning, 32*, 58–64.
Vallascas, F., & Hagendorff, J. (2011). The impact of European bank mergers on bidder default risk. *Journal of Banking and Finance, 35*, 902–915.
Vallascas, F., & Keasey, K. (2012). Bank resilience to systemic shocks and the stability of banking systems: Small is beautiful. *Journal of International Money and Finance, 31*, 1745–1776.
Vander Vennet, R. (2002). Cost and profit efficiency of financial conglomerates and universal banks in Europe. *Journal of Money, Credit and Banking, 34*, 254–282.
Wagner, W. (2008). The homogenization of the financial system and financial crises. *Journal of Financial Intermediation, 17*, 330–356.
Wagner, W. (2010). Diversification at financial institutions and systemic crises. *Journal of Financial Intermediation, 19*, 373–386.
Walter, I. (1997). Universal banking: A shareholder value perspective. *European Management Journal, 15*, 344.
Walter, I. (2009). Economic drivers of structural change in the global financial services industry. *Long Range Planning, 42*, 588–613.
Weiß, G. N. F., Neumann, S., & Bostandzic, D. (2014a). Systemic risk and bank consolidation: International evidence. *Journal of Banking and Finance, 40*, 165–181.

Weiß, G. N. F., Bostandzic, D., & Neumann, S. (2014b). What factors drive systemic risk during international financial crises? *Journal of Banking and Finance, 41*, 78–96.

Wheelock, D. C., & Wilson, P. W. (2001). New evidence on returns to scale and product mix among U.S. commercial banks. *Journal of Monetary Economics, 47*, 653–674.

Zhou, C. (2009). *Are banks too big to fail? Measuring systemic importance of financial institutions*. SSRN working paper, available at: http://ssrn.com/abstract=1546384

Zhou, C. (2013). The impact of imposing capital requirements on systemic risk. *Journal of Financial Stability, 9*, 320–329.

4

Banks' Business Models in Europe

Rym Ayadi and Willem Pieter de Groen

Introduction

Since the onset of the 2007–8 financial crisis, the banking sector has been in the spotlight. The previous decades saw a frenetic race to high returns on equity coupled with excessive risk-taking, encouraged by a lax monetary policy and accommodating banking regulations. This led to major changes in the way banks conduct business. A large number of banks stretched the conventional intermediating role up beyond its limits and also extended their proprietary activities. This resulted in a ballooning banking sector that attached less value to financing the real economy and put systemic stability at risk. The failures of several banks with unsustainable business models, such as Lehman Brothers and Northern Rock to name a few, spurred contagion and contributed to the global financial and Eurozone economic crises. Crises episodes have been widely documented and have sparked a fundamental overhaul of regulation and supervision.[1]

[1] See Acharya et al. (2013), Blundell-Wignall et al. (2008), Brunnermeier (2009), Dewatripont et al. (2010), Gorton and Metrick (2012), Hellwig (2009), Reinhajrt and Rogoff (2009), etc.

R. Ayadi (✉)
HEC Montreal International Business School, HEC Montreal,
Montreal, QC, Canada
e-mail: rym.ayadi@hec.ca

W.P. de Groen
Financial Institutions and Prudential Policy Unit, Centre for European Policy Studies (CEPS), Brussels, Belgium
e-mail: willem.pieter.degroen@ceps.eu

T. Beck, B. Casu (eds.), *The Palgrave Handbook of European Banking*,
DOI 10.1057/978-1-137-52144-6_4

However, not all types of bank faced the same challenges and/or responded in the same way to crises because of their diverse business models. Ayadi et al. (2011) screened a sample of 26 large European banks to identify and assess their business models covering the years 2006–9. The analysis, using a set of asset and liability balance sheet indicators and a clustering methodology, showed that these banks are grouped broadly into three business models: retail, wholesale and investment. When assessing the performance and risk of the three business models, the paper concluded that the retail-banking model has seemingly fared better through the crisis but the market has not accounted for the higher riskiness of the other business models, namely investment banking, so that a moral hazard problem was suspected to exist. In addition, the paper advised against a heavy reliance on risk-adjusted capital requirements, because these indicators may not reflect the underlying risks of the different business models.

This chapter, which expands on Ayadi et al. (2011), attempts to address this diversity of banks in Europe by identifying their business models using a novel definition and methodology. The analysis is performed on 147 European banks accounting for more than 80 % of total assets during the period 2006–13. The results on the structural and financial attributes, the interaction with ownership structure, the extent of internationalization and the degree of migration are provided per business model.

Identifying Business Models in European Banking

The Banks' Business Models Analysis for Europe identified the business models of 147 banks that cover more than 80 % of assets of the EU banking industry. Using a novel definition and a careful selection of multi-dimensional attributes and developing state-of the art clustering methodologies, the Business Models Analysis provides a coherent approach to screen a set of banks and to monitor their behaviour over time (from 2006 to 2013). In what follows, we present the definition, the sample, the methodology and the results.

Definition

The business models definition used in this chapter distinguishes primarily between the key banking activities (i.e. retail versus market or mixed) and the funding strategies (i.e. retail versus market or mixed), which broadly builds on an asset-liability approach (Fig. 4.1). This approach allows a clear understanding of the behaviour of a bank within its sector, the financial system and the economy as a whole.

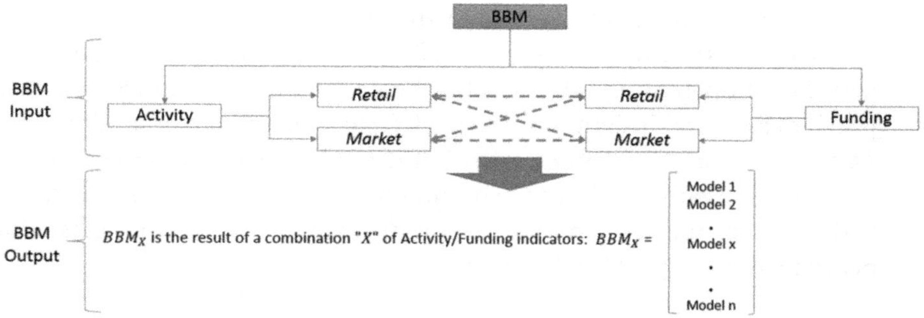

Fig. 4.1 Bank business model definition (First used in Ayadi and De Groen (2014a))
Source: Authors

To constitute the defining activity/funding features of a business model in banks from an asset and liability stand point, several factors or instruments are used collectively, without over-representing any particular factor, which were used to form the clusters or models.

These are the six instruments that were used to form the clusters.[2]

1. *Loans to banks (as % of assets).* The indicator measures the scale of wholesale and interbank activities, which proxy for exposures to risks arising from interconnectedness in the banking sector.
2. *Trading assets (as % of assets).* These are defined as non-cash assets other than loans; a greater value would indicate the prevalence of investment activities that are prone to market and liquidity risks.
3. *Bank liabilities (as a % of assets).* This indicator identifies the share of liabilities of other banks, including deposits, issued debt, and funds obtained from central banks. Banks with greater interbank funding requirements, often due to an excessive reliance on short-term funding, faced severe problems in the earlier phases of the crisis.
4. *Customer deposits (as % of assets).* This indicator identifies the share of deposits from non-bank and private customers, e.g. households or enterprises, in the total balance sheet, indicating a reliance on more traditional funding sources.
5. *Debt liabilities (as % of assets).* Calculated by netting customer deposits, bank liabilities, total equity and negative fair values of all derivative trans-

[2] Alternative instrument combinations were also considered. In many cases, using a different set of instruments led to an unrealistically large number of clusters, with many comprising a single bank/year. Removing any one of the six indicators from the clustering exercise also led to an indistinct clustering. In turn, using a larger set did not change the results substantially, as long as the named indicators were included.

actions from total liabilities, this instrument is strongly (and negatively) correlated with customer deposit funding. While bank liabilities are comprised of short-term interbank debt, the broader debt liabilities indicator provides a general insight into the bank's exposure to market funding.
6. *Derivative exposures (as % of assets).*[3] This measure aggregates the carrying value of all negative derivative exposures of a bank, which are often identified as one of the key (and most risky) financial exposures of banks with heavy investment and trading activities.

Control is made for financial and risk exposures.

More sub-instruments can be used depending on the level of granularity of data available under each of the five instruments chosen. More granular data will allow a better understanding of business models in banking. This exercise was, however, subject to data limitations but, yet, can offer a useful encompassing framework to do more research on this topic in the future, when data becomes available.

Sample

The European banking sector incorporates a rich array of banks with diverse business models and ownership structures. Apart from the larger commercial banks, which mostly follow the shareholder value (SHV) type, which focus on a broad mix of banking activities, a large number of stakeholder value (STV) institutions with different ownership structures (public banks, cooperatives, and savings institutions) co-exist in a diversified market (see also Fig. 4.2).

The sample under study in this chapter is comprised of 147 large European Economic Area (EEA) banking groups and subsidiaries of non-EEA banking groups (up from 74 covered in our earlier study, Ayadi et al. 2012) and of 26 covered in Ayadi et al. 2010. These banks together account for around 80 % of the EU's banking assets (See also Fig. 4.3 which indicates the coverage across banking groups.).[4] The sample consists of the banks subject to at least one of the Committee of European Banking Supervisors (CEBS) and European Banking Authority (EBA) exercises conducted between 2010 and

[3]Total derivative exposures are defined as the summation of positive and negative fair values of all derivative transactions, including interest, currency, equity, over the counter (OTC), hedge and trading derivatives.

[4]Except for Norwegian DnB NOR Bank, all banking groups and banks are domiciled in the EU. These EU banking groups and banks had total assets of €34.7 trillion in 2012. Hence, the sample represents around 80 % of the EU total banking assets (€43.6 trillion), using ECB (2014) consolidated banking data. The sample covers at least 50 % of the banking assets in each of the EU member states.

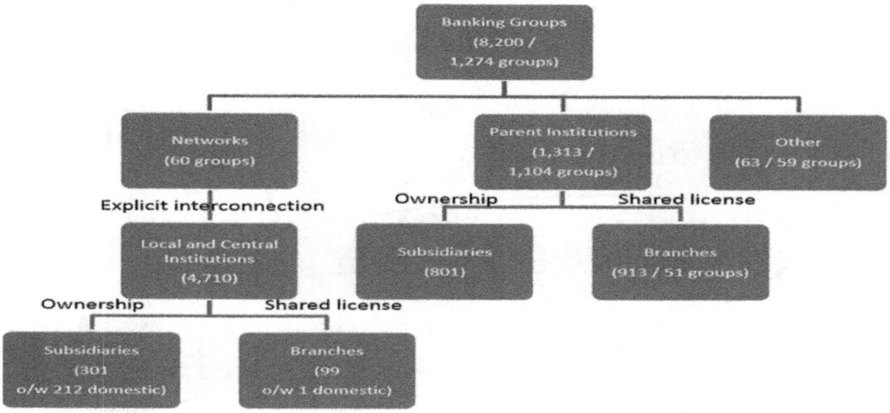

Fig. 4.2 European banking sector structure framework (December 2012) (The figure shows the order in credit institutions and branches across the European Economic Area (EEA). In total there are 8,200 credit institutions and branches in this region. However, these are often strongly related through ownership (i.e. subsidiaries and branches) or networks (i.e. groups of credit institutions that are jointly liable for each others' losses and/or having integrated organizations). When taking this into account, the number of distinct banking groups in the EEA is 1,274.)
Note: The numbers in the figures are the number of unconsolidated credit institutions and/or branches in the EEA unless stated otherwise
Source: Authors

2014,[5] the credit institutions identified for the comprehensive assessment of the European Central Bank (ECB),[6] EU based banks identified by the FSB as global systemically important banks (GSIBs),[7] and the EU-based cooperative banking groups and central institutions included in the private Database on Institutions of the IOFSC at HEC Montreal. The sample covers the years 2006–2013 and includes 1,126 bank-year observations (up from 352 in Ayadi et al. 2012).

The list of the sampled banks, their ownership structure, total assets and the growth of assets for recent years is given in Ayadi and De Groen (2014a).

[5] See Ayadi and De Groen (2014b) for a comprehensive overview of the banks subject to the CEBS EU-Wide Stress Testing Exercise in 2010 and the 2011 EU-wide stress test, EU Capital exercise 2011, and 2013 EU-wide transparency exercise conducted by EBA. See https://www.eba.europa.eu/documents/10180/669262/Methodological+Note.pdf for the sample of the 2014 EU-banks stress test.

[6] See http://www.ecb.europa.eu/pub/pdf/other/en_dec_2014_03_fen.pdf?21d953cb19106056a509a22888c646a8 for the full list of credit institutions that is subject to the first comprehensive assessment of the European Central Bank (ECB). The subsidiaries of banking groups included in the CEBS/EBA exercises are assessed at the group level, e.g. to avoid double counting.

[7] See http://www.financialstabilityboard.org/publications/r_131111.pdf for the GSIBs-list as of November 2013.

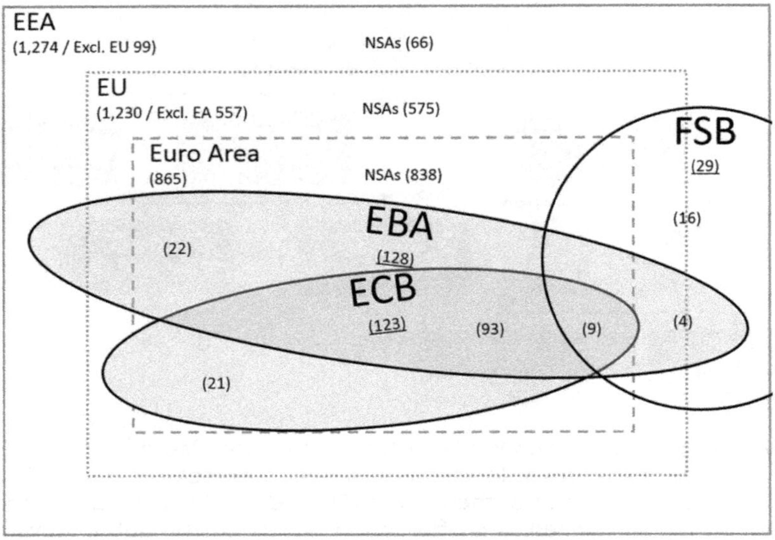

Fig. 4.3 Banking groups active in EEA by supervisor and area (December 2012)
Note: The grey areas in the figure correspond with the banks covered in this report. The amounts behind NSAs provide the cumulative number of banking groups supervised by National Supervisory Authorities. The amounts in the left-hand corner express the consolidated number of banking groups in the total area. The remaining figures express the number of supervised institutions. Only an exact overlap is considered. Hence, the subsidiaries of EBA supervised banking groups are not considered as overlap. The list of ECB supervised banks includes 12 subsidiaries of EBA stress-tested banks (SEB AB (3x), DNB BANK, Swedbank (2x), Danske, Nordea, HSBC (2x) and RBS (2x))
Source: Authors

To account for mergers that have taken place in recent years, all the large pre- and post-merger and acquired entities that qualify as the largest banks have been included in the database. In particular, the list covers the French Caisse d'Epargne and Banque Populaire, which merged in 2009 to form the BPCE Group, the Italian Banca Intesa and Sanpaolo IMI, which merged in 2007 to form the Intesa Sanpaolo and the British HBOS, which was acquired by Lloyds Banking Group in 2009. In addition, there is a large number of Spanish savings banks (or *cajas de ahorro*) that merged or were absorbed by other banks during and after the Spanish banking crisis that started in 2009.

Methodology

To identify the business models, we used a cluster analysis, which is a statistical technique for assigning a set of observations (i.e. a particular bank in a particular year) into distinct clusters (i.e. business models). By definition, observations that are assigned to the same cluster share a certain degree of similarity, as measured by a set of instruments (that are considered relevant). The formation of clusters ensures that they are sufficiently dissimilar among themselves, identifying different distinguishing characteristics of the observations they represent. To create the clusters, the initial step is to determine a set of instruments to identify any similarities or distinctions. The second step—more technical in nature—is to determine the methods for measuring similarities, for partitioning the clusters, and for determining the appropriate number of clusters (i.e. the 'stopping rule').

One of the key problems often encountered in clustering is the presence of missing values. When a particular observation has one or more missing instrument values, it has to be dropped from the cluster analysis since the similarity measures cannot be computed. The sample used in the study contains some such cases, despite efforts to choose indicators with high coverage ratios. In order to accommodate the entire sample of observations, missing values were filled with 'regression method' estimates using the existing set of indicators as predictors. In addition, when the 'intangible assets' and 'negative carrying values of derivatives exposures' were not reported, they were assumed to be zero in the calculation of 'trading assets' and 'derivative exposures', since banks are not required to report both balance sheet items unless significant.

Assuming that banks consciously choose their business models, any cluster analysis should be based on instruments over which the banks can have a direct influence. For example, a bank is likely to have a great degree of choice over its general structure, financial position and some of the risk indicators.[8] In turn, most of the performance indicators are related to instruments that are beyond the bank's control, such as market conditions, systemic risks and consumer demand. This was one of the principal reasons why details on income sources (i.e. interest vs. non-interest income) were not used as instruments in the creation of the clusters.

Ward's (1963) procedure to calculate the distance between clusters was used to form the technical aspects. The procedure form partitions in a hierarchical manner, starting from the largest number of clusters possible (i.e. all bank/years in a separate cluster) and merging clusters by minimizing the within-cluster sum-of-squared-errors for any given number of clusters. Several studies found that the Ward clustering methods perform better than other clustering procedures for instruments that involve few outliers and in the presence of overlaps.[9] Moreover, to diagnose the appropriate number of clusters, Calinski

[8] All the instruments used for clustering were standardized so that each indicator had a mean of zero and a standard deviation of one. This was done to prevent any potential biases arising from the choice of units, i.e. use of percentages rather than basis points.

[9] See Milligan (1981) and references therein for an assessment of different clustering methods.

and Harabasz's (1974) pseudo-F index, i.e. the 'stopping rule', was used. The index is a sample estimate of the ratio of between-cluster variance to within-cluster variance.[10] The configuration with the greatest pseudo-F value was chosen as the most distinct clustering.

All the multiple imputation and clustering procedures were conducted using SAS's built-in and user-contributed functions.[11]

It is important to highlight once again that cluster analysis is an inexact science. The assignment of individual banks to a specific cluster, or model, depends crucially on the choice of instruments and procedures, such as the proximity metric, procedures for forming clusters and the stopping rules used. Although the literature on the technical aspects of cluster analysis is relatively well developed, there is little theory on why certain procedures perform better than others.[12] In choosing instruments, attention was given to testing a variety of alternative configurations. The six indicators mentioned above led to the most consistent and distinct clustering. Dropping or adding variables resulted in a substantial worsening of the statistical measures of distinct clustering, which suggests that the chosen set adequately identifies the main distinguishing characteristics of the sampled banks. As the discussion below makes clear, the characteristics of the business models that are identified by the cluster analysis are by and large in line with expectations. Despite these efforts, it is certainly true that the outcomes may change with other configurations. For these reasons, the results of the present analysis should be interpreted with care.

Results

The clustering procedures summarized in the previous section lead to highly consistent results. In particular, the results show that the pseudo-F indices attain a single maximum, pointing to the four-cluster configuration as the most distinct one (see Table 4.1).

The descriptive details for the four clusters are given below in Table 4.2 and Fig. 4.4.

The clustering analysis identified four models as the most distinct form of clustering. Table 4.2 gives the descriptive statistics for the four models result-

[10] Evaluating a variety of cluster stopping rules, Milligan and Cooper (1985) single out the Calinski and Harabasz index as the best and most consistent rule, identifying the sought configurations correctly in over 90 % of all cases in simulations.

[11] The model was computed in close collaboration with HEC Montreal through its Observatory on Financial Services Cooperatives and the International Initiative for Sustainable Financial Systems (ISFS) under the International Institute of Cooperatives Alphonse and Dorimène-Desjardins (IICADD).

[12] See Everitt et al. (2001) for a highly readable introduction to cluster analysis and some of the practical issues in the choice of technical procedures.

Table 4.1 Pseudo-F indices for clustering configurations

Number of clusters	Pseudo-F index (Calinski & Harabasz)	Number of clusters	Pseudo-F index (Calinski & Harabasz)
1		6	279
2	269	7	270
3	281	8	268
4	**294**	9	271
5	292	10	269

Note: The Calinski and Harabasz (1974) pseudo-F index is an estimate of the between-cluster variance divided by within-cluster variance
Source: Authors

ing from the cluster analysis based on the six selected balance sheet indicators. Next, an overview of the main structural and financial attributes of the clusters is provided.

Model 1 groups together large investment-oriented banks and contains the largest banks, both in terms of total and average assets (see Table 4.3).[13] The average size of a bank in this cluster was approximately €583 billion in 2013, about quadruple for an average wholesale or focused retail bank and almost double the amount of a diversified retail bank.

In what follows, Model 1 will be referred to as the cluster of 'investment banks'. As is clear from the name, these banks have substantial trading activities. The cluster averages for trading assets and derivative exposures—representing 51.2 % and 15.2 % of total assets, respectively—stand between 1.3 and 1.5 standard deviations above the relevant sample means. In funding, the focus is on less stable and less traditional sources, such as debt liabilities and, more importantly, repurchase agreements, which came under severe stress during the financial crisis (Gorton and Metrick 2012). The investment banks also tend to be highly leveraged, with an average tangible common equity ratio of 3.9 %.

Model 2 includes banks with a heavy reliance on interbank funding and lending.[14] The liabilities of an average bank under this bank model to other banks, including both deposits and other interbank debt, represent, on average, 37.4 % of the total balance sheet, towering above the interbank liabilities of other bank models. In turn, traditional customer deposits represent only

[13] Three-quarters of the banks included in Ayadi et al. (2012) have been identified in the same cluster in this exercise. 85 % to 90 % of the banks identified as investment, diversified retail or focused retail in the previous study have been identified as such again. In turn, a large share of the formerly identified wholesale banks are now identified as investment banks.

[14] The group of banks identified as wholesale banks have changed substantially from Ayadi et al. (2012). In particular, only 41 % bank/year observations identified as wholesale banks in the earlier study were identically grouped here. An important explanation for this might be the fact that the number of banks and years covered have been increased, which has changed the composition of the sample.

Table 4.2 Descriptive statistics for four clusters

		Bank loans (% assets)	Customer loans (% assets)	Trading assets (% assets)	Bank liabilities (% assets)	Customer deposits (% assets)	Debt liabilities (% assets)	Derivative exposures (% assets)	Tang. Comm. eq. (% tang. assets)
Model 1—Investment (188 obs.)	Mean	9.5 %	37.4 %	51.2 %	14.3 %	23.1 %	44.8 %	15.2 %	3.9 %
	St. dev.*	0.075***	0.163***	0.168***	0.088***	0.14***	0.185***	0.109***	0.076***
	Min.	0.5 %	0.0 %	13.8 %	0.0 %	0.0 %	1.7 %	0.0 %	0.2 %
	Max.	46.6 %	77.2 %	99.5 %	44.7 %	86.5 %	99.4 %	53.9 %	94.1 %
Model 2—Wholesale (145 obs.)	Mean	38.4 %	31.4 %	28.1 %	37.4 %	19.1 %	32.6 %	4.5 %	5.9 %
	St. dev.*	0.254***	0.168***	0.154**	0.255***	0.16***	0.22***	0.035***	0.083***
	Min.	1.0 %	0.1 %	0.4 %	0.4 %	0.0 %	0.0 %	0.0 %	0.1 %
	Max.	96.7 %	63.2 %	65.7 %	99.9 %	78.5 %	84.4 %	14.4 %	50.8 %
Model 3—Diversified retail (303 obs.)	Mean	6.2 %	67.5 %	23.3 %	8.5 %	34.2 %	48.0 %	3.4 %.	4.7 %
	St. dev.*	0.046**	0.12***	0.102***	0.055***	0.159***	0.151***	0.033***	0.025***
	Min.	0.1 %	38.7 %	2.9 %	0.0 %	0.0 %	22.7 %	0.0 %	0.6 %
	Max.	28.0 %	91.9 %	56.6 %	32.4 %	66.4 %	94.3 %	15.5 %	14.2 %
Model 4—Focused retail (490 obs.)	Mean	7.4 %	60.8 %	27.9 %	13.1 %	62.8 %	14.3 %	2.8 %	5.5 %
	St. dev.*	0.068**	0.136***	0.112**	0.095***	0.154***	0.102***	0.034***	0.031***
	Min.	0.3 %	0.9 %	4.3 %	0.0 %	27.2 %	−40.2 %	0.0 %	−6.3 %
	Max.	43.2 %	91.7 %	94.3 %	51.5 %	96.2 %	38.8 %	16.0 %	15.9 %
All banks (1126 obs.)	Mean	11.4 %	54.9 %	30.6 %	15.2 %	42.9 %	30.8 %	5.1 %	5.1 %
	St. dev.*	0.151	0.195	0.158	0.149	0.239	0.214	0.069	0.05
	Min.	0.1 %	0.0 %	0.4 %	0.0 %	0.0 %	−40.2 %	0.0 %	−6.3 %
	Max.	96.7 %	91.9 %	99.5 %	99.9 %	96.2 %	99.4 %	53.9 %	94.1 %

Notes: The independence of clusters was tested using non-parametric Wilcoxon-Mann-Witney two-sample tests at 5 % significance. According to the results of these tests, the number of asterisks (*, **, or ***) stands for the statistical difference of any given cluster from that number of other clusters for that indicator. For example, two asterisks (**) implies that the cluster is statistically different from two other clusters but not the third (closest) one.

Source: Authors

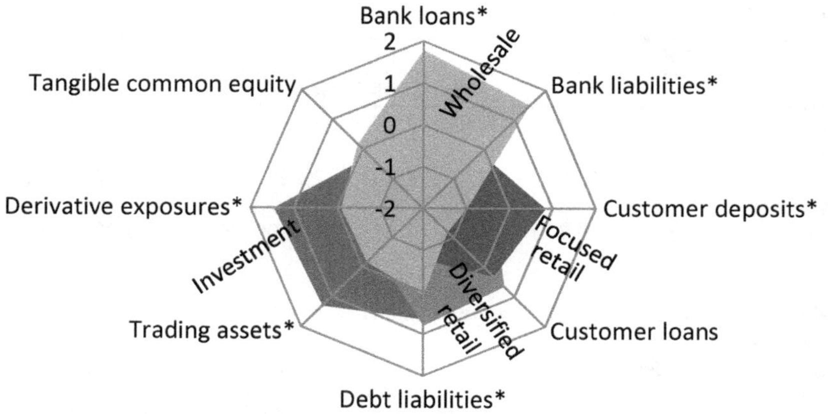

Fig. 4.4 Comparison of clusters, standardized scores
Notes: Indicators marked with an asterisk (*) were used as instruments in the cluster analysis. The figures represent the number of standard deviations from the sample mean. *Customer loans* and *customer deposits* represent the balance sheet share of deposits from and loans to non-bank customers, respectively. *Bank liabilities* and *bank loans* identify the share of liabilities of and loans to other banks, including bank deposits, issued debt, interbank transactions, and received funding from central banks. *Debt liabilities* are calculated by netting customer deposits, bank liabilities, total equity and negative fair values of all derivative transactions from total liabilities. *Derivative exposures* captures all negative carrying values of derivative exposures. *Trading assets* are defined as total assets minus liquid assets (cash & deposits at central bank) minus total loans and intangible assets. *(Tangible) common equity* is defined as common equity minus intangible assets and treasury shares as a share of tangible assets (i.e. total assets minus intangible assets)
Source: Authors

16.0 % of the total balance sheet—the lowest among the four groups. Other funding sources come from debt liabilities, which exclude traditional deposits and interbank funding.

The Model 2 banks, which will henceforth be referred to as 'wholesale', are also very active in non-traditional uses of these funds, including trading assets (i.e. all assets excluding cash, loans and intangible assets). On average, trading assets account for 28.1 % of their balance sheets and interbank lending represents 38.4 % of total assets. These banks are substantially less leveraged than their peers, with the highest tangible common equity ratio of 5.9 % among the four clusters studied. The total size of the wholesale banking group, which is the smallest group, has declined over time, partly as a result of shrinking average sizes in the midst of the financial crisis in 2008 and partially due to a migration to other business models. Lastly, the expenditures on staff are the lowest in the wholesale banking group, with median personnel expenditures remaining at €3.0 per €1,000 of assets, less than half of the sample median.

Table 4.3 Evolution of the sizes of business models

	2006	2007	2008	2009	2010	2011	2012	2013
	Sum of total assets (€ billion)							
Model 1. 'Investment'	10,900	15,200	18,100	15,700	15,900	17,200	16,500	11,100
Model 2. 'Wholesale'	2,318	2,689	3,475	2,192	2,225	1,959	2,022	1,501
Model 3. 'Diversified retail'	9,528	10,300	8,486	7,683	10,500	8,899	8,265	9,529
Model 4. 'Focused retail'	4,162	4,227	4,700	6,467	5,298	7,319	8,143	9,358
All banks	26,900	32,400	34,800	32,100	33,900	35,400	35,000	31,500

	2006	2007	2008	2009	2010	2011	2012	2013
	Total assets of average bank (€ billion)							
Model 1. 'Investment'	496	726	726	629	690	638	636	583
Model 2. 'Wholesale'	122	128	165	115	117	115	119	125
Model 3. 'Diversified retail'	203	223	212	202	238	287	306	318
Model 4. 'Focused retail'	95	85	89	110	83	98	112	130
All banks	204	235	250	227	226	236	245	237

Note: All figures correspond to the year-end observations for the relevant sub-sample
Source: Authors

Model 3 is composed of retail-oriented banks, which use relatively non-traditional funding sources. Hence, customer loans and debt liabilities account for 48.0 % and 67.5 % of the total balance sheet on average, surpassing the sample averages. The greater diversification of funding sources is most likely an attempt to maintain a larger size. In line with this description, the Model 3 banks have, after a hiccup in 2009, continued to expand during the crisis, implying that the reliance on multiple sources of financing has reinforced the group's growth prospects.

Model 4 shares several similarities with Model 3. First, and foremost, the group is comprised of retail-oriented banks, with traditional customer loans representing on average 60 % or more of the balance sheet totals in both groups. Moreover, the ratio of cash and cash-like liquid assets remains above the sample average. Models 3 and 4 also spend about twice as much as investment and wholesale banks on staff, with median personnel expenditures at €7.5 and €8.8 per €1,000 of assets, respectively. The higher staff costs may possibly reflect a larger geographical coverage through a larger number of branches and personnel.

However, the two models differ in funding sources. While Model 3 banks have a greater reliance on debt markets, Model 4 banks rely primarily on customer deposits. The average size of predominantly focused retail banks under Model 4, as measured by average total assets, tends to be around half of the sample average, the smallest banks in the sample. The quest for a larger size of Model 3 banks is also expressed in higher leverage ratios; the average tangible common equity ratios are 4.7 and 5.5 for Model 3 and 4 banks, respectively.

In order to distinguish between the two retail-oriented groups, models 3 and 4 will be referred to as the 'diversified retail' and 'focused retail' models, respectively.

Bank Business Models, Ownership Structure, Internationalization and Migration

After identifying the business models in European banks, we examine the interaction with the ownership structure, the internationalization and migration.

Turning to the variation in ownership structures, Table 4.4 shows that investment banks are mostly owned by profit-maximizers. In turn, wholesale banks are mostly stakeholder banks, which is reflected in the highest share of cooperatives and state-owned banks. From all business models, block owners have the largest say. The shares are mostly privately held, since wholesale banks are less often listed. Hence, only 14 % of the wholesale banks are listed, while on average, half of the banks in the sample have publicly listed shares. The retail banks are close to the sample average. Most of the diversified retail banks are not owned by public institutions.

Figure 4.5 shows that the wholesale banking business models category contains the most diverse types of banks. Most of the wholesale banks are cooperative banks, while of all other business models, about half or more are commercial banks. It has the least savings banks and nationalized banks among the models, while it has by far the largest share of public banks. Hence, some of the cooperative banks included in this Monitor are the central institutions of cooperative banking networks (See Box 4.1). These central institutions serve the local banks,[15] which results in more interbank exposures that typically characterize the wholesale banks. On the other hand, many of the public banks also rely more on interbank funding, when they do not have

[15] The public data on these local banks is often scarce. Many of the local banks are rather small and therefore have to comply with less extensive reporting requirements. This makes the analysis of this group of banks, which make up a significant part of the banking sector, more challenging.

Table 4.4 Ownership attributes of business models

	Model 1 - Investment (%)	Model 2—Wholesale (%)	Model 3 – Diversified retail (%)	Model 4—Focused retail (%)	ALL (%)
SHV banks	64.4***	30.3***	46.9**	52.0**	49.9
Cooperative banks	11.7***	33.8***	23.1**	20.4**	21.4
Savings banks	19.7	19.3	24.1	25.1	23.2
State-owned banks[a]	18.6**	31.7***	11.6***	22.0**	19.9
Private block owners[b]	34.1*	51.9***	34*	31.7*	35.6
Banks listed on stock exchange	60.1*	13.8***	55.5*	52.0*	49.4

Notes: [a]At least 50 % owned by public authorities; [b]Private block owners are those who own more than a 5 % stake, excluding the stake of EU public authorities

All figures are the mean values for the year-end observations for the relevant sample. The independence of cluster subsamples was tested using the Wilcoxon-Mann-Whitney non-parametric two-sample tests at 5 % significance. According to the results of these tests, the number of asterisks (*, **, or ***) stands for the statistical difference of any given cluster from that number of other clusters for that indicator

Source: Authors

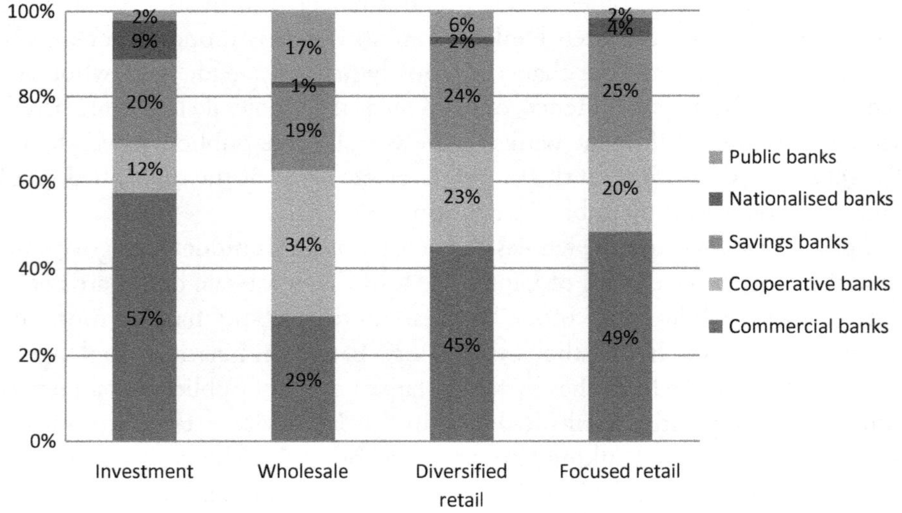

Fig. 4.5 Distribution of types of ownership across business models, 2006–13
Source: Authors

access to deposits. In turn, cooperative and public banks rely relatively less on asset trading, which is reflected in low shares of these types of banks among investment banks. The largest share of nationalized banks is among investment banks. Lastly, all the business models have more or less an equal share of savings banks.

Box 4.1 Cooperative Banks

The European banking sector is a mix of different types of banks. Besides the most studied commercial banks, there are also public-, savings-, and cooperative banks. The cooperative banks might have the most diverse organizational model. However, there is no common model that fits all cooperative banks in Europe.

The cooperative banks are, in principle, client-owned. Clients own the nominal valued shares in a local cooperative bank, which usually owns, together with other local cooperatives, a regional or central institution. These central institutions mostly act as central service providers for the local cooperative banks and serve clients that are too large for the local bank or undertake cross-border activities.

Depending on the level of integration of the cooperative banking group, the local banks and the regional and central institutions either report consolidated figures or report separately. For example, the integrated cooperative banking groups in the Netherlands and Finland report consolidated figures for the whole group, including the local cooperatives and the central institution, while the central institutions and local cooperatives in Germany report separately.

This also has an impact on exercises like this business model monitor, which monitors the largest banks. The consolidated cooperative banking groups are included as a whole, while of the less integrated groups, only the central- and regional- institutions are included. The exposures of the latter consist primarily of loans to and deposits from the local cooperative banks. The activities of the local banks affiliated to these central institutions itself are not analysed. Although these institutions are, in general, relatively small when assessed separately, taken together they are, in many cases, of systemic proportions.

The research on these local cooperatives, which often have similar characteristics, is relatively scarce. Ayadi et al. (2010) performed a comprehensive assessment on the performance of local cooperative banks in the years leading up to the 2007–9 global financial crisis. But the impact of the period thereafter with the 2010–12 Eurozone sovereign debt crisis on local cooperative banks still needs to be studied. The research on these local cooperatives is more difficult due to data limitations. The local cooperatives have to comply with less extensive public reporting requirements than the larger banks.

Source: Authors

On the extent of internationalization, investment and diversified retail banks are the most internationally active. Table 4.5 shows that the median banks of these models have credit institutions and/or branches in seven EEA countries. This is significantly more than wholesale and focused retail banks which cover, respectively, one and two countries. Most of the non-domestic countries are served using branches. The median investment and diversified retail banks have three branches, while focused retail banks and wholesale banks have one or no branches, respectively. The median investment and diversified retail banks also have subsidiaries, which are often used to conduct more substantial international activities. The median investment bank has two subsidiaries, while the diversified retail has one. However, these numbers are not significantly different.

Finally, in terms of migration, although the composition of banks under the different models remains relatively steady over time, transitions do occur and more so in some models than in others.[16] Figure 4.6 provides the transition matrix for the four models during the years 2006–13. The assignment of banks to the focused retail model shows a striking persistence. In particular, the vast majority of the focused retail banks remained within the same model throughout the sampled years (95 %). Moreover, a large part of the remainder of the focused retail banks migrated to diversified retail, while no single bank became a wholesale bank from the entire sample. However, the transition probabilities are relatively high for the investment and diversified retail banks, with around 15 % of all banks that start in one group moving to the other model in the subsequent period. While almost all migrating diversified retail banks have moved to focused retail, the majority of investment banks migrated to either wholesale or focused retail. Hence, only 3.2 % of focused retail banks later became diversified retail, while 12.2 % of all banks that started out as diversified retail moved to focused retail. In addition, approximately 1.5 % of focused retail banks have moved to the investment model, while the opposite is true for 6.1 % of investment banks. The migration between the investment bank and the wholesale model is more balanced. 7.0 % of all banks that started out as investment banks become wholesale banks, while the opposite is true for 6.1 % of wholesale banks.

Since the financial crisis erupted, many European governments have supported their banks in order to safeguard financial stability. These aided banks have had to fulfil certain conditions in order to become economically sound, prevent a distortion of the market, and break the lending chain. Most of the restructuring plans that contained the bank specific

[16] See Appendix I for a complete list of banks surveyed, grouped by business model.

Table 4.5 International activities of business models

	Model 1—Investment	Model 2—Wholesale	Model 3—Diversified retail	Model 4—Focused retail	ALL
International activities (nr of unique EEA countries)	7**	1**	7**	2**	3
Internationalization through subsidiaries (nr of unique EEA countries)	2**	0*	1*	0**	1
Internationalization through branches (nr of unique EEA countries)	3**	0**	3**	1**	1

Notes: Number of unique EEA countries in which the bank had banking activities at year-end 2012, i.e. parent institution, subsidiaries and branches with credit institution licence or passport

All figures are the median values for the year-end observations for the relevant sample. The independence of cluster subsamples was tested using the equality-of-medians two-sample tests at 5 % significance. According to the results of these tests, the number of asterisks (*, **, or ***) stands for the statistical difference of any given cluster from that number of other clusters for that indicator

Source: Authors

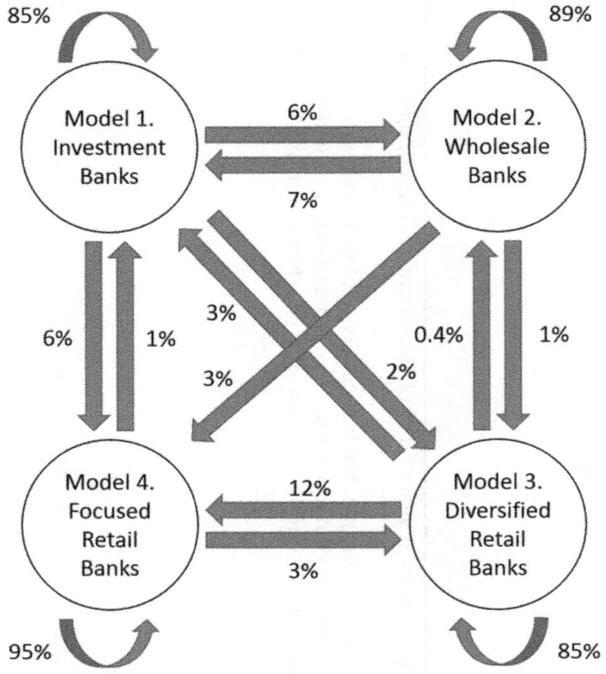

Fig. 4.6 Model transition matrix, share of banks (%)
Note: The figures give the share of banks that belong to a specific model in one period switching to another model (or remaining assigned to the same model) in the next period
Source: Authors

conditions foresaw a focus on more traditional banking activities, that is, lending to the real economy using customer deposits. For many of the banks this meant a shift towards more focused retail-like business models. Table 4.6 shows that about two-thirds of the banks that were identified as wholesale-, investment-, or diversified retail banks in 2006 and received public capital support changed business models. Of the banks identified in 2006 as investment banks, a third became focused retail in 2013 and 17 % became diversified retail. Half of the aided wholesale banks turned into focused retail banks in the period from 2006 to 2013. Moreover, of the diversified retail banks, two-thirds changed to retail focused. In turn only a quarter of the aided focused retail banks were identified as belonging to a different business model in 2013. Most of the focused retail banks that changed business models became diversified retail.

Overall, the number of focused retail banks increased substantially, while the number of banks identified as investment, wholesale, and diversified retail

Table 4.6 Model transition matrix aided banks (2006–13)

		Business model in 2013				
		Model 1—Investment (%)	Model 2—Wholesale (%)	Model 3—Diversified retail (%)	Model 4—Focused retail (%)	ALL (%)
Business Model in 2006	Model 1—Investment	42	8	17	33	29
	Model 2—Wholesale	25	25	0	50	10
	Model 3—Diversified retail	0	0	31	69	32
	Model 4—Focused retail	8	0	17	75	29
	ALL	17	5	20	59	

Note: The figures show the migration of banks that have received State aid in the period 2007 –August 2014. The business model in the pre-crisis year (2006) and most recent year covered in the sample (2013) are compared. Only banks that have benefitted from re-capitalization measures are included. Only banks that received capital support were bound to restructure the activities, while banks that only received liquidity support (i.e. credit guarantees and loans) were not. Variables in bold highlight the instruments used in formingthe clusters

Source: Authors

has decreased between 2006 and 2013, also confirmed by the increase in the size of the focused retail group over time (see Table 4.3).[17]

The results provided above give an insight into the main areas of activity and inherent characteristics of the four different bank business models: on the one hand are banks that engage in riskier and less stable funding and trading activities; on the other hand are banks which remain closer to their traditional roots, relying more on retail funding and customer loans.

Conclusions

The Business Model analysis of the European banking sector assesses the banking sector structure pre and post financial crisis and in light of the establishment of different new international supervisors. It also attempts to get better insights into the interaction between business models, corporate structures, the extent of internationalization and migration.

Focusing on the large and systemic banking groups that are supervised by the international supervisors, the Business Model analysis covers 147 banking groups between 2006 and 2013, that account for around 80 % of the EU banking assets, and uses a novel clustering model using SAS programming. For the analysis, the 1,126 bank-year observations were clustered into four broad categories: investment, wholesale, diversified retail and focused retail banks.

The banks identified as investment-oriented are, on average, the largest and most internationally oriented banks among the four models. The investment banks also include the largest share of profit-maximizing banks, that is, the highest share of shareholder value banks. These banks engage extensively in trading activities while relying on debt securities and derivatives for funding.

Wholesale banks have, on average, the smallest and most domestically oriented models. The banks primarily engage in interbank lending and borrowing and are primarily categorized as stakeholder value banks. These include, among others, central institutions of cooperative- and savings banks that provide liquidity and other services to local banks. Hence, the wholesale banks include most cooperative and state-owned banks. Moreover, the model contains the least listed and the largest shares of block-ownership.

[17] An analysis of the year-by-year transitions (not provided here) shows that the transitions from the investment and diversified retail to the focused retail model were particularly high in 2011, in the midst of the Eurozone crisis when non-deposit funding was more difficult to attract.

Diversified retail banks have a modest size and are internationally oriented. The ownership structure is close to the sample average, with the exception of the lowest share of state-owned banks. In particular, the diversified retail banks lend to customers using primarily debt liabilities and customer deposits.

Focused retail banks have an ownership structure that is close to the sample average. About half of these small domestically oriented institutions are SHV banks, while about a fifth are cooperative- and a quarter savings banks. Most institutions providing traditional services such as customer loans are funded by customer deposits.

The number of banks that were identified as focused retail increased during the crises. Most of the banks that received state aid have, for example, reoriented towards focused retail, which was in many cases supported by the conditions for obtaining capital support.

References

Acharya, V. V., Schnabl, P., & Suarez, G. (2013). Securitization without risk transfer. *Journal of Financial Economics, 107*(3), 515–536.

Ayadi, R., & De Groen, W. P. (2014a). *Banking business models monitor—2014*. Montreal: CEPS and IOFSC.

Ayadi, R., & de Groen, W. P. (2014b). Stress testing, transparency and uncertainty in European banking: What impacts? In J. Forssbaek & L. Oxelheim (Eds.), *The Oxford handbook of economic and institutional transparency*. New York: Oxford University Press.

Ayadi, R., Llewelyn, D. T., Schmidt, R. H., Arbak, E., & de Groen, W. P. (2010). *Investigating diversity in the banking sector in Europe: Key developments, performance and role of cooperative banks*. Brussels: Centre for European Policy Studies (CEPS).

Ayadi, R., Arbak, E., & de Groen, W. P. (2011). *Business models in European banking: A pre-and post-crisis screening*. Brussels: Centre for European Policy Studies (CEPS).

Ayadi, R., Arbak, E., & de Groen, W. P. (2012). *Regulation of European banks and business models: Towards a new paradigm?* Brussels: Centre for European Policy Studies (CEPS).

Blundell-Wignall, A., Atkinson, P., & Lee, S. G. (2008). The current financial crisis: Causes and policy issues. In*OECD Financial Market Trends*. Paris: OECD.

Brunnermeier, M. K. (2009). Symposium: Early stages of the credit crunch: Deciphering the liquidity and credit crunch 2007–2008. *Journal of Economic Perspectives, 23*(1), 77–100.

Calinski, R. B., & Harabasz, J. (1974). A dendrite method for cluster analysis. *Communications in Statistics, 3*(1), 1–27.

Dewatripont, M., Rochet, J.-C., & Tirole, J. (2010). *Balancing the banks: Global lessons from the financial crisis*. Princeton/Oxford: Princeton University Press.

Everitt, B. S., Landau, S., & Leese, M. (2001). *Cluster analysis* (4 ed.). West Sussex: Wiley, John & Sons Ltd..

Gorton, G. B., & Metrick, A. (2012). Securitized banking and the run on repo. *Journal of Financial Economics, 104*(3), 425–451.

Hellwig, M. (2009). Systemic risk in the financial sector: An analysis of the subprime-mortgage financial crisis. *De Economist, 157*(2), 129–207.

Milligan, G. W. (1981). A review of Monte Carlo tests of cluster analysis. *Multivariate Behavioral Research, 16*(3), 379–407.

Milligan, G. W., & Cooper, M. C. (1985). An examination of procedures for determining the number of clusters in a data set. *Psychometrika, 50*(2), 159–179.

Reinhart, C. M., & Rogoff, K. (2009). *This time is different: Eight centuries of financial folly*. Princeton: Princeton University Press.

Ward, J. H. (1963). Hierarchical grouping to optimize objective function. *Journal of the American Statistical Association, 58*(301), 236–244.

5

Ownership in European Banking

John Goddard, Donal G. McKillop, and John O.S. Wilson

Introduction

The European banking industry comprises commercial, mutual and public banks. The categorizations refer to differences in ownership form. Commercial banks are primarily shareholder based institutions. In most European countries they are the main providers of credit to the household and corporate sector and operate the payments system. Mutual banks are owned by their members and include savings banks, building societies and cooperative banks. Savings banks focus on savings and savings mobilization. At a stage in the past these were viewed as public banks, but in many countries there has been a shift towards private ownership with many savings banks now providing a universal banking service. The early building societies were founded on self-

J. Goddard
Bangor Business School, Bangor University, Bangor, UK
e-mail: j.goddard@bangor.ac.uk

D.G. McKillop
Queen's Management School, Queen's University Belfast, Belfast, UK
e-mail: dg.mckillop@qub.ac.uk

J.O.S. Wilson (✉)
Centre for Responsible Bankig & Finance, School of Management,
University of St Andrews, St Andrews, UK
e-mail: jsw7@st-andrews.ac.uk

T. Beck, B. Casu (eds.), *The Palgrave Handbook of European Banking*,
DOI 10.1057/978-1-137-52144-6_5

help principles and were dedicated to addressing the housing needs of the newly urbanized population created by industrial society. Today, building societies continue to provide housing, but have expanded their reach into retail financial services. Cooperative banks typically offer retail and small business banking services. They have a regional orientation and tend to be part of networks that facilitate cooperation. Public banks are those where public authorities have a significant share in ownership either in terms of an influence on voting rights or in terms of outright share ownership. Public banks do not form a distinct homogeneous group, and this ownership form may overlap with others: for example, mutual banks and commercial banks may all be partly publicly owned.

Business objectives may depend upon ownership form. Commercial banks maximize profit for shareholders, while mutual banks pursue the interests of multiple stakeholders (borrowers, savers and employees). The voting rights of owners, the marketability of ownership stakes, and the strength of capital market discipline also differ across different ownership forms. Residual risk and principal-agent conflict are also a function of ownership form. The ownership form may have implications for lending relationships and the bank's choice between a relationship or transaction based lending model.

Differences in ownership form are likely to lead to differences in strategies pursued, although many large institutions across each ownership form have evolved to a full-service banking model. As a consequence, some large institutions now compete in the same markets and are subject to the same regulatory and supervisory arrangements.

Evidence suggests that more diverse financial systems (in terms of size and ownership form) are more resilient in the face of changing conditions over the business cycle (Ayadi et al. 2009, 2010). Finally, the business model may differ not only across ownership forms, but also within (Ayadi and de Groen, 2016 provide a detailed discussion of this issue).

The rest of this chapter is structured as follows. The section "Shareholder and Stakeholder-Oriented Financial Institutions" examines agency issues across different ownership forms. The "Ownership Forms" section provides a brief discussion of the extent and evolution of public, commercial, and mutual banks, which co-exist in various European countries. "Performance, Risk and Lending" provides a selective review of research which examines the importance of ownership form for the efficiency, profitability, risk and lending of financial institutions. "Concluding Comments" draws the chapter to a close.

Shareholder and Stakeholder-Oriented Financial Institutions

Financial institutions may be classified as either shareholder or stakeholder-oriented (Llewellyn 2006). Shareholder-owned firms exist primarily to maximize shareholder value or the rate of return on equity. According to Friedman (1970, p. 7) 'there is one and only one social responsibility of business – to use its resources to engage in activities designed to increase its profits as long as it stays within the rules of the game, which is to say, engages in open and free competition, without deception or fraud…' Shareholders, the ultimate owners and the primary risk-takers, delegate the management of the bank to a management team lead by the chief executive officer (CEO). Shareholder-owned banks are reliant on capital markets for funding. Commercial banks are most clearly identified with shareholder value theory.

Stakeholder-oriented financial institutions endeavour to balance the interests of various stakeholders who, depending on the constitution of the institution, may include some or all of the following groups: shareholders, customers, employees, local communities and government (Jensen 2010). The organizational objective may be characterized as creating value for stakeholders, not just shareholders (NEF 2014). Mutual banks are usually classed as stakeholder-oriented in that they share a tradition of stakeholder governance that empowers their boards, instead of delegating to a professional management team as in the case of a shareholder-owned bank. Commercial banks whose shares are partly or wholly in public ownership may also be viewed as stakeholder-oriented. Management of public banks can involve participation of stakeholders such as employees, public officials and social and political representatives.

The ownership of shareholder-owned banks can be highly dispersed, or relatively concentrated if large institutional investors maintain significant shareholdings. An income stream accrues to the shareholders in the form of dividends. Ownership is easily transferable through the sale of equity in secondary markets and additional capital can be raised through the sale of new equity. Capital market discipline is exerted via the threat of takeover. Remuneration of senior managers that is linked to the share price may help align the interests of owners and managers.

In mutual organizations members are the owners and exercise control on the basis of one vote per person irrespective of their ownership share. In contrast to shareholder-owned banks, members of mutual financial institutions cannot, in general, sell their stake to a third party as ownership entitlements are non-transferable. Members do not have any legal claim on the profits or capital accumulation of the bank. Cumulative profits are owned by the mutual itself and used to reinvest in the business. Current members of the mutual can be viewed as having inherited the communal wealth from past members under an implicit contract that such communal wealth should be built upon and passed on to future members (Davis 2014). It is more difficult for a mutual to raise capital outside retained earnings.[1] Difficulty in raising capital may deter mutual banks from pursuing risky ventures. In that there is no externally held capital and no tradable ownership rights that can be bought in a hostile bid, this also implies that mutuals face no (or weak) discipline from the market in corporate ownership and control. Set against this, management in mutuals cannot be awarded bonuses that are linked to shareholder value, which reduces the incentive to engage in risky investment and unsafe lending practices to maximize short-term returns.

While mutual banks have typically focused on serving households, public banks have often been viewed as taking on a more economic development role (Sawyer 2014). In the case of public-owned firms, as Shleifer and Vishny (1997) state, while they are technically controlled by the public, they are run by bureaucrats who can be viewed as having highly concentrated control rights, but no significant cash flow rights.

Following the global financial crisis of 2007–8, many European banks were bailed out by their national governments, which has revived the debate concerning the state ownership of financial institutions (Iannotta, Nocera and Sironi, 2013). Development and political views are often put forward as rationales for public ownership of financial institutions. According to the development view, public ownership responds to institutional deficiencies and market failures and can result in the financing of projects that other institutions are unable or unwilling to finance (Schmit et al. 2011). In contrast, in the political view, public control may be driven by political motives with lending behaviour influenced by the political needs of the public entity with the controlling stake.

Agency theory investigates conflicts of interest between the principal and the agent. In a shareholder-owned bank, for example, the owners may seek to maximize profit, but the managers may be content to sacrifice profit so as to pursue other objectives such as growth, reduce risk by avoiding investments with uncertain payoffs, or maximize their own utility through expense-preference behaviour (Berger and Hannan 1998; Goddard, Molyneux and Wilson, 2004).

[1] In certain cases they may have an option of raising capital from their members through issuing various types of subordinated shares that pay interest but do not carry voting rights (Birchall 2013).

Features of shareholder-owned banks may help to minimize the principal-agent problem and reduce agency costs.[2] Concentrated ownership in the hands of institutional investors creates incentives to keep risk-averse managerial behaviour in check. Executive compensation can be arranged in such a way so as to align managerial and shareholder interests. The threat of takeover can deter managers from deviating from profit maximization.

Mutuals are not reliant on capital markets for funding, and are therefore not subject to capital market discipline. Typically, ownership is spread across large numbers of members, who may have insufficient incentives to devote effort to monitoring, since their ability to exert control is weak, and the potential rewards are small. Managers of mutuals may have more freedom than those of shareholder-owned banks to avoid risk, and mutuals may consequently adopt lower risk profiles. A further factor ameliorating principal-agent relationships in all financial institutions is that of competition. Competition, rather than corporate structure, may well dominate the behaviour of financial institutions when mutuals, public banks and shareholder-owned banks operate in the same markets in competition with each other (Drake and Llewellyn 1997; Llewellyn 2005).

The lack of market monitoring and the non-option of selling the value of the bank on the market can also be arguments applied to public-owned banks to suggest lower levels of efficiency and profitability relative to shareholder-owned banks. Additionally, managers of publicly owned banks may face political interference which may not coincide with the desire to maximize the value of the institution.

A further agency issue that may emerge is the potential conflict between customers (borrowers and depositors) and owners. In shareholder-owned banks, customers want competitively priced financial products while the owners want as high a return as possible on their capital investment. Given limited liability (which implies that potential for profit is unlimited while the potential for losses is limited); owners may prefer a higher risk profile than savers. An implicit assumption is that shareholder-owned banks aim to maximize profits and prioritize the objectives of owners over customers. In mutual organizations the owners in many instances are the customers and consequently this agency issue is not as prevalent. The simultaneous presence of depositors and borrowers forms the basis for a self-sufficient or balanced

[2] Jensen and Meckling (1976) define agency costs as the sum of monitoring costs, bonding costs, and residual loss. Monitoring costs refer to the costs the principal incurs to constrain the activities of the agent. Bonding costs refer to the costs the agent incurs in an attempt to convince the principal of her commitment. The welfare loss for the principal, as compared with a situation of complete utility alignment, is called the residual loss.

financial intermediary. However, the same source of intermediation balance produces conflicts in the interests of the two sets of owners. Borrowers will demand low loan rates and transactions costs, while depositors demand high deposit rates and strong prudential discipline.

Ownership Forms

This section describes the evolution of various ownership forms in European banking, including public, commercial and mutual banks (savings banks, building societies and cooperative banks).

Public Banks

A public bank is a bank whose outstanding stock is partly or fully owned by public authorities.[3] Public banks do not form a distinct homogeneous group, and this ownership form today may overlap with others: for example, savings banks, cooperative banks and commercial banks may all be partly publicly owned.

Public banks are typically not profit oriented, but may instead pursue other objectives. Public officials may instruct the bank to adopt policies in support of objectives such as economic development and financial inclusion. Through public ownership, public officials may seek to correct forms of market failure associated with abuses of market power, externalities or asymmetric information, or they may seek to avoid wasteful competition or excessive risk-taking. However, the public provision of financial services raises several difficult issues. Public banks may be partially sheltered from competitive discipline, with little or no threat of insolvency or acquisition, as losses are effectively underwritten or subsidized using taxpayer funds. There may be little or no incentive for the pursuit of efficiency savings, especially if managers' remuneration is not directly linked to financial performance. There may be a tendency for banks established and governed by politicians to allocate credit based on political favour. Poor lending decisions may lead to problems with non-performing loans, financial fragility and a misallocation of productive resources (Andrianova, Demetriades and Shortland, 2010).[4]

[3] The literature offers no authoritative definition of what is meant by the term 'public bank'. Most studies use some variants of share ownership by public authorities as a criterion for defining public banks, yet neither the nature of such ownership, nor the term 'public authorities' are further defined in the literature (Schmit et al. 2011).

[4] Political bureaucrats often have goals that are in conflict with social welfare improvements and are dictated by political interests (Ianotta et al. 2013). Public ownership, and with it the perception of preferen-

In the nineteenth and early twentieth centuries public (state) banking became firmly established in many European countries. For example, the Ottoman government created an agricultural fund in 1863 to support farmers. This fund eventually evolved to Ziraat Bank (Marois 2013). The French Caisse de Dêpots (1816) and Crédit Mobilier (1852) were established to finance railways and industry (Kindleberger 1984).

The involvement of public banks in development and public infrastructure projects peaked during the early and mid-twentieth century. Development banks were established to manage industrial reconstruction across war-torn Europe (Marois and Güngen 2013). After the Second World War, for example, the Kreditanstalt fur Weidaraufbau (Reconstruction Credit Agency, KfW) channelled funds for reconstruction and development in West Germany (von Mettenheim and Butzbach 2012). From the 1970s, there was a trend towards the privatization of public banks. This trend was reversed, perhaps temporarily, during the global financial crisis of 2007–9, when governments throughout Europe acquired ownership stakes in distressed privately owned banks in dire need of recapitalization. In the UK, for example, banking industry assets under public ownership increased from 1 % in 2008 to 26 % in 2010 (Marois and Güngen 2013). In Ireland, the corresponding increase was from zero in 2008 to 21 % in 2010. Public banks are particularly prominent in Germany and France but also have a strong presence in Spain, Switzerland, and in Eastern Europe (Schmit et al. 2011).[5]

Public banks in Germany are represented by the Association of German Public Sector Banks (Bundesverband Öffentlicher Banken Deutschlands, VÖB). It was founded in 1916 and represents 63 member institutions including the regional savings banks (Landesbanken) as well as the development banks owned by the federal and state governments. The public banking sector is organized territorially and vertically: cities and local authorities own local *Sparkassen*, while *Länder* (regions) own Landesbanken (see subsection on mutual banks for more details). The development banks (Förderbanken) objective is to "complement the market where the state regards free market outcomes as insufficient and hence not socially acceptable" (VÖB 2014). Examples of development banks include Kreditanstalt fur Weidaraufbau (KfW)

tial government support, may also encourage excessive risk-taking behaviour on the part of management in the belief that the cost of such risk will be covered by public bodies. La Porta, Lopez-de-Silanes and Shleifer (2002) find a negative association between government ownership of banks and average growth rates.

[5] The European Association of Public Banks (EAPB) represents about 100 financial institutions consisting of public banks and funding agencies at the European level. EAPB members have a market share of approximately 15 %, a balance sheet of about €3,500 billion and around 190,000 employees (see www.eapb.eu).

which is 80 % owned by the German federal government. It lends to export-oriented firms and small and medium-sized enterprises. Landwirtschaftliche Rentenbank, provides loans for agriculture and other rural borrowers. L-Bank, the state bank of Baden-Württemberg, provides finance to small and medium-sized enterprises.

In France one of the major public banks providing retail financial services is La Banque Postale. La Banque Postale was created in 2006 and provides a banking service through a network of more than 10,000 post offices. Banque Publique d'Investissement, in contrast is a public sector development bank which provides soft loans for innovation, undertakes risk-sharing in support of bank financing and private equity investments and co-finances loans. Other smaller public banks include Caisse de Dêpots, a financial and investment group that supports economic development projects and Société de Financement Local, a 75 % publicly owned bank that provides medium and long-term loans to local authorities, hospitals and other healthcare institutions.

Commercial Banks

Commercial banks typically pursue a primary objective of profit maximization. Commercial banks are the dominant financial intermediaries in almost all European countries, acting as the main providers of credit to the household and corporate sectors. Commercial banks offer a broad range of financial services to their retail and corporate clients, and operate the payments system. Traditionally commercial bank have been brick-and-mortar institutions, but more recently an increasing number do not have any physical branches, but instead provide services by phone or through the internet. Many of the largest commercial banks also provide investment banking, insurance and other financial services; and some are internationally focused, operating in multiple jurisdictions (De Haas and van Horen, this volume, examine cross-border banking).

Modern-day commercial banking can be traced back to medieval and early Renaissance Italy, where privately owned merchant banks, constituted as partnerships, were established to finance trade and public expenditure. The gradual acceptance that banks could be shareholder-owned and subject to limited liability law was crucial to the evolution of modern commercial banks during the nineteenth century. Shareholder-owned commercial banks could grow much larger than partnerships, simply by expanding their shareholder capital base; while limited liability placed an upper limit on the funds any individual shareholder could lose in the event of insolvency.

For much of the twentieth century and in most countries, the scope of commercial banking was defined either broadly or narrowly, depending upon national regulations and historical inheritance. As a typical feature, traditionally the production and distribution of banking products and services was vertically integrated. From the 1980s onwards, however, this structure has been challenged, as financial deregulation has lowered the barriers separating commercial banks from other financial institutions. Financial innovation and technological change have reshaped the production and distribution of financial services. Commercial banks, in common with other financial institutions, have sought opportunities to diversify or re-focus their portfolios of services in line with their relative competitive advantage.

In all major European countries the distinction between the traditional financial intermediation services of accepting deposits and granting loans and other capital market activities has been eroded. The growth of the retail mutual fund sector, as well as sectors specializing in savings and investment vehicles such as life insurance and pensions, created new sources of competition for commercial banks in their traditional lines of business. Commercial banks collectively lost market share in deposit-taking and lending. Financial innovation, technological change and financial deregulation, as well as limited growth opportunities in traditional lines of business, and a proliferation of new financial services providers all contributed towards these developments. The term disintermediation refers to diversification on the part of commercial banks away from traditional intermediation activity, towards the provision of a broader range of financial services, with commensurate growth in the share of fees and commissions in net income. As a consequence, the traditional separation between commercial banking, insurance, investment banking, and brokerage and asset management no longer exists.

Starting with the First Banking Directive in 1977, EU legislation has been directed consistently towards the reduction of barriers to cross-border banking. Financial deregulation at national level has helped facilitate cross-border competition between commercial banks. Many commercial banks expanded the scale of their operations, in some cases through merger and acquisition (M&A), while mutual banks for the most part remained focused on providing traditional products in localized geographic areas. Consolidation was motivated by the objectives of realizing scale and scope economies, reducing labour and other variable costs, eliminating operational inefficiencies, and risk-spreading through product or geographic diversification. Rapid growth in the loan portfolios of some banks was financed by the securitization of prospective cash flows from sources such as mortgages and credit-card debt, commonly recorded off-balance sheet. Rapid growth of non-interest income reflected the growing use of securities-based financing by private-sector companies, and the increase in demand for protection products (insurance and personal pensions), and investment in mutual funds, by the household sector.

The geographic aspect to diversification involves expansion of cross-border banking activity. Expansion by banks into other EU countries has taken place mainly through the establishment of subsidiaries. Changes embodied in the European Company Statute (passed in 2004) allowed banks to form single legal entities that can operate freely across EU national borders, enabling the conversion of subsidiaries to branches. However, subsidiaries remain the predominant cross-border organizational form, reflecting the benefits of risk-spreading between different legal entities within a banking group; see De Haas and Van Horen, this volume).

The failure in 2007 of Northern Rock, a commercial bank (that had previously been a building society) led to a serious financial crisis that afflicted the UK banking industry. In the United States, the Lehman failure triggered a spectacular sequence of events that brought the global financial system to the very brink of collapse. Large banks across Europe incurred heavy losses resulting in numerous bank rescues through the intervention of central banks and governments. Initial responses to the financial crisis of 2007–9 included: government purchase of distressed assets; changes to the rules concerning the types of asset accepted as collateral; nationalization or part-nationalization of financial institutions considered too-big-to-fail; and government guarantees of consumer deposits and bank liabilities (Goddard, Molyneux and Wilson, 2009a, b). These attempts to bail out distressed banks during the financial crisis fuelled a sovereign debt crisis in the UK and elsewhere as distressed banks' assets transferred from bank balance sheets into public ownership (Correa and Sapriza 2015).

Table 5.1 lists the 20 largest commercial banks in Europe, ranked by total assets, in 2015. HSBC is the largest financial institution in Europe with assets of €2.3 trillion. The top ten banks include four UK banks, four French banks and one bank each from Germany and Spain. All banks in this top 20 are shareholder based institutions listed on major exchanges. Table 5.2 lists the 20 largest banks by market capitalization. Here the top ten banks include four UK banks, two Spanish banks, one bank each from France, Italy, the Netherlands and Switzerland. Commercial banks can also be unlisted but in general they have a much smaller asset base and lie outside the top 40 European banks in terms of asset size.

Table 5.1 Largest commercial banks by asset size, 2015

Bank name	Total assets (€000)	Country
HSBC Holdings Plc	2,283,476,608	UK
BNP Paribas SA	2,145,416,000	France
Deutsche Bank AG	1,719,374,000	Germany
Crédit Agricole Group	1,701,100,000	France
Barclays Plc	1,677,411,028	UK
Crédit Agricole SA	1,524,000,000	France
Société Générale SA	1,351,800,000	France
Banco Santander, SA	1,320,427,087	Spain
Royal Bank of Scotland Group Plc	1,188,913,998	UK
Lloyds Banking Group Plc	1,109,266,992	UK
UBS AG	900,393,344	Switzerland
UniCredit SpA	873,506,000	Italy
ING Groep N.V.	862,039,000	Netherland
Credit Suisse Group AG	787,170,525	Switzerland
Banco Bilbao Vizcaya Argentaria, SA	746,476,777	Spain
Nordea Bank AB	679,877,000	Sweden
Intesa Sanpaolo SpA	668,235,000	Italy
Commerzbank AG	563,852,000	Germany
KfW	499,200,000	Germany
Danske Bank A/S	448,804,431	Denmark

Source: SNL Financial

Table 5.2 Largest commercial banks by market capitalization, 2015

Institution name	Market capitalization (€000)	Country
HSBC Holdings Plc	132,348,119	UK
Lloyds Banking Group Plc	72,853,847	UK
Banco Santander, SA	67,777,056	Spain
BNP Paribas SA	65,275,978	France
UBS Group AG	61,978,765	Switzerland
Barclays Plc	55,571,444	UK
Intesa Sanpaolo SpA	52,963,997	Italy
Royal Bank of Scotland Group Plc	49,345,255	UK
ING Groep N.V.	48,937,790	Netherlands
Banco Bilbao Vizcaya Argentaria, SA	47,730,813	Spain
Nordea Bank AB	40,133,313	Sweden
Credit Suisse Group AG	35,086,074	Switzerland
UniCredit SpA	33,250,732	Italy
Deutsche Bank AG	33,179,848	Germany
Société Générale SA	31,742,437	France
Crédit Agricole SA	27,008,553	France
Danske Bank A/S	26,489,406	Denmark
Svenska Handelsbanken AB	24,425,276	Sweden
KBC Group NV	23,550,295	Belgium
PAO Sberbank of Russia	22,143,795	Russia

Source: SNL Financial

Mutual Banks

Mutual banks are member owned institutions and include both savings banks, building societies and cooperative banks. Credit unions, a subset of cooperative banks, are the purest form of cooperative as all customers must also be members of the credit union. Each of these mutual groups is now reviewed in more detail.

Savings Banks

Savings banks are mutually owned by their members, who are usually the bank's depositors or savers. Savings banks often pursue objectives relating to the social and economic development of the geographic region or locality in which they operate. Historically, savings banks were viewed as public banks, owned or sponsored and governed by a regional or local public body. Recently, in many countries, there has been a shift towards private ownership. Acknowledging that there are differences in ownership structure and business models between savings banks, (Ferri, Kalmi, and Kerola, 2013) identify three common features. First, savings banks are not-for-profit financial institutions. Second, savings banks, or the entities that own them, have a social mission. Third, savings banks may be decentralized elements of some larger system or network.

European savings banks have their origins in specific local regions. The ideological roots of the savings bank movement date back to the Age of Enlightenment, when the 'enlightened', the intellectual elite, thought it their task to communicate the benefits of the middle-class virtue of thrift to the lower classes. Initially, savings banks were established either by associations of individuals or by foundations set up by local authorities or ecclesiastical bodies. The association form was pioneered in the UK, while the foundation route was developed in Germany (Revell 1989). The first savings bank was founded in Hamburg, Germany in 1778. In the UK Priscilla Wakefield founded a benefit society in 1798 in London, to which a savings bank was added in 1801. In several European countries such as Italy and Spain savings banks grew with the aid of government and private action (WSBI-ESBG 2015). Savings banks have a regional or local focus, and tend not to compete with each other. Cooperative arrangements between groups of savings banks were common (Gardener et al. 1997, 1999; Bulbul et al. 2013).

Savings banks have a significant presence today in a number of European countries. In Germany there are two different types of institutions. The *Sparkassen* which are locally focused institutions and the *Landesbanken*, which have a regional dimension. There is also a national central institution, *Dekabank Deutsche Girozentrale (Dekabank),* which acts as a national Landesbank and is owned by the *Landesbanken* and by the national association of savings banks *(Deutscher Sparkassen und Giroverband*).

The *Sparkassen* are public institutions. These institutions are not permitted to operate outside their local area, and are tasked with serving the public interest in that area. Their primary role is to encourage savings and provide credit to small and medium-sized enterprises. For the most part, capital is raised through retained earnings. However, some capital takes the form of preference shares. *Landesbanken* may be joint-stock companies, or public law institutions. They are owned by local savings banks, regional public authorities and, in some cases, other *Landesbanken* (Martín and Sevillano 2011). The *Landesbanken* were originally designed to act as central banks for the savings banks. In recent years, however, the *Landesbanken* have increasingly become involved in wholesale funding, investment banking and international banking, and have been drawn into direct competition with commercial banks.

In 2015 there were 417 *Sparkassen* (562 in 2000) and eight *Landesbanken* employing 244,000 employees and 94,000 employees respectively. These institutions serve 50 million customers. Approximately, three-quarters of small and medium-sized enterprises (SMEs) had a working relationship with either a *Sparkasse* or a *Landesbank* (Savings Banks Finance Group 2015). *Sparkassen* and Landesbanken accounted for 21 and 16 % of the loans market in Germany, respectively.

During the global financial crisis, several *Landesbanken* required state support, and there were a number of mergers involving *Sparkassen* in financial distress. However, many German savings banks remained stable and profitable throughout the crisis. Their resilience has been attributed to their strong deposit base, and close established relationships with business clients (Bulbul, Schmidt and Schuwer, 2013).

The origins of savings banks (*cajas de ahorros*) in Spain can be found in the 'Mount of Mercy' (*Montes de Piedad*) thrift institutions established in the eighteenth century, whose main objective was to channel individual savings into socially-beneficial investments in their respective geographic areas. Until the 1970s, the Spanish savings banks were publicly owned, and their operations were restricted to a specific geographical area. Their governing bodies consisted of a general assembly, a board of directors, and a control committee. The board of directors was broken up into two broad categories: insiders (bank employees, depositors and private funders) and outsiders (regional politicians and representatives of other public authorities) (IMF 2012). During the 1970s the savings banking sector was transformed by privatization, deregulation and the abolition of geographic restrictions. The savings banks expanded their range of products, and extended their branch networks throughout Spain.[6] In the late 2000s the global financial crisis had a profound effect on the savings banks, mainly as a consequence of their heavy exposure to commercial real estate. Initially, many were the subject of publicly-funded bailouts. Government legislation, in the form of Royal Decrees in 2010 and 2013, effectively decimated the savings banks. The number dropped from 45 in 2010 to only two in 2015: Caixa Ontinyent and Caixa Pollença. The others were either acquired, or transferred their banking business into newly created commercial banks, separating their banking business from other socially responsible activities (FROB 2013). For example, CaixaBank, a financial services company that holds an 81 % stake in the savings bank Caixa, was founded in 2007 and changed its name to CaixaBank in 2011. In 2014 it was the third-largest Spanish bank, after Banco Santander and BBVA.

Building Societies

Building societies are mutual financial institutions with over 250 years of history. They were first established in the UK but can also be found elsewhere in Europe. Originally these early mutual societies were founded on self-help principles and were dedicated to addressing the housing needs of the newly urbanized population created by the industrial society. The logic of these early societies was a simple one where 20 to 30 members banded together to regularly contribute funds in order to finance house building. Once all members had been housed, the society was terminated.

If structure is a purpose of function, then the development of permanent societies can be viewed as a consequence of the need to speed up the provision of housing. First appearing in the middle of the nineteenth century, permanent societies paid interest to investors and charged interest to borrowers who required funds for house purchase. As the title implies, permanent societies expected to be enduring societies. In the UK there were 540 permanent societies and 959 terminating societies in 1873 (Cleary 1965). At the start of the twentieth century there were 2,286 building societies in the UK with terminating societies constituting about 20 % of all societies (Drake 1989). The last UK terminating society was dissolved in 1980.

[6] Savings banks opened so many branches outside of their traditional catchment areas that the branch density in Spain became twice as high as the Eurozone average (IMF 2012).

For most of their history, building societies have operated within a well-defined segment of the UK financial services market. In recent years, competition and innovation has dramatically affected the contours of the financial services sector and has made it increasingly difficult to view it as comprising of distinct segments. The Building Societies Act 1986 currently governs both the powers and constitution of building societies and is exclusive to them. As a restrictive piece of legislation, building societies are able to do only those things laid down in the 1986 Act and subsequent statutory instruments made under the Act. Any society with aspirations to undertake activities outside the legal parameters of the Act, and not wishing to be frustrated by ultra vires, must convert to public limited company status (Ferguson and McKillop 1993).[7]

In 1989, Abbey National was the first building society to exercise the option and convert to a bank. At that stage there were 109 building societies in the UK. There followed in subsequent years many more demutualizations. Many of the large players opted to reconstitute as commercial banks (Alliance and Leicester, Bradford and Bingley, Halifax, Northern Rock, Woolwich). Some commentators have branded the demutualization as a large failure, as the demutualized building societies have played a large part in the UK banking crisis (Casu and Gall 2016). At the end of 2014 there were 44 building societies operating in the UK.

Building societies have operated elsewhere in Europe. In Ireland the number of building societies peaked at 40 in the 1950s. Most of these societies were small and merged or dissolved as Irish commercial banks began to offer residential mortgages. The financial crisis took a final toll on the remaining two building societies. EBS Building Society became a subsidiary of AIB Bank in July 2011. Irish Nationwide Building Society deposits were sold to Irish Life and Permanent. In July 2011 all of Irish Nationwide's remaining assets and liabilities (including the branch network) were transferred to Anglo Irish Bank.[8] In Finland the Mortgage Society of Finland, a permanent building society, was founded in 1860. It is the oldest private credit institution in Finland. It is now part of the Hypo Group along with the deposit bank Suomen AsuntoHypoPankki which is a licensed bank owned by the society.

Elsewhere in Europe house finance tends to be provided by specialist mortgage banks. For example, in Germany housing finance tends to be provided through

---

[7] The 1986 Act has been amended over time, most notably in 1997, which changed the prescriptive nature of the 1986 Act to a permissive regime whereby a building society could engage in a wide range of commercial activities subject to a building society's principal purpose, as well as so-called balance sheet 'nature limits' and restrictions on powers. These changes increased the commercial freedom of societies, with the aim of enhancing competition and consumer choice (Casu and Gall 2016).

[8] In June 2011, Irish Life and Permanent itself collapsed into full state ownership.

Bausparkassen (European Office, German Bausparkassen 2013). There are 10 public *Bausparkassen* which operate within regionally defined markets and 12 private *Bausparkassen* which operate nationally. The public law *Bausparkassen* are either divisions of public banks or institutions incorporated under public law with their own legal personality, or public limited companies. The private *Bausparkassen* operate exclusively as public limited companies.

Cooperative Banks

Cooperative banks are mutually owned by their members. In many instances the members are also the bank's customers. Some cooperatives have a geographically dispersed membership, while others have a membership that is highly localized (Birchall 2013). Typically, cooperative banks offer retail and small business banking services. In 2015 cooperative banks operated in 19 European countries, notably France, the Netherlands, Austria, Italy, Finland and Germany. In several countries there has been significant consolidation of small cooperative banks to form larger institutions. In aggregate cooperative banks in Europe held €6,797 billion in assets at the end of 2013, served 205 million customers of whom 58 million were members, and they have an average domestic share of the loan market of approximately 20 % (EACB 2014).

The Rochdale Society of Equitable Pioneers was formed in Rochdale, England in 1844. Its rules established the essential principles of the cooperative movement (McKillop and Wilson 2015). Three cooperative principles shape the structure of cooperative banks. The first is *self-help*: cooperatives are self-governed private organizations, owned by their members who are also the providers of equity. The second is the principle of *identity*: the members are the primary customers. The third principle is *democracy*: each member has only one vote, irrespective of how many shares they hold. Hermann Schulze-Delitzsch, a politician and judge, founded the first urban credit cooperative in 1850 in Germany to meet the needs of small traders. Friedrich Wilhelm Raiffeisen, a mayor in Germany's Western Rhineland, formed the first rural credit cooperative in 1864 to meet the needs of small farmers. The Schulze-Delitzsch and Raiffeisen credit cooperatives were focused upon groups under pressure from economic change (Guinnane 1994; Vittas 1996). From Germany, cooperative financial institutions spread to several other European countries: Austria, Italy, Switzerland and the Netherlands initially, then west to France, Belgium and Spain, and north to Finland and Sweden (Birchall 2013).

Today, cooperative banks share many of the characteristics of savings banks prior to the 1970s.[9] Cooperative banks are typically regional banks, and form

[9] Cooperatives are private banks while savings banks tend to be linked with public institutions with many savings banks in public ownership.

part of broader cooperative networks (Bulbul et al. 2013). In many European countries, cooperative banks have developed prominent central institutions and formed network alliances. Networks range from loose associations to cohesive groups, and can be multi-levelled (Fonteyne 2007). The level of integration ranges from centralization of common services (strategic advice, basic support or group representation) to pooled executive functions (risk and liquidity management, supervision, or advice on merger and acquisition). Finland, France and the Netherlands are characterized by high levels of centralization and integration. Austrian and German cooperative banks have centralized fewer functions, while Italian and Spanish cooperative banks are almost entirely decentralized (Ayadi et al. 2010). Some cooperative banks have sold some activities to investors or have become partially listed, leading to the emergence of a hybrid form of financial cooperative (see Table 5.3).

In Germany there are 17.7 million cooperative bank members and 30 million customers, accounting for 30 % and 15 % of the totals for all European countries, respectively (see Table 5.3). The cooperative network Bundesverband der Deutschen Volksbanken und Raiffeisenbanken (BVR) is structured as a federation, and provides its members, 1100 legally-independent individual cooperative banks, access to common clearing, liquidity and risk-sharing facilities through the cooperative central banks, DZ Bank and WGZ Bank. The individual cooperative banks cater to retail and small and medium-sized enterprises within specific geographical areas. DZ Bank, the sector's main central bank, provides local cooperative banks, as its key client group, with competitive products and services, allowing the sector to offer a complete range of financial services, such as insurance, commercial real estate finance, private banking, mutual funds, and leasing (Standard & Poor's, 28 November 2014). The cooperative network operates its own deposit protection scheme, for which each bank pays a risk-related levy. Cooperative principles apply not only within individual banks but also to the sector as a whole, with stronger banks supporting weaker ones. German cooperative banks required no public funding during the global financial crisis. Those cooperative banks that did fail were resolved by the cooperative sector (Coppola, 27 February 2015).

In France the cooperative movement has 23.7 million members and 115.4 million customers, which represent 41 % and 56 % of the total for all European cooperative banks respectively (see Table 5.3). In France several of the largest banks, including Crédit Agricole, BCPE and Crédit Mutuel, are constituted as cooperative banks; and the cooperative banking sector as a whole has an estimated 59 % share of the domestic loans market. Crédit Agricole and BPCE are classed as Global Systematically Important Banks. Crédit Agricole is a network of cooperative and mutual banks comprising 39 Crédit Agricole Regional Banks. Crédit Agricole has evolved into an interna-

Table 5.3 Cooperative banks and national associations for cooperative banks in Europe

	Total assets (€ million)	No. employees	No. customers	No. of independent cooperative banks	No. of branches – home country	No. members	Domestic market share loans (%)
Austria							
Österreichische Raiffeisenbanken	281,609	26,000	3,600,000	490	1,646	1,700,000	27.3
Österreichischer Volksbanken	40,602	6,785	900,000	59	512	688,000	6.1
Bulgaria							
Central Cooperative Bank	1,915	2,042	1,474,650	n.a.	271	6,818	2.95
Cyprus							
Cooperative Central Bank	15,209	2,973	600,000	19	349	554,363	23.9
Denmark							
Nykredit	189,994	4,052	1,093,000	1	755	270,000	31
Finland							
OP Cooperative, Financial Group	100,991	10,806	4,252,000	183	457	1,404,229	34.6
France							
Crédit Agricole	1,706,326	150,000	49,000,000	39	9,099	7,400,000	20.9
Crédit Mutuel	658,618	78,482	30,400,000	18	5,920	7,500,000	17.2
BPCE	1,123,520	115,000	36,000,000	36	7,530	8,800,000	21
Germany							
BVR	1,080,565	191,243	>30,000,000	1,078	13,056	17,712,774	19.1
Greece							
Association of Cooperative Banks of Greece	3,158	905	385,571	10	129	157,835	0.8
Hungary							

National Federation of Savings Cooperatives	6,386	7,326	1,150,000	105	1,484	84,000	4.44
Italy							
Associazione Nazionale fra le Banche Popolari	460,000	82,200	12,300,000	72	9,256	1,336,000	26.4
FEDERCASSE	206,289	31,565	6,000,000	385	4,454	1,173,668	7.1
Luxembourg							
Banque Raiffeissen	6,354	559	100,000	13	46	10,241	13
Netherlands							
Rabobank Nederland	674,139	56,870	10,000,000	129	722	1,947,000	n.a.
Poland							
National Union of Cooperative Banks	31,195	33,084	n.a.	571	4,816	1,034,448	6.3
Portugal							
Crédito Agrícola	12,969	3,834	1,220,075	83	683	400,000	3.6
Romania							
Creditcoop	199	2,235	919,467	763	46	660,000	n.a.
Slovenia							
Dezelna Banka Slovenije d.d.	856	355	85,000	1	85	260	2.22
Spain							
Unión Nacional de Cooperativas de Crédito	135,019	18,910	10,713,548	65	4,651	2,764,746	6.21
Sweden							
Landshypotek	9,105	130	70,000	1	19	45,000	2.0
United Kingdom							
The Cooperative Bank p.l.c.	52,093	6,704	4,700,000	n.a.	294	2,000,000	1.8
Total	6,797,111	832,060	204,963,311	4,121	66,280	57,649,382	

Source: European Association of Cooperative Banks: Key statistics, end 2013

(*continued*)

tional full-service banking group. It was listed on the Paris stock exchange in December 2011 and forms part of the CAC 40 stock market index. BPCE has a federal structure, bringing together 17 regional Banques Populaires, two specialist national lenders (including Crédit Coopératif, which lends to producer cooperatives), and 17 savings banks. BPCE was formed in 2009 from the merger of two cooperative banks, Groupe Caisses d'Epargne and Groupe Banque Populaire. Crédit Mutuel comprises 18 regional federations, which coordinate business within their respective jurisdictions, encompassing 2,131 local mutual banks serving 7.5 million members and 30.4 million customers. The French local cooperative banks emerged largely unscathed from the global financial crisis. However, their central institutions encountered serious financial difficulties and required government financial support, which has subsequently been repaid (Bulbul, Schmidt and Schuwer, 2013).

Credit Unions

Credit unions are not for profit cooperative financial institutions which provide financial services to a membership defined on the basis of a common bond. Unlike cooperative banks, credit unions are fully mutual which means that all customers must be members. Due to the common bond, credit unions are often viewed as well positioned to provide financial services to those who are excluded by mainstream financial institutions. The common bond mitigates information deficiencies inherent in financial transactions and enables credit unions to provide banking facilities and credit to financially excluded members where it would be deemed too risky by mainstream financial institutions (McKillop and Wilson 2011).

Credit unions can trace their origin to Schulze-Delitzsch and Raiffeisen in Germany. The concept of a credit cooperative crossed form Europe to Canada at the start of the twentieth century with Alphonse Desjardins, a parliamentary reporter, establishing the first *caisse populaire* (people's bank) in his home town of Levi, Quebec in 1900. The first credit union in the USA was established in Manchester, New Hampshire in 1909. The credit union movement in North America now dominates the credit union landscape and the process of diffusion, well tested in the transfer of the cooperative ideal from Europe to North America, has subsequently operated in reverse with Canada and US providing significant support to credit union establishment and development in a number of European countries (McKillop et al. 2006).

Table 5.4 provides descriptive statistics on credit unions by country for 2014. Information is presented on the number of credit unions, their membership, asset under their control and membership as a percentage of the population (penetration). Overall within Europe there are 2,371 credit unions with a total membership of over 8 million which represents a population penetration of 3.4 %. Although the credit union movement owes its cooperative origins to Europe it is now dwarfed by the development of the movement in other regions. Worldwide, there are 57,480 credit unions with 217 million members and a penetration level of 8.2%. Credit unions are particularly significant in North America which has 13% of credit union numbers, 51.7% of worldwide members, 79% of total assets and a penetration rate of 45.92% (World Council of Credit Unions 2015). The fact that cooperative banks have a significant presence in Europe, but are almost non-existent in the US may explain the relative weakness of the credit union movement in Europe.

Table 5.4 shows that credit unions have significant acceptance by the general population in Ireland, Poland, Lithuania and Moldova. The average asset size of credit unions in Moldova and Lithuania is extremely small but is much larger in Ireland and Poland (€38 million and €70 million respectively). Credit unions in both Poland and Ireland are currently facing significant difficulties.

Prior to 1992, there were no operating credit unions in Poland. Today the sector is a primary source of funds for over 2 million poor and working-class people, mainly in rural areas and smaller cities. In Poland credit unions account for about 1.2 % of banking assets. Unfortunately, approximately 50

Table 5.4 Credit unions in Europe, 2014

Country	Credit unions 2014	Members	Assets €m	Penetration (%)
Albania	117	48,410	43.6	2.3
Belarus	6	500	0.14	0.01
Estonia	22	5,627	36.34	0.7
Ireland[a]	378	2,600,000	14,200.0	63.0
Latvia	31	25,788	25.35	1.7
Lithuania	63	142,603	60.29	5.9
Macedonia	1	7,838	40.61	0.5
Moldova	303	121,104	28.97	4.7
Netherlands	20	400	6.70	0.004
Poland	52	2,192,287	3,617.56	8.1
Romania	20	65,938	54.80	0.4
Russia	250	330,481	336.90	0.3
Ukraine	589	821,600	138.12	2.6
United Kingdom[b]	519	1,769,003	3,713.6	3.0
Total (Europe)	2,371	8,131,579	22,302.98	3.4

Source: World Council of Credit Unions (Statistical data, 2014) unless otherwise specified

[a]Central Bank of Ireland, Credit Union Annual Statistics: 2014

[b]Bank of England, Credit Union Annual Statistics: 2014

% of all Polish credit unions are currently close to bankruptcy. The Polish regulator, Komisja Nadzoru Finansowego, estimates that there is a capital shortfall for the sector of €386 million (Foy 2015).

In Ireland credit unions have a population penetration of 63 % (see Table 5.4). Credit union loans make up only 4 % of aggregate loans to Irish households, but they are a significant player in the Irish household sector for unsecured loans with duration of less than five years, accounting for approximately 25 % of that market. The Irish credit union movement was established in the 1950s when both unemployment and emigration were at high levels, and there had been a significant increase in the activity of money lenders. The first credit union was established in 1958 and a year later there were three credit unions with a total of 200 members and €530 in savings. In 2007, prior to the financial and economic crisis in Ireland there were 422 credit unions with approximately €12 billion in assets.

The adverse economic conditions following the financial crisis have resulted in a decline in the performance of Irish credit unions and have made it difficult for some credit unions to replenish reserves through retained earnings. A Commission on Credit Unions was established in 2011 to review the sector. Based on the recommendations of the Commission new legislation was introduced (Credit Union and Cooperation with Overseas Regulators Act 2012) and a Restructuring Board (ReBo) was established to facilitate mergers and restructuring.[10] By the end of 2015 the number of credit unions had fallen to 378 (see Table 5.4). Most of this decline was through mergers although a small number of credit unions were also liquidated by the Central Bank of Ireland. It is anticipated that there will be a further steady decline in credit union numbers over the coming years.[11]

Performance, Risk and Lending

Comparing the relative performance of public, commercial and mutual banks is not without problems. As highlighted previously these institutions may pursue different objectives; profit maximization in the case of shareholder-owned commercial banks and more varied objectives (focusing on improving the well-being of key stakeholders in the case of mutual and public banks). A further complicating factor is that the business model

[10] Report of the Commission on Credit Unions was published in March 2012. The Credit Union and Cooperation with Overseas Regulators Act was published in December 2012. The Restructuring Board was established in January 2013.

[11] During 2015, 40 credit unions transferred engagements reducing the number of credit unions to 338.

may differ not only across ownership structures but within ownership forms (Ayadi and de Groen, this volume). Many early studies chose not to control for such differences (Fonteyne 2007). More recent studies adopt a more rounded approach and rather than concentrating on for example profitability also consider the riskiness of business activities, cost efficiency and loan quality (Ferri et al. 2014a, b).

Efficiency

There is a large empirical literature on the measurement of cost structure and efficiency in European banking. The early literature, reviewed by Goddard, Molyneux and Wilson (2001) and Goddard, Molyneux, Wilson and Tavakoli (2007) was concerned with identifying the potential for achieving cost savings by selecting the optimal firm size and product mix and by maximising operational or productive efficiency. This literature for the most part ignores differences in scale, scope and operational efficiency across ownership types.[12] Some notable exceptions exist, albeit the results emanating from these studies are rather mixed and inconclusive. For example, Altunbas, Evans and Molyneux (2001) find that savings and cooperative banks in Germany are slightly more profit and cost efficient than their commercial bank counterparts. For Spain, Hasan and Lozano-Vivas (2002) find that mutual banks suffer from higher cost inefficiency than their shareholder-owned competitors supporting the hypothesis of expense-preference behaviour of mutual banks' management. Across Eastern European countries, Fries and Taci (2005) find that shareholder-owned banks are more efficient than publicly owned counterparts. However, there is variation across shareholder owned banks. Specifically, majority foreign owned privatized banks are less efficient that de novo domestic and foreign banks, and banks that are domestically owned. More recently, using a large cross-country sample of mutual and commercial banks, Girardone, Nankervis and Velentza (2009) find that mutual banks are more cost inefficient than shareholder-owned banks. Finally, Makinen and Jones (2015) compare the relative efficiency of European commercial banks with that of savings and cooperative banks over the period 1994–2010. The authors find that cooperative banks are more efficient (less inefficient) than savings and commercial banks.

[12] Seminal work comparing the efficiency of US shareholder and mutual financial institutions finds that mutuals are more efficient than shareholder-owned banks (O'Hara 1981; Mester 1989, 1993).

Profitability

Most early literature examining differences in profitability was based on the application of the Structure-Conduct-Performance (SCP) paradigm to European bank-level data (Molyneux and Thornton 1992; Goddard, Molyneux and Wilson, 2001). The empirical models used typically contained a large number of industry- and bank-specific variables, but often explained little of the variation in profitability across banks. Furthermore, differences in ownership were for the most part neglected.

A small number of empirical studies have attempted to establish a systematic relationship between ownership type and bank profitability. For example, Goddard, Molyneux and Wilson (2004) find little evidence that ownership type matters in explaining profitability differences across banks in Denmark, France, Germany, Italy, Spain and the UK. In a cross-country study, Fernández, Fonseca and González (2004) find that public and mutual banks had higher interest margins than shareholder-owned banks, but that this difference disappeared when net income was considered. This suggested that mutual and public banks have higher non-interest expenses than shareholder-owned banks.

Iannotta, Nocera and Sironi (2007) examine the relationship between ownership form and the performance and risk of a sample of large banks from 15 European countries over the period 1999–2004. In spite of their lower cost base, cooperative and savings banks exhibit lower profitability than shareholder-owned banks. Goddard, Liu, Molyneux and Wilson (2013) investigate the determinants and convergence of bank profitability in eight European Union member countries, between 1992 and 2007. By ownership form, the results of the empirical analysis suggest that savings banks were more profitable than commercial banks in Germany, the Netherlands, Spain and the UK. Savings banks in Denmark were less profitable than commercial banks. Cooperative banks were more profitable than commercial banks in Germany, Italy, the Netherlands and Spain.

In a recent contribution, Casu and Gall (2016) conduct an analysis of the relative performance of commercial banks and building societies in the UK over the period 2000–14. The authors find that the average level and variability of profit is higher for banks than for building societies. Furthermore, following a decline during the financial crisis, the profitability of building societies recovered more quickly than commercial banks.

Risk

Bank ownership can also originate differences in bank risk exposure. Mutual banks are likely to have different risk-taking incentives to commercial banks, since they pursue social and economic development objectives, rather than shareholder value maximization. Mutual banks may be less fragile than their commercial banking counterparts because they have a stable deposit base and pursue business strategies that aim to build up capital for future generations. However, mutual banks are less diversified and have less option to raise capital at short notice. Consequently, these banks are less able to absorb demand- or supply-side shocks to their balance sheets (Fonteyne 2007). Furthermore, mutual bank borrowers may have incentives to free ride in taking risky loans, since the losses will be shared among all the members of the bank (Delgado, Salas and Saurina, 2007). Hower (2009) notes that firms that have a main banking relationship with a cooperative or savings bank are less likely to exit upon the onset of financial distress than counterparts whose main bank relationship is with a commercial bank.

Results from extant empirical studies appear to suggest that savings and cooperative banks are less risky than their commercial banking counterparts. For example, Iannotta, Nocera and Sironi (2007), in a study of banks across Europe, find that mutual banks have better loan quality and lower asset risk than shareholder-owned banks. Using a large sample of commercial, savings and cooperative banks from 29 Organisation for Economic Co-operation and Development (OECD) countries, Hesse and Čihak (2007) find that while cooperative banks are less profitable and capitalized than commercial banks, they enjoy more stable returns. In a study of Spanish banks, Garcia-Marco and Robles-Fernandez (2008) also find that shareholder owned commercial banks are riskier than their savings bank counterparts. In a recent contribution Chiaramonte, Poli and Oriani (2015) find that cooperative banks appear to be more stable than commercial banking counterparts during stressed periods. The opposite appears to be true under normal economic conditions.

The increasing role of the state in European banking industries since the onset of the financial crisis in 2007 has motivated researchers to investigate whether there are differences between shareholder-owned commercial banks and public banks. Hau and Thum (2009) in an analysis of the 29 largest German banks show a systematic underperformance of publicly owned banks in the recent banking crisis. Adjusted for size, asset write-downs and losses from the first quarter of 2007 to the third quarter of 2008 are on average three times as large for publicly owned banks compared to shareholder-owned banks. In a recent contribution, Ianotta, Nocera and Sironi (2013) examine the relationship between government ownership, and bank default risk and bank operating risk. Using a cross-country dataset of large European banks, the authors find that government owned banks have a lower default risk and higher operating risk than their privately owner banking counterparts.

Lending

How banking lending responds to shocks has attracted the attention of academic and policy makers. The effects of unexpected shocks to bank balance sheets and resultant liquidity constraints during financial crises have been studied in some detail. Differences in lending across ownership form are evident in a number of studies with mutual and publicly owned banks typically providing some stability to the supply of credit during crisis periods. For example, Sapienza (2004) considers bank lending relationships in Italy and finds that publicly owned banks tend to charge lower interest rates than shareholder-owned banks. Using a sample of public-owned and privately owned banks from 50 countries (including Europe) over the period 1994–2009, Brei and Schclarek (2013) find that in response to financial crises, public-owned banks increase lending, while private banks decrease lending. Bolton, Freixas, Gambacorta and Mistrulli (2013) study how relationship lending and transaction lending vary over the business cycle. During normal times, relationship lenders (mutuals) tend to incur higher costs and therefore charge higher lending rates than transaction-based lenders (shareholder-owned banks). However, as relationship banks learn more about their borrowers over time, they can continue to lend at more favourable terms when a crisis hits and suffer fewer defaults.

In Eastern Europe evidence suggests that state-owned and cooperatively owned banks provide more stable forms of credit over the business cycle. For Russia, Fungacova, Herrala and Weill (2013) find that overall credit supply diminishes following the financial crisis, and that foreign-owned banks and private-owned domestic banks reduced credit supply more than state-controlled banks. Hasan, Jackowicz, Kowalewski and Kozłowski (2014) find that local cooperative banks in Poland lend more to small businesses than do large domestic banks and foreign-owned banks. Finally, Ferri Kalmi and Kerola (2014a, b) analyse differences in lending policies between stakeholder and shareholder EU banks to detect possible variations in bank lending supply responses to changes in monetary policy.

Following a monetary policy contraction, stakeholder banks are found to decrease their loan supply to a lesser extent than shareholder banks. A detailed analysis of the effect among stakeholder banks reveals that cooperative banks continued to smooth the impact of tighter monetary policy on their lending during the crisis period (2008–11), whereas savings banks did not. Stakeholder banks' propensity to smooth their lending cycles suggests that their presence in the economy has the potential to reduce credit supply volatility.

Concludings Comments

The banking industry in Europe has a rich array of banks with different ownership forms which coexist together as part of the wider financial system. Commercial banks are primarily shareholder-based institutions which aim to maximize profits for their respective owners, while mutual financial institutions (such as savings banks, building societies, cooperative banks and credit unions) are primarily stakeholder institutions that seek to balance the interests of various stakeholders (including shareholders, customers, employees and local communities) while performing financial intermediation functions. These different objective functions have led to differences in both the behaviour and performance across different types of financial institution.

Prior to the financial crisis, deregulation reduced or eliminated many of the lines of demarcation between different ownership forms. This facilitated both domestic and cross-border competition. The financial crisis of 2007–8 and the more recent European sovereign debt crisis of 2009–13, resulted in large losses and the bailouts of commercial and savings banks. This has led in many countries to consolidation and a reduction in the number of banks, and an enhanced role for partial public ownership of many of Europe's largest banks.

Empirical research that attempts to assess differences in the efficiency, profitability, risk and lending strategies of commercial banks and mutual financial institutions produces rather mixed results, which vary depending on the geographic area or time period under consideration. However, some evidence appears to suggest mutual financial institutions' investments in gathering soft information and establishing close relationships with borrower during periods of economic buoyancy allows them to continue to lend to borrowers during stressed periods. This suggests that stakeholder banks are likely to continue in future to play an important role alongside commercial banks in providing credit to households and firms across Europe.

References

Altunbas, Y., Evans, L., & Molyneux, P. (2001). Bank ownership and efficiency. *Journal of Money, Credit and Banking, 33*, 926–954.

Andrianova, S., Demetriades, P., & Shortland, A. (2010). *Is government ownership of banks really harmful to growth?* Berlin: German Institute for Economic Research.

Ayadi, R., & de Groen W. P. (2016). Bank business models. In T. Beck & B. Casu (Eds.), *Handbook of European banking*. Basingstoke: Palgrave.

Ayadi, R., Llewellyn, D., Schmidt, R. H., Arbak, E., & de Groen, W. P. (2010). *Investigating diversity in the banking sector in Europe: Key developments, performance and role of cooperative banks*. Brussels: Centre for European Policy Studies.

Ayadi, R., Schmidt, R. H., & Carbo-Valverde, S. (2009). *Investigating diversity in the banking sector in Europe: The performance and role of savings banks*. Brussels: Centre for European Policy Studies.

Berger, A., & Hannan, T. (1998). The efficiency cost of market power in the banking industry: A test of the 'quiet life' and related hypotheses. *Review of Economics and Statistics, 80*, 454–465.

Birchall, J. (2013). *Resilience in a downturn*. Geneva: International Labour Organization.

Bolton, P., Freixas, X., Gambacorta, L., & Mistrulli, P. E. (2013). *Relationship and transaction lending in a crisis* (Bank of Italy discussion paper No. 917).

Brei, M., & Schclarek, A. (2013). Public bank lending in crisis times. *Journal of Financial Stability, 9*, 820–830.

Bulbul, D., Schmidt, R. H., & Schuwer, U. (2013). *Savings banks and cooperative banks in Europe* (SAFE white paper No. 5).

Casu, B., & Gall, A. (2016). *Building societies in the financial services industry*. London: Building Societies Association.

Chiaramonte, L., Poli, F., & Oriani, M. (2015). Are cooperative banks a lever for promoting bank stability? Evidence from the recent financial crisis in OECD countries. *European Financial Management, 21*, 491–523.

Cleary, E. J. (1965). *The building society movement*. London: Elek.

Coppola, F. (2015, February 27). What lessons can the UK learn from Germany's cooperative banking sector? *Cooperative News*. http://www.thenews.coop/

Correa, R., & Sapriza, H. (2015). Sovereign debt crises. In A. Berger, P. Molyneux, & J. O. S. Wilson (Eds.), *Oxford handbook of banking*. Oxford: Oxford University Press.

Davis, K. (2014). *Changing organizational form: Demutualization and the privatization of communal wealth – Australian credit union experiences* (University of Melbourne working paper). http://kevindavis.com.au/secondpages/workinprogress/credit%20union%20demutualization%20cases%20Feb2015.pdf

De Haas, R., & Van Horen, N. (2016). N. Recent trends in cross-border banking in Europe. In T. Beck & B. Casu (Eds.), *Handbook of European banking*. Basingstoke: Palgrave.

Delgado, J., Salas, V., & Saurina, J. (2007). Joint size and ownership specialization in bank lending. *Journal of Banking & Finance, 31*, 3563–3583.

Drake, L. (1989). *The building society industry in transition*. London: Macmillan.

Drake, L., & Llewellyn, D. T. (1997). *The economics of mutuality*. London: Building Societies Association.

European Association of Cooperative Banks (EACB). (2014). *Last key figures on the sector*. http://www.eacb.coop/en/cooperative_banks/key_figures/last_key_figures.html

European Office, German Bausparkassen. (2013). *The Bauspar system in Germany Rue Jacques de Lalaing 28 1040 Brussels*. http://www.bausparkassen.de/fileadmin/user_upload/english/Bausparen_in_Deutschland_en_130109.pdf

Ferguson, C., & McKillop, D. G. (1993). *Building societies: Structure, performance and change*. Norwell: Kluwer academic Publishers Group.

Fernández, A. I., Fonseca, A. R., & González, F. (2004). The effect of government ownership on bank profitability and risk. In R. Roll (Ed.), *Focus on financial institutions and services*. New York: Nova Science Publishers.

Ferri, G., Kalmi, P., & Kerola, E. (2013). Governance and performance: Reassessing the pre-crisis situation of European banks. In S. Goglio & Y. Alexopoulos (Eds.), *Financial cooperatives and local development*. Abingdon: Routledge.

Ferri, G., Kalmi, P., & Kerola, E. (2014a). *Organizational structure and performance in European banks: A post-crisis reassessment* (LUMSA University working paper).

Ferri, G., Kalmi, P., & Kerola, E. (2014b). Does bank ownership affect lending behavior? Evidence from the Euro area. *Journal of Banking & Finance, 48*, 194–209.

Fonteyne, W. (2007). *Cooperative banks in Europe—policy issues* (IMF working paper, European department).

Foy, H. (2015, January 5). Bankruptcy fears for Poland's credit unions. *Financial Times*. http://www.ft.com/cms/s/0/bc5c4fea-94cd-11e4-8341-00144feabdc0.html#axzz41Cfa8fAV

Friedman, M. (1970, September 13). The social responsibility of business is to increase its profits. *New York Times Magazine*.

Fries, S., & Taci, A. (2005). Cost efficiency of banks in transition: Evidence from 289 banks in 15 post-communist countries. *Journal of Banking & Finance, 29*, 55–81.

Fund for Orderly Bank Restructuring (FROB). (2013). *Savings banks today, Fondo de Reestructuración Ordenada Bancaria*. Available at: http://www.frob.es/financiera/docs/20130425%20_Presentacion_abril2013.pdf

Fungacova, Z., Herrala, R., & Weill, L. (2013). The influence of bank ownership on credit supply: Evidence from the recent financial crisis. *Emerging Markets Review, 15*, 136–147.

Garcia-Cestona, M., & Surroca, J. (2008). Multiple goals and ownership structure: Effects on the performance of Spanish savings banks. *European Journal of Operational Research, 187*, 582–599.

Garcia-Marco, T., & Robles-Fernandez, M. D. (2008). Risk-taking behaviour and ownership in the banking industry: The Spanish evidence. *Journal of Economics & Business, 60*, 332–354.

Gardener, E. P. M., Molyneux, P., & Williams, J. (1999). *European savings banks, coming of age? Exploring the role of savings banks in European financial services*. Dublin: Lafferty Publications.

Gardener, E. P. M., Molyneux, P., Williams, J., & Carbo, S. (1997). European savings banks: Facing up the new environment. *International Journal of Bank Marketing, 15*, 243–254.

Giradone, C., Nankervis, J. C., & Velentza, E. F. (2009). Efficiency, ownership and financial structure in European banking: A cross-country comparison. *Managerial Finance, 35*, 227–245.

Goddard, J., Liu, H., Molyneux, P., & Wilson, J. O. S. (2013). Do bank profits converge? *European Financial Management, 19*, 345–365.

Goddard, J., Molyneux, P., & Wilson, J. O. S. (2001). *European banking: Efficiency, technology and growth*. Chichester: John Wiley and Sons.

Goddard, J., Molyneux, P., & Wilson, J. O. S. (2004). The profitability of European banks: A cross-sectional and dynamic panel analysis. *Manchester School, 72*, 363–381.

Goddard, J., Molyneux, P., & Wilson, J. O. S. (2009a). Crisis in UK banking: Lessons for public policy. *Public Money and Management, 29*, 276–284.

Goddard, J., Molyneux, P., & Wilson, J. O. S. (2009b). The financial crisis in Europe: Evolution, policy responses and lessons for the future. *Journal of Financial Regulation and Compliance, 17*, 362–380.

Goddard, J., Molyneux, P., Wilson, J. O. S., & Tavakoli, M. (2007). European banking: An overview. *Journal of Banking and Finance, 31*, 1911–1935.

Guinnane, T. W. (1994). A failed institutional transplant: Raiffeisen's credit cooperatives in Ireland, 1894–1914. *Explorations in Economic History, 31*, 38–61.

Hasan, I., & Lozano-Vivas, A. (2002). Organizational form and expense preference: Spanish experience. *Bulletin of Economic Research, 54*, 135–150.

Hasan, I., Jackowicz, K., Kowalewski, O., & Kozłowski, Ł. (2014). *Bank ownership, SME lending and local credit markets* (Bank of Finland discussion paper No. 22).

Hau, H., & Thum, M. (2009). *Subprime crisis and board (in-) competence: Private vs. public banks in Germany* (CESifo working paper No. 2640).

Hesse, H., & Cihak, M. (2007). *Cooperative banks and financial stability* (IMF working paper No. 07/02).

Hower, D. (2009). *From soft and hardnosed bankers: Bank lending strategies and the survival of financially distressed firms* (ZEW Centre for European economic research discussion paper No. 09–059).

Iannotta, G., Nocera, G., & Sironi, A. (2007). Ownership structure, risk and performance in the European banking industry. *Journal of Banking & Finance, 31*, 2127–2149.

Iannotta, G., Nocera, G., & Sironi, A. (2013). The impact of government ownership on bank risk. *Journal of Financial Intermediation, 22*, 152–176.

IMF. (2012, June). *Spain: The reform of Spanish savings banks technical notes* (IMF country report No. 12/141).

Jensen, M. C. (2010). Value maximization, stakeholder theory, and the corporate objective function. *Journal of Applied Corporate Finance, 22*, 32–42.

Jensen, M., & Meckling, W. (1976). Theory of the firm: Managerial behavior, agency costs and ownership structure. *Journal of Financial Economics, 3*, 305–360.

Kindleberger, C. (1984). *A financial history of Western Europe*. London: George Allen & Unwin.

La Porta, R., Lopez-de-Silanes, F., & Shleifer, A. (2002). Government ownership of banks. *Journal of Finance, 57*, 265–301.

Llewellyn, D. T. (2006). Globalization and convergence on the shareholder value model in European banking. *BIS Papers, 32*, 20–30.

Llewellyn, D. T. (2005). Competition and profitability in European banking: Why are British banks so profitable? *Economics Notes, 34*, 279–311.

Makinen, M., & Jones, D. C. (2015). Comparative efficiency between cooperative, savings and commercial banks in Europe using the frontier approach. *Annals of Public & Cooperative Economics, 86*, 401–420.

Martín R., A & Sevillano J. M. M. (2011) Cooperative and Savings Banks in Europe: Nature, Challenges and Perspectives. *Banks and Bank Systems, 6*, 121–135

Marois, T. (2013). *State-owned banks and development: Dispelling mainstream myths* (Municipal Services Project, occasional paper No. 21). Cape Town: Municipal Services Project.

Marois, T., & Güngen, A. R. (2013). *Reclaiming Turkey's state-owned banks* (Municipal Services Project occasional paper No. 22). Cape Town: Municipal Services Project.

McKillop, D. G., & Wilson, J. O. S. (2011). Credit unions: A theoretical and empirical overview. *Financial Markets, Institutions and Instruments, 20*, 79–123.

McKillop, D. G., & Wilson, J. O. S. (2015). Credit unions as cooperative institutions: Distinctiveness, performance and prospects. *Social & Environmental Accountability Journal, 35*, 96–112.

McKillop, D. G., Goth, P., & Hyndman, N. (2006). *The structure, performance and governance of Irish credit unions*. Dublin: Institute of Chartered Accountants in Ireland.

Mester, L. (1989). Testing for expense preference behavior: Mutual versus stock savings and loans. *RAND Journal of Economics, 20*, 483–498.

Mester, L. J. (1993). Efficiency in the savings and loan industry. *Journal of Banking & Finance, 17*, 267–286.

Molyneux, P. & Thornton, J. (1992). Determinants of European bank profitability: A note. *Journal of Banking and Finance, 16*, 1173–1178.

NEF. (2014). *Stakeholder banks benefits of banking diversity*. London: New Economics Foundation.

O'Hara, M. (1981). Property rights and the financial firm. *Journal of Law and Economics, 24*, 317–332.

Revell, J. (1989). *The future of savings banks: A study of Spain and the rest Europe*. Bangor: Institute of European Finance.

Sapienza, P. (2004). The effects of government ownership on bank lending. *Journal of Financial Economics, 72*, 357–384.

Sawyer, M. (2014). Concept paper on effects of finance on industry under different financial systems, mimeo.

Schmit, M., Gheeraert, L., Denuit, T., & Warny, C. (2011). *Public financial institutions in Europe*. Brussels: European Association of Public Banks.

Shleifer, A., & Vishny, R. W. (1997). A survey of corporate governance. *Journal of Finance, 52*, 737–783.

Standard and Poors. (2014, November 28). www.standardandpoors.com/ratingsdirect

Vittas, D. (1996). *Thrift deposit institutions in Europe and the United States*. Washington: World Bank.

VÖB, Association of Public German Banks. (2014). *Promotional banks in Germany, acting in the public interest*. Available online at: http://www.voeb.de/de/ueber_uns/

Von Mettenheim, K., & Butzbach, O. (2012). Alternative banking: Theory and evidence from Europe. *Brazilian Journal of Political Economy, 32*, 580–596.

World Council of Credit Unions (WOCCU). (2015). *Statistical report*. World Council of Credit Unions.

WSBI-ESBG. (2015). *Roots of savings and retail banks*. http://www.savings-banks.com/Who-we-are/History/Pages/portal.aspx

6

Pay Structures in European Banks

Jens Hagendorff and Abhishek Srivastav

Introduction

Recent episodes of bank failures and financial instability have given attempts to understand the factors that contribute to excessive risk-taking renewed impetus. Ongoing academic research and policy debates have widely argued that the design of executive compensation contracts resulted in misaligned incentives and contributed to financial instability (Bebchuk and Spamann 2009; Financial Stability Board 2009; DeYoung et al. 2013; IMF 2014). The focus of this chapter is to explore the pay structures of senior managers at European banks with a special emphasis on the implications of pay for risk-taking.

Typically, the compensation structure of senior bank managers consists of a large fraction of equity-like instruments in the form of common stocks and stock options. When managers are paid with such instruments, their wealth is tied to that of shareholders, thereby causing them to engage in additional risk-taking. This is particularly relevant in the banking industry where equity makes up only a small proportion of a bank's balance sheet. Another potential

J. Hagendorff (✉)
Cardiff Business School, Cardiff University, Cardiff, UK
e-mail: HagendorffJ@cardiff.ac.uk

A. Srivastav
Leeds University Business School, University of Leeds, Leeds, UK
e-mail: A.Srivastav@leeds.ac.uk

T. Beck, B. Casu (eds.), *The Palgrave Handbook of European Banking*,
DOI 10.1057/978-1-137-52144-6_6

channel through which managerial compensation has exacerbated risk-taking is the use of performance-based bonuses that induce managers to pursue risky policies that yield short-term payoffs (Bebchuk and Spemann 2009; Federal Reserve et al. 2010).

Recent proposals to reform pay in the banking industry highlight the need to understand better how to structure managerial compensation in a way that it can mitigate risk-taking behaviour and align the interests of managers and shareholders while also ensuring financial stability. For instance, the Financial Stability Board (2009) recommends that compensation structure should be consistent with the goal of risk alignment where the instruments used to compensate executives should be sensitive to the overall impact on bank risk and to the time horizon over such risks materialize. Similarly, the European Banking Authority (2015) proposes explicit caps on bonus payments such that at least 40–60 % of variable compensation (including bonus payments) should be deferred.

The objective of these and similar executive compensation guidelines at banks is to find a balancing point between long-term bank performance and prudent risk-taking. Pay structures that promote excessive risk-taking at the cost of bank stability can easily subordinate the interests of (risk-averse) regulators and taxpayers to those of (risk neutral) shareholders. Against this background, the focus of this chapter is on the pay structures of senior European bank managers and the implications of pay for risk-taking.

Before the financial crisis of 2007, academic research largely looked at the role of equity-based compensation in influencing bank risk (e.g., Houston and James 1995; Chen et al. 2006; Mehran and Rosenberg 2007). However, given the media and regulatory scrutiny given to executive compensation practices in the banking industry, there has been a shift towards understanding alternate pay mechanisms that make managerial pay-offs sensitive to a bank's financial condition and stability. For instance, emerging research has argued that chief executive officers (CEOs) may be compensated with debt-like components that vest after a CEO retires (Edmans and Liu 2011; Bolton et al. 2015) and that CEO pay should be deferred over longer time periods and be subject to risk-adjusted performance criteria (Bebchuk and Spamann 2009; Bhagat and Romano 2009). The aim of this chapter is to provide an understanding of trends in executive compensation and establish a connection between ongoing policy reforms and executive pay structures in European banks.

This chapter is organized as follows. The section "Theoretical Background" discusses the theoretical background behind executive compensation and its implication for the banking industry. The section "The Structure of Managerial Compensation" discusses the various components of executive compensation, while "Impact of European Policy Developments on Pay Characteristics" assesses the link between recent policy developments and academic research. Next, "Contrasting Compensation Reforms in the US to the European Approach" contrasts the regulatory approach followed in the US to that in Europe, and the section "Are There Costs Associated with Regulating Executive Pay?" highlights some of the unintended consequences of cross-country differences in pay rules. The "Conclusion" brings the chapter to a close.

Theoretical Background

Executive compensation serves as a mechanism to reduce conflicts between managers and shareholders over the deployment of corporate resources and the riskiness of the firm. Jensen and Meckling (1976) posit that paying CEOs with firm equity, instead of fixed compensation in the form of salary, induces managers to exert effort and pursue actions that increase shareholder value, while mitigating incentives to extract perquisites.

However, the idea of paying managers with instruments that are sensitive to shareholder value instead of firm value results in a theoretically well-defined moral hazard problem in the banking industry. This is because banks are highly leveraged institutions and, given the call option properties of equity, bank shareholders face limited downside risk but stand to benefit more from high-risk strategies (Jensen and Meckling 1976; John and John 1993; Noe et al. 1996). By contrast, creditors have fixed claims on the value of bank assets and they prefer low volatility and are concerned about the long-term solvency of a bank. Clearly, managers aligned more with shareholders are more likely to pursue policies that may increase firm risk, even though this may be detrimental for other stakeholders.

Shareholder incentives to increase risk are further aggravated by deposit insurance and the operation of implicit bailout policies, which act as a taxpayer-funded put option (Merton 1977). Bank shareholders may maximize the value of this put by engaging in additional risk-taking at the expense of bank creditors and the deposit insurer. The extant literature has provided ample evidence of moral hazard arising from the safety net as well as from government guarantees more generally (e.g., Hovakimian and Kane 2000; Dam and Koetter 2012; Freixas and Rochet 2013).

Shareholders are likely to use their control over CEO pay to encourage managerial risk-taking and the shifting of risk to regulators and bondholders (Benston et al. 1995; Hubbard and Palia 1995; Bolton et al. 2015). For instance, Bolton et al. (2015) posit that shareholders may induce CEOs to pursue shareholder-friendly policies by granting them higher equity-based compensation in the form of stock grants and stock options. These incentives may motivate bank CEOs to pursue riskier policies, in order to maximize their payoffs. By contrast, emerging evidence has shown that CEO pay may also consist of some debt-like instruments that motivate managers to also assess long-term stability of the company (Edmans and Liu 2011; Bolton et al. 2015). We explore different components of CEO's compensation structure and assess their implications for risk-taking behaviour in the next section.

The Structure of Managerial Compensation

Managerial compensation broadly consists of three different components: cash-based compensation, equity-based compensation and debt-based compensation. This section critically reviews existing empirical work on the different components of pay and their implications for bank risk-taking.

Cash-Based Compensation

Cash bonuses are generally awarded to executives when they achieve certain performance threshold over a short time horizon, such as a one-year period (Murphy 2000). These bonus payments are strictly increasing as the performance reaches different thresholds, wherein performance measures could be based on objectives linked to financial performance such as earnings per share or return on equity. Figure 6.1 illustrates this payoff through the shape of a typical bonus function.

Historically, cash bonuses have formed a significant component of executive pay. Figure 6.2 shows for a sample of senior managers at large European banks that bonus payments represented nearly 70 % of cash-based compensation in the pre-crisis era. Bebchuk et al. (2010) also note that the CEO in Lehmann Brothers and Bear Stearns received more than $61 million and $87 million in the form of cash bonuses during 2000–8, respectively. Thanassoulis (2012) shows that the bonuses granted to bank executives are substantial, with the remuneration bill at Merrill Lynch and Morgan Stanley accounting for 50 % of shareholder equity.

However, this trend has reversed after the financial crisis with the fraction of bonuses falling to less than 30 % of cash-based compensation after the introduction of regulatory reforms arguing for explicit caps on bonuses in the post-crisis era. This is in line with the discussion below where it is argued that excessive use of cash bonuses induce risk-taking incentives.

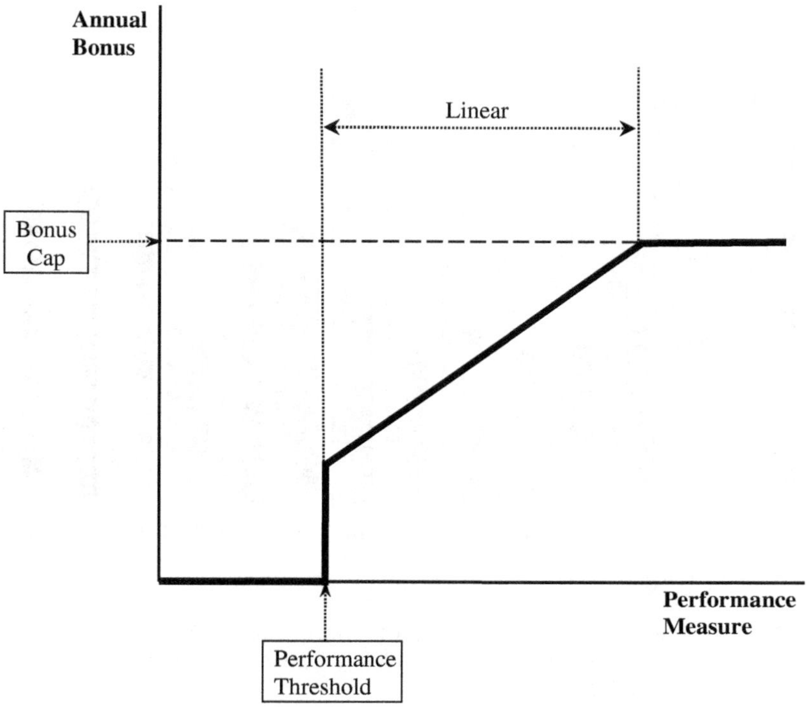

Fig. 6.1 Payoffs from a typical bonus function

Prior theoretical work provides some evidence in regard to the risk implications of bonuses. In a theoretical model, Smith and Stulz (1985) show that as long as cash bonuses increase linearly with corporate performance, the payoffs linked to a bonus plan are non-convex and, therefore, not inherently risk-rewarding. However, when performance is below the earnings-based threshold at which bonuses become payable, bonus plans resemble a call option on the performance measure. In this case, bonus plan payoffs will be convex and offset the concavity of the CEO's risk-averse utility function.

Edmans and Liu (2011) argue that since CEO cash bonuses are only paid in states of solvency, CEOs at distressed firms may engage in risk-shifting to "gamble for solvency" with little regard for the liquidation value of a firm. When senior management knows that there is a high likelihood a bank could fail, they are likely to undertake riskier strategies in an effort to boost short-term performance. While such behaviour may increase the probability of bank default, managers expect to benefit in terms of continuous employment and future pay should their gamble payoff.

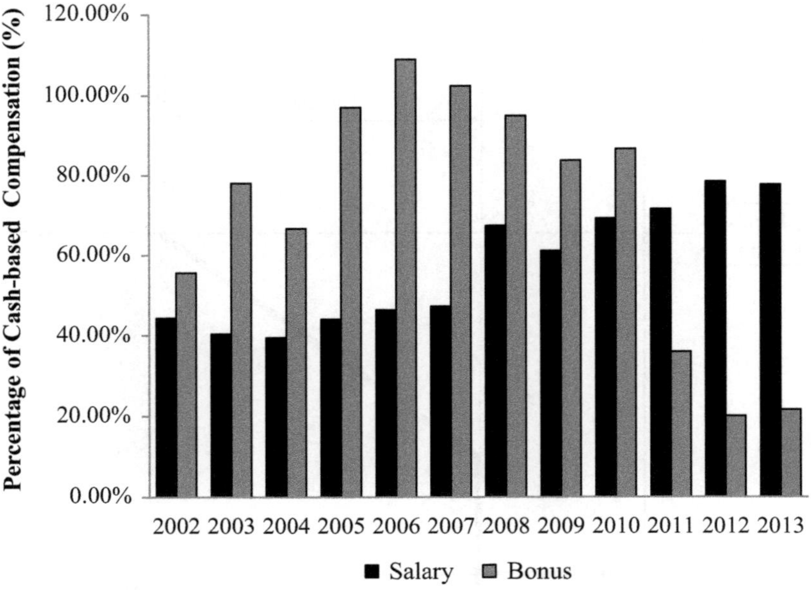

Fig. 6.2 Cash-based compensation (Salary and bonus) in 2002–2013 for the five highest-paid senior bank managers at 14 large European banks. Authors' calculations with data from Boardex

Another factor that may moderate the bonus–risk relationship is the overall strength of the bank regulatory regime. When the prospect of regulatory intervention is low, cash bonuses may lose their risk-reducing effect (Noe et al. 1996). Webb (2008) suggests that as regulatory monitoring weakens, bank executives become less risk averse. Similarly, Hakenes and Schnabel (2014) argue show that one implication of increased bailout expectations is that it motivates shareholders to grant steeper bonus payments, resulting in further exacerbating risk-taking concerns. Consequently, it could be argued that when regulatory environments are less strict and the probability of bailout is high, CEOs may be become more responsive to incentives to shift risk to regulators.

The narrow empirical evidence available on the impact of bonuses on bank risk reaches conflicting conclusions on the role of CEO bonus payments and bank risk. Harjoto and Mullineaux (2003) report a positive association between bonus payments and return volatility. Balachandran et al. (2010) proffer some evidence that the sum of bonus and other cash incentives reduces the probability of bank default. Vallascas and Hagendorff (2013) find that CEO bonuses at European and US banks are associated with higher default risk amongst the riskiest of banks, although this relationship does not exist in less risky banks where bonuses may instead improve bank stability. More recently, Thanassoulis (2012) build a theoretical model to show that competition for managerial talent results in banks resorting to higher bonuses in order to attract and retain talented managers. However, this competition results in negative externalities since the equilibrium pay for all executives in the market goes up and rewards more risk-taking. More recently, Efing et al. (2015) show that employee bonuses in the capital market and investment banking divisions for European banks are positively correlated to the volatility of trading income.

Evidently, cash bonuses are not the only form of incentive compensation that may affect CEO risk-taking. Stock and stock options may cause CEOs to overcome their risk aversion and incentivize them to engage in risk-increasing projects (Smith and Stulz 1985; Coles et al. 2006). We discuss these equity-based incentives in the following section.

Equity-Based Compensation

Equity-based compensation takes the form of grants of the firm's shares as well as call options on the firm's equity. Since the 1990s, the use of equity-linked compensation has increased rapidly. As shown in Fig. 6.3, typically equity-based pay represented more than 46 % of total compensation in a sample of European bank executives in 2006. Generally, the increasing use of performance-sensitive compensation is consistent with agency theory, which suggests that optimal executive compensation needs to align the interests

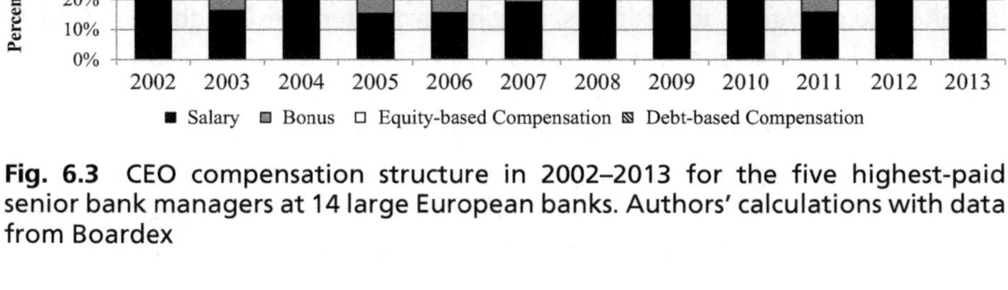

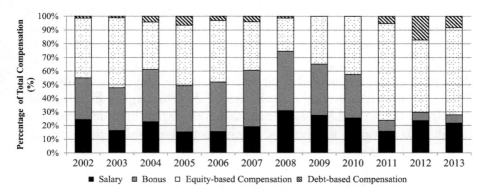

Fig. 6.3 CEO compensation structure in 2002–2013 for the five highest-paid senior bank managers at 14 large European banks. Authors' calculations with data from Boardex

of risk-averse managers with those of risk-neutral shareholders (Jensen and Meckling 1976; Smith and Stulz 1985).

Equity instruments results in embedding two types of incentive. First, equity instruments induce CEOs to exert greater effort by making compensation more sensitive to performance (also known as pay-performance sensitivity or Delta incentives). Second, equity instruments motivate CEOs to pursue risky policies by making compensation more sensitive to risk (also known as pay-risk sensitivity or Vega incentives). These pay-based incentives are captured by a method described in Guay (1999). The measure captures the partial derivative of the value of the CEO's portfolio of options (estimated using the dividend-adjusted Black–Scholes value) or stock holdings, respectively.

$$\text{vega} = \frac{\partial \text{value}}{\partial \sigma} \times .01 = e^{-dT} N'(Z) S \sqrt{T} \times .01 \tag{6.1}$$

$$\text{delta} = \frac{\partial \text{value}}{\partial S} \frac{S}{100} = e^{-dT} N(Z) \frac{S}{100} \tag{6.2}$$

where $Z = \left[\ln(S / X) + \left(r_f - d + 0.5\sigma^2\right)T \right] / \sigma\sqrt{T}$. $N'(.)$ and $N(.)$ are the normal probability density function and the cumulative normal distribution respectively. S is the closing stock price at the fiscal year end, X is the exercise price of the option, σ is the annualized standard deviation of daily stock returns, r is the risk-free rate for a maturity value equal to that of the option contract, d is the dividend yield, and T is the time to maturity of the option grant.

The impact of higher levels of pay-performance sensitivity (delta) on bank risk is ambiguous since high levels of delta incentives may exacerbate managerial risk aversion. For instance, high levels of stock ownership (a primary component of Delta incentives) may result in poorly diversified managers and thus result in inducing conservative behaviour by managers (Amihud and Lev 1981; Smith and Stulz 1985). DeYoung et al. (2013) find some evidence that delta reduces the riskiness of bank activities, while Mehran and Rosenberg (2007) do not detect any robust influence of delta on bank risk-taking. Bliss and Rosen (2001) and Minnick et al. (2011) show that high-delta banks are less likely to engage in acquisitions, which is consistent with high-delta CEOs forgoing risky investment projects such as mergers and acquisitions.

Previous evidence on the impact of risk-taking (Vega) incentives on bank policies has produced a range of findings. Mehran and Rosenberg (2007) show that high-vega banks are positively associated with equity and asset volatility. DeYoung et al. (2013) show that high-vega banks engage in riskier types of business policies, such as a higher fraction of non-interest income and use of mortgage-backed securities. Bai and Elyasiani (2013) also show that CEO vega incentives are associated with higher bank instability, indicating that the use of risk-taking incentives in equity contracts results in promoting risk-taking. By contrast, Fahlenbrach and Stulz (2011) do not find that CEO vegas explain the performance of bank stocks (i.e. previous managerial risk-taking) during the recent financial crisis. Hagendorff and Vallascas (2011) find that CEOs are responsive to the vega embedded in their compensation, with higher vega incentives resulting in bank acquisitions that resulted in increasing default risk. Thus, higher pay risk sensitivity causes CEOs to engage in risk-increasing deals, even beyond that desirable to creditors and regulators.

To alleviate these shortcomings, various researchers have raised the need for the compensation incentives of bank managers to be structured in a manner that also results in aligning their interests with the interests of creditors, taxpayers and depositors (Adams and Mehran 2003; Macey and O'Hara 2003). More specifically, Bebchuk and Spamann (2009) suggest the use of instruments that are correlated with equity value as well as with the value of debt. One such mechanism is the use of debt-based compensation that results in tying managerial wealth with the wealth of creditors (Sundaram and Yermack 2007; Edmans and Liu 2011). The next section provides a discussion of this mechanism and how CEO's pay can be restructured using debt-like instruments.

Debt-Based Compensation

Debt-based compensation consists of deferred compensation and pension benefits (Sundaram and Yermack 2007; Edmans and Liu 2011). These instruments resemble debt in two aspects: first, inside debt is a fixed obligation for a firm to make ongoing payments to a manager commencing upon retirement and continuing throughout retirement. Second, inside debt is an unsecured firm obligation. In the event of bankruptcy, a manager stands in line with other unsecured creditors to recover some fraction of her inside debt holdings. With the payoffs of CEO's wealth tied to creditors, managers may shift their focus to long-term solvency of the firm (Edmans and Liu 2011).

The idea of compensating managers with debt-like instruments was first assessed by Jensen and Meckling (1976) who proposed that "inside debt" can help attenuate conflicts of interest between shareholders and creditors that arise when managers hold only firm equity. However, the authors were not able to incorporate this formally in their model and proposed that firm managers may not transfer wealth from creditors to shareholders if they own equal fractions of firm debt and equity. Edmans and Liu (2011) later formalized the role of inside debt as an efficient instrument to prevent equity-aligned managers from pursuing policies which increase shareholder wealth at the cost of increasing risk beyond that desirable to creditors. The authors posit that managers who own a larger fraction of firm debt, relative to percentage of firm equity, are more likely to pursue conservative firm policies and reduce firm risk.

More recently, Bolton et al. (2015) develop a theoretical framework to show that compensating bank executives with debt-like instruments results in mitigating excessive risk-taking behaviour. The authors argue that CEO compensation should be linked with credit default swap spreads, thereby suggesting that CEO wealth should automatically decrease if a bank becomes riskier.

A growing empirical literature has shown that compensating CEOs with this so-called "inside debt" can mitigate risk-taking. Tung and Wang (2012) show that bank CEOs with higher inside debt holdings engaged in less risk-taking before the financial crisis (as indicated by better stock market performance during the financial crisis). Bennett et al. (2015) show a negative association between inside debt and a market-based measure of default risk. Similarly, Van Bekkum (2016) reports a negative relation between CEO and chief financial officer (CFO) inside debt and measures of subsequent market volatility and tail risk. Srivastav et al. (2014) show that bank CEOs with higher inside debt are associated with more conservative bank payout policies.

Although the idea of including debt-like instruments in a CEO's compensation structure is not new, there is only a limited amount of evidence to lend credible support to the notion that debt-based pay is effective in reducing bank risk. As a result, policy reforms have been ambiguous with regards to formalizing a role of debt instruments in executive pay contracts. Pay guidance issued by the European Banking Authority (2015) suggests that pension benefits should consist of instruments that reflect the credit quality of a financial institution. Similarly, the Liikanen Report (2012) proposes that senior bank employees should hold bonds issued by the institution that they work for to induce more conservative behaviour. Future research into this area can pave the way for informing policy research with specific guidelines regarding the use of such pay components.

Impact of European Policy Developments on Pay Characteristics

The focus of this section is to highlight recent developments in the pay practices of European banks and an attempt to relate these developments to academic research. European pay reforms have largely adopted a prescriptive format to address the risk-taking incentives embedded in compensation contracts.

For instance, the Capital Requirements Directive – IV (CRD-IV) was implemented by the European Union in 2013 to reform the European banking sector. The directive proposes an upper limit on the fraction of performance-based compensation and that a substantial proportion of variable pay should consist of long-term instruments (e.g. equity) that should be deferred over a period of at least three years.

The shift in regulatory attitudes towards performance-based pay in European banks is also evident in the fraction of bonuses in terms of managerial pay. Figure 6.4 shows for a sample of large European banks that bonus payments have fallen from 37 % of total compensation in the pre-crisis period (2002–7) to 9 % of total compensation in 2008–13. Although, the fraction of equity-based compensation has increased over the same period, this shift has largely been towards long-term deferred equity awards. As a result, the wealth of European bank executives has become more aligned with long-term bank stability.

Interestingly, academic opinion regarding the implementation of pay reforms in the spirit of the reforms detailed above is equivocal. For instance, Bolton et al. (2015) argue that *ex ante* shareholders lack the incentives to restructure CEO pay in order to protect the interests of the government and taxpayers (who might be called upon to finance a bailout and instead reward managers for excessive risk-taking). The authors call for regulators to require executive pay to contain debt-like components. Similarly, John et al. (2000) propose that regulatory practices surrounding the design of deposit insurance

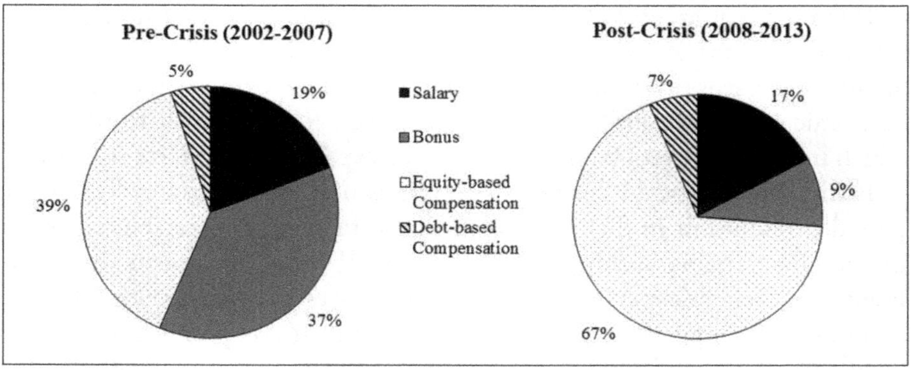

Fig. 6.4 CEO compensation structures pre-crisis (2002–7) and post-crisis era (2008–13) for the five highest-paid senior bank managers at 14 large European banks. Values shown are in percentage of total compensation. Authors' calculations with data from Boardex

premia should be explicitly linked to executive pay incentives. This should influence executive behaviour and mitigate risk-taking concerns.

By contrast, attempts to regulate CEO pay have been criticized on the grounds that there may be excessive regulatory intervention and such interference may drive away talent into less-regulated sectors (IMF 2014). Core and Guay (2010) also assess the differences between executive pay in financial and non-financial sectors and do not find any evidence that bank executives have higher risk-taking incentives than executives in other industries. They argue that pay reforms should not neglect the pay-setting process where the supervisory board and remuneration committees are actively involved instead of regulating the level and structure of executive pay.

The section attempts to relate pay developments in European banks to academic research. The section starts below by discussing the impact of embedding time- and performance-based characteristics in CEO equity contracts in the section "Long-term Deferred Equity Awards" followed by a brief review of bonus caps mandated by CRD-IV in the "Bonus Caps" section before discussing the role of other internal governance mechanisms in the design of executive pay structures in the section "Pay and the Governance Context of Banks".

Long-Term Deferred Equity Awards

During the financial crisis, various academics and policymakers have argued that a key issue in bank remuneration practices is that the equity holdings of many CEOs had short vesting schedules which aligned CEO wealth to short-term performance (e.g. Federal Reserve et al. 2010). Mehran, Morrison, and Shapiro (2011) note that around 49 % of CEOs hold option awards that vest within one year. If equity awards vest within a short time, the payoffs to bank CEOs are no longer sensitive to the time horizon over which many of the underlying economic risks materialize. This may incentivize CEOs to pursue bank policies which maximize current equity payoffs at the expense of long-term stability.

Partly in response to concerns of these issues, the European Parliament passed a resolution in 2013 urging banking regulators to establish deferral periods for variable compensation that extend up to an executive's retirement age. Deferrals result in long-term incentives and incentivize CEOs to account for the impact of their policies on the future risk profile of a bank. As detailed above, the Capital Requirements Directive – IV (CRD-IV) also sets out explicit criteria that establish minimum thresholds for certain pay characteristics. For instance, 40–60 % of variable compensation should be deferred over three years or more.

Emerging academic evidence also supports calls for longer vesting periods and deferral of larger parts of executive pay. For instance, Edmans et al. (2012) propose that deferring pay to a longer time horizon results in deterring short-termism since deferred equity awards are now sensitive to long-term performance and prevent CEOs from pursuing policies that maximize their short-term pay. Similarly, Bhagat and Romano (2009) posit that bank executive pay should consist of equity awards that cannot be cashed out for a period of two to four years after their retirement. However, Fahlenbrach and Stulz (2011) note that there is a lack of evidence to show that bank CEO pay resulted in short-termism. The authors find that bank CEOs held on to vested equity and option grants before the crisis and subsequently bore huge wealth losses. This is in conflict with the widespread notion of pervasive short-termism inherent in CEO pay.

Another aspect about equity awards that receives increasing regulatory scrutiny is the argument that equity awards are conditional upon meeting certain performance criteria that would typically be market-based (shareholder returns) or accounting-based (e.g. profitability). Simply employing performance measures that are not risk relevant may motivate managers to pursue projects that maximize bank performance without affecting a bank's risk profile. Bebchuk and Spamann (2009) argue that the performance thresholds underlying bonus contracts should be based on a broader set of accounting measures such as a bank's operating income before payments to creditors instead of shareholder-focused profit measures. An important policy reform agenda has therefore been to select performance criteria that employ risk-adjusted performance measures, for example risk-adjusted return on capital or a bank's risk-adjusted cost of funding (European Banking Authority 2015).

Bonus Caps

CEO bonus contracts produce asymmetric payoffs since bonus payments are partly based on performance gains which have yet to fully materialize at the time the bonus becomes payable. Therefore, managers have strong incentives to pursue higher risk-taking strategies to achieve these short-term goals. Consequently, CRD-IV mandates that variable pay components (including bonuses) are to be capped at 100 % of a CEO's fixed remuneration with the possibility that this threshold can reach up to 200 % subject to shareholder approval. Similarly, both the UK and France introduced a 50 % tax on bonuses paid during 2009.[1]

[1] See, for instance, 'FSA Unveils Tough New Pay and Bonus code', *Financial Times*, July 30 2010; 'Big Bonuses Face Curbs', *Financial Times*, 17 May 2010.

Jokivuolle et al. (2015) provide evidence for supporting a mandatory cap on executive bonuses by showing that there is a positive association between the fraction of bonus payments to fixed salary and bank risk. Hakenes and Schnabel (2014) also posit that regulating bank bonuses may help in mitigating the excessive risk-taking incentives of bank managers and shareholders, especially for banks that pose a systemic threat and that rely on non-traditional banking activities. However, Thanassoulis (2012) argues that implementing a rigid limit may increase bank risk because banks may have to continue distributing these bonuses regardless of the bank's financial condition. Instead, Thanassoulis argues for applying a flexible threshold limiting the amount of bonuses given to bankers as a fraction of bank assets.

Pay and the Governance Context of Banks

The Committee of European Banking Supervisors (2010) report argues that an important feature of reforming executive pay is the need to take into account the corporate governance context in which pay incentives are set. For instance, in countries with a two-tier board structure, the supervisory board holds ultimate responsibility for designing and overseeing the implementation of executive compensation policies and for ensuring that compensation policies meet broader principles that foster financial stability. However, bank boards may also distort managerial incentives. In this regard, DeYoung et al. (2013) show that boards actively restructured the compensation contracts of bank executives towards a greater amount of risk-taking incentives in order to take advantage of new business opportunities arising from industry deregulation in the USA.

Another governance dimension that feeds into the executive compensation policies are a bank's risk management function and internal controls. Critical inputs from the risk management function include accounting for the impact of a CEO's choice of bank policies on bank risk and thereby assessing if this behaviour is a consequence of CEO pay structure. Similarly, the internal control function (e.g. via the audit committee) also needs to communicate and establish that performance-based criteria in executive pay cannot be manipulated to inflate performance.

Peng and Roell (2015) argue that compensating managers with instruments that focus on short-term performance-based pay may result in incentivizing them to manipulate firm performance measures. Cornett et al. (2009) show that bank CEOs with higher pay-performance sensitivity (or Delta incentives) were more likely to engage in earnings management, in an attempt to inflate performance and increase their personal wealth. Therefore, the compensation policies for executives should account for the internal governance mechanisms of a bank in order to account for the overall impact of managerial pay on both the performance and risk-profile of a bank.

Contrasting Compensation Reforms in the US to the European Approach

The previous section highlights how European regulators have largely followed a prescriptive approach that introduced caps on the level and structure of executive pay. This section describes how US regulators have followed a different and more principle-based approach and have given banks more flexibility to decide on their optimal mix of pay.

Specifically, US regulators have followed a principle-based approach by issuing broad guidelines that guide banks in deciding on their remuneration policies. Among those, the Federal Reserve (2010) issued guidance that outlined key compensation principles for remunerating top executives. The first principle focused on encouraging banks to adopt pay instruments that account for the impact of each executive on overall bank risk and that take into account the time horizon over which financial risks may materialize. The second and third principles highlighted the role of the risk management division in providing inputs during the pay setting process and the role of the board of directors in designing pay structures that ensure an appropriate balance between bank risk and performance. More importantly, banks were urged to tailor compensation policies to the ability of individuals to expose their institutions to extreme negative risk events, bank complexity and size.

Another key development in the US regulatory landscape was the passing of the Dodd Frank Wall Street Reform and Consumer Protection Act (Dodd-Frank Act) in July 2010. Dodd-Frank reiterated the already established principle that banks should limit those types of incentive pay that may result in excessive risk-taking. Moreover, banks were encouraged to disclose the structure of executive compensation to their respective regulatory agencies. Further, Dodd-Frank required shareholder approval through say-on-pay votes and safeguarded the independence of compensation committees. While such policies help in directing remuneration practices in the right direction, they do not directly interfere or and restrict executive pay arrangements. Each bank can decide on their compensation based on idiosyncratic factors that affect the bank. The following section further discusses this issue by highlighting some limitations of EU regulatory reforms.

Are There Costs Associated with Regulating Executive Pay?

Introducing executive pay restrictions in the form of explicit bonus caps and mandating certain forms of compensation has led to further debate amongst academics and banking professionals over the costs of doing so. Fundamentally, the notion of regulating executive pay is in conflict with a vast literature that advocates competitive pay to attract scarce talent (Gabiax and Landier 2008; Tervio 2008). In a competitive market, banks compete for talent and efficient sorting of executives into banks will result in long-term performance gains. Therefore, for an executive with superior ability, firms will be willing to pay a premium. Recent research has shown that higher wages in the financial sector are partially explained by increased demand for skill in complex jobs (Philippon and Reshef 2012) and by competition for workers with superior ability (Célérier and Vallée 2013).

By directly regulating the structure of pay and by introducing explicit pay restrictions, European regulatory reforms may well distort an efficient matching in the labour market and entail economic costs. In support of this, Kleymenova and Tuna (2015) show that the stock market reaction to the announcement of the EU bonus cap was significantly negative. This implies that shareholders anticipate some detrimental effects of regulatory interference in compensation policies. Moreover, the authors show that UK banks experienced greater levels of executive turnover in comparison to US banks in the post-2010 period.

Along the same lines, Murphy (2013) argues that EU pay regulations may result in reducing managerial incentives to exert effort owing to the upper limit on performance-based pay that can be granted for each unit of effort. Similarly, Hakenes and Schnabel (2014) argue that while imposing caps on bank bonuses may make bank managers reluctant to engage in risk-shifting, it may also curb their incentives to exert effort. However, the authors show that it is optimal to impose regulatory caps when the risk-shifting problem is sufficiently large.

Another potential implication is that the banking sector could lose some of the most talented (and most highly-remunerated) individuals to other sectors. If banks are restricted in terms of the level and structure of remuneration contracts they can offer, less regulated financial institutions may poach talent by offering more lucrative pay deals (Murphy 2013; Hakenes and Schnabel 2014; IMF 2014). This may result in a talent drain and undermine the competitiveness of the EU banking sector relative to industries or jurisdictions with fewer restrictions.[2]

[2] In support of this view, recent media reports have highlighted the view that regulating pay will drive away talented bankers to either less regulated sectors or countries with less restrictive regulatory regime.

In sum, cross-country differences in regulatory responses have resulted in creating an unequal playing field in the market for talent in banking. Whether cross-country and cross-industry differences in the regulatory approach to reform compensation will drive talented bankers to less regulators jurisdictions or sectors is yet to be seen.

Conclusion

The structure of compensation and design of incentives embedded in CEO pay contracts shape CEO behaviour and bank policies. Clearly, it is in the interest of regulators and taxpayers that bank executives are concerned about the impact of their policies on long-term bank solvency. Frequently, however, these concerns are neglected by bank executives in an attempt to boost short-term profit or pursue risky policies that may increase shareholder value. This is primarily due to the fact that the incentive structures of senior bank managers do not take into account the risk horizon of their policies.

Emerging academic research and heated policy debates have advocated many changes into the design of compensation. This chapter contributes to the ongoing conversation on reforming executive pay structures by establishing a connection between policy and executive pay structures in European banks. CEO pay structures that consist of a disproportionate amount of cash bonuses and equity compensation may result in misaligned incentives that promote risk-taking. To mitigate this issue, compensation should consist of debt-like instruments that are contingent on the credit quality of the bank, such as a measure of pay that is related to bank's CDS spread or a manager's unsecured pension benefits.

The chapter also discusses the use of risk-adjusted criteria to assess CEO performance and the long-term deferral of equity instruments as key factors for striking a balance between pursuing risky projects that maximizing shareholder value subject to sound risk management.

Arguably, the design of compensation contracts does not happen in a vacuum and relies on important inputs from various internal governance mechanisms. Taking this into account, draft guidelines issued by the Committee of European Banking Supervisors (2010) require that the board of directors work in collaboration with a bank's risk management function, remuneration committee and other control functions to devise sound compensation policies.

See for example: 'Bankers fear new UK rules will scare off talent', *Financial Times*, 2014; 'Banks warn of hiring handicap under EU bonus rules', *Financial Times*, 2015.

However, an important issue that may arise in the future is uncertainty regarding the applicability of compensation rules and guidelines. For instance, small banks may find it time-consuming and costly to comply with an ever changing and more complex set of compensation rules. Further, banks that are deemed too-big-to-fail and have ready access to higher safety net benefits may require particular regulatory scrutiny in ensuring that compensation practices do not exacerbate the risk-taking incentives that senior managers at these institutions already have. Whether or not the pay proposals applying to European banks discussed in this chapter will result in enhanced financial stability or spur a new round of creative risk-taking instruments is yet to be seen.

References

Adams, R. B., & Mehran, H. (2003). Is corporate governance different for bank holding companies? *Federal Reserve Bank of New York Economic Policy Review, 9*(1), 123–142.

Amihud, Y., & Lev, B. (1981). Risk reduction as a managerial motive for conglomerate mergers. *The Bell Journal of Economics, 12*, 605–617.

Bai, G., & Elyasiani, E. (2013). Bank stability and managerial compensation. *Journal of Banking & Finance, 37*(3), 799–813.

Balachandran, S., Harnal, H., & Kogut, B. (2010). *The probability of default, excessive risk, and executive compensation: A study of financial services firms from 1995 to 2008* (Columbia Business School working paper).

Bebchuk, L. A., & Spamann, H. (2009). Regulating bankers' pay. *Georgetown Law Journal, 98*, 247–287.

Bebchuk, L. A., Cohen, A., & Spamann, H. (2010). Wages of failure: Executive compensation at Bear Stearns and Lehman 2000–2008. *Yale Journal on Regulation, 27*, 257–282.

Bennett, R. L., Güntay, L., & Unal, H. (2015). Inside debt, bank default risk, and performance during the crisis. *Journal of Financial Intermediation, 24*(4), 487–513.

Benston, G. J., Hunter, W. C., & Wall, L. D. (1995). Motivations for bank mergers and acquisitions: Enhancing the deposit insurance put option versus earnings diversification. *Journal of Money, Credit and Banking, 27*, 777–788.

Bhagat, S., & Romano, R. (2009). Reforming executive compensation: Simplicity, transparency and committing to the long-term. *Yale Journal on Regulation, 26*, 359–372.

Bliss, R. T., & Rosen, R. J. (2001). CEO compensation and bank mergers. *Journal of Financial Economics, 61*, 107–138.

Bolton, P., Mehran, H., & Shapiro, J. (2015). Executive compensation and risk taking. *Review of Finance, 19*, 2139–2181.

Célérier, C., & Vallée, B. (2013). *Are bankers worth their pay? Evidence from a talent measure* (Working paper). HEC Paris.

Chen, C. R., Steiner, T. L., & Whyte, A. M. (2006). Does stock option-based executive compensation induce risk-taking? An analysis of the banking industry. *Journal of Banking & Finance, 30*, 915–945.

Coles, J. L., Daniel, N. D., & Naveen, L. (2006). Managerial incentives and risk-taking. *Journal of Financial Economics, 79*, 431–468.

Committee of European Banking Supervisors. (2010, December 10). *Guidelines on remuneration policies and practices*. https://www.eba.europa.eu/documents/10180/106961/Guidelines.pdf.

Core, J. E., & Guay, W. R. (2010). *Is there a case for regulating executive pay in the financial services industry?* (MIT working paper).

Cornett, Marcia Millon, Jamie John McNutt, and Hassan Tehranian, 2009. "Corporate governance and earnings management at large US bank holding companies." *Journal of Corporate Finance 15*, 412-430.

Dam, L., & Koetter, M. (2012). Bank bailouts and moral hazard: Evidence from Germany. *Review of Financial Studies, 25*, 2343–2380.

DeYoung, R., Peng, E. Y., & Yan, M. (2013). Executive compensation and business policy choices at US commercial banks. *Journal of Financial and Quantitative Analysis, 48*, 165–196.

Edmans, A., & Liu, Q. (2011). Inside debt. *Review of Finance, 15*, 75–102.

Edmans, A., Gabaix, X., Sadzik, T., & Sannikov, Y. (2012). Dynamic CEO compensation. *Journal of Finance, 67*, 1603–1647.

Efing, M., Hau, H., Kampkotter, P., & Steinbrecher, J. (2015). Incentive pay and bank risk-taking: Evidence from Austrian, German and Swiss banks. *Journal of International Economics, 96*, 123–140.

European Banking Authority. (2015, March 4). *Consultation paper for draft guidelines on sound remuneration policies*.

Fahlenbrach, R., & Stulz, R. M. (2011). Bank CEO incentives and the credit crisis. *Journal of Financial Economics, 99*, 11–26.

Federal Reserve (2010). "*Guidance on Sound Incentive Compensation Policies*". June 25 2010, http://www.fdic.gov/news/news/press/2010/pr10138a.pdf

Financial Stability Board. (2009). *Principles for sound compensation practices*. Basel, Switzerland. http://www.financialstabilityboard.org/publications/r_0904b.pdf.

Freixas, X., & Rochet, J. c. (2013). Taming systemically important financial institutions. *Journal of Money, Credit and Banking, 45*, 37–58.

Gabaix, X., & Landier, A. (2008). Why has CEO pay increased so much? *Quarterly Journal of Economics, 123*, 49–100.

Guay, W. R. (1999). The sensitivity of CEO wealth to equity risk: An analysis of the magnitude and determinants. *Journal of Financial Economics, 53*, 43–71.

Hagendorff, J., & Vallascas, F. (2011). CEO pay incentives and risk-taking: Evidence from bank acquisitions. *Journal of Corporate Finance, 17*, 1078–1095.

Hakenes, H., & Schnabel, I. (2014). Bank bonuses and bailouts. *Journal of Money, Credit and Banking, 46*, 259–288.

Harjoto, M. A., & Mullineaux, D. J. (2003). CEO compensation and the transformation of banking. *Journal of Financial Research, 26*, 341–354.

Houston, J. F., & James, C. (1995). CEO compensation and bank risk is compensation in banking structured to promote risk taking? *Journal of Monetary Economics, 36*, 405–431.

Hovakimian, A., & Kane, E. J. (2000). Effectiveness of capital regulation at US commercial banks, 1985 to 1994. *Journal of Finance, 55*(1), 451–468.

Hubbard, R. G., & Palia, D. (1995). Executive pay and performance evidence from the US banking industry. *Journal of Financial Economics, 39*(1), 105–130.

IMF. (2014). *Risk-taking by banks: The role of governance and executive pay, in: Global financial stability report: Risk-taking, liquidity, and shadow banking: Curbing excess while promoting growth.* Washington D.C.

Jensen, M. C., & Meckling, W. H. (1976). Theory of the firm: Managerial behavior, agency costs and ownership structure. *Journal of Financial Economics, 3*, 305–360.

John, T. A., & John, K. (1993). Top-management compensation and capital structure. *Journal of Finance, 48*, 949–974.

John, K., Saunders, A., & Senbet, L. W. (2000). A theory of bank regulation and management compensation. *Review of Financial Studies, 13*, 95–125.

Jokivuolle, E., Keppo, J., & Yuan, X. (2015). *Bonus caps, deferrals and banks' risk-taking* (Bank of Finland research discussion paper).

Kleymenova, A., & Tuna, I. (2015). *Regulation of compensation* (University of Chicago Booth School of Business working paper).

Liikanen Report. (2012, October 2). *High-level expert group on reforming the structure of the EU banking sector.* Brussels. http://ec.europa.eu/internal_market/bank/docs/high-level_expert_group/report_en.pdf.

Macey, J. R., & O'hara, M. (2003). The corporate governance of banks. *Federal Reserve Bank of New York Economic Policy Review, 9*, 91–107.

Mehran, H., & Rosenberg, J. V. (2007). *The effect of employee stock options on bank investment choice, borrowing, and capital* (Federal Reserve Bank of New York Staff Report 305).

Mehran, H., Morrison, A. D., & Shapiro, J. D. (2011). *Corporate governance and banks: What have we learned from the financial crisis?* (Federal Reserve Bank of New York Staff Report 502).

Merton, R. C. (1977). An analytic derivation of the cost of deposit insurance and loan guarantees an application of modern option pricing theory. *Journal of Banking & Finance, 1*, 3–11.

Minnick, K., Unal, H., & Yang, L. (2011). Pay for performance? CEO compensation and acquirer returns in BHCs. *Review of Financial Studies, 24*, 439–472.

Murphy, K. J. (2000). Performance standards in incentive contracts. *Journal of Accounting and Economics, 30*, 245–278.

Murphy, K. J. (2013). *Regulating banking bonuses in the European Union: A case study in unintended consequences* (USC Marshall School of Business working paper).

Noe, T. H., Rebello, M. J., & Wall, L. D. (1996). Managerial rents and regulatory intervention in troubled banks. *Journal of Banking & Finance, 20*, 331–350.

Peng, Lin, Ailsa Röell, 2015 "*CEO Incentives: Measurement, Determinants, and Impact on Performanc*e." unpublished working paper.

Philippon, T., & Reshef, A. (2012). Wages and human capital in the U.S. finance industry: 1909–2006. *Quarterly Journal of Economics, 127*, 1551–1609.

Smith, C. W., & Stulz, R. M. (1985). The determinants of firms' hedging policies. *Journal of Financial and Quantitative Analysis, 20*, 391–405.

Srivastav, A., Armitage, S., & Hagendorff, J. (2014). CEO inside debt holdings and risk-shifting: Evidence from bank payout policies. *Journal of Banking & Finance, 47*, 41–53.

Sundaram, R. K., & Yermack, D. L. (2007). Pay me later: Inside debt and its role in managerial compensation. *Journal of Finance, 62*, 1551–1588.

Tervio, M. (2008). The difference that CEOs make: An assignment model approach. *American Economic Review, 98*, 642–668.

Thanassoulis, J. (2012). The case for intervening in bankers' pay. *Journal of Finance, 67*, 849–895.

Tung, F., & Wang, X. (2012). *Bank CEOs, inside debt compensation, and the global financial crisis* (Boston University School of Law working paper).

Vallascas, F., & Hagendorff, J. (2013). CEO bonus compensation and bank default risk: Evidence from the US and Europe. *Financial Markets, Institutions & Instruments, 22*, 47–89.

Van Bekkum, Sjoerd (2016). "Inside Debt and Bank Risk". *Journal of Financial and Quantitative Analysis 51*, pp. 359-385.

Webb, E. (2008). Regulator scrutiny and bank CEO incentives. *Journal of Financial Services Research, 33*, 5–20.

Part II

Performance and Innovation in European Banking

7

European Retail Payments Systems: Cost, Pricing, Innovation and Regulation

Wilko Bolt, Nicole Jonker, and Mirjam Plooij

Payments are absolutely essential for the smooth operation of an economy. Recent developments in European retail payments have included changes in instrument composition, payment costs, innovations, new players and the regulatory framework. How do these factors interact and shape the payment landscape? What conditions result in the most efficient payment systems for the greatest economic good? An outline of major shifts in European payments over the past two decades can set a framework for approaching these questions.

More specifically, in this chapter we examine the structure of European payment markets in terms of payment composition, behaviour and cost. Next, the operation of a typical payment network is described, which illustrates the so-called two-sidedness of payment markets. This specific network structure underlies many aspects of the "economics of payments". Payment pricing, incentives, competition and cooperation are analysed within this

We thank Hans Brits for valuable comments. The views expressed are those of the authors and do not necessarily represent the views of De Nederlandsche Bank or the European System of Central Banks.

W. Bolt (✉)
Economics and Research Division, De Nederlandsche Bank,
1000 AB, Amsterdam, P.O. Box 98, The Netherlands
e-mail: w.bolt@dnb.nl

N. Jonker • M. Plooij
Payments Policy Division, De Nederlandsche Bank, Amsterdam, The Netherlands
e-mail: n.jonker@dnb.nl; mirjam.plooij@ecb.europa.eu

T. Beck, B. Casu (eds.), *The Palgrave Handbook of European Banking*,
DOI 10.1057/978-1-137-52144-6_7

two-sided markets framework. A discussion of payment innovations, the growing importance of "non-banks" in all segments of the payment chain and the European regulatory framework affecting the future of retail payments completes this overview.

Structure of European Retail Payments Markets

The way we pay for goods and services has been changing. Since the 1990s', a major change in Europe was the increasing replacement of cash and paper-based payments to electronic forms of payment. Besides a change in payment behaviour, this shift to electronic payments was also accommodated by large advances in computing power, data storage and the advent of the Internet. Nevertheless, cash use has fallen but has not disappeared: Europe's cash ratio still lies at 10 % in 2014.[1] Going forward, the Internet will probably drive expectations and capabilities in speeding up payments from end to end at lower costs, both for individuals and businesses. The UK has already started down this road with their Internet-based 24/7 faster payment initiative.[2]

This section discusses the development of payment usage of the most commonly used instruments in the Eurozone, the differences in payment behaviour of consumers from different euro area countries as well as the costs associated with paying with different means of payment for society as a whole.

Payment Use and Composition

Consumers and businesses use several payment instruments to transfer funds to each other. In retail, we often discern point-of-sale payments ("face to face") and remote payments ("at a distance"). Cash, cheques, debit cards and credit cards are used for making payments at the point of sale—in shops, restaurants or petrol stations—whereas instruments such as credit cards, credit transfers and direct debits can be used to make remote payments, such as bill payments and online payments (see Box 7.1).

[1] As measured by banknotes and coins over nominal gross domestic product (GDP). In the USA the cash ratio lies around 5 %, however, at the same time, they process a high number of paper-based instruments (cheques) and online credit transfer payments are still lagging behind and often at high user cost.

[2] Denmark and Sweden have also developed "instant payment" systems where payment processing only takes seconds. For an in-depth analysis of the digitization of retail payments, the reader is referred to Bolt and Chakravorti (2012). See also Schwienbacher (2016) in this Handbook for an analysis how the Internet and crowdfunding shape the banking industry.

Box 7.1 Retail Payments

Technically, a payment is a transfer of funds which discharges an obligation of a payer vis-à-vis a payee. As a broad distinction, retail payments are of lower value and urgency than interbank (or large-value) payments. A payment instrument is viewed as a tool/procedure enabling the transfer of funds from the payer to the payee. Different classifications of retail payment instruments are possible: cash vs non-cash, paper-based vs electronic, point-of-sale vs remote. These classifications are often not mutually exclusive, e.g. a credit card can be used at the point-of-sale but also as remote instrument for an online payment.

Main retail payment instruments in the Euro area

	Function	Main type	
Point of sale			
Cash	Enables holder to make purchases by transferring money in the physical form of currency, such as banknotes and coins	Cash	Paper/coins
Debit card	Enables holder to have his purchases directly charged to funds on his account at a deposit-taking institution	Non-cash	Electronic
Credit card	Enables the holder to make purchases to a pre-arranged ceiling; the credit granted can be settled in full by the end of a specified period or can be settled in part, with the balance taken as extended credit.	Non-cash	Electronic
Stored-value card	Enables holder to make purchases using a prepaid card in which the record of funds can be increased as well as decreased; also called an electronic purse	Non-cash	Electronic
Remote			
Credit transfer	Payment order made for the purpose of placing funds at the disposal of the payee; both the payment instructions and the funds described therein move from the bank of the payer/originator to the bank of the payee possibly via several other banks as intermediaries	Non-cash	Electronic/paper
Direct debit	Preauthorised debit on the payer's bank account initiated by the payee	Non-cash	Electronic
Cheque	Payment order from the drawer to the drawee (i.e., a bank) requiring the drawee to pay a specified sum on demand to the drawer or to a third party specified by the drawer	Non-cash	Paper

Source: BIS Glossary (2003) *Notes*: payment cards are also used for ATM withdrawals to allow cash payments

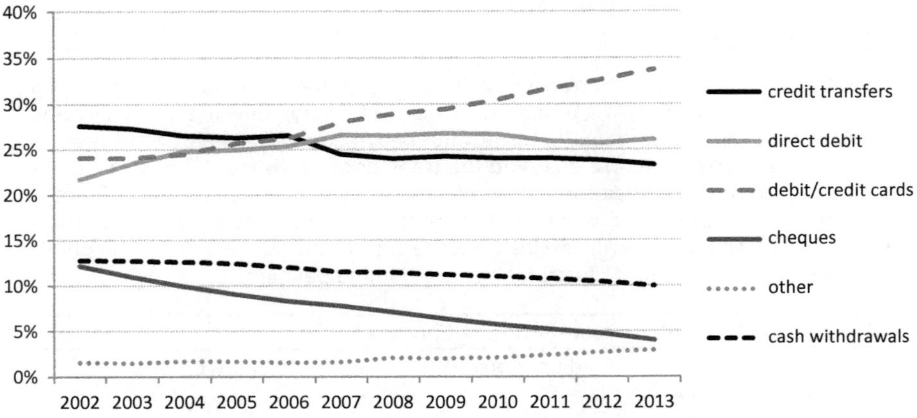

Fig. 7.1 Relative usage non-cash payment instruments in the Eurozone, 2002–13 (*Source*: ECB statistical data warehouse)

Since the introduction of the euro in 2002 the way consumers in the Eurozone pay has changed notably. Figure 7.1 presents the relative usage of different means including cash withdrawals at automated teller machines (ATMs). The usage of debit and credit cards by European consumers has increased most strongly, reflecting the ongoing substitution of cash by card payments at the point-of-sale. Its share in the total number of (non-cash) transactions went up by 10 percentage points from 24 % to 34 %, whereas the relative share of cash withdrawals at ATMs fell by 3 percentage points from 13 to 10 percentage points. Furthermore, the relative usage of cheques has declined considerably to 4 % of all transactions in 2013. Cheques are in fact the only means of payment for which usage has fallen in both relative and absolute terms. The decline has taken place in all cheque-intensive countries such as France, Ireland and Italy, probably due to promotion of less costly means of payment by payment service providers such as card companies (Kokkola 2010).

Regarding remote payments, there was a gradual shift from the usage of the credit transfer to the usage of the direct debit, suggesting an ongoing substitution process. From 2006 onwards, Eurozone consumers used direct debits more frequently for remote payments than credit transfers. Since 2010, the share of direct debits has remained 2–3 percentage points higher than that of credit transfers. Figure 7.1 also reveals the slow but steady increase of the importance of other payment instruments in the total number of payment transactions: the proportion has risen from approximately 1.5 % to 3 %, including e- money transactions such as payments using prepaid cards.[3]

[3] Electronic money is broadly defined as an electronic store of monetary value on a device that may be widely used for making payments to third parties. It can be issued by both traditional credit institutions

In the wake of the financial crisis of 2007–8, the ongoing shift from cash towards electronic forms of payment may lose some of its momentum when monetary policy authorities are forced to implement negative interest rates to further stimulate economic growth. Currently in Europe, the European Central Bank (ECB) and central banks in Sweden, Switzerland and Denmark have been setting negative policy rates and many more central banks have rates which are at historically very low levels. When nominal interest rates turn negative (for a longer period of time), paper currency becomes increasingly attractive as a store of value since it promises a zero return.

To break through this "zero lower bound" problem, various solutions have been proposed to deal with the effect of negative rates on the demand for cash but they are either considered politically controversial or administratively difficult. These solutions vary from abolishing paper currency altogether, to taxing cash (using e.g. bar codes on bank notes) and decoupling the fixed exchange rate between cash and central bank reserves (Agarwal and Kimball 2015; Buiter and Rahbari 2015; Goodfriend 2000; Rogoff 2014). Probably the most viable way to mitigate the incentive for banks to withdraw cash from their central bank balance is by charging a sufficiently high fee on a bank's net cash withdrawal. Similar procedures can then be applied to businesses and consumers to limit the incentive to withdraw cash (Humphrey 2015).[4]

Differences in Payment Behaviour

Despite the introduction of the euro and the unification of the European payments area, there are still considerable discrepancies in payment habits between citizens of different Eurozone countries, see Fig. 7.2.

The Greek mainly use cash for all their transactions: 47 % of transactions are cash withdrawals at ATMs, and each cash withdrawal represents several cash transactions. So, the relative share of cash payments on all payments well exceeds 47 %. People in Estonia on the other hand use payment cards for 60 % of their payments.

Focusing on differences in usage of credit transfers and direct debit which are used for remote payments only, it becomes clear that in most Eurozone countries consumers and businesses either have a clear preference for either

as well as by a new type of (non-bank) payment institutions called electronic money institutions (EMIs).

[4] It may be comforting to note that, not only has cash demand remained finite, but its response to negative rates has been quite subdued in countries that currently face negative policy rates.

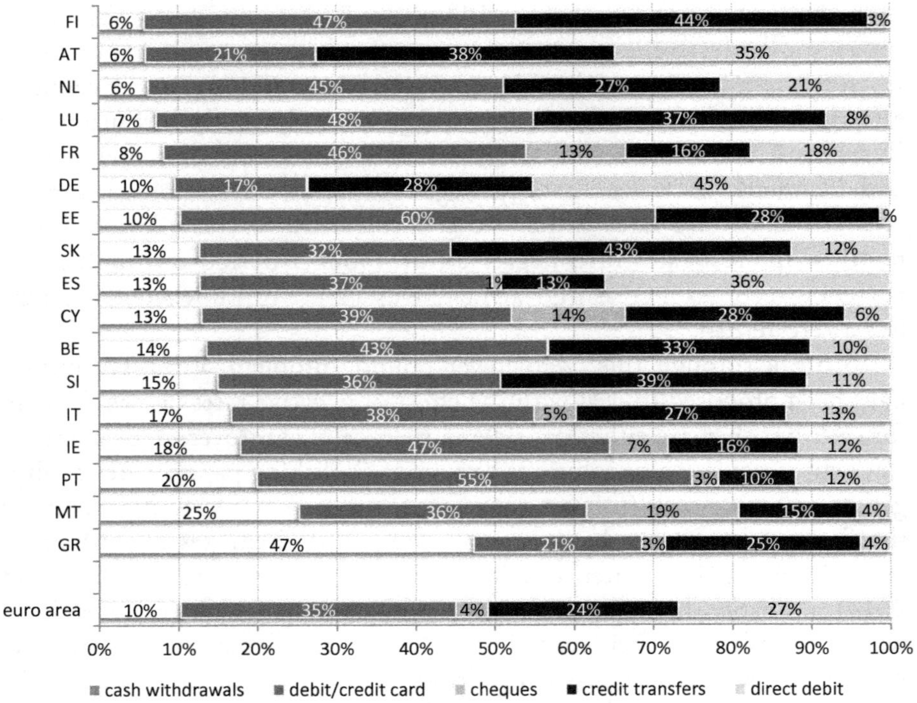

Fig. 7.2 Differences in relative usage payment instruments in the euro area, 2013 (*Source*: ECB statistical warehouse)

credit transfers or direct debits. Only in Austria, France, Germany, the Netherlands and Portugal is usage of these means of payment roughly the same. Another notable difference is that in France, Ireland and Italy cheques are still frequently used—mostly for remote payments like rent and utilities—whereas in most other countries its usage has been abolished or has become negligible (Germany and Spain).

Some factors may partly explain differences in payment behaviour between countries, such as demographic factors, transaction sizes or venue (Bagnall et al. 2015). However, these factors are not sufficient to explain all variations in observed payment patterns between countries. Other factors such as differences in consumption patterns, consumer access to banking services, density of payment infrastructure, pricing of payment transactions (Bolt et al. 2010; Borzekowski et al. 2008) acceptance by businesses and decisions by payment service providers to offer or stop offering specific payment instruments may also be important (Jonker 2011).

Payment Cost and Scale Economies

As payment instruments differ in total social cost, differences in payment habits lead to differences in cost efficiency of retail payment systems between countries. Surveying countries for which the overall cost of their payment system has been estimated, Hayashi and Keeton (2012) found it to range from 0.5 % to 0.9 % of gross domestic product (GDP) annually. Their findings corroborate a recent ECB study, based on a sample of 13 European countries, showing that the total social cost of retail payment instruments comprised around 1 % of total GDP and the cost of cash was found to represent the largest component (Schmiedel et al. 2012).[5]

In practice, the use of any payment instrument has trade-offs with other considerations. For example, the availability of terminals is a clear precondition for the use of cards; consumer cash flow considerations and reward programmes influence the use of credit cards; with cash some merchants do not accept high-value notes due to counterfeiting concerns; and some merchants exclude card use for low-value payments to avoid high merchant discounts on those transactions. On the supply side, cost considerations have induced banks to shift consumer cash acquisition away from branch offices to cheaper ATMs and away from cheques and cash to less expensive debit cards or more profitable credit cards. In addition, banks have outsourced some of the payment services related activities to non-banks in order to bring costs down (CPMI 2014).[6] Due to their specialized nature, these non-banks may enjoy economies of scale and scope by offering their services to several banks.

Payment cost differs widely, depending not only on payment habits but also on the size of the country—showing the influence of payment scale economies—and partly on the size of the transaction. Generalizing from various studies, it seems safe to say a debit card is less costly than a cheque, which, in turn, is less costly than a credit card, and that cash costs rise significantly with higher transaction values. Data from the European Union (EU) ranks the social costs as: cash (lowest), to debit card, to credit card (highest) which is basically the same as that for the USA for transactions under $50 (Garcia-Swartz et al. 2006). However, within the EU there is some heterogeneity regarding the social cost of payment instruments. In countries where debit card usage is high, such as in Denmark, the Netherlands, Norway and

[5] Social cost usually contains bank cost, merchant cost and central bank cost. Consumer ("shoeleather") costs are often ignored in these payment cost studies because they are difficult to measure.

[6] According to a fact-finding study by CPMI (2014) "non-banks participate in all stages in the payment process and across all payment instruments".

Sweden, the social cost of debit card payments are lower than cash payments due to payment scale economies (Danmarks Nationalbank 2012; Gresvik and Haare 2009; Jonker 2011; Segendorf and Jansson 2012). Scandinavian countries turn out to have the most cost-effective retail payments systems (costs 0.80 % of GDP). Their payment behaviour is characterized by low cash usage, high card and credit transfer usage, low or no cheque usage and intermediate usage of direct debits (Schmiedel et al. 2012).

Some economies of scale exist in paper-based payments, but they are much greater for electronic payments because the fixed expenses (building, computer, software, and other overhead expenses) are large relative to their variable costs (labour, telecommunications, and materials expenses). If all costs were variable and none were fixed, then the scale measures would equal 1.00 indicating that a doubling of payment transactions would also double total cost, resulting in constant average cost as transactions expanded.

Estimates of payment scale economies in Europe based on bank and processor data are quite large, in the order of 0.30 for electronic instruments so a doubling of output results in only a 30 % rise in total cost (Bolt and Humphrey 2007; Beijnen and Bolt 2009). This implies that consolidation of payment processors across countries in Europe could generate substantial reductions in payment costs, similar to those in the USA following the Federal Reserve's consolidation of its separate US regional wire transfer operations into a centralized facility (Hancock et al. 1999). Lower payment costs should facilitate the emergence of a more competitive cross-country product market as envisioned by the European Commission and the system of European central banks' Single Euro Payments Area policy.

However, even with large economies of scale and technological advances, card payments have remained expensive for merchants in many countries. Apparently, in the payment industry greater cost efficiency does not necessarily go hand in hand with lower merchant discounts. This disparity, further discussed below, has triggered a great deal of merchant dissatisfaction and led to some spectacular antitrust litigation in Australia, Europe and the United States.

Some Economics of Payment Systems

Network structure is important to understand the underlying economics of retail payment systems. Most electronic transactions occur in three- or four-party networks. These networks are composed of consumers and their banks, known as issuing banks, as well as merchants and their banks, known as acquiring banks. Issuing and acquiring banks are part of a network that sets the rules and procedures for clearing and settling electronic payments among its members. In a three-party network the issuer and the acquirer are of the same identity.

Payment Networks

Although a similar network structure applies to other electronic payment instruments, card payment networks are typically the most complex in terms of market participants, flow of funds, and fee structures. The network structure for the card payment industry is described below.

In Fig. 7.3, the four main players are shown along with interactions with one another in the card payment industry. First, a consumer establishes a relationship with an issuer (usually a bank) and receives a debit card or a credit card or both. Consumers often pay annual card membership fees to their issuers. They generally are not charged a per transaction fee by their banks and some payment card issuers give their customers a reward for each transaction, such as cash back or airline miles.

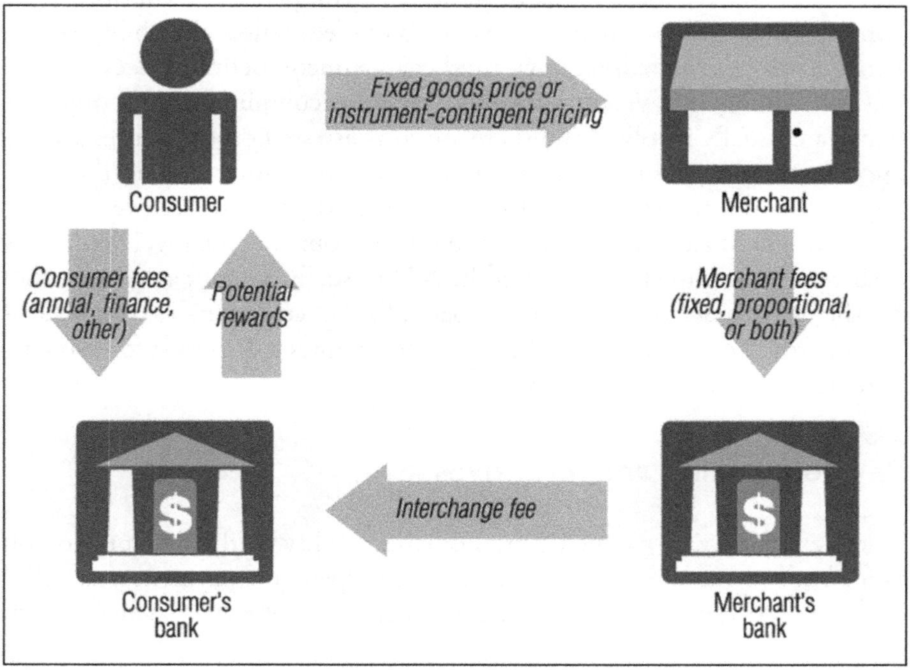

Fig. 7.3 Main players in a card payment network (*Source*: Bolt and Chakravorti (2008b))

Second, a consumer makes a purchase from a merchant. Typically, merchants have been restricted (by legislation or by contract with the card firm) from charging consumers more for purchases that are made with payment cards instead of cash. These are called no-surcharge rules. However, merchants may use price discounts to steer consumers to use payment instruments that are less costly.

Third, if a merchant has established a relationship with an acquirer, it is able to accept payment card transactions. Merchants' costs of card acceptance involve fees that are divided among issuers and acquirers. Broadly speaking, the merchant pays either a fixed per transaction fee (more common for debit cards) or a proportion of the total purchase value (more common for credit cards), but more complicated tariff schemes are possible.[7] These fees, known as merchant discounts, are paid to the acquiring bank. For payment cards, the merchant discount can range from 0.5 % to 5 % depending on the type of transaction (debit or credit card), the product class sold by the merchant (luxury versus low value items), the type of card (reward or not), and if the card is present for the merchant to physically swipe.

Fourth, the acquirer pays an interchange fee to the issuer, which generally makes up a large portion of the merchant discount. Interchange fees have recently attracted a lot of antitrust scrutiny by competition authorities as real concerns exist over whether the level of these fees reflect the ability of card networks to exercise market power and charge uncompetitive prices.

Check and giro payment networks are not as complicated. Although two banks are usually involved and there are costs assessed on the parties sending and receiving funds, there is usually no revenue transfer among the banks engaged in the transaction as there is for a card payment. However, direct debit and ATM fee structures may also involve some interchange. With ATM cash withdrawals the bank owning the ATM usually receives a compensation for the use of a customer of another bank. Often, customers are charged differently for "home" and "guest" use, and sometimes a direct fee for using the teller machine is applied on top.

Payment Pricing and Incentives

A key externality in payments pricing is the ability of the network to convince both consumers and merchants to participate in a payment network. A "chicken-and-egg problem" arises: consumers will not use a payment instru-

[7] Shy and Wang (2011) suggest that proportional fees may not only be more profitable for card networks but also socially efficient when card networks and merchants enjoy some market power.

ment if merchants do not accept it, and merchants will not accept an instrument when consumers do not see value in using it.

In a seminal paper, Baxter (1983) argued that pricing the consumer and merchant side of the market separately, based on each side's incurred marginal cost, need not yield the socially optimal allocation because the usage externality has not been taken into account. Therefore, an interchange fee that transfers revenues between the issuer and the acquirer may be required to "get the network going". It is unclear whether this arrangement is still necessary given that most consumers and merchants now have and accept cards. If merchants imposed a surcharge on card transactions to share the cost, cards would not disappear even though their growth may be initially reduced. Convenience and habit would, over time, offset the likely negative influence of the surcharge because cash must be acquired to be used and writing a cheque takes time and requires record-keeping. Use of a payment card takes less time and record-keeping is provided in the monthly statement.

To study the optimal structure of fees between consumers and merchants in payment markets, economists have developed the two-sided market framework.[8] In a two-sided market one or more platforms enable transactions between two different groups of end-users—consumers and merchants—such that the price structure affects the total volume of transactions. Rochet and Tirole (2002) considered strategic interactions of consumers and merchants. In their two-sided model, issuers have market power, but acquirers operate in competitive markets. Thus, any increase in interchange fees is passed onto merchants completely. Rochet and Tirole found that the profit-maximizing interchange fee for the issuers may be more than or equal to the socially optimal interchange fee. Moreover, merchants are willing to pay more than their net benefit if they can attract customers from their competitors. This reasoning was valid when early on few merchants accepted cards. Today, it is a more matter of retaining customers when most merchants already accept cards.

There is minimal evidence on how strongly consumers respond to price incentives in the payments area because they generally do not face direct fees per transaction. Consumers typically view their transaction as being "free".[9] However, Norway has broadly implemented per-transaction fees for both

[8] A large body of literature on two-sided market theory has been developed to evaluate payment pricing and card market competition issues, see e.g., Schmalensee (2002), Rochet and Tirole (2002, 2003, 2006), Gans and King (2003), Wright (2003, 2004), Guthrie and Wright (2007), Kahn and Roberds (2009), Prager et al. (2009), Rysman (2009), Verdier (2011), Evans (2011), McAndrews and Wang (2012), Wang (2012), Wright (2012) and Bedre and Calvano (2013).

[9] This does not apply to business payments that regularly carry per transaction fees and are not "free" on the margin. The different treatment for business transactions is because payment volumes differ considerably across firms so, unlike the situation for consumers where this variance is much smaller, banks need

consumers and businesses. It overcame antitrust concerns by coordinating only the timing of when per-transaction pricing of consumer payments would start—not the level of prices to be charged. The largest banks started by implementing a positive charge while other banks kept them at zero, expecting to gain market share. When this did not generate much of a gain, the zero fees were raised to values charged by other banks. Bolt et al. (2008) analysed the effect that consumer transaction-based pricing had on the adoption rate of electronic payments in Norway in contrast to the Netherlands, which did not have per-transaction pricing for consumers. Controlling for country-specific influences, explicit per-transaction payment pricing (as expected) induced consumers to shift more rapidly to lower-cost electronic payment instruments.

Payment Steering

In many countries and jurisdictions, merchants are often not allowed to surcharge card payments because of legal or contractual restrictions even though the merchant cost of accepting a credit card is generally higher than for different payment instruments. Conventional wisdom holds that if merchants were able to recover the cost of accepting different payment instruments directly from consumers—applying price differentiation—the initial impact on card-based payments would be significant but cards would not disappear.[10]

The Netherlands offers an interesting case. In 2006, a significant number of Dutch merchants were surcharging debit transactions for purchases below €10. Those surcharges were, on average, four times the debit card merchant interchange fee. Once they were removed, consumers started using their debit cards for smaller payments. They were encouraged to do so by a nationwide public campaign, that started in 2007. The campaign's aim was to improve the efficiency and safety of the retail payment system by increasing debit card usage for small amounts at the expense of cash. It stimulated small merchants to accept debit card payments and to remove any surcharges for small debit card payments, and it encouraged consumers to use their debit card more often. The campaign was a joint initiative of banks and retailers. This strategy turned out to be successful. It contributed to the growth in debit card volume in 2007 and 2008; a large share of the growth came from payments below €10 (Bolt et al. 2010; Jonker et al. 2015).

per transaction fees to recover their costs—not charge all firms the same fee based on the average number of business transactions across all firms.

[10] Gans and King (2003) prove that when surcharges are allowed the impact of the interchange fee on card usage is neutralized. However, excessive surcharges may shy consumers away from using cards.

Recent legislation and court settlements allow US merchants to use price discounts to steer customers to pay with means of payment that are less costly to merchants. Briglevics and Shy (2014) found that steering consumers to debit and cash via simple price discounts reduces most merchants' card processing cost. However, this reduction is small and may be insufficient to offset the increase in the cost of administering price menus that vary by payment instrument, which may be one reason why such discounts have not been offered more widely in the USA.

In an imperfect-information framework, Bourguignon et al. (2014) analysed the impact of card surcharging and cash discounting and its potential regulation. They concluded that, if given the choice, merchants always opt for a card surcharge that brings in additional revenue over a cash discount that benefits customers. As a result, surcharging may generate too few card transactions from the point of view of social economic efficiency. This corroborates the Bolt et al. (2010) estimate that removing debit card surcharges should increase the share of debit card payments in the Netherlands on average from 36 % to 44 %.

Payment Competition and Cooperation

Due to its two-sidedness, competition in the payments market is different from competition in most other markets. On the one hand, payment service providers (mostly banks) that either act as issuer or acquirer of a specific payment instrument within a payment network need to agree on certain standards in order to ensure an efficient and secure processing of the transactions initiated by payers and accepted by payees. This requires close cooperation between issuers and acquirers within a network. On the other hand, issuers need to compete with each other in order to attract payers and acquirers need to compete with each other in order to attract payees. They can do so by competing on fee levels or by offering additional benefits for end-users in the form of new services next to the core services offered by all service providers within the network. There has been an intense debate between payment service providers and competition authorities on how wide the "collaborative space" may be (Uittenbogaard 2007). Regulatory clarity is needed to avoid lack of innovation and underinvestment in payment infrastructure.

Competition authorities examine whether the extent to which service providers cooperate within a network is necessary for its secure and efficient functioning or whether it tends to reduce competition without leading to sufficient benefits for end-users. In that respect, recent regulatory, legal, and legislative actions in the USA, Europe, and Australia have targeted payment fees and practices deemed inefficient, unfair, or uncompetitive. Unfortunately, the effects of competition in payment markets are difficult to determine since available data on bank payment costs are very limited. Economic theory has shown that competition among suppliers of goods and services generally reduces prices, increases output, and improves welfare. However, "two-sided" payment competition may yield an inefficient price structure. In particular, payment competition may result in low or negative consumer fees (i.e., offer a reward) if issuers compete too vigorously on the consumer side, tilting pricing heavily against merchants (Bolt and Tieman 2008; Wright 2012). Moreover, determining the degree of competition (or substitution) between payment instruments—such as cards versus cheque or giro payments—is limited because not all instruments can easily substitute with others at the point of sale or for bill payments.

Payment competition brings additional complexities. Consumers and retailers may participate in different networks at the same time. In particular, many consumers carry cash, debit and credit cards in their wallet, while many merchants accept cash, debit and credit cards in their store. When end-users participate in more than one network, they are said to be "multihoming"; if they connect to only one network, they "singlehome". As a general finding, competing networks try to attract end-users who tend to singlehome, since—in a two-sided market—attracting them determines which network has the greater volume of business (Guthrie and Wright 2007). However, if a retailer's customer is viewed to be temporary some merchants may at the point of sale choose to decline payment cards even when they signed an acquiring contract to accept them. This phenomenon forms the basis for the so-called Tourist Test (Rochet and Tirole 2011). The tourist test defines the interchange fee level that leaves a merchant indifferent between different means of payment, say between a payment card and cash, when an incidental customer (the "tourist") enters the store and pays at the counter. This test provides a general basis for interchange fee regulation as applied by the European Commission (Schwimann 2009).

There can be a perverse side-effect, however, especially in countries such as the Netherlands where debit card volumes are still strongly increasing over cash. Due to economies of scale, the average cost of accepting a debit card transaction continues to fall for merchants while the average cost of accepting a cash payment is flat or even increasing. Straightforward application of the tourist test methodology would then predict higher (future) interchange fees so as to maintain the indifference level between cash and cards (Bolt et al. 2013).

Banks and merchants can also influence consumer choice when consumers have access to three competing payment forms—cash, debit card and credit card. Unlike most two-sided market models, where benefits are exogenous, Bolt and Chakravorti (2008a) showed how consumers' utility and merchants' profits increase from additional sales resulting from greater security and access to credit. They found that bank profit rises when merchants are unable to pass on payment costs to consumers because the bank is better able to extract merchant surplus. Moreover, in their model, the relative cost of providing debit and credit cards determines whether banks will provide both or only one type of payment card.

Payment Innovation

Since the early 2000s, various retail payment innovations have seen the light of day. Contactless payments, mobile payments, digital wallets are currently mentioned as the future payment media of a "cashless society". These innovations will certainly affect the retail payment market in terms of consumer behaviour and merchant acceptance and by reshaping payment processes. Key drivers for payment innovation are technological change, end-user preferences, the increasing number of non-banks offering payment services and regulatory framework.

Network Effects, Incentives and Lock-In

Since funds have to flow from A to B in an efficient, safe and sound way, payment innovation requires cooperation between competing players. This may cause adverse incentives and lock-in effects. An important question arises who captures the rents from innovation. This will largely depend on the market structure of the payment industry determining (ex ante) incentives to invest in innovation. Pure cost-based approaches to payment pricing may limit incentives to innovate and payment providers may require years to recoup investments in new payment products. In the end, they may not introduce new products but just upgrade existing "rails". In a recent paper, Bourreau and Verdier (2012) argue that interchange fees may be necessary for providing the right incentives to innovate, in particular when merchants do not exert strong externalities on consumer adoption.

A network good can provide large benefits to providers and users, but network economies can also make replacing old technologies difficult. Adoption is often slow. An innovation will be preferred to the existing technology only if sufficient numbers of providers and end-users adopt it. In such cases, regulation or market intervention may be necessary to facilitate a transition and provide legal clarity and level playing fields. However, imposing regulations mandating the use of new technology usually imposes high costs on some market participants, but alternatively, if the intervention is too "light" and open-ended, the transition may be delayed or even postponed indefinitely, forgoing its benefits (Bauer and Gerdes 2012).

Interoperability and Fragmentation

The Bank for International Settlements (BIS) Committee on Payment and Settlement Systems (CPSS) has identified five different categories of payment innovation, i.e. (i) innovations in card payments, (ii) internet payments, (iii) mobile payments, (iv) electronic bill presentment and payment, and (v) infrastructure and security improvements (CPSS 2012). Whereas earlier innovations in European CPSS countries were mainly focused on card, internet and mobile payments, more recently a higher proportion of innovations were aimed at improving infrastructure and security (Deutsche Bundesbank 2012). In particular, infrastructure improvements in order to speed up processing ("instant payments" and "blockchain technology") have gained a prominent place on the European retail payments agenda.[11]

Providing for interoperability of the old and new payment technologies can ease the transition by lowering the cost of adoption. Users with the largest net benefits adopt first, and as more agents adopt, positive network effects enhance the new technology, increasing incentives for non-adopters to also switch, accelerating further adoption (Bauer and Gerdes 2012). However, European payment infrastructure innovations are difficult to implement due to the complexity of existing domestic infrastructures. Investment costs are high and it is often unclear how these costs will be recouped in the short term. Moreover, many different national players with possibly conflicting interests are involved in the European payment market where end-users across euro area countries may have different preferences as well. There is a risk that similar payment solutions will be developed in different locations that are not fully compatible. Multiple non-interoperable solutions may yield "renewed" market fragmentation.

Recently, businesses from other sectors—non-banks—are also starting to move into offering payment services to end-users. They include large technology companies, such as Facebook, Apple and Google, but also a growing group of smaller financial technology ("FinTech") firms. FinTech firms tend to special-

[11] See Schwienbacher (2016) in this Handbook for a discussion on the rise of digital currencies.

ize in a limited number of products or services, with which they compete with incumbents (mainly banks) who offer a complete package of related products and services, not all of which are profitable on their own: for example, offering payment services in order to cross-sell other products such as savings accounts or consumer loans.[12] The payments-related services offered by FinTech firms are often end-user solutions, which make use of the underlying infrastructure of existing payment service providers such as banks. Examples include payment initiation services, which allow users to initiate a payment from an account held at another provider, digital wallets in which users can store the details of one or more payment cards issued by other providers, and solutions for making person-to-person payments via a mobile devices.

The entrance of new providers increases competition and diversity of supply, which should in general lead to lower costs and more choice for consumers, but in the absence of cooperation there is an additional risk of market fragmentation (Segendorf and Wretman 2015). To avoid fragmentation and adverse incentives to innovate, additional thoughtful regulation may be necessary to increase economic surplus. The BIS Committee on Payment and Market Infrastructures (CPMI) also identified a number of risks associated with the increasing role of non-banks, including concentration risk, outsourcing risk, operational complexity risk and consumer protection issues. In addition, the CPMI puts forward two efficiency issues, i.e. level playing field issues between banks and non-banks and stakeholder involvement issues relating to non-banks' interests not being adequately represented in industry bodies that prepare industry arrangements (CPMI 2014). According to the CPMI the extent to which the abovementioned risks and efficiency issues may materialize differs per jurisdiction, due to differences in the type of non-banks that are active, the regulatory and institutional framework and the mandates of public authorities with respect to non-banks. Consequently, additional regulatory measures, if necessary, to mitigate these risks and issues may differ across jurisdictions.

Regulatory Framework

Since the 1990s, the EU has called upon banks to harmonize and integrate national payment markets into a European payment market in order to stimulate cross-border trade within the EU, to improve cost efficiency and competi-

[12] Some examples of European FinTech firms are Transferwise (an international money transfer service), iZettle (which makes card readers for mobile devices) and Adyen (an online payments platform that allows customers to accept many payment methods).

tion in the retail payment market, and to simulate innovation at an EU-scale. A key step in this process was the introduction of the euro as a common currency on 1 January 1999 by 12 EU member states, creating a single money market. Subsequently, on 1 January 2002, euro banknotes and coins replaced the national banknotes and coins in Eurozone countries. People could use the same set of coins and banknotes in all countries that had adopted the euro. However, cross-border non cash payments were still costly, both in terms of time and money. Initially, progress in the harmonisation and integration was slow and European payment markets remained fragmented. More regulatory stimulus was needed.

Since 2000, additional legislation has been adopted by the EU in order to further the development of an efficient, competitive and innovative EU-wide retail payments market (see Kokkola 2010, for an overview of legal acts adopted until 2010). Five main legal acts that underpin the current regulatory framework are discussed below in more detail.

E-Money Directive

Directive 2000/46 (EC), also known as the E-Money Directive was adopted on 18 September 2000; see European Commission (2000). The directive aimed at promoting the provision of e-money in the EU by introducing a harmonized set of prudential rules for electronic money institutions (EMIs) and a "single passport" for the provision of e-money services throughout the EU. By regulating market access of EMIs the EU attempted to create a level playing field for the issuance of e-money between traditional credit institutions and the EMIs.

After evaluating the impact of the directive the Commission concluded that the e-money market had not grown as fast as expected. The prudential requirements for the EMIs were more stringent than needed in view of the risks associated with issuing e-money. The Commission (2009a) therefore proposed a revised directive which was adopted on 16 September 2009. The revised E- Money Directive (2009/110/EC) aims at removing unnecessary or disproportionate barriers to market entry for EMIs. A fundamental change with the original directive concerns the introduction of proportionate prudential requirements facilitating market access to newcomers, including a reduction of capital requirements, new rules on the calculation of own-funds and the abolition of the exclusivity principle. The latter is intended to stimulate EMIs active in other sectors to develop innovative services in the payments market as well.

Regulation on Cross-Border Payments

In 2000, banks and automated clearing houses (ACHs) were not capable of processing cross-border non-cash transfers in a fully automated way, as they did with otherwise similar domestic payments, because the European payment infrastructure had not reached the same level of standardisation as the domestic payment infrastructures. This relative inefficiency was reflected in longer processing times for cross-border than for domestic payments in euro. Cross-border payments were also more costly than domestic payments for the banking community, and banks passed on these higher costs to their customers by charging them relatively higher payment fees for cross-border payments than for domestic payments.

The difference in fee level was hampering cross-border trade, and was therefore considered as an obstacle to the proper functioning of the internal market in the EU. In order to remove this barrier the Regulation on cross-border payments in euros (2560/2001/EC) was adopted on 19 December 2001; see European Commission (2001). This regulation stipulates that fees which banks levy on cross-border payments in euros up to an amount of EUR 50,000 cannot be higher than those levied on payments in euros within a member state. The regulation covered transactions by credit transfer, cheque, credit card, debit card and ATM withdrawal. In case of credit transfers, in order to pay the charges that apply to domestic payments, customers were required to indicate the international bank account number (IBAN) of the beneficiary and the Business Identifier Code (BIC) of the beneficiary's institution.

On 16 September 2009 regulation EC no. 924/2009 on cross-border payments in the Community was adopted, which modified Regulation 2560/2001 (EC); see European Commission (2009b). One of the changes was the extension of the scope to direct debit payments. In addition, it introduced temporary rules until November 2012 on multilateral interchange fees (MIFs) for direct debit payments and from November 2010 onwards it required banks in the Eurozone that offered direct debits to be reachable for cross-border direct debit collections in euro. These changes where an initiative of the banks to create a Eurozone-wide payment system for payments in euros in accordance to the Single Euro Payments Area (SEPA).

Due to Regulation on Cross-border Payments in euros (2560/2011 EC) banks' revenues out of cross-border payments were substantially reduced, but their costs had not. As a reaction the European banking community decided in 2002 to establish the Single Euro Payments Area in order to improve the efficiency of the European retail payment system. It envisaged the implementation of SEPA by 2010. To this end a decision making and coordinating body was set up in June 2002, called the European Payment Council (EPC), representing the largest banks in Europe. The objective of SEPA was to turn all national payment markets into one euro retail payment market, so that there would no difference anymore between processing domestic or cross-border payments in euro, made with the three most used non-cash means of payment (credit transfer, direct debit and payment cards).

Although the Regulation on Cross-border Payments led to the alignment of fee levels of domestic and cross-border payments at national levels, it did not harmonize national price levels of payment transactions. So, there are still large differences in fee levels between member states, which hamper the reduction of the fragmentation between member states. The Interchange Fee Regulation is an attempt to further harmonize fee levels for card payments in the EU.

Payment Services Directive (1 and 2)

The Directive on Payment Services 2007/64/EC (PSD) was adopted on 13 November 2007 (European Commission 2007), and its follow up Directive (EU) 2015/2366, also dubbed as PSD2, was adopted on 25 November 2015 (European Commission 2015b). The PSD provides the legal basis of SEPA. One of its main target is to ensure that cross-border payments would not differ between euro area countries from the perspective of consumers and businesses in terms of user friendliness, efficiency and security. It harmonizes national legislation regarding consumer protection, information requirements as well as the rights and obligations for consumers and businesses and payment providers.

The PSD also aims at fostering competition and innovation in the European retail payment by facilitating the entrance of newcomers in the payment market. It establishes a new category of non-bank payment service providers, named payment institutions which could compete with existing payment service providers. These payment institutions are licensed to provide payment services across the EU and fall under a lighter supervisory regime than banks. Member states had until 1 November 2009 to implement the PSD into their national law.

According to the impact assessment of the European Commission, some of PSD's provisions needed adjustment. In particular, the PSD was adjusted in order to bring two new types of payment service providers within its scope: payment initiation service providers (PISPs) and account information service providers (AISPs).[13] These new providers will for the most part have to follow the same rules as other non-banks who provide payment services in the EU. In addition, the "new" PSD2 imposes stricter security requirements on all parties providing online payment services. PSD2 has come into force on 13 January 2016, and the measures taken by member states to comply with this directive will apply (with some exceptions) from 13 January 2018.

SEPA Regulation

In 2014 SEPA became a reality, four years later than initially envisaged by the European banking community. International bank account numbers (IBANs) have replaced national bank account numbers and national payment instruments for credit transfers and direct debit payments have gradually been replaced by European counterparts. Since 1 August 2014 there are no differences between making payments in euro with these payment instruments within one's own country or to another European country.

As the self-regulatory efforts of the European banking sector did not lead to a swift and smooth changeover towards a pan-European payment system the EU stepped in and adopted on 14 March 2012 Regulation EU 260/2012 "Establishing technical and business requirements for credit transfers and direct debits in euro", also known as the SEPA Regulation (European Commission 2012). The SEPA regulation set 1 February 2014 as end date for the SEPA migration in order to urge the national market to migrate. In particular, from 1 February 2014 onward, the regulation stipulated that (i) all national bank account numbers are converted into their European counterpart, the (longer) international bank account number (IBAN), (ii) all credit transfers in euro are executed using the same standard: the SEPA credit transfer and (iii) all direct debits in euro are executed under the same standard: the SEPA direct debit. In addition, the regulation prohibits the usage of multilateral interchange fees (MIFs) for direct debit payments in order to reduce transaction fees for businesses and thus stimulate direct debit usage at a European level.

The migration towards SEPA was a very complex and time consuming process. Not only did the payment industry itself have to migrate, but also large

[13] "Account information services" refer to services provided to consumers that collect and consolidate information on the different current accounts of consumers a single place. These services provide consumers with more than one account to get insight into their net balance and to make payments from various accounts. "Payment initiation services" refer to services to facilitate the use of online banking to make online payments. Payment initiation service providers prepare online credit transfers by transmitting a consumer's security code to their bank with the credit transfer and inform the merchant that the transaction has been initiated.

corporations, small and medium sized enterprises, and software developers needed to prepare themselves. The Eurosystem was closely monitoring the migration process in all countries in the euro area. At the end of 2013 many credit transfers and the majority of the direct debit payments were still made using the legacy payment schemes. The European Commission therefore considered it highly unlikely that the SEPA migration would be fully completed by 1 February 2014. Nor could it exclude the possibility that consumers and businesses would be affected by an incomplete migration to SEPA (payment delays, market distortions, etc.). On 9 January 2014 it therefore published a proposal for a regulation amending the original SEPA Regulation by introducing a transition period of six months. This Regulation EU 248/2014 was adopted on 26 February 2014 (European Commission 2014). Until 1 August 2014 payment service providers were still allowed to continue processing credit transfers and direct debits in euro using legacy schemes alongside the processing of SEPA compliant credit transfers and direct debits.

Interchange Fee Regulation

With the migration to SEPA most of the legal and technical barriers in retail payments between countries have been removed for credit transfers and direct debits. However, this does not hold yet for card payments. The Regulation on Interchange Fees for Card-based Payment Transactions (the "IFR") was adopted on 29 April 2015 and entered into force on 8 June 2015. Its aim is to promote an EU-wide market for card-based payments. It intends to give payment service providers legal clarity and a level playing field for offering EU-wide card-payment services, to reduce costs for merchants and consumers and to promote efficiency and innovation in the payment cards market at the point-of-sale and in e-commerce, including mobile payments.

The key element of the IFR is a cap on interchange fees of debit and credit card transactions made by consumers with payment cards issued in the EU. Merchants' banks pass the cost of an interchange fee on to merchants. Thus, interchange fees exercise upward pressure on merchant discount fees for card payments, who pass on these costs to consumers via consumer prices. As the level of interchange fees varies between member states so do the merchant discounts. Hence, these fees affect card acceptance by merchants and card usage by consumers. As interchange fees for cross-border card payments used to be relatively high, they discouraged merchants to accept card payments from international brands. The IFR intends to stimulate card acceptance and card usage at an EU-wide scale by setting maximum fee levels for interchange fees—based on the Tourist Test methodology—for domestic and cross-border usage at the same level. There are different caps for debit and credit card transactions, which entered into force on 9 December 2015. First, interchange fees for cross-border debit cards payments are capped at 0.2 % of the transaction value, for domestic debit card payments member states may either define an ad valorem cap (default) or impose a fixed per transaction cap. The ad valorem cap is 0.2 % of the transaction value and the fixed per transaction cap is five eurocents, provided that the sum of interchange fees does not exceed 0.2 % of the annual transaction value of the domestic debit card transactions within each payment card scheme.[14] Second, interchange fees for credit card payments are capped at 0.3 % of the transaction value. This holds for both domestic and cross-border payments. For domestic credit card transactions member states may define a lower per transaction interchange fee cap.

These caps attempt to remove the interchange fee controversy. This controversy exists because (i) merchant costs of accepting payment cards tend to be much higher than for other payment instruments and (ii) interchange fees have often not fallen as volume has expanded. Although many economists and competition authorities agree that an interchange fee may be necessary to balance the demands of consumers and merchants resulting in higher social benefit, the "right" level of the fee remains a subject of debate. Caution is required: well-intended regulation may have unintended consequences. The USA presents an interesting example. Although the US cap on debit card interchange fees was intended to lower merchant card acceptance costs, some merchants find that their fees have risen instead. In order to recoup lost revenues, debit card networks raised the interchange fee on small value transactions that previously cost merchants much less as they were effectively cross-subsidized by other merchants where the fees were much higher (Wang 2012).

Conclusion

We have outlined some recent changes in the European retail payment system, focusing on changes in payment composition, cost and pricing,and regulation. The EU has adopted several legal acts to lower the entry barriers for new providers of payment services and to provide the market the regulatory

[14] Member states may apply two other options. Firstly, they may impose lower caps for domestic card payments. Secondly, during a five-year transition period they may allow banks and card schemes to apply a weighted average interchange fee of no more than the equivalent of 0.2 % of the annual average transaction value of all domestic debit card transactions.

stimulus to further the development of an efficient, competitive and innovative EU-wide retail payments market.

As the migration to electronic forms of payment and in particular mobile solutions continues, globally operating, high-tech non-banks are attempting to enter the European retail payment market and get a piece of the "payment pie". Their entrance has the potential to increase competition and to lead to a more diversified supply of payment services, which should in general lead to lower costs and more choice for consumers and merchants. However, these non-banks with their innovative potential may also lead to further market fragmentation of the European payment market in case cooperation with incumbent players, mostly banks, turns out to be problematic. Incumbents for their part are facing a dilemma: should they compete with these new players by offering innovative end-user solutions, or rather focus on their role as providers of payment accounts services and payment infrastructures?

Looking at current trends, different future scenarios are possible, in which either the incumbents, or large technology firms, or many small FinTech firms turn out to be the dominant blocks. In the end, the central issue remains whether further European public policy or market intervention is necessary to avoid inefficient fragmentation, increase incentives to innovate and mitigate potential security risks so as to improve economic surplus on the whole.

References

Agarwal, R., & Kimball, M. (2015). *Breaking through the zero lower bound.* IMF working paper, 15–224.

Bagnall, J., Bounie, D., Huynh, K., Kosse, A., Schmidt, T., Schuh, S., & Stix, H. (2015). Consumer cash usage: a cross-country comparison with payment diary survey data, *International Journal of Central Banking*, Forthcoming.

Bauer, P. & Gerdes, G. (2012). *Network economies and innovation: Lessons from the transition to check, 21.* Working paper.

Baxter, W. (1983). Bank interchange of transactional paper: Legal and economic perspectives. *Journal of Law and Economics, 26*(3), 541–588.

Bedre, O., & Calvano, E. (2013). Pricing payment cards. *American Economic Journal: Microeconomics, 5*(3), 206–231.

Beijnen, C., & Bolt, W. (2009). Size matters: Economies of scale in European payments processing. *Journal of Banking and Finance, 33*(2), 203–210.

BIS. (2003). *A glossary of terms used in payments and settlement systems.* Bank for International Settlements.

Bolt, W., & Chakravorti, S. (2008a). *Consumer choice and merchant acceptance of payment media.* Federal Reserve Bank of Chicago working paper, 08–11.

Bolt, W., & Chakravorti, S. (2008b). *Economics of payment cards: A status report.* Federal Reserve Bank of Chicago Economic Perspectives, Fourth quarter, 15–27.

Bolt, W., & Chakravorti, S. (2012). Digitization of retail payments. In M. Peitz & J. Waldfogel (Eds.), *Oxford handbook of the digital economy.* New York: Oxford University Press.

Bolt, W., & Humphrey, D. (2007). Payment network scale economies, SEPA, and cash replacement. *Review of Network Economics, 6*(4), 453–473.

Bolt, W., & Tieman, A. (2008). Heavily skewed pricing in two-sided markets. *International Journal of Industrial Organization, 26*(5), 1250–1255.

Bolt, W., Humphrey, D., & Uittenbogaard, R. (2008). Transaction pricing and the adoption of electronic payments: A cross-country comparison. *International Journal of Central Banking, 4*(1), 89–123.

Bolt, W., Jonker, N., & van Renselaar, C. (2010). Incentives at the counter: An empirical analysis of surcharging card payments and payment behavior in the Netherlands. *Journal of Banking and Finance, 34*(8), 1738–1744.

Bolt, W., Jonker, N., & Plooij, M. (2013). *Tourist test or tourist trap: Unintended consequences of debit card interchange fee regulation.* DNB working paper no. 405.

Borzekowski, R., Kiser, E., & Ahmed, S. (2008). Consumers' use of debit cards: Patterns, preferences and price response. *Journal of Money Credit and Banking, 40*(1), 149–172.

Bourguignon, H., Gomes, R., & Tirole, J. (2014). *Shrouded transaction costs.* Mimeo.

Bourreau, M., & Verdier, M. (2012). *Interchange fees and innovation in payment systems.* Working paper.

Briglevics, T., & Shy, O. (2014). Why don't most merchants use price discounts to steer consumer payment choice? *Review of Industrial Organization, 44*(4), 367–392.

Buiter, W., & Rahbari, E. (2015, April 9). High time to get low: Getting rid of the lower bound on nominal interest rates. *Global Economics View*, Citi Research.

CPMI. (2014, March). *Non-banks in retail payments.* Report of the working group on non-banks in retail payments. Available via http://www.bis.org/cpmi/publ/d118.pdf

CPSS. (2012, May). *Innovations in retail payments.* Report of the working group on innovations in retail payments. Available via http://www.bis.org/cpmi/publ/d102.pdf

Danmarks Nationalbank. (2012). *Costs of payments in Denmark.* Danmarks: Nationalbank.

Deutsche Bundesbank. (2012, September). *Innovations in payment systems.* Monthly report, 47–60.

European Commission. (2000, October 27). Directive 2000/46/EC on the taking up, pursuit of and prudential supervision of the business of electronic money institutions. *Official Journal of the European Union.*

European Commission. (2001, December 28). Regulation EC no. 2560/2001 on cross-border payments in euros. *Official Journal of the European Union.*

European Commission. (2007). *Report of the retail banking industry.* Commission staff working document, SEC 106, Brussels.

European Commission. (2009a, October 10). Directive 2009/110/EC on the taking urp, pursuit of and prudential supervision of the business of electronic money institutions. *Official Journal of the European Union.*

European Commission. (2009b, October 9). Regulation EC no. 924/2009 on cross-border payments in the community. *Official Journal of the European Union.*

European Commission. (2012, March 30). Regulation 260/2012 (EU) on establishing technical and business requirements for credit transfers and direct debits in euro. *Official Journal of the European Union.*

European Commission. (2014, March 20). Regulation EU 248/2014 as regards the migration to Union-wide credit transfers and direct debits. *Official Journal of the European Union.*

European Commission. (2015a, June 8). Regulation 2015/751 interchange fees for card-based payment transactions. *Official Journal of the European Union.*

European Commission. (2015b, December 23). Directive (EU) 2015/2366 on payment services in the internal market. *Official Journal of the European Union.*

Evans, D. (2011). *Interchange fees.* Competition Policy International.

Gans, J., & King, S. (2003). "The neutrality of interchange fees in payment systems," Topics in Economic Analysis & Policy, 3(1), article 1. Available at www.bepress.com/bejeap/topics/vol3/iss1/art1

Garcia-Swartz, D., Hahn, R., & Layne-Farrar, A. (2006). The move toward a cashless society: Calculating the costs and the benefits. *Review of Network Economics, 5,* 199–228.

Goodfriend, M. (2000). Overcoming the zero bound on interest rate policy. *Journal of Money, Credit, and Banking, 32*(4), 1007–1035.

Gresvik, O., & Haare, H., (2009). *Costs in the Norwegian payment system.* Norges Bank, Staff memo, No. 4.

Guthrie, G., & Wright, J. (2007). Competing payment schemes. *Journal of Industrial Economics, 55*(1), 37–67.

Hancock, D., Humphrey, D., & Wilcox, J. (1999). Cost reductions in electronic payments: The roles of consolidation, economies of scale, and technical change. *Journal of Banking and Finance, 23*(2–4), 391–421.

Hayashi, F., & Keeton, W. (2012). Measuring the costs of retail payment methods. *Federal Reserve Bank of Kansas City Economic Review*, Second quarter: 37–77.

Humphrey, D. (2015). Negative interest rates and the demand for cash. *Journal of Payments Strategy & Systems*, WINTER 2015–16, *10*, 280–289.

Jonker, N. (2011). Card acceptance and surcharging: The role of costs and competition. *Review of Network Economics, 10*(2), article 4.

Jonker, N., Plooij, M., & Verburg, J. (2015). *Does a public campaign influence debit card usage? Evidence from the Netherlands.* DNB working paper, no. 470.

Kahn, C., & Roberds, W. (2009). Why pay? An introduction to payments economics. *Journal of Financial Intermediation, 18*(1), 1–23.

Kokkola, T. (ed.) (2010). *The payment system: Payments, securities and derivatives, and the role of the Eurosystem*, European Central Bank. Available at: https://www.ecb.europa.eu/pub/pdf/other/paymentsystem201009en.pdf

McAndrews, J., & Wang, Z. (2012). The economics of two-sided payment card markets: Pricing, adoption and usage. *Federal Reserve Bank of Richmond*, 12-06.

Prager, R., Manuszak, M., Kiser, E., & Borzekowski, R. (2009). *Interchange fees and payment card networks*. Board of Governors of the Federal Reserve System Finance and Economics discussion paper, 09–23.

Rochet, J.-C., & Tirole, J. (2002). Cooperation among competitors: Some economics of payment card associations. *RAND Journal of Economics, 33*(4), 549–570.

Rochet, J.-C., & Tirole, J. (2003). Platform competition in two-sided markets. *Journal of the European Economic Association, 1*(4), 990–1029.

Rochet, J.-C., & Tirole, J. (2006). Two-sided markets: A progress report. *RAND Journal of Economics, 37*(3), 645–667.

Rochet, J.-C., & Tirole, J. (2011). Must-take cards: Merchant discounts and avoided costs. *Journal of the European Economic Association, 9*(3), 462–495.

Rogoff, K. (2014). *Costs and benefits to phasing out paper currency*. In J. Parker & M. Woodford (Eds.), *NBER Macroeconomics Annual 2014* (Vol. 29). Chicago: University of Chicago Press.

Rysman, M. (2009). The economics of two-sided markets. *Journal of Economic Perspectives, 23*(3), 125–143.

Schmalensee, R. (2002). Payment systems and interchange fees. *Journal of Industrial Economics, 50*(2), 103–122.

Schmiedel, H., Kostova, G., & Ruttenberg, W. (2012). *The social and private costs of retail payment instruments: A European perspective*. European Central Bank occasional paper, 12–137.

Schwienbacher, A. (2016). The internet, crowdfunding and the banking industry. In T. Beck & B. Casu (Eds.), *The Palgrave handbook for European Banking*. Palgrave Macmillan UK Publisher (forthcoming).

Schwimann, I. (2009). European Union competition policy and payment systems: A review of recent developments. *Journal of Payments Strategy & Systems, 3*(3), 243–252.

Segendorf, B., & Jansson, T. (2012). *The cost of consumer payments in Sweden*. Sveriges Riksbank working paper, no. 262.

Segendorf, B., & Wretman, A.-L. (2015). The Swedish payment market in transformation. *Sveriges Riksbank Economic Review, 2015*(3), 48–68.

Shy, O., & Zhu, W. (2011). Why do payment card networks charge proportional fees? *American Economic Review, 101*(4), 1575–1590.

Uittenbogaard, R. (2007). Turkeys voting for Christmas? How self-regulation makes the European payments market more competitive. *Journal of Payments Strategy and Systems, 1*(4), 318–330.

Verdier, M. (2011). Interchange fees in payment card systems: A review of the literature. *Journal of Economic Surveys, 25*(2), 273–297.
Wang, Z. (2012). *The distributional effects of price cap regulation: Learning from a two-sided market.* Mimeo.
Wright, J. (2003). Optimal card payment systems. *European Economic Review, 47*(4), 587–612.
Wright, J. (2004). The determinants of optimal interchange fees in payment systems. *Journal of Industrial Economics, 52*(1), 1–26.
Wright, J. (2012). Why payment cards fees are biased against retailers. *RAND Journal of Economics, 43*(4), 761–780.

8

Competition in EU Banking

Olivier De Jonghe, Maaike Diepstraten, and Glenn Schepens

Introduction

This chapter discusses recent EU-wide movements in bank competition and concentration. We start with a concise overview of the most frequently used competition and concentration measures. Given that different measures may capture different aspects of bank competition, we focus on the differences and similarities between concentration and competition measures for a broad sample of EU banks. We show that a high level of bank concentration does not necessarily imply a low level of competition and that competition measures such as the Boone indicator (Boone 2008) and the H-statistic (Panzar and Rosse 1987) might capture different aspects of bank competition. Next, we discuss the evolution of bank competition in the EU over time. We end with an overview of recent findings on three important issues concerning bank competition: the impact of bank competition on bank risk-taking, the relationship between bank competition and systemic risk and the relationship between bank competition and switching costs for bank customers.

O. De Jonghe (✉) • M. Diepstraten
Department of Finance, Tilburg University, Tilburg, The Netherlands
e-mail: O.deJonghe@uvt.nl; m.diepstraten@tilburguniversity.edu

G. Schepens
Financial Research Division, European Central Bank, Frankfurt, Germany
e-mail: Glenn.Schepens@ecb.europa.eu

T. Beck, B. Casu (eds.), *The Palgrave Handbook of European Banking*,
DOI 10.1057/978-1-137-52144-6_8

Bank Competition and Market Concentration

Indicators

The most frequently used competition measures in banking can be divided into two broad categories. Firstly, the use of traditional concentration measures, such as the Herfindahl–Hirschman Index (HHI) or concentration ratios for *n* banks, finds its origin in the Structure-Conduct-Performance (SCP) model, originally developed by Bain (1956). The main idea behind the SCP model is that the structure or the concentration of firms in an industry will determine the pricing behaviour of firms (conduct), which will then have an impact on profits. More precisely, higher concentration will make it easier for firms to collude, leading to higher profits. Berger et al. (2004) provide an excellent overview of the many empirical banking studies on this topic, discussing their main findings and potential shortcomings. The main shortcoming of these types of measure is that high concentration could simply be a reflection of market share gains of efficient firms, making the SCP scenario less likely to hold and thus casting doubt on the usefulness of concentration indicators as competition measures. This is often referred to as the efficient structure hypothesis and was first brought forward by Demsetz (1973) and Peltzman (1977).

The main reason why existing academic studies as well as policy institutions still rely heavily on concentration measures as proxies for competition is the limited amount of data needed to calculate them and the fact that they are easy to calculate. This is especially true for the *n*-bank concentration measures (CR_n), which equal the sum of the market shares (*MS*) of the *n* largest banks in a market:

$$CR_n = \sum_{n}^{i=1} MS_i$$

Alternatively, the HHI indicator accounts for the market shares of all banks in the system and assigns a larger weight to the biggest banks. The indicator is defined as the sum of the squared market shares of all banks:

$$HHI = \sum_{n}^{i=1} MS_i^2$$

Depending on the exact question one wants to answer, these indicators are typically calculated based on total assets, total loans or total deposits. If there is only a single bank, HHI will equal 10,000. If there are a large number of small banks that all have a market share close to zero, HHI will be close to zero.

The aforementioned weaknesses in the SCP framework—and more specifically the questionable relationship between concentration proxies and actual competition—have led to the development of measures that try to capture market conduct directly by focusing on either bank pricing behaviour or market power. This approach is often referred to as the New Empirical Industrial Organization (NEIO) approach and includes competition measures such as the Panzar–Rosse H-statistic and the Lerner index. The main advantage of these indicators is that they allow for a more direct measurement of bank competition and that they are firmly grounded in competition theory. The disadvantage is that they require a substantial amount of data, that they are more complicated to calculate compared to traditional concentration measures and that they rely on specific theoretical assumptions in order to be interpretable.

Panzar and Rosse (1987) developed the H-statistic, which is based on the elasticity of a firm's revenue to its input prices and allows for discrimination between perfect competition, monopolistic competition and monopoly. The starting point for calculating the H-statistic is a reduced form revenue equation which relates an income variable (e.g. total interest revenues) to a number of factor input prices (w_i) and—optionally—a number of control variables (X_j):

$$\text{In}(\text{revenues}) = \alpha + \sum_{n}^{i=1} \beta_i \ln(w_i) + \sum_{n}^{j=1} \delta_j \ln(X_j) + \varepsilon$$

In banking studies, income is often proxied by total interest revenues scaled by total assets, while the input factors being considered are typically deposits, labour and fixed assets. Prices of these input factors are often proxied by interest expenses over total assets (or over total deposits), personnel expenses over total assets and non-interest expenses over total assets. The control variables included are bank-specific variables that capture business model and risk characteristics of the bank, such as the equity ratio, loan ratio and diversification measures. After estimating this equation for the relevant market under consideration, the H-statistic can be computed as the sum of the elasticities (β_i) of the revenue variable with respect to their input prices:

$$\text{H} = \sum_{n}^{i=1} \beta_i$$

The H-statistic effectively allows one to discern three particular market situations, given that the market is in long-run equilibrium: perfect competition, monopolistic competition and monopoly. An H-statistic equal to one indicates that increases in input prices are followed by similar changes in marginal costs and total revenues, and thus corresponds to a situation of perfect competition. For a monopolist, an increase in input prices will lead to lower revenues (given that a profit maximizing monopolist will always operate on the price elastic part of the demand curve). As such, the H-statistic will be negative or equal to 0 in a monopolistic market. The vast majority of empirical banking studies employing this measure, however, find an H-statistic between 0 and 1, which is indicative of a situation of monopolistic competition.[1] Bikker and Haaf (2002) use the Panzar-Rosse H-statistic to measure competition in a sample of 23 European and non-European countries for the period 1988–1998.[2] Focusing on the European countries, they find that all large banks operate in highly competitive environments except in Finland, Norway and Spain. De Bandt and Davis (2000) focus on the period 1992–1996 and find evidence of monopolistic competition among large banks in France, Germany and Italy. For small banks they provide evidence of monopoly in France and Germany and monopolistic competition in Italy. In a more recent analysis, Weill (2013) finds that, using the H-statistic, competition on the aggregate level decreased for the 27 EU countries between 2002 and 2010.

The Lerner index (Lerner 1934) measures pricing power and captures the extent to which banks can increase the marginal price beyond the marginal cost. It is derived from the monopolist's profit maximization condition as price minus marginal cost, divided by price:

$$\text{Lerner}_{i,t} = \frac{P_{i,t} - MC_{i,t}}{P_{i,t}}$$

For a monopolist, the index will be equal to one, while under perfect competition the index will be equal to zero as prices and marginal costs should be equal. Marginal costs are either calculated using a cost function or proxied by average costs. An important advantage of the Lerner index is that it allows the researcher to assess the market power of an individual bank, making it possible to compare market power between banks without having to make

[1] We refer to Liu et al. (2010) for a review of studies using the H-statistic.

[2] The sample includes Australia, Austria, Belgium, Canada, Denmark, Finland, France, Germany, Greece, Ireland, Italy, Japan, Korea (South), Luxembourg, the Netherlands, New Zealand, Norway, Portugal, Spain, Sweden, Switzerland, United Kingdom and United States.

assumptions about the relevant market for which the indicator should be calculated. A potential disadvantage is that more market power for a bank does not necessarily correspond with a less competitive market (see e.g. Stiglitz 1987, 1989; Bulow and Klemperer 2002). Weill (2013) uses the Lerner index to assess the evolution of competition in European countries. He finds that the Lerner index increased for 23 of the 27 EU countries in the years prior to the crisis (2002–2006), pointing towards a reduction in competition. On the aggregate level the value decreased during the crisis (2006–2010) but is still above the mean Lerner index of 2002, indicating that competition is still lower than in 2002.

A more recent measure of bank competition, fitting in the NEIO approach, is the Boone indicator (Boone 2008). The reasoning behind this indicator is that (1) more efficient firms will gain higher market shares and higher profits and (2) this effect is stronger in more competitive markets. This relates back to the efficiency hypothesis (Demsetz 1973), which predicts that more efficient firms will be more profitable and will ultimately gain more market share. Boone (2008) shows that this reallocation effect from inefficient to efficient firms increases with competition. In practice, the Boone indicator is often estimated using the following equation (see e.g. Van Leuvensteijn et al. 2011; Schaeck and Cihák 2014):

$$\ln s_i = \alpha + \beta \ln mc_i$$

where s_i is the profitability or the market share of bank i and mc_i is the marginal cost of bank i (either estimated using a cost function or proxied by average costs). The Boone indicator is then equal to the β coefficient. The Boone indicator is expected to be negative, and expected to be lower for more competitive markets. The fact that the indicator is easy to interpret, relies on a simple linear regression and has minimal data requirements (market share and average costs) makes it appealing to use. On the other hand, efficiency gains may not be directly translated into higher profits and higher market share in the short term, which could distort the measurement of the Boone indicator (see e.g. Van Leuvensteijn et al. 2011).

Comparing Indicators

The discussion above clearly illustrates that different competition and concentration measures start from different assumptions and may capture different aspects of bank competition. In order to get a better idea of how different these measures are in practice, we analyse the summary statistics and the correlations between different competition and concentration measures for banks operating in EU-28 countries between 2000 and 2015. All data used to construct the graphs and tables in this chapter is taken from Bureau Van Dijk's Bankscope database. We only include commercial banks and bank holding companies and use unconsolidated data whenever available.

Table 8.1 reports the summary statistics for the inverse of the number of banks, three concentration measures (CR3, CR5 and HHI, all based on total assets) and three structural competition indicators (H-statistic, Lerner index and Boone indicator). Apart from the Lerner index, all indicators are calculated at the country-year level. The Lerner index is calculated at the bank-year level and then averaged at the country-year level in order to make it comparable with the other measures. Table 8.2 reports the pairwise correlations between these measures. In order to make it easier to interpret and compare the different correlations, we use the negative value of the H-statistic and the inverse of the number of banks, such that for all indicators a lower value means more competition.

Table 8.1 Summary statistics for various competition and concentration variables

Variable	Variation	Mean	Std. Dev.	Min.	Max.	Observations		
1 / (Nr. of Banks)	Overall	0.057	0.046	0.007	0.200	N	=	420
	Between		0.045			n	=	28
	Within		0.015			T	=	15
HHI(TA)	Overall	0.211	0.121	0.039	0.696	N	=	420
	Between		0.115			n	=	28
	Within		0.044			T	=	15
CR3(TA)	Overall	0.653	0.169	0.231	0.989	N	=	420
	Between		0.162			n	=	28
	Within		0.055			T	=	15
CR5(TA)	Overall	0.793	0.142	0.357	1.000	N	=	420
	Between		0.138			n	=	28
	Within		0.043			T	=	15
Lerner	Overall	0.204	0.047	0.078	0.356	N	=	420
	Between		0.030			n	=	28
	Within		0.037			T	=	15
H-statistic	Overall	0.691	0.236	0.127	1.336	N	=	355
	Between		0.143			n	=	25
	Within		0.191			T-bar	=	14.2
Boone indicator	Overall	−0.009	0.008	−0.034	0.005	N	=	375
	Between		0.007			n	=	25
	Within		0.002			T	=	15

Source: Own calculations based on Bankscope data (sample: EU-28 countries)

Table 8.2 Pairwise correlations between various indicators of competition and concentration

	1 / (Nr. of Banks)	HHI(TA)	CR3(TA)	CR5(TA)	Lerner	-(H-statistic)
HHI(TA)	**0.584**					
	0.000					
	420					
CR3(TA)	**0.585**	**0.888**				
	0.000	0.000				
	420	*420*				
CR5(TA)	**0.586**	**0.783**	**0.942**			
	0.000	0.000	0.000			
	420	*420*	*420*			
Lerner	**0.266**	**0.198**	**0.225**	**0.170**		
	0.000	0.000	0.000	0.001		
	420	*420*	*420*	*420*		
H-statistic	−0.020	**−0.135**	−0.058	−0.040	**0.121**	
	0.701	0.011	0.280	0.459	0.023	
	355	*355*	*355*	*355*	*355*	
Boone indicator	**−0.213**	**−0.158**	**−0.271**	**−0.212**	**−0.215**	**−0.273**
	0.000	0.002	0.000	0.000	0.000	0.000
	375	*375*	*375*	*375*	*375*	*347*

Source: Own calculations based on Bankscope data (sample: EU-28 countries)
Correlation coefficient / *p*-value / *Observations*

The summary statistics of the concentration measures indicate moderate average levels of bank concentration, with an average HHI of 0.21 and average concentration ratios of 0.65 (CR3) and 0.79 (CR5). These averages, however, hide some large underlying heterogeneity. The HHI, for example, ranges between 0.039 and 0.696. Interestingly, this heterogeneity is mainly driven by a large variation between countries, while the variation over time within a country is far more limited. The between (countries) variation is 11.5% for the HHI, whereas the within (countries) variation is only 4.4%. For the CR3, the CR5 and the (inverse of the) number of banks in a country, we also observe that the between variation is about three times as large as the within variation. Furthermore, the correlation table indicates that all three concentration indices are highly correlated, with significant correlation coefficients ranging between 0.78 and 0.94. This indicates that the choice of the exact concentration indicator should be of little concern when analysing the impact of bank concentration.

The structural competition measures behave somewhat less coherently. The Lerner index and the H-statistic both vary more within countries over time than between countries, while the opposite holds for the Boone indicator. For the latter, the sources and extent of variation (i.e. relative magnitudes of within versus between) are more similar to the concentration measures.

Additionally, the Lerner index and minus the H-statistic are positively correlated (i.e. when one indicator suggests that there is more competition, the other points in the same direction), while they are both negatively correlated with the Boone indicator. They do have in common that, on average, they all point at some level of monopolistic competition, with an average H-statistic, Lerner index and Boone indicator of respectively 0.69, 0.20 and −0.008. Overall, while the outcomes for H-statistic and the Lerner index seem to be relatively similar, this is not necessarily the case for the Boone indicator, which is potentially capturing a very different aspect of bank competition. Finally, looking at the correlation between concentration and competition measures shows that high concentration does not necessarily imply low competition (and vice versa). This result confirms the doubts discussed earlier about the usefulness of employing concentration measures to gauge competition. The competition indicator that is most closely related to bank concentration is the Lerner index, which has a significantly positive correlation with all concentration measures. Correlations between the H-statistic and various concentration measures are almost always non-significant, except once when it is even negative. The latter findings have also been documented by Claessens and Laeven (2004) in a regression setup covering 50 countries over the period 1994–2001. They regress a competitiveness indicator (H-statistic) on a large number of country characteristics and find no evidence that banking system concentration is negatively associated with competitiveness. To the contrary, if anything, they find that more concentrated banking systems have a higher H-statistic (recall that we take the opposite of the H-statistic). Similarly, they also find that the degree of competitiveness relates negatively to the number of banks, although never significantly so. Our correlation table shows that the Boone indicator is consistently negatively correlated with bank concentration as well as other measures of conduct. This finding is in line with Liu et al. (2013b) who also find negative (though insignificant) correlations between the Boone indicator and other measures of concentration and competition. They conclude from their correlation table that while the Boone is conceptually valid, its effectiveness is suspect.[3]

[3] Schiersch and Schmidt-Ehmcke (2011) also express their doubts on the empirical applicability of the Boone indicator, albeit in a different setup for non-financial firms. They test the robustness of the measure by focusing on cartel cases in German manufacturing enterprises and expect to find an increase in competition after the debunking of a cartel. The authors conclude that the Lerner index indicates changes in competition as expected, but state that the Boone indicator is not an empirically robust indicator.

EU-Wide Movements

We continue by showing and discussing the time series evolution of banking sector concentration and competition in the European Union as a whole as well as in two subregions consisting of the initial EU with 15 member states and the group of 13 more recent accession countries. For the sake of space, we focus on only one indicator of concentration (the CR5, panel A) and one indicator of market power (the Lerner index, panel B) as these are most commonly used. The average level of concentration of the EU-28 countries shows a V shape, as it was declining in the early 2000s before starting to slowly increase as of 2007. In 2014, CR5 exceeds its previous peak (which was in 2001). When we look at the two subgroups of countries, we notice fairly similar average levels and trends until 2006. In 2007, the parallel trends disappear as the level of concentration remains more or less constant in the sample of newly acceded countries, whereas it increases quickly and substantially in the subset of the original 15 EU member states. The graph also confirms, especially from 2006 onwards, that the between countries variation is larger than the variation over time.

Panel B, on the other hand, shows much more time variation rather than between group variation. In general, the lines of the group of the initial 15 EU member states and the 13 most recent accession countries are close to each other. The exceptions to that trend are the years 2006, 2007 and 2008. In 2006 and 2007, the average Lerner index is still increasing in the 13 Central and Eastern European (CEE) EU members, whereas it drops substantially in the 15 original EU members. In 2009, however, the rebound in the Lerner index in the EU15 is so large that the two groups of countries again exhibit similar levels of bank pricing power as of 2009. On the aggregate level, the pricing power increased for all three subgroups during the sample period.

A final interesting observation comes from comparing the two subgroups in the two panels. While the CR5 indicates that on average the EU15 countries' banking markets are more concentrated than the banking markets of the 13 most recently acceded countries, they nevertheless have on average lower market power. Again, this indicates that measures should be chosen carefully and that one should use different measures to gauge concentration and competition (Fig. 8.1).

Numerous studies examine bank competition in Europe using the measures described and documented above. One strand of the literature examines the relationship between competition and efficiency. Maudos and de Guevara (2007) find a positive relationship between efficiency and market power (the Lerner index) for EU15 countries for the period 1993–2002. Carbo et al.

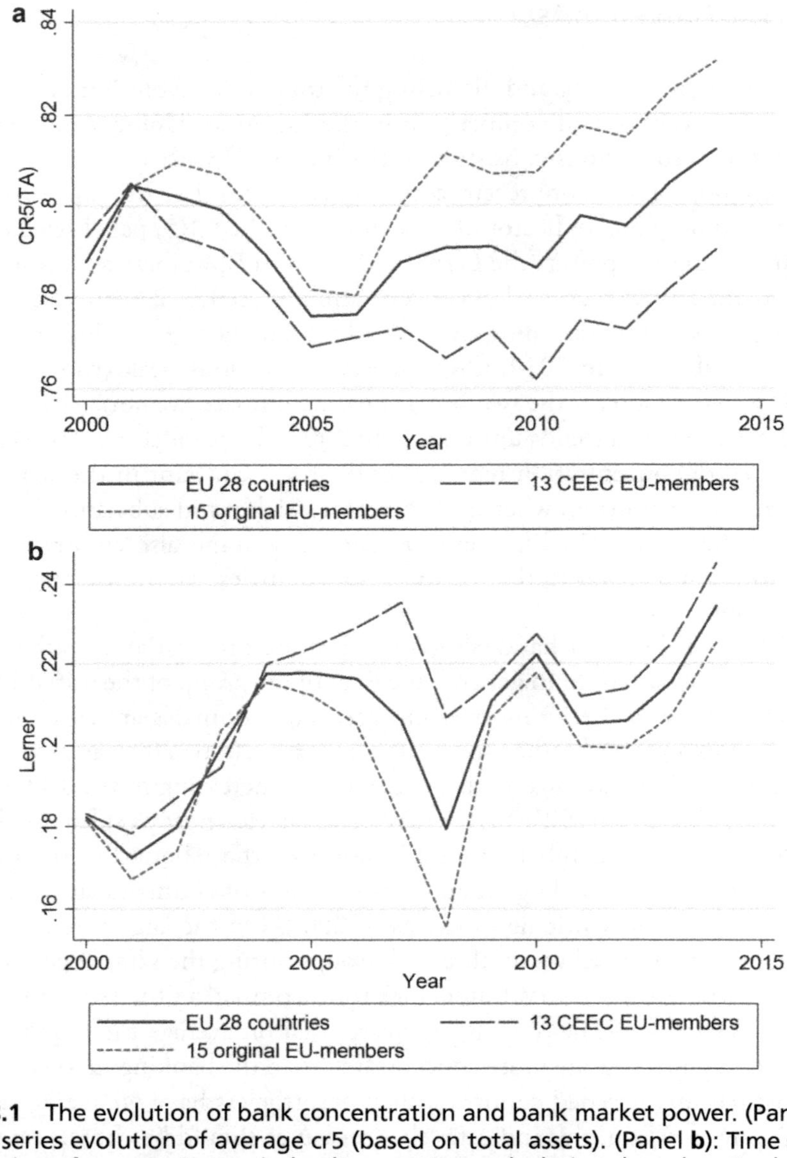

Fig. 8.1 The evolution of bank concentration and bank market power. (Panel **a**): Time series evolution of average cr5 (based on total assets). (Panel **b**): Time series evolution of average Lerner index (*Source*: Own calculations based on Bankscope data)

(2009) confirm the positive relationship between cost efficiency and competition, providing evidence for the efficient structure hypothesis. Schaeck and Cihák (2014) find that competition (Boone indicator) increases cost efficiency. Others (e.g. Schaeck and Cihák 2012) investigate the relationship between competition and capital ratios. By studying commercial, savings and cooperative banks from ten European countries from 1999 to 2005, Schaeck and Cihák (2012) find that banks operating in more competitive environments have higher capital ratios.

Another strand of the literature focuses on the link between competition and stability. Schaeck and Cihák (2014) find that competition (Boone indicator) leads to soundness as it has a positive impact on the distance to default. They find that this effect is even stronger for small banks than for large banks. Liu et al. (2013a) focus on regional competition in ten European countries in the period 2000–2008 and find an inverted U-shaped relationship between competition and stability. In uncompetitive markets, an increase in competition leads to an increase in stability, whereas in competitive markets increased competition results in more fragility. We elaborate on this last issue in more detail in the following subsections.

Capita Selecta

Competition and Bank Risk-Taking

In contrast to other industries where debates on competition are mainly focused on the link between competition and firm efficiency, discussions on bank competition also have to take into account the potential consequences for bank stability. Given the important role that banks play as financial intermediaries in the modern economy, the social cost of bank failure could be very high. If competition has an impact on bank risk-taking incentives, it is important that these consequences are taken into account by competition policy makers. As a consequence, a large body of the competition literature in banking has been devoted to the relationship between bank competition and stability.

Before diving into that literature, let us first have a look at the relationship between bank competition and bank risk-taking in the sample used in this chapter. Figure 8.2 suggests that bank market power and bank stability are positively correlated in the European banking sector over the period 2000–2014.

In particular, the upper panel of Fig. 8.2 shows the evolution of both the Lerner index (pricing power) and the Z-score (bank soundness) over time. The Lerner index captures the extent to which banks can increase the marginal price beyond the marginal cost and the Z-score measures the distance from insolvency (Roy 1952). The Z-score can be interpreted as the number

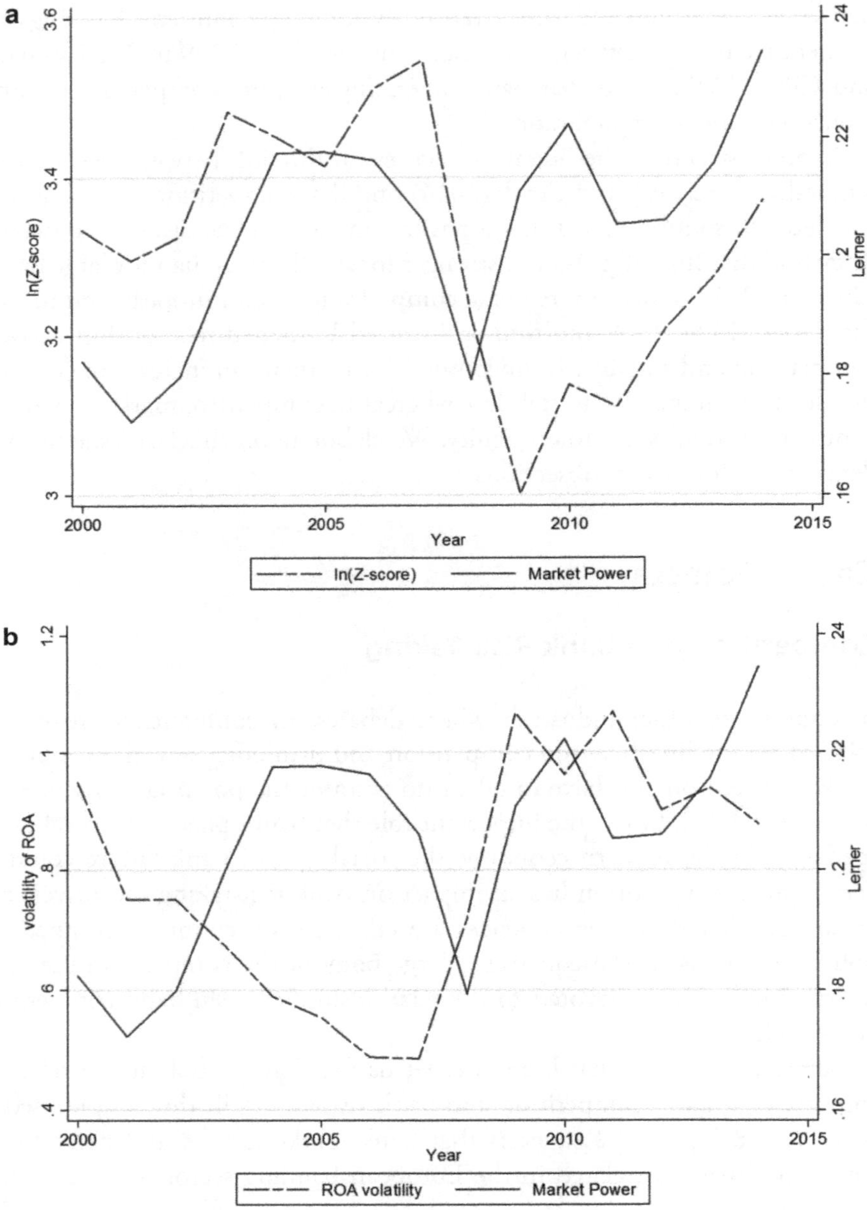

Fig. 8.2 The evolution of bank stability, bank power and profit volatility. (Panel **a**): Time series evolution of risk (ln(Z-score)) and average market power. (Panel **b**): Time series evolution of volatility of ROA and average market power (*Source*: Own calculations based on Bankscope data. Similar to Beck et al. (2013))

of standard deviations by which returns would have to fall from the mean to wipe out all equity in the bank (Boyd and Runkle 1993). A higher Z-score implies a lower probability of insolvency, providing a more direct measure of soundness than, for example, simple leverage measures.

As the lines follow a similar pattern we can conclude that there is a positive relationship between the two. That is, bank soundness (Z-score) and market power (Lerner) are positively correlated over time. However, as both measures include profitability in the numerator, this relationship can be mechanical rather than economically meaningful. Therefore we plot in the lower panel of Fig. 8.2 the evolution of Lerner and the standard deviation of returns on assets, which is the denominator in the Z-score. This figure shows that an increase in market power leads to a drop in profitability volatility. Hence the former finding is confirmed, indicating that the relationship between bank soundness and market power is not spuriously created by profitability in the numerator.

Figure 8.2 may suggest a positive relationship between market power and bank risk-taking. There is not yet a consensus, however, on the generalizability and robustness of this finding across different samples, risk measures and competition proxies.

What guidance does theory provide? Broadly speaking, there are two main views on the impact of competition on bank stability. On the one hand, the competition–fragility view posits that more competition among banks leads to more fragility. This charter value view of banking, as theoretically modelled by Marcus (1984) and Keeley (1990), sees banks as choosing the risk of their asset portfolio. Bank owners have incentives to shift risks to depositors, as in a world of limited liability they only participate in the upside of this risk-taking. In a more competitive environment with more pressure on profits, banks have higher incentives to take more excessive risks, resulting in higher fragility. In addition, in a more competitive environment, banks earn fewer informational rents from their relationship with borrowers, reducing their incentives to properly screen borrowers, again increasing the risk of fragility (Boot and Thakor 1993; Allen and Gale 2000; Allen and Gale 2004). The competition–stability hypothesis, on the other hand, argues that more competitive banking systems result in more rather than less stability. Specifically, Boyd and De Nicolo (2005) show that lower lending rates reduce the entrepreneur's cost of borrowing and increase the success rate of entrepreneurs' investments. As a consequence, banks will face lower credit risk on their loan portfolios in more competitive markets, which should lead to increased banking sector stability.

Since the 2008 financial crisis, however, attention has shifted more towards (1) trying to explain why competition is deteriorating for bank stability in some markets while having a positive impact in others, (2) taking into account the consequences for systemic risk and (3) incorporating other types of bank-specific risks next to credit risk.

Firstly, recent extensions of the Boyd and De Nicolo (2005) model allow for imperfect correlation in loan defaults (Martinez-Miera and Repullo 2010; Hakenes and Schnabel 2011) and show that the relationship between competition and risk is U-shaped. On the empirical front, Beck et al. (2013) document large cross-country variation in the relationship between bank competition and stability for a large sample of banks in 79 different countries and assess how regulation, supervision and other institutional characteristics impact this relationship. Their results indicate that an increase in competition will have a larger impact on bank risk-taking in countries with stricter activity restrictions, lower systemic fragility, better developed stock exchanges, more generous deposit insurance and more effective systems of credit information sharing. Similarly, Forssbaeck and Shehzad (2015) show that higher quality of regulation and supervision reduces the risk-increasing impact of competition.

Secondly, while traditional theoretical models and empirical work typically focus on bank credit risk, some recent papers have started looking at other bank risk concepts. Carletti and Leonello (2013) develop a theory that links bank competition to liquidity risk. They show that increased credit market competition reduces the opportunity cost to banks of holding liquid assets on their balance sheet, thus improving a bank's ability to survive liquidity crises. Freixas and Ma (2014) study the impact of competition on portfolio risk, default risk, liquidity risk and systemic risk. Crucially, they highlight that the impact of competition will depend on a bank's liability structure.

Taken together, both the empirical and theoretical work on this topic over the last five years implies that there is no one-size-fits-all approach to regulatory initiatives to ensure that too much or too little competition would endanger bank (systemic) stability. The usefulness of curbing or stimulating bank competition will depend heavily on both institutional and bank-specific characteristics, and might have different consequences for different types of risks.

Competition and Systemic Risk

In response to the financial crisis that emerged in 2008, the European Commission pursued a number of initiatives to create a safer and sounder financial sector for the single market. Among other things, the creation of the Banking Union implied establishing the Single Supervisory Mechanism (SSM) to ensure consistent supervision across EU countries and to enhance the safety and soundness of the European banking system.[4] Additionally, the European Systemic Risk Board was created in order to contribute to the prevention or mitigation of systemic risks to financial stability in the European Union, while several country-level macro-prudential authorities also activated a range of measures aimed at reducing systemic financial stability risk, such as extra capital buffers for systemically important banks. What makes a bank systemically important is a multifaceted question, but two important determinants are the size of the bank and the scope of its activities.

The general conclusion from recent empirical studies is that larger banks have higher (conditional) tail risk and that diversification (scope of bank activities) leads to higher systemic risk. Barth and Schnabel (2013) present an overview of the direct and indirect channels through which large banks affect or are affected by systemic risk. Empirical evidence on the size–systemic risk relationship can be found in Demirguc-Kunt and Huizinga (2013), Fahlenbrach et al. (2012), Brunnermeier et al. (2012) and Adrian and Brunnermeier (2015). The impact of bank scope (or diversification) on systemic risk is investigated by, for example, Wagner (2010), Ibragimov et al. (2011), Boot and Ratnovski (2016), De Jonghe (2010) and Brunnermeier et al. (2012). A recent study by De Jonghe et al. (2015) shows, in addition, that the two dimensions (size and diversification) should not be considered in isolation. More specifically, the impact of non-interest income on banks' systemic risk exposures and contributions depends on the size of the bank. They show that the dark side of diversification (complexity leading to systemic risk) dominates for small banks, whereas the bright side effects of diversification and innovation (scope for risk-sharing) dominate for medium and large banks.[5]

While the literature on bank competition and risk-taking is large and growing, far less empirical evidence is available on the relation between bank competition and systemic risk. One notable exception is Anginer et al. (2014), who investigate the impact of competition on systemic risk for a worldwide sample of banks. Their main finding is that greater competition leads to banks that take on more diversified risks, which makes the banking system less sensitive to shocks. In line with the latest papers on competition and individual bank risk, they also show that the exact impact will depend on the institutional and regulatory setting in a country. A lack of competition will have a larger impact in countries with weak investor protection, generous safety nets and limited diversification guidelines from the relevant authorities.

[4] All Eurozone countries participate automatically in the SSM. Other EU countries that do not yet have the euro as their currency can choose to participate. To do so, their national supervisors enter into "close cooperation" with the European Central Bank.

[5] For more in-depth reading on the banking union, we refer to Chap. 17 of this handbook. Chapter 4 deals with various issues of banks' business models, of which size and scope are crucial determinants.

Two recent papers blend the two aforementioned issues, that is, bank business models and systemic risk as well as bank concentration and systemic stability. Engle et al. (2014) on the one hand, and De Jonghe et al. (2015) on the other hand, suggest that the impact of banking sector concentration on the diversification–systemic risk relationship should not be ignored. The former paper by Engle et al. (2014) analyses the relationship between concentration, the shift to non-interest income activities and systemic risk in a global context. Their results are threefold. Firstly, the level of non-interest income is higher for banks in low concentration banking systems. They also document that competition among banks to obtain higher shareholder returns (higher franchise value) creates this relationship. Secondly, they show that the relationship between non-interest income and systemic risk is not homogeneous in concentration—on the contrary. In the regressions with bank fixed effects, they obtain that non-interest income actually reduces systemic risk for banks in concentrated banking markets, while it has no effect on systemic risk in low or moderately concentrated banking sectors.

De Jonghe et al. (2015) find that diversification may lead to less systemic risk for large banks. However, they show that this bright side of diversification for large banks crucially depends on country characteristics that facilitate the creation of conflicts of interest.[6] Their empirical setup (using information on listed banks across the globe) allows one to analyse the impact of country-specific characteristics such as bank concentration on the relationship between non-interest income and systemic risk, while taking into account that the impact could differ for either small or large banks.

To facilitate the interpretation and to provide insights into the economic magnitude of their effects, we graphically present the obtained marginal effects of a change in non-interest income on the marginal expected shortfall. Marginal expected shortfall (MES) is a measure of systemic risk exposure proposed by Acharya et al. (2015). It shows a bank's equity loss per dollar in a given year conditional on the banking sector experiencing one of its 5% worst trading days in that year. A higher value of MES indicates a higher contribution of bank *i* to the risk of the banking system. Following common practice, we flip the sign of MES such that a higher value indicates a larger systemic risk exposure.

[6] According to Saunders and Cornett (2014), three factors affect the likelihood with which potential conflicts of interest in financial conglomerates turn into realized conflicts of interest. They are (1) imperfect information on banks, (2) the level of concentration in the banking sector, and (3) the value of reputation. De Jonghe et al. (2015) find empirical support for each of these three channels, but we focus here only on the role of bank concentration.

The graph represents the marginal effect of a change in diversification on systemic risk exposures for countries that have a low (10th percentile), median (50th percentile) or a high (90th percentile) level of bank concentration. At the same time, we calculate the effect for each subgroup for three types of banks (small, median, large) based on the 10th, 50th and 90th percentile of bank size. The results in Fig. 8.3 reveal a couple of interesting patterns. Firstly, diversification into non-interest income activities will lead to higher systemic risk exposures in countries with more concentration, irrespective of the size of the bank. There is no statistically significant difference in the impact of the non-interest income (NII) share on MES for large versus small banks in countries with high levels of concentration. Secondly, for large banks (which are subject to the scrutiny of the European Central Bank since the start of the SSM), the effect of non-interest income and MES varies across countries with different levels of concentration. There is a significant positive relationship for banks operating in institutional settings conducive to conflicts of interest (e.g. high concentration, 1.93) and a significant and large negative relationship for banks operating in institutional settings mitigating conflicts of interest (e.g. low concentration, −3.773).

The economic magnitude of the effects is also large. The difference in impact between high and low concentrated markets is always positive and significant, and ranges between 1.25 for small banks and 5.70 for large banks. More specifically, a standard deviation increase in the non-interest income ratio for large banks operating in a concentrated banking environment leads a to jump in the MES of 0.27, which corresponds with an increase of around 14% for

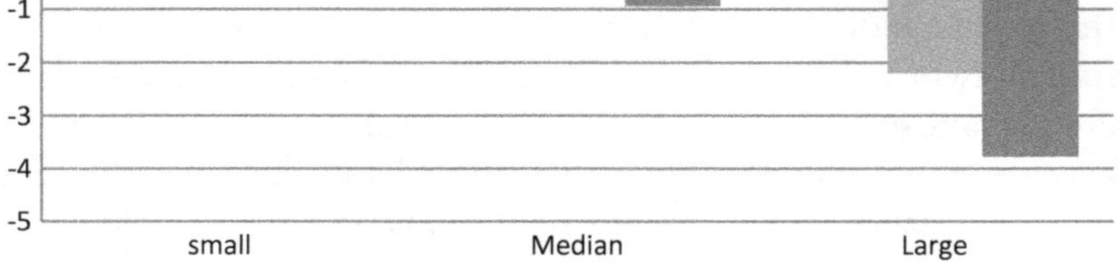

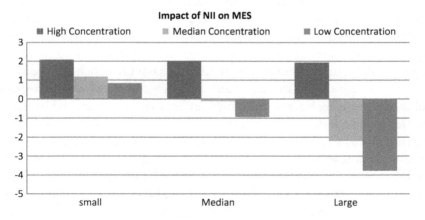

Fig. 8.3 Impact of an increase in non-interest income on marginal expected shortfall for different bank sizes and different levels of concentration (*Source*: Figure based on results in De Jonghe et al. (2015))

the average bank in our sample. On the other hand, when a similar large bank operates in an unconcentrated banking market, a standard deviation increase in the non-interest income ratio leads to a change in the MES of −0.53 (drop with almost 28%). This lends support to the idea that concentrated banking markets can suffer from too-important-to-fail problems, which will give banks an incentive to opt for more risky assets when they decide to (further) diversify their revenue stream. This may make supervision and enforcement of actions in a banking union with different banking structures potentially more complex. Given that the SSM implies that a single supervisor is monitoring banks from various countries that have widely different banking structures and levels of concentration, these results imply that it is important to take these cross-country differences into account.

Bank Customer Inertia: Barriers to Switching

Explicit or implicit barriers to switching banks may lead to welfare losses. Firstly, locked-in borrowers may be faced with higher (than competitive) interest rates, leading to either under-investment or more risk-taking. Secondly, depositor discipline is less effective when customers face difficulties upon moving deposit and savings accounts from one bank to another. These explicit and implicit barriers to switching are affected by the bank market structure as well as the existence of barriers to entry.

However, promoting competition in the banking sector is a necessary but insufficient condition to convince customers (firms and households) to switch banks. Even in a competitive market, customers may not switch if the actual or perceived costs are too high. In order to encourage customer poaching, regulators and banks must understand what drives a customer's decision to stay or switch. Focusing on households, several studies have been undertaken to gain insight into customers' switching behaviour, which can be divided into two categories. On the one hand, there are studies which are backward-looking by focusing on *actual* (non-)switches that have occurred in the past. On the other hand, there are forward-looking studies which focus on the *intention* to switch. Different studies use different types of independent variables to explain switching behaviour: socio-economic variables (Kiser 2002; Chakravarty et al. 2004; Brunetti et al. 2015), bank characteristics (Brunetti et al. 2015), relationship characteristics (Chakravarty et al. 2004; Brunetti et al. 2015), customer service quality dimensions (Chakravarty et al. 2004) and reasons to stay at the main bank (Kiser 2002).

Kiser (2002) uses US survey data to study households' past bank switching behaviour. She finds that younger (age < 35) and older (age > 65) households are equally likely to not change banks, pointing towards a cohort effect rather than an age effect. Moreover, she finds that prices are an important factor that triggers switches, and that location and service quality impact the decision to switch. In contrast, perceived switching cost (trouble) does not explain why some households never switched banks. Lastly, Kiser concludes that switchers and non-switchers are equally satisfied with their banks.

Chakravarty et al. (2004) find that the duration of the relationship, empathy, responsiveness, reliability and age have a negative impact on the propensity to switch.[7] In contrast, whether one has had problems with the bank during the past six months and whether one has switched before have a positive impact on the propensity to switch.

A more recent study from Brunetti et al. (2016) focuses on Italy. They argue that Italy is a good case to study switching behaviour as on average 25% of the households changed their main bank between two successive waves of the survey. They find, among other things, that having a relationship with a single bank reduces the probability of switching, and that having more services at the main bank reduces the probability of switching. Hence, this study shows the importance of the relationship between the household and the bank.

The aforementioned studies do not distinguish between banking products, even though banking products have different characteristics. Van der Cruijsen and Diepstraten (2015) argue that switching costs differ across banking products and therefore they test whether the propensity to switch and the factors that explain variation in intentions vary across banking products. Their analyses include savings accounts, current accounts, mortgage loans and revolving credit, enabling them to study both consumers' assets and liabilities. By conducting a survey among the CentER panel, a representative panel of the Dutch-speaking population in the Netherlands, they find that the propensity to switch savings accounts in the next 12 months is the highest. Moreover, they document that variation in the propensity to switch current accounts is best explained by the bank–customer relationship and socio-psychological factors. Variation in switching savings accounts is best explained by the bank–customer relationship, followed by switching experience. Lastly, variation in the propensity to switch mortgage loans is best explained by switching experience and personal characteristics. As both switching intentions and the factors that explain switching intentions vary across banking products, this study shows the importance of studying banking products separately.

[7] Empathy is defined as "the perception that a business has the consumers' needs at the core of its behavior", p. 514. Responsiveness is defined as "the willingness to help customers and provide prompt service", p. 514. Reliability is defined as "the ability to perform the promised service dependably", p. 514.

In contrast to Italy, in many other European countries switching is not that common. The Dutch Authority for Consumers and Markets (ACM) concluded in 2014 that there is inertia on the Dutch retail market for savings accounts and checking accounts. It is documented that 50% of holders of a savings account have never switched to another bank in their life. In addition, 73% of holders of a checking account who are18 years and older has never switched. This inertia can be viewed as a barrier for new entrants as it will be hard to attract customers. This inertia is not specific to the Netherlands, but is also found in the UK where the Competition and Markets Authority (2016) conclude in their retail banking market investigation that almost 60% of account holders have been with their main personal current accounts provider for more than ten years. In addition, banks are aware of this. Given that current and checking accounts often act as "gateway" products for the sale of other banking products (i.e. after opening up a current account one is more likely to take out other bank products as well), this product is very important to banks. A major stumbling block for most customers is the time and effort it takes to arrange a switch. Beyond opening and closing an account, one also needs to inform other stakeholders if the account number changes (as is usually the case). A solution to this last barrier would be number portability, which means that one can retain the same account number when switching banks. A 2015 report by the Financial Conduct Authority (in the UK) revealed that 35% of consumers and 40% of businesses "would be much more likely or more likely to switch if they had portable account details".

Next to time and effort, trust in the bank and safety of deposits might also be important, as well as loyalty to the bank and feeling at home at the bank.

Inertia is not specific to the consumer market, but is also found in the corporate market. In 2010, the Office of Fair Trading (UK) found low levels of switching among small and medium enterprises (SMEs). More recently, the ACM arrived at the same conclusion when focusing on the Netherlands (2015). The market for SME funding is very concentrated as the market is dominated by three large banks, there are severe barriers to entering the market and the income margin on financing to SMEs has increased in recent years, pointing towards a decrease in competition. As a result, the committee recommends that the government stimulate new entry as well as alternative ways of funding. Moreover, banks should be more transparent about the costs involved in order to simplify comparisons.

In the academic literature we also find work on firms' bank switching behaviour. It is widely believed that private information plays a prominent role in the relationship between banks and its customers. The longer the relationship, the more private information can be gathered and therefore it is believed that customers can be locked in. Ongena and Smith (2001) test this conjecture empirically and find that the probability of a firm terminating the relationship with the bank increases with the duration of the relationship, implying that the value of the relationship declines over time. Hence this finding contradicts the idea of lock-in effects. Gopalan et al. (2007) find a non-monotonic relationship between a firm's informativeness and its propensity to switch banks. They find that the most opaque firms and the most transparent firms are least likely to switch. Ioannidou and Ongena (2010) focus on loan conditions when switching to a new bank. That is, they compare loan conditions of firms that obtain a new loan from both the current (inside) bank and an outside bank. They find, among other things, that a new loan from an outside bank carries an interest rate that is 89 basis points lower than a new loan from the firm's current bank. In addition, the interest rate offered by the outside bank is 87 basis points lower than the interest rate of comparable loans granted to existing customers of the outside bank. The first one and a half year after granting the loan, the interest rate decreases even more, but after this period the interest rate increases and after three to four years the interest rate equals the rate offered by the inside bank.

Conclusion

In this chapter, we have shown that the measurement and the implications of competition in banking are multidimensional. The extent of concentration and competition in the banking sector can be gauged by looking at indicators of the structure of the market on the one hand, and indicators capturing bank behaviour or conduct on the other hand. Examples of the former are the number of banks, the share of assets held by the *n* largest banks or the Hirschman–Herfindahl index. Examples of the latter are the Lerner index, the Panzar-Rosse H-statistic and the recently developed Boone indicator. We document a positive and significant correlation between the various concentration measures, but also show that only one measure of conduct, that is, the Lerner, is positively and significantly related to market structure measures. The H-statistic does not correlate significantly. The market structure measures are more suitable for a cross-market comparison rather than a time series analysis, as the variation over time is rather limited. The Lerner, on the other hand, can be used to analyse both conduct within the same bank or country over time as well as across banks and countries.

Not only is the measurement of concentration and competition in banking multidimensional, but analysing the potential implications is an arduous task as well. When analysing market structure and market power for non-financial firms, one is generally concerned with the implications for consumer pricing and firm efficiency. When it comes to banks and other financial intermediaries, one also needs to take into account that there might be a trade-off between competition and bank risk-taking as well as financial stability. We also discussed the implications for consumer switching behaviour. In other chapters of this book, other aspects are touched upon. In particular, bank competition may have an impact on access to credit and small business financing (Chap. 9), cross-border banking and the banking union (Chaps. 17 and 18). Relatedly, the institutional framework (Chap. 12) or government intervention by means of state aid and guarantees (Chap. 14) may have unintended consequences by affecting the level of competition.

References

Acharya, V.V., Pedersen, L.H., Philippon, T., & Richardson, M.P. (2016). Measuring systemic risk. *Review of Financial Studies*, forthcoming.

Adrian, T., & Brunnermeier, M.K. (2016). *CoVaR, American Economic Review, 106*(7), 1705–1741.

Allen, F., & Gale, D. (2000). *Comparing financial systems*. Cambridge, MA: MIT Press.

Allen, F., & Gale, D. (2004). Competition and financial stability. *Journal of Money, Credit and Banking, 36*(3), 453–480.

Anginer, D., Demirguc-Kunt, A., & Zhu, M. (2014). How does competition affect bank systemic risk? *Journal of Financial Intermediation, 23*(1), 1–26.

Bain, J. S. (1956). *Barriers to new competition: Their character and consequences in manufacturing industries*. Cambridge: Harvard University Press.

Barth, A., & Schnabel, I. (2013). Why banks are not too big to fail – Evidence from the CDS market. *Economic Policy, 28*(74), 335–369.

Beck, T., De Jonghe, O., & Schepens, G. (2013). Banking competition and stability: Cross-country heterogeneity. *Journal of Financial Intermediation, 22*, 218–244.

Berger, A. N., Demirguc-Kunt, A., Levine, R., & Haubrich, J. G. (2004). Bank concentration and competition: An evolution in the making. *Journal of Money, Credit and Banking, 36*(3), 433–451.

Bikker, J. A., & Haaf, K. (2002). Competition, concentration and their relationship: An empirical analysis of the banking industry. *Journal of Banking & Finance, 26*, 2191–2214.

Boone, J. (2008). A new way to measure competition. *The Economic Journal, 118*(531), 1245–1261.

Boot, A.W. A., & Ratnovski, L. (2016). Banking and trading. *Review of Finance, 20*(6), 2219–2246.

Boot, A. W. A., & Thakor, A. V. (1993). Self-interested bank regulation. *The American Economic Review, 83*(2), 206–212.

Boyd, J. H., & De Nicolo, G. (2005). The theory of bank risk taking and competition revisited. *Journal of Finance, 60*(3), 1329–1343.

Boyd, J. H., & Runkle, D. E. (1993). Size and performance of banking firms: Testing the predictions of theory. *Journal of Monetary Economics, 31*(1), 47–67.

Brunetti, M., Ciciretti, R., & Djordjevic, Lj. (2016). *The determinants of household's bank switching. Journal of Financial Stability, 26*, 175–189

Brunnermeier, M.K., Dong, G.N., & Palia, D. (2012). *Banks' non-interest income and systemic risk.* AFA 2012 Chicago meetings paper.

Bulow, J., & Klemperer, P. (2002). Prices and the winner's curse. *The RAND Journal of Economics, 33*(1), 1–21.

Carbó, S., Humphrey, D., Maudos, J., & Molyneux, P. (2009). *Cross-country comparisons of competition and pricing power in European banking. Journal of International Money and Finance, 28*(1), 115–134.

Carletti, E., & Leonello, A. (2013). *Credit market competition and liquidity crises.* CEPR discussion paper No. DP9311.

Chakravarty, S., Feinberg, R., & Rhee, E.-Y. (2004). Relationship and individuals' bank switching behaviour. *Journal of Economic Psychology, 25*, 507–527.

Claessens, S., & Laeven, L. (2004). What drives bank competition? Some international evidence. *Journal of Money, Credit and Banking, 36*, 563–583.

Competition and Markets Authority. (2016). *Retail banking market investigation: Final report.* https://assets.publishing.service.gov.uk/media/57ac9667e5274a0f6c00007a/retail-banking-market-investigation-full-final-report.pdf

De Bandt, O., & Davis, E. P. (2000). Competition, contestability and market structure in European banking sectors on the eve of EMU. *Journal of Banking & Finance, 24*, 1045–1066.

De Jonghe, O. (2010). Back to the basics in banking? A micro-analysis of banking system stability. *Journal of Financial Intermediation, 19*(3), 387–417.

De Jonghe, O., Diepstraten, M., & Schepens, G. (2015). Banks' size, scope and systemic risk: What role for conflicts of interest? *Journal of Banking and Finance, 61*, S3–S13.

Demirguc-Kunt, A., & Huizinga, H. (2013). Are banks too big to fail or too big to save? International evidence from equity prices and CDS spreads. *Journal of Banking & Finance, 37*(3), 875–894.

Demsetz, H. (1973). Industry structure, market rivalry, and public policy. *The Journal of Law & Economics, 16*(1), 1–9.

Engle, R.F., Moshirian, F., Sahgal, S., & Zhang, B. (2014). *Banks non-interest income and global financial stability.* Centre for International Finance and Regulation WP 015/2014.

Fahlenbrach, R., Prilmeier, R., & Stulz, R. M. (2012). This time is the same: Using bank performance in 1998 to explain bank performance during the recent financial crisis. *The Journal of Finance, 67*(6), 2139–2185.

Financial Conduct Authority. (2015). *Making current account switching easier: The effectiveness of the Current Account Switch Service (CASS) and evidence on account number portability*.

Forssbaeck, J., & Shehzad, C. T. (2015). The conditional effects of market power on bank risk – Cross-country evidence. *Review of Finance, 19*, 1997–2038.

Freixas, X., & Ma, K. (2014). *Banking competition and stability: The role of leverage*. CentER discussion paper series No. 2014-048 and European Banking Center discussion paper series No. 2014-009.

Gopalan, R., Udell, G.F., & Yerramilli, V. (2007). *Why do firms switch banks*? AFA 2008 New Orleans meetings paper.

Hakenes, H., & Schnabel, I. (2011). Capital regulation, bank competition, and financial stability. *Economics Letters, 113*(3), 256–258.

Ibragimov, D., Jaffee, J., & Walden, J. (2011). Diversification disasters. *Journal of Financial Economics, 99*(2), 333–348.

Ioannidou, V., & Ongena, S. (2010). "Time for a change": Loan conditions and bank behaviour when firms switch banks. *The Journal of Finance, 65*(5), 1847–1877.

Keeley, M. C. (1990). Deposit insurance, risk, and market power in banking. *The American Economic Review, 80*(5), 1183–1200.

Kiser, E. K. (2002). Predicting household switching behaviour and switching cost at depository institutions. *Review of Industrial Organization, 20*, 349–365.

Lerner, A. P. (1934). The concept of monopoly and the measurement of monopoly power. *The Review of Economic Studies, 1*(3), 157–175.

Liu, H., Molyneux, P., & Wilson, J.O.S. (2010). *Measuring competition and stability: Recent evidence for European banking*. BBSWP/10/020.

Liu, H., Molyneux, P., & Wilson, J. O. S. (2013a). Competition and stability in European banking: A regional analysis. *The Manchester School, 81*(2), 176–201.

Liu, H., Molyneux, P., & Wilson, J. O. S. (2013b). Competition in banking: Measurement and interpretation. In A. R. Bell, C. Brooks, & M. Prokopczuk (Eds.), *Handbook of research methods and applications in empirical finance* (pp. 197–215). Northampton: Edward Elgar Publishing.

Marcus, A. J. (1984). Deregulation and bank financial policy. *Journal of Banking & Finance, 8*(4), 557–565.

Martinez-Miera, D., & Repullo, R. (2010). Does competition reduce the risk of bank failure? *Review of Financial Studies, 23*(10), 3638–3664.

Maudos, J., & de Guevara, J. F. (2007). The cost of market power in banking: Social welfare loss vs. cost inefficiency. *Journal of Banking & Finance, 31*, 2103–2125.

Netherlands Authority for Consumers and Markets. (2014). *Barriers to entry into the Dutch retail banking sector*. https://www.acm.nl/en/publications/publication/13257/Barriers-to-entry-into-the-Dutch-retail-banking-sector/

Ongena, S., & Smith, D. C. (2001). The duration of bank relationships. *Journal of Financial Economics, 61*, 449–475.

Panzar, J. C., & Rosse, J. N. (1987). Testing for "monopoly" equilibrium. *The Journal of Industrial Economics, 35*(4), 443–456.

Peltzman, S. (1977). The gains and losses from industrial concentration. *The Journal of Law & Economics, 20*(2), 229–263.

Roy, A. D. (1952). Safety first and the holding of assets. *Econometrica, 20*(3), 431–449.

Saunders, A., & Cornett, M. M. (2014). *Financial institutions management: A risk management approach* (8th ed.). New York: McGraw-Hill.

Schaeck, K., & Cihák, M. (2012). Banking competition and capital ratios. *European Financial Management, 18*(5), 836–866.

Schaeck, K., & Cihák, M. (2014). Competition, efficiency, and stability in banking. *Financial Management, 43*(1), 215–241.

Schiersch, A., & Schmidt-Ehmcke, J. (2011). Is the Boone-Indicator applicable?—Evidence from a combined data set of German manufacturing enterprise. *Jahrbücher für Nationalökonomie und Statistiek, 231*(3), 336–357.

Stiglitz, J. E. (1987). Competition and the number of firms in a market: Are duopolies more competitive than atomistic markets? *Journal of Political Economcy, 95*(5), 1041–1061.

Stiglitz, J. E. (1989). Imperfect information in the product market. *Handbook of Industrial Organization, 1*, 769–847.

Van der Cruijsen, C., & Diepstraten, M. (2015). *Banking products: You can take them with you, so why don't you?* De Nederlandsche Bank working paper No. 490.

Van Leuvensteijn, M., Bikker, J. A., van Rixtel, A. A. R. J. M., & Kok Sorensen, C. (2011). A new approach to measuring competition in the loan markets of the euro area. *Applied Economics, 43*(23), 3155–3167.

Wagner, W. (2010). Diversification at financial institutions and systemic crisis. *Journal of Financial Intermediation, 19*(3), 373–386.

Weill, L. (2013). Bank competition in the EU: How has it evolved? *Journal of International Financial Markets, Institutions and Money, 26*, 100–112.

9

The Internet, Crowdfunding and the Banking Industry

Armin Schwienbacher

Introduction

In the early 2000s, a few researchers were interested in whether and how the Internet would affect financial markets (Economides 2001; Claessens et al. 2002). At the time, Claessens et al. (2002) identified the arrival of different providers of financial services, such as pure online banks, online lenders, aggregators, online brokers, financial portals, enablers and providers of e-payment services. Today, well-established, Internet-enabled service providers exist for each of these functions and directly compete with traditional banks. Similarly, new functions have appeared on the Internet, notably due to the rise of social networks, which facilitate horizontal communications even more among individual economic players, including depositors, investors and borrowers. In the past few years, large amounts of capital have been invested in "fintech" ventures to develop solutions for the financial industry of the future (Arner et al. 2015). This recent surge in investments is likely to accelerate the impact of Internet-enabled solutions on the traditional financial industry players. Moreover, it is likely to expand the range of available services and solutions in the future.

One of the first occasions the banking industry made use of the Internet was the adoption of Internet banking, in which banks began offering their clients

A. Schwienbacher (✉)
SKEMA Business School, Avenue Willy Brandt, Euralille 59777, France
e-mail: armin.schwienbacher@skema.edu

T. Beck, B. Casu (eds.), *The Palgrave Handbook of European Banking*,
DOI 10.1057/978-1-137-52144-6_9

the ability to carry out their banking operations online at any time of the day. While this innovation affected the structure of banks and their need for local subsidiaries, these services did not require social media, so Internet banking was developed before most other activities related to the Internet. Although researchers have investigated whether Internet banking helped banks improve their performance (see e.g. Lin et al. 2011), the focus of this chapter is on the latest wave of impacts, notably through the emergence of social media, which has facilitated communications even more between end users of the Internet and thereby also affected other forms of banking activities.

In terms of market structure, the reduction in search costs due to use of the Internet has led to the entry of new players, generated more competition among incumbents (including established banks) and reduced the need for intermediation (Lenz 2015). The impact of the Internet on the banking industry is also a result of network effects (Economides 2001), as the Internet enables the creation of large networks of individuals who can be contacted directly. Network effects generate gains that increase with the number of users: the more users there are, the larger are the gains of a network (Easley and Kleinberg 2010; Belleflamme et al. 2015). The impact may even become non-linear, in that network effects may disrupt existing markets if networks become sufficiently large. Indeed, the disappearance of transaction costs and other barriers often gives significant benefits to actors that have competitive advantages, even if these advantages are small. Thus, the Internet has become a powerful tool to connect a large number of buyers and sellers at almost no cost and, thereby, to create new, large marketplaces (Einav et al. 2015). This situation, in turn, makes it difficult for local "champions" to survive in a global, well-connected economy. At the same time, greater collaboration and a broader range of offers that target more tailored needs and preferences may arise, as global solutions tend to be standardized as a way to benefit from scale economies and thus offer solutions and services at lower costs. A good example of increased collaboration among decentralized individuals is the phenomenon of crowdsourcing, a concept introduced and defined by Howe (2008) as "the act of taking a task once performed by an employee and outsourcing it to a large, undefined group of people external to the company in the form of an open call" (Bayus 2013, p. 226). Community members (e.g. dispersed non-experts or consumers) can then propose ideas or comment on those of others. Some of these crowdsourcing ideas are organized as a one-shot contest, others as a continuous event that promotes collaboration over a longer period. Crowdfunding can also be regarded as belonging to this phenomenon, in which the contribution of the crowd is in the form of financing (Schwienbacher and Larralde 2012).

This chapter discusses some of the aforementioned issues that are at the crossroads between the Internet and banking. Note, however, that it does not cover all the topics, even though many others likely deserve equal coverage. One reason is that many of these topics are still poorly covered by researchers, as we discuss later in this chapter. The topics covered here are those for which academic research is available, at least partially. This chapter focuses on the impact of the Internet on the banking industry. As the topic is still very broad and the available space limited, only a select number of more specific themes are covered. The section "The Internet, Network Effects and the Horizontalization of Organizations" discusses network effects and the horizontalization of established organizations and communications that arise from the Internet and social media, and how such horizontalization may ultimately affect market structure. The section "Loan-Based Crowdfunding, Peer-to-Peer Lending and the Banking Industry" covers the main theme of the chapter, namely loan-based crowdfunding and peer-to-peer lending. This new form of corporate finance for smaller businesses is likely to affect banks' core activities in several ways, some of which have already been studied in recent years. The section "Related Issues" discusses a few other topics related to the Internet and the banking industry that have attracted attention among researchers and for which data have become available. "Concluding Remarks" draws the chapter to a close.

The Internet, Network Effects and the Horizontalization of Organizations

According to Mishkin (1995), banks play an important role as financial intermediaries if they possess either technologies to reduce transaction costs (notably through scale economies) or informational advantages, such that they are able to mitigate adverse selection and moral hazard problems of borrowers. In such cases, banks are better able to play a crucial role in allocating financial resources to firms and, in doing so, to promote economic growth more efficiently. Similarly, Freixas and Rochet (2008) describe four main functions of banks: offer liquidity and payment services, transform assets, manage risks, and process information and monitor borrowers. New players have entered the market through the Internet and begun offering services that directly compete with traditional banks, with the latter acting as incumbents. These players typically offer only one specific function, such as payment services (e.g. PayPal). In addition, these newcomers face no cannibalization effects, in contrast with traditional banks, for which offering similar services on the

Internet negatively affects their offline activities. This can create comparative advantages to newcomers and reshape existing markets profoundly.

Economides (2001, p. 8) offers a useful definition of the Internet in the context of financial markets: "The Internet is a multi-purpose, multi-point digital interactive worldwide telecommunications network. By its nature, the Internet facilitates multi-point information flows and all the processes that are based on information flows." As this definition emphasizes information flows, it is directly linked to the very nature of financial markets and the role of financial intermediaries in modern finance. Financial transactions are based on the exchange of information. Therefore, it becomes apparent that the Internet significantly affects the banking industry and financial markets in general. The market structure may also be affected through price competition in standardized goods and services that may have existed before because of, for example, geographical barriers.

Because the Internet operates as a network that directly connects a very large number of participants (Easley and Kleinberg 2010), the economic outcome tends to generate a few large players for which even small advantages are magnified, leaving very small market shares for others. In other words, we are likely to end up with "winners-take-most" situations (Economides 2001). Network effects lead to collective gains from using new technologies, which increase when the number of users grows. Eventually, these may even lead to the disruption of existing markets, as we have experienced in many other, non-financial markets that have incorporated the Internet into their business models. Even absent major disruptions, small differences between providers of financial services may generate large market shifts, as the large number of participants connected through the Internet can easily shift their demands for such services quickly. For example, Economides (2001, p. 9) argues that "small advantages tend to be magnified [...] as the Internet smoothes out flows and removes frictions that used to support early egalitarian market structures". In contrast, transaction costs that exist in the absence of the Internet generate either local monopolists or limited competition. According to several recent studies (Philippon 2015; Hanson et al. 2015), financial intermediation costs banks 2–3 % of assets. The Internet could enable new market players to enter the market if they can offer better, quicker services or similar services at lower costs. In that case, they may force banks to give up market share or adapt to new entrants.

According to Economides (2001), the impact of the Internet on financial markets is threefold: it (1) enhances information flows, leading to greater and quicker information transfers; (2) facilitates direct interactions among economic agents; and (3) gives economic agents access to more markets. One major challenge is that the Internet crosses national borders, which makes it difficult for national regulators to retain oversight. An illustrative example is crowdfunding, in which startups in Europe are now raising funds across borders where regulation offers more opportunities and flexibility. Eventually, this may lead to regulatory arbitrage in the absence of regulatory harmonization at the European Union level, as the existence of different national regulations is an impediment to achieving a level playing field in Europe. Whether regulatory arbitrage is good or bad in this context is an open question. However, this concern was also raised by the European Banking Authority (European Banking Authority 2015) in connection with lending-based crowdfunding, in which little is harmonized at the European Union level. But similar trends are likely to arise for other financial services provided on the Internet. While earlier technological innovations created network effects and affected the financial industries (including the telephone and fax machine), the Internet brings the scope of networking to the next level (Economides 2001), as it creates a global network in which information can be exchanged virtually instantaneously, giving more economic agents access to any available market on Earth.

Information technologies enable the processing of information in a decentralized way, providing new benefits to more flexible and horizontal organizations. Rifkin (2014) conjectures an important shift in paradigm, with economies and society as a whole, through the Internet and especially the Internet of Things, moving toward collaborative commons in which individuals collaborate. The main underlying source of this shift, according to the author, is that through the Internet, society is approaching near-zero marginal costs of many of the services and goods that society is demanding. Whether this extreme prediction will truly occur is still an open question, but certainly the marginal costs of many goods and services, including financial ones, have drastically decreased since the adoption of the Internet, and the Internet of Things (which we discuss later in this chapter) is likely to induce a further shift toward even lower marginal costs. As Rifkin convincingly argues, hierarchical organizations become less important through the Internet, as individuals can more easily communicate with each other directly. This, in turn, affects their capacity to decide on their own what is best for them, including which entrepreneurial project or firm they wish to sponsor. Moreover, the Internet, and especially Web 2.0, has made participation easier and more multidimensional for individuals, by allowing them to post comments, share opinions on blogs and elsewhere, and even transfer money. Therefore, new forms of collaboration have emerged, such as the sharing economy (Airbnb and Uber are striking examples), crowdsourcing and crowdfunding (discussed subsequently).[1]

[1] This shift also creates problems (Rifkin 2014), which we do not directly discuss here, including the increased risk of individualism becoming more important (decisions based on Pareto efficiency, not wel-

An important distinction between network-enabled transactions and banks is that the former typically rely on spot transactions (Einav et al. 2015), while banks typically rely on relationship building in which individual information is collected over time to overcome information asymmetries (Boot and Thakor 2000). Matching on networks relies instead on mechanisms such as auctions or first-come, first-served mechanisms. They also rely more on reputation and feedback effects to solve informational issues (Einav et al. 2015) than ex ante screening and certification. The crowd is responsible for screening lending opportunities, analysing the information disclosed by borrowers and collecting extra information on borrowers.

The Internet also allows providers of online services to capture financial benefits in other ways that banks cannot, so they are able to offer some services at much lower prices or even for free. For example, online service providers can earn additional revenues from advertisements shown when individuals visit their website and even broker information on individual behaviour (Lambrecht et al. 2014). Similarly, individuals interested in online services may pay in money (as in banks that charge fees), personal information or time. Banks that meet clients personally cannot collect the same type of information.

As a global network that facilitates information flows, the Internet can induce changes that are likely to profoundly affect existing markets (Economides 2001) and lead to the emergence of new service providers but also the elimination of some intermediaries (because direct channels are now created and transaction-specific information can be made available through the Internet). One of these is crowdfunding, which we discuss in the section titled "Loan-Based Crowdfunding, Peer-to-Peer Lending and the Banking Industry". Crowdfunding, as it has developed in recent years, could only have emerged from the Internet, which made it possible for individuals and small firms to reach a large audience at virtually no transaction costs (Belleflamme et al. 2015; Schwienbacher 2015).

Loan-Based Crowdfunding, Peer-to-Peer Lending and the Banking Industry

Some online social networks on the Internet have evolved in recent years to become Internet-based two-sided markets, with potential network effects on both sides of the market (Belleflamme et al. 2015; Morse 2015). One strik-

fare efficiency) and unstable coalitions/collaborations among individuals, because collaborations are more often project-specific.

ing example in finance is crowdfunding, in which many small individuals (the "crowd") pool their monetary contributions to fund the projects of an individual or even a company. The crowd may then receive some compensation in return for its contribution. This compensation may take the form of interest (in which case it is called "crowdlending", "loan-based crowdfunding" or, for consumer loans, "peer-to-peer lending"), dividends and capital gains (also called "crowd-investing", "investment-based crowdfunding" or "equity crowdfunding"), the good generated by the production of the project ("reward-based crowdfunding") or nothing more than a thank you ("donation-based crowdfunding"). Several studies discuss differences between these forms of crowdfunding, including Agrawal et al. (2013), Belleflamme et al. (2015) and Schwienbacher and Larralde (2012). As these studies show, the different forms need to be examined separately because crowd participation is based on distinct incentives, and the requests for funding are fundamentally different among the types of crowdfunding. In this section, we primarily focus on lending-based crowdfunding because it is closely related to the primary business activities of banks.

Lending-based crowdfunding (or loan-based crowdfunding) is broader than peer-to-peer lending, which involves individuals lending to other individuals and thus primarily involves consumer finance. In contrast, lending-based crowdfunding also includes peer-to-business lending (European Banking Authority 2015; Colaert 2016). Thus, lending-based crowdfunding involves the financing of small businesses that raise money from the crowd instead of traditional lenders such as commercial banks. The matching between borrowers and lenders occurs on online platforms that act as intermediaries between the two groups. Borrowers advertise their financing needs on the platform, where lenders can compare the different investment opportunities and decide whether to invest. Crowdfunding campaigns typically last a few weeks, unless the borrower can raise the necessary money before the end and decides to close the fundraising campaign. Platforms are generally remunerated, based on successful closing and (sometimes) servicing of loans or investments. Platforms typically organize the fundraising as either an "all-or-nothing" or a "keep-it-all" funding model (Cumming et al. 2015). In the first case, the borrower only receives pledged money if a pre-specified minimum is achieved; in the second case, the borrower receives any pledged money even if the pre-specified minimum is not achieved. Cumming et al. (2015) show that the all-or-nothing model can serve as a costly signal mechanism because lenders commit not to undertake the project if insufficiently funded. In contrast, the crowd bears higher risks that the project may fail under the keep-it-all model, as the project may be undertaken even if the desired funding is not achieved. If the project fails, the crowd is left with nothing.

In this form of dis-intermediated financing, the crowd gets to decide how financial resources are allocated in the economy (i.e. which projects should receive funding) (Mollick and Nanda 2014), so that banks no longer play the intermediary role of channelling financial resources of individuals (depositors) to financing investments. However, crowdfunders are responsible for collecting information and making their own financing decisions. Iyer et al. (2010) show that on peer-to-peer lending platforms, lenders use a broad range of quantitative and qualitative information to assess borrowers' creditworthiness.

Platforms generally offer their own risk assessment based on their internally developed risk model. One possible reason for the attractiveness of these platforms to borrowers is their simplicity, particularly in light of the often-used, complex teaser rates and hidden fees charged by banks. Although teaser rates and various fees may follow specific economic rationales, they add costs and risks to borrowers. Rates charged on lending-based crowdfunding platforms are often determined by auctions, so that the most attractive projects may obtain very low rates.

The few studies that have examined crowdfunding have mostly focused on reward-based crowdfunding. There is, however, a more developed literature on online peer-to-peer lending, including Duarte et al. (2012), Freedman and Jin (2014), Herzenstein et al. (2011), Hildebrand et al. (2014), Michels (2012) and Lin et al. (2013). Such peer-to-peer lending has found especially significant growth in consumer lending and funding of social projects. For consumer lending, individuals often refinance their existing loans held by traditional banks by raising the money on online platforms, such as Lending Club and Prosper. Other individuals raise new funds instead. According to Fitch Ratings (Morse 2015), the five largest peer-to-peer platforms in the United States originated $3.5 billion of new loans in 2013. Furthermore, the market is expected to grow to $114 billion a few years from now, according to Fitch Ratings.

Loan-based crowdfunding is regulated differently by national financial authorities across countries. In Europe, the development of such platforms has been difficult because banks often enjoy a monopoly as a result of the regulation in place. This explains why there are still no platforms in some countries such as Austria and Belgium. For example, peer-to-peer lending remains problematic in Belgium because of a specific Belgian bank law (Colaert 2016) that prohibits candidate-borrowers from seeking funds from more than 50 people. Moreover, platforms' use of a broad range of business models creates great complexity in the applicability of current regulations (European Banking Authority 2015). While some business models only require compliance with a small set of regulations, others require specific bank licences and compliance with a broad range of regulations (including on capital requirements, payment services, consumer and mortgage credit, electronic money and anti-money laundering; for a comprehensive discussion, see European Banking Authority 2015). France has recently lifted the monopoly of banks as a way to facilitate loan-based crowdfunding, authorizing people to invest directly up to €1,000 per project. However, project initiators need to comply with specific information disclosure requirements by providing pre-specified documentation.

From an economic and financial perspective, a crucial question is whether the crowd has certain advantages over traditional lenders such as commercial banks. The latter generally use screening mechanisms to sort out bad borrowers and, thus, to improve the average quality of borrowers. Similarly, banks may have accumulated experience and proprietary knowledge that give them a comparative advantage over less informed individuals. As such, crowdlending may be perceived as arm's-length finance, similar in spirit to capital markets (Allen and Gale 1999). Because of these benefits, different studies therefore argue that bad borrowers will seek crowdfunding that appears to be populated, as the argument goes, by unsophisticated individuals (Griffin 2012; Hazen 2012; Hildebrand et al. 2014; Mollick 2014). According to traditional economic and finance theory, the emergence of crowdfunding is at first glance not obvious (Agrawal et al. 2013). What, then, are the advantages of crowdfunding over banks? One benefit is reduced operating risks (Schwienbacher 2015). Borrowers can reduce their operating risks by setting the pre-specified minimum in an all-or-nothing funding model at what they would need to cover their fixed costs. In this case, the value of running the campaign resembles a call option, as the project would be discontinued in the absence of sufficient positive feedback from backers who are also likely to be consumers. This explains why a crowdfunding campaign may also be considered a marketing campaign and market feasibility study.

Another possible reason is that the crowd may be wiser than experts, at least in certain areas. Crowdfunding involves the aggregation of information (or preferences, depending on the type of crowdfunding; Schwienbacher 2015) held by a large number of individuals. Hakenes and Schlegel (2014) show that under certain conditions, an unsophisticated crowd may do better than an expert, because the commitment of each individual may result in better information. Mollick and Nanda (2014) compare funding decisions of art projects made on Kickstarter and evaluations of a panel of experts; they find no significant quantitative or qualitative differences between crowdfunders and experts, suggesting that experts are not better than the crowd for projects in which personal preferences matter. Whether similar conclusions can be drawn for investment opportunities such as crowdlending or crowdinvesting remains to be tested. Sociologists have long assessed differences between individual and collective decisions, showing that collective decisions may be better in some situations but worse in other situations (for a comprehensive overview, see Larrick et al. 2011). In their study on collective outcomes and social media, Chen et al. (2014) show that comments on stocks provided by retail investors on social media offer good predictions of future stock returns and earnings surprises.

Similarly, Larrick et al. (2011) note that combining judgements of many helps cancel out outliers or errors or, as they write, smooth "the rough edges to isolate the collective's view of the truth". Sociologists have long been interested in examining differences between decisions made by a crowd and those made by a single person (Zhang and Liu 2012; Lyon and Pacuit 2013). Lyon and Pacuit (2013) explore how individual information can be aggregated to obtain a collective output. Different forms of information aggregation may, however, lead to different outcomes (see Surowiecki 2004).

Whether a single person is wiser than a crowd depends on the degree of expertise of that person and the diversity of the crowd (Larrick et al. 2011). Firstly, expertise in the needed field generally helps achieve a better outcome more quickly, as then a collective decision may arise with a smaller number of individuals. In contrast, a complete lack of knowledge would be similar to tossing a coin. Secondly, greater diversity allows more perspectives to be taken into account. The way the crowd is sampled is therefore crucial. Differences in perspective are likely to arise when each member of the crowd first thinks independently and then, only afterward, shares his or her analysis with others (Larrick et al. 2011). In other instances, crowd decisions may lead to biases such as herding behaviour, anchoring effects, bias against the minority and the creation of bubbles (Zhang and Liu 2012; Lyon and Pacuit 2013), all of which are well documented in financial markets. Crowdfunding is likely to be exposed to these biases as much as financial markets and perhaps even more so if the crowd lacks sufficient financial knowledge to make sound investments. Whenever they occur, these effects may impair the crowd's capacity to collectively decide wisely. Relatedly, Mannes (2009) offers results on how individuals revise their own beliefs, indicating that crowds have a stronger impact than individuals. It is also not clear whether the crowd is best at predicting the "next big thing", which is difficult to predict even with distinct knowledge (Denrell and Fang 2010).

While crowdfunding remains a small market, it has been growing significantly in recent years, achieving impressive growth rates and becoming a serious market in which traditional intermediaries, such as venture capitalists, banks and other financial institutions, become interested. In the United States, Prosper, one of the leading peer-to-peer lending platforms, has enabled $5 billion of borrowing from more than two million lenders since its start in 2006.[2] According to Prosper's statistics, for all loans originated between July 2009 and November 2013 (67,290 loans), the average rate of return was 9.33 %, with an actual loss rate of 6.62 %.[3] Another example is Lending Club, also started in 2006, through which more than $13.4 billion in loans have already originated.[4] Average rates of return are similar to those reported by Prosper. However, whether individual investors can actually achieve that return is unclear. These high rates may merely be the result of information asymmetry in the market, similar to the initial public offering (IPO) market, such that under-pricing (or higher rates in the case of loan-based crowdfunding) is necessary to induce less informed individuals to participate. Indeed, it is well documented that IPO issuances are significantly under-priced, even on NASDAQ and NYSE, such that the average first-day return on any IPO issuance is remarkably high. For example, the average first-day return of all the IPOs on NASDAQ, NYSE and AMEX during the 1980–2003 period was 18.7 % (Loughran and Ritter 2004). While several theories can help explain this remarkable first-day return, a well-known explanation is that a high return is required to ensure the participation of uninformed investors who cannot determine which issuances are good and bad (Rock 1986). In contrast, better informed investors strategically only participate in good issuances, and participation in good issuances then becomes more difficult than in bad issuances. A high under-pricing helps uninformed investors cover their losses. The same rationale may be at play in loan-based crowdfunding platforms, meaning that the true return that the uninformed crowds really achieve is much lower than the rate advertised by the platform, as they can easily participate in bad loans but hardly in good loans (due to over-subscriptions). Whether this is the case is an interesting research question to investigate.

From a macroeconomic perspective, crowdfunding and peer-to-peer lending platforms also differ from commercial banks in a very important way. While banks are highly interconnected and thus prone to systemic risk, platforms exhibit no interconnections (Lenz 2015). Systemic risk occurs when there is a risk that intermediaries are linked (e.g. through inter-bank loans in the case of banks), in that risk may spill over to other intermediaries. However, crowdfunding is dis-intermediated, and platforms themselves are not connected through liabilities. A platform that becomes insolvent spreads the losses across its own platform users but not to other platforms. As Lenz (2015) notes, "while banks accumulate risks, platforms decentralise the risks". This distinction implies that crowdfunding is risky for the crowd, while platforms only act as intermediaries that match borrowers and lenders.

[2] Source: https://www.prosper.com/ (last viewed: 30 October 2015).

[3] Source: https://www.prosper.com/invest/marketplace-performance (last viewed: 30 September 2015).

[4] Source: https://www.lendingclub.com/ (last viewed: 30 October 2015).

Further Issues

Many other topics related to the impact of the Internet and social media on the banking sector are important, because many more new types of service providers have appeared that either compete directly with banks and other financial intermediaries or offer new services. While we cannot cover them extensively in this chapter, we nevertheless briefly introduce two of these topics here to highlight key research questions that have recently been addressed.

The Rise of Digital Currencies

One important topic is the emergence of new forms of payment, one of which is digital currencies (also called "cyber-currencies"). These currencies are traded on online platforms, which makes them possible payment systems, though different from services such as PayPal. Legal scholars have begun investigating regulatory issues related to digital currencies (Turpin 2014; Marian 2015), highlighting the fact that these are not issued by a central bank or government and thus remain largely unregulated. Similar to "regular" currencies issued by central banks, digital currencies are often also fiat money. The most well-known digital currency is the Bitcoin, which made its first appearance in 2009 (Mittal 2012), in which monetary creation occurs through "mining" by individuals who support the operating network (Turpin 2014). This makes Bitcoin a fully decentralized currency, such that those who request transactions enable rewarding miners through the creation of new Bitcoins. These rewards can be viewed as transaction costs (as these extra Bitcoins are awarded for free to miners) that are borne collectively by everyone who holds Bitcoins (since they get diluted). Transfers can be done simply through the Internet, without relying on banks or having a bank account. Thus, if digital currencies become more widely used over time, they will directly affect banking activities in several ways, as these currencies enable payments through an encrypted online communication protocol, thereby bypassing current payment systems that are supported by banks.

Digital currencies have not attracted much research attention so far. One exception is the work by Yermack (2014), who argues that Bitcoins more closely resemble speculative investments in a currency, given their high volatility and very low volume. These properties make Bitcoins unattractive as a substitute for existing currencies issued by central banks and used as primary currency units by traditional financial institutions.

Bitcoin trading platforms themselves do not generate loans in the way that banks do (Lenz 2015), as they play no immediate role in lending available money. Therefore, they do not facilitate the circulation of money through loans as banks do. Indeed, Bitcoins are exchanged and traded. They are not kept in accounts of financial intermediaries that can then lend that money to others but are held in individual "digital wallets", conferring an equity-like investment asset instead of a safe asset (cash is typically considered a safe asset in finance).

Big Data, Internet of Things and the Banking Industry

Massive amounts of data can be collected online in different forms and from different sources, such as from actual transactions, web data trails and cookies, contents of e-mail exchanges, videos and photos posted on websites and Facebook, search queries conducted on search engines, health records collected through mobile apps and social networking activities (Geslevich-Packin and Lev-Aretz 2015). Much of this information is potentially relevant to financial service providers, and many of the fintech ventures that have received funding in recent years aim to develop data-driven solutions for the financial industry (Arner et al. 2015). The next step toward increased connectivity and network effects arises with the Internet of Things, which connects "things" with each other, allowing anything to exchange information with any other "thing" through small, embedded sensors. For example, connected home appliances may provide valuable information about future purchases of consumer products and services but also enable financial institutions and insurance companies to improve the precision of risk profiles of individuals. Therefore, the Internet of Things will generate even more big data, enabling better predictions about future needs and optimized offers of services, including financial services (for examples, see Geslevich-Packin and Lev-Aretz 2015).

Eventually, by accessing individual profiles, firms and banks can make offers with individualized prices and thereby price discriminate, reducing competition. Geslevich-Packin and Lev-Aretz (2015) argue that data collected by online and mobile companies, including Google, Amazon.com, Apple, Facebook and Twitter, will be used in the future for the provision of financial services, either by existing players in the financial market or by the companies that collect the data themselves (e.g. Google, with its transfer payment service Google Wallet). The collection of proprietary information on their subscribers may grant these firms substantial informational advantages.

The increased collection of risk-relevant information of borrowers may affect how risk of loan borrowers is assessed. Einav et al. (2013) document how the automation of credit scorings affects pricing of consumer loans in a given auto finance company. The availability of more individual-based information and the capacity to store and process the information have enabled the use of data-driven econometric models to better assess prices and risk of borrowers. Overall, the authors find an improvement in the risk classification of borrowers (through better screening) and enhanced profitability for lenders. The arrival of big data and the Internet of Things is likely to bring automation of individual-based data to the next level of sophistication, including for the provision of financial investment advice.

Concluding Remarks

This area of research is still developing, and we expect it to grow exponentially in the next few years, following the growth rates of these new financial markets. Many of the studies discussed in this chapter are still at the working paper stage. As this review of the literature has shown, broad areas of research still need to be addressed. Further research is clearly required to assess the true impact of the Internet on banks, but also to understand the opportunities for banks to become active players and collaborate with newcomers to shape the financial markets of the future.

Internet-enabled financial products and services have the ability to disrupt many activities that traditional banks currently provide. Even insurance companies and asset management companies face competitive threats from fintechs, which develop solutions to help customers more easily compare products and provide data-driven advice for asset management services (so-called algo-banking and robo-advisers). These dramatic changes will offer further opportunities for research in those areas. Therefore, the topics covered in this chapter are likely to be active research areas in the coming years.

References

Agrawal, A. K., Catalini, C., & Goldfarb, A. (2013). *Some simple economics of crowdfunding* (NBER working paper 19133). Available at NBER: http://www.nber.org/papers/w19133

Allen, F., & Gale, D. (1999). *Comparing financial systems*. Cambridge, MA: MIT Press.

Arner, D. W., Barberis, J., & Buckley, R. P. (2015). *The evolution of FinTech: A new post- crisis paradigm?* (University of Hong Kong Faculty of Law Research Paper No. 2015/047). Available at: http://ssrn.com/abstract=2676553

Bayus, B. L. (2013). Crowdsourcing new product ideas over time: An analysis of the Dell IdeaStorm community. *Management Science, 59*(1), 226–244.

Belleflamme, P., Omrani, N., & Peitz, M. (2015). The economics of crowdfunding platforms. *Information Economics and Policy, 33*, 11–28.

Boot, A., & Thakor, A. V. (2000). Can relationship banking survive competition? *Journal of Finance, 55*(2), 679–713.

Chen, H., De, P., Hu, Y., & Hwang, B.-H. (2014). Wisdom of crowds: The value of stock opinions transmitted through social media. *Review of Financial Studies, 27*(5), 1367–1403.

Claessens, S., Glaessner, T., & Klingebiel, D. (2002). Electronic finance: Reshaping the financial landscape around the world. *Journal of Financial Services Research, 22*(1–2), 29–61.

Colaert, V. (2016). *On the absence of peer-to-peer lending in Belgium*. Available at: http://ssrn.com/abstract=2721645

Cumming, D., Leboeuf, G., & Schwienbacher, A. (2015). *Crowdfunding models: Keep-it-all vs. all-or-nothing*. Available at: http://ssrn.com/abstract=2447567

Denrell, J., & Fang, C. (2010). Predicting the next big thing: Success as a signal of poor judgment. *Management Science, 56*(10), 1653–1667.

Duarte, J., Siegel, S., & Young, L. (2012). Trust and credit: The role of appearance in peer-to-peer lending. *Review of Financial Studies, 25*(8), 2455–2484.

Easley, D., & Kleinberg, J. (2010). *Networks, crowds, and markets: reasoning about a highly connected world*. Cambridge: Cambridge University Press.

Economides, N. (2001). The impact of the internet on financial markets. *Journal of Financial Transformation, 1*(1), 8–13.

Einav, L., Jenkins, M., & Levin, J. (2013). The impact of credit scoring on consumer lending. *RAND Journal of Economics, 44*(2), 249–274.

Einav, L., Farronato, C., & Levin, J. (2015). *Peer-to-peer markets* (NBER Working Paper No. 21496).

European Banking Authority. (2015). *Opinion of the European banking authority on lending-based crowdfunding* (Discussion paper EBA/Op/2015/03).

Freedman, S., & Jin, G. Z. (2014), *The signaling value of online social networks: Lessons from peer-to-peer lending* (Working paper). Available at: http://kuafu.umd.edu/~ginger/research/freedman_jin_networks_submitted_012014.pdf

Freixas, X., & Rochet, J.-C. (2008). *Microeconomics of banking*. Cambridge, MA: MIT Press.

Geslevich-Packin, N., & Lev-Aretz, Y. (2015). *Big data and social netbanks: Are you ready to replace your bank?* (Columbia Law School Public Law & Legal Theory Working Paper No. 14-460).

Griffin, Z. J. (2012). *Crowdfunding: Fleecing the American masses* (Working paper). Available at: http://ssrn.com/abstract=2030001

Hakenes, H., & Schlegel, F. (2014). *Exploiting the financial wisdom of the crowd* (Working paper). Available at: http://ssrn.com/abstract=2475025

Hanson, S. G., Shleifer, A., Stein, J., & Vishny, R. W. (2015). Banks as patient fixed-income investors. *Journal of Financial Economics, 117*(3), 449–469.

Hazen, T. L. (2012). Crowdfunding or fraudfunding? Social networks and the securities laws – why the specially tailored exemption must be conditioned on meaningful disclosure. *North Carolina Law Review, 90*(5), 1735–1770.

Herzenstein, M., Dholakia, U. M., & Andrews, R. L. (2011). Strategic herding behavior in peer-to-peer loan auctions. *Journal of Interactive Marketing, 25*(1), 27–36.

Hildebrand, T., Puri. M., & Rocholl, J. (2014). Adverse incentives in crowdfunding. *Management Science*, forthcoming.

Howe, J. (2008). *Crowdsourcing: Why the power of the crowd is driving the future of business*. New York: Crown Publishing Group.

Iyer, R., Ijaz, A., Erzo, K., Luttmer, F. P., & Shue, K. (2010). *Inferring asset quality: Determining borrower creditworthiness in peer-to-peer lending markets* (Working paper).

Lambrecht, A., Goldfarb, A., Bonatti, A., Ghose, A., Goldstein, D. G., Lewis, R. A., Rao, A., Sahni, N. S., & Yao, S. (2014), *How do firms make money selling digital goods online?* (Rotman School of Management Working Paper No. 2363658).

Larrick, R. P., Mannes, A. E., & Soll, J. B. (2011). The social psychology of the wisdom of crowds. In J. I. Krueger (Ed.), *Frontiers in social psychology: Social judgment and decision making* (pp. 227–242). New York: Psychology Press.

Lenz, R. (2015). *Banking 2025: The bank of the future* (Working paper). Available on SSRN: ssrn.com/abstract=2613155.

Lin, M., Lucas, H. C., & Bailey, J. (2011). *'Banking' on the internet: Does internet banking really improve bank performance?*. Available at SSRN: http://ssrn.com/abstract=1989838

Lin, M., Prabhala, N. R., & Viswanathan, S. (2013). Judging borrowers by the company they keep: Friendship networks and information asymmetry in online peer-to-peer lending. *Management Science, 59*(1), 17–35.

Loughran, T., & Ritter, J. (2004). Why has IPO underpricing changed over time? *Financial Management, Autumn*, 5–37.

Lyon, A., & Pacuit, E. (2013). The wisdom of crowds: Methods of human judgement aggregation. In P. Michelucci (Ed.), *Handbook of human computation* (pp. 599–614). New York: Springer.

Mannes, A. E. (2009). Are we wise about the wisdom of crowds? The use of group judgments in belief revision. *Management Science, 55*(8), 1267–1279.

Marian, O. (2015). A conceptual framework for the regulation of cryptocurrencies. *University of Chicago Law Review, 82*(53), 53–68.

Michels, J. (2012). Do unverifiable disclosures matter? Evidence from peertopeer lending. *Accounting Review, 87*(4), 1385–1413.

Mishkin, F. (1995). *The economics of money, banking, and financial markets*. New York: Harper Collins College Publishers.

Mittal, S. (2012). Is Bitcoin money? Bitcoin and alternate theories of money (Working paper).

Mollick, E. (2014). The dynamics of crowdfunding: An exploratory study. *Journal of Business Venturing, 29*(1), 1–16.

Mollick, E., & Nanda, R. (2014). *Wisdom or madness? Comparing crowds with expert evaluation in funding the arts* (HBS Working Paper 14-116).

Morse, A. (2015). Peer-to-peer crowdfunding: Information and the potential for disruption in consumer lending. *Annual Review of Financial Economics, 7*, 463–482.

Philippon, T. (2015). Has the U.S. finance industry become less efficient? On the theory and measurement of financial intermediation. *American Economic Review, 105*(4), 1408–1438.

Rifkin, J. (2014). *The zero marginal cost society: The internet of things, the collaborative commons, and the eclipse of capitalism*. New York: Palgrave Macmillan.

Rock, K. (1986). Why new issues are underpriced. *Journal of Financial Economics, 15*, 187–212.

Schwienbacher, A. (2015). Financing the business. In T. Baker & F. Welter (Eds.), *Routledge companion on entrepreneurship* (pp. 193–206). New York: Routledge.

Schwienbacher, A., & Larralde, B. (2012). Crowdfunding of small entrepreneurial ventures. In D. Cumming (Ed.), *The Oxford handbook of entrepreneurial finance* (pp. 369–391). New York: Oxford University Press.

Surowiecki, J. (2004). *The wisdom of crowds: Why the many are smarter than the few and how collective wisdom shapes business, economies, societies, and nations*. New York: Doubleday.

Turpin, J. B. (2014). Bitcoin: The economic case for a global, virtual currency operating in an unexplored legal framework. *Indiana Journal of Global Legal Studies, 21*(1), 335–368.

Yermack, D. (2014). *Is Bitcoin a real currency? An economic appraisal* (Working paper). Available on SSRN: http://ssrn.com/abstract=2361599

Zhang, J., & Liu, P. (2012). Rational herding in microloan markets. *Management Science, 58*(5), 892–912.

10

Small Business Lending

Santiago Carbo-Valverde
and Francisco Rodríguez-Fernández

Introduction

Small business lending is at the core of the theory of financial intermediation. This theory relies on the information asymmetries that arise in screening the quality of potential borrowers. These market imperfections are well explained in the seminal contributions of, inter alia, Ramakrishnan and Thakor (1984), Bhattacharya and Thakor (1993) or Allen and Santomero (1998). Even if the nature and determinants of the related moral hazard and adverse selection problems have been revised in different contributions, they have guided a considerable strand of the financial intermediation literature over the past two decades. Specifically, most theoretical models justify the existence of financial intermediaries based on their ability to lower information production costs. In the standard framework, a borrower needs to raise capital from a number of investors, and lenders act as intermediaries to provide this capital. Given the relative informative opaqueness of small and medium-size enterprises (SMEs), they become a particularly illustrative case of asymmetric information problems. Considering the relevance

S. Carbo-Valverde
Bangor Business School, Bangor University, Bangor, UK
e-mail: s.carbo-valverde@bangor.ac.uk

F. Rodríguez-Fernández (✉)
Department of Economics, University of Granada, Granada, Spain
e-mail: franrod@ugr.es

T. Beck, B. Casu (eds.), *The Palgrave Handbook of European Banking*,
DOI 10.1057/978-1-137-52144-6_10

of SMEs in the economic activity and employment of many countries, it is not surprising that many banking studies have paid substantial attention to small business lending over the last 40 years.

Ramakrishnan and Thakor (1984) show that without an intermediating information broker, there would be enormous duplication in information production as each investor attempted to screen each company. This problem becomes even more acute if the number of firms evaluated is particularly large, as is the case with SMEs. In a way, this shortcoming can be solved if specialized intermediaries (banks) certify the firm's economic worth (or the borrower's likelihood of default). Thus, the intermediary is not simply a broker that gathers individual information but an agent that pools information from a large number of applicants to reduce costs and to identify those with greater creditworthiness. The larger the volume of information pooled, the smaller the cost of screening each borrower. As noted by Udell (2015), this modern banking theory has generated a considerable academic interest in SME finance because "it implicitly pointed out that the best place to look for the effect of asymmetric information on financial contracting is likely to be in the SME sector".

In this chapter we analyse small business lending in Europe from both the theoretical and empirical perspectives. We generally refer to SME lending, as most of the literature specifically looks not only to small but also to medium-sized firms as particularly vulnerable in terms of access to external finance.

There are a limited number of overview papers on SME finance. Notable examples are Beck et al. (2013), Berger and Udell (1998, 2002, 2006) and Udell (2015). They show that multiple characteristics of SME financing have been considered in extant studies, with lending technologies and SME credit channels probably being the most important ones.

SME lending is particularly relevant in Europe. Although the specific figures may vary to some extent depending on the source (as we will show later on), SMEs account for around two-thirds of private employment in Europe (compared, for example, with half in the USA). Additionally, most studies identify a "funding gap" whereby credit demand exceeds supply, and in recent years a particularly large number of studies have shown evidence of this gap in Europe.

SME funding has become a matter of public policy interest as well. In the case of Europe, EU-wide initiatives have been established. Specifically, the European Commission launched the so-called project for a Small Business Act (SBA) in 2011. It aims to improve the approach to entrepreneurship in Europe by simplifying the regulatory and policy environment for SMEs, removing barriers to their development and enhancing access to markets and internationalization. The SBA was under consultation in 2014. As the crisis has been severe in many European economies, many governments have also launched domestic initiatives to improve the financial conditions of SMEs.[1]

The policy interest has also coincided with a growing academic attention in Europe. From a microeconomic analysis point of view, this special consideration is explained by the relative lack of microeconomic data on SMEs in the USA compared to Europe. The lack of data in the US is particularly important for relationship lending variables. Recent studies offer many interesting insights, as they show not only particular features of SME funding in Europe, but also suggest that the dynamics of SME lending may be changing with technology, bank relationships, competition and other related matters.

The chapter comprises three sections following this introduction. The section "A Growing Academic Interest" explains the growing academic interest in SME funding. The section "Recent Evolution of SME Finance in Europe" shows the main descriptive figures for Europe making use of the Survey of Access to Finance of Enterprises (SAFE) jointly provided by the European Commission and the European Central Bank. The section "Small Business Lending Technologies in Europe: A Diagnosis" surveys the role of technology in SME lending and how the taxonomy of funding alternatives for SMEs has been changing over time. It also revises some of the most recent contributions on SME lending in Europe. "Conclusions" draws the chapter to a close.

A Growing Academic Interest

There has been a growing academic interest in SME finance since the mid-1970s. A discipline has been created whereby the knowledge of how to alleviate financial restrictions on small businesses has improved considerably. Both the corporate finance and the banking research have come closer to the real world.

Probably the most complete overview paper on SME lending was Berger and Udell (1998), but the last two decades have also witnessed a large number of contributions. Berger and Udell (2002), for example, revise the conceptual framework of SME finance. In this revised framework, lending technologies are shown to be the key conduit through which government policies and national financial structures affect credit availability. The authors stress the relevance of a "causal chain from policy to financial structures". In this regard, they try to assess the feasibility and profitability of different lending technologies. They also show that financial structures include the presence

[1] These initiatives go beyond the aims of this chapter but many of them can be checked here: http://ec.europa.eu/growth/smes/business-friendly-environment/performance-review/index_en.htm.

of different financial institution types and the conditions under which they operate. Importantly, they argue that the framework implicit in most of the extant contributions is frequently over-simplified, neglecting key elements of the casual chain. One of the most common simplifications identified is the treatment of transactions technologies as a homogeneous group. This would imply that transaction-based lending is unsuitable for opaque SMEs, while this is not the case in practice.

According to Udell (2015), the growing research interest in small business lending has gone through four stages. The first stage took place during the 1980s and early 1990s, when the financial intermediation theory based on asymmetric information problems was mostly developed. In this theory, informationally opaque borrowers are the central paradigm (e.g. Diamond 1984; Boyd and Prescott 1986). At that time, the corporate finance literature was also acknowledging the relevance of information-related problems for the external funding choices of small firms (e.g. Myers 1984; or Myers and Majluf 1984).

A second stage was mainly developed during the early 1990s and refers to what Udell (2015) labels "the emphasis on contract terms". These terms include collateral (as in Boot 2000), covenants (as, for example, Berlin and Mester 1992) or loan commitments (as in Avery and Berger 1991).

The third stage refers to the substantial expansion of research on relationship lending during the 1990s, with the seminal contributions of Petersen and Rajan (1994, 1995), and Berger and Udell (1995) as prominent examples.

A fourth and final stage refers to the studies since the begining of the 2000s and is characterized by more specific microeconomic studies that incorporate complexity in the analysis by looking at a variety of dimensions, such as the role of the institutional framework (which is described later in this chapter), the application of transactions lending to SMEs (de la Torre et al. 2010) or the impact of technology (e.g. Petersen and Rajan 2002).

Some of these distinctive features of small business lending are described in the following sections, with a focus on recent contributions to the European case. Some studies might be missing from the references, but our aim is not to offer a comprehensive survey but rather a guide to the relevance of some work within the European framework.

Recent Evolution of SME Finance in Europe

A simple analysis of some basic statistics on the demography and representativeness of SMEs across European countries (Table 10.1) gives an idea of how relevant those firms are for economic activity and employment. With very small variation across countries, SMEs represent 99.8 % of firms in the European Union. Differences are larger when the share of total employment is shown.

The average percentage of employment corresponding to SMEs in the EU is 67 %, ranging from 53 % in the United Kingdom or 62.5 % in Germany to over 78 % in Estonia, Latvia or Malta.

Contribution to gross value added (GVA) also varies across countries, ranging from 51.8 % in Poland and 53.8 % in Croatia to over 70 % in countries like Spain or Ireland.

Table 10.1 Representativeness of SMEs across Europe (2012)

	Enterprises		Persons employed		GVA (million euro)	
Country	Total	%SME	Total	%SME	Total	%SME
European Union	22,346,729	99.8	133,767,348	67.0	6,184,826	57.5
Belgium	566,006	99.8	2718,355	70.1	189,086	62.2
Bulgaria	312,608	99.8	1872,997	75.5	18,246	62.3
Czech Republic	1,007,441	99.9	3521,520	69.8	84,142	56.0
Denmark	21,358	99.7	1,602,105	65.0	119,936	62.5
Germany	2,189,737	99.5	26,401,395	62.5	1,385,501	53.3
Estonia	58,408	99.7	393,545	78.1	9,338	74.9
Ireland	146,741		1097,444		88,360	
Greece	726,581	99.9	2,198,986	86.5	54,703	72.8
Spain	2,385,077	99.9	10,923,323	73.9	434,156	63.0
France	2,882,419		15,495,621		890,597	
Croatia	148,573	99.7	1002,905	68.3	19,115	54.8
Italy	3,825,458		14,715,132		646,476	
Cyprus	46,139	99.9	224,915		7,864	
Latvia	91,939	99.8	573,580	78.8	9,269	69.2
Lithuania	141,893	99.8	835,630	76.2	12,155	68.5
Luxembourg	29,265	99.5	242,533	68.3	19,250	70.7
Hungary	528,519		2,430,618		46,497	
Malta	26,796	99.8	119,224	79.3	3,548	74.9
Netherlands	862,697	99.8	5,359,446	66.7	310,022	62.9
Austria	308,411	99.7	2,671,477	68.0	164,976	60.5
Poland	1,519,904	99.8	8,326,839	68.9	171,627	50.1
Portugal	793,235	99.9	2,942,895		66,360	
Romania	425,731	99.6	3,837,868	66.4	48,432	
Slovenia	119,644	99.8	474,479	72.3	17,140	62.8
Slovakia	398,392	99.9	1,417,228	69.7	32,922	60.5
Finland	226,373	99.7	1,457,599	63.0	86,957	69.6
Sweden	661,822	99.8	3,025,006	65.4	210,589	58.5
United Kingdom	1,703,562	99.7	17,784,620	53.0	1,037,293	50.9
Norway	278,899	99.8	1,510,838	67.6	230,661	58.6

Source: Eurostat business statistics

Among the EU-wide efforts to provide homogeneous statistical sources on a number of SME funding dimensions, the main one is the Survey of Access to Finance of Enterprises (SAFE) of the European Commission (EC) and the European Central Bank (ECB).[2] An investigation by both the ECB and the EC showed that comparable, timely and frequent data do not exist for SMEs in the European Union. To fill this gap, the EC and the ECB decided in 2008 to collaborate on a survey on access to finance of enterprises in the European Union. The survey covers micro, small, medium-sized and large firms and provides evidence on the financing conditions faced by SMEs compared with those of large firms during the past six months.

In addition to a breakdown into firm size classes, SAFE offers evidence across branches of economic activity, Eurozone countries, firm age, financial autonomy of the firms and ownership of the firms. The first wave of the survey was held in June–July 2009. Part of the survey is run by the ECB every six months to assess the latest developments in the financing conditions of firms in the Eurozone. The more comprehensive survey has been run every year since 2013 (previously every two years) in cooperation with the EC.[3]

SAFE offers data from 2009 to 2014. For the descriptive purposes of this section we will exploit the semi-annual frequency of the database. Importantly, SAFE provides descriptive information not only on financing conditions, but also on how firms perceive these conditions. In the analysis of each indicator, two groups of firms are compared: SMEs and large firms. In this way we can have an idea of how financial conditions differ depending on firm size. A potential limitation of the analysis is that the sample period coincides to a large extent with crisis years. However, the positive side of that restriction is that we can have a better picture of how financing conditions changed for SMEs after the severe credit shock suffered during that period.

Figure 10.1 offers a first look at the magnitude of the SME funding problem. It shows the evolution of the percentage of SMEs that consider access to

[2] Along with SAFE, there are other recent significant efforts by public institutions to provide data on SMEs in Europe. Particularly relevant is the Business Environment and Enterprise Performance Survey (BEEPS), a joint initiative of the European Bank for Reconstruction and Development (EBRD) and the World Bank Group. BEEPS is a firm-level survey of a representative sample of an economy's private sector whose objective is to gain an understanding of firms' perception of the environment in which they operate. BEEPS covers a broad range of business environment topics including access to finance, corruption, infrastructure, crime, competition and performance measures. It covers approximately 4,100 enterprises in 25 countries of Eastern Europe and Central Asia (including Turkey) to assess the environment for private enterprise and business development. The use of BEEPS seems particularly sensible for analysing SME restrictions in Eastern European countries where SME funding problems have been found to be particularly acute and there are different lending technologies in play.

[3] Full details on SAFE can be obtained here:
https://www.ecb.europa.eu/stats/money/surveys/sme/html/index.en.html.

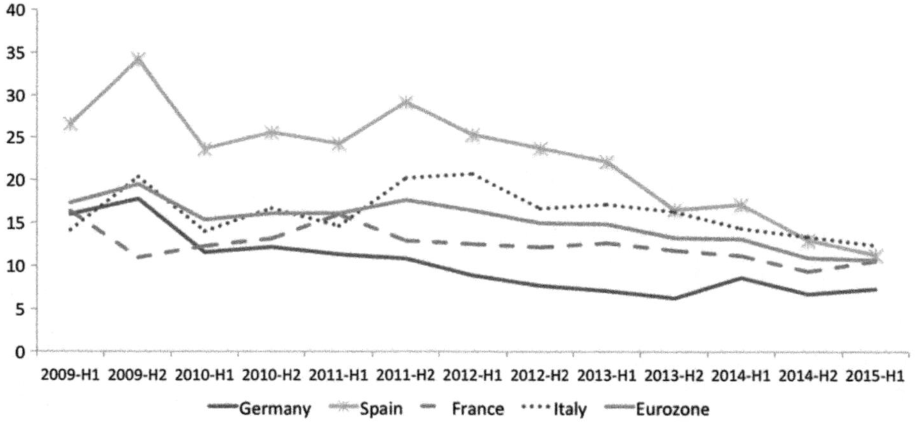

Fig. 10.1 Percentage of SMEs that consider access to funding as their most important problem (*Source*: European Commission and European Central Bank Survey on the access to finance of SMEs and own elaboration)

funding as among their more important problems. This percentage has gone down as the financial crisis has been progressively left behind. It reached a maximum of 34 % in Spain in 2009, while the average for the Eurozone was highest in 2011 at 18 %. Among the countries considered, the lowest value is observed for Germany, ranging from 16 % in 2009 to 7 % in 2015.

Figure 10.2 compares the reported external financing needs of SMEs and large companies in the EU. The figure summarizes survey responses to the question "For each of the following types of external financing, please indicate if your needs increased, remained unchanged or decreased over the past six months."

It appears that aggregate demand conditions dominate the external financing needs of European companies. Around 30 % of the EU SMEs considered that their need for bank loans would increase in 2009, while only 25 % of large firms expected a rise in their need for bank loans. Similarly, the number of SMEs stating a decreasing need for bank loans has been slightly below 20 % for SMEs and around 25 % for large firms, being larger in the post-crisis years. In the case of trade credit, however, an increasing percentage of European large firms reported increasing funding needs in 2010 and 2011, when debt markets were relatively closer for large EU companies due to the sovereign debt tensions.

Figure 10.3 looks at the actual availability of external funding (irrespective of the perceived funding needs). It shows the percentage of answers to the question: "For each of the following types of financing, would you say that their availability has improved, remained unchanged or deteriorated for your

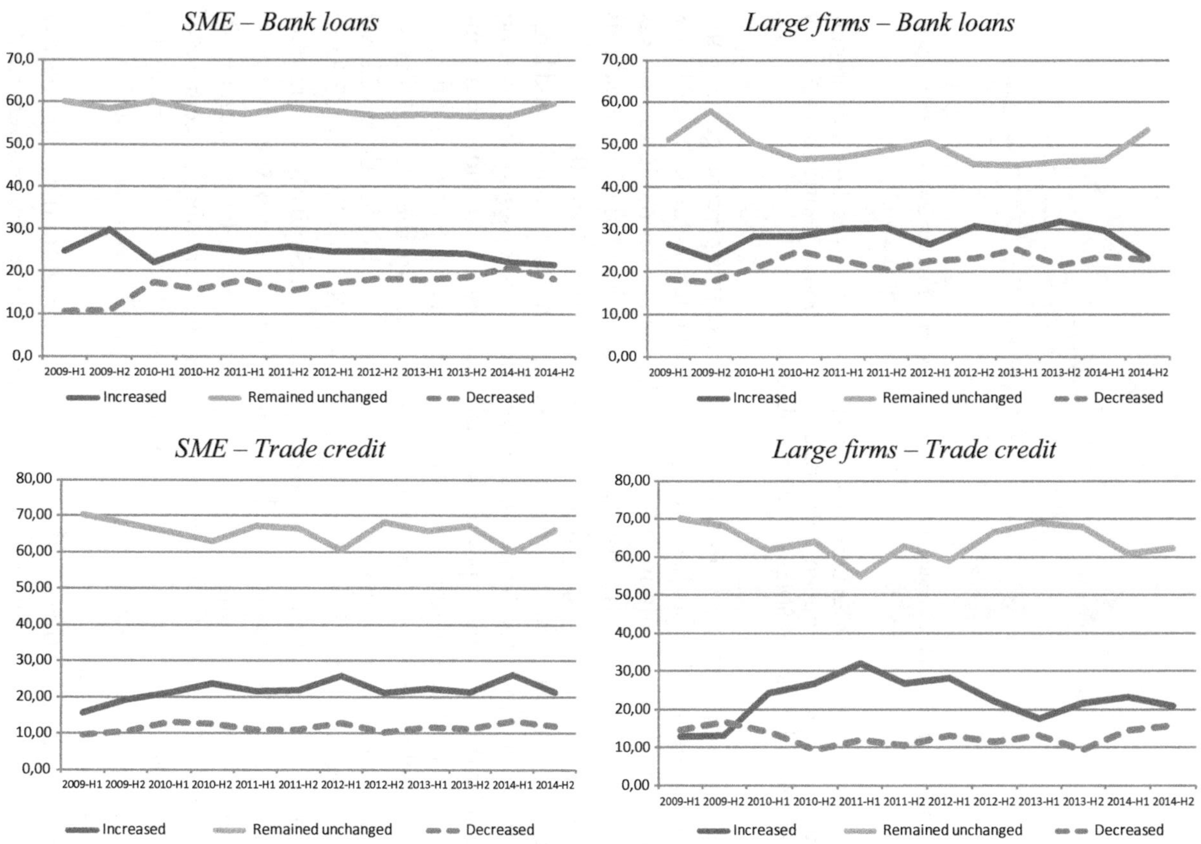

Fig. 10.2 Comparison of reported external financing needs of SMEs vs large companies in the EU (%) (*Source*: European Commission and European Central Bank Survey on the access to finance of SMEs and own elaboration)

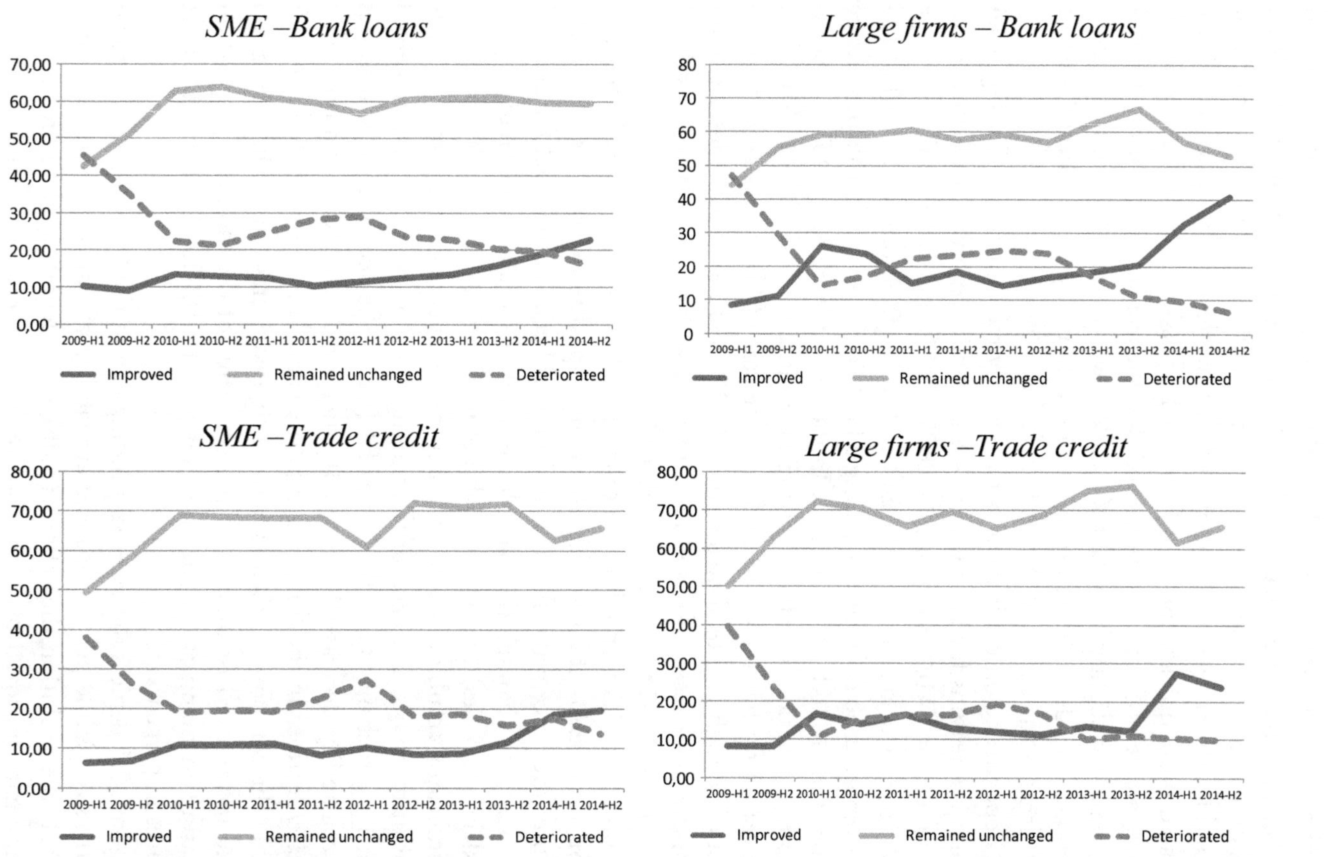

Fig. 10.3 Availability of external funding in the EU (%) (*Source*: European Commission and European Central Bank Survey on the access to finance of SMEs and own elaboration)

enterprise over the past six months?" The main two instruments considered were "bank loans" and "trade credit", the breakdown shown in Fig. 10.3. Interestingly, SMEs reported slow growth in the percentage of firms that reported improved availability of bank loans, while availability seems to have increased more quickly for large firms in the post-crisis period. As of 2014, the percentage of SMEs that perceived that the availability of funds deteriorated remained slightly below 20 %, while it was around 8 % for large firms. In the case of trade credit, improvement in accessibility has also been faster for larger firms as the effects of the crisis have faded away.

As dependence on bank loans is particularly relevant for SMEs, Fig. 10.4 explores the reasons for having a bank loan denied at SMEs and large firms. The survey for SMEs was done in 2009, 2011 and 2013, while for large firms it is only available for 2011 and 2013. By 2009, only one-third of EU SMEs reported no obstacles to getting a bank loan approved. This percentage improved to around 40 % in 2013. In the case of large firms, 45 % of companies reported no obstacles to getting a loan in 2011 and 52 % in 2013. The main reason for having a loan denied in the case of SMEs was lack of collateral or of enough collateral quality (for 20–25 % of them) while interest rates where the main reason for around 20 %. Large firms, however, considered interest rates (12–15 %) the main obstacle.

A summary indicator of how funding conditions change in the EU depending on firm size is the so-called financing gap. The external financing gap measures the perceived difference at firm level between the need for external funds across all channels (i.e. bank loans, bank overdrafts, trade credit, equity and debt securities) and the availability of funds. Therefore, the financing gap indicator combines both financing needs and availability from a variety of instruments. For each of the instruments, an indicator of a perceived financing gap change takes the value of 1 (−1) if the need increases/decreases and availability decreases/increases. If enterprises perceive only a one-sided increase/decrease in the financing gap, the variable is assigned a value of 0.5 (−0.5). The composite indicator is the weighted average of the financing gap related to the five instruments. A positive value of the indicator suggests an increasing financing gap. Values are multiplied by 100 to obtain weighted net balances in percentages.

Figure 10.5 depicts the external funding gap in the EU with a breakdown by firm size. While perceptions and availability of funds were at their worst in 2011, the evolution thereafter has differed widely depending on size. The funding gap improved over time but remained positive for micro firms. In 2014, it fell to negative values for SMEs although it was still close to zero. In

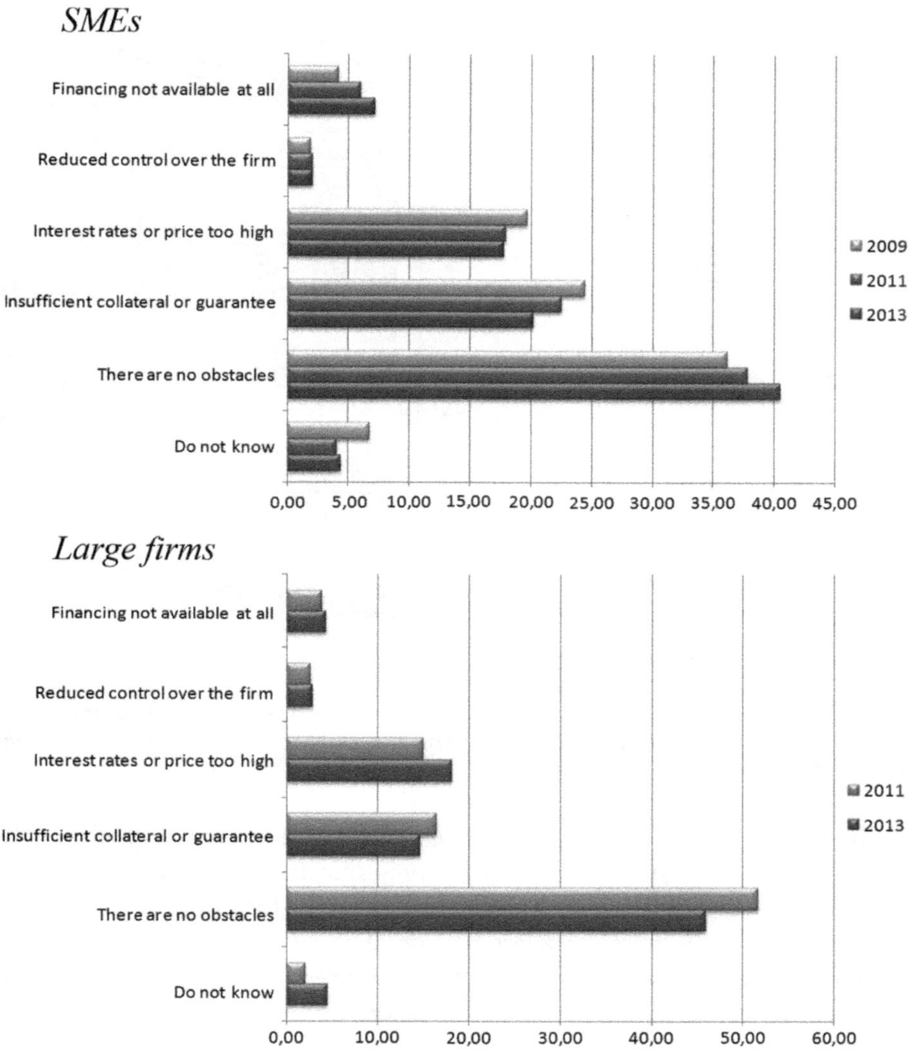

Fig. 10.4 Reasons for having a loan denied (% of answers) (*Source*: European Commission and European Central Bank Survey on the access to finance of SMEs and own elaboration)

any event, medium-sized and large firms enjoyed a much shorter funding gap (larger negative value in absolute terms).

Part of the reason for a larger funding gap for smaller firms is the application of larger interest rates in their loan contracts, as revealed in Fig. 10.6, where rates applied on credit lines and overdrafts are shown across firm sizes. Rates paid by micro firms in 2014 (the only year available) were double those of large firms.

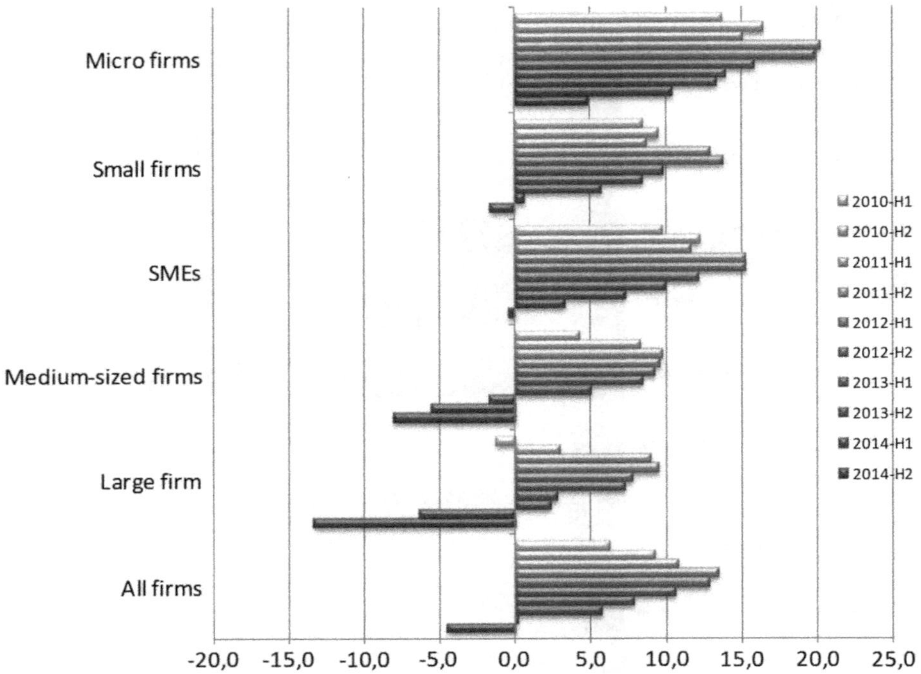

Fig. 10.5 Financing gap perceived by EU firms (*Source*: European Commission and European Central Bank Survey on the access to finance of SMEs and own elaboration)

These figures suggest a persistent disadvantage in access to finance for SMEs in Europe. Although the situation is applicable to most EU SMEs, these conditions may vary across countries. Kaya (2014), for example, shows that SMEs in Germany represent a larger share of small and medium-sized firms relative to micro firms than in other EU countries. This is due, inter alia, to the German SMEs' greater export orientation, and fewer obstacles to corporate growth in other EU partners. This could have made German SMEs more resilient to adverse financial conditions in recent years. In France, the defining characteristic of the SME financing environment has been well-established public support schemes, although this has not prevented SMEs from facing increasing financing constraints in recent years. In Italy—where SMEs represent almost half of the economy's total employment—the overwhelmingly large share of micro enterprises has made access to finance tougher for Italian SMEs in recent years. The case of Spain is similar to that of Italy, as SMEs account for 40 % of employment. As Kaya (2014) emphasizes, Spanish SMEs comprise low-tech manufacturing and less knowledge-intensive services that focus on domestic markets. These features have made them less competitive and particularly vulnerable to changes in domestic demand.

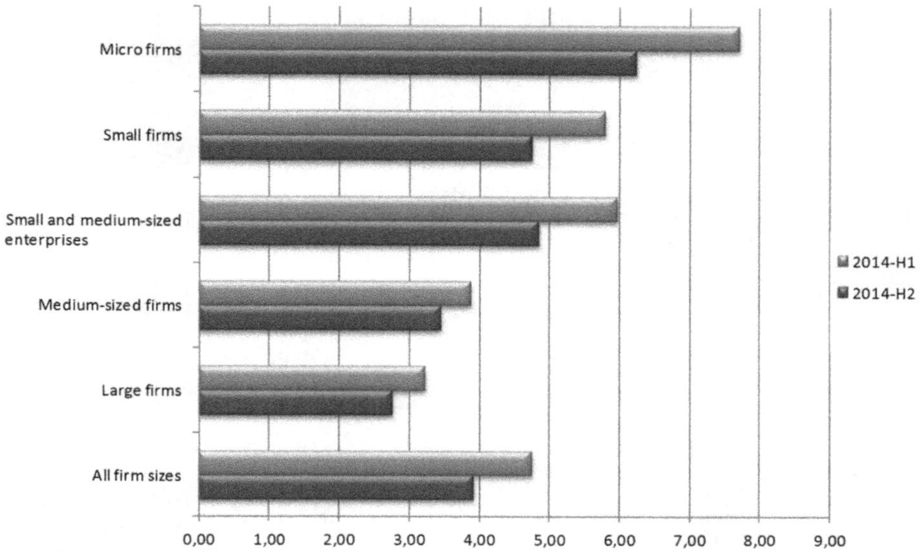

Fig. 10.6 Interest rates applied on credit lines and overdrafts (*Source*: European Commission and European Central Bank Survey on the access to finance of SMEs and own elaboration)

Small Business Lending Technologies in Europe: A Diagnosis

The Universe of Lending Technologies

The contributions to the field reveal that SME lending is a more diversified and complex topic than it may at first seem. One of the reasons is that there are different information-related dimensions to this type of lending. One of them is the extent to which the information produced by these firms is explicit and easily verifiable. When this is the case, information is labelled as "hard". Hard information is quantifiable and can be transmitted (e.g. audited financial statements). Conversely, the information is "soft" when it is not easily quantifiable or transmitted within the hierarchy of a financial institution. As shown in Fig. 10.7, this distinction frequently leads to two different sets of lending technologies. A lending technology is a "unique combination of the primary source of information, screening and underwriting policies/procedures, structure of the loan contracts, and monitoring strategies and mechanisms" (Berger and Udell 2006, p. 2948). The main distinction refers to those technologies that are typically based on soft information as "relationship lending" and those based on hard information as "transactions lending".

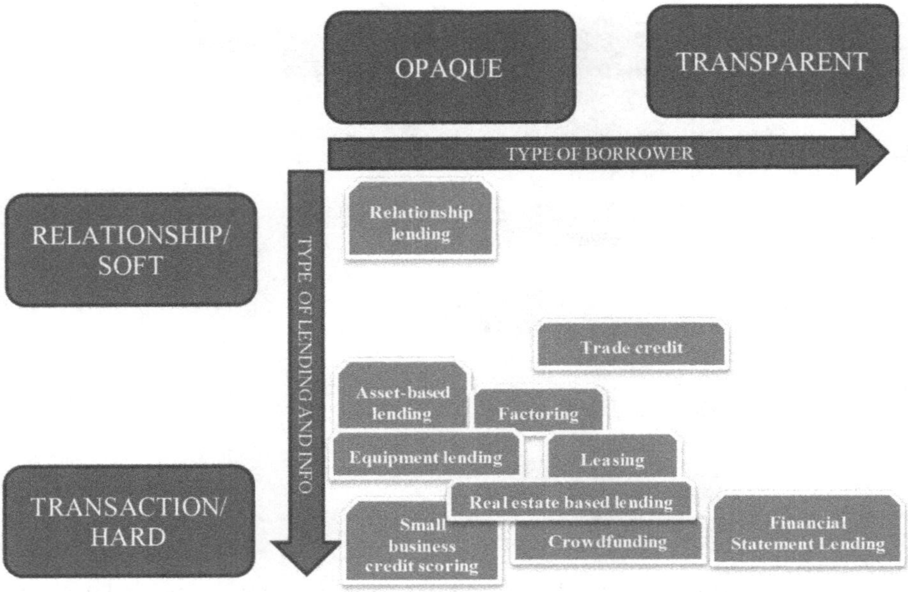

Fig. 10.7 The universe of lending technologies (*Source*: Udell (2015) and own elaboration)

Another dimension is given by the degree of transparency (vs opaqueness) of the borrower. As also shown in Fig. 10.7, the universe of SME lending technologies can be distributed between these two dimensions. In the top left corner of the diagram, "relationship lending" refers to the collection of soft information about the borrower over time, and this information is used to underwrite and monitor a loan. This technology is frequently used when no other alternative is available, which is frequently the case with SMEs.

There are also some technologies for relatively opaque borrowers that incorporate some kind of asset or audited statement. This makes the information processed a bit "harder" than in relationship lending. This is the case of asset-based lending—when the loan is often discounted or backed by receivables and/or inventory as collateral; equipment-based lending—when the loan is tied to equipment and the payment depends on the value and the amortization of such asset; and real estate lending—when a real estate asset is used as collateral. There are also other similar technologies that can be undertaken by banks or other intermediaries, such as factoring—where the intermediary acts as a "factor" that purchases account receivables from the borrower; or leasing—when the lender acts as a "lessor" and provides financing based on equipment that the lender owns.

Other forms of SME funding are characterized by dealing with transaction-based technologies but different degrees of borrower opaqueness. A first case is "small business credit scoring", where the lenders use statistical methods to evaluate relatively small loans for opaque businesses. Another case is crowdfunding, where small businesses/individuals borrow from other individuals through a peer-to-peer (P2P) platform, where each member of the platform provides a small amount of the total loan. The degree of borrower opaqueness may vary significantly in crowdfunding.

"Financial statement lending" is shown at the bottom right corner of Fig. 10.7, as the borrower is characterized as transparent and the information is transaction-based. This technology involves a set of accounting statements whose quality has been verified/certified by reputable auditors.

A particular case among SME lending technologies is "trade credit", which is depicted at the centre of the figure. This is credit extended by vendors to purchase raw materials and it is shown as "accounts payable" on the borrower's balance sheet and as "accounts receivable" on the lender's balance sheet. It incorporates some relevant features such as a maximum maturity and a limited discount period. As we will show later on in this chapter, the information properties of trade credit and its relationship (as a complement or a substitute) to bank loans have been explored recently by academics, with some mixed findings.

The array of technologies shown in Fig. 10.7 is frequently available in the USA and, to a lesser extent, in other countries like Japan. However, the variety of funding sources is frequently more limited across European countries. It is important to note that the financial crisis that started in 2007 has also had an impact on the way these technologies are considered. In particular, the realization that diversification of funding sources helps alleviate financial tensions at times of crisis has elevated the importance of alternative funding instruments. However, there seems to be substantial confusion over what "alternative" really means. Traditionally, "alternative" described the funding of firms and individuals beyond banks and standard debt and equity markets. In the current business environment, there are more restrictive definitions that just refer to financial activities that are developed through entirely new channels, such as business-to-business (B2B) online lending or P2P crowdfunding.

Alternative finance may grow significantly in the future. Allen et al. (2012) suggest that financing from non-market, non-bank external sources will likely become as important as bank funding globally. Moreover, alternative finance appears to be the dominant source of funds for firms in fast-growing economies. However, it seems that the current role of alternative sources of SME funding has been overstated.

In European countries such as Spain, Italy or Germany banks have been allowed to offer a wider range of services under what is called a "universal banking model". Therefore, rather than dis-intermediation, many European banks enjoyed a "reoriented intermediation". Some 20 years later, the European SMEs still depend to a significant extent on bank funding. Analysts and policy makers have traditionally advocated for a wider array of funding sources for households and firms, in particular in private equity and debt markets.

Considering this emphasis by private and public sources on the growing importance of alternative financing channels, it could be argued that banks will have a diminishing role in the economy in the near future. However, this is not necessarily true. Alternative financing may emerge as a complement rather than a substitute for bank lending. The anecdotal evidence suggests that banks have been finding new ways of building lending relationships with firms and also that the same banks have developed technologies such as factoring, leasing and other forms of financing that are not frequently attributed to them.

As shown in Fig. 10.8, the crisis may have introduced some disruption in SME lending. As many countries on both sides of the Atlantic have been affected by a significant increase in private debt (with large firms being hit especially hard), lending based on hard information (most typical of large firms) is expected to lose some ground in favour of relationship lending. Trade credit may grow as well, as many small firms will still find it hard to access bank financing. Other technologies such as leasing or factoring also seem to have been negatively affected by the crisis—although the post-crisis evolution may differ across countries. As for "alternative finance", it is growing but the current volume is still too low to think of it as a solid substitute for more

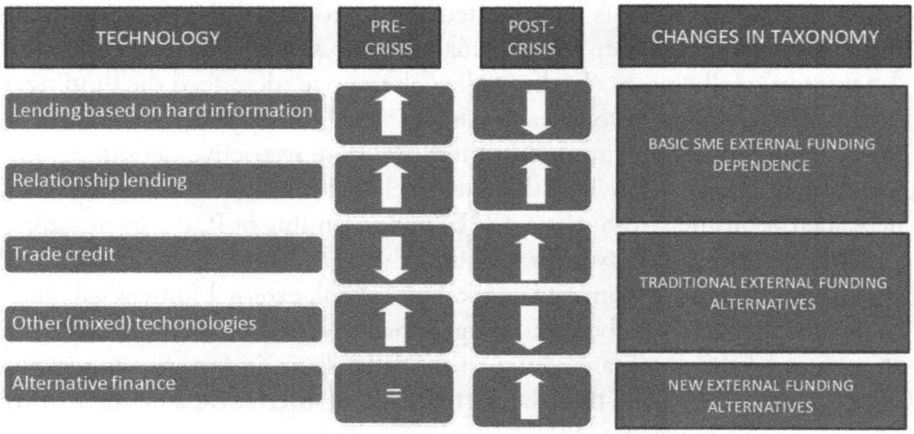

Fig. 10.8 Disruption in SME lending technologies (*Source*: own elaboration)

conventional funding sources. Wardrop et al. (2015) provide an estimate of the new alternative finance channels. The highest values (by far) are shown in the UK (2.3 billion euros), followed by France (154 million euros), Germany (140 million euros), Sweden (107 millions euros) and the Netherlands (78 million euros).

Relationship Lending and Other Technologies: European Evidence

Relationship lending is perhaps the most widely studied topic within small business lending. A relatively early literature review can be found in Elyasiani and Goldberg (2004). They note that most studies show that relationships increase funds availability and reduce loan rates. They argue, however, that the evidence on the direction and magnitude of the length of relationships is mixed and that multiple relationships (getting funding from various lenders) reduce the value of any single borrower–lender relationship. They also suggest that small banks can maintain the advantages of relationship banking in spite of technological changes.

In a recent and empirically exhaustive contribution, Kysucky and Norden (2015) use hand-collected information from 101 studies in the United States, Europe, Asia and Latin America from 1970–2010. They find that strong relationships are generally beneficial for borrowers but that lending outcomes differ across various relationships' dimensions. Long-lasting, exclusive and synergy-creating bank relationships are associated with higher credit volume and lower loan rates. They find, however, that these benefits are more likely to occur in the USA (rather than Europe) and in countries where bank competition is high. They also suggest that the benefits are not related to the importance of SMEs in an economy. Overall, these empirical findings suggest that a higher prevalence of relationship lending does not necessarily come with higher benefits for borrowers.

Other recent studies for Europe suggest that relations are fundamental, although the way they are settled is changing. This is the case of Presbitero et al. (2014). They use detailed data on loan applications and decisions for a large sample of manufacturing firms in Italy during the recent financial crisis. Their findings suggest the credit crunch was more acute in provinces with a large share of branches owned by distantly managed banks. Surprisingly, they do not find evidence that economically weaker firms (such as SMEs) suffered more during the crisis. What they suggest is that financially healthier firms were affected more in functionally distant credit markets than in markets populated by less distant banks.

The impact of lending relationships is also changing as other sources of funding are evolving in Europe. For example, Berger and Schaeck (2011) investigate the nexus of the use of venture capital and bank lending relationships using SME finance information from Italy, Germany and the UK. They find that entrepreneurial firms substitute venture capital for multiple banking relationships. They suggest that this finding is indicative of venture capital being used to avoid rent-extracting behaviour by the firm's main bank. Hence, venture capital funds are used if bank funding is deemed not appropriate, and firms do seem to be aware of which type of financing is more appropriate for them.

When other sources of small business funding are considered along with relationship banking, trade credit is particularly relevant. Uchida et al. (2013) underscore that given its ubiquitous nature, it is not surprising that trade credit has garnered considerable attention in the academic literature. They underscore that some theories reveal that trade creditors (either product sellers or suppliers) have a special ability to provide credit to debtors (either buyers or customers) that is different from what financial institutions have. The authors believe strong transactional relationships explain this special ability and connection between trade creditors and debtors. They test the hypothesis that trade creditors are relationship lenders using SME data from Japan and find that the validity of the relationship-lending hypothesis depends on the relative bargaining power between the buyer and seller.

A look at recent contributions suggests the role of trade credit may have changed during the financial crisis both in the USA and in Europe. Garcia-Appendini and Montoriol-Garriga (2013) suggest that in the USA, stronger larger firms extended more trade credit and weaker smaller firms received more trade credit. Carbo-Valverde et al. (2015b) explore the real effects of trade credit as compared to bank loans during the crisis in Spain. They find that (bank lending) unconstrained firms depend more on bank financing to fund capital expenditure while (bank lending) constrained firms depend more on trade credit. More precisely, for unconstrained firms, bank funding predicts capital expenditure (but not trade credit) and for constrained firms, trade credit predicts capital expenditure (but not bank loans). They also find that the magnitude of these effects increased during the credit crunch.

There is also recent evidence for Italy comparing relationship-based technologies with more transaction-based ones, as in Bartoli et al. (2013). They find that banks lend to SMEs by using both relationship and transactions technologies, independently of the size and proximity of borrowers. Their findings also indicate that the use of soft information decreases the probability of firms being credit rationed.

With a broader and deeper focus, other recent contributions such as Bolton et al. (2013) and Beck et al. (2014) explain how different lending techniques co-vary with firms' financing constraints in good and bad times. The evidence suggests that relationship lenders incur higher costs and therefore charge higher lending rates than transaction-based lenders in normal times. However, the information gains that relationship lenders gather over time make them more suitable as lenders during bad times.

Other recent evidence for Europe points at other interesting dimensions of SME lending. In particular, it shows that trust in SME managers is a fundamental and frequently forgotten dimension of relationship lending by banks. Moro and Fink (2013) explore data on corporate cultural information from six German banks and three Italian banks and find that SMEs that enjoy a high level of trust among loan managers obtain more credit and are less credit constrained.

There is also evidence that banks may have changed their attitudes towards relationship banking with the crisis in Europe. Puri et al. (2011), for example, employ loan application data at German savings banks in the period 2006–2008. They investigate whether savings banks that are exposed to shocks from Landesbanken (whom they own) stemming from the USA behave differently than non-exposed savings banks, that is, those who own Landesbanken without exposure to the US financial crisis. They find evidence consistent with a supply side effect, as affected banks reject substantially more loan applications than do non-affected banks. Furthermore, bank relationships mitigate supply side effects, as firms with longer relationships are less likely to be rejected even when their bank is exposed to a financial shock. Carbo-Valverde et al. (2015a) find evidence for Spain that banks that are more involved in securitization activities relax SME credit constraints in normal periods. They also find that while a relationship with a firm's main bank that covered bonds reduces credit rationing during crisis periods, the issuance of asset-backed securities by a firm's main bank aggravates these firms' credit rationing in crisis periods.

Institutional Features and Market Structure: European Evidence

In a Handbook on European Banking, institutional features are essential, including market structure, regulation, and their quality. A survey and some evidence on the impact of institutional features at the international level is provided in La Porta et al. (2002) and Beck et al. (2005, 2006). Beck et al. (2005)

examine the impact of financing conditions on firm growth. Using a unique firm-level survey database covering more than 50 countries, they analyse the effects of financial, legal and corruption problems on firms' growth rates, paying particular attention to SMEs. They find that whether these factors constrain growth depends on firm size. In particular—as may be expected—they suggest that the smallest firms are consistently the most constrained and that institutional quality is positively and significantly related to the availability of funding. They also find that financial and institutional development weakens the constraining effects of financial, legal and corruption obstacles.

In the European case, one of the most studied institutional features has been the role of publicly owned versus privately owned banks. The case of Germany has been a particularly relevant one in this context.

The baseline reference here is the work of La Porta et al. (2002) who argue that public ownership of banks is associated with lower gross domestic product (GDP) growth. However, this finding seems to be far from conclusive in the European case. Körner and Schnabel (2011) also employ an international sample and empirically show that this relationship does not hold for all countries but depends on a country's initial conditions, with particular influence from economic development and political institutions. They suggest public ownership is harmful only if a country has low financial development and low institutional quality.

Altunbas et al. (2001) explore the case of Germany and find that public savings banks are more cost and profit efficient than German private commercial banks. Similarly, Behr et al. (2010) suggest German savings banks reduce corporate financial constraints and the volatility of economic activity. These results are consistent with a differential effect of public ownership in developed and developing countries.

Behr et al. (2013) study whether financial constraints of private firms depend on bank lending behaviour. They look at specific factors such as the scale, scope and timing of loans. Using a sample of German SMEs, they show that an increase in relative borrowing from local state-owned banks significantly reduces firms' financial constraints, while there is no such effect for privately owned banks. They also show that improved credit availability and private information production are the main channels that explain that finding. It is also suggests that the lending behaviour of local state-owned banks in Germany can be sustainable because it is less cyclical and does not lead to either more risk-taking or under-performance.

As in any other industry, market structure—including competition—has also been found to have a significant impact on small business lending, with some interesting findings for Europe in recent times that we explore in this section.

The potential impact of financial market structure on access to external finance and economic growth has garnered considerable interest recently among researchers as well as policy makers (e.g. Rajan and Zingales 1998; Boot and Thakor 2000). A particularly interesting dimension of financial market structure is the competitiveness of the banking industry. The traditional market power view has been that less competitive banking markets are associated with less credit availability and a higher price for credit. However, an alternative view has emerged over the past decade that argues that the impact of competition on credit may be related to the level of asymmetric information in the market (Dell'Ariccia and Marquez 2006). This is particularly relevant in the context of SMEs because they are more vulnerable to information problems. Notably, Petersen and Rajan (1994, 2002) suggest that a larger bank concentration may imply better financing conditions for SMEs and concentration enables more relationship banking.

However, the extent to which the "market power hypothesis" dominates over the "information hypothesis" (or the opposite) is an open question that depends on specific market conditions. Carbo-Valverde et al. (2009) find that the market power hypothesis seems to be in play in Spain when bank contestability, demand elasticity and information production are considered. This suggests that researchers and policy makers need to be very careful in drawing strong conclusions about market power and credit availability based on analyses that rely exclusively on concentration as a measure of market power without introducing other necessary controls to disentangle, inter alia, the market power effects and the information production effects.

Another important structural feature is the relationship between bank size and bank involvement in SME financing. The standard view during the 1990s was that small banks with local or regional ties are more able to build lending relationships than their larger counterparts. However, some recent studies are challenging this view. De la Torre et al. (2010) find that the "conventional wisdom" that large and foreign banks generally are not interested in serving SMEs is far from accurate. Using bank-level information from various countries, they show banks perceive SMEs as a core and strategic business and seem well positioned to expand their links with SMEs. They find that intensification of bank involvement with SMEs in various emerging markets is neither led by small or niche banks nor highly dependent on relationship lending.

Again, the organizational structure emerges as fundamental to explain banks' involvement in SME lending beyond their size. Canales and Nanda (2012) study the case of Mexico and find that the organizational structure of banks impacts small business lending. They find that decentralized banks—where branch managers have greater autonomy over lending decisions—give larger loans to small firms and those with "soft information". However, decentralized banks are also more responsive to their own competitive environment. They are more likely to expand credit when faced with competition but also to cherry pick customers and restrict credit when they have market power. This evidence also seems to be in line with Uchida et al. (2012) for Japan, as they show that loan officers play a critical role in relationship lending by producing soft information about SMEs. They find that loan officers at small banks produce more soft information than at large banks, but large banks appear to have the equivalent potential to underwrite relationship loans.

Conclusions

Small businesses are particularly vulnerable to external funding conditions. They usually exhibit a substantial dependence on bank loans. In this chapter, we surveyed some of the main funding sources of SMEs, how the taxonomy of the instruments is changing in recent years and a number of particular features of the European case.

SMEs account for two-thirds of private employment in Europe as compared to half in the USA. Several academic and policy studies have identified a "funding gap" problem in the EU—where credit demand exceeds supply—that may have been exacerbated during the crisis years.

In this chapter we analysed the most common technologies for SME funding and the evolution of small business lending in Europe. The variety and availability of funding sources have been limited in Europe and this has motivated policy makers to advocate for a wider array of funding sources for these firms. Although the emergence of new alternative financing channels may represent an opportunity, these instruments will still have a partial impact for some time. These limitations have led governments to launch support initiatives for SMEs at both domestic and EU levels. On this front, the European Commission released the so-called project for a Small Business Act (SBA) in 2011. The SBA aims to improve small business entrepreneurship in Europe by simplifying the regulatory and policy environment and enhancing access to markets and internationalization.

We have also shown that there has been a growing academic interest in SME financing in Europe, with topics such as relationship lending, and institutional factors such as competition and the relationship between bank size and SME funding, being particularly relevant. As for the recent evolution of SME funding in Europe, the homogeneous information provided by the

Survey on Access to Finance of Enterprises (SAFE) suggests that EU SMEs remain significantly dependent on bank loans. It also indicates an expanding role for trade credit in SME financing during and after the crisis. Additionally, although the funding gap has significantly shortened since the crisis, it still remains larger for smaller firms compared to their larger counterparts. Loan terms are also found to be persistently and significantly different, with large firms paying half the loan rates faced by micro firms.

References

Allen, F., & Santomero, A. M. (1998). The theory of financial intermediation. *Journal of Banking and Finance, 21*, 1461–1485.

Allen, F., Gu, X., & Kowalewski, O. (2012). Financial crisis, structure and reform, *Journal of Banking and Finance, 36*, 2960–2973.

Altunbas, Y., Evans, L., & Molyneux, P. (2001). Ownership and efficiency in banking. *Journal of Money, Credit and Banking, 33*(4), 926–954.

Avery, R. B., & Berger, A. N. (1991). Risk-based capital and deposit insurance reform. *Journal of Banking and Finance, 15*, 847–874.

Bartoli, F., Ferri, G., Murro, P., & Rotondi, Z. (2013). SME financing and the choice of lending technology in Italy: Complementarity or substitutability? *Journal of Banking and Finance, 37*(12), 5476–5485.

Beck, T., Demigüç-Kunt, A., & Maksimovic, V. (2005). Financial and legal constraints to growth: Does firm size matter? *The Journal of Finance, 60*(1), 137–177.

Beck, T., Demirguc-Kunt, A., Laeven, L., & Maksimovic, V. (2006). The determinants of financing obstacles. *Journal of International Money and Finance, 25*, 932–952.

Beck, T., Demigüç-Kunt, A., & Singer, D. (2013). Is small beautiful? Financial structure, size and access to finance. *World Development, 52*, 19–33.

Beck, T, Degryse, H., De Haas, R., & N. Van Horen. (2014). *When arm's length is too far: Relationship banking over the business cycle* (EBRD Working Paper 169).

Behr, Patrick, Schmidt, Reinhard H., & Xie, Ru. (2010). Market Structure, Capital Regulation, and Bank Risk Taking. *Journal of Financial Services Research, 37*, 131–158.

Behr, P., Norden, L., & Noth, F. (2013). Financial constraints of private firms and bank lending behaviour. *Journal of Banking and Finance, 37*(9), 3472–3485.

Berger, A. N., & Schaeck, K. (2011). Small and medium-sized enterprises, bank relationship strength, and the use of venture capital. *Journal of Money, Credit and Banking, 43*(2–3), 461–490.

Berger, A. N., & Udell, G. F. (1995). Relationship lending and lines of credit in small firm finance. *The Journal of Business, 68*(3), 351–381.

Berger, A. N., & Udell, G. F. (1998). The economics of small business finance: The role of private equity and debt markets in the financial growth cycle. *Journal of Banking and Finance, 22*, 613–673.

Berger, A. N., & Udell, G. F. (2002). Small business credit availability and relationship lending: The importance of bank organisational structure. *Economic Journal, 112*, 32–53.

Berger, A. N., & Udell, G. F. (2006). A more complete conceptual framework for SME finance. *Journal of Banking and Finance, 30*(11), 2945–2966.

Berlin, M., & Mester, L. J. (1992). Debt covenants and renegotiation. *Journal of Financial Intermediation, 2*(2), 95–133.

Bhattacharya, S., & Thakor, A. V. (1993). Contemporary banking theory. *Journal of Financial Intermediation, 3*, 2–50.

Bolton, P., Freixas, X., Gambacorta, L., & Mistrulli, P.E. (2013). Relationship and transaction lending in a crisis. BIS working paper n. 4017.

Boot, A. W. A. (2000). Relationship banking: What do we know? *Journal of Financial Intermediation, 9*, 7–25.

Boot, A. W. A., & Thakor, A. V. (2000). Can relationship banking survive competition? *The Journal of Finance, 55*, 679–713.

Boyd, J. H., & Prescott, E. C. (1986). Financial intermediary-coalitions. *Journal of Economic Theory, 38*(2), 211–232.

Canales, R., & Nanda, R. (2012). A darker side to decentralized banks: Market power and credit rationing in SME lending. *Journal of Financial Economics, 105*, 2.

Carbo-Valverde, S., Rodriguez-Fernandez, F., & Udell, G. F. (2009). Bank market power and SME financing constraints. *Review of Finance, 13*, 309–340.

Carbo-Valverde, S., Rodriguez-Fernandez, F., & Udell, G. (2016). Trade credit, the financial crisis and firms access to finance. *Journal of Money, Credit and Banking, 97*, forthcoming.

Carbo-Valverde, S., Degryse, H., & Rodriguez-Fernandez, F. (2015b). The impact of securitization on credit rationing: empirical evidence. *Journal of Financial Stability, 20*, 36–50.

De la Torre, A., Martínez Pería, S., & Schmukler, S. L. (2010). Bank involvement with SMEs: Beyond relationship lending. *Journal of Banking and Finance, 34*(9), 2280–2293.

Dell'Ariccia, G., & Marquez, R. (2006). Lending booms and lending standards. *The Journal of Finance, 61*(5), 2511–2546.

Diamond, D. W. (1984). Financial intermediation and delegated monitoring. *The Review of Economic Studies, 51*(3), 393–414.

Elyasiani, E., & Goldberg, L. G. (2004). Relationship lending: A survey of the literature. *Journal of Economics & Business, 56*(4), 315–330.

Garcia-Appendini, E., & Montoriol-Garriga, J. (2013). Firms as liquidity providers: Evidence from the 2007–2008 financial crisis. *Journal of Financial Economics, 109*(1), 272–291.

Kaya, O. (2014). SME financing in the euro area. New solutions to an old problem. EU Monitor Global Financial Markets. Deustche Bank Research.
Körner, T., & Schnabel, I. (2011). Public ownership of banks and economic growth—The role of heterogeneity. Economics of. *Transition, 19*(3), 407–441.
Kysucky, V., & Norden, L. (2015). The benefits of relationship lending in a cross-country context: A meta-analysis. *Management Science, 62*(1), 90–110.
La Porta, R., Lopez-de-Silanes, F., Shleifer, A., & Vishny, R. (2002). Government ownership of banks. *Journal of Finance, 57*(1), 256–301.
Moro, A., & Fink, M. (2013). Loan managers' trust and credit access for SMEs. *Journal of Banking and Finance, 37*(3), 927–936.
Myers, S. C. (1984). The capital structure puzzle. *The Journal of Finance, 39*(3), 574–592.
Myers, S. C., & Majluf, N. S. (1984). Corporate financing and investment decisions when firms have information that investors do not have. *Journal of Financial Economics, 13*(2), 187–221.
Petersen, M. A., & Rajan, R. G. (1994). The benefits of lending relationships: Evidence from small business data. *The Journal of Finance, 49*, 3–37.
Petersen, M. A., & Rajan, R. G. (1995). The effect of credit market competition on lending relationships. *Quarterly Journal of Economics, 110*, 407–443.
Petersen, M. A., & Rajan, R. G. (2002). Does distance still matters? The information revolution in small business lending. *Journal of Finance, 57*, 2533–2570.
Presbitero, A., Udell, G. F., & Zazzaro, A. (2014). The home bias and the credit crunch: A regional perspective. *Journal of Money, Credit and Banking, 46*(1), 53–85.
Puri, M., Rocholl, J., & Steffen, S. (2011). Global retail lending in the aftermath of the US financial crisis: Distinguishing between supply and demand effects. *Journal of Financial Economics, 100*(3), 556–578.
Rajan, R., & Zingales, L. (1998). Financial dependence and growth. *American Economic Review, 88*(3), 559–586.
Ramakrishnan, R. T. S., & Thakor, A. V. (1984). Information reliability and a theory of financial intermediation. *The Review of Economic Studies, 51*(3), 415–432.
Uchida, H., Udell, G. F., & Yamori, N. (2012). Loan officers and relationship lending to SMEs. *Journal of Financial Intermediation, 21*(1), 97–122.
Uchida, H., Udell, G. F., & Watanabe, W. (2013). Are trade creditors relationship lenders? *Japan and the World Economy, 25–26*, 24–38.
Udell, G. F. (2015). SME access to intermediated credit: What do we know and what don't we know? Conference Vol. Federal Reserve Bank of Australia.
Wardrop, R. Zhang, B., Rau, R., & Gray, M. (2015). The European alternative finance benchmarking report. Cambridge University and Ernst and Young.

11

European Bank Efficiency and Performance: The Effects of Supranational Versus National Bank Supervision

Rients Galema and Michael Koetter

Introduction

In the 2000s the European banking market has been severely tested. In the run-up to the financial crisis of 2007–8 countries like Ireland and Spain experienced large bank-financed housing booms. The financial crisis of 2007–8 necessitated the bailing out of banks on a large scale, and the dust of these policies had not settled when Europe was confronted with the sovereign debt crisis. This crisis made painfully clear how intertwined Europe's banks and sovereigns actually are. In response, a Banking Union was proposed to help decouple the sovereign debt–bank risk nexus and to generally strengthen the resilience of the financial system in Europe.

The period leading up to the financial crisis witnessed increasing integration of European banking markets. In 2004, the new EU Takeover Directive provided a common framework for cross-border takeover bids. Basel II was also

We are very grateful for feedback received from Thorsten Beck and Barbara Casu. Manuela Storz provided excellent research assistance.

R. Galema
School of Economics, Utrecht University, Utrecht, The Netherlands
e-mail: r.j.galema@uu.nl

M. Koetter (✉)
Department of Financial Markets, Halle Institute for Economic Research, Halle, Germany
e-mail: Michael.Koetter@iwh-halle.de

T. Beck, B. Casu (eds.), *The Palgrave Handbook of European Banking*,
DOI 10.1057/978-1-137-52144-6_11

proposed in 2004 and subsequently implemented in the European Union via the Capital Requirements Directive in 2006. A notable part of Basel II is that it features risk sensitivity of regulatory capital. The crisis of 2007–8quickly revealed the weakness of this feature, as especially European banks that were subject to Basel II held many highly rated subprime assets that, ex post, turned out to be much riskier than anticipated, leaving European banks severely under-capitalized when losses on these assets materialized.

The many publicly funded bank bailouts that followed quickly led to a deterioration of public debt ratios in many European countries. The rescue package for the Greek government in May 2010 marked an important turning point in the sovereign debt crisis in the European (Monetary) Union (E(M)U) because it set a fundamental change to the financial architecture into motion. It constituted the third phase of global financial turmoil following the subprime mortgage meltdown in the USA and the subsequent banking crisis sparked by the failure of Lehman Brothers. Already at the inception of the EMU, numerous scholars warned about the potentially vicious nexus between the surrendering of exchange rate policy in a monetary union to bolster financial and macroeconomic shocks without establishing and strengthening alternative mechanisms (see, for example, Lane 2012). The most important of such missing alternative mechanisms, besides a fiscal union called for by many economists, was presumably the absence of a Banking Union (O'Rourke and Taylor 2013; Chap. 17 of this Handbook). Supranational monetary policy conducted by the European Central Bank (ECB) for economies with at times vastly different credit cycles paired with national responsibility for the prudential supervision of banks by national competent authorities (NCAs) gave rise to a series of undesirable side effects. Recent literature demonstrates, for example, how excess central bank liquidity sparked lending by risky banks to risky customers (Jiménez et al. 2012, 2014) and liquidity hoarding (Benmelech and Bergman 2012; Acharya and Merrouche 2013). Similarly, the preferential treatment of EMU sovereign debt regarding risk weights and resulting capital requirements has induced carry trade behaviour (Acharya and Steffen 2015) and additional risk-taking (Buch et al. 2013a, b).

In response to the sovereign debt–bank risk nexus and to generally strengthen the resilience of the financial system in Europe, proposals for a Banking Union were put forward at the EU summit in June 2012 with the aim to complete the legislative process by December of the same year. The proposal featured a three-pillar approach that consisted of the Single Supervisory Mechanism (SSM), the Single Resolution Mechanism (SRM) and the Single Deposit Guarantee Scheme, of which only the first two eventually passed legislation. As aptly noted by policy observers such as Véron (2015), the reallocation of supervisory responsibility and power to the SSM at the supranational level constitutes a major change to the architecture of the European financial system. The SSM is part of the ECB and responsible for the supervision of approximately 6,000 banks in the EMU. The objective of the SSM is to ensure a harmonized development and application of supervisory rules and procedures in the EMU, thereby restoring trust in the banking system and ensuring efficient yet stable operations. Prior to assuming this responsibility, these banks were subject to a comprehensive assessment of their business conducted by the ECB in close cooperation with NCAs. As of November 2014 the SSM is operational and focuses on the direct supervision of 122 systemically relevant financial institutions, which together account for around 82 % of total assets. Whereas the SSM is the organization responsible for supervision, most banks thus continue to be supervised by NCA.

Table 11.1 provides some general trends for selected average performance indicators of a 2004–13 sample of European banks that is further discussed below. In this period, average return on equity (ROE) declined continuously, while return on assets (ROA) remained roughly constant. This is consistent with banks having to deleverage as a result of recent crises and regulatory efforts to recapitalize banks. Average banks' cost–income ratios do not show a clear trend over time, having decreased a bit during the 2007–8 crisis and rebounding to their pre-crisis levels in recent years. European bank revenues still depend to a large extent on interest income, albeit with a declining trend. This pattern reflects in part policy rates that declined dramatically, mimicked by interest expenses on deposits and other interest expenses that show a declining trend. Finally, consistent with more stringent regulation, banks' z-score measured as the number of standard deviations from default shows an upward trend, although credit risk in terms of loan impairment charges over gross loans has remained fairly constant over time.

Table 11.2 takes a more detailed look and shows average return on equity, capitalization and credit risk for a set of European countries in three subperiods: 2004–6, 2007–9 and 2010–13 (all variables winsorized at 1 % and further described below). It shows quite some heterogeneity across countries. For instance, Ireland's average return on equity declined from 19.3 % to 6.8 % from 2004–6 to 2010–13 as its capitalization also increased with a factor three across this period. Greece's average ROE halved, even though capitalization only dropped by 2.5 percentage points. Credit risk in most countries increased when comparing 2004–6 with either 2007–9 or 2010–13. The only exception is Germany which shows a decline in credit risk.

Table 11.1 Performance of European banks—selected indicators

Year	2004	2005	2006	2007	2008	2009	2010	2011	2012	2013
Efficiency and performance										
Return on equity (%)	18.4	16.3	18.1	15.2	13.9	14.9	14.8	13.6	13.1	13.4
Return on assets (%)	1.1	1.1	1.3	1.1	1.0	1.1	1.1	1.0	1.1	1.1
Cost–income ratio (%)	45.8	48.5	44.2	41.0	37.8	43.1	46.3	44.8	44.1	44.0
Income structure (% of total revenues)										
Interest income on loans	65.8	64.4	62.3	65.3	66.8	63.6	62.3	62.9	60.7	59.3
Other interest income	24.4	26.7	25.8	23.5	23.2	21.5	20.9	20.9	20.7	19.3
Non-interest operating income	17.6	19.3	21.2	17.5	14.6	18.7	20.2	19.4	21.0	23.1
Expense structure (% of total expenses)										
Interest expenses—customer deposits	33.0	25.4	27.4	27.0	27.3	19.6	16.5	17.9	19.6	20.4
Other interest expenses	43.3	38.4	40.1	43.9	46.6	40.5	36.2	36.7	35.7	31.8
Personnel expenses	30.4	32.2	30.8	27.5	25.2	30.4	33.1	32.5	32.6	33.8
Other operating expenses	22.4	24.1	22.7	20.7	18.4	22.0	24.7	24.2	24.6	25.8
Risk and capitalization										
Capitalization	6.7	7.8	7.9	8.0	7.9	8.0	8.2	8.4	8.6	8.8
Credit risk	4.6	4.5	4.6	4.4	4.6	4.7	4.6	4.1	4.4	4.5
Z-score	32.4	34.7	35.3	34.2	32.7	33.9	35.3	37.6	39.2	39.1

This table reports selected indicators per country and period for the cost frontier estimation sample, column 4 of Table 11.3. Efficiency and performance and risk and capitalization indicators are defined in Table 11.3. Total revenues are defined as the sum of interest income on loans, other interest income, dividend income and non-interest operating income. Total expenses equal operating costs (TOC): the sum of interest expenses, loan impairment charges, other operating expenses and personnel expenses. All ratios are winsorized at 99 %

These descriptive statistics underpin the challenging environment with low interest rates and increasing non-performing loans in selected countries faced by European banks. Technological advancements pose both opportunities in terms of increased bank productivity and threats in terms of disruptive start-ups threatening banks' existing business models. Simultaneously, increased regulation through Basel III and the SSM place increasingly large burdens on banks. Questions related to many of these developments are related to bank productivity and efficiency, for which there exists an extensive literature.

In the remainder of this chapter we set out to do two things. First, we provide an overview of the key estimation methods for efficiency and discuss selected applications to the European banking sector. Second, we apply stochastic frontier analysis to investigate the extent to which the reallocation of supervisory powers is associated with efficiency differences between European banks. In doing so, we are particularly interested in whether direct supervision by the SSM as opposed to NCA is related to cost and profit efficiency.

Table 11.2 Performance European banks – selected indicators per country and period

	Return on equity			Capitalization			Credit risk		
Country / period	2004–2006	2007–2009	2010–2013	2004–2006	2007–2009	2010–2013	2004–2006	2007–2009	2010–2013
Austria	16.4	15.0	11.8	7.6	7.5	7.4	4.5	4.7	4.7
Belgium	11.1	11.9	11.6	6.5	7.0	6.8	3.9	4.2	4.2
Cyprus	22.1	18.8	22.2	7.9	8.8	8.0	4.6	4.9	5.7
Denmark	16.2	10.0	11.7	14.1	12.6	11.8	4.0	5.2	5.9
Estonia	15.9	17.3	13.2	16.5	12.3	15.6	3.9	5.6	6.0
Finland	13.7	14.8	12.7	8.4	10.6	8.9	4.0	4.5	4.3
France	17.5	15.3	14.6	9.1	9.3	9.8	4.2	4.4	4.4
Germany	18.8	14.8	14.5	6.1	6.3	7.6	4.8	4.6	3.9
Greece	18.1	17.6	9.1	12.5	10.6	9.9	4.6	4.9	6.3
Ireland	19.3	17.1	6.8	4.2	6.9	11.4	3.9	5.6	6.8
Italy	13.2	13.1	12.6	11.3	11.0	10.0	4.3	4.5	5.0
Latvia	24.1	20.1	13.3	9.2	9.5	9.8	4.2	6.0	6.2
Lithuania	14.6	14.4	11.4	9.2	9.3	10.3	4.4	5.8	5.5
Luxembourg	19.9	18.7	15.2	6.4	6.1	8.2	3.9	4.2	4.1
Malta	19.1	14.6	13.1	9.7	14.8	11.0	4.2	4.0	4.2
Netherlands	16.1	13.5	13.2	9.5	9.1	10.0	4.2	4.5	4.8
Portugal	19.6	18.1	12.4	8.8	9.6	10.2	4.4	4.6	4.8
Slovakia	15.0	15.0	14.5	10.7	12.0	12.7	4.4	5.3	4.9
Slovenia	18.1	17.9	15.3	9.1	8.2	7.8	4.4	4.8	6.4
Spain	16.1	17.4	12.6	7.8	8.3	8.0	4.2	4.5	5.0

This table reports selected indicators per country and period for the cost frontier estimation sample, column 4 of Table 11.3. Variable definitions of return on equity, capitalization and credit risk are provided in Table 11.3

Using Bankscope data for approximately 27,000 bank-year observations of European banks between 2004 and 2013, our main results suggest that SSM-supervised banks are both less cost and less profit efficient compared with non-SSM-supervised financial institutions. The cost efficiency difference is insignificant as of 2010. Specifying an indicator variable equal to one when a bank is supervised by the SSM as a covariate confirms the positive effect of SSM membership on the distribution of inefficiency also after controlling for observable bank traits. The analysis of banks that switched their SSM status indicates no significant effects for profit efficiency. However, for those banks that were already on the SSM list in 2013 and continued to be on the one published in 2015 we find a negative interaction term, indicating that these banks experienced lower cost inefficiency. Overall, we thus find evidence that supranational supervision by the SSM coincides with larger inefficiencies. This result may indicate an additional administrative burden, at least during the run-up towards a more homogeneous approach to banking supervision in the EMU.

Methodological Trends and Applications to Banking

Do economic agents employ and allocate scarce resources optimally to accomplish their objectives? This is the capstone question underlying a rich and continuously growing literature on the measurement of efficiency. The contributions by Koopmans (1951), Debreu (1951), Farrell (1957) and Leibenstein (1966) were pivotal in sparking the development of a more formal measurement of (in)efficiency.

Two main approaches emerged for gauging deviations of agents, such as banks, non-financial firms or households, from an optimal benchmark, such as output, profit or cost, conditional on their input choices, say capital and labour used in order to produce output. The first approach is deterministic and solves optimization problems with non-linear programming methods, such as Data Envelopment Analyses. A comprehensive review is Simar and Wilson (2013). The second approach is stochastic and imposes structure on the observable data to fit a benchmark function econometrically, the so-called stochastic frontier. Deviations from this benchmark are decomposed into a systematic inefficiency component and random deviations. An introduction to the foundations of stochastic frontier analysis (SFA) is available in Kumbhakar and Lovell (2000), and a comprehensive discussion of more recent methodological developments can be found in Parmeter and Kumbhakar (2014).

Given the scope of the extant efficiency literature, we will focus in this chapter on selected recent methodological trends in SFA and their applications to European bank efficiency.

Methodological Developments

Aigner, Lovell and Schmidt (1977) and Meeusen and van den Broeck (1977) developed independently the following "workhorse" stochastic production frontier model:

$$y_i = T(x_i;\beta) - u_i + v_i, \tag{11.1}$$

where y denotes the output of firm i generated by employing production factors x with a common production technology T( ). The difference to a canonical production function are the two error components $-u_i + v_i = \varepsilon_i$, which denote non-random deviations from the estimated log-linear function and random noise, respectively. The random error is assumed to be normally distributed with mean zero, whereas the most simple parametric assumption regarding the inefficiency component is a half-normal distribution with a mean μ, often equal to zero, and a standard deviation σ. Systematic deviations gauge inefficiency that may arise because of over-employing factors (technical efficiency, TE) and/or an inefficient allocation of resources at given factor prices (allocative efficiency, AE).

The modern SFA literature developed numerous advances in how to specify such models in terms of functional forms assumed for the kernel of Eq. (11.1), functional form and distributional assumptions regarding the error term components, methods to account for confounding factors in the environment or selection bias and many more. We limit ourselves here to a selection of these mostly methodological advances.

Firstly, the assumptions concerning the error term can influence firm-specific measures of inefficiency substantially. Beyond the most commonly employed (truncated) half-normal model, alternatives include a wide range, such as the gamma distribution suggested by Greene (1990) or more recently the treatment of inefficiency as a double-truncated normal (Almanidis et al. 2014). Horrace and Parmeter (2014) assume v to be Laplace-distributed and u to be distributed as truncated Laplace, which is particularly well suited for data featuring many firms close to full efficiency. Hafner et al. (2013) suggest a generalized SFA model, which generates well-defined efficiency measures even if the skew of errors is theoretically wrong, for example positive in a production model where inefficiencies should be strictly negative.

Secondly, the modelling of technical efficiency requires a careful definition of the outputs of the firm. Especially a multi-output setting is challenging because it requires a system approach of both the objective as well as factor demand functions to estimate TE and AE separately. Tsionas et al. (2015b) develop such a system approach in terms of a cost minimization instead of output maximization problem. They account for endogenous factor demand in the input distance functions by means of a flexible system employing first order conditions as restrictions. Their estimator generates both TE as well as AE and detects inefficiencies that remain unobserved in a conventional single-frontier model. Imprecise efficiency estimates might also arise from including "bad outputs", such as pollution. Kumbhakar and Tsionas (2015) develop a so-called by-product model, which combines directional distance functions and single efficient frontier approaches and allows for bad outputs. They use Baysian estimation methods to separate TE from environmental reasons to deviate from optimal output of "good" outputs taking into account endogenous factor demand and the presence of undesirable co-production of bad outputs. Related developments are the use of Baysian Generalized Methods of Moments techniques to allow for endogenous inputs and outputs (Agee et al. 2014), endogeneity corrections of quadratic directional distance functions (Atkinson and Tsionas 2015) or the specification of separate production functions for desirable und undesirable outputs (Murty et al. 2012).

Thirdly, when firm-specific efficiency scores inform policy making, for example in banking applications, it is crucial to ensure that they do not confound inefficient behaviour with environmental differences and unobservable differences across studied subjects. Bos et al. (2009) showed that already fairly simple single-technology SFA models that account for such heterogeneity controls z in the kernel, the error term components, or both lead to significantly different levels of inefficiency and, at times, rank orders of firms. To relax the assumption in the basic SFA that all firms are inefficient to some degree, Kumbhakar et al. (2013) develop a zero-inefficiency with single technology frontier, which can also accommodate fully efficient firms. A related model by Rho and Schmidt (2013) allows one to test for the assumption of zero inefficiency. Another alternative to the specification of controls z in exiting single-frontier models is to allow for parameter heterogeneity in the kernel. Greene (2005) suggests to this end a latent-class SFA, where subjects are sorted into different technology regimes. Bos et al. (2010) show that this approach can reconcile the absence of economic convergence in many growth studies due to the existence of different convergence clusters in cross-country such that countries converge only with respect to their relevant production frontier. Another reason for confounding inefficiency with unobservable alternative factors is systematic sample selection. Greene (2010) proposes a simple and straightforward extension of the normal half-normal SFA model and demonstrates that accounting for selection bias leads to qualitatively different inference in a cross-country study on the efficiency of national health systems.

Fourthly, to the extent that inefficiency measures gauge properly the ability and/or willingness of a firm's management skill in optimal decision making, any static measurement falls short in investigating the effects, for example how policy changes affect TE and AE. Therefore, panel data models that help to identify time-varying inefficiency have been developed. The composite nature of the error term, however, poses a challenge to the proper specification of a true panel data estimator due to an incidental parameter problem. Greene (2005) develops a fixed-effect panel estimator that relies on maximum likelihood estimation (MLE). This model is extended by Chen et al. (2014). They utilize the joint density of the deviations from means to remedy the incidental parameter problem. Similarly, Colombi et al. (2011, 2014) apply closed-skew distributional assumptions for the error term components to develop random effects panel estimators that allow the generation of time-variant measures of, for example, short-run and firm-specific efficiency scores.

Fifthly, an important challenge in SFA compared to alternative methods is the need for parametric assumptions in general, which are usually hard to motivate by economic theory. An important methodological development therefore pertains to approaches that leave increasingly many of these assumptions unnecessary. Martins-Filho and Yao (2015), for example, extend earlier studies by Kumbhakar et al. (2007) and suggest a non-parametric frontier, which hinges on an error density function characterized by a known, finite parameter vector. Kousmanen and Kortelainen (2012) suggest a two-step approach that combines deterministic data envelopment analysis (DEA) with parametric SFA. The first step gauges the shape of the benchmark frontier without having to impose any parametric form a priori. Inefficiency is then obtained in the second stage as conditional expectations relative to the residuals from this first stage. Along a related train of thought, Battese et al. (2004) suggest a so-called meta-frontier, which envelops separately estimated stochastic frontiers, say for firms in different countries, with a non-deterministic encompassing benchmark, the meta-frontier. Simar et al. (2014) use a local polynomial least-squares technique to obtain the frontier, which is computationally substantially less demanding compared to local MLE. Other developments focus on the specification of the error term instead of obtaining parameters of the production kernel as such. For example, Parmeter et al. (2014) estimate the determinants of inefficiency non-parametrically and Horrace and Parmeter (2011) relax distributional assumptions on the inefficiency component u.

This highly selective review of some of the recent methodological advances highlights the continuous and fast-growing nature of the econometrics literature, which focuses on the determination of efficient frontiers and associated inefficiency scores. Important strides have been made towards increasingly less rigid assumptions, important concerns about possible endogeneity of frontier components, as well as adequately separating firm inefficiency from other observable and unobservable factors. Next, we review a similarly selective set of papers that apply SFA to the European banking industry.

SFA in European Banking

Much of the policy effort prior to the financial crisis of 2007–8 was dedicated to the establishment of a single banking market in the European Union. This approach reflects the notion that a level playing field should strengthen competition, thereby eliminating existing inefficiencies in the provision of financial services and products, and ultimately fostering the integration of European banking markets.

A number of studies test whether national banking markets indeed converged. Weill (2009) uses panel SFA methods for a sample of European banks from ten countries to test for β- and σ-convergence between 1994 and 2005. He reports that cost efficiency improved in all countries for different banking sectors, that is, commercial, savings and cooperative banks. Moreover, banking systems that started out from lower levels of cost efficiency improve faster and the dispersion of inefficiency declines over time. Thus, he provides important evidence for both β- and σ-convergence. Casu and Girardone (2010) ask the same research question, but expand the country coverage significantly to banks from 26 EU countries between 1997 and 2003. They use non-parametric DEA to obtain cost efficiency measures and model their convolution over time more explicitly using dynamic panel generalized method of moments (GMM) estimators. Whereas they confirm both β- and σ-convergence, in contrast to Weill (2009) they report declining efficiency levels, thereby corroborating possibly important changes in inference due to methodological choices.

Alternatively, excessive cross-country heterogeneity in terms of environmental factors may be the main driver of diverging results. Koutsomanoli-Filippaki et al. (2009), for example, focus on just a subsample of banking markets in ten Central and Eastern European (CEE) countries between 1998 and 2003.

Using directional distance functions, they generate a Luenberger productivity indicator, which is decomposed into efficiency changes and technological change. They report generally a low level of cost efficiency, which does not improve over time. Productivity gains are instead driven mainly by technological progress. Correspondingly, they also find that foreign banks consistently outperform domestic ones. This result for CEE banking markets indicates the existence of barriers to how foreign banking may aid market integration. Correspondingly, Fang et al. (2011) report for six South-Eastern European banking markets that such efficiency gaps also exist between domestic and foreign banks. But on the basis of cost and profit efficiency estimated with SFA, they report in contrast that efficiency differences converge over time and that efficiency generally improves, mostly due to the development of institutions and a concentration of market power among fewer banks.

These diverging results highlight the need to account adequately for heterogeneity in efficiency measurement by allowing for different transformation technologies, which constitute the benchmark against which inefficiency indicators are measured. Already for a sample of US banks only, for example, Kumbhakar et al. (2013) show that an estimator allowing for fully efficient banks yields significantly different efficiency levels and rankings for individual banks compared to more conventional single-frontier estimates. Likewise, Koetter and Poghosyan (2009) apply the latent-class model of Greene (2005) to show that already within German banking only three different technology regimes exist. These technology regimes cannot be identified solely with institutional differences, such as bank types like commercial, savings and cooperatives, and therefore have to be modelled econometrically. Since they show for each of the regimes significantly different profiles in terms of efficiency, market power and risk-taking, it seems reasonable to expect such differences to exist at the European, cross-country level as well. Bos and Schmiedel (2007) take these into account by applying the meta-frontier method of Battese et al. (2004) to a sample of banks from all major European countries to test for the existence of a single, that is, integrated market frontier in the EU between 1993 and 2004. They do confirm the existence of such a single meta-frontier.

The proper measurement of banking market integration and the associated effects on bank efficiency and competition are important beyond the implications for financial markets alone. Extending the extant literature on the nexus between finance and growth, a number of studies have shown for both national (Koetter and Wedow 2010) as well as regional markets in different European economies (Hasan et al. 2009) that a sheer expansion of credit alone did not spark significant additional economic growth. Using cost and profit efficiency measures obtained with a latent-class SFA model in the case of Germany and a single-frontier SFA method accounting for heterogeneity in the inefficiency distribution for the explanation of regional growth at the European level, they show that the quality of intermediaries in terms of bank efficiency matters for growth, while the seminal measure of financial development, credit over gross domestic product (GDP), does not.

At the same time, additional competitive pressure arising from an increasingly integrated banking market might also induce banks to take excessive individual risks, ultimately contributing to an increase of systemic risk (see Chap. 7 of this Handbook).

Fiordelisi et al. (2011) estimate accordingly the cost, profit and revenue efficiency of commercial banks from EU-26 prior to the crisis. For a sample ranging from 1995 to 2007 they subsequently use Granger causality tests to show that higher cost and revenue efficiency Granger causes lower probabilities of bank defaults (PD). Although better bank capitalization precedes cost efficiency improvements, they find no evidence for Granger causality between capital ratios and bank risk. Thus, efficiency might be an important channel by which policies aiming to strengthen the resilience of the banking system by means of higher capital requirements help accomplish the ultimate objective of lower probabilities of bank default.

An open question from their work remains, however, whether results can be generalized to banks for which implied PDs based on rating information is not available. This is particularly important in studying European banking markets, where the vast majority of financial institutions are neither listed on capital markets nor do they issue rated debt. As an alternative, Assaf et al. (2013) resort to an accounting-based, well-established measure of bank risk, namely non-performing loans (NPL). For a sample of Turkish commercial banks, they use Baysian estimation techniques and specify NPL as a bad output in the vein of Kumbhakar and Tsionas (2015). Accounting for credit risk in the form of bad (NPL) outputs alters efficiency estimates significantly. They find evidence of productivity growth due to technical change but a decline in efficiency, and report as well that foreign banks are both more productive and efficient.

Against the backdrop of the more recent turmoil in European banking markets due to the financial crisis of 2007–8 and especially the sovereign debt crisis that started in 2010, further research on the relationship between bank efficiency and risk in more recent years is particularly important. Two studies in this regard are Tsionas et al. (2015a) and Matousek et al. (2015). The former employ Baysian dynamic frontier models to estimate both technical and allocative efficiency among banks from 15 European countries between 2005 and 2012. Impulse response functions show a difference in the short-

and long-term dynamics of efficiency. Their results suggest only a mild drop in efficiency in the short run after the crisis, which rebounds soon after. An important insight for policy makers is furthermore that allocative efficiency depends positively on the capitalization of banks. The latter study also treats NPL explicitly as an undesirable output using parametric distance functions when investigating possible convergence in terms of bank efficiency before and after the shock represented by the financial crisis. They provide evidence not only that efficiency declined in the aftermath of the crisis, but also that it halted integration and convergence. Instead, they show that their findings indicate the formation of separate convergence clubs.

In the light of these developments, it is startling that so far no research exists on the efficiency implications of the pervasive regulatory measures passed after 2007–8 in pursuit of establishing a common regulatory framework in the form of the European Banking Union. Therefore, we provide next a simple exercise to test for the implications of introducing supranational microprudential supervision in the form of the Single Supervisory Mechanism.

Specification and Data

Specification

We focus here on the efficiency effect of being a bank that is supervised by the SSM according to the latest list of the ECB (2015) while controlling for observable bank traits that gauge the profitability, risk and size of the banking firms. To this end we use the conditional mean model, suggested initially by Coelli (1995).

More specifically, we specify a cost frontier where we explain the operating cost *TOC* of bank i in year t as a function of output quantities y_k, input factor prices w_l and further controls z, which includes our variable of interest, namely an indicator equal to one if the bank is supervised by the SSM. To control for technical change we also specify next to country fixed effects a time trend t, its squared term t^2 and interactions with the direct production terms y and w:[1]

$$\ln TOC = \alpha_{\text{country}} + \sum_k \beta_k \ln y_k + \sum_l \beta_l \ln w_l + \frac{1}{2}\sum_k \sum_m \beta_{k,m} \ln y_k \ln y_m$$
$$+\frac{1}{2}\sum_l \sum_m \beta_{l,m} \ln w_l \ln w_m + \sum_k \sum_l \beta_{k,l} \ln y_k \ln w_l + \eta t \qquad (11.2)$$
$$+\lambda t^2 \sum_k \beta_{t,k} \ln y_k t + \sum_l \beta_{t,l} \ln w_l t + yz + \mathbf{v} + \mathbf{u}.$$

For the profit frontier, we replace the log of total cost by the log of total operating profits before tax *PBT*.[2] As is common in many bank efficiency studies, we choose a translog functional form and define variables below. For our purposes, it is more relevant to note that contrary to ordinary least squares (OLS) estimation, the error term in Eq. (11.1) features two components. The first term v is random noise and normally distributed with an expected value of zero. The second term u captures inefficiency. In line with Coelli (1995), we assume that it is drawn from a truncated half-normal distribution with mean μ. We furthermore specify this mean of the inefficiency distribution to depend also on the control variables z:

$$\mu = \gamma z. \qquad (11.3)$$

Parameters are estimated by maximizing the joint-likelihood function after imposing the necessary restrictions, such as homogeneity of degree one, by dividing all factor prices and the dependent variables by one of the factor prices. Given estimated parameters, we obtain bank-specific point estimates of cost and profit efficiency (CE and PE) using the method by Jondrow et al. (1982) as $E_i = E\{\exp(u_i)|\varepsilon_i\}$, where $\varepsilon = u \pm v$. Hence, inefficiency leads to higher than optimal cost and lower than optimal profits, respectively.

Bank Data

We obtain balance sheet and profit and loss account information for all universal banks that are active in 20 member states of the European Union from the Bankscope database for the time period 2004 until 2013.[3] We select all banks with specializations equal to those in the lists of SSM-supervised banks. All variables are defined in Table 11.3. Total operating cost equals the sum of interest expenses, loan impairment charges, other operating expenses and personnel expenses. Total profits before tax is the profit before impairment charges. To specify an according cost and profit frontier, we follow the intermediation approach of Sealey and Lindley (1977) and assume that banks hold

Table 11.3 Variable definition and sources

Name	Acronym	Description	Source
Total securities	y1	Total securities in € millions	Bankscope
Gross loans	y2	Gross loans in € millions	Bankscope
Off-balance sheet activities	y3	The sum of managed securitized assets, other off-balance sheet exposures, guarantees, acceptances and documentary committed credit lines in € millions	Bankscope
Cost of fixed assets	w1	Operating expenses divided by fixed assets	Bankscope
Cost of labour	w2	Personnel expenses divided by number of employees	Bankscope
Cost of borrowed funds	w3	The sum of interest expenses and other interest expenses divided by total deposits and money market funding	Bankscope
Significant supervised entity 16-03-2015	SSE	Dummy variable indicating a significant supervised entity, as indicated by the European Central Bank on their list of 16 March 2015	European Central Bank
Significant supervised entity 10-10-2013	SSE_oct2013	Dummy variable indicating a significant supervised entity, as indicated by the European Central Bank on their preliminary list of 10 October 2013	European Central Bank
Equity	Z	Total equity in € millions	Bankscope
Operating costs	TOC	The sum of interest expenses, loan impairment charges, other operating expenses and personnel expenses	Bankscope
Profits before tax	PBT	Pre-impairment operating profit in € millions	
Return on equity	ROE	Pre-impairment operating profit as a percentage of total equity	Bankscope
Capitalization	CAPITAL	Equity as a percentage of total assets	
Z-score	ZSCORE	Sum of CAPITAL and returns on assets, defined as PBT over Total Assets, divided by the standard deviation of ROA	Bankscope
Credit risk	CREDITRISK	Loan impairment charges as a percentage of gross loans	Bankscope
Cost–income ratio	CI_RATIO	The sum of personnel and other operating expenses divided by total revenues	Bankscope
Total assets	Total_assets	Total assets in € millions	Bankscope
Size indicator	SIZE	A quartile indicator indicating the quartile of total assets distribution a bank belongs to in each year	Bankscope

securities (y_1), originate loans (y_2) and engage in off-balance sheet activities (y_3) to generate income. As is common in the bank efficiency literature, we also specify the log level of equity capital because it can be used as a netput to fund bank assets. Banks employ fixed assets, labour and borrowed funds to generate output. We approximate the rental price of fixed assets (w_1) by dividing fixed assets by operating expenses. The price of labour (w_2) is obtained as the sum of personnel expenditure divided by the number of employees. The rental price of funds (w_3) results from dividing interest expenses by interest-bearing liabilities.

Table 11.4 depicts descriptive statistics for the cost frontier sample in panel A and for the profit frontier sample in panel B. We show the distributional properties for the entire sample, the group of banks supervised by the SSM according to the March 2015 list and those supervised by NCAs. Both cost and frontier data show clearly that SSM banks are significantly larger, directly reflecting the focus on size to define systemically relevant financial institutions. Whereas SSM banks exhibit higher mean factor cost for both labour and borrowed funds, these differences are not statistically significant.

Aside from the bank production technology data, we also specify further controls in logs to gauge systematic differences across banks other than the responsible supervisor. Empirical banking studies that measure the stability and soundness of banks by capturing risk and return traits, such as Wheelock and Wilson (2000), inspire our choice of controls. The capital ratio is measured as the ratio of equity to total assets to measure possible differences of banks' risk–return preferences. To measure risk more explicitly, we furthermore include the z-score as in Laeven and Levine (2009) as the sum of return on equity and capitalization divided by the (time-invariant) standard deviation of each bank's returns. This measure therefore grasps the bank's distance to default. In addition, we specify the ratio of loan impairment charges to gross total loans as an indicator of credit risk. As a metric of operational cost efficiency we also include the cost-to-income ratio in the profit frontier. In the cost frontier, we specify instead the return on equity to gauge the profitability of the bank explicitly. Finally, we account for size differences as another source of systemic deviations from both optimal cost and profits by means of an ordinal indicator per quartile of the annual asset distribution. All factor prices and control variables expressed in ratios are winsorized at the 1st and 99th percentile. Data expressed in monetary terms that are used to generate variables are deflated by country-specific consumer price indices to price levels in 2005.

Clearly, many of these covariates are correlated with another, adding to inherent multicollinearity issues that result from the specification of the many interaction terms in a translog functional form. Therefore, we present our

Table 11.4 Summary statistics, cost and profit frontier

	Full sample					SSEs					All others				
	mean	sd	p5	p95	N	mean	sd	p5	p95	N	mean	sd	p5	p95	N
Panel A: Cost frontier															
SSE	0.03	0.17	0.00	0.00	27,301										
y1	3,629.74	37,543.68	9.80	5,616.64	27,301	76,045.56	193,596.33	294.29	316,996.78	784	1,488.70	13,594.93	9.60	3,102.79	26,517
y2	5,556.08	31,537.30	44.76	17,309.81	27,301	88,311.31	132,249.44	1,902.00	396,465.56	784	3,109.34	17,293.59	44.15	10,805.40	26,517
y3	3,368.01	30,500.01	6.00	6,537.03	27,301	59,263.51	147,841.79	421.99	322,174.03	784	1,715.41	14,738.35	5.84	4,003.57	26,517
w1	184.68	419.67	31.11	700.00	27,301	182.59	332.92	33.08	512.53	784	184.74	421.97	31.04	708.48	26,517
w2	68.13	32.27	39.34	134.46	27,301	71.92	41.62	25.05	153.01	784	68.01	31.95	39.86	134.01	26,517
w3	2.77	2.06	1.04	5.80	27,301	4.39	3.44	1.04	13.27	784	2.73	1.99	1.04	5.60	26,517
Z	542.43	3,061.09	7.29	1,727.25	27,301	8,384.45	13,776.11	289.60	43,436.00	784	310.58	1,473.49	7.10	1,178.76	26,517
TOC	468.60	2,864.86	4.09	1,294.62	27,301	7,621.70	12,627.19	140.13	37,591.75	784	257.12	1,477.91	4.07	798.88	26,517
PBT	81.88	579.61	0.94	238.36	27,301	1,357.30	2,809.62	13.31	7,022.30	784	44.17	251.51	0.94	167.64	26,517
ROE	30.79	8.84	18.56	45.62	27,301	32.34	10.56	17.03	49.51	784	30.75	8.78	18.63	45.31	26,517
CAPITAL	8.06	4.26	3.46	15.70	27,301	6.01	3.69	1.79	11.78	784	8.12	4.26	3.63	15.76	26,517
ZSCORE	35.40	26.09	8.22	81.18	27,301	31.50	29.64	6.62	87.06	784	35.51	25.97	8.32	81.00	26,517
CREDITRISK	4.50	1.10	3.37	6.30	27,301	4.61	1.17	3.80	6.74	784	4.50	1.10	3.36	6.29	26,517
CI_RATIO	43.85	15.24	17.66	68.24	27,301	30.12	14.95	3.93	53.17	784	44.25	15.05	18.80	68.58	26,517
Total_assets	11,493.71	78,214.20	90.52	29,920.57	27,301	199,473.75	359,724.94	4,312.68	967,359.43	784	5,935.91	37,436.52	89.74	17,782.23	26,517
Panel B: Profit frontier															
SSE	0.03	0.17	0.00	0.00	26,228										
y1	3,481.72	36,187.58	11.12	5,375.00	26,228	74,660.64	187,693.70	272.03	320,695.03	754	1,374.91	12,349.33	10.78	2,990.23	25,474
y2	5,526.80	31,557.16	49.46	17,178.48	26,228	88,800.36	134,076.92	1,902.00	397,777.00	754	3,062.00	16,810.52	48.98	10,805.40	25,474
y3	3,309.71	30,587.95	6.35	6,453.79	26,228	60,277.80	150,374.46	410.34	332,614.59	754	1,623.52	13,998.93	6.25	3,983.65	25,474
w1	175.14	399.62	31.28	615.44	26,228	174.63	305.38	32.16	486.93	754	175.15	402.07	31.28	620.00	25,474
w2	67.28	31.40	39.53	131.09	26,228	71.84	41.94	25.02	158.30	754	67.15	31.02	39.99	130.47	25,474
w3	2.75	2.00	1.05	5.70	26,228	4.31	3.34	1.00	11.56	754	2.70	1.93	1.05	5.48	25,474
Z	543.85	3,087.15	7.84	1,720.08	26,228	8,542.51	13,974.73	280.12	44,521.27	754	307.10	1,445.61	7.69	1,176.38	25,474
TOC	454.29	2,812.30	4.40	1,246.01	26,228	7,484.50	12,572.55	137.78	37,788.00	754	246.20	1,401.51	4.35	779.93	25,474

(continued)

Table 11.4 (continued)

	Full sample					SSEs					All others				
	mean	sd	p5	p95	N	mean	sd	p5	p95	N	mean	sd	p5	p95	N
PBT	88.30	579.80	1.01	248.77	26,228	1,450.27	2,812.33	41.25	7,270.06	754	47.98	236.19	1.01	174.48	25,474
ROE	31.62	7.90	21.59	45.86	26,228	33.41	9.22	19.60	50.10	754	31.57	7.85	21.59	45.71	25,474
CAPITAL	8.01	4.10	3.55	15.32	26,228	6.09	3.71	1.93	11.80	754	8.06	4.10	3.72	15.38	25,474
ZSCORE	36.31	26.03	10.07	82.40	26,228	32.07	28.91	7.29	87.06	754	36.43	25.93	10.28	82.27	25,474
CREDITRISK	4.50	1.07	3.39	6.21	26,228	4.56	1.08	3.80	6.47	754	4.50	1.07	3.37	6.21	25,474
CI_RATIO	42.90	13.63	17.88	64.29	26,228	29.90	13.84	4.12	51.74	754	43.28	13.43	19.03	64.53	25,474
Total_assets	11,243.19	77,003.21	97.84	29,045.16	26,228	198,582.11	358,050.81	4,052.93	1,005,473.39	754	5,698.18	35,294.87	96.36	17,554.85	25,474

This table reports summary statistics for the cost and profit frontier estimation samples, respectively columns 4 of Tables 11.5 and 11.6

results below in four steps, gradually adding these control variables to both the kernel of the frontiers shown in Eq. (11.1) as well as determinant of the mean of the inefficiency distribution shown in Eq. (11.2).

Single Supervisory Mechanism Data

The four criteria to select which banks are directly supervised emphasize the size of financial institutions, either in absolute terms or relative to the size of the host economy.[4] Recent studies indeed find that larger European banks tend to be more efficient in terms of scale economies (Beccalli et al. 2015), but also caution that part of these efficiencies may be due to implicit too-big-to-fail subsidies (Davies and Tracey 2013), which might even be increased when officially considered systemically important by the SSM. Therefore, we estimate the effect of being a bank supervised by the SSM on both cost and profit efficiency using a simple stochastic frontier analysis model by Coelli (1995), thereby essentially comparing banks with NCA supervision to those supervised by the ECB.

We also analyse the fact that the list of systemically relevant banks changed over time. Specifically, the ECB published together with the procedure of the comprehensive assessment in preparation of the SSM a list of included banks in October 2013. The final list of SSM-supervised banks that was published, in turn, in March 2015 contained some additional banks, but also omitted a few from this initial list. While these changes might merely reflect changes to the fulfilment of the defined criteria to be considered systemically relevant, such as Lithuania joining the SSM, these changes might also partly reflect a political bargaining process (De Rynck 2014). Although we are not aiming to explain this political bargaining process, we want to test whether exposure to different supervisory styles, and possibly alternative objectives of NCA compared to those of the SSM, influence bank efficiency.[5] A more rigid approach to regulation might reduce the efficiency of bank operations if it imposes excessive administrative burdens on banks, as representatives of the financial industry frequently claim. Therefore we are particularly interested to test if efficiency differentials exist for banks that switched from SSM supervision status into NCA status or vice versa.

Our main variable of interest is an indicator equal to one whether a bank was supervised by the SSM according to the latest list of systemically relevant financial institutions (ECB 2015). All banks that are chartered in member countries of the EMU are automatically subject to micro-prudential supervision by the SSM. Most of these are, however, in practice supervised by

NCA. The SSM report indicates that 122 entities are directly supervised, covering 82 % of total assets in the EMU banking industry (ECB 2015). From this report, we are able to match for up to 108 banks the identity and the required cost frontier data. For the profit frontier sample, we are able to match up to 107 banks listed by the SSM with Bankscope data.

In addition, we compare the contemporary list of SSM-supervised banks to the preliminary one published in March 2013 during the preparations for the comprehensive assessment conducted by the ECB.[6] Thereby, we can account for possible efficiency differences if banks either entered the list or were re-allocated to the supervisory authority at the national level. For both the cost and the profit frontier samples we find that seven banks disappeared from the list and six new ones were added.[7] To test whether these changes from supranational to national responsibility, or vice versa, for supervision can also explain efficiency differences, we specify in Eq. (11.2) an interaction term of the indicator variables whether a bank was part of the SSM list in 2013 and 2015, respectively. We realize that whether a bank is supervised by the SSM is clearly not exogenous to a bank's costs and profits. In particular, it is likely that there are omitted variables driving both. We leave it to future work to solve these issues as it would benefit from having both a period before and after the implementation of the SSM.

Results

Frontier Estimation Results

Consider first the parameter estimates of the cost frontier depicted in Table 11.5. To conserve on space, we only show in each pair of columns (1) through (4) the effect of the vector of control variables z on the kernel of the cost frontier in the left subcolumn (CF) and the mean of the inefficiency distribution in the right subcolumn (μ), respectively. Results for all direct and interaction terms of cost frontier arguments shown in Eq. (11.1) are available upon request.

When we control only for the size and profitability of banks, column pair (1) shows neither an effect of SSM supervision on the cost kernel nor one on the inefficiency distribution. Larger banks that are more profitable exhibit larger cost *ceteris paribus*, but the effect on the location of the first moment of the inefficiency distribution has opposing effects. Whereas size correlates with a higher average inefficiency, more profitable banks are found to yield a lower mean inefficiency.

Table 11.5 Cost frontier estimates

	(1)		(2)		(3)		(4)	
	CF	μ	CF	μ	CF	μ	CF	μ
SSE	−0.0008	0.2028	−0.0909***	1.6103***	−0.0713***	1.5655***	−0.0323*	1.9513***
	[0.969]	[0.350]	[0.000]	[0.000]	[0.001]	[0.000]	[0.061]	[0.000]
lnSIZE	0.3075***	0.6453***	0.0773***	1.3173***	0.0678***	1.3028***	0.0890***	2.6297***
	[0.000]	[0.000]	[0.000]	[0.000]	[0.000]	[0.000]	[0.000]	[0.000]
lnROE	0.3514***	−1.5067***	0.2364***	−1.4872***	0.1902***	−0.6081***	0.0133**	−0.0884
	[0.000]	[0.000]	[0.000]	[0.000]	[0.000]	[0.000]	[0.039]	[0.167]
lnCAPITAL			−0.8073***	1.4018***	−0.7979***	1.6520***	−0.7551***	2.1802***
			[0.000]	[0.000]	[0.000]	[0.000]	[0.000]	[0.000]
lnZSCORE					−0.0042	−1.5946***	0.0235***	−2.6725***
					[0.311]	[0.000]	[0.000]	[0.000]
lnCREDITRISK							0.7927***	−2.9731***
							[0.000]	[0.000]
Observations	27,497	27,497	27,497	27,497	27,301	27,301	27,301	27,301
# Banks	3,789	3,789	3,789	3,789	3,648	3,648	3,648	3,648
# SSEs	108	108	108	108	106	106	106	106
# Countries	20	20	20	20	20	20	20	20
σ(v)	0.3159	0.3159	0.2871	0.2871	0.2781	0.2781	0.2191	0.2191
σ(u)	0.7547	0.7547	0.7404	0.7404	0.7665	0.7665	0.9913	0.9913

This table shows the cost frontier estimations of Eq. 11.1 for 2004–2013 using a truncated normal distribution for the inefficiency term. Columns labelled CF show the coefficients of the kernel of the cost frontier; those labelled μ show coefficients for the mean of the inefficiency distribution. For brevity we only show the results on the control variables *z* included in the kernel and the mean of the inefficiency distribution. All estimations include country fixed effects in the cost function. σ(v) and σ(u) indicate the standard deviation of the error term and technical efficiency, respectively. P-values are reported in square brackets: *** $p < 0.01$, ** $p < 0.05$, * $p < 0.1$

The insignificance of the SSM indicator variable in both the kernel and the inefficiency distribution might reflect the fact that it was the primary criterion for the ECB to select banks that ought to be supervised at the supranational level. To differentiate between alternative bank traits in a more detailed fashion, we therefore gradually add in columns (2) through (4) as further controls. We specify the log of the equity capital ratio, the z-score and a measure of credit risk results in parameter estimates of the SSM indicator that consistently indicate two effects. Firstly, banks that are supervised by the SSM exhibit significantly lower cost levels compared to banks supervised at the national level. The magnitude of this effect varies between nine and three basis points and is therefore rather small. This effect may indicate that the exposure to homogenous supervisory practices exerts cost discipline on supervised banks. Secondly, the effect on the mean of the inefficiency distribution is in turn significantly positive throughout. The economic magnitude associated with these coefficients is not straightforward to interpret because the marginal effects depend on the distribution of the estimated total error ε given that inefficiency scores are obtained as conditional means according to the Jondrow et al. (1982) method. We therefore discuss below estimated efficiency scores that we average across all banks per year, separated by SSM versus non-SSM-supervised institutions.

All the additional controls are also statistically significant, underpinning the importance of controlling for environmental factors in both the cost frontier as well as the determination of the inefficiency distribution's location and shape. Our results indicate lower costs for banks that are better capitalized and are exposed to lower credit risk while simultaneously yielding lower z-scores, that is, those that are less distant from default in terms of capital and earnings buffers relative to earnings volatility. The results also show that the mean of the cost inefficiency distribution depends positively on higher capitalization ratios, but negatively on more credit risk and more stable banks in terms of the z-score. The first finding is in line with the notion that capital is an expensive source of funding for banking activities. The second result underscores the danger of mistakenly identifying more risky loan portfolios as efficient banking operations. Overall, the results corroborate the importance of accounting explicitly for risk factors, which are likely to capture very different aspects of banking risk such as the z-score and credit risk, to avoid confounding effects on estimated inefficiency.

Table 11.6 shows parameter estimates for the profit frontier. Across all specifications in column pairs (1) through (4) we estimate a positive effect of the SSM indicator variable on both the level of profits before tax, but also the mean of the profit inefficiency distribution.

Table 11.6 Profit frontier estimates

	(1)		(2)		(3)		(4)	
	PF	μ	PF	μ	PF	μ	PF	μ
SSE	0.2342***	0.5512***	0.2119***	0.4176***	0.1808***	0.3449***	0.1949***	0.3903***
	[0.000]	[0.000]	[0.000]	[0.000]	[0.000]	[0.001]	[0.000]	[0.000]
lnSIZE	0.3575***	2.5278***	0.2807***	2.2662***	0.2736***	1.7108***	0.2817***	1.7178***
	[0.000]	[0.000]	[0.000]	[0.000]	[0.000]	[0.000]	[0.000]	[0.000]
lnCI	−0.5947***	−2.1500***	−0.6077***	−1.8324***	−0.5634***	−1.6327***	−0.5195***	−1.5552***
	[0.000]	[0.000]	[0.000]	[0.000]	[0.000]	[0.000]	[0.000]	[0.000]
lnCAPITAL			−0.3290***	−0.6704***	−0.2703***	−0.3039***	−0.2447***	−0.2137***
			[0.000]	[0.000]	[0.000]	[0.000]	[0.000]	[0.000]
lnZSCORE					−0.1349***	−0.8542***	−0.1300***	−0.9453***
					[0.000]	[0.000]	[0.000]	[0.000]
lnCREDITRISK							0.1875***	−0.8982***
							[0.000]	[0.000]
Observations	26,328	26,328	26,328	26,328	26,228	26,228	26,228	26,228
# Banks	3,704	3,704	3,704	3,704	3,606	3,606	3,606	3,606
# SSEs	107	107	107	107	105	105	105	105
# Countries	20	20	20	20	20	20	20	20
σ(v)	0.3258	0.3258	0.3166	0.3166	0.2877	0.2877	0.2831	0.2831
σ(u)	1.2249	1.2249	1.1456	1.1456	1.1292	1.1292	1.1396	1.1396

This table shows the profit frontier estimations of Eq. 11.1 for 2004–2013 using a truncated normal distribution for the inefficiency term. Columns labelled PF show the coefficients of the kernel of the profit frontier; those labelled μ show coefficients for the mean of the inefficiency distribution. For brevity we only show the results on the control variables *z* included in the kernel and the mean of the inefficiency distribution. All estimations include country fixed effects in the kernel. σ(v) and σ(u) indicate the standard deviation of the error term and technical efficiency, respectively. P-values are reported in square brackets: *** $p < 0.01$, ** $p < 0.05$, * $p < 0.1$

Regarding the former result, banks that are supervised by the SSM tend to exhibit, according to our estimation results, 18 and 23 basis points higher profit levels. Supranational supervision might in fact aid banks to boost profits, potentially due to imposing risk management discipline and requiring banks to report in a more granular fashion details of their operations, even after we control explicitly for size, profitability and risk.

The latter estimation result also indicates, however, that banks under the supervision of the SSM exhibit significantly higher means of the profit inefficiency distribution. This finding might indeed confirm practitioners' claims of an increased regulatory burden of systemically relevant financial institutions compared to smaller and less relevant competitors that are supervised at the national level. But given that the interpretation of these coefficients is a bit cumbersome, we turn next to a discussion of estimated mean cost and profit efficiency levels.

Mean Efficiency of SSM Versus Non-SSM Banks Over Time

Figure 11.1 depicts the dynamics of average cost inefficiency developments of banks that are supervised by the SSM compared to those that are not, where higher cost inefficiency scores indicate less efficient banks, that is, a score of one indicates no inefficiencies.

At the beginning of the sample period, those banks that eventually were supervised by the SSM exhibit significantly higher levels of cost inefficiency on the order of almost 50 % above optimal cost compared to the smaller banks eventually supervised by national authorities. The latter group of banks exhibits around 20 % higher costs in excess of estimated optimal cost levels and also a much more narrow dispersion of cost inefficiency. Starting in 2010, the year of the European sovereign debt crisis and the beginning of Banking Union initiatives, these differences continued to exist but were no longer statistically significant. This development might indicate that the inception and the progress of the Banking Union also marked the start of converging cost efficiency, possibly due to efforts to homogenize banking supervision rules and in particular their application in practice in member states of the EMU. The development of cost inefficiency also indicates, however, that banks tended to become increasingly cost inefficient irrespective of where supervisory authority rests. One interpretation of this result is that increased supervisory burden is one of the reasons for these cost efficiency losses. Put differently, regulators might face a trade-off between incurring some slack in terms of operational efficiency of banks when tightening regulation with the aim to enhance the resilience and financial stability of the banking industry. Further research

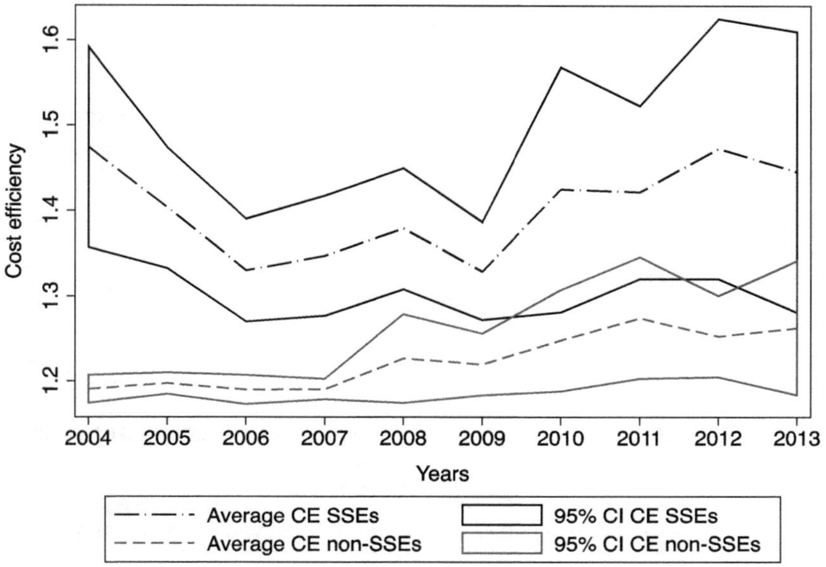

Fig. 11.1 Cost inefficiency of SSEs vs non-SSEs. This figure shows average cost inefficiency (CE) and its 95 % confidence interval (CI) for significant supervised entities (SSEs) and non-SSEs. Cost inefficiency is calculated as average technical inefficiency in each year. Technical inefficiency is derived from the cost function estimates in column (4) of Table 11.5

in such an efficiency–financial stability trade-off is warranted. An alternative explanation is that banking supervision in an increasingly materializing Banking Union forced banks to reveal inefficient operations independently of whether supervision is actually conducted centrally or decentralized. Future research seeking to identify the causal relationship between the organization of supervision and bank efficiency, which is beyond the scope of this chapter, is therefore warranted.

Figure 11.2 depicts the corresponding dynamics for estimated profit efficiency across SSM and non-SSM banks over time, where higher profit efficiency indicates more efficient banks, that is, a score of one indicates no inefficiencies. As before, non-SSM-supervised banks exhibit significantly higher levels of profit efficiency. They realize around 70 % of estimated optimal, potential profits compared to a mere 50 % realized by the larger, SSM-supervised competition. Lower profit efficiency scores among larger banks are to some extent in line with earlier bank efficiency studies. This result is also consistent with more recent evidence on the role of organizational complexity in large banks that prevents the efficient (internal) allocation of capital and optimal realization of profitable project opportunities, as discussed, for example, in Cetorelli and Goldberg (2014).

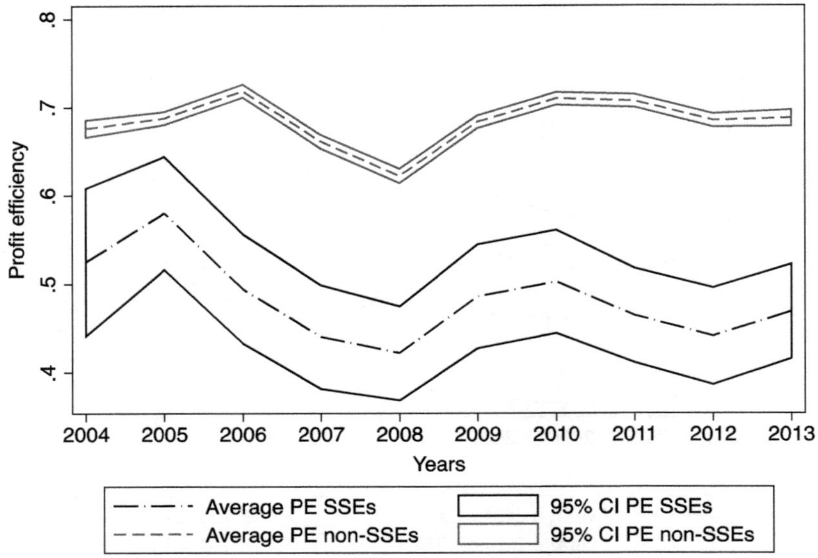

Fig. 11.2 Profit efficiency of SSEs vs non-SSEs. This figure shows average profit efficiency (PE) and its 95 % confidence interval (CI) for significant supervised entities (SSEs) and non-SSEs. Profit efficiency is calculated as average technical efficiency in each year. Technical efficiency is derived from the profit function estimates in column (4) of Table 11.6

Contrary to cost inefficiency, the differences between SSM and non-SSM-supervised banks are persistent. This development may indeed indicate a sustained higher regulatory burden for systemically relevant banks facing more detailed reporting requirements. Alternatively, this persistent difference may also indicate an excessively favourable treatment of banks by NCA, akin to the extreme forms of regulatory capture experienced during the S&L crisis in the USA during the late 1980s and early 1990s (see Kane 1990).

Switching Supervisory Regimes

We therefore investigate next the effects of inclusion and exclusion from the list of systemically relevant financial institutions published in ECB (2015) relative to the one published by the ECB (2013) in preparation for the Comprehensive Assessment preceding the handover of supervisory authority from national authorities to the ECB. Specifically, in Table 11.7 we show results from cost frontier (panel A) and profit frontier (panel B) estimations where we include next to the indicator of systemically relevant banks

Table 11.7 Frontier estimates, SSEs vs SSEs 2013

	(1)		(2)		(3)		(4)	
	CF/PF	μ	CF/PF	μ	CF/PF	μ	CF/PF	μ
Panel A: Cost frontiers								
SSE	−0.6719***	2.8036***	−0.4894***	2.0122***	−0.4995***	2.3120***	−0.2870***	1.3753*
	[0.000]	[0.000]	[0.000]	[0.000]	[0.000]	[0.000]	[0.000]	[0.059]
SSE_2013	0.2957***	−2.3613	0.1860*	−5.2160	0.0881	0.4755	−0.0983	2.3543***
	[0.010]	[0.679]	[0.064]	[0.676]	[0.285]	[0.706]	[0.131]	[0.000]
SSE × SSE_2013	0.4231**	−0.4752	0.2504*	4.7711	0.3834***	−1.3015	0.3799***	−1.7820*
	[0.010]	[0.934]	[0.057]	[0.702]	[0.001]	[0.336]	[0.000]	[0.065]
Observations	27,497	27,497	27,497	27,497	27,301	27,301	27,301	27,301
# Banks	3,789	3,789	3,789	3,789	3,648	3,648	3,648	3,648
# SSEs	108	108	108	108	106	106	106	106
# SSEs 2013	109	109	109	109	107	107	107	107
Panel B: Profit frontiers								
SSE	−0.3060***	−1.2547	−0.3252***	−0.9719	−0.2889***	−0.7135	−0.2621**	−0.7131
	[0.003]	[0.168]	[0.002]	[0.225]	[0.005]	[0.276]	[0.011]	[0.297]
SSE_2013	0.2754**	0.5821	0.1917	0.5504	0.1844*	0.3011	0.1944*	0.4537
	[0.022]	[0.297]	[0.116]	[0.257]	[0.090]	[0.481]	[0.071]	[0.291]
SSE × SSE_2013	0.3104*	1.2838	0.3938**	0.8902	0.3257**	0.7953	0.2997**	0.6860
	[0.055]	[0.232]	[0.016]	[0.345]	[0.034]	[0.313]	[0.049]	[0.399]
Observations	26,328	26,328	26,328	26,328	26,228	26,228	26,228	26,228
# Banks	3,704	3,704	3,704	3,704	3,606	3,606	3,606	3,606
# SSEs	107	107	107	107	105	105	105	105
# SSEs 2013	108	108	108	108	106	106	106	106

This table shows cost and profit frontier estimations that correspond to those in Tables 11.5 and 11.6, respectively. In this table we add an indicator variable, SSE_2013, equal to one when a bank is on the preliminary list of significant supervised entities as published by the ECB in 2013, and zero otherwise. We also add an interaction between SSE and SSE_2013. All estimations include country fixed effects in the kernel of the cost and profit functions. P-values are reported in square brackets: *** $p < 0.01$, ** $p < 0.05$, * $p < 0.1$

according to the 2015 list also an indicator of when the bank was included on the preliminary list published in 2013, as well as the according interaction term.

The four pairs of columns correspond to the gradual inclusion of additional control variables in the tables above, which we, however, no longer report to conserve on space.

The results for the cost frontier in panel A confirm across columns, first of all, the importance of controlling for observable bank traits gauging their size, risk and return profile. In the most saturated specification in the pair of columns (4), the indicators for both SSM supervision according to the 2013 and the 2015 list, respectively, confirm the baseline results of a higher mean cost inefficiency. The interaction term is significantly negative, indicating that the large group of banks that remained throughout the process of setting up the SSM as part of the Banking Union exhibited a lower mean cost inefficiency relative to those banks that either entered the contemporary list of systemically relevant institutions or were excluded from it since the announcement of the comprehensive assessment in 2013. We tabulate below mean cost inefficiency levels across all four categories of banks.

Consider first the effects for the level of cost reflected by the estimated coefficients specified in the kernel of the cost frontier. We find that banks eventually supervised by the SSM exhibited lower levels of cost relative to the time when they were not part of the SSM list. The effect for those banks on the 2013 list is in turn not significant. The significantly positive interaction term in subcolumn CF/PF in (4), the kernel, indicates that banks switching between national and supranational supervision had operating costs, *ceteris paribus*, 28 basis points lower compared to those banks that stayed in their supervisory regime. Together, these results suggest that clarity about which authority supervises a bank reduces cost inefficiencies, that is, the ability to attain optimal cost, but is associated with banks generally exhibiting slightly higher levels of operating cost.

With regards to the effects of SSM versus non-SSM supervision on profit efficiency, the bottom panel B of Table 11.7 shows that the statistical significance is much weaker once we include an interaction term. In the most saturated specification in column (4), only the effects on the kernel of the optimal profit frontier are significantly different from zero. Contrary to the baseline effects reported above, banks that are eventually supervised according to the regime communicated in 2015 incur lower levels of profit, whereas banks that were already on the 2013 list exhibit a slightly positive effect on their level of profits before tax. Relative to the group of switching banks, profit levels of non-switchers are also significantly higher. Therefore, in particular, banks that entered the supranational supervisory regime only in the course of events after 2013 appear to generate lower levels of profits.

Table 11.8 Cross tabulation, SSEs vs SSEs 2013

Panel A: Cost frontier			
	SSE_2013 = 0	SSE_2013 = 1	Total
SSE = 0			
Average CE	1.225	1.454	1.225
SD CE	1.225	0.598	1.225
# Observations	26,477	40	26,517
# Banks	3,535	7	3,542
SSE = 1			
Average CE	1.284	1.413	1.404
SD CE	0.327	0.545	0.534
# Observations	53	731	784
# Banks	6	100	106
Total			
Average CE	1.225	1.415	1.230
SD CE	1.224	0.547	1.211
# Observations	26,530	771	27,301
# Banks	3,541	107	3,648
Panel B: Profit frontier			
	SSE_2013 = 0	SSE_2013 = 1	Total
SSE = 0			
Average PE	0.684	0.586	0.684
SD PE	0.204	0.267	0.204
# Observations	25,434	40	25,474
# Banks	3,494	7	3,501
SSE = 1			
Average PE	0.479	0.477	0.478
SD PE	0.189	0.266	0.261
# Observations	53	701	754
# Banks	6	99	105
Total			
Average PE	0.684	0.483	0.678
SD PE	0.204	0.267	0.208
# Observations	25,487	741	26,228
# Banks	3,500	106	3,606

This table reports tabulations of cost inefficiency (CE) and profit efficiency (PE) calculated from the cost frontier estimations and profit frontier estimations in, respectively, columns 4 of Tables 11.5 and 11.6. Cost inefficiency and profit efficiency are calculated as technical efficiency

To compare the levels of cost and profit efficiency more directly, we show in Table 11.8 the according mean levels of efficiency across groups of banks.

Consistent with Fig. 11.1, Panel A illustrates that the largest group of banks, which continued to be supervised by NCAs throughout, exhibit the lowest cost inefficiency on the order of 22 %. The 100 banks that were consistently allocated to the supervisory regime at the supranational level, in turn, exhibit mean cost inefficiency of around 41 %, although these differences are not statistically significantly different from zero. Potentially more interesting are the seven banks that were not included in the communication of 2013, but listed in ECB (2015). These banks were on average also more cost inefficient (45 %) compared to nationally supervised banks. Likewise, those banks that used to be included in the ECB (2013) communication but were excluded from the contemporary list of systemically relevant institutions exhibit a lower mean cost inefficiency compared to currently SSM-supervised banks on the order of 28 %, which is in turn slightly larger than the continuously non-SSM-supervised banks.

Again, it is important to note that we cannot infer from our analysis whether larger foregone cost savings are the consequence of SSM supervision, for example due to a higher regulatory burden for these banks, or whether a potentially more objective supranational supervision that is facing fewer entrenchment challenges compared to NCAs causes these differences, corroborating once more the need for future research into the causal relationship between supervisory setups and bank efficiency.

The bottom panel B of Table 11.8 sketches a similar picture for the comparison of mean profit efficiency scores. Those 3,494 banks consistently considered to be supervised by NCAs are on average more profit efficient (68 %) compared to any other group. The 99 banks indicated in both ECB communications to be supervised by the SSM exhibit the lowest profit efficiency (48 %). The seven banks coming under SSM supervision are, contrary to the cost efficiency case, better able on average to realize optimal profits, exhibiting a mean profit efficiency on the order of 59 % compared to an average of 48 % for those banks that were excluded from the list since 2013. Importantly, these differences are once more not statistically significant and therefore provide only a qualitative indication.

Conclusion

The (regulatory) need to increase capital buffers in the aftermath of the financial crisis exerted considerable pressure on bank profitability in many European countries. Whereas the resilience of the average bank in the system might have increased due to increasing mean capitalization, simple descriptive statistics also show that credit risk was not subdued in all countries after the financial and/or the sovereign debt crisis similarly. One reason might be related to the trade-off faced by regulators between financial stability and bank efficiency. Imposing rules and regulation that enhance the resilience of the entire system, for instance higher capital requirements, might burden the relative ability of European banks to efficiently transform savings into credit and other financial services.

This chapter provides a selective review of methodological advances in the parametric efficiency measurement literature to obtain firm-specific measures of efficiency, taking into account in particular environmental factors and unobserved heterogeneity that might be confounded with inefficient behaviour. The subsequent review of applications to European banking provides little evidence of convergence among European banking systems once heterogeneity across national banking systems is accounted for more explicitly. We also show that so far little empirical work exists on the effects of recent micro-prudential regulation at the European level, which might have fostered exactly such lacking integration.

Against the backdrop of the commencement of the European Banking Union in general and the inception of supranational banking supervision by the Single Supervisory Mechanism (SSM) in particular, we therefore estimate the cost and profit efficiency of European banks conditional on an indicator under which prudential regime they fall: SSM or national competent authority (NCA). Our results indicate that banks supervised by the SSM according to the list of systemically relevant financial institutions published in ECB (2015) exhibit both lower cost and profit efficiency compared to banks supervised by NCAs.

Besides the around 100 banks continuously indicated to fall under SSM supervision since the first announcement of banks included in the comprehensive assessment, we identify around six to seven banks that either were excluded from SSM supervision and relegated back to NCAs or came under SSM supervision according to ECB (2015) without having been listed in the notes preceding the comprehensive assessment, which prepared the grounds for the handover of supervisory responsibility starting in 2013. These switches of supervisory regime are informative because they might indicate the outcome of a political power struggle over where to locate the primary de facto authority to audit the financial soundness of financial institutions despite the *de jure* responsibility of the SSM. We find that banks that are supervised by the SSM according to the ECB (2013) list, but are excluded from the ECB (2015) list, exhibit higher cost inefficiency compared to both banks that switched to SSM supervision and those that have stayed on the SSM list. Banks switching into the SSM regime exhibit lower profit efficiency compared to those switching back into NCA supervision, whereas the levels of profit efficiency are generally lower for banks that were announced to fall under SSM supervision throughout.

The empirical outcomes might be due to two competing explanations. Banks under SSM supervision might face a significantly larger regulatory burden, which reduces their ability to attain minimal cost and hampers the realization of optimal profits. This explanation would be in line with frequent concerns voiced by the financial industry. Alternatively, a more homogeneous supervisory approach by supranational teams that are possibly less sensitive and therefore less able to transparently address any possible shortcomings at former national champions could be the reason why the larger, systemically relevant banks exhibit efficiency losses. The scope of this chapter does not yet permit any inference on the causal nature of the relationship between the regulatory architecture and efficiency, which warrants important future research.

Notes

1. We suppress bank and time subscripts throughout to conserve on space.
2. We excluded banks that incurred losses because the logarithm of negative numbers is not defined.
3. The sampled countries are: Austria, Belgium, Cyprus, Denmark, Estonia, Finland, France, Germany, Greece, Italy, Ireland, Latvia, Lithuania, Luxembourg, Malta, Netherlands, Portugal, Slovakia, Slovenia, Spain.
4. According to article 39 and related articles of the SSM Framework Regulation ECB (2014), a supervised entity can be classified as SSE if the following hold: firstly, its total assets exceed more than €30 billion or 20 % of national GDP; secondly, the bank is one of the three most significant credit institutions in a member state; thirdly, the bank received funds from the European Stability Mechanism; and fourthly, total assets exceed €5 billion and cross-border assets relative to liabilities in more than one other participating member state relative to the ratio of total assets to liabilities is larger than 20 %.
5. Different supervisory cultures among European NCA are documented by Carretta et al. (2015), who analyse the speeches of the heads of supervisory authorities in 15 EU countries between 1999 and 2011 and relate these scores to observed risk-taking behaviour by banks. They report, for example, that a more directional approach to supervision with narrow interpretation and strict enforcement of rules induced additional risk-taking by banks.
6. Note that the criteria used to define SSEs in ECB (2013) are very similar to the final criteria in ECB (2014) on the basis of which the list of SSEs in 2015 was constructed (ECB 2015).
7. The banks initially included in the comprehensive assessment, but excluded from the list in 2015, are: Banco de Caja Espana de Inversiones Salamanca y Soria SA (ES), Wüstenrot & Württembergische (DE), KfW Ipex Bank (DE), Credito Valtellinese Soc Coop (IT), Clearstream Banking SA (LU), Credito Emiliano SpA-

CREDEM (IT), SID—Slovene Export and Development Bank (SV). The banks not inlcuded in the 2013 list, but supervised by the SSM according to ECB (2015), are: Sberbank Europe AG (AT), VTB Bank AG (AT), UniCredit Banka Slovenija (SV), AB DNB Bankas (LT), AB SEB Bankas (LT), and Swedbank AB (LT).

References

Acharya, V. V., & Merrouche, O. (2013). Precautionary hoarding of liquidity and inter-bank markets: Evidence from the sub-prime crisis. *Review of Finance, 17*, 107–160.

Acharya, V., & Steffen, S. (2015). The "greatest" carry trade ever? Understanding Eurozone bank risks. *Journal of Financial Economics, 115*, 215–236.

Agee, M. D., Atkinson, S. E., Crocker, T. D., & Williams, J. W. (2014). Non-separable pollution control: Implications for a CO_2 emissions cap and trade system. *Resource and Energy Economics, 36*(1), 64–82.

Aigner, D. J., Lovell, C. A. K., & Schmidt, P. (1977). Formulation and estimation of stochastic frontier production functions. *Journal of Econometrics, 6*(1), 21–37.

Almanidis, P., Qian, J., & Sickles, R. C. (2014). Stochastic frontier models with bounded inefficiency. In *Festschrift in honor of Peter Schmidt* (pp. 47–81). New York: Springer.

Assaf, A. G., Matousek, R., & Tsionas, E. G. (2013). Turkish bank efficiency: Bayesian estimation with undesirable outputs. *Journal of Banking and Finance, 37*(2), 506–517.

Atkinson, S. E., & Tsionas, M. G. (2015). Directional distance functions: Optimal endogenous directions. *Journal of Econometrics, 190*.

Battese, G. E., Rao, D. S. P., & O'Donnell, C. (2004). A metafrontier production function for estimation of technical efficiencies and technology gaps for firms operating under different technologies. *Journal of Productivity Analysis, 21*, 91–103.

Beccalli, E., Anolli, M., & Borello, G. (2015). Are European banks too big? Evidence on economies of scale. *Journal of Banking and Finance, 58*, 232–246.

Benmelech, E., & Bergman, N. K. (2012). Credit traps. *American Economic Review, 102*, 3004–3032.

Bos, J. W. B., & Schmiedel, H. (2007). Is there a single frontier in a single European banking market? *Journal of Banking and Finance, 31*, 2081–2102.

Bos, J. W. B., Koetter, M., Kolari, J. W., & Kool, C. J. M. (2009). Effects of heterogeneity on bank efficiency scores. *European Journal of Operational Research, 195*, 251–261.

Bos, J. W. B., Economidou, C., Koetter, M., & Kolari, J. W. (2010). Do all countries grow alike? *Journal of Development Economics, 91*(1), 113–127.

Buch, C. M., Koch, C. T., & Koetter. (2013a). Do banks benefit from internationalization? Revisiting the market power-risk nexus. *Review of Finance, 17*, 1401–1435.

Buch, C. M., Koetter, M., & Ohls, J. (2013b). *Banks and sovereign risk: A granular view* (Bundesbank discussion paper, 29).

Carretta, A., Farina, V., Fiordelisi, F., Schwizer, P., & Lopes, F. S. S. (2015). Don't stand so close to me: The role of supervisory style in banking stability. *Journal of Banking and Finance, 52*, 180–188.

Casu, B., & Girardone, C. (2010). Integration and efficiency convergence in EU banking markets. *Omega, 38*(5), 260–267.

Cetorelli, N., & Goldberg, L. (2014). Measuring complexity in global banks. *Federal Reserve Bank of New York Economic Policy Review, 20*.

Chen, Y. Y., Schmidt, P., & Wang, H. J. (2014). Consistent estimation of the fixed effects stochastic frontier model. *Journal of Econometrics, 181*(2), 65–76.

Coelli, T. J. (1995). Estimators and hypothesis tests for a stochastic frontier function: A Monte Carlo analysis. *Journal of Productivity Analysis, 6*, 247–268.

Colombi, R., Martini, G., & Vittadini, G. (2011). *A stochastic frontier model with short-run and long-run inefficiency random effects.* (No. 1101), Department of Economics and Technology Management, University of Bergamo.

Colombi, R., Kumbhakar, S. C., Martini, G., & Vittadini, G. (2014). Closed-skew normality in stochastic frontiers with individual effects and long/short-run efficiency. *Journal of Productivity Analysis, 42*(2), 123–136.

Davies, R., & Tracey, B. (2013). Too big to be efficient? The impact of implicit subsidies on estimates of scale economies for banks. *Journal of Money, Credit and Banking, 46*, 219–253.

De Rynck, S. (2014). *Changing banking supervision in the Eurozone: The ECB as a policy entrepreneur.* (Bruges political research papers 38).

Debreu, G. (1951). The coefficient of resource utilization. *Econometrica, 19*, 273–292.

European Central Bank. (2013, October). *Note comprehensive assessment.* Frankfurt a.M.

European Central Bank. (2014, April 16). *Regulation of the European central bank* (SSM Framework regulation).

European Central Bank. (2015). *List of significant supervised entities.* Frankfurt a.M.

Fang, Y., Hasan, I., & Marton, K. (2011). Bank efficiency in South-Eastern Europe. *Economics of Transition, 19*(3), 495–520.

Farrell, M. J. (1957). The measurement of productive efficiency. *Journal of the Royal Statistical Society, Series A, General, 120*(Part 3), 253–281.

Fiordelisi, F., Marques-Ibanez, D., & Molyneux, P. (2011). Efficiency and risk in European banking. *Journal of Banking and Finance, 35*(5), 1315–1326.

Greene, W. H. (1990). A gamma-distributed stochastic frontier model. *Journal of Econometrics, 46*, 141–161.

Greene, W. (2005). Reconsidering Heterogeneity in Panel Data Estimators of the Stochastic Frontier Model. *Journal of Econometrics, 126*, 269–303.

Greene, W. (2010). A stochastic frontier model with correction for sample selection. *Journal of Productivity Analysis, 34*(1), 15–24.

Hafner, C. M., Manner, H., & Simar, L. (2013). *The "wrong skewness" problem in stochastic frontier models: A new approach*. Institut de Statistique, Biostatistique et Sciences Actuarielles (ISBA), Université Catholique de Louvain, Bélgica.

Hasan, I., Koetter, M., & Wedow, M. (2009). Regional growth and finance in Europe: Is there a quality effect of bank efficiency? *Journal of Banking and Finance, 33*, 1413–1422.

Horrace, W. C., & Parmeter, C. F. (2014). *A Laplace stochastic frontier model.* (No. 166), Center for Policy Research, Maxwell School, Syracuse University.

Jiménez, G., Ongena, S., Saurina, J., & Peydró, J.-L. (2012). Credit supply and monetary policy: Identifying the bank balance-sheet channel with loan applications. *American Economic Review, 102*, 2301–2326.

Jiménez, G., Ongena, S., Saurina, J., & Peydró, J.-L. (2014). Hazardous times for monetary policy: What do twenty-three million bank loans say about the effects of monetary policy on credit risk? *Econometrica, 82*, 463–505.

Jondrow, J., Lovell, C. A. K., Van Materov, S., & Schmidt, P. (1982). On the estimation of technical inefficiency in the stochastic frontier production function model. *Journal of Econometrics, 19*, 233–238.

Kane, E. (1990). Principal-agent problems in S&L salvage. *Journal of Finance, 20*, 755–764.

Koetter, M., & Poghosyan, T. (2009). The identification of technology regimes in banking: Implications for the market power-fragility nexus. *Journal of Banking and Finance, 33*, 1413–1422.

Koetter, M., & Wedow, M. (2010). Finance and growth in a bank-based economy: Is it quantity or quality that matters? *Journal of International Money and Finance, 29*, 1529–1545.

Koopmans, T. C. (1951). An analysis of production as an efficient combination of activities. In T. C. Koopmans (Ed.), *Activity analysis of production and allocation*. Cowles Commission for Research in Economics, Monograph No. 13. New York: Wiley.

Koutsomanoli-Filippaki, A., Margaritis, D., & Staikouras, C. (2009). Efficiency and productivity growth in the banking industry of Central and Eastern Europe. *Journal of Banking and Finance, 33*(3), 557–567.

Kumbhakar, S. C., & Lovell, C. A. K. (2000). *Stochastic frontier analysis*. Cambridge: Cambridge University Press.

Kumbhakar, S. C., & Tsionas, E. G. (2015). The good, the bad and the technology: Endogeneity in environmental production models. *Journal of Econometrics, 1*.

Kumbhakar, S., Park, B., Simar, L., & Tsionas, E. (2007). Nonparametric stochastic frontiers: A local maximum likelihood approach. *Journal of Econometrics, 137*, 1–27.

Kumbhakar, S. C., Parmeter, C. F., & Tsionas, E. G. (2013). A zero inefficiency stochastic frontier model. *Journal of Econometrics, 172*(1), 66–76.

Kuosmanen, T., & Kortelainen, M. (2012). Stochastic non-smooth envelopment of data: semi-parametric frontier estimation subject to shape constraints. *Journal of Productivity Analysis,* (2012), 11–28.

Laeven, L., & Levine, R. (2009). Bank governance, regulation, and risk taking. *Journal of Financial Economics, 93*, 259–275.

Lane, P. R. (2012). The European sovereign debt crisis. *Journal of Economic Perspectives, 26*, 49–67.

Leibenstein, H. (1966). Allocative efficiency vs. 'X-efficiency'. *American Economic Review, 56*, 392–415.

Martins-Filho, C., & Yao, F. (2015). Semiparametric stochastic frontier estimation via profile likelihood. *Econometric Reviews, 34*(4), 413–451.

Matousek, R., Rughoo, A., Sarantis, N., & Assaf, A. G. (2015). Bank performance and convergence during the financial crisis: Evidence from the 'old' European Union and Eurozone. *Journal of Banking Finance, 52*, 208–216.

Meeusen, W., & van den Broeck, J. (1977). Efficiency estimation from Cobb-Douglas production functions with composed error. *International Economic Review, 18*(2), 435–444.

Murty, S., Russell, R. R., & Levkoff, S. B. (2012). On modeling pollution-generating technologies. *Journal of Environmental Economics and Management, 64*(1), 117–135.

O'Rourke, K. H., & Taylor, A. M. (2013). Cross of Euros. *Journal of Economic Perspectives, 27*, 167–191.

Parmeter, C. F., & Kumbhakar, S. C. (2014). Efficiency analysis: A primer on recent advances. *Foundations and Trends in Econometrics, 7*(3–4), 191–385.

Rho, S., & Schmidt, P. (2013). Are all firms inefficient? *Journal of Productivity Analysis, 43*(3), 327–349.

Sealey, C. W., & Lindley, J. T. (1977). Inputs, outputs, and a theory of production and cost and depository financial institutions. *Journal of Finance, 32*, 1251–1265.

Simar, L., & Wilson, P. W. (2013). Estimation and inference in nonparametric frontier models: Recent developments and perspectives. *Foundations and Trends in Econometrics, 5*(2), 183–337.

Simar, L., Van Keilegom, I., & Zelenyuk, V. (2014). *Nonparametric least squares methods for stochastic frontier models.* (No. WP032014), School of Economics, University of Queensland, Australia.

Tsionas, E. G., Assaf, A. G., & Matousek, R. (2015a). Dynamic technical and allocative efficiencies in European banking. *Journal of Banking Finance, 52*, 130–139.

Tsionas, E. G., Kumbhakar, S. C., & Malikov, E. (2015b). Estimation of input distance functions: A system approach. *American Journal of Agricultural Economics, 97*.

Véron, N. (2015). *Europe's radical banking union*. Bruegel Essay and Lecture Series. Brussels.

Weill, L. (2009). Convergence in banking efficiency across European countries. *Journal of International Financial Markets, Institutions and Money, 19*(5), 818–833.

Wheelock, D. C., & Wilson, P. W. (2000). Why do banks disappear? The determinants of U.S. bank failures and acquisitions. *Review of Economics and Statistics, 82*, 127–138.

Part III

Financial Stability and Regulation

12

Regulatory Reforms in the European Banking Sector

Elena Carletti and Agnese Leonello

The 2007 Crisis and the New Regulatory Reforms

The banking sector, historically, has been one of the most regulated industries in the economy. In almost all countries around the world, an articulated system of institutions and authorities regulates and supervises banks, and more generally, the financial industry. The need for such a special treatment is motivated by the key role that financial intermediaries play in the economy, as well as some inherent and unique features distinguishing banks from all other companies.

Traditionally, the core activity of a commercial bank is to take funds from individuals who have a surplus of resources and to allocate these resources to productive activities. Banks thereby provide payment and settlement services to households and firms and allow a multitude of small and disperse savers to access profitable (long-term) investment opportunities, while still being able to obtain liquidity when needed. To achieve this, banks raise most of their funding in the form of short-term debt. Furthermore, savers providing funds

The views expressed here are the authors' and do not reflect those of the ECB or the Eurosystem.

E. Carletti
Department of Finance, Bocconi University, Milan, Italy
e-mail: elena.carletti@unibocconi.it

A. Leonello (✉)
Financial Research Division, European Central Bank, Frankfurt, Germany
e-mail: Agnese.Leonello@ecb.europa.eu

T. Beck, B. Casu (eds.), *The Palgrave Handbook of European Banking*,
DOI 10.1057/978-1-137-52144-6_12

to banks are not only banks' creditors, but also their customers. While this may also be the case for public companies, banks are special as only banks' claims are used as means of payment and the debt-to-assets ratio is usually larger for banks than for other companies.

Pooling funds from many different creditors and investing in a wide range of activities allow financial intermediaries to minimize costs and inefficiencies associated with the information and incentives problems between savers and borrowers and exploit the benefits of diversification and economy of scale. However, these functions also entail some risks and represent potential sources of fragility, which, in turn, may lead to banks' failures. Unlike other sectors, the costs associated with those failures can be very large and go beyond the individual failing banks. Banks' failures may produce severe negative consequences for their borrowers, the rest of the financial sector and the real economy. The reason is twofold.

Firstly, as financial intermediation is a high information content activity, a bank's failure may have severe negative consequences for its borrowers, in that it may become difficult for them to obtain credit from other banks or, even if they can, the conditions may be tougher (e.g., Petersen and Rajan 1994). Impaired credit provision, in turn, undermines growth and economic development, as it limits the investment possibilities of existing firms and new businesses creation. The costs in terms of output losses associated with financial crises have been estimated to be significant (Cerra and Saxena 2008) and long-lasting (Reinhart and Rogoff 2009).

Secondly, a bank's failure is often detrimental rather than beneficial to its competitors. The reason for this is that banks trade among each other much more than other companies do. They are linked either through common portfolio exposures or via their reciprocal claims in the interbank market. The high degree of interconnectedness in the financial industry implies that a bank's failure or distress can rapidly spread to other financial institutions, to their borrowers and creditors, with negative effects for the economy as a whole.

The recent financial and Eurozone crises are clear examples of how disruptive banks' failures and, more generally, financial distress can be. The financial crisis started in August 2007 in the subprime mortgage market in the USA and propagated rapidly across the world. As argued by Brunnermeier (2009), one of the major causes of the crisis was the bursting of the housing bubble in the USA in 2007. This was followed by a deterioration in the credit quality of the subprime mortgages and an increase in delinquency rates. The turmoil spread from the subprime mortgage market to other securitized products, leading to the downgrading of many mortgage-related products as well as other structured finance products and to a general loss of confidence in the financial markets. Market participants, including banks, became reluctant to lend to each other, with the consequence of a liquidity dry-up and a consequent sharp increase in London Interbank Offered Rate (LIBOR) spreads (Brunnermeier 2009; Heider et al. 2015). The decline in asset prices led to numerous write-offs in the balance sheets of banks and other financial institutions, pressures on funding costs and instruments, and severe declines in the market equity values of many financial institutions.

In order to stop the downward spiral in asset prices and to restore confidence in the solvency of financial institutions, governments and central banks around the world implemented extraordinary emergency measures, ranging from recapitalization, loans, implicit and explicit guarantees to mergers among private institutions (e.g., Lloyds and HBOS; Merrill Lynch and Bank of America). While successful in restoring the stability in the banking sector, the implementation of these emergency measures entailed huge costs for governments implementing them, to the point, in some cases, of undermining the stability of the sovereigns.

These measures and the consequent large exposure of sovereigns to their own banking sectors can be enumerated among the causes of the recent sovereign debt crisis in Europe.[1]

Owing to the absence of a supra-national support mechanism and of any form of mutualization within the Eurozone, every national country had to rely exclusively on their own fiscal capacity when taking actions and intervening in their financial system, despite the fact that, in some cases, the size of the banking system outgrew the fiscal capacity of their countries. In 2012, although for different reasons, several countries experienced a steep increase in their sovereign bond yields as well as in their banks' cost of funding. This became known as the "vicious circle" between sovereigns and banks, whereby banks' poor solvency conditions put pressure on their countries' fiscal positions, and pressure on highly indebted sovereigns led to the increasing cost of funding for banks headquartered in these countries (see e.g., Acharya et al. 2015; Cooper and Nikolov 2013; Farhi and Tirole 2015; Leonello 2016), thus leading to a re-fragmentation of the Single Market.

[1] The most extreme example in terms of the negative impact of the emergency actions taken to rescue the banking system on the stability of the sovereign is Ireland. Starting in the autumn of 2008, the Irish government implemented major measures to support the banking sector, such as blanket guarantees for all the liabilities of the six major banks, as well as additional measures in the form of recapitalization and the purchase of toxic assets and rescue intervention. All these measures contributed significantly to a deterioration in Irish public finance.

The Eurozone sovereign crisis also had significant negative consequences for non-financial companies. One consequence of the sovereign distress was a significant reduction in credit provision. A series of recent papers (see e.g., Correa et al. 2012; Adelino and Ferreira 2015; De Marco 2015) show a tightening in bank lending to the private sector following a sovereign shock to their balance sheet.

The severity of the financial and sovereign debt crises has led to a wave of reforms of the existing regulatory framework. In Europe, the key elements of the new regulatory framework are the implementation of Basel III regulatory standards, for capital, liquidity and activities restrictions through the Capital Requirement Directive (CRD IV) and the creation of the Banking Union, which defines a new and European-wide supervisory and resolution mechanism and delineates the need for a common, pan-European deposit insurance scheme.

The primary objective of these reforms is to limit the occurrence of crises, their severity and the associated costs for the taxpayers. In order to achieve that, these regulatory reforms aim at curbing banks' and sovereigns' behaviours and risk-taking incentives, which are the sources of instability in the banking sector.

We will discuss each area of these regulatory reforms in turn. Specifically, we will present the new (1) capital regulation; (2) liquidity regulation, and (3) activities restrictions, as featured in the CRD IV, and the three pillars of the banking union (i.e., the Single Supervisory Mechanism, the Resolution Mechanism and the common deposit insurance scheme).[2] For each of the new regulatory tools, we will highlight the rationale behind it and the institutional details, and we will identify the possible challenges and open issues related to its design and implementation.

The remainder of this chapter is structured as follows. The section "Market Failures in the Banking Industry and the Purpose of Financial Regulation" identifies the market failures in the financial system that lead to fragility, so highlighting the rationale for regulation, and the section "Regulatory Reforms" presents the recent regulatory reforms in the wake of the Global Financial Crisis. The section "Concluding Remarks" draws the chapter to a close.

[2] While the Single Supervisory Mechanism and the Single Resolution Mechanism are already in place and well defined, the third pillar of the Banking Union—the creation of a pan-European deposit insurance scheme—is still under discussion at the time of writing.

Market Failures in the Banking Industry and the Purpose of Financial Regulation

Fragility and risk are inherent features of the functions that banks perform in the economy. Preventing banks from taking risks is not necessarily efficient as it often leads to inefficient credit provision and limits financial innovation. The purpose of financial regulation, then, should not be minimizing fragility per se, but rather finding an optimal balance between fragility and the provision of credit and risk-sharing. In other words, regulation should aim at tackling the market failures and inefficiencies that prevent the system from reaching the efficient levels of risk-sharing and credit provision to firms and households.

The current structure of financial regulation, however, does not seem to address specific market failures, but is rather the response to specific issues that emerged in past crises. Looking back at the past hundred years, an historical pattern emerges: regulation becomes stricter following periods of instability and looser following periods of stability. Since the Great Depression, many countries adopted a whole range of regulatory measures and some—such as France and Italy—even nationalized their financial institutions. These measures were successful in containing instability and, in the period from 1945 to the 1970s, there were almost no financial crises. However, the costs in terms of reduced credit provision and financial innovation motivated a process of financial liberalization in the 1970s, which led to a revival of crises around the world (see, e.g., Boyd et al. 2009) and culminated with the 2007 financial crisis.

What about the recent wave of regulatory reforms? What is the rationale behind their design? Which market failures are they meant to address?

In order to answer these questions, it is key to first identify the market failures in the financial industry that lead to financial crises and, in turn, to the disruptive consequence for the real economy. We restrict our attention to the main market failures being:

- Vulnerability to runs
- Moral hazard and excessive risk-taking
- Build-up of systemic risk

Vulnerability to Runs

As highlighted in the previous section, banks provide useful liquidity services to savers, while still allowing them to access long-term profitable investment opportunities. Banks achieve this goal by offering creditors demandable deposit contracts. These contracts improve savers' welfare relative to autarky, but they also represent an important source of fragility for banks as they expose them to panic or self-fulfilling runs.

A first formal analysis of panic runs dates back to the seminal papers by Bryant (1980) and Diamond and Dybvig (1983). In Diamond and Dybvig (1983), the use of demandable deposit contract leads to multiple equilibria. There is a good equilibrium in which all depositors withdraw according to their consumption needs and banks can meet their demands without costly liquidation of their assets. The other equilibrium, instead, features a massive withdrawal of funds by depositors (i.e., a run) before the maturity of the bank's investment, thus forcing it into costly liquidation and default. In their framework, a run results from the strategic complementarity between depositors' withdrawal decisions; a depositor's incentive to run increases monotonically with the number of other depositors running. In other words, when a depositor expects others to withdraw, it is rational for him to do the same in the attempt to avoid being the "last in the queue" and, thus, being served when the bank's resources have been already depleted.

In Diamond and Dybvig (1983), runs are only the result of a coordination failure between depositors. The situation in the real world, however, is often more complex and banking crises can also be related to a bad realization of the banks' investment projects or, more generally, to downturns in the business cycle (see evidence in Gorton 1988; Calomiris and Gorton 1991; Calomiris and Mason 2003). In this case, bank runs are triggered by information about a low realization of the banks' investment projects or about the underlying fundamentals of the economy—that is, they are triggered by fundamental reasons, concerns about the solvency of the bank, rather than panic.

The dynamic behind fundamentals-driven runs has been analysed in several theoretical papers (see, e.g., Chari and Jagannthan 1988; Jacklin and Battacharya 1988) and it works as follows. When depositors receive information about a fall in the value of banks' assets, they have an incentive to withdraw their funds prematurely and run, as they expect that banks will no longer be able to meet their commitments and make the promised repayments.

Unlike panic-based runs, fundamental ones are triggered by the arrival of negative information about banks' solvency. This leads to an important difference. Panic runs are inefficient as they are only the result of a coordination failure and not related to the "health" of banks' investment projects. They are spurred by liquidity problems and drive solvent banks into default. When panic runs occur, banks' creditors forgo higher returns of banks' assets at maturity and banks are forced into a costly premature liquidation.

Fundamental-driven crises, instead, are not necessarily inefficient. By preventing the continuation of insolvent banks, they can improve creditors' situation in various ways. On the one hand, creditors may be able to obtain a higher payoff by forcing the bank into an early liquidation and default rather than waiting until the maturity of its projects. On the other hand, the fear of a run may have a disciplining effect on banks, thus inducing better and less risky investment choices. This disciplining role of bank runs is emphasized in Calomiris and Kahn (1991) and Diamond and Rajan (2001), where the threat of a run prevents bank owners from diverting resources for personal use and guarantees that loans are repaid.

The distinction between panic- and fundamental-driven crises plays a crucial role in the design and implementation of regulation. However, in the banking literature, panic and fundamental-based approaches to bank runs have mostly moved on parallel trails. A remarkable exception to this is the paper by Goldstein and Pauzner (2005).

Goldstein and Pauzner (2005) develop a global game model of bank runs. The use of global games allows them to reconcile the panic- and fundamental-based view of bank runs and, at the same time, to characterize a unique equilibrium to determine whether a run will occur or not and its nature (panic- or fundamentals-driven).[3]

In their setting, depositors receive a slightly noisy signal about the fundamentals of the economy and, in turn, the realization of the banks' investment projects. Based on the signal, a depositor decides whether to run or not, as the signal gives him information not only about the realization of the banks' investment but also about the action of the other agents. Runs occur when the fundamentals are below a specific threshold and, in the range in which they occur, they can be distinguished between panic and fundamental ones. Goldstein and Pauzner (2005) also analyse how the probability of panic and fundamental runs interact with the deposit contract. They show that both types of crises become more likely when banks offer more liquidity (i.e., a higher repayment to early withdrawing depositors) and prove that, anticipating this, banks offer less liquidity than would be optimal.

Regulation can play an important role in reducing banks' vulnerability to runs. Historically, the main tool to limit runs (mainly panic-driven ones) has been deposit insurance. The literature on deposit insurance is very large and different conclusions have been reached about its effectiveness in reducing the

---

[3] The global game literature dates back to Carlsson and van Damme (1993), who show the possibility of deriving a unique equilibrium in contexts characterized by strategic complementarity when agents have noisy information. Since then, global games have been widely used in finance to study, among others, currency crises (Morris and Shin 1998), issues of contagion (Goldstein and Pauzner 2004), the effect of large traders on the occurrence of currency crises (Corsetti et al. 2004), twin crises (Goldstein 2005) and central bank lending (Rochet and Vives 2004).

occurrence of runs, depending on the type of crisis considered (panic- versus fundamental- based). In a more recent paper, Allen et al. (2015a) analyse the effect of deposit insurance on bank runs and show that different schemes may significantly differ in terms of their effectiveness in preventing runs, distortions in the banks' choice of the deposit contract and the costs for the government providing them. Their framework builds on Goldstein and Pauzner (2005), thus sharing with them the use of global games to uniquely pin down the probability of a run and to distinguish between panic and fundamental crises. Specifically, Allen et al. (2015a) enrich the framework in Goldstein and Pauzner (2005) by accounting for government intervention, which allows the study of how government guarantee policy interacts with the banking contract and the probability of a run.

As we will discuss in detail in the section "Regulatory Reforms", other regulatory tools have been designed to reduce banks' vulnerability to runs. The new liquidity requirements serve this purpose by reducing the scope for costly liquidation of banks' assets. Capital requirements may also play a (indirect) role in the occurrence of runs, by affecting banks' risk-taking incentives and, thus, banks' exposure to fundamental-driven crises.

Moral Hazard and Excessive Risk-Taking

Credit provision always entails information and incentives problems. Lenders usually have less information about the initial quality of the borrowers' investment projects, as well as its final realization. Moreover, they can neither induce nor effectively oversee the borrowers' effort for the project to succeed. Monitoring and screening borrowers may require specific technologies, skills and competencies, which are not accessible to savers. Moreover, they may entail large costs, which, in the case of small investors, may prevent them from providing credit in the first place.

Intermediation by banks reduces the severity of these problems by allowing a more efficient monitoring and screening of investment projects (Diamond 1984). However, such information and incentives problems do not disappear with financial intermediation. Still, there is asymmetric information between banks and their lenders, in that banks screen and monitor the investment projects on the behalf of their creditors and have access to superior information.

Limited liability and the nature of debt contracts, on which banks mostly rely for their funding, also contribute to moral hazard and excessive risk-taking. If investment projects fail bank owners' losses are only limited to the paid-in capital, while in the case of success they fully enjoy the upside of banks. This reduces their incentives to monitor and screen projects effectively and also makes it profitable to engage in asset substitution by choosing riskier projects over safer ones.

These moral hazard and excessive risk-taking problems become even more severe in the presence of public guarantees protecting banks' creditors against the adverse realizations of banks' investment projects or negative shocks. The reason is twofold. On the one hand, being guaranteed by the government, banks' creditors no longer have an incentive to discipline banks (see e.g., Cooper and Ross 2002). On the other hand, guarantees premia do not (fully) reflect the increase in banks' risk and banks do not (fully) internalize the effects of their risk-taking decisions. As a consequence, in the presence of public guarantees, risks taken by the banks are shifted onto the insurer and this overall leads to an increase in bank's risk-taking and fragility (see Allen et al. 2015b for a survey on moral hazard associated with government guarantees).

Public guarantees are not the only factor exacerbating the information and incentives problems associated with financial intermediation. Asset prices dynamics and their determinants—such as credit expansion and financial liberalization—also have a significant impact on bank's risk-taking incentives and, in turn, on the occurrence of crises.

Financial crises often follow the collapse in asset prices after what appears to have been a bubble. The 2007 financial crisis is not an exception. In the USA, Ireland, UK and Spain, real estate prices rose significantly up to 2007 and the crisis was triggered precisely when they collapsed. Several papers have documented that a large credit expansion anticipates the occurrence of a crisis (see, among others, Kaminsky and Reinhart 1999; Reinhart and Rogoff 2011; Schularick and Taylor 2012).

Consistent with the mechanism for the creation of bubbles described in Allen and Gale (2000a), large credit availability and expectations about the future path of credit expansion sustain an increase in the demand for risky assets, which is further reinforced by a subsequent increase in prices, thus triggering an upward spiral (i.e., a bubble) with prices above the fundamental values. As a consequence, banks become overexposed to such assets. This was precisely the case in the real estate and stock markets in numerous countries before 2007.

When the bubble bursts, either because returns are low or because the central bank tightens credit, markets collapse and banks that are significantly exposed to those markets face huge losses. As it was the case in the recent crisis, given the high degree of interconnectedness of the financial system, the distress of a few institutions rapidly spreads to the rest of the financial system.

Regulation can affect the severity of these information and incentives problems in different ways. Firstly, specific regulatory tools could be designed to improve transparency and so reduce the asymmetric information problem between banks and their creditors.

Secondly, capital and liquidity requirements may affect banks' risk-taking incentives. A large literature has discussed the role of capital requirements in reducing banks' risk-taking incentives as well as distortions and costs associated with the provision of public guarantees. A recent view in the literature (see, e.g., Furlong and Keeley 1989; Repullo 2004; Dell'Ariccia and Marquez 2006; Allen et al. 2011) is that capital requirements represent an effective tool to curb banks' moral hazard. The premise of these papers is that stringent capital requirements induce banks to internalize the costs associated with their risk-taking decisions by giving them "skin in the game". By doing this, they allow the limitation of the scope of the moral hazard problem described in this section. Better capitalized banks are more resilient to crises, as shown by Beltratti and Stulz (2012) and Berger and Bouwman (2013).

An opposite view regarding the effect of capital on banks' risk-taking incentives emerges in earlier papers (e.g., Kareken and Wallace 1978; Kahane 1977; but also, more recently, Boot and Greenbaum 1993; Hellman et al. 2000). These papers show that capital requirements can be either ineffective in limiting risk-taking or even counterproductive, inducing bankers to choose riskier assets. The premise behind these papers is that capital requirements, by having a negative effect on banks' franchise values, remove (one of) the main reason for banks to behave prudently.

A recent paper by Calomiris et al. (2015) shows that liquidity requirements can also be effective in curbing banks' risk-taking incentives in the presence of deposit insurance, where banks' behaviour is not disciplined by the threat of run.

Finally, as emerged from the discussion about bubbles and asset prices dynamics, it is important that regulation is not only designed to reduce individual institutions' risk-taking incentives and so improve their own stability, but also to prevent the build-up of systemic risk and banks' overexposure to common risk factors and aggregate shocks. As we discuss in the section that follows, this aspect has obtained a prominent role in the current debate about regulatory reforms and is the rationale behind the macro-prudential approach to regulation.

Build-Up of Systemic Risk

The high degree of interconnectedness is a key feature of the banking system, which differentiates it from other sectors of the economy. A relevant implication of the high degree of interconnectedness is that banking crises, when they occur, are systemic in that they involve several institutions rather than just individual intermediaries.

Systemic risk in the banking sector can originate from two sources. It can be the consequence of aggregate adverse shocks hitting several institutions simultaneously or contagion, that is the propagation of an individual bank's failure (or shock) to the rest of the system in a sequential fashion. In both cases systemic risk is the product of the high degree of interconnectedness in the banking sector and materializes when banks do not fully internalize the effects that their choices and failures have on others.

The most common form of aggregate shocks is the burst of an asset price bubble described in the previous section, widespread panic or cash-in-the-market pricing due to aggregate liquidity shortage.[4]

The literature on contagion is vast and highlights the existence of various mechanisms through which the distress of individual institutions spreads throughout the entire system (see, Allen et al. 2009 for a survey). These propagation mechanisms refer for example to information spillovers (Chen 1999), interbank connections via interbank deposits (Allen and Gale 2000b) or payment systems (Freixas and Parigi 1998; Freixas et al. 2000), portfolio diversification and common exposures (Goldstein and Pauzner 2004; Wagner 2011), common assets and funding risk (Allen et al. 2012), transmission of fire sales prices through interdependency of banks' portfolios (Allen and Carletti 2006) and the use of mark-to-market accounting standards (e.g., Allen and Carletti 2008).

Allen and Gale's paper (2000b) is one of the first to analyse the propagation of a small shock within the banking sector. It assesses how the banking system responds to liquidity shocks when banks exchange interbank deposits. Specifically, in their study, banks are linked to each other as they swap deposits. Two main results emerge from their analysis. Firstly, the creation of a financial network allows banks to insure each other against idiosyncratic liquidity shocks but, at the same time, they expose the system to contagion as soon as some frictions, such as a small aggregate liquidity shock, emerge. Secondly, the structure of the network is crucial to the resiliency of the system. Incomplete networks, where all banks are connected but each bank exchanges deposits only with a group of other banks, turn out to be more prone to contagion than complete structures. Similar results concerning the resiliency of more complete networks are present also in Freixas et al. (2000) and more recently in Acemoglou et al. (2015), where the resiliency of different networks is analysed also as a function of the size of shocks.

[4] Cash-in-the-market pricing refers to the dependence of asset prices on the amount of liquidity available in the market. When liquidity in the market is scarce relative to the amount of assets on sale, asset prices do not any longer reflect the fundamental value of the assets, but they are determined by demand and supply of liqudiity, that is by the amount of liquidity held by market participants in aggregate.

According to Allen and Gale (2000b), a shock spreads within the system as banks hold direct deposit claims. Other channels of contagion based on direct balance sheet linkages rely on fire sales and accounting standards. When some intermediaries are forced to sell their assets, due to idiosyncratic liquidity reasons and there is price volatility and fire sales in some states of the world, then other intermediaries holding similar assets are also affected because of the lower market prices. This is the case either because the drop in prices affects the evaluation of their assets due to mark-to-market accounting (Allen and Carletti 2006) or because it forces them to sell more assets to satisfy their liquidity needs (Allen and Carletti 2008; Carletti and Leonello 2016; Luck and Schempp 2014).

While direct balance sheet linkages are relevant channels of contagion, shocks also spread among banks via indirect balance-sheet linkages. In this context, as shown by Lagunoff and Schreft (2001), de Vries (2005) and Cifuentes et al. (2005), portfolio readjustments represent a very relevant channel. The basic idea in these papers is that a bank's portfolio return depends on the portfolio allocations of the other banks. When a negative shock hits and some banks decide to readjust their portfolio in response to such a shock, this produces negative externalities and may negatively affect the return on other banks' portfolios. As a consequence, other banks may decide to abandon those investments in the attempt of limiting contagion and larger future losses.

The relevance of systemic risk and the importance of clearly identifying its determinants have been well understood after the recent crisis by regulators. This emerges clearly from the current macro-prudential approach applied to the design of the new regulatory framework and tools. It has been well understood that the soundness and safety of individual institutions does not guarantee or imply the stability of the whole system. This is what some scholars have defined as "fallacy of composition" (Brunnermeier et al. 2009), that is, the impossibility of making the system as a whole safe by making sure individual banks are safe. The reasons are multiple. Firstly, as explained above, there are risks such as those due to the interconnections among banks which go beyond the preservation of individual stability. Secondly, it may happen that in trying to make themselves safer, banks behave in a way that collectively undermines the system. Asset sales and fire sale prices are an example of this. Banks start selling assets when they need to deal with idiosyncratic shocks. But doing so, they disregard the effect that their sale will have on asset prices and thus on the stability of the other institutions. A similar argument applies to diversification. Banks choose their diversification strategies by taking account of their own individual risk-sharing and hedging motives, disregarding the effects of increasingly more correlated portfolios on systemic risk. These are just two forms of the more general and well-known problem of individual agents not being able to internalize externalities.

Such concerns have played a prominent role in recent policy and academic debate and in the design of the new regulatory framework, which features prominently a macro-prudential approach. It thereby entails specific regulatory tools aimed at reducing the build-up of systemic risk, as we will discuss in detail in the section that follows.

Regulatory Reforms

Having described the market failures leading to banks' fragility and crises, we now present the key elements of the current regulatory reforms in Europe and discuss how their design and implementation curb banks' vulnerability to runs, moral hazard and risk-taking problems as well as the build-up of systemic risk in the banking sector.

Basel III and CRD IV

Basel III accord is a set of reforms designed to strengthen the regulation, supervision and risk management of banks. In Europe, it is implemented via the Capital Requirement Directive IV (CRD IV), whose main objectives are to improve the stability and resilience of single institutions, and the whole banking sector, to shocks and to create a level playing field across countries.

Such objectives are pursued with substantial reforms to the existing capital regulation, as well as with the introduction of a new liquidity regulation and restrictions on banks' activities. A key and new feature of the new regulatory framework is the macro-prudential approach, in that it includes regulatory tools that are specifically intended to tackle the build-up of systemic risk.

In what follows, we present in detail regulatory reforms on (1) capital requirements; (2) liquidity requirements; and (3) assets and activities restrictions.

Capital Requirements

According to the new regulation, minimum capital requirements are still set to 8% of risk-weighted assets. However, banks are required to increase Common Equity Tier 1 (CET 1) from the current 2% to 4.5% of risk-weighted assets.

While the minimum capital requirements are unchanged relative to the previous regulation, Basel III and thereby the CRD IV expand substantially the set of capital-based requirements by including buffers to make banks more resilient to adverse aggregate shocks, as well as to limit contagion within the system.

To serve these purposes, the new regulation prescribes mandatory capital buffers for global systemically important institutions (G-SIIs), a capital conservation buffer, as well as countercyclical capital buffers.

Concerning the implementation of capital surcharges for systemically important institutions, G-SIIs are divided into five subcategories, depending on their systemic importance. A progressive additional CET 1 capital requirement, ranging from 1% to 2.5%, will be applied to the first four groups, while a buffer of 3.5% will be applied to the highest subcategory. Each member state will maintain flexibility concerning the stricter requirements to impose on domestic systemically important institutions (D-SIIs).

A capital conservation buffer aims at making banks more resilient to adverse shocks. This takes the form of additional common equity for 2.5% of risk-weighted assets. Finally, banks may be required a further increase in their capital in the range of 0–2.5% of common equity in the presence of excessive credit growth and signals of systemic risk build-up.

In summary, the new capital requirements lead to both higher quantity and quality of capital and complement the previous regulatory framework (mostly micro-prudential-based) with a macro-prudential approach. In the new regulation, this emerges, for example, from the specific requirements for institutions that, because of their size, could represent a potential threat to the stability of the system—systemically important financial institutions (SIFIs). In the new regulatory framework the importance assigned to the prevention of the build-up of systemic risk also clearly emerges from the introduction of countercyclical capital buffers.

There are two important issues that are worth discussing regarding the implementation of the new capital-based measures. One refers to the costs for the banks of these requirements, and so their incentives to comply with them; the other concerns the systemic effects of the new capital regulation, and specifically its effectiveness in limiting the build-up of systemic risk.

The literature on bank capital usually assumes that equity is more costly than other forms of finance (see, for example, Gorton and Winton 2003). This also justifies the need for capital regulation as, in its absence, banks would simply minimize their capital holdings and hold more debt. However, it is not at all clear what this higher cost is due to. One simple answer is that it is privately more costly because in many countries debt interest is tax deductible at the corporate level but dividends are not. One important shortcoming of this explanation though is that it does not explain the difference in capital holdings across industries. Simple evidence shows indeed that non-financial firms hold around 30–40% of their liabilities in the form of capital whereas the financial firms operate with approximately 10% of capital on average in normal times (Flannery and Rangan 2008). Given this, another, more plausible, explanation is that debt is implicitly subsidized in the financial industry through government guarantees and bailouts (see also Admati et al. 2010). If this is the case, the removal of the public guarantees and the design of clear resolution schemes would enhance financial stability substantially as it would improve banks' incentives to take risks and induce higher capital holdings. A more recent explanation for the higher cost of equity capital in banks is based on the market segmentation between deposits and capital and the positive role of capital as a way to reduce the bankruptcy costs of deposit-taking institutions (Allen et al. 2015). This discussion, thereby, suggests the convenience of complementing capital regulation with other measures so as to improve its effectiveness and reduce its burden for banks.

Regarding the new macro-prudential approach to capital regulation, an important point concerns the effectiveness of capital in preventing the build-up of systemic risk. While the literature focusing on the micro-prudential role of capital is vast and, as noted above, seems to suggest a positive role of capital in curbing bank's moral hazard and risk-taking incentives, the literature on the macro-prudential role of capital is, instead, still in its infancy although quickly developing.[5] Acharya (2009) and the 3D model developed in the context of the Macroprudential Research Network (MaRS) of the European System of Central Banks by Clerc and colleagues (2015), as well as Repullo and Suarez (2013), Martinez-Miera and Suarez (2014) and Malherbe (2015) are recent studies focusing on the macro effects of capital regulation. Acharya (2009) develops a theoretical framework with multiple banks, thus being able to assess the effects of prudential regulation, taking into account both individual and systemic failure risk.

The 3D model was designed to conduct quantitative analysis of the welfare implications of macroprudential policies and, in particular, capital regulation. It is a dynamic stochastic general equilibrium model (DSGE) in which financial intermediation and banks' instability play a central role. Unlike other recent DSGE models incorporating financial frictions, the 3D model provides a clear rationale for capital regulation and features a key role for banks' default, which arises from both aggregate and idiosyncratic risk.

[5] See "Literature Review on the integration of regulatory capital and liquidity instruments"(2016) by the Basel Committee on Banking Supervision for a complete survey of the general equilibrium models analysing macroeconomic implications of capital requirements.

Repullo and Suarez (2013), Martinez-Miera and Suarez (2014) and Malherbe (2015) analyse the cyclical properties of capital requirements. Repullo and Suarez (2013) develop a dynamic equilibrium model to analyse the optimal degree of cyclicality in capital regulation. Using this model, they compare and evaluate different capital regulations regimes. According to their analysis, Basel III regulation represents a positive improvement relative to Basel II, as the newly introduced capital conservation buffer and countercyclical buffers make capital requirements less sensitive to the cycle.

Martinez-Miera and Suarez (2014) focus on the socially optimal level of the capital requirements and the extent to which such a level should or should not be adjusted over the credit cycle. The key ingredient of their model is what they refer to as the "last-bank-standing effect", that is, the existence of rents that a surviving bank can earn after a large share of bank capital is wiped out. In choosing their exposure to shocks, banks trade-off these rents with the standard risk-shifting gains. In this framework, capital requirements reduce credit and output, but, as a consequence of the last-bank-standing effect, they also reduce systemic risk-taking. An important implication of their analysis is that systemic risk-taking may worsen if capital requirements are countercyclical, since such adjustment diminishes bankers' prospects of appropriating high scarcity rents by avoiding the exposure of their capital to the systemic shock.

Malherbe (2015) also focuses on the design of optimal capital requirements. The theoretical model hinges on two key ingredients: socially costly defaults and diminishing returns to physical capital. In his paper, optimal capital requirements depend negatively on aggregate productivity and positively on aggregate capital. The second effect, however, always dominates. If banks were allowed to increase their lending proportionally to an increase in productivity, this would magnify economic fluctuations, since more lending would lead to lower returns and, in turn, to more and more costly failures.

Liquidity Requirements

Liquidity requirements represent another important and novel feature of the new regulatory framework. Basel III and the CRD IV regulation in Europe introduce two liquidity requirements: the liquidity coverage ratio (LCR) and the net stable funding ratio (NSFR).

The LCR requires banks to hold sufficient liquidity to withstand a severe liquidity freeze of at least 30 days. Its main goal is to limit the occurrence of fire sales and, thus, contagion. In this respect, it belongs to the group of new macro-prudential tools introduced under the recent regulation.

The NSFR, instead, imposes a mandatory ratio between banks' deposits and equity and weighted long-term assets. It is then designed to contain the maturity mismatch between assets and liabilities and to reduce the vulnerability of an institution to runs. In this respect, it is more of a micro-prudential tool, aimed at strengthening the safety and soundness of an individual institution rather than containing the negative spillovers for the rest of the system, which are associated to its failure.

Although the role of liquidity requirements stills need to be investigated in detail, the new liquidity requirements are meant to reduce the occurrence of panics in individual institutions and the occurrence of fire sales and, in turn, limit contagion within the system.

However, liquidity requirements could also have broader and potentially negative effects on banks' stability. One way of thinking about these effects is to go back to the frameworks described above (Diamond and Dybvig 1983; Goldstein and Pauzner 2005), where banks act as providers of liquidity insurance and expose themselves to maturity transformation by choosing the appropriate mix of the long- and short-term assets they want to invest in.

Introducing liquidity requirements in such frameworks would lead to the following effects. On the one hand, as already mentioned, liquidity requirements reduce the premature liquidation (or sale) of the long-term assets, thus reducing depositors' incentives to run in the case of coordination problems and panics. However, by forcing banks to invest more in shorter-term assets, which are typically less profitable than longer-term assets, liquidity requirements also reduce banks' profitability in the longer run. This, in turn, may lead depositors and investors more generally to run at the bank out of worries of inadequate resources of the bank in the long run, that is out of fundamental driven reasons. Given these two contrasting effects, the overall implications of liquidity regulation on bank stability is unclear. Much more work is needed in this direction in the upcoming years, and also in looking at the interaction between capital and liquidity requirements.

Assets and Activities Restrictions

Another important set of reforms includes assets, activities, size and bonus restrictions. The CRD IV envisages a set of asset-based tools allowing the European Central Bank (ECB) and/ or the national authorities to prevent banks from being excessively exposed to single counterparties (either banks or other financial institutions), single borrowers or sectors (such as the real estate sector).

Regarding activities restrictions, the proposals are contained in two reports: the Vickers report in the UK and the Liikanen report in Europe. Both reports hinge on the separation between banking and trading activities, with the goal of making banks safer and, in turn, reducing the burden for taxpayers associated with their failures. However, they differ in terms of the activities that have to be separated. For example, trading activities are treated differently in the two reports. The Liikanen report suggests to separate trading activities from other activities only when they amount to a significant share of bank's business. This is not the case in the Vickers' report, which supports the complete separation of trading activities under any circumstances. Similar differences also apply to deposits from and loans to large corporations.

Banking Union

Another key element of the new regulatory framework in Europe is the Banking Union. It consists of three pillars: (1) the Single Supervisory Mechanism (SSM); (2) the Single Resolution Mechanism (SRM); and (3) the European deposit insurance scheme (EDIS). The main driver behind the establishment of the Banking Union was the willingness to break the vicious circle between banks and sovereigns, reduce the burden and costs for the taxpayers associated with bank distress and failure, and to harmonize rules and standards across countries so to improve the quality and the effectiveness of the supervisory and regulatory frameworks.[6]

Single Supervisory Mechanism

In October 2013, the Council Regulation (EU) 1024/2013 conferred to the ECB, and specifically to the newly created SSM, the powers related to prudential supervision of credit institutions. As stated in the regulation, the ultimate objective of the SSM is to guarantee the safety and soundness of credit institutions as well as financial stability.

To achieve these goals, the SSM directly supervises the largest 129 banks in the Eurozone, which account for about 82% of all assets of the banks in the euro area, and indirectly, via the national central banks, all the remaining institutions. Banks located in other countries in the European Union (EU) may voluntarily decide whether to be supervised by the SSM or by their national authority.

The primary objectives attributed to the SSM by the council regulation—safety and soundness of credit institutions and financial stability—reflect the

---

[6] For a broader discussion about the Banking Union, the rationale behind it, its architecture and solved and unsolved issues, refer to Chap. 17 by D. Schoenmaker.

importance of both a micro-prudential and a macro-prudential perspective, which is perfectly in line with the new approach that has characterized the entire package of regulatory reforms implemented after the crisis.

The SSM shares its tasks and powers as macro-prudential supervisors with the national authorities, and the available tools to conduct macro-prudential policies are defined in the CRD IV, which we have described in the previous section, such as some capital buffers, the net stable funding ratio, the leverage ratio and some other assets restrictions.

As discussed above in the framework of capital regulation, the implementation of macro-prudential policies by the SSM features the interaction between the SSM and the national authorities. The new supervisory framework in Europe states that the SSM is empowered to apply more stringent measures than those applied by the member states, if deemed necessary for addressing systemic risk and other macro-prudential risks. However, this only applies to measures and tools covered in the CRD IV, as national authorities are solely responsible for all other measures (e.g., caps on loan-to-value ratios and debt-service-to-income ratios). Still related to this macro-prudential perspective, the SSM has the role of ensuring a consistent implementation within the Eurozone, accounting for potential spillovers.

Regarding its role as micro-prudential supervisors, the SSM supervises banks' compliance with the minimum requirements set in the relevant EU regulation and can set more stringent requirements for individual institutions in the case that their situation and behaviour pose excessive risks. Besides this, the SSM grants and withdraws authorizations. It can, moreover, require institutions to reinforce arrangements, mechanisms and strategies; to limit the variable remuneration as a percentage of net revenues and restrict distributions to shareholder; to present a plan to restore compliance with the supervisory requirements; and to require individual institutions to dismiss specific assets and business activities that are perceived to be too risky.

Finally, it can intervene in the internal governance of credit institutions by requiring banks to remove members from the management bodies and ensuring that institutions have proper internal governance arrangements in place.

Single Resolution Mechanism

The second pillar of the banking Union concerns the Single Resolution Mechanism (SRM), whose implementation and rules are contained in the Bank Recovery and Resolution Directive (BRRD). The SRM applies to all banks supervised by the SSM, that is all banks in the Eurozone plus those in the member states that opt to participate. It consists of two main bodies: the Single Resolution Board (SRB) and the Single Resolution Fund (SRF).

The SRB, which started to operate on 1 January 2015 and became fully operational on 1 January 2016, works in close cooperation with the national resolution authorities of the participating member states. It is backed up by the SRF. This fund is financed by the banking sector and is expected to have a target level of at least 1% of all banks' assets in the participating member states. It also has the option to borrow from the market, if deemed necessary by the SRB.

The main goal of the SRM is to limit the costs of banks' failure for both the taxpayers and the real economy. To achieve this goal, the SRM establishes the rules to ensure an orderly resolution of failing banks and identifies specific resolution tools—for example, the sale of the business private sector, the creation of a bridge bank, the separation of the bank's assets, and bail-in instruments such as the conversion into equity and write-downs.

European Deposit Insurance Scheme

The third pillar of the Banking Union is the creation of a pan-European deposit insurance scheme. Unlike the SSM and SRM, which are already operational and well defined, the design and implementation of the European Deposit Insurance Scheme (EDIS) is still under discussion.

The main goal of the guarantee scheme is to provide additional financial resources in case of large shocks that member state deposit guarantee schemes are not sufficiently funded to handle. In doing this, the scheme pursues two main objectives. Firstly, it contributes to reduce the reliance of the national deposit guarantee scheme on the financial support of their respective sovereigns. Secondly, it increases depositors confidence, thus, as discussed in the previous section, it reduces banks vulnerability to panic-driven crises.

The details about the current structure and implementation of an EDIS are presented in a recent legislative proposal by the European Commission.[7]

Based on the proposal, the guarantee scheme provides that banks' deposits in the participating member states are covered up to 100,000 euros per depositor per bank if the bank fails. Unlike the current set-up, where national government are solely responsible for the provision of the insurance, the proposal envisages the creation of a common system, disconnected from the sovereigns, where EDIS emerges as a natural complement to the other two pillars of the Banking Union.

[7] See the document "Proposal for a regulation of the European Parliament and of the Council amending Regulation (EU) 806/2014 in order to establish a European Deposit Insurance Scheme" at https://ec.europa.eu/transparency/regdoc/rep/1/2015/EN/1-2015-586-EN-F1-1.PDF.

One of the key element in the proposal is the creation of a European Deposit Insurance Fund, set up at the level of the Banking Union and managed by a Board representing all members of the Banking Union. The Fund will be filled by contributions from banks operating in the participating member states. Unlike the current set-up, the risk of a given institution would be assessed relative to the other banks in the Banking Union, rather than to the banks at the national banking sector.

The proposal envisages that the establishment of EDIS follows a gradual process consisting of three phases: (1) reinsurance; (2) co-insurance; and (3) full insurance. In the reinsurance phase, funding will be provided only if there is a liquidity shortfall in the national deposit insurance scheme and it will cover only 20% of the shortfall. Differently, in the co-insurance phase, funding will be provided to cover only a percentage of the liquidity need of a national insurance scheme in the case of a pay-out event or request to participate in the resolution. The share of the liquidity need borne by the EDIS will gradually increase with the co-insurance period. Finally, in the full insurance phase, the EDIS will provide full funding (i.e., 100%) of the liquidity need and cover all losses associated with a pay-out event or a request to contribute to resolution. The proposal also envisages a series of measures (such as exclusion from the EDIS in the case that the national deposit guarantee scheme does not observe the obligations set out in the regulation) to limit the moral hazard problem at the level of a national deposit insurance scheme that could potentially arise as a consequence of the full mutualization.

The Banking Union is the response to the shortcomings that emerged in the recent crisis and it is specifically designed to counter regulatory arbitrage and to promote an equal treatment across the participating member states. In the words of ECB President Draghi, one of the main goals of the Banking Union is to guarantee that "deposits, which are the most widespread form of money, have to inspire the same level of confidence wherever they are located".[8]

The Banking Union is well structured to achieve this goal. A central supranational authority, applying uniform and sound supervisory practices, reduces the risk of forbearance and is also better suited to identify systemic and macroprudential risks and to internalize externalities stemming from cross-border banking in the Eurozone. This, in turn, allows for better and prompter intervention, thus potentially reducing the likelihood and costs associated with banks' failures. Having common and harmonized rules for resolution also contributes to reduce the likelihood and costs of banking crises.

---

[8] See "One year of ECB Banking Supervision" (2005), speech by ECB President Draghi at the SSM Banking Supervision Forum, 4 November 2015.

Despite the advantages of a centralized approach to supervision and resolution, still some issues remain related to the specific design of the SSM and SRM. Concerning the SSM, its architecture features a "hub and spoke system", where local supervisors still play an important role, for example, in the collection of information. A few recent papers (see e.g., Carletti et al. 2015; Colliard 2015) have investigated the optimal supervisory architecture. Carletti et al. (2015) highlight the potential drawbacks of this specific design. In their framework, an inefficient level of information collection may emerge when supervision is centralized in a "hub and spoken system", due to the separation between decision-making bodies (central supervisor) and information-collection bodies (national supervisors) and the misalignment of incentives between the two.

Another relevant aspect of the current architecture of the Banking Union is that, while supervision is completely centralized, this is not the case for the resolution mechanism. Moreover, there are other issues concerning the common funding scheme for the resolution and also for the common deposit insurance scheme.

As we discussed above, despite the existence of a set of harmonized resolution practices and rules, the size of the resolution fund is limited. Regarding the common deposit insurance scheme, instead, the exact design is still under discussion. These are important issues as the existence of a fiscal backstop is necessary to achieve the objectives for which the Banking Union was created. In particular, in order to restore confidence in the banking sector and, in turn, avoid failures and financial contagion, banks' creditors and, most importantly depositors, need to be sure that, even in the case of distress, their money is safe. This is also important for breaking the vicious circle between banks and sovereigns that, as we mentioned above, represents one of the main goals of the Banking Union. The uncertainty about the availability of common funds as well as of the details of the common deposit insurance scheme may induce investors to think that little has changed relative to before the crisis and that, still, the ultimate responsibility in the case of banks' failures and distress is in the hands of the national government, with all the incentives problems and other issues that this implies.

Finally, a related issue refers to the introduction of bail-in instruments. They have two main objectives: (1) reducing the burden of banks' failures on taxpayers; and (2) enhancing financial stability. The introduction of "bail-inable" debt allows both of these goals to be achieved by improving market discipline of banks' creditors and, in turn, curbing the moral hazard and excessive risk-taking of banks. However, there are a few important caveats and issues that deserve deeper discussion, such as the identity of the creditors holding bail-inable debt and how such instruments should be marketed.

Regarding the identity of the creditors holding bail-inable debt, the choice between institutional investors and retail investors does not seem straightforward. On the one hand, in order to improve market discipline, it would be desirable that institutional investors, which are financially literate, would hold the bail-inable debt rather than retail investors, which are less likely to have the knowledge and the instruments to exert the same level of market discipline. However, there are risks associated with such a possibility, which have to do with the credibility of bail-in and, in turn, its effectiveness in curbing excessive risk-taking. If, despite the exerted market discipline, a bad outcome materializes and bail-in rules need to be triggered, then the losses faced by institutional investors may be transferred within the system, generating the risk of systemic crises. Systemic risk triggered by the losses on the bail-inable debt may prevent the regulator from implementing bail-in rules, with the consequence of undermining its credibility and, in turn, effectiveness.

From this perspective, the systemic risk triggered by losses on the bail-inable debt leads to a time inconsistency problem similar to that characterizing ex post bailouts. Bail-in tools are optimally ex ante, but not ex post, exactly like authorities' commitment not to bail out banks is optimal ex ante but not ex post. As a result, no investor would have an incentive to exercise market discipline effectively if he anticipates that the bail-in will actually not take place.

The opposite case—selling bail-inable debt to retail investors—also entails problems and may not achieve the two main goals described above as a consequence of the limited market discipline that those investors are able to exert. Moreover, in this case, there is an additional concern regarding consumers' protection, which may not be achieved.

An additional issue concerns the amount and quality of information available to bail-inable creditors. Bail-in rules make a bank safer from the perspective of taxpayers; they also make it riskier from the perspective of creditors. It is then important that the bail-inable debt holders are well informed about the risk that they take. This is not always the case, as the recent events in Italy have shown, because often those investors are not financially knowledgeable and are not able to assess the risks associated with their investments.

Finally, the separation between supervision and resolution authority, as well as the current architecture featuring central and decentralized component, may still be subject to incentives problems, forbearance risks and conflicts of interests.

Concluding Remarks

This chapter takes stock of the recent regulatory reforms in Europe and link them to the market failures inherent in the role that banks perform in the economy that were analysed in the banking literature over the past thirty years. We have discussed the rationale behind the various regulatory reforms, their effectiveness in curbing information and incentives problems that the sources of fragility of individual banks and of the system as a whole.

As emerged from our discussion, a lot has been done with the recent wave of regulatory reforms, although some critical points remain. Moreover, looking ahead, there are other challenges and open issues for the policy-makers stemming from the change in the border between regulated and non-regulated institutions, and the emergence of shadow banking, as well as the increasing complexity of the banking system due to financial innovation, which will require the regulatory framework to evolve and adapt to those changes.[9]

References

Acemoglu, D., Ozdaglar, A., & Tahbaz-Saleh, A. (2015). Systemic risk and stability in financial networks. *American Economic Review, 105*(2), 564–608.

Acharya, V. (2009). A theory of systemic risk and design of prudential bank regulation. *Journal of Financial Stability, 5*(3), 224–255.

Acharya, V., Drechsler, I., & Schnabl, P. (2015). A Pyrrhic victory? – Bank bailouts and sovereign credit risk. *Journal of Finance, 69*(6), 2689–2739.

Adelino, M., & Ferreira, M.. (2015). Bank ratings and lending supply: Evidence from sovereign downgrades. *Review of Financial Studies*, forthcoming.

Admati, A., DeMarzo, P., Hellwig, M., & Pfleiderer, P. (2010). *Fallacies, irrelevant facts, and myths in the discussion of capital regulation: Why bank equity is not expensive.* Stanford University working paper, No. 86.

Allen, F., & Carletti, E. (2006). Credit risk transfer and contagion. *Journal of Monetary Economics, 53*, 89–111.

Allen, F., & Carletti, E. (2008). Mark-to-market accounting and liquidity pricing. *Journal of Accounting and Economics, 45*, 358–378.

Allen, F., & Gale, D. (2000a). Bubbles and crises. *The Economic Journal, 110*(460), 236–255.

Allen, F., & Gale, D. (2000b). Financial contagion. *Journal of Political Economy, 108*(1), 1–33.

Allen, F., Babus, A., & Carletti, E. (2009). Financial crises: Theory and evidence. *Annual Review of Financial Economics, 1*, 97–116.

[9] See Beck et al. (2016), "Financial Regulation in Europe: Foundations and Challenges".

Allen, F., Carletti, E., & Marquez, R. (2011). Credit market competition and capital regulation. *Review of Financial Studies, 24*(4), 983–1018.

Allen, F., Babus, A., & Carletti, E. (2012). Asset commonality, debt maturity and systemic risk. *Journal of Financial Economics, 104*, 519–534.

Allen, F., Carletti, E., & Marquez, R. (2015a). Deposits and bank capital structure. *Journal of Financial Economics*, forthcoming.

Allen, F., Carletti, E., Goldstein, I., & Leonello, A. (2015b). *Government guarantees and financial stability*. CEPR discussion paper 10560.

Allen, F., Carletti, E., Goldstein, I., & Leonello, A. (2015c). Moral hazard and government guarantees in the banking industry. *Journal of Financial Regulation, 1*, 1–21.

Basel Committee on Banking Supervision. (2016). *Literature review on the integration of regulatory capital and liquidity instruments, BIS working paper 30*.

Beck, T., Carletti, E., & Goldstein, I. (2016). *Financial regulation in Europe: Foundations and challenges*. CEPR Discussion paper 11147.

Beltratti, A., & Stulz, R. M. (2012). The credit crisis around the globe: Why did some banks perform better. *Journal of Financial Economics, 105*(1), 1–17.

Berger, A. N., & Bouwman, C. H. S. (2013). How does capital affect bank performance during financial crises? *Journal of Financial Economics, 109*, 146–176.

Boot, A., & Greenbaum, S. I. (1993). Bank regulation, reputation and rents: Theory and policy implications. In C. Mayer & X. Vives (Eds.), *Capital markets and financial intermediation* (pp. 262–285). New York: CEPR, Cambridge University Press.

Boyd, J., De Nicoló, G., & Loukoianova, E. (2009). *Banking crises and crisis dating: Theory and evidence, IMF working paper 09/141*. Washington, DC: International Monetary Fund.

Brunnermeier, M. K. (2009). Deciphering the liquidity and credit crunch 2007–2008. *Journal of Economic Perspectives, 23*(1), 77–100.

Brunnermeier, M. K., Crockett, A., Goodhart, C. A., Persaud, A., & Shin, H. S. (2009). *The fundamental principles of financial regulation* (Vol. 11). London: Centre for Economic Policy Research.

Bryant, J. (1980). A model of reserves, bank runs and deposit insurance. *Journal of Banking & Finance, 4*, 335–344.

Calomiris, C., & Gorton, G. (1991). The origins of banking panics, models, facts, and bank regulation. In R. G. Hubbard (Ed.), *Financial markets and financial crises* (pp. 109–173). Chicago: University of Chicago Press.

Calomiris, C., & Kahn, C. M. (1991). The role of demandable debt in structuring optimal banking arrangements. *American Economic Review, 81*(3), 497–513.

Calomiris, C., & Mason, J. (2003). Fundamentals, panics and bank distress during the depression. *American Economic Review, 93*(5), 1615–1647.

Calomiris, C., Heider, F., & Hoerova, M. (2015). *A theory of bank liquidity requirements*. Columbia Business School research paper No. 14–39.

Carletti, E., & Leonello, A. (2016). *Credit market competition and liquidity crises.* ECB working paper 1932.

Carletti, E., Dell'Ariccia, G., & Marquez, R. (2015). *Supervisory incentives in a banking union.* Mimeo.

Carlsson, H., & van Damme, E. (1993). Global games and equilibrium selection. *Econometrica, 61*, 989–1018.

Cerra, V., & Saxena, S. C. (2008). Growth dynamics: The myth of economic recovery. *American Economic Review, 98*(1), 439–457.

Chari, V. V., & Jagannthan, R. (1988). Banking panics, information, and rational expectations equilibrium. *Journal of Finance, 43*(3), 749–761.

Chen, Y. (1999). Banking panics: The role of the first-come, first-served rule and information externalities. *Journal of Political Economy, 107*(5), 946–968.

Cifuentes, R., Ferrucci, G., & Shin, H. (2005). Liquidity risk and contagion. *Journal of the European Economic Association, 3*, 556–566.

Clerc, L., Derviz, A., Mendicino, C., Moyen, S., Nikolov, K., Stracca, L., et al. (2015). Capital regulation in a macroeconomic model with three layers of default. *International Journal of Central Banking, 11*(3), 9–63.

Colliard, J. E. (2015). *Optimal supervisory architecture and financial integration in a banking nion, ECB working paper 1786.* Luxembourg: Publications Office.

Cooper, R., & Nikolov, K. (2013). *Government debt and banking fragility: The spreading of strategic uncertainty, NBER working paper 19278.* Cambridge, MA: National Bureau of Economic Research.

Cooper, R., & Ross, T. W. (2002). Bank runs, deposit insurance and capital requirements. *International Economic Review, 43*(1), 55–72.

Correa, R., Sapriza, H., & Zlate, A. (2012). *Liquidity shocks, dollar funding costs, and the bank lending channel during the European sovereign crisis* (International Finance discussion papers 1059). Washington, DC: Board of Governors of the Federal Reserve System.

Corsetti, G., Dasgupta, A., Morris, S., & Shin, H. S. (2004). Does one Soros make a difference? A theory of currency crises with large and small traders. *Review of Economic Studies, 71*(1), 87–113.

De Marco, F. (2015). *Bank lending and the European sovereign debt crisis.* Mimeo.

De Vries, C. G. (2005). The simple economics of bank fragility. *Journal of Banking & Finance, 29*(4), 803–825.

Dell'Ariccia, G., & Marquez, R. (2006). Lending booms and lending standards. *Journal of Finance, 61*(5), 2511–2546.

Diamond, D. (1984). Financial intermediation and delegated monitoring. *Review of Economic Studies, 51*(3), 393–414.

Diamond, D. W., & Dybvig, P. H. (1983). Bank runs, deposit insurance and liquidity. *Journal of Political Economy, 91*(3), 401–419.

Diamond, D., & Rajan, R. (2001). Liquidity risk, liquidity creation and financial fragility: A theory of banking. *Journal of Political Economy, 109*, 2431–2465.

Draghi, M. (2015, November 4). *One year of ECB banking supervision*. Speech by Mario Draghi, President of the ECB, at the ECB Forum on Banking Supervision. Frankfurt.

Farhi, E., & Tirole, J. (2015). *Deadly embrace: Sovereign and financial balance sheets doom loops*. Mimeo.

Flannery, M. J., & Rangan, K. P. (2008). What caused the bank capital build-up of the 1990s? *Review of Finance, 12*(2), 391–429.

Freixas, X., & Parigi, B. (1998). Contagion and efficiency in gross and net interbank payment systems. *Journal of Financial Intermediation, 7*(1), 3–31.

Freixas, X., Parigi, B., & Rochet, J. C. (2000). Systemic risk, interbank relations and liquidity provision by the central bank. *Journal of Money, Credit and Banking, 32*, 611–638.

Furlong, F. T., & Keeley, M. C. (1989). Capital regulation and bank risk-taking: A note. *Journal of Banking & Finance, 13*(6), 883–891.

Goldstein, I. (2005). Strategic complementarities and the twin crises. *The Economic Journal, 115*, 368–390.

Goldstein, I., & Pauzner, A. (2004). Contagion of self-fulfilling financial crises due to diversification of investment portfolios. *Journal of Economic Theory, 119*, 151–183.

Goldstein, I., & Pauzner, A. (2005). Demand-deposit contracts and the probability of bank runs. *Journal of Finance, 60*, 1293–1327.

Gorton, G. (1988). Banking panics and business cycles. *Oxford Economic Papers, 40*(4), 751–781.

Gorton, G., & Winton, A. (2003). Bank liquidity provision and capital regulation in transition economies. In A. Meyendorff & A. Thakor (Eds.), *William Davidson Institute conference volume on "Financial sectors in transition"*. Cambridge, MA: MIT Press in press.

Heider, F., Hoerova, M., & Holthausen, C. (2015). Liquidity hoarding and interbank market spreads: The role of counterparty risk. *Journal of Financial Economics, 118*, 336–354.

Hellman, T. F., Murdock, K. C., & Stiglitz, J. E. (2000). Liberalization, moral hazard in banking, and prudential regulation: Are capital requirements enough? *American Economic Review, 90*(1), 147–165.

Jacklin, C. J., & Battacharya, S. (1988). Distinguishing panics and information-based bank runs: Welfare and policy implications. *Journal of Political Economy, 93*(3), 568–592.

Kahane, Y. (1977). Capital adequacy and the regulation of financial intermediaries. *Journal of Banking & Finance, 1*(2), 207–218.

Kaminsky, G. L., & Reinhart, C. M. (1999). The twin crises: The causes of banking and balance-of-payments problems. *American Economic Review, 89*(3), 473–500.

Kareken, J. H., & Wallace, N. (1978). Deposit insurance and bank regulation: A partial-equilibrium exposition. *Journal of Business, 51*(3), 413–438.

Lagunoff, R., & Schreft, S. (2001). A model of financial fragility. *Journal of Economic Theory, 99*, 220–264.

Leonello, A. (2016). *Government guarantees and the feedback loop between banking and sovereign debt crises*. Mimeo.

Luck, S., & Schempp, P. (2014). *Banks, shadow banking, and fragility, ECB Working Paper 1726*. Frankfurt am Main: European Central Bank.

Malherbe, F. (2015). *Optimal capital requirements over the business and financial cycle, ECB working paper 1830*. Luxembourg: European Central Bank.

Martinez-Miera, D., & Suarez, J. (2014). *A macroeconomic model of endogenous systemic risk taking*. Mimeo.

Morris, S., & Shin, H. S. (1998). Unique equilibrium in a model of self-fulfilling currency attacks. *American Economic Review, 88*(3), 587–597.

Petersen, M. A., & Rajan, R. (1994). The benefits of lending relationships: Evidence from small business data. *Journal of Finance, 49*(1), 3–37.

Reinhart, C. M., & Rogoff, K. S. (2009). *This time is different: Eight centuries of financial follies*. Princeton: Princeton University Press.

Reinhart, C. M., & Rogoff, K. S. (2011). From financial crash to debt crisis. *American Economic Review, 101*(5), 1676–1706.

Repullo, R. (2004). Capital requirements, market power, and risk-taking in banking. *Journal of Financial Intermediation, 13*(2), 156–182.

Repullo, R., & Suarez, J. (2013). The procyclical effects of bank capital regulation. *Review of Financial Studies, 26*, 452–490.

Rochet, J. C., & Vives, X. (2004). Coordination failures and the lender of last resort: Was Bagehot right after all? *Journal of the European Economic Association, 2*(6), 1116–1147.

Schularick, M., & Taylor, A. M. (2012). Credit booms gone bust: Monetary policy, leverage cycles, and financial crises, 1870–2008. *American Economic Review, 102*(2), 1029–1061.

Wagner, W. (2011). Systemic liquidation risk and the diversity–diversification trade-off. *Journal of Finance, 66*(4), 1141–1175.

13

Complexity in Regulation

Andrew Haldane and Tobias Neumann

A Journey Towards Complexity

Modern banking regulation started in Europe. This is true in two senses: firstly, European countries were the first to write into law which prudential metrics were being used and enforced by supervisors; secondly, risk-weighted regulation—the central pillar of the international regulatory framework—started in Germany and was further refined there and in the UK. This section describes how banking regulation became ever more complex, evolving from a number of simple metrics into one highly complex ratio defined by the Basel Committee on Banking Supervision.

European Banking Regulation Before Basel

The origin of risk-weighted banking regulation can be traced back to 1930s Germany. The German Banking Act of 1934 defined various ratios in law that had to be met by banks, though the threshold values were left to be defined by the Reichsbank on a bank-by-bank basis. On only 12 pages it defined an embryonic risk-weighted capital ratio, a liquidity coverage ratio and a large

A. Haldane • T. Neumann (✉)
The Bank of England, London, UK
e-mail: Andy.Haldane@bankofengland.co.uk; Tobias.Neumann@bankofengland.co.uk

T. Beck, B. Casu (eds.), *The Palgrave Handbook of European Banking*,
DOI 10.1057/978-1-137-52144-6_13

exposure limit (complete with a sovereign exemption). It also defined what "capital" and "liquid assets" were to begin with; and it included such modern ideas as distribution restrictions if requirements were breached and bonus deferrals for senior management (Reichsgesetzblatt 1943). Denmark can lay claim to the first formalized leverage ratio: it mandated that banks hold equity of at least 10% of their total liabilities in 1930 (Moe 1955).

The main innovation in Germany compared to the more liquidity-focused laws in other early adopters of statutory banking regulation such as Denmark was that the Act defined an embryonic risk-weighted capital ratio: total liabilities less liquid asset should not exceed a percentage of regulatory capital prescribed by the supervisory authority. Subtracting liquid asset is the same as giving them a 0% risk weight, making this the first risk-weighted capital ratio defined in law (Reichsgesetzblatt 1943). It is not clear why they were given a 0% risk weight, but a reasonable supposition is that the Reichsbank did not want to make it more difficult for the banking system to lend to the government. Similar considerations led the Federal Reserve to exclude sovereign debt from its first risk-weighted ratio (Alfriend 1988). The German Banking Act also included a simple but precise definition of capital: equity. And it enumerated precisely which types of reserves were eligible for inclusion in addition to paid-in share capital.

In addition to relying on a risk-weighted capital ratio, the Act allowed the supervisory office to define a large exposure limit, excluding loans made to or guaranteed by the *Reich*. The final metric in the act was a type of liquidity coverage ratio. Banks would have to hold bonds with a maturity of 90 days or less, or other assets accepted as collateral by the Reichsbank, to cover a percentage of their liabilities (Reichsgesetzblatt 1943). These types of metrics were already in other banking laws at the time. For example, Denmark required a liquidity coverage ratio that was very close to the Basel liquidity coverage ratio: banks had to hold liquid assets to cover 15% of all debt maturing within the next month. Denmark also introduced a large exposure limit in its Banking Act of 1930 (Deumer 1933).

The German Banking Act of 1934 followed the German Banking Crisis of 1931. Its provisions mirrored the shortcomings in the German banking system that had made it vulnerable to a crisis: it was under-capitalized, over-risked and illiquid. The average capital-to-asset ratio had fallen from 24% in 1913 to 8.5% in 1930 as a result of war and inflation. Though this was in line with the capital ratios of British and French banks at the time, German banks' assets were on average riskier (von Bissing 1933). In Britain and France, banks mostly provided short-term credit to corporate clients and bridge financing; long-term financing, especially in Britain, tended to be carried out via highly development capital markets (Collins 1988).

In Germany, in contrast, banks were tasked with providing longer-term financing. The need for capital was immense as a result of war, war reparation and hyperinflation; there was no deep capital market to provide this financing. At the same time, the state of corporate interwar Germany was weak. This resulted in a considerable number of illiquid and high-risk assets on German banks' balance sheets (Fischer 1933). The risky loans on German banks' balance sheets, and their default in the crisis, caused regulators to realize that the asset side of the balance sheet matters beyond providing liquid assets: its composition directly affects a bank's riskiness and capital can be used to mitigate this risk. This sounds obvious now. But this peculiar nature of the German banking system may explain why risk-weighted capital regulation had its origin in Germany and not elsewhere. Despite the riskiness of their balance sheets, German banks mostly financed the demand for credit by issuing debt rather than equity. To quote Dr W. M. von Bissing, a professor at Königsberg business school at the time:

> Since the tightness of the German capital markets places strict limitations on the issuance of new shares; and since refinancing was limited because of write-downs and the necessity to pay appropriate dividends, banks were forced to largely rely on debt, in particular on foreign debt. (p. 73, von Bissing 1933)

In 1930, 35% of debt on German banks' balance sheets was owed to foreigners. These, and most domestic liabilities, were largely short-term loans: 41.4% of total liabilities had a maturity of seven days or less; 51.5% had a maturity between seven days and three months; and only 7.1% had a maturity of three months or more (Fischer 1933). Banks only held on average 1.7% of their liabilities in cash in 1930. This compares to an average of 9.5% for English banks (Nordhoff 1933).

The failure of the Austrian Creditanstalt in May 1931 was the trigger that led to a run on German wholesale funding (Hasse 1933). But it was the failure of Darmstädter und Nationalbank (Danatbank) that led to a run of domestic creditors and really brought the crisis to Germany. Danatbank was the second largest bank in Germany and somewhat notorious for aggressive lending practices; its failure was triggered by the bankruptcy of Nordwolle to which it had lent RM 48 million, representing 40% of its equity capital (Schnabel 2004). That is a large exposure by anyone's standard, and reining in this type of lending was likely a motivation of the large exposure limit in the Banking Act.

By the end of 1932 German banks had made losses equivalent to RM 525 million, equivalent to 40% of their equity capital. As observed at the time: "It is only due to the intervention of the state that there has not been a greater reduction in capital as a result of the 1931 crisis" (p. 59, von Bissing 1933). The public purse recapitalized banks to the tune of RM 410 million; adding other means of assistance such as guarantees brings the total to RM 1920 million (Hasse 1933).

In summary, German banks entered the Great Depression with little capital relative to the riskiness of their assets and flighty (because foreign) short-term funding that was not matched with commensurate liquid assets. The trigger for the crisis was the default of a large-exposure obligor. The Banking Act's three provisions of a capital ratio, a liquidity requirement and large exposure limit appear a natural response to the German experience.

Though some European countries such as Sweden and Denmark had introduced more formal banking regulation by the 1930s, neither France nor the UK had done so. The Vichy regime introduced the first banking act on French soil in 1941, introducing the concept of a minimum capital requirement, but without going into much detail on the definition of the ratio (Legifrance n.d.). Supervision in the UK in the 1930s remained informal—largely relying on the Governor's "raised eyebrow" (p.71, Norton 1995). The Bank of England did take into account certain ratios when assessing bank health but they were considerably more flexible than in Germany (Dessauer 1935). There appears no reference to anything resembling risk weighting; in fact, the focus was primarily on liquidity rather than capital (Norton 1995).

In the English-speaking world, risk weighting can be traced back to the USA shortly after World War II. American banks' balance sheet had ballooned, mostly as a result of investing in US government bonds to finance the war. To avoid penalizing banks for this effort, the Federal Reserve Board removed US government bonds from the denominator of the capital-to-asset ratio—essentially assigning them a 0% weight (Alfriend 1988). That said, prior to 1983 the US regulators did not have the statutory power to issue capital directives; so risk-weighted ratios were only examination tools not legally enforceable minimum criteria (Norton 1995).

But risk-weighted assets were never adopted with much gusto by US regulators other than the Federal Reserve. The Comptroller of the Currency dismissed the risk-weighting approach in the 1960s as arbitrary and incomplete. Instead, a number of factors such as liquidity and management quality were relied on to arrive at an internal rating for the bank. That is significant because at the time the Comptroller was the main regulator; the Federal Reserve Board's modern-day pre-eminence in banking regulation was only cemented during the 1970s (Norton 1995). The Federal Deposit Insurance Corporation (FDIC) relied on a simple capital-to-asset ratio throughout this period. (Alfriend 1988). Over time, the risk-weighted approach gained in importance—along with the Federal Reserve Board's importance as a regulator—but it was by no means the primary means of assessing capital adequacy for US banks prior to the Basel Accord (Norton 1995).

European countries continued formalizing banking regulation after World War II, with risk-weighted capital regulation in particular gaining importance. Again, Germany led the pack. In 1961, the Banking Act was revised and the Federal Banking Supervisory Office was charged with developing "principles" for assessing capital adequacy (Bundesgesetzblatt 1961). The principles were first published in 1961, establishing a maximum ratio of credit asset to capital of 18 (implicitly risk weighting certain other assets at 0%), as well as liquidity ratios and the large exposure limit stipulated in the Banking Act (Bundesbank 1962). The revised version of 1972 included the next step in the evolution of risk weights by explicitly assigning weights of 50%, 20% and 0% to certain credits (Bundesbank 1973). Together with the 1961 Banking Act, the 1972 principles weighed in at 21 pages.

During the 1970s the Bank of England started to throw its weight behind risk weighting when it published the outcomes of a joint working party it had formed with London and Scottish clearing banks to develop regulatory ratios. To quote George Blunden, the chief supervisor at the time:

> We should relate capital and reserves [...] to the purpose for which they are required. There should [...] be a margin of shareholders' funds available to provide coverage, in addition to the coverage provided by the current earnings and by past provisions, against the risks of loss. In assessing a bank one needs to relate these three sources of protection against loss to the volume of risk assets and contingent liabilities. (p.193, Bank of England 1975)

In 1980, the Bank of England made its expectations on capital adequacy more precise in response to having received statutory responsibility for banking supervision the year before. It established two ratios: a gearing (i.e., leverage) ratio and a risk asset ratio (Bank of England 1980). The risk asset ratio included seven risk weights ranging from 0% to 200%. It did not establish a minimum ratio.

The risk asset ratio was viewed as the more useful by the Bank. But it was nevertheless thought to be too crude to be applied as a single, uniform standard across institutions: "the Bank considers that to prescribe a precise numerical guideline for the capital needs of all institutions or for groups of institutions would be inappropriately inflexible. Such an approach would endorse overtrading by some companies and be harmfully restrictive to others" (p. 324, Bank of England 1980). Consideration was also given to whether it should incorporate operational or concentration risks. But the Bank of England concluded that to encompass all these elements within a single calculation would "involve the construction of an excessively elaborate model whose appearance of accuracy could be dangerously misleading" (p. 328, Bank of England 1980).

By the late 1970s, five out of the nine member states of the European Economic Community (EEC) used a risk-weighted approach. All except Italy had formal capital regulation; most of them used it alongside liquidity regulation and large exposure limits (Inter-Bank Research Organisation 1978).

With capital adequacy regulation coming into greater focus the question of the definition of capital became more important. Here, too, complexity steadily increased over time; but in contrast to risk-weighted assets, the origin of the complexity lies in the USA. In 1962, the Comptroller of the Currency, James Saxon, ruled that subordinated debt be allowed into the definition of capital, subject to suitable limits. The reasoning was that it is sufficiently loss absorbing and had the advantage of being tax-efficient:

> The use of preferred stock enables business firms to provide additional capital without dilution of the equity position of the common shareholders. The use of debentures accomplishes the same result and has the additional advantage that interest costs are deductible for income tax purposes. There is no sound reason why National Banks should be deprived of any legitimate capital-raising method that is available to corporations generally. (p. 82, Office of the Comptroller of the Currency 1962)

Thus was born the possibility of non-equity capital to count for regulatory purposes. European countries followed suit. By the late 1970s seven out of the nine ECC countries allowed subordinated debt to count as capital—Denmark allowing up to 40%; Luxembourg up to 50%. The exceptions where Germany and Italy (Inter-Bank Research Organisation 1978). The FDIC, too, did not allow anything but equity in its definition of capital (Norton 1995). Neither did Japan (Goodhart 2011).

Basel: Singularly Complex

The pre-Basel world was roughly one of multiple—fairly simple—constraints on banks. These would often include a risk-weighted ratio, but this was far from universally accepted outside Europe. A similar picture existed for including subordinated debt in the definition of capital. In 1988 the Basel Committee on Banking Supervision (BCBS) harmonized this to a single risk-weighted ratio with multiple tiers of capital. Though national jurisdictions were free to continue to rely on other ratios, and many did, the focus of banking regulation shifted to a single ratio.

The Basel standard that was eventually published bore a great semblance to a proposal drafted by the Bank of England and the US authorities; an excellent history of these early developments can be found in Goodhart (2011). The 1988 Basel Accord defined a single risk-weighted capital ratio across 11 countries. It did not include a leverage ratio or liquidity metrics. A bank's assets were allocated to one of five broad risk categories, each with a fixed risk weighting that ranged from 0% to 100%. A portfolio of corporate loans, for instance, received a risk weight of 100%, while retail mortgages—perceived to be safer—received a more favourable weighting of 50%. Only credit risk was covered.

Minimum capital was set in proportion to the weighted sum of these assets, called "risk-weighted assets" (RWA). Capital came in two flavours: Tier 1 was defined as equity and reserves and needed to constitute at least 4% of RWA. The remainder of the 8% overall ratio could be met by lesser quality instruments such as hybrid and subordinated debt, so-called Tier 2 capital. This was similar in spirit to the definition of capital found in the majority of ECC countries at the time—though very much against German opinion in particular (Goodhart 2011). The document ran to 30 pages with a word count of around 10,000—roughly the length of this chapter (Basel Committee on Banking Supervision 1988).

Regulators were aware that the 1988 Basel Accord was not the be-all and end-all of banking regulation. For example, it did not cover market risk. But it framed the debate on how to regulate banks for two decades: use a risk-weighted capital ratio. This was a departure from earlier schools of thoughts that put greater emphasis on liquidity regulation, and, subsequently, on a suite of ratios. All later additions and revisions to the Basel Accord elaborated on this basic principle but none challenged it until the advent of Basel III 20 years later.

Perhaps the most significant such elaboration was the Market Risk Amendment of 1996. Banks were, for the first time, allowed to model capital requirements themselves. The Basel Committee used the then state-of-the-art "value-at-risk" (VaR) methodology, which had only been popularized two years earlier when JPMorgan published the methodology in 1994. In order to investigate how much to constrain banks' internal models, the Committee conducted a hypothetical portfolio exercise in which 15 major banks calculated VaR on the same portfolio (BCBS 1995). A third to one-half of the 15 banks fell outside a range of plus or minus 25% of the median estimate. The

Committee concluded that "a moderate amount of supervisory guidance […] could substantially reduce the dispersion in the results" (p. 280, Goodhart 2011). On this count it appears to have been overly optimistic, as shown in the section "Risk Weights".

The Market Risk Amendment also introduced a third tier to the definition of capital—short-term subordinated debt. Banks were allowed to meet up to roughly 70% of their market risk capital requirements using this so-called Tier 3 capital as long as the sum of Tier 2 and Tier 3 capital was less than that of Tier 1.

The Market Risk Amendment was followed by an analogous attempt to replicate best practice in credit risk modelling. The main reason for this was that the fairly simple approach to credit risk was heavily arbitraged by banks. For example, since it only imposed a flat risk weight on all corporates, banks could increase their net interest margin by lending to riskier corporates without having to fund the loans with more capital. Since capital did not always increase with risk, this approach was criticized as insufficiently "risk-sensitive" (Jackson 1999).

Concerns about risk sensitivity led to the Basel Committee publishing a revised set of rules in 2004, called "Basel II". The new accord widened the scope of internal models to include all risk classes, including credit risk. Banks lacking the capacity to model these risks were required to use the so-called "standardized approaches", under which capital requirements were based on external agency ratings. Basel II was considerably more comprehensive than its predecessor: it ran to 347 pages, or 140,000 words—roughly the length of two PhD theses or a Dickens novel (*A Tale of Two Cities* appears to be the closest match). Basel II was transposed into European law via the Capital Requirements Directive in 2006.

But the increase in the length of the Basel rulebook, if anything, understates its increase in complexity. If we trace the evolution of complexity by how many parameters have to be estimated, we notice two trends: on the one hand, the number has gone down because Basel only relied on one ratio—in contrast to the multiple ratios typically employed before then. On the other hand, the calculation of the risk-weighted ratio became ever more complicated. The second effect far outweighed the first.

The move to internal models, and from broad asset classes to individual loan exposures, had resulted in a ballooning in the number of estimated risk weights. For a large, complex bank, this has meant a rise in the number of calculations required from single figures a generation ago to several million today (Haldane 2011). It is close to impossible to determine with complete precision the size of the parameter space for a large international bank's banking book. That, by itself, is revealing. Across the banking book, a large bank might need to estimate several thousand default probability and loss-given-default parameters. To turn these into regulatory capital requirements, the number of parameters increases by another order of magnitude (Haldane 2012). A rough guess would put it at thousands, perhaps tens of thousands, of estimated and calibrated parameters. That is three, perhaps four, orders of magnitude greater than Basel I.

If that sounds large, the parameter set for the trading book is almost certainly larger still. A large firm would typically have several thousand risk factors in its VaR model. Estimating the covariance matrix for all of the risk factors means estimating several million individual risk parameters. Multiple pricing models are then typically used to map from these risk factors to the valuation of individual instruments, each with several estimated pricing parameters. Taking all of this together, the parameters used in a large bank's banking and trading books could easily run to several millions.

This increase in density and complexity of financial regulation has had predictable consequences for the scale and scope of regulatory resources. One metric for that would be the number of human resources devoted to financial regulation. In the UK up until the late 1970s, bank supervision was performed by the Bank of England on an informal basis, with a team of around 30 employees. Even when the Bank was given statutory responsibility in 1979, fewer than 80 people were engaged in the supervision of financial firms (Haldane 2012).

In the period since, the number of UK financial supervisors has increased dramatically, rising almost fortyfold. In response to the global financial crisis of 2007–8, regulatory numbers have risen further. Over the same period, the number of people employed in the UK financial services sector has only edged up. In 1980, there was one UK regulator for roughly every 11,000 people employed in the UK financial sector. By 2011, there was one regulator for every 300 people employed in finance (Haldane 2012).

How Complexity Failed in the Crisis

The Basel Accord aimed to capture the increasing complexity of modern banking in its rules. The global financial crisis suggests that at least three aspects of this ever-increasing complexity were misguided. The first was the definition of capital, which consisted of six different layers each with interdependent minimum and maximum requirements. The second is risk weighting, which did not sufficiently capture the underlying risks of financial instruments. Finally, the Basel Accord assumed that it is possible and sufficient to condense the myriad of risks that may lead to bank failure into on (complex) minimum capital requirement. This section discusses each fault line in turn.

Definition of Capital

The Basel Accord allowed three tiers of capital, two of which had sub-tiers. These were: Core Tier 1, Non-Innovative Tier 1, Innovative Tier 1, Upper Tier 2, Lower Tier 2 and Tier 3. In addition, there was a fairly complex set of rules establishing minimum and maximum levels acceptable to meet the overall 8% minimum ratio.

Tier 1 capital was meant to absorb losses and had to constitute at least 50% of the 8% minimum; the other tiers were meant to be available after resolution. Straightforward common equity absorbs losses with certainty because there is no legal obligation to pay dividends or to pay back any principal. If losses occur and are covered by the equity cushion, equity just gets written off without a default.

Common equity was represented in the Accord as Core Tier 1 capital. It had to constitute at least half of the minimum Tier 1 requirement—that is, 2 percentage points of the overall 8% minimum. That meant that only 25% of the minimum requirement had to be met with common equity. It also meant a step-change away from the earliest capital requirements that insisted on common equity.

Non-core Tier 1 capital was defined as perpetual, non-cumulative preference shares. The intention was to absorb losses by deferring coupon payment. Any non-payment of coupons would mitigate the losses in a stressed period, without the bank's defaulting. Some banks also issued preferred shares with a further loss-absorbing feature in form of principal write-down. These are called silent, or profit, participation notes. Typically, the reporting of a loss would trigger a reduction in a bond's principal. This would generate a profit, and coupons, if paid, would be based on the new principal. In all cases, it was the bank's responsibility to pull the trigger.

At least 70% of the total Tier 1 requirement had to be "non-innovative". Innovative Tier 1 capital added complexity by including step-up clauses or other features that legally meant they were regarded as debt. Overall, the flexibility of non-core Tier 1 instruments made them difficult to price: not only did investors have to price default (or in the case of equity, model future cash flows), but also the bank's option of payment deferral or other option features.

Tier 2 capital was divided in Upper and Lower Tier 2. Upper Tier 2 consisted of undisclosed reserves, some provisions that were assigned there as a result of the risk-weighting process, perpetual cumulative preference shares and perpetual cumulative subordinated debt. Lower Tier 2 consisted of non-perpetual subordinated debt with a minimum time to maturity of five years. It was limited to a maximum of 50% of Tier 1 capital (so more Tier 1 capital allowed banks to use more Lower Tier 2). Tier 3 capital was shorter-term subordinated debt which could be used up to a proportion of 2.5 the amount of Tier 1 capital used to support market risk.

This was a baffling array of minima and limits. It was coupled with an over-optimistic view on loss absorbency in times of stress. In addition, the various deductions of regulatory capital were not harmonized across jurisdictions and there were no disclosure requirements on banks' structure of capital (Hannoun 2010). Banks took advantage of this. The years before the crisis saw a shift away from "core Tier 1" to more innovative forms of Tier 1 and Tier 2 capital (Bank of England June 2009).

When the crisis hit, the complexity of this framework collapsed. In the eyes of financial markets nothing mattered but core Tier 1 equity in ensuring solvency. The more complex Tier 1 capital instruments disappointed. They were meant to absorb losses and keep distressed banks alive, but banks were reluctant to cancel coupons or otherwise cancel or defer payments (Her Majesty's Treasury 2009). Tier 2 and Tier 3 capital were also irrelevant: bailed-out banks did not go legally bankrupt, due to governments' capital injections which meant that some fairly large stocks of subordinated capital were of little use for absorbing losses.

Risk Weights

All in all, how has the more complex risk-weighted approach fared in the crisis? To test this Haldane and Madouros (2012) take a sample of about 100 large, complex global banks, defined as those with total assets over $100 billion at the end of 2006. Out of these 37 defaulted. These large banks are likely to hold a diverse array of assets and in the case of market risk to have used complex internal models to calibrate regulatory capital against these assets. So at least in principle, risks to these banks should be better captured by granular, risk-sensitive capital measures. The authors test whether the amount of risk-weighted capital could distinguish ex ante between default and survival. It did not. Other studies come to a similar conclusion—for example Aikman and colleagues (2014), Demirguc-Kunt, Detragiache and Merrouche (2013) and

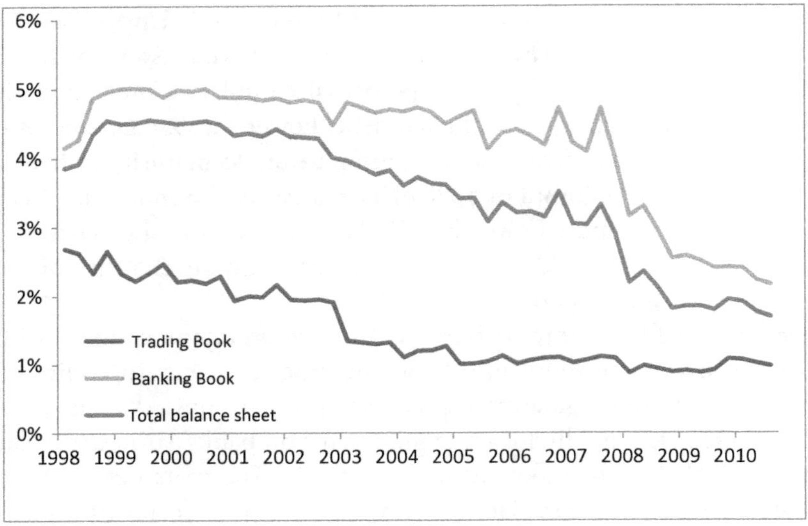

Fig. 13.1 Capital requirements divided by relevant assets in the UK since 1998 (*Source*: Regulatory returns. Sample includes all UK-regulated firms, which changes over time. Banking (trading) book capital is divided by banking (trading) book assets)

Blundell-Wignall and colleagues (2014). Mariathasan and Merrouche (2013) suggest that the risk-weighted ratio fails when it is arguably needed most: in times of stress.

What can explain this apparent failure of the risk-weighted approach? One clue is that there has been a secular fall in risk weights over time. In the UK, we saw UK banks' capital requirements relative to total assets fall from just under 5% in 1998 to around 2.2% at the end of 2010 (Fig. 13.1). Since risk-weighted requirements were held constant over the period, a fall in risk weights over time explains this secular shift. This decline in average risk weights is not confined to the UK but occurred across most countries (Haldane 2013).

One explanation for this fall is that banks invested in ever-safer assets. The crisis experience suggests that this is not the whole story. A more likely explanation is that banks exploited weaknesses in the framework by investing in assets where risk weights were low relative to returns. Trading book exposures are an example. From the early 2000s, banks seem to have taken advantage of the relatively low trading book risk weights and expanded trading activities at a much faster pace than traditional banking book activities (Fig. 13.2). Banks clearly had an incentive to do so as the average risk weight were lower than in the banking book. But they also had the opportunity to do so: they were free to assign positions based on "intent to trade".

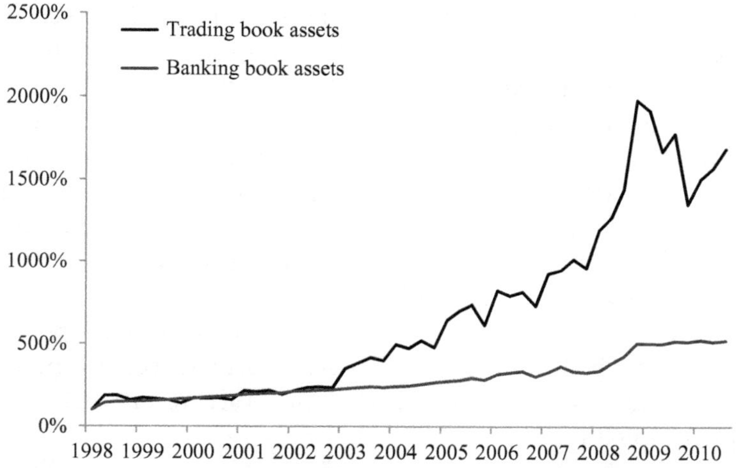

Fig. 13.2 Change in trading book and banking book assets in the UK (1998 = 100) (*Source*: Regulatory returns. Sample includes all UK-regulated firms, which changes over time)

Trading intent essentially means the bank expects to trade-out of the position in the short term. Intent is of course not verifiable, so supervisors had little to no scope to prevent banks from allocating positions to the regulatory book where risk weights were lower. During booms, where markets are not very volatile, this tended to favour the trading book because it models capital requirements based on changes in prices. During the crisis, the opposite happened. Volatility increases and trading book capital requirements may well have exceeded banking book requirements. The ability to put positions where capital requirements were lowest was one factor that contributed to the under-capitalization of banks ahead of the financial crisis (Basel Committee on Banking Supervision 2016a, b).

A final explanation for the fall in risk weights is that banks may "game" internal models. As time passes, banks may become more adept at this and we see a decline in internally modelled risk weights. Though Basel II had not been in place before the crisis, internal models were widely used by large banks in their trading books, which experienced large losses relative to capital during the crisis. For UK banks, trading book capital requirements were as little as one-sixth that of trading book losses during the crisis (Haldane 2011).

There is evidence that this may be part of the story. The US Senate's hearing into a loss of $6.2 billion at JPMorgan Chase that followed a change of the bank's VaR model found that "a key motivation for developing the new VaR models was to produce lower VaR and Risk Weighted Assets (RWA) results" and that "efforts to manipulate RWA results to artificially lower the bank's capital requirements were both discussed and pursued by the bank's quantitative experts" (Levin and McCain, 2013: 196).

Another piece of evidence that suggests that the flexibility associated with internal models can well affect some banks' risk assessment is given by Behn and colleagues (2014). They compare modelled estimates of banks that used internal models for capital purposes and those that had submitted a model application form but whose capital requirement was still driven by the standardized approach. They find that banks on internal models under-estimated risk systematically compared to those on the standardized approach. The interest rates the banks on internal models charge reflect risk more closely. This suggests that they took the relative risk into account in their pricing, but not in their capital models.

In a similar vein, Plosser and Santos (2014) find that internally modelled risk weights vary systematically across banks for syndicated loans. In their words: "some banks hold less capital for a given credit by reporting lower credit risk" (p.3). Moreover, the probability of systematic under-reporting increases for less well capitalized banks, which are the banks that would have the greatest incentives to under-estimate capital requirements. The authors also find that this report is strongest for privately held borrowers where the bank is likely to have a greater scope for under-reporting because there are fewer external benchmarks.

The variability in risk weights that Plosser and Santos (2014) found has also been seen in numerous so-called "hypothetical portfolio exercises". In these exercises banks are asked to estimate the risk weights on a portfolio designed by regulators using their regulatory capital models—so all participating banks estimate their capital requirements on identical risk. The Basel Committee conducted two studies on the trading book, both of which found risk estimates to vary by more than an order of magnitude between the most and least conservative bank.

The reports also found that more complex models exhibited greater variability. Consistent with the result from Plosser and Santos (2014), this variability does not disappear if the individual trades are combined into a much bigger portfolio suggesting that some banks systematically report lower risk weights than others (Basel Committee on Banking Supervision 2013a). The Basel Committee's hypothetical portfolio exercise on the banking book came to similar conclusions. This study also showed that variability is greater where data are sparse because defaults are rare, for example for sovereigns and banks (Basel Committee on Banking Supervision 2014).

This apparent arbitrage or gaming is intriguing. The point of increasing complexity in the Basel framework was because simpler rules appeared too easy to arbitrage, in particular by "risk shifting". Risk-shifting refers to incentives to shift portfolios towards higher-risk, higher-return assets. These incentives are likely to be strongest when risk is not well aligned with return—for example, under an equally weighted leverage ratio. Indeed, this powerful logic was one of the reasons for choosing a risk-weighted capital standard rather than the leverage ratio in the first place (Basel Committee on Banking Supervision 2013c).

There is evidence of risk-shifting in the past. For example, the movement by banks into Latin American debt in the 1980s; the loading-up on zero risk-weighted Organisation for Economic Co-operation and Development (OECD) sovereign debt in the 1990s; and the extension of zero risk-weighted 364-day lines of credit in the 2000s. Yet in these cases, the problems seem to have been caused by the miscalibration of risk weights (Haldane 2013).

Few studies have looked at the evidence on risk-shifting more systematically. For example, Furlong (1988) looked at the behaviour of around 100 US bank holding companies after the introduction of the leverage ratio in 1981. While banks' average riskiness increased, there was no difference in behaviour between regulatory-constrained and unconstrained banks. This suggests risk-shifting was not too potent a factor. Sheldon (1996) reaches the same conclusion when considering the move by international banks to Basel I.

The evidence from other areas of public policy suggests that complexity may bring about its own arbitrage problems. Take the tax system. Simple linear tax schedules are typically found to be more robust to problems of tax arbitrage than complex rules (Hindriks et al. 1999). Why? Because complexity increases the number of loopholes through which the tax-avoider can slip. Indeed, evidence suggests that the complexity of the tax system may be the single largest determinant of tax avoidance across countries (Richardson 2006).

The same logic carries across to financial regulation. Regulatory complexity can create loopholes. At a macro level, cross-country studies suggest that regulatory complexity, in particular the use of internal models, appears to have had an important bearing on bank failure (Cihak et al. 2012). At a micro level, the parts of the regulatory framework which have been most prone to arbitrage before the crisis are those where complexity and opacity has been greatest—for example, the trading book.

Incentives will always exist to shift risk to where it is cheapest. No tax or regulatory system can fully avoid those incentives. But some regimes may be better at constraining those incentives than others. The mix of complexity and self-regulation under Basel I and II appears to have provided too few constraints. Rather than matching risk with capital, complexity may have meant in practice that avoidance and arbitrage flourished behind a curtain of opacity.

In addition to concerns about arbitrage, any variability of RWAs unrelated to risk is a cause of concerns for regulators. The reason is simple: if RWAs are too noisy they fail as a predictor for bank failure (which they have, as described above). Neumann (2015) suggests that even in the absence of regulatory arbitrage internal models can be problematic because of inherent statistical problems: complexity of models and scarcity of data. More complex models are more likely to mistake noise for signal—and may do so in many different ways—which results in greater variability of risk estimates. Where there is little data, internal models also tend to result in greater risk-weighted variability simply because available samples are smaller. Both hypotheses are consistent with the results in the hypothetical portfolio exercises mentioned above, which found higher variability for more complex portfolios and those where data are sparse.

The problems associated with internal models means that simpler approaches can outperform more complex models. Neumann (2015) shows how a simple but false model can outperform a model that is a true but more complex representation of the underlying risk process. The reason is that simpler models tend to deliver less variable predictions than more complex models, even though the simpler model may on average be more biased (Gigerenzer and Brighton 2009).

This idea is applied to banking regulation in Aikman and colleagues (2014). The authors compare the performance of "standardized approaches"—essentially risk weights fixed by regulators—with an internal model in estimating capital requirements on a simulated portfolio of corporate loans. They find that losses exceed estimated capital requirements less often for the standardized approach than for the internal model even where the standardized approach is calibrated to deliver as much capital as the internal model on average. The authors found that the performance of internal models could be improved considerably by applying floors to the input parameters, reducing the discretion banks have.

In summary, not only may the more complex internal models introduced until Basel II have failed to decrease risk shifting and increase risk sensitivity; they may in some cases have had the opposite effect than intended by the Basel Committee.

Lack of Other Ratios

As mentioned in the previous section, a considerable number of studies found that—in contrast to the risk-weighted ratio—the leverage ratio did predict bank failure better than the risk-weighted ratio. Other studies, for example Berger and Bouwman (2012) and Mayes and Stremmel (2012) find that the risk-weighted ratio and leverage ratio have similar predictive power. Interestingly, in the latter study, the leverage ratio is more informative for banks supervised by the Federal Reserve, which tend to be more complex.

These studies suggest that something was amiss in the focus on a single, risk-weighted ratio. Figure 13.3 shows the leverage and average risk weight of 27 large banks before the financial crisis. Highly leveraged banks were more likely to fail than others—even though they held less risky assets as assessed by the risk-weighted ratio.

If we could assess risk perfectly, this would not be the case. In reality, though, we cannot assess risk perfectly. Even the best models—be they banks' own models or regulators'—can only try to infer future risk from past data. They are limited in their usefulness to "known knowns": the risks we know we have seen and can quantify.

The leverage ratio may help with dealing with "unknown unknowns"; those risks for which there doesn't exist a sample large enough to estimate, or for which we simply do not have the faintest idea that they lurk outside. This may be particularly relevant to the financial system because it includes complexity at several layers, the individual bank level, the banking system level and the wider economy level (Haldane 2015). Just because we can't—by definition—quantify these risks does not mean they are not there. Something

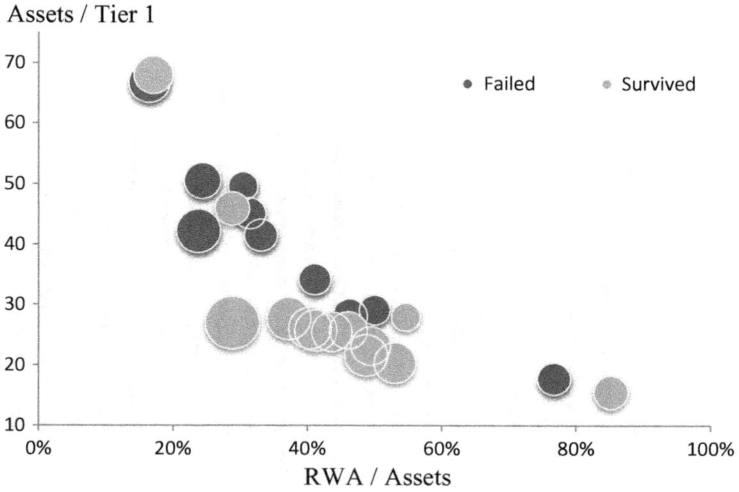

Fig. 13.3 Leverage and average risk weights for large banks at the end of 2007 (*Source*: Bloomberg, FDIC)

similar may be said about stress testing. Their forward-looking nature helps deal with "known unknowns" and "what ifs". In addition, imposing several parallel constraints makes it more difficult for banks to cross the threshold from capital optimization to capital arbitrage.

The crisis also shows that capital regulation alone was not sufficient. The global financial crisis was, in a sense, a re-discovery of the lessons learnt in previous crises—for example, the German banking crisis of 1931. Recall that German banks were vulnerable not just because they were under-capitalized, but also because of their dependence on flighty funding and the large concentrated loans they had made.

The 2008–2009 financial crisis was, at least in part, a crisis of liquidity. Figure 13.4 shows the precipitous fall of Bear Stearn's liquidity position shortly before it failed and was subsequently acquired by rival bank JPMorgan on 16 March 2008. This was despite its high capital ratio (it had a capital ratio well in excess of the Basel standard). Only four days later the chairman of the Security and Exchange Commission wrote to his counterpart at the Basel Committee: "These events illustrate just how critical not just capital, but liquidity is to the viability of financial firms and how the evaporation of market confidence can lead to liquidity being impaired" (Cox 2008).

Recent research backs up this point. Lallour and Mio (2016) examine the predictive power of a particular type of liquidity regulation, the "net stable funding ratio". This class of liquidity regulation aims to match longer-term

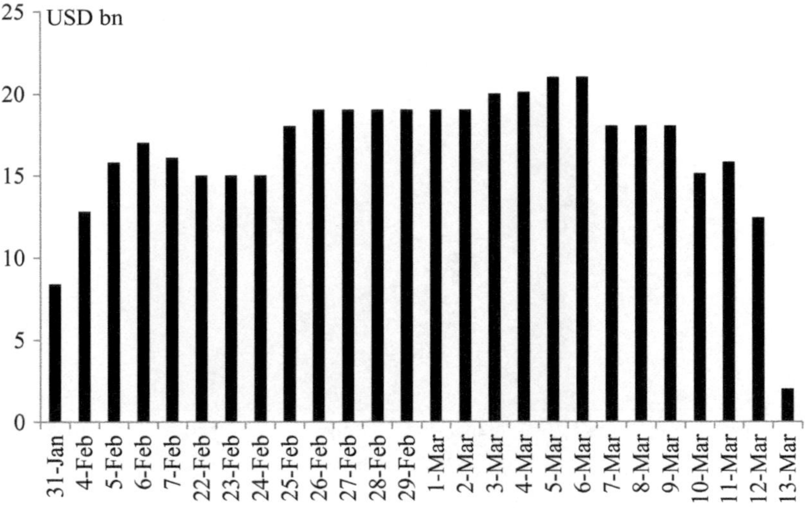

Fig. 13.4 Bear Stearns liquidity pool (Chart based on data in (Cox 2008))

assets with more stable funding, for example long-term wholesale funding. The authors find that banks' liquidity position were a statistically significant predictor of subsequent stress, even controlling for capital regulation.

Intriguingly, they find that net stable funding ratios that weigh assets more uniformly—as the final Basel definition of the ratio does—have a better predictive power than other weighting schemes. And, the funding metric that works best is a simple deposit-to-asset ratio. Again, these results suggest that simplicity can outperform more complex regulatory approaches.

What's Been Done and Where to Go from Here

In response to the crisis, the Basel Committee drew up a new framework: Basel III. The first aspects of the Basel III framework the Basel Committee finalized were a new definition and level of capital requirements (Basel Committee on Banking Supervision December 2010). The reforms were threefold: the taxonomy of capital was simplified by removing innovative Tier 1 and Tier 3, and unifying upper and lower Tier 2; the definition of the remaining capital tiers was tightened to increase loss absorbency; and the overall level of capital was increased.

The new Tier 1 capital is composed of Common Equity Tier 1 (CET1) and Additional Tier 1 (AT1). And, the new accord introduced a set of principles to harmonize and increase deductions from common shares, notably on deferred tax assets and participations in financial institutions. Overall, it is a stricter definition of equity than the old Core Tier 1. The European Banking Authority estimates that capital decreased by 17.6% on average for large European banks and 22.5% for smaller banks as a result of the definitional change (European Banking Authority 2015).

Additional Tier 1 consists of instruments that are subordinated, have fully discretionary non-cumulative dividends or coupons and have neither a maturity date nor an incentive to redeem. Those instruments that are classified as debt for accounting purposes must either automatically convert to equity after breaching a pre-specified trigger point, or have a write-down mechanism that allocates losses at a specific trigger point. In the European Union (EU), in contrast to the USA, all AT1 instruments are subject to conversion or write-down with a minimum trigger rate set at 5.125% of the CET1 risk-weighted ratio.

Tier 2 capital is subordinated debt with a maturity of at least five years, no incentive to redeem and redemption permitted only in limited circumstances after five years from date of issue.

Firms continue to face a minimum risk-weighted capital requirement of 8%. The minimum CET1 requirement increases to 4.5%; AT1 capital is limited to 1.5% and Tier 2 capital is limited to 2%. In addition, the Basel Committee introduced a capital conversation buffer: banks would have to hold an additional 2.5% of CET1 capital or face automatic distribution restrictions. The largest, and therefore most systemically important, banks would be subject to an additional buffer ranging from 1% to 2.5%. The changes to the definition and level of capital were introduced in the EU as part of the Capital Requirements Directive 4 / Capital Requirements Regulation package (CRD4/CRR). Again, though aspects of the framework have become simpler, the framework as a whole became more complex. The CRD4/CRR package is twice as long as Basel II, with a word count of about 260,000. Whereas Basel II was the length of a Dickens novel, CRD4/CRR has surpassed the length of the New Testament and is entering the territory of the great Russian novelists.

Fixing risk weights, in contrast to capital, has taken a longer time. The BCBS introduced a quick fix to market risk in 2009, dubbed Basel 2.5. In 2010, this was implemented in Europe as the Capital Requirements Directive 3 (and therefore retained in CRD4/CRR). In January 2016, the BCBS published revised market risk rules. This fixes major weaknesses in the previous regime. Notably, it increases average capital requirements for traded risk by 40% beyond the level introduced as part of Basel 2.5 (Basel Committee on Banking Supervision 2016). It also tightens the rules for what is allowed in banks' trading books—the combination of low capital requirements and weak rules was a major fault line identified during the crisis. What the new framework does not do is noticeably simplify the framework for market risk. The framework continues to rely on banks' internal models, for example. Continuing using length as a rough guide complexity, the word count for the market risk framework doubled in length from about 20,000 words to 40,000.

The Basel Committee has also acted on concerns about risk-weighted asset variability by removing internal models from some aspects of the framework. Internal models will be removed where they result in excessive variability and complexity. One example is operational risk. It is worth quoting the Basel Committee in full on the reasons of removing the internal model for operational risk, the so-called "Advanced Measurement Approach" (AMA):

> Supervisory experience with the AMA has been mixed. The inherent complexity of the AMA and the lack of comparability arising from a wide range of internal modelling practices have exacerbated variability in risk-weighted asset

> calculations, and have eroded confidence in risk-weighted capital ratios. The Committee has therefore determined that the withdrawal of internal modelling approaches for operational risk regulatory capital from the Basel Framework is warranted. (p.1, Basel Committee on Banking Supervision 2016)

At time of writing the Basel Committee was consulting on also removing internal models from exposures to financial institutions, commercial real estate and credit-valuation adjustment risk. Where models remain, the Basel Committee has decided to apply a series of floors; this decision is consistent with the findings of Aikman and colleagues (2014). The Basel Committee intends to finalize the new risk-weighted framework by the end of 2016. Overall, the approach to calculating RWAs will be somewhat simpler than in Basel II, with more constraints on banks' discretion. But it will remain considerably closer in spirit to Basel II than Basel I—that is to say, it remains very complex.

Perhaps what increases the robustness of the framework most is the introduction of several metrics in addition to the risk-weighted capital ratio—a framework of "multi-polar regulation" (Haldane 2015). In 2014, the BCBS finalized the definition for a leverage ratio (an international definition is needed because it cannot rely on accounting measures because they differ across countries). The BCBS is planning to finalize the calibration of the international leverage ratio standard in 2016. The UK and the Netherlands are the only EU countries to have introduced a leverage ratio requirement as of the time of writing.

In addition, the BCBS added the first international standards on liquidity and large exposures. The first liquidity ratio, finalized in 2013, was the liquidity coverage ratio. Banks will now have to hold liquid assets to cover at least 30 days of liquidity stress. The second, finalized in 2015, is the net stable funding ratio which requires banks to fund illiquid assets with more "stable" funding such long-term wholesale funding. Large exposure limits were finalized in 2014 limiting the exposure to a given counterparty to 25% of Tier 1 capital. A tighter limit of 15% applies to exposures between the largest and most systemically important banks.

A major innovation in the post-crisis regulatory landscape that was not driven by the BCBS has been the introduction of regular, supervisory-run stress tests. A number of authorities internationally—including the Federal Reserve, the European Banking Authority (EBA) and the Bank of England—now conduct regular, public stress tests as a tool for assessing the capital adequacy of individual banks and the system as a whole (see Chap. 16 for more detail).

Stress tests are a way of evaluating how a set of adverse shocks would affect banks' health—and their ability to continue providing financial services to households and businesses. They ask questions like: how big could losses be if house prices fell sharply? What would happen to banks' profitability if funding costs were to increase abruptly? How would banks' ability to supply credit to the real economy be affected if their capital position deteriorated in the face of an unexpected recession? On the back of the test, policy-makers can reach a judgement around the resilience of individual banks—and the system as a whole—and take actions to bolster resilience if needed.

The introduction of regular, supervisory-run stress tests is filling an important gap of the pre-crisis regulatory infrastructure. They reduce its reliance on any one regulatory metric and on any particular calibration of risk weights. This will add to the robustness of the regime. That said, they add complexity: scenarios need to be designed and the impact of hypothetical shocks on banks' balance sheets needs to be modelled. Stress tests can also be opaque—in some cases intentionally so. In addition, the fact that stress tests are not internationally harmonized (and it is difficult to see how this could be done) adds further layers of complexity.

Where does this leave us? We started our journey with multiple simple metrics. Then the Basel Accord replaced them with one metric that became increasingly complex over time. This metric failed spectacularly in the financial crisis of 2008–2009. The emerging framework is now one of multiple metrics; some are simple, many are complex. We have little historical precedent or data, nor do we have much in terms of compelling theory, to assure us that this is a robust resting place for regulation. More research will be needed on this framework if future systemic crises are to be avoided.

References

Aikman, D., Galesic, M., Gigerenzer, G., Kapadia, S., Katsikopoulos, K., Kothiyal, A., … Neumann, T.. (2014, May). *Taking uncertainty seriously: Simplicity versus complexity in financial regulation* (Financial stability paper 28). London: Bank of England.

Alfriend, M. C. (1988). International risk-based capital standard: History and explanation. *Economic Review, 74*, 28–34 Federal Reserve Bank of Richmond.

Bank of England. (1975). The supervision of the UK banking system. *Quarterly Bulletin, 2*, 188–194.

Bank of England. (1980). The measurement of capital. *Quarterly Bulletin, 3*, 324–330.

Bank of England. (2009, June). *Financial stability report.* London: Bank of England.

Basel Committee on Banking Supervision. (1988). *International convergence of capital measurement and capital standards*. Basel: Bank for International Settlements.

Basel Committee on Banking Supervision. (2010, December). *Basel III: A global regulatory framework for more resilient banks and banking systems*. Basel: Bank for International Settlements.

Basel Committee on Banking Supervision. (2013a). *Regulatory consistency assessment programme (RCAP): Analysis of risk-weighted assets for market risk*. Basel: Bank for International Settlements.

Basel Committee on Banking Supervision. (2013b). *Regulatory consistency assessment programme (RCAP): Second report on risk-weighted assets for market risk in the trading book*. Basel: Bank for International Settlements.

Basel Committee on Banking Supervision. (2013c). *The regulatory framework: Balancing risk sensitivity, simplicity and comparability*. Basel: Bank for International Settlements.

Basel Committee on Banking Supervision. (2014). *Regulatory consistency assessment programme (RCAP): Analysis of risk-weighted assets for the banking book*. Basel: Bank for International Settlements.

Basel Committee on Banking Supervision. (2016a). *Minimum capital requirements for market risk*. Basel: Bank for International Settlements.

Basel Committee on Banking Supervision. (2016b). *Standardised measurement approach for operational risk*. Basel: Bank for International Settlements.

BCBS. (1995). *An internal-model based approach to market risk capital requirements*. Basel: Basle Committee on Banking Supervision.

Berger, A. N., & Bouwman, C. H. (2013). How does capital affect bank performance during financial crises?. *Journal of Financial Economics, 109*(1), 146–176.

Behn, M., Haselmann, R., & Vig, V. (2014). *The limits of model-based regulation*. Working paper.

Blundell-Wignall, A., Atkinson, P., & Roulet, C. (2014). Bank business models and the Basel system: Conplexity and interconnectedness. *OECD Journal: Financial Market Trends, 2013*, 43–68.

Bundesgesetzblatt (1961). Gesetz über das Kreditwesen. *Cologne: Bundesanzeiger Verlag*. Number 49.

Cihak, M., Demirguc-Kunt, A., Peria, M. S., & Mohseni-Cheraghlou, A. (2012). *Bank regulation and supervision around the world : A crisis update*. Washington, DC: World Bank.

Collins, M. (1988). English bank development within a European context, 1870–1839. *The Economic History Review, 51*, 1–24.

Cox, C. (2008, March, 20). *www.sec.gov*. Retrieved October 2015, from https://www.sec.gov/news/press/2008/2008-48.htm

Demirguc-Kunt, A., Detragiache, E., & Merrouche, O. (2013, September). Bank capital: Lessons from the financial crisis. *Journal of Money, Credit and Banking, 45*(6), 1147–1164.

Dessauer, M. (1935). The German Bank Act of 1934. *The Review of Economic Studies, 2*, 214–224.

Deumer, D. R. (1933). Die Gesetzgebung des Auslandes auf dem Gebiete der Kreditbanken. *Untersuchung des Bankwesens, 1*(2), 271–310. Berlin: Heymann.
Deutsche Bundesbank (1962). *Geschäftsbericht der Deutschen Bundesbank für das Jahr 1961.*
Deutsche Bundesbank (1973). *Geschäftsbericht der Deutschen Bundesbank für das Jahr 1972.*
European Banking Authority. (2015, February). *Overview of the potential implications of regulatory measures for banks' business models.*
Fischer, D. O. (1933). Die fehlerhafte Kreditpolitik. *Untersuchung des Bankwesens, 1*(1), 493–538. Berlin: Heymann.
Furlong, F. (1988). Changes in bank risk-taking. *Federal Reserve Bank of San Francisco Economic Review.*
Gigerenzer, G., & Brighton, H. (2009). Homo heuristicus: Why biased minds make better inferences. *Topics in Cognitive Science, 1*, 107–143.
Goodhart, C. (2011). *The Basel Committee on Banking Supervision: A history of the early years 1974–1977.* Cambridge: Cambridge University Press.
Haldane, A. (2011). *Capital discipline.* Based on a speech given at the American Economic Association, Denver. London: The Bank of England.
Haldane, A., & Madouros, V. (2012). *The dog and the frisbee.* London: Bank of England.
Haldane, A. (2013). *Constraining discretion in bank regulation.* London: Bank of England.
Haldane, A. (2015). *Multi-polar regulation.* London: Bank of England.
Hannoun, H. (2010, November). The Basel III capital framework: A decisive breakthrough. *BoJ-BIS High Level Seminar on Financial Regulatory Reform: Implications for Asia and the Pacific.* Hong Kong SAR.
Hasse, E. (1933). Die Krisenmaßnahmen des Jahres 1931. *Untersuchung des Bankwesens, 1*(2), 67–88. Berlin: Heymann.
Hindriks, J., Keen, M., & Muthoo, A. (1999). Corruption, extortion and evasion. *Journal of Public Economics, 70*, 395–430.
Jackson, P. (1999). *Capital requirements and bank behaviour: The impact of the Basel Accord.* BCBS working papers.
Lallour, A., & Mio, H. (2016, May). *Do we need a net stable funding ratio? Banks' funding in the global financial crisis.* Bank of England staff working paper.
Legifrance. (n.d.). *Loi n°41-2532 du 13 juin 1941 relative à la réglementation et à l'organisation de la profession bancaire.* Retrieved 2015, from Legifrance.gouv.fr.
Levin, C., & McCain, J. (2013). *JPMorgan chase whale trades: A case history of derivatives risk and abuse.* Washington: Permanent Subcommittee on Investigations, United States Senate.
Mariathasan, M., & Merrouche, O. (2013, May). *The manipulation of Basel risk-weights. Evidence from 2007–2010.* CEPR discussion paper No. DP9494.

Mayes, D. G., & Stremmel, H. (2012, December). *The effectiveness of capital adequacy measures in predicting bank distress*. In 2013 Financial Markets & Corporate Governance Conference.

Moe, J. (1955). *Bankloven og banklovforslaget*. Retrieved 2015, from https://tidsskrift.dk/index.php/nationaloekonomisktidsskrift/article/view/22154/42383

Neumann, T. (2015, August 12). *It's a model: but is it looking good? When banks' internal models may be more style than substance*. Retrieved March 2016, from http://bankunderground.co.uk/2015/08/12/its-a-model-but-is-it-looking-good-when-banks-internal-models-may-be-more-style-than-substance/

Nordhoff, D. K. (1933). Über die Liquiditätsfrage. *Untersuchung des Bankwesens* (pp. 475–491). Berlin: Heymann.

Norton, J. J. (1995). *Devising international bank supervisory standards*. Dordrecht: Martinus Nijhoff Publishers.

Office of the Comptroller of the Currency. (1962). *National banks and the future; Report to the comptroller of the currency*. Washington: U.S. Treasury Department.

Organisation, I.-B. R. (1978). *The regulation of banks in the member states of the ECC*. London: Sijthoff & Noordhoff.

Plosser, M., & Santos, J. (2014). *Banks' incentives and the quality of internal risk models*. Federal Reserve Bank of New York staff reports.

Reichsgesetzblatt. (1943). Reichsgesetz über das Kreditwesen vom 5. Dezember 1934. *Nr. 132*, pp. 1203–1214.

Richardson, G. (2006). Determinants of tax evasion: A cross-country investigation. *Journal of International Accounting, Auditing and Taxation, 15*, 150–169.

Schnabel, I. (2004). The German twin crisis of 1931. *The Journal of Economic History, 64*, 822–871.

Sheldon, G. (1996). Capital adequacy rules and the risk-seeking behavior of banks: A firm-level analysis. *Swiss Journal of Economics and Statistics, 132*, 709–734.

Treasury, H. M.'s. (2009). *Risk, reward and responsibility: The financial sector and society*. London: HM Treasury.

von Bissing, D. W. (1933). Die Schrumpfung des Kapitals und seine Surrogate. *Untersuchung des Bankwesens, 1*(1), 57–112. Berlin: Heymann.

14

State Aid and Guarantees in Europe

Reint Gropp and Lena Tonzer

Motivation

The financial crisis of 2008–9 resulted in massive government intervention in the banking sector. To stabilize the banking system and to avoid the risk of spillovers, national governments have massively intervened by providing liquidity guarantees and capital support to banks in distress. Public interventions have been aimed at restoring confidence and stabilizing the financial system. In particular, the rescue of large and systemically important banks was intended to reduce systemic risk in the financial system. This is important for a proper functioning of financial intermediation, the provision of credit to the real sector and, consequently, economic growth.

While state aid and guarantees are implemented to take out risks in the financial system, they also come at a cost. Often taxpayers' money is used to bail out

JEL Codes: G21, G28, G32
The authors thank Felix Noth for helpful comments and suggestions. Annika Bacher has provided highly efficient research assistance. All errors and inconsistencies are solely our own.

R. Gropp (✉)
Halle Institute for Economic Research (IWH), Member of the Leibniz Association, Kleine Maerkerstraße 8, 06108 Halle, Germany

Otto von Guericke, University Magdeburg

L. Tonzer (✉)
Otto von Guericke, University Magdeburg, Kleine Maerkerstraße 8, 06108 Halle, Germany e-mail: reint.gropp@iwh-halle.de

T. Beck, B. Casu (eds.), *The Palgrave Handbook of European Banking*,
DOI 10.1057/978-1-137-52144-6_14

banks. Also, the bailout of banks can have implications for the market structure in the banking system as well as affect monitoring and risk-taking incentives (Hakenes and Schnabel 2010; Cordella and Yeyati 2003). At the micro level, two opposing effects can be at work. Firstly, the prevalence of state aid and guarantees can reduce *market discipline*. Investors, shareholders and depositors have fewer incentives to monitor or adjust risk premia in response to higher bank risk, if they anticipate future bailouts. This is likely to result in increased risk-taking by protected banks: the upside of projects benefits current bank stakeholders of banks; the downside is borne by taxpayers ("moral hazard"). Secondly, banks subject to implicit guarantees might face a funding cost advantage. Lower funding costs increase interest margins and thus banks' *charter value*. This reduces banks' incentives to invest in risky projects because they would like to preserve future rents (Keeley 1990; Hakenes and Schnabel 2010).

At the macro level, public interventions can have detrimental consequences for the sovereign's budget. States that bail out fragile banks shift the risks to the fiscal budget. This erodes the sustainability of the budget and drives up sovereign credit risk spreads. A weaker fiscal position undermines the credibility of public guarantees, makes them less effective in ensuring financial stability and leads to higher funding costs for banks, but may also restore some market discipline. Negative feedback effects between the sovereign and the banking system might cause a banking crisis to be followed by a sovereign debt crisis much like the one recently experienced by some European countries (Acharya et al. 2014; Alter and Schüler 2012; Gennaioli et al. 2014; Leonello 2014). This raises the question to which extent governments should make use of state aid and guarantees to safeguard financial stability, and, if they intervene, which type of instrument should be chosen.

Bank guarantees can be of *explicit* and *implicit* nature. *Explicit* guarantees are guarantees made explicit by the government in a law or an official statement. This is similar to the establishment of explicit deposit insurance with the objective to reduce the risk of panic-based runs on banks causing the failure of illiquid but solvent banks (Diamond and Dybvig 1983). While deposit insurance schemes are introduced *to prevent bank distress*, the provision of capital support and liquidity guarantees are used by governments *once banks are in distress*. However, in most countries explicit rules on the use of these instruments are missing. In this case, market participants form expectations about future bailouts giving rise to the *implicit* nature of state aid and guarantees. For example, large and highly interconnected banks are likely to be rescued by the government due to their systemic relevance ("too-big-to-fail", "too-interconnected-to-fail").[1] This causes them to be protected by *implicit* public guarantees which

[1] In 1984, the term "too-big-to-fail" (although already existing) gained prominence in the context of the rescue of Continental Illinois Bank due to the congressman Stewart B. McKinney who said: "We have a

can give them a funding cost advantage. In this case, the pure expectation that the state may bail out banks can affect market outcomes.

As a response to the experiences during the recent financial and sovereign debt crisis, regulatory and supervisory changes at the national and supranational level have been implemented. Within the European Union (EU), the establishment of the Banking Union consisting of the Single Resolution Mechanism (SRM), the Single Supervisory Mechanism (SSM) and a harmonization of deposit insurance schemes across countries was driven by the desire of policy-makers to reduce bailout expectations and ultimately the granting of state aid to banks.

The main objectives of the Banking Union are to reduce systemic risk in the financial system and to prevent excessive risk-taking. Furthermore, it should lower costs for taxpayers of future financial crises and mitigate the negative feedback loop between bank and sovereign risk (European Commission 2014). In this respect, the build-up of a European restructuring fund to resolve and restructure banks in distress might reduce the need for state aid and guarantees at the national level. Given these developments, we take a closer look at the benefits and risks of state aid and guarantees provided to the banking system. Furthermore, we address resulting policy implications and discuss in how far current changes in the financial architecture such as the establishment of the Banking Union affect this trade-off. For example, the establishment of the SRM which foresees the option of a bail-in of shareholders can reduce implicit guarantees.

The main strand of related literature analyses risk-taking incentives of banks in the presence of state aid and guarantees. The central question is whether there is evidence for the market discipline or the charter value hypothesis (Cordella and Yeyati 2003; Dam and Koetter 2012; Gropp et al. 2014; Keeley 1990). This literature has been extended by asking whether the relationship between public bailout guarantees and banks' risk-taking is affected by the size or number of banks to be rescued as well as the market structure (Acharya and Yorulmazer 2007; Brown and Dinç 2009; Gropp et al. 2011). In the presence of public guarantees, banks might also change their lending behaviour keeping inefficient non-financial firms in the market. This can have real effects if allocative efficiency is affected (Gropp et al. 2015).

Understanding the effects of public interventions on financial stability and macroeconomic outcomes is thus important. On the one hand, state interventions can ensure the functioning of the financial system and clearly

new kind of bank. It is called too big to fail. TBTF, and it is a wonderful bank" (Farber 2012). The term "too-interconnected-to-fail", in contrast, became prominent during the recent crisis following the failure of Lehman Brothers or the collapse of Bear Stearns and the resulting spillovers (Taylor 2014).

a well-developed financial system is important for economic growth (King and Levine 1993). On the other hand, public guarantees can increase risk-taking, lead to the build-up of imbalances in the banking system and result in banking crises. Reinhart and Rogoff (2009) show that banking crises are often followed by large and long-lasting declines in asset prices, output and employment as well as surges in public debt. Furthermore, public interventions during crisis times can shift risks from the banks to the sovereign and erode fiscal sustainability (Acharya et al. 2014; Alter and Schüler 2012).

This chapter is structured as follows. In the next section, "State Aid and Guarantees During the Recent Financial Crisis", we provide an overview of state aid and public guarantees provided during the recent financial crisis in Europe. The third section, "Theoretical Results", analyses the effects of state aid and guarantees on financial stability from a theoretical perspective, while the fourth section, "Empirical Evidence" summarizes the empirical evidence on the topic. In the fifth section, "Institutional Design and Policy Implications", we ask whether the provision of state aid and guarantees is linked to political considerations like the electoral cycle and discuss the consequences for public intervention. In the sixth section, "The European Banking Union", we describe the elements of the European Banking Union intended to resolve and restructure banks in distress and to lower the need for public intervention. Based on our analysis, we investigate which conclusions can be drawn regarding the new design.

State Aid and Guarantees During the Recent Financial Crisis

The European Case

During the financial crisis starting in 2007–8, the European Commission authorized national governments to provide state aid and guarantees to financial institutions. The objective was to prevent bank failures and possible contagious effects with severe systemic impacts that could have led to the drying up of liquidity in the interbank-lending market and, ultimately to the collapse of the European financial system. Such a scenario would have involved sharp declines of real economic activity and, hence, a painful fall in living standards among the average European.

Reinhart and Rogoff (2009) show that financial crises are followed by large increases in unemployment and public debt as well as large declines in real growth. For advanced economies, Laeven and Valencia (2013) find that output losses cumulatively amount to 32.4% of gross domestic product (GDP) and

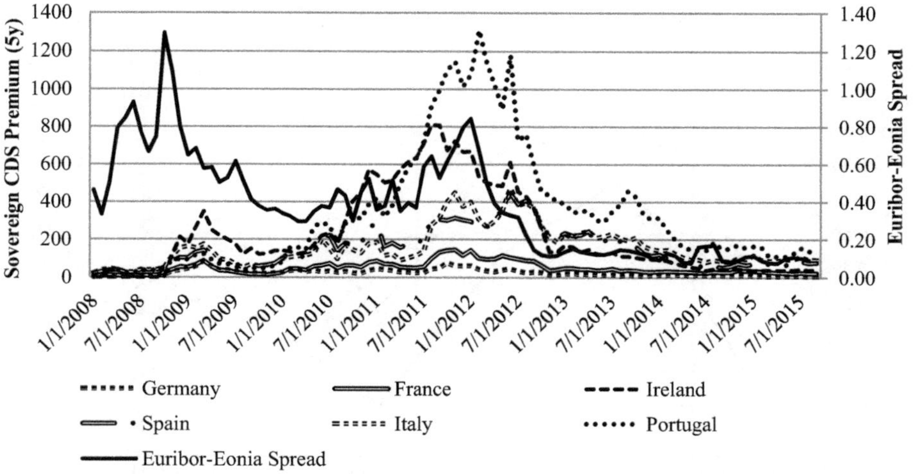

Fig. 14.1 Distress in financial markets and sovereign risk. This figure shows the evolution of the Euribor (Euro Interbank Offered Rate—three-month)–Eonia (Euro Overnight Index Average) spread (right axis) and sovereign Credit Default Swaps (CDS) premium (five years) for selected countries of the Eurozone (*Source*: Datastream)

public debt increases by 23.6% of GDP. While state interventions prevented the failure of systemically important banks during the financial crisis of 2007–8, public debt positions have dramatically worsened. Figure 14.1 shows that tensions in financial markets reflected by a higher Euribor–Eonia spread increased significantly with the failure of Lehman Brothers in September 2008. As a response to distress in financial markets, governments intervened and provided liquidity guarantees and capital support to banks. This reduced tensions in the banking sector but transferred risks to the sovereign. This is reflected by an increase in sovereign Credit Default Swaps (CDS) spreads.

In the European Union (EU), state aid was mainly provided through four main instruments: recapitalization, asset relief interventions, the provision of guarantees and other liquidity support measures. Guarantees on liabilities were the most commonly used instrument, as they accounted for around 7% of the EU's GDP at their peak in 2009 (Fig. 14.2).[2] Through such instruments, the government gives the debtors of the bank an implicit guarantee that in case the bank fails to repay its debt, the state will cover it. This helps restoring confidence in the market. Since 2009, such guarantees were steadily declining in their amount to about 2.7% of EU GDP in 2013. In total, the

[2] Data come from the State Aid Scoreboard of the European Commission: http://ec.europa.eu/competition/state_aid/scoreboard/financial_economic_crisis_aid:en.html.

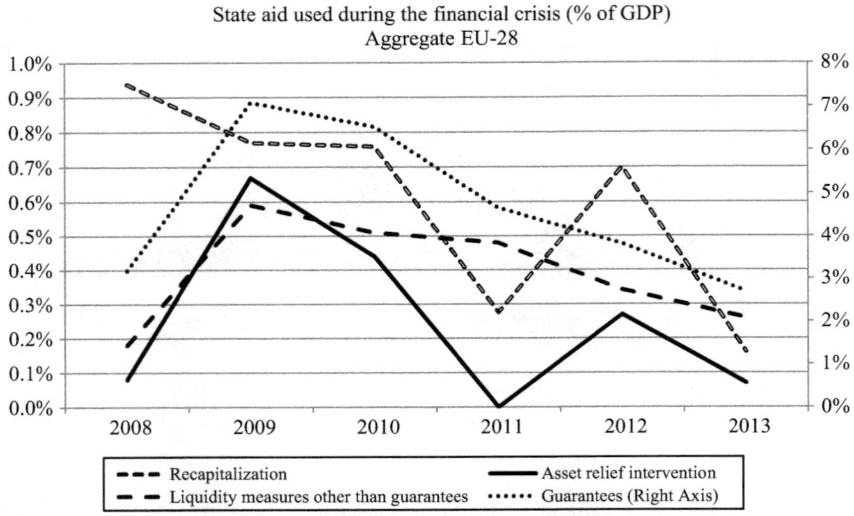

Fig. 14.2 State aid during the financial crisis in the European Union. This figure shows the evolution of state aid used in the European Union from 2008 to 2013 as percentage of GDP. It covers four types of instruments: recapitalization measures, asset relief interventions, liquidity measures other than guarantees and the provision of guarantees (right axis) (*Source*: European Commission)

Commission authorized 3892.6 billion euros to be used for guarantees on liabilities, around one-third of EU GDP.

The second most used instrument was recapitalization measures, being at their highest at around 1% of EU GDP in 2008 and declining since then. During the European sovereign debt crisis, they rose again to 0.7% of EU GDP in 2012. Recapitalization measures usually aim at improving the debt-to-equity ratio by restructuring banks' debt. Further actions taken by governments to stabilize their countries' financial sector were asset relief interventions (governments relieving banks from assets that are regarded as "toxic") and liquidity measures other than guarantees. These instruments did not account for more than 1% of EU GDP at any point in time.

Disaggregating the amounts used by country group reveals that the Eastern European Countries (Baltic States, Slovakia and Slovenia) spend the least amount of money on state aid with 7.99 billion euros in contrast to the GIIPS countries (Greece, Ireland, Italy, Portugal and Spain) with 771.61 billion euros (non-Eurozone: 513.52 billion euros; remaining Eurozone: 626.31 billion euros).[3] Figure 14.3 shows that the largest share of recapitalization and asset

[3] We define the country groups as follows: *GIIPS* comprises Greece, Ireland, Italy, Portugal and Spain; *Eastern Euro* comprises Latvia, Lithuania, Estonia, Slovakia and Slovenia; *Remaining Euro* comprises

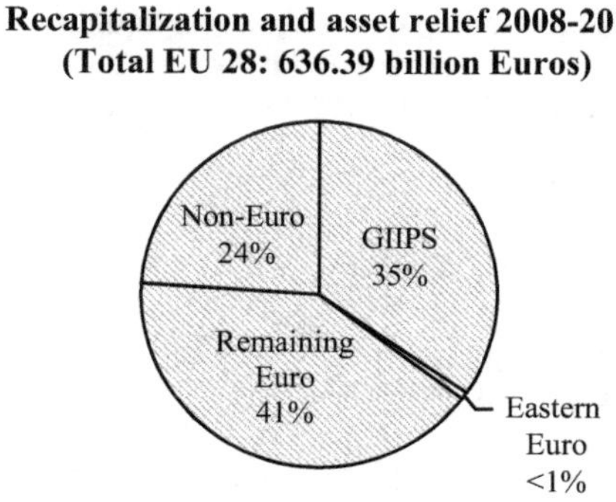

Fig. 14.3 Recapitalization and asset relief measures by country group. This figure shows the amount of used recapitalization and asset relief measures by country group and as a percentage of the total amount provided in the European Union in the period 2008–13. The country groups are defined as follows: *GIIPS* comprises Greece, Ireland, Italy, Portugal and Spain; *Eastern Euro* comprises Latvia, Lithuania, Estonia, Slovakia and Slovenia; *Remaining Euro* comprises Belgium, Germany, France, Cyprus, Luxembourg, Malta, the Netherlands, Austria and Finland; *Non-Euro* comprises Bulgaria, Czech Republic, Denmark, Croatia, Hungary, Poland, Romania, Sweden and the UK (*Source*: European Commission)

relief measures of totally used amounts in the EU was granted by Eurozone countries excluding the GIIPS countries.[4] However, the highest share of liquidity support, 43% of total liquidity support measures used in the EU in the period 2008–13, was provided by the GIIPS countries (Fig. 14.4), which were all suffering from great instabilities during the financial crisis and were hit hardest by the European sovereign debt crisis.

The used amounts of state aid and guarantees have been of different size not only across different country groups but also across individual countries (Fig. 14.5). Ireland had, with 173.27%, the highest amount of outstanding guarantees relative to its GDP, the Irish government provided blanket guarantees for the six largest banks (Allen et al. 2015a), followed by Denmark with 58.24% of GDP, which reflects the government interventions after the failure of Roskilde Bank in 2008 and increasing distress in the Danish banking system. Recapitalization and asset relief measures have been highest in Ireland

Belgium, Germany, France, Cyprus, Luxembourg, Malta, the Netherlands, Austria and Finland; *Non-Euro* comprises Bulgaria, Czech Republic, Denmark, Croatia, Hungary, Poland, Romania, Sweden and the UK. To calculate the total amount used, we take the sum of (1) recapitalization measures and asset relief measures over the period 2008–13, and (2) outstanding guarantees and other liquidity support measures in the EU-28 peak year 2009.

[4] Looking at either asset relief measures or recapitalization measures separately reveals that the share of asset relief (recapitalization) measures of GIIPS countries amounted to 21% (40%) compared to 58% (34%) for the remaining Eurozone countries.

Fig. 14.4 Outstanding guarantees and liquidity support by country group. This figure shows the used amount of outstanding guarantees and liquidity measures by country group and as a percentage of the total amount provided in the European Union (EU) in the peak year 2009. The country groups are defined as follows: *GIIPS* comprises Greece, Ireland, Italy, Portugal and Spain; *Eastern Euro* comprises Latvia, Lithuania, Estonia, Slovakia and Slovenia; *Remaining Euro* comprises Belgium, Germany, France, Cyprus, Luxembourg, Malta, the Netherlands, Austria and Finland; *Non-Euro* comprises Bulgaria, Czech Republic, Denmark, Croatia, Hungary, Poland, Romania, Sweden and the UK (*Source*: European Commission)

(39.9% of GDP) followed by Greece (22.4% of GDP) and Cyprus (10.9% of GDP). Table 14.1 shows a more detailed overview for different types of instruments used by EU countries.

Eventually, by far, more money was approved for the stabilization of the financial sector than ultimately used by the respective national governments (Fig. 14.6). This applies for all four instruments of state aid, with the largest gap between used and approved amounts occurring for guarantees. However, one should consider that the used amount in this case displays the maximum amount outstanding in the peak year 2009 whereas the approved amounts by the European Commission cover the total amount authorized over the period from January 2008 to October 2014.

The US Experience

As a reaction to the international financial crisis, the US government also agreed upon the need for financial state aid. The emergency measures included the purchase of mortgage-backed securities, liquidity facilities by the Federal Reserve and the establishment of the Troubled Asset Relief Program (TARP). TARP was established by Congress in October 2008 through the Economy Emergency Stabilization Act (EESA) and US$700 billion were authorized for

a) Outstanding guarantees as of 2009

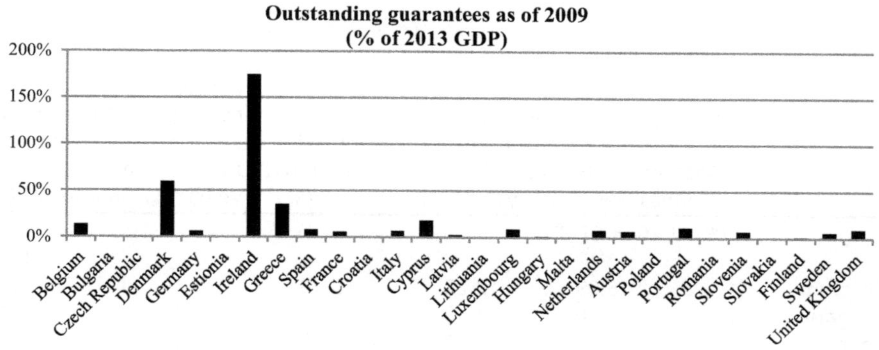

b) Recapitalization and asset relief (2008-2013)

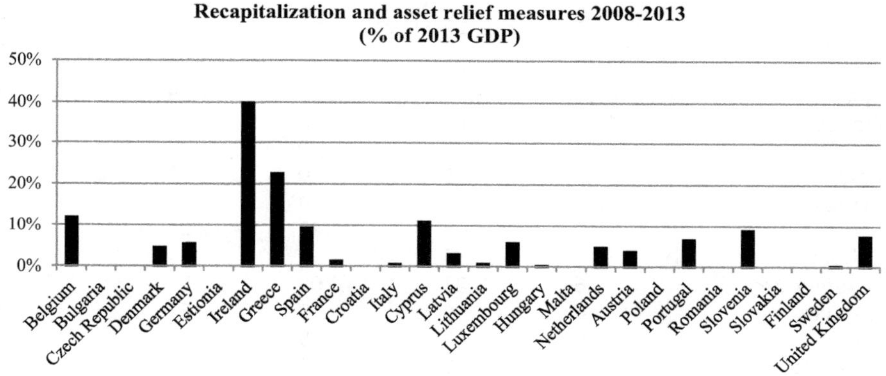

Fig. 14.5 Comparison of state aid measures across individual countries. This figure shows state aid measures used in individual countries. Panel (a) depicts the amount of outstanding guarantees (percentage of 2013 GDP) in the year 2009 which was the EU peak year. Panel (b) depicts recapitalization and asset relief measures (per cent of 2013 GDP) over the period 2008–13 (*Source*: European Commission)

the stabilization of five areas such as housing and credit markets. Thereof, US$250 billion were allocated to the "Bank Investment Programs", with the objective to lower distress in the financial sector and restore confidence in the solvency of banks.[5] This should, furthermore, ensure the availability of liquidity in the interbank lending market and loan supply to the real economy. Of

[5] Detailed information on TARP can be found at: http://www.treasury.gov/initiatives/financial-stability/about-tarp/Pages/default.aspx, with the distribution of the granted money across the five programmes described here: http://www.treasury.gov/initiatives/financial-stability/about-tarp/Pages/where-did-the-money-go.aspx

Table 14.1 Overview of state aid and guarantees used in the EU

	Recapitalization measures (%)	2009 outstanding guarantees (EU-28 peak year) (%)	Asset relief interventions (%)	2009 outstanding liquidity measures other than guarantees (EU-28 peak year) (%)	Total revenues: asset relief and recapitalization measures (%)
	(% of 2013 GDP)				(% of 2012 GDP)
Belgium	6.09	12.22	5.70	0	0.8
Bulgaria	0	0	0	0	0.0
Czech Republic	0	0	0	0	0.0
Denmark	4.33	58.24	0.13	0.79	1.4
Germany	2.34	4.93	2.92	0.17	1.0
Estonia	0	0	0	0	0.0
Ireland	38.27	173.27	1.58	0.55	3.8
Greece	22.44	34.22	0.00	3.79	3.3
Spain	6.05	7.04	3.22	1.89	0.4
France	1.22	4.50	0.06	0	0.1
Croatia	0	0	0	0	0.0
Italy	0.51	5	0	0	0.0
Cyprus	10.91	17.12	0	0	0.2
Latvia	2	1.63	1.23	2.89	1.0
Lithuania	1	0	0	0	0.0
Luxembourg	6	8.27	0.00	0.31	1.1
Hungary	0	0	0	2.51	0.1
Malta	0	0	0	0.00	0.0
Netherlands	3.82	6.79	0.83	5.04	1.0
Austria	3.54	6.18	0.16	0	0.4
Poland	0	0	0	0	0.0
Portugal	5	10.02	1.87	2.30	0.5
Romania	0	0	0	0	0.0
Slovenia	8.94	6.09	0	0	0.8
Slovakia	0	0	0	0	0.0
Finland	0	0.06	0	0	0.0
Sweden	0	4.73	0	0	0.1
United Kingdom	5	8.33	2.13	1.75	2.5
Total EU 28	**3.43**	**6.39**	**1.44**	**0.54**	**0.8**

Source: European Commission

This table shows state aid and guarantee measures (percentage of 2013 GDP) for the countries in the European Union (EU) as well as the aggregate amount for the EU-28. Recapitalization measures and asset relief interventions refer to the amounts used in the period 2008–13. Outstanding guarantees and other liquidity measures refer to the EU peak year 2009. The last column shows total revenues from asset relief and recapitalization measures

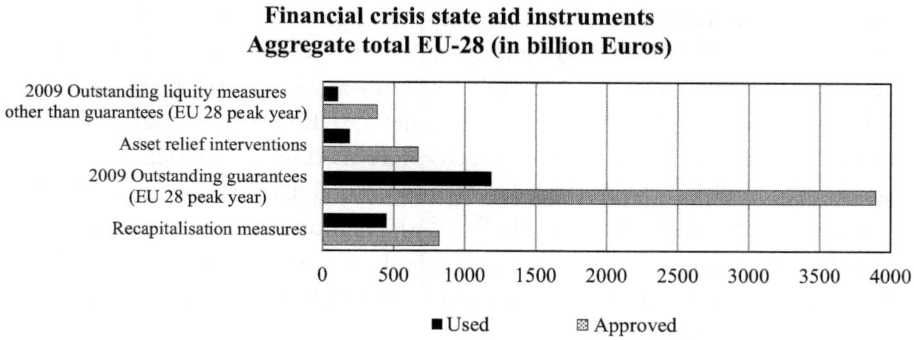

Fig. 14.6 Comparison of approved and used amounts of state aid in the EU. This figure shows the amounts of state aid which have been approved by the European Commission compared to the amounts used by EU countries (in billion euros). State aid instruments used comprise 2009 outstanding liquidity measures, asset relief interventions in the period 2008–13, 2009 outstanding guarantees, and recapitalization measures in the period 2008–13. For all four instruments the approved amounts refer to the period from 2008 to 01 October 2014 (*Source*: European Commission)

the approved amount, the Treasury invested a total of US$245.1 billion of which it had recovered US$274.9 billion in the form of repayments, dividends and interest payments by 31 May 2015.

In contrast, in the EU approved amounts have been much higher than used amounts of state aid and guarantees. This might go back to the choice of the instrument and how it was applied. In the USA, capitalization was used much more often and banks were partly required to take the bailouts, whereas in the EU the approval of guarantees dominated.[6] It might also reflect that within a single country, it is easier to coordinate state aid measures. Finally, this observation might be due to data reasons as we can only compare used amounts outstanding in the EU in the peak year 2009 with approved amounts in the period 2008–14. Fees and revenues from asset relief and recapitalization measures in the EU amount to 0.8% of GDP compared to amounts used of 4.87% of GDP.

Similar to the European case, different types of instruments have been used, which have been divided in five subareas: Asset Guarantee Program (AGP); Supervisory Capital Assessment Program (SCAP) and Capital Assistance Program (CAP); Capital Purchase Program (CPP); Community Development Capital Initiative (CDCI); and Targeted Investment Program (TIP).[7] Hence, systemically

[6] See, for example, http://www.theguardian.com/business/blog/2008/oct/15/banking.

[7] The Bank Investment Programs are explained at: http://www.treasury.gov/initiatives/financial-stability/TARP-Programs/bank-investment-programs/Pages/default.aspx

important banks under distress could receive asset guarantees by the AGP or funding through the TIP. Both larger and smaller banks could receive capital through the CPP. In contrast to the EU, recapitalization was a key instrument in the USA with the CCP being the largest program under TARP. From the original US$250 billion USD authorized, 204 billion USD were used for the stabilization of 707 banking organizations (with the latest investment made in December 2009). Out of this investment sum, more than half (US$125 billon) was assigned to nine large financial institutions such as Citigroup or Bank of America. Similarly, large banks in the EU have benefited from state aid measures with the top receivers being RBS, Anglo Irish Bank and Bankia.[8]

Theoretical Results

State aid and guarantees are often criticized because they cause incentives for banks to behave less prudently. However, governments would not intervene in the banking sector if these interventions had only shortcomings. This section discusses the benefits and risks of state aid and guarantees from a theoretical perspective.

Deposit Insurance and Moral Hazard

The earliest strand of related literature focuses on the effects of explicit public guarantees, namely deposit insurance, and starts with the seminal work by Diamond and Dybvig (1983).[9] In their study, the key task of banks is financial intermediation, meaning that banks transform liquid liabilities into illiquid assets. Hence, banks provide liquidity insurance to the depositors. This comes, however, at the risk of a panic-based run. Depending on depositors' beliefs, a good or a bad equilibrium may occur. In the good equilibrium, depositors are confident such that only those with liquidity needs withdraw their money from the bank. In the bad equilibrium, depositors fear that the bank may run out of money, because other depositors withdraw. Hence, a self-fulfilling panic ensues, a bank run occurs and all depositors simultaneously withdraw their funds, even those without liquidity needs. The crucial mechanism is that they collectively believe that all other depositors withdraw. In this situation, the bank is forced to sell illiquid assets at a loss making it impossible to fulfil

[8] See http://ec.europa.eu/competition/state_aid/scoreboard/financial_economic_crisis_aid:en.html.

[9] See also the section "Vulnerability to Runs" in Chap. 12.

withdrawal demands of all depositors. Hence, for a depositor it is optimal to withdraw early to avoid being late and receive nothing. The introduction of a deposit insurance scheme helps rule out the bad equilibrium. This is due to the fact that a deposit insurance scheme guarantees repayment to each depositor individually irrespective of other depositors' behaviour, eliminating the incentive to run the bank.

The results by Diamond and Dybvig (1983) are derived from a model which relies on various assumptions.[10] An important assumption is that banks invest only in riskless projects. Hence, the existence of government guarantees does not affect the risk-taking behaviour and generate a moral hazard problem. Furthermore, the paper does not discuss a concrete design of the guarantee scheme. This is not necessary because government guarantees are considered to be fully feasible and credible. This implies that their mere announcement is sufficient to avoid bank runs. Without doubt, these assumptions fall short in capturing relevant real world characteristics. While the literature has been extended into various directions, our focus is on the moral hazard problem which becomes prevalent once banks can invest in risky projects.[11] The reason for this is that deposit insurance acts as a safety net which insures against possible losses. This reduces monitoring incentives of depositors and causes moral hazard if the deposit insurance scheme is risk-insensitive and not fairly priced (Merton 1977).

Adapting the *design* of the deposit insurance scheme can be one option to mitigate the moral hazard problem. For example, the pricing can be risk-adjusted. This requires, however, that the regulator can adequately evaluate the risk of banks. Alternatively, Gropp and Vesala (2004) show that, compared to a scheme with implicit guarantees, the establishment of an explicit deposit insurance scheme can reduce moral hazard if it credibly excludes some creditors. This arises because the exclusion of some creditors from the safety net increases their monitoring efforts. Another option is to complement the regulatory framework with an instrument that reduces moral hazard by increasing the "skin in the game" and the loss absorption capacity of the bank—for example, through high capital requirements (Cooper and Ross 2002).

[10] Allen et al. (2015a) provide an excellent discussion of these assumptions and resulting limitations.

[11] For example, there are papers which study panic- and fundamentals-based runs (see, for example, Gorton 1988; Jacklin and Bhattacharya 1988; Allen et al. 2015b; see also Chap. 12 of this book). The effect of limited commitment is studied in Cooper and Kempf (2016). Competition for deposits under deposit insurance or the pricing of deposit insurance is analysed by Matutes and Vives (1996) and Freixas and Rochet (1998). A more detailed overview of the literature is provided by Allen et al. (2011).

Market Discipline and Charter Value

A more recent strand of literature analyses the effects of public bailouts of banks and/or of market participants' expectations regarding future bailout probabilities. In contrast to an explicit guarantee scheme such as deposit insurance, bailout rules are often not explicitly specified. Market participants instead form bailout expectations that translate into implicit guarantees for protected banks. One prominent example relates to the existence of implicit guarantees for large banks. Due to their systemic importance, market participants expect that the government will intervene to avoid a failure. This occurs even if the government has not committed to do so ex ante and we will discuss the underlying reasons in detail below. A key contribution of this literature is to show that government guarantees do not only cause a moral hazard problem. In contrast, banks can have incentives to reduce their risk-taking. Two opposing hypothesis are behind this trade-off:

Firstly, under the **market discipline hypothesis** , the existence of government bailout guarantees reduces creditors' incentives to monitor banks or to adjust funding costs to banks' riskiness if debt is insured through public guarantees. This is likely to result in higher risk-taking by banks.[12] Similar to the effects under a deposit insurance scheme, expectations of public bailouts can cause creditors to feel protected against future losses which leads to a reduction in market discipline (Flannery and Sorescu 1996; Sironi 2003; Gropp et al. 2006).

Secondly, under the **charter value hypothesis**, banks reduce their risk-taking due to public guarantees. Keeley (1990) was one of the first to raise this issue. He noticed that despite the existence of a deposit insurance scheme in the USA, banks did not necessarily engage in excessive risk-taking. The reason for this is that protected banks face reduced risk premium and lower refinancing costs. Hence, the higher interest margins resulted in a higher charter value. As banks would like to benefit from higher charter values and the future rents associated with high margins, this reduces moral hazard and results in more prudent behaviour. In this line of argument, Cordella and Yeyati (2003) show that the central bank as a lender of last resort can announce and commit to a bailout policy without necessarily increasing banks' risk-taking if the charter value effect prevails.

[12] Further factors behind moral hazard and bank risk-taking are discussed in the section "Moral Hazard and Excessive Risk-Taking" in Chap. 12.

Bailout Expectations, Time Consistency and Competitive Effects

In how far banks, shareholders, investors and depositors form bailout expectations which in turn affect their risk-taking and monitoring incentives can be affected by various determinants. For example, differences between ex ante announced and ex post executed bailout policies can affect bailout expectations and generate a problem of *time inconsistency*. In the case of explicit guarantees, such as a deposit insurance scheme, these policies are only effective given it is actually optimal for the government to intervene ex post, meaning once a period of distress occurs. If there is an ex ante lack of credibility that the government commits to its policy ex post, this hampers the effectiveness of the instrument (Allen et al. 2011). In the case of implicit guarantees, it might not be optimal for the government to commit to a bailout policy from an ex ante perspective due to the effects on risk-taking. However, this might not hold true any more ex post. Whether the government finds it optimal to bailout a bank ex post, which generates in turn bailout expectations ex ante, can depend on a bank's type, including characteristics like ownership or bank size.

For example, the *ownership status* might matter: if government-owned banks are deemed to be more likely to receive funds from the government than privately owned banks, bailout expectations will be higher for those banks.[13] Implicit guarantees can also be high for large and systemically important banks if investors assume that the regulator will bail them out because their failure might lead to systemic disruptions.[14] Implicit subsidies might result in lower monitoring incentives of investors, as well as reduced funding costs and increased risk-taking for these "too-big-to-fail" banks. Governments might also find it optimal to bail out smaller banks when the number of failing banks is large, resulting in a "too-many-to-fail" problem (Mitchell 2001). Acharya and Yorulmazer (2007) show that ex ante the government might not find it optimal to rescue a small bank, which can still be acquired by another bank in the market. However, a bailout policy is optimal ex post if many small banks are in trouble simultaneously. This provides incentives for small banks to herd, for example, by investing in the same risky asset because it increases the probability to be bailed out during a systemic event but leads

[13] Agency problems due to ownership status and effects on profitability, risk and lending are presented in more detail in Chap. 3.

[14] Freixas et al. (2000) provide a model in which banks with a key position in interbank markets are subject to a "too-big-to-fail" policy and rescued by the central bank to ensure the functioning of payment flows.

to a higher number of systemic crises.[15] Similarly, Farhi and Tirole (2012) argue that banks collectively engage in maturity mismatch if they anticipate that the need for public interventions will be most prevalent once a shock occurs.

A large literature analyses the moral hazard problem for banks that benefit from bailout guarantees, such as large banks or publicly owned banks. However, public bailout policies which protect only some banks might also change the *competitive structure* in the banking market, and thus affect unprotected banks.[16] Hakenes and Schnabel (2010) focus on these competitive effects of public bailout policies and show that bailout guarantees for a restricted set of banks increase the risk-taking of the protected banks' competitors. This occurs due to the fact that depositors demand a lower default premium from the protected banks which leads those banks to expand their deposit volume. As a consequence, the deposit rate increases and competition is reinforced. This reduces rents for the protected banks' competitors and causes them to take more risk. Hence, asymmetric bailout policies can have long-lasting effects for the risk-taking behaviour of both the protected banks and their competitors.

Interpreting their results in the context of the recent crisis, Hakenes and Schnabel (2010) point out that a large number of countries rescued their "too-big-to-fail" banks, which might change the competitive structure and bear implications for future risk-taking. This is important because the degree of competition in the banking market can also affect whether the market discipline or charter value channel dominate banks' risk-taking incentives. The net outcome of these two opposing effects determines whether expectations of public bailouts cause serious negative distortions regarding banks' risk-taking behaviour. The underlying driver is that a more competitive market reduces banks' charter value. This undermines the incentives to behave prudently and gives more scope to the moral hazard component (Keeley 1990).

In sum, government guarantees can change the behaviour of the individual bank but also the market structure as a whole. Distorted competition and increased risk-taking incentives are detrimental if they affect banks' lending decisions negatively and, thus, allocative efficiency. However, government guarantees may not always increase risk-taking. While banks have incentives

[15] Acharya and Yorulmazer (2008) propose that instead of directly bailing out banks, the government should grant liquidity to surviving banks such that they acquire failed banks. This lowers banks' incentives to herd and the probability of banking crises. However, this support should be conditional on surviving banks' liquidity holdings, otherwise they might have incentives to hold less liquid resources (Acharya et al. 2011).

[16] For a general discussion on the relation between competition and banking stability see Chap. 7.

to take more risk based on the market discipline hypothesis, the opposite effect holds following the charter value hypothesis (Cordella and Yeyati 2003). The outcome of this trade-off can be influenced by the market structure, bank ownership and bank size. The effect of government guarantees on risk-taking depends crucially on the theoretical modelling, and the implications with regard to their effectiveness depends on the assumptions about the government's commitment or the feasibility of the guarantee scheme (Allen et al. 2015a). Which effect prevails in the real world remains an empirical question and will be discussed in the next section.

Empirical Evidence

The theoretical literature on state aid and guarantees is large. In contrast, empirical evidence on Europe is rather scarce. The reason for this is that the European banking system has been relatively stable before the recent financial crisis. Furthermore, finding a convincing empirical strategy to identify effects of state aid and guarantees is challenging. In the following, we begin by discussing identification issues before providing an overview of the empirical literature which follows the structure of the theoretical section.

Identification Issues

The credibility of empirical results crucially relies on the strength of the econometric approach. Identifying effects of state aid and guarantees convincingly has to overcome various problems. Firstly, implicit guarantees are difficult to measure because neither interventions have occurred yet nor the government has made explicit announcements of intended measures. This requires the *correct measurement* of bailout expectations of market participants. Various studies thereby make use of distress events or ratings to extract bailout expectations (Dam and Koetter 2012; Damar et al. 2014).

Dam and Koetter (2012), for example, do not rely on safety net membership as a proxy for bailout expectations. They argue that safety net membership does not yet indicate whether a bank will indeed be bailed out and thus may be a poor proxy for bailout expectations. In contrast, they use a dataset that contains information on actual bank bailouts and distress events. In a first step, they estimate expected bailout probabilities for the sample of distressed banks. These estimates are then used to make out-of-sample predictions and to obtain bailout expectations for the sample of distressed *and* non-distressed banks. In a second step, these estimates are used to analyse the effect of bailout expectations on risk-taking. Damar et al. (2014) exploit the introduction of a new ratings system that incorporates the probability of government support. Thereby, the change in the ratings has not been influenced by changes in other variables underlying the ratings and it has been introduced without being announced ex ante. Thus, this newly revealed information can be taken as a reliable proxy for investors' bailout expectations.

Secondly, state aid instruments tend to be used disproportionately in the midst of a financial crisis. However, in a period of financial distress, many events are happening at the same time. For example, governments intervene into the banking sector but simultaneously central banks change conditions for liquidity provision to banks. Consequently, it is difficult to disentangle the effects of different rescue measures due to *confounding events*. Quasi-natural experiments, such as exogenous policy changes during non-crisis times, can help to circumvent this problem. For example, Gropp et al. (2014) exploit the removal of public guarantees on a set of German banks for their identification strategy.

Thirdly, even during tranquil times, capturing the effect of a public bailout is not trivial but can be subject to an endogeneity problem. If a bank is in distress and the government steps in to rescue the bank, this can have implications for the bank's risk-taking. However, the reason for which the bank entered into trouble can, on the one hand, be due to "bad luck". On the other hand, it might be due to "bad behaviour" and have its roots in the bank's expectation to receive state aid resulting in fewer incentives to behave prudently (see Dam and Koetter 2012). If the former is the case, higher risk does not necessarily reflect moral hazard. If the latter is the case, this questions the *direction of causality*. Dam and Koetter (2012) solve this issue by choosing an instrumental variables approach and exploiting that political factors affect bailout probabilities but have no direct impact on bank risk.

Deposit Insurance and Moral Hazard

Deposit insurance is primarily implemented to promote financial stability. Yet as theory has shown, an unintended side-effect can be that, in the presence of a safety net, depositors are likely to monitor less, which causes banks to behave more riskily. This effect has been confirmed in a large number of empirical studies.[17] For a sample of 61 countries from 1980 to 1997, Demirgüç-Kunt

[17] For example, Keeley (1990) shows for US banks that if competition increases, risk-taking increases under a deposit insurance scheme due to reduced interest margins. Wheelock (1992) or Wheelock and Wilson (1995) find a higher probability of failure for US banks in the 1920s and 1930s due to member-

and Detragiache (2002) show that deposit insurance increases the probability of financial crises. The effect is conditional on the design of the deposit insurance scheme and the institutional environment. A larger coverage, a government-funded scheme and weak institutions increase the negative effect of deposit insurance. Similar results are found by Hovakimian et al. (2003). For 56 countries from 1991 to 1999, these authors show that risk-shifting is reduced if risk-sensitive premium or coverage limits are part of the deposit insurance scheme but reinforced in countries with low degrees of political and economic freedom or with a high level of corruption.

In contrast, few studies find that deposit insurance has positive effects on bank stability. One example is the paper by Gropp and Vesala (2004). For European data, they find that the introduction of an explicit guarantee scheme such as a deposit insurance system reduces risk-taking if the scheme credibly excludes non-deposit creditors. Uninsured subordinated debt holders have incentives to monitor such that banks behave more prudently. The effect holds in particular for smaller banks with a large share of subordinated debt holders whereas larger banks might still benefit from a "too-big-to-fail" guarantee. The discrepancy in results compared to earlier work can stem from the fact that the focus is on developed rather than emerging market countries. In the former, there might be strong expectations about implicit guarantees because debt holders assume that governments intervene once a bank is in distress. These will be removed by the introduction of an explicit scheme which credibly excludes some debt holders.

Even if deposit insurance increases risk-taking in the banking sector, it might still stabilize the system during a financial crisis. Anginer et al. (2014) analyse the effect of deposit insurance on bank risk before the recent crisis (2004–06) and during the financial crisis (2007–09) for 4109 publicly traded banks in 96 countries. Their results provide evidence for moral hazard in the period leading to the crisis but higher stability during the crisis in countries with deposit insurance, whereas this stabilizing effect is smaller than the negative impact in tranquil times. These results suggest that deposit insurance serves the purpose in crisis times. In general, the above-mentioned results suggest that various factors can impact on risk-taking incentives in the presence of deposit insurance. A strong institutional environment, reliable resolution mechanisms and the design of the deposit insurance scheme are key in safeguarding the financial stability objectives underlying the establishment of a deposit insurance scheme.

---

ship in the deposit insurance system. Ioannidou and Penas (2010) show that after the introduction of deposit insurance in Bolivia in 2001, banks grant riskier loans without asking for higher collateral.

Market Discipline and Charter Value

Empirical evidence using cross-country data suggests that market discipline declines and risk-taking increases given a public safety net (Hryckiewicz 2014; Marques et al. 2013). For example, Nier and Baumann (2006) use bank-level data for 32 countries from 1993 to 2000 and show that uninsured liabilities and disclosure increase market discipline and cause banks to hold larger capital buffers to insure themselves against the risk of insolvency. In contrast, banks reduce capital buffers the more government support is provided. Whether protected banks' risk-taking behaviour differs during calm and crisis times is analysed by Damar et al. (2014). Making use of a new rating methodology which captures the probability of government support, their results suggest that in calm times higher bailout probabilities cause moral hazard. However, during crisis times, they observe the opposite: Banks with ex ante *lower* expectations of government support exhibit higher risk-taking. This might arise from worse funding conditions and depressed charter values compared to protected banks.

Studies based on data for single countries tend to confirm moral hazard effects in the presence of bailout expectations. For the German banking system in the period 1995–2006, Dam and Koetter (2012) show that the probability of bank distress increases with higher bailout expectations. Their results are based on a structural estimation for which they exploit that political factors determine bailout expectations but have no direct impact on bank risk-taking. Augmenting their model by supervisory actions such as warnings, restrictions on certain activities and management interventions, they find that soft measures such as warnings either do not reduce the moral hazard problem or make it even worse. Some evidence for mitigating effects is only found for more direct interventions like restrictions.

Gropp et al. (2014) exploit the *removal* of public guarantees which protected creditors of German savings banks for their empirical identification scheme and find evidence for reduced moral hazard and increased market discipline. The former arises because banks decrease credit risk by cutting credit supply to their riskiest borrowers. The latter is reflected by banks adjusting their funding side towards less risk-sensitive liabilities and facing higher bond yield spreads.[18] The same policy change is used by Fischer et al. (2014) who focus on the risk-taking behaviour of the eight affected German Landesbanken over

---

[18] In a related study, Koerner and Schnabel (2013) also document an increase in funding costs for German savings banks. They assign this to spillovers from German Landesbanken, which have also been affected by the removal of guarantees and transmitted increased costs within the network of interrelated savings banks.

the transition period from the announcement in 2001 to the implementation in 2005. During this period, German Landesbanken experienced a drop in their charter value due to higher funding costs and provided more loans to riskier borrowers. This suggests that in contrast to the savings banks, the loss in charter value dominated for the German Landesbanken. To outweigh declines in charter value, these banks increased their risk-taking during the transition period in which they still benefited from guarantees.

Bailout Expectations, Time Consistency and Competitive Effects

Market participants anticipate public bailouts even if the government does not make any official announcement or explicit commitment. This can give rise to *time inconsistencies* as described in the section "Theoretical Results". Without clear guidelines that rule out a bailout or credible statements that an insolvent bank will be resolved ex post, expectations about public rescue measures are formed ex ante. Whether bailout expectations are formed ex ante can depend on the *bank type*. The importance of *ownership* is empirically analysed in Acharya et al. (2014) who show for a sample of Indian banks that weak private banks restricted their activities during the recent crisis compared to less vulnerable private banks, whereas the opposite happened in the case of state-owned banks. They argue that weak government-owned banks could expand as they benefited from public guarantees resulting into a funding cost advantage and reduced market discipline compared to private banks.[19]

Furthermore, market participants are likely to anticipate the bailout of an individual bank if its failure endangers systemic stability because it is "too-big-to-fail". In this sense, Acharya et al. (2015) show for a sample of US banks that bond credit spreads are insensitive to risk for large financial institutions. The required compensation for higher credit risk is thus lower due to the perceived guarantee.[20] For actually granted state aid and guarantees to banks in the Eurozone during the recent crisis, Buch et al. (2015) find a positive correlation between banks' contribution to systemic risk and received state aid. A bank's contribution to systemic risk is measured by SRISK developed by Brownless and Engle (2016) and captures an institution's propensity to

[19] Also, Sironi (2003) shows that subordinated debt holders price risk appropriately except for public banks suggesting that they benefit from public guarantees. However, De Nicoló and Loukoianova (2007) do not find that public banks behave in a more risky manner than private banks.

[20] The funding cost advantage for "too-big-to-fail" banks has also been shown by Ueda and Weder di Mauro (2013). Boyd and Gertler (1994) find higher risk-taking among the largest banks in the USA.

be under-capitalized when the whole market experiences a capital shortfall. Bailout expectations can also apply to smaller banks exposed to common risks. Brown and Dinç (2009) show that insolvent banks are less likely to be closed by the government if the banking system is fragile as such. This "too-many-to-fail" phenomenon can provide incentives for banks to behave strategically and coordinate their risk-taking if a future bailout due to system-wide effects is anticipated.

Bailout expectations due to public guarantees can have *competitive effects*. The theoretical predictions by Hakenes and Schnabel (2010) are tested by Gropp et al. (2011), who analyse the relationship between public guarantees and the behaviour of protected banks' competitors in a sample of banks in Organisation for Economic Co-operation and Development (OECD) countries. Rating information is used to approximate bailout guarantees of banks and to identify protected banks. They then proceed to construct the market share of protected banks in each country. They show that a higher market share of protected banks significantly increases non-insured banks' risk-taking and demonstrate that the effect comes through the depressed margins of unprotected banks. Protected banks themselves do not increase their risk-taking, except if they are under public ownership, pointing toward the charter value effect. Hence, state aid and guarantees can affect the competitive conditions for individual banks but also the degree of competition in the banking sector as such. State aid and guarantees are directed towards weak banks facing the immediate risk of failure and market exit. A public bailout thus means that these banks stay in the market. This immediately has implications for the degree of competition.

Calderon and Schaeck (2016) look at the effect of blanket guarantees, liquidity support, recapitalizations and nationalizations on the degree of competition of a country's banking sector for a sample of 124 countries, 41 of them experiencing a banking crisis in the period 1996–2010. They find that public interventions increase competition because the exit of bankrupt banks is prevented. However, their results might be driven by the choice of bailout measures. While liquidity support, recapitalizations and nationalizations indeed reduce exits, this would not hold true for mergers and acquisitions or orderly resolutions. However, in the latter case data limitations can undermine reliable empirical evidence. In a theoretical model, Perotti and Suarez (2002) show that banks might have incentives to reduce speculative lending and stay solvent in an environment in which failing banks are rather subject to takeovers than rescue measures that keep them in the market. The possible exit of failing banks reduces competition and the solvent bank benefits from larger charter values. As such, the prospects of a lower degree of competition and a policy that favours exits and mergers have positive effects on financial stability.

Understanding the link between state aid instruments and competition is important also in terms of *real outcomes*. Banks which anticipate public bailouts have incentives to change their risk-taking and lending decisions toward non-financial firms. This can affect allocative efficiency in the corporate sector. Allocative efficiency refers to the idea that banks should channel resources to the most productive firms and away from unproductive ones. Gropp et al. (2015) exploit the removal of guarantees for a set of German banks and evaluate how this affects the allocation of capital in the economy and the efficiency within the non-financial sector. Using matched bank/firm data, they show that guarantees benefit poorly performing and technologically inefficient firms. These firms invest more, have higher sales growth and better access to funding reflecting reduced screening and monitoring efforts of banks which are protected by public guarantees. Importantly, this suggests that public guarantees can distort competition not only in the banking sector but also in the corporate sector.[21] Favourable conditions for weak firms which borrow from protected banks facilitate them to stay in the market and finance their investment. New and more efficient firms have difficulties in entering which might affect overall growth options.

The Effects of TARP in the USA

The US regulatory authority has been successful in recovering its outlays arising from TARP. However, if one takes market distortions such as incentives for moral hazard and non-economic, social costs into account, it is unclear whether taxpayers ultimately had a positive net return through TARP. Calomiris and Khan (2015) argue that TARP, though it represented a net cash flow gain, had impacts on the broader economy that should not be overlooked. On the one hand, the implementation of TARP calmed down financial markets as the interest payment on bank-to-bank overnight lending fell and thereby revived borrowing and lending. On the other hand, it is hard to isolate the contributions made exclusively by TARP from those of other programmes or to tell to what extent the markets would have recovered on their own.

In terms of banks' risk-taking, Duchin and Sosyura (2014) provide evidence that banks accepted for the programme shifted lending and investing towards riskier assets rather than expanding their credit volume. Consequently, their probability of default has risen instead of stabilizing the market. This points

[21] For a sample of Italian banks, Sapienza (2004) shows that government-owned banks grant cheaper loans to larger firms, providing evidence for a misallocation of financial resources.

toward moral hazard. An approval for funds might increase the chance of being rescued in the future leading to increased risk-taking today. In contrast, a recent study by Berger et al. (2016) finds evidence for decreased risk-taking of German banks following capital support. Yet they focus not on public capital injections but support coming from the bankers associations' insurance schemes.Unintended costs may also arise due to market distortions. The risk premium for unprotected banks may increase whereas rescued ones are indirectly subsidized through a lower risk-premium. Koetter and Noth (2016) test if the mere bailout expectation distorts competition by affecting interest rates of unsupported banks (as a proxy for the risk premium) for borrowing and lending. They find that increased bailout expectations have indeed an effect on loan and deposit rates, whereas the overall economic effect remained rather small and was only statistically measurable in the immediate aftermath of the crisis. They conclude that TARP did not give room for substantial competitive distortions but may have aggravated already existing differences in banking competition. In contrast, Berger and Roman (2015) look at the competitive power of protected banks and show that TARP had an amplifying impact on market shares and market power, measured by local market shares of assets and the Lerner index. Banks receiving financial assistance experienced competitive advantages which may lead to further misallocation. According to their results, the increased market share and market power was due to the fact that those banks were perceived as safer. This applies particularly for banks that repaid their funds early.

The *real consequences* of TARP have been analysed by Berger and Roman (2016). Considering net job creation, net hiring establishments, business bankruptcies and personal bankruptcies, they find that conditions in areas in which more banks received TARP were significantly better than in those areas with fewer recipients. This difference is mainly driven by an enhancement of lending activities and an increase in off-balance-sheet guarantees. An analysis of subsamples suggests that the observed effects especially apply to medium–large banks, banks who did not repay early, and banks that are located in states with poor economic conditions and less economic freedom.

Calomiris and Khan (2015) point out that there exists evidence for *political influence* when selecting the banks that receive funds. Institutions located in the election districts of members of the finance committee had a higher chance of being chosen. Such decisions guided by political considerations might lead to the misallocation of resources and a mistrust of financial institutions and rescue programmes such as TARP.

Institutional Design and Policy Implications

State aid and guarantees can be useful to safeguard financial stability; however, the following considerations have to be kept in mind. Firstly, the use of state aid and guarantees should be based on economic rather than political reasoning to avoid further distortions. That this does not always hold true is demonstrated by Brown and Dinç (2005) and Calomiris and Khan (2015). For a sample of emerging market countries, they find that bailout probabilities depend on the electoral cycle: in the pre-election period, bailouts tend to be delayed. The link between political considerations and bailout probabilities is not limited to emerging markets with weak institutions but can be extended to advanced economies—see, for example, Liu and Ngo (2014) or Behn et al. (2015). This interconnection between politics and bailout decision could be weakened by reallocating supervisory power to a supra-national level as is currently done for the largest Eurozone banks within the European Banking Union. A supra-national supervisor is more independent from political considerations. The disadvantage is that information gathering can become more difficult than at the national level, and homogeneous rules have to be applied to banks from heterogeneous banking markets which might affect efficiency.

Secondly, the choice of the public guarantee scheme is crucial. The presence of implicit guarantees is most likely to give rise to bailout expectations which reduce market discipline and create moral hazard. An explicit scheme, which credibly excludes some market participants from the safety net can, thus, be a solution to ensure monitoring. The establishment of a restructuring and resolution scheme with a bail-in clause in the context of the European Banking Union is one step into this direction. The moral hazard problem can be mitigated by complementary regulation such as capital requirements and systemic surcharges. This could also align the level playing field among protected banks which benefit from a funding cost advantage and their unprotected competitors.

Thirdly, policy-makers who use state aid instruments today to rescue banks in distress have to be aware that this might have implications tomorrow, both for the market structure and for market participants' bailout expectations. Bailout expectations are only tackled effectively if strong institutions ensure the enforcement of explicitly established rules. Strong resolution schemes can thereby reduce the costs of liquidating banks. This reduces ex post incentives for governments to bail out a bank and makes the announced resolution policy ex ante more credible (Gimber 2015).[22]

---

[22] A more detailed discussion on resolution schemes can be found in Chap. 12.

Fourthly, if governments decide to remove public guarantees or change the institutional setting regarding the provision of state aid, the timing matters. In the case of the removal of public guarantees for German banks, it became apparent that if the transition period is long, banks might exploit this and behave less prudently as long as they are still protected (Fischer et al. 2014).

Finally, the European banking market is largely integrated and operates under a common monetary policy. However, the provision of state aid and guarantees has been in the mandate of national authorities. This can give rise to competition or coordination failures among national regulators if internationally active banks are in distress (Dell'Ariccia and Marquez 2006; Niepmann and Schmidt-Eisenlohr 2013). Furthermore, differences in national (bailout) policies can lead to cross-border regulatory arbitrage and international transmission of the effects of rescue measures (Buch et al. 2011; Houston et al. 2012). As a response, the establishment of the European Banking Union is under way and the section that follows discusses possible implications.

The European Banking Union

The European Banking Union consists of three main pillars: the Single Supervisory Mechanism (SSM), the Single Resolution Mechanism (SRM) and the harmonization of deposit insurance schemes. All three pillars contain elements that affect the interplay between public guarantees and market participants' incentives, as well as the feedback between bank and sovereign risk. In the following, we will touch on these issues insofar as they are relevant for public guarantees and state support. For more details on the Banking Union, we refer the reader to the section "Banking Union" in Chap. 12 and to Chap. 17.[23]

The first pillar, the SSM, entered fully into force in November 2014, and grants the European Central Bank supervisory power for large and systemically important banks in the Eurozone, with a focus on the adherence of capital and liquidity requirements. Delegating supervision to the supranational level implies that a common set of rules is applied. This increases transparency and mitigates the influence of political decisions at the national level. Stricter monitoring can reduce banks' risk-taking incentives. Furthermore, it aligns the level playing field across banking systems in Eurozone countries and

---

[23] Summary information on the structure of the Banking Union can be found at: http://bankinglibrary.com/e/fdz/IntBankLib/regulation/monitoring.asp; http://ec.europa.eu/finance/general-policy/banking-union/index_en.htm.

reduces possibilities for regulatory arbitrage. As a supranational supervisor has oversight over the largest banks in all Eurozone countries, the build-up of common risks which threaten systemic stability can be detected at an initial stage. This can reduce the probability of systemic crises which usually come at large costs. However, it is to ask whether banks that fall under the supervision of the SSM are assigned the status of being "too-big-to-fail" by market participants resulting into implicit guarantees.

The second pillar, the SRM, came into effect in January 2015 and has been fully operational since January 2016 with the objective to build an effective and uniform framework for the resolution and restructuring of insolvent banks. The SRM is directed by the Single Resolution Board (SRB), with the power to take rapid decisions about whether a bank should be resolved or restructured. The presence of explicit rules for resolution and restructuring can reduce implicit guarantees (compare Gropp and Vesala 2004). If market participants believe that a bank in distress will not receive a bailout but will be resolved, this might reduce bailout expectations. Lower bailout expectations and the threat of resolution can result in higher monitoring incentives and reduce moral hazard. This depends on the credibility of the restructuring and resolution scheme. Weak institutions undermine the positive effect on financial stability while the same holds for large coverage of insurance schemes (Demirgüç-Kunt and Detragiache 2002). Given that the SRM foresees the establishment of a resolution fund equipped by a final amount of 55 billion euros and is backed by the European Stability Mechanism (ESM) during the transition period,[24] market participants might still expect available resources to be used to rescue banks which are too systemic as that they could be resolved. Hence, a stringent enforcement of the new rules would benefit credibility and reduce bailout expectations. Weak restrictions or soft warnings might not be sufficient to mitigate moral hazard (Dam and Koetter 2012).

To finance bank resolution and restructuring, one important element of the SRM is the Single Resolution Fund (SRF) financed by bank levies. The establishment of the SRF implies that, firstly, resources are generated which limit the costs of future banking crises for the sovereign. Like this, the negative feedback loop between the banking sector and the state can be broken. Secondly, banks have to pay a levy, whereas the amount to be paid depends on banks' characteristics such as size and asset quality. This can be interpreted as a systemic surcharge making banks internalize their contribution to systemic risk. It can also reduce competitive distortions given that these banks benefit from a funding advantage due to implicit guarantees (compare, e.g., Hakenes

[24] See http://www.consilium.europa.eu/en/policies/banking-union/single-resolution-mechanism/

and Schnabel 2010). However, as applies to all regulatory measures, the design determines effectiveness. In the case of the German bank levy, banks did not seem to adjust their balance sheet toward less risky positions as a response to the levy (Buch et al. 2016). Thirdly, before the resources of the SRF can be used, a bail-in of at least 8% of total assets is required. This restricts the safety net and ensures that shareholders participate in the losses which can, in turn, increase their monitoring incentives (Gropp and Vesala 2004).

The third pillar foresees a harmonization of national deposit insurances and the underlying directive 2014/49/EU of April 2014 instructs institutions of the member states to secure deposits of at least 100,000 euros per depositor per bank. The main purpose of such insurance systems is the prevention of bank runs. This depends on the credibility and feasibility of the deposit insurance scheme (Allen et al. 2011). The main drawback of explicit guarantees is that depositors have fewer incentives to monitor such that banks take more risk. On the one hand, the restriction of deposit insurance to the national level can hamper credibility and feasibility if depositors doubt that single member states with weak public budgets have the resources to maintain such a scheme. On the other hand, a Europe-wide insurance scheme with a large loss-absorbing capacity and the possibility to shift losses across borders might have reduced market discipline, resulting in higher moral hazard.

Conclusion

In this chapter, we have attempted to show the trade-offs policy-makers face when dealing with public guarantees. On the one hand, public guarantees may increase the probability of financial crises through moral hazard; on the other hand, they may be a useful stabilizer once a financial crisis actually takes place, preventing banking distress to spread or deepen. They also may distort the competitive interaction in the banking sector, as only some banks generally will benefit from a guarantee, and possibly even in the corporate sector, where public guarantees may undermine competition between firms due to poor screening and monitoring decisions induced by public guarantees, which in turn may hamper an efficient allocation of capital.

We also emphasized that which effects dominate may strongly depend on the specific institutional setting in a country, the strength and credibility of fiscal policy, the intervention of other players (especially the central bank as a potential lender of last resort) and the specific nature and underlying cause of the ensuing financial instability. Further, we pointed to the time inconsistency problem when dealing with public guarantees. Even if the policy-maker ex ante publicly commits to not bailing out a bank, ex post it may be optimal to do so anyway, which in turn will be incorporated into the expectations of financial market participants. Recently, the reverse problem has gained prominence. Even if the government tries to commit to bailing out a bank ex ante, market participants may doubt the ability of the government to do so (due to perhaps already very high levels of public debt) and, hence, guarantees may fail to stabilize the financial system.

At the root of the problem is the *reason* for bailing out banks in the first place. It is (generally) not to save the bank per se, but to contain the damage that may result; the strongest motivation is to protect other parts of the economy from the failure of the bank. Hence, reducing the potential damages to the real economy from bank failures would serve a number of purposes simultaneously. Firstly, it would reduce the *need* for public guarantees. Secondly, it would increase the *credibility* of governments to abstain from bailouts. Thirdly, it would enhance *market discipline*, because the likelihood of shifting losses to the taxpayer would be greatly reduced. These considerations support a number of recent policy initiatives that focus on orderly bank resolution, such as the SRM in the EU or the requirement for banks to draw up "living wills".[25] If a bank, even a large bank, can be resolved with minimal externalities to other parties outside the bank (i.e., with minimal cost to the real economy and the financial system), public guarantees, whether explicit or implicit, may no longer be necessary or expected by the market.

References

Acharya, V. V., and Yorulmazer, T. (2007). Too many to fail—An analysis of time-inconsistency in bank closure policies. *Journal of Financial Intermediation, 16*, 1–31.

Acharya, V. V., and Yorulmazer, T. (2008). Cash-in-the-market pricing and optimal resolution of bank failures. *The Review of Financial Studies, 21*(6), 2705–2742.

Acharya, V. V., Shin, H. S., and Yorulmazer, T. (2011). Crisis resolution and bank liquidity. *The Review of Financial Studies, 24*(6), 2166–2205.

Acharya, V. V., Drechsler, I., & Schnabl, P. (2014). A pyrrhic victory? Bank bailouts and sovereign credit risk. *The Journal of Finance, 69*(6), 2689–2739.

Acharya, V.V., Anginer, D., and Warburton, A.J. (2015) *The end of market discipline? Investor expectations of implicit government guarantees.* Available at https://ssrn.com/abstract=1961656

[25] See for example: http://www.federalreserve.gov/bankinforeg/resolution-plans.htm.

Allen, F., Carletti, E., & Leonello, A. (2011). Deposit insurance and risk taking. *Oxford Review of Economic Policy, 27*(3), 464–478.

Allen, F., Carletti, E., Goldstein, I., & Leonello, A. (2015a). Moral hazard and government guarantees in the banking industry. *Journal of Financial Regulation, 1*, 30–50.

Allen, F., Carletti, E., Goldstein, I., and Leonello, A. (2015b). *Government guarantees and financial stability* (CEPR discussion papers No. 10560). London: Centre for Economic Policy Research.

Alter, A., & Schüler, Y. S. (2012). Credit spread interdependencies of European states and banks during the financial crisis. *Journal of Banking & Finance, 36*(12), 3444–3468.

Anginer, D., Demirgüç-Kunt, A., & Zhu, M. (2014). How does deposit insurance affect bank risk? Evidence from the recent crisis. *Journal of Banking & Finance, 48*, 312–321.

Behn, M., Haselmann, R., Kick, T., and Vig, V. (2015). *The political economy of bank bailouts* (Institute for Monetary and Financial Stability working paper No. 86). Frankfurt am Main: Goethe University.

Berger, A., & Roman, R. (2015). Did TARP banks get competitive advantages? *Journal of Financial and Quantitative Analysis, 50*(06), 1199–1236.

Berger, A., and Roman, R. (2016). Did saving wall street really save main street? The real effects of TARP on local economic conditions. *Journal of Financial and Quantitative Analysis*, forthcoming. Available at SSRN: https://ssrn.com/abstract=2442070

Berger, A., Bouwman, C. H. S., Kick, T., & Schaeck, K. (2016). Bank liquidity creation following regulatory interventions and capital support. *Journal of Financial Intermediation, 26*, 115–141.

Boyd, J. H., & Gertler, M. (1994). The role of large banks in the recent U.S. banking crisis. *Federal Reserve Bank of Minneapolis, Quarterly Review, 18*, 2–21.

Brown, C. O., & Dinç, I. S. (2005). The politics of bank failures: Evidence from emerging markets. *The Quarterly Journal of Economics, 120*, 1413–1444.

Brown, C. O., & Dinç, I. S. (2009). Too many to fail? Evidence of rgulatory forbearance when the banking sector is weak. *Review of Financial Studies, 24*(4), 1378–1405.

Brownlees, C., & Engle, R. (2016). *SRISK: A conditional capital shortfall index for systemic risk measurement. Review of Financial Studies*, doi:10.1093/rfs/hhw060

Buch, C. M., Koch, C. T., & Koetter, M. (2011). *Crises, rescues, and policy transmission through international banks* (Discussion paper series 1: Economic studies 2011, 15). Frankfurt am Main: Deutsche Bundesbank, Research Centre.

Buch, C. M., Hilberg, B., and Tonzer, L. (2016) *Taxing banks: An evaluation of the German bank levy. Journal of Banking and Finance, 72*, 52–66.

Buch, C. M., Krause, T., & Tonzer, L. (2015). *Drivers of systemic risk: Do national and European perspectives differ?* Halle (Saale): Mimeo.

Calderon, C., and Schaeck, K. (2016). The effects of government interventions in the financial sector on banking competition and the evolution of zombie banks, *Journal of Financial and Quantitative Analysis, 51*(4), 1391–1436.

Calomiris, C., & Khan, U. (2015). An assessment of TARP assistance to financial institutions. *Journal of Economic Perspectives, 29*, 53–80.

Cooper, R., & Kempf, T. W. (2016). Deposit insurance and banks liquidation without commitment. Can we sleep well? *Economic Theory, 61*(2), 365–392.

Cooper, R., & Ross, T. W. (2002). Bank runs: Deposit insurance and capital requirements. *International Economic Review, 43*(1), 55–72.

Cordella, T., & Yeyati, E. L. (2003). Bank bailouts: Moral hazard vs. value effect. *Journal of Financial Intermediation, 12*, 300–330.

Dam, L., & Koetter, M. (2012). Bank bailouts and moral hazard: Empirical evidence from Germany. *Review of Financial Studies, 25*(8), 2343–2380.

Damar, E., Gropp, R., & Mordel, A. (2014). The ex-ante versus ex-post effect of public guarantees. In D. Evanoff, C. Holthausen, G. Kaufman, & M. Kremer (Eds.), *The role of central banks in financial stability: How has it changed? World Scientific studies in international economics* (Vol. 30). Hackensack: World Scientific.

De Nicoló, G., & Loukoianova, E. (2007). *Bank ownership, market structure and risk (International Monetary Fund working paper no. 07/215).* Washington, DC: IMF.

Dell'Ariccia, G., & Marquez, R. (2006). Competition among regulators and credit market integration. *Journal of Financial Economics, 79*(2), 401–430.

Demirgüç-Kunt, A., & Detragiache, E. (2002). Does deposit insurance increase banking system stability? An empirical investigation. *Journal of Monetary Economics, 49*, 1373–1406.

Diamond, D. W., & Dybvig, P. H. (1983). Bank runs, deposit insurance and liquidity. *Journal of Political Economy, 91*(3), 401–419.

Duchin, R., & Sosyura, D. (2014). Safer ratios, riskier portfolios: Banks' response to government aid. *Journal of Financial Economics, 113*, 1–28.

European Commission. (2014). Banking Union: Restoring financial stability in the Eurozone, MEMO/14/294.

Farber, A. (2012). Historical echoes: "Too big to fail" is one big phrase. *Liberty Street Economics.* http://libertystreeteconomics.newyorkfed.org/2012/10/historical-echoes-too-big-to-fail-is-one-big-phrase.html#.VfGDhpfbzsY

Farhi, E., & Tirole, J. (2012). Collective moral hazard, maturity mismatch, and systemic bailouts. *American Economic Review, 102*(1), 60–93.

Fischer, M., Hainz, C., Rocholl, J., & Steffen, S. (2014). *Government guarantees and bank risk taking incentives* (CESifo working paper series 4706). Munich: CESifo Group.

Flannery, M. J., & Sorescu, S. M. (1996). Evidence of bank market discipline in subordinated debenture yields: 1983–1991. *Journal of Finance, 51*(4), 1347–1377.

Freixas, X., & Rochet, J. C. (1998). Fair pricing of deposit insurance. Is it possible? Yes. Is it desirable? No. *Research in Economics, 52*, 217–232.

Freixas, X., Parigi, B. M., & Rochet, J.-C. (2000). Systemic risk, interbank relations, and liquidity provision by the Central Bank. *Journal of Money, Credit and Banking, 32*(3), 611–638.

Gennaioli, N., Martin, A., & Rossi, S. (2014). Sovereign default, domestic banks, and financial institutions. *Journal of Finance, 69*(2), 819–866.

Gimber, A. (2015). *Bank resolution, bailouts and the time inconsistency problem.* Available at http://apps.eui.eu/Personal/Researchers/Gimber

Gorton, G. (1988). Banking panics and business cycles. *Oxford Economic Papers, 40*(4), 751–781.

Gropp, R., & Vesala, J. (2004). Deposit insurance, moral hazard and market monitoring. *Review of Finance, 8*, 571–602.

Gropp, R., Hakenes, H., & Schnabel, I. (2011). Competition, risk-shifting, and public bailout policies. *Review of Financial Studies, 24*, 2084–2120.

Gropp, R., Gruendl, C., & Guettler, A. (2014). The impact of public guarantees on bank risk-taking: Evidence from a natural experiment. *Review of Finance, 18*(2), 457–488.

Gropp, R., Gruendl, C., and Saadi, V. (2015). *Public bank guarantees and allocative efficiency* (IWH discussion paper No. 7–15). Available at: https://ideas.repec.org/p/iwh/dispap/7-15.html

Gropp, R., Vesala, J., & Vulpes, G. (2006). Equity and bond market signals as leading indicators of bank fragility. *Journal of Money, Credit and Banking, 38*, 399–428.

Hakenes, H., & Schnabel, I. (2010). Banks without parachutes: Competitive effects of government bail-out policies. *Journal of Financial Stability, 6*, 156–168.

Houston, J. F., Lin, C., & Ma, Y. (2012). Regulatory arbitrage and international bank flows. *Journal of Finance, 67*(5), 1845–1895.

Hovakimian, A., Kane, E. J., & Laeven, L. (2003). How country and safety-net characteristics affect bank risk-shifting. *Journal of Financial Services, 23*(3), 177–204.

Hryckiewicz, A. (2014). What do we know about the impact of government interventions in the banking sector? An assessment of various bailout programs on bank behavior. *Journal of Banking & Finance, 46*, 246–265.

Ioannidou, V. P., & Penas, M. F. (2010). Deposit insurance and bank risk-taking: Evidence from internal loan ratings. *Journal of Financial Intermediation, 19*, 95–115.

Jacklin, C., & Bhattacharya, S. (1988). Distinguishing panics and information-based bank runs: Welfare and policy implications. *Journal of Political Economy, 96*(3), 568–592.

Keeley, M. C. (1990). Deposit insurance, risk, and market power in banking. *American Economic Review, 80*, 1183–1200.

King, R. G., & Levine, R. (1993). Finance and growth: Schumpeter might be right. *The Quarterly Journal of Economics, 108*(3), 717–737.

Koerner, T., and Schnabel, I. (2013), Abolishing public guarantees in the absence of market discipline (Ruhr economic papers 437). Rheinisch-Westfälisches Institut für Wirtschaftsforschung, Essen.

Koetter, M., and Noth, F. (2016). Did TARP distort competition among sound unsupported banks? *Economic Inquiry, 54*(2), 994–1020.

Laeven, L., & Valencia, F. (2013). Systemic banking crises database. *IMF Economic Review, 61*, 225–270.

Leonello, A. (2014). *Government guarantees and the two-way feedback between banking and Sovereign debt crises*. Philadelphia: Mimeo.

Liu, W.-H., & Ngo, P. T. H. (2014). Elections, political competition and bank failure. *Journal of Financial Economics, 112*, 251–268.

Marques, L.B., Correa, R., and Sapriza, H. (2013). *International evidence on government support and risk taking in the banking sector (IMF working paper 13/94)*. Washington, DC: IMF.

Matutes, C., & Vives, X. (1996). Competition for deposits, fragility and insurance. *Journal of Financial Intermediation, 5*, 184–216.

Merton, R. C. (1977). An analytic derivation of the cost of deposit insurance and loan guarantees: An application of modern option pricing theory. *Journal of Banking and Finance, 1*, 3–11.

Mitchell, J. (2001). *Too many to fail and regulatory response to banking crises, Working paper*. Brussels: Facultes Universitaires Saint-Louis.

Niepmann, F., & Schmidt-Eisenlohr, T. (2013). Bank bailouts, international linkages, and cooperation. *American Economic Journal: Economic Policy, 5*(4), 270–305.

Nier, E., & Baumann, U. (2006). Market discipline, disclosure and moral hazard in banking. *Journal of Financial Intermediation, 15*, 332–361.

Perotti, C. E., & Suarez, J. (2002). Last bank standing: What do I gain if you fail? *European Economic Review, 46*, 1599–1622.

Reinhart, C. M., & Rogoff, K. S. (2009). The aftermath of financial crises. *American Economic Review, 99*(2), 466–472.

Sapienza, P. (2004). The effects of government ownership on bank lending. *Journal of Financial Economics, 72*, 357–384.

Sironi, A. (2003). Testing for market discipline in the European banking industry: Evidence from subordinated debt issues. *Journal of Money, Credit and Banking, 35*, 443–472.

Taylor, M. W. (2014). Regulatory reform after the financial crisis: Twin Peaks revisited. In R. Huang & D. Schoenmaker (Eds.), *Institutional structure of financial regulation: Theories and international experiences, Routledge research in finance and banking law*. London: Routledge.

Ueda, K., & Werder di Mauro, B. (2013). Quantifying structural subsidy values for systematically important financial institutions. *Journal of Banking & Finance, 37*, 3830–3842.

Wheelock, D. C. (1992). Deposit insurance and bank failures: New evidence from the 1920s. *Economic Inquiry, 30*(3), 530–543.

Wheelock, D. C., & Wilson, P. W. (1995). Explaining bank failures: Deposit insurance, regulation, and efficiency. *The Review of Economics and Statistics, 77*(4), 689–700.

15

The Bank Lending Channel of Monetary Policy: A Review of the Literature and an Agenda for Future Research

Mintra Dwarkasing, Narly Dwarkasing, and Steven Ongena

That monetary policy, the tool with which central banks control the supply of money, can have concurrent effects on bank lending and behaviour and has been the subject of research in a large body of literature. In this chapter we aim to provide an overview of the empirical literature on two specific channels through which monetary policy can affect banks and in particular their lending behaviour: the bank lending and risk-taking channels of monetary policy. In relation to the bank lending channel, we discuss two distinct features of the existing bank lending channels: the *local* and *international* bank lending channels, especially the *international* bank lending channels, where domestic monetary policy can have far-reaching effects on cross-border lending or, through which, foreign monetary policy can influence domestic bank lending and can be of great importance for European economies when assessing the overall

M. Dwarkasing
Department of Business Economics, Erasmus University Rotterdam, Rotterdam, The Netherlands
e-mail: dwarkasing@ese.eur.nl

N. Dwarkasing
Department of Economics, IFS, Bonn University, Bonn, Germany
e-mail: ndwarkas@uni-bonn.de

S. Ongena (✉)
Department of Banking and Finance, University of Zurich, Zürich, Switzerland
e-mail: steven.ongena@bf.uzh.ch

T. Beck, B. Casu (eds.), *The Palgrave Handbook of European Banking*,
DOI 10.1057/978-1-137-52144-6_15

effect of monetary policy on the banking sector. This is particularly of interest given the globalization of the banking sector (Berger et al. 2000) and the accompanying interconnectedness of economies around the globe. In particular we will relate the existing findings on the pass-through of monetary policy via the banking sector onto the real economy to the institutional differences within Europe. As members of the European monetary Union are characterized by the same monetary policy but yet different institutional settings, this chapter will analyse the different institutional factors among member states of the EU, and will try to explain as to how these factors can be determining in how large the pass through of monetary policy via the bank lending channel is by reviewing the existing work on this topic.

We start by outlining the concepts of the bank lending channel, comprising of the local and international lending channel, and the bank risk taking channel (see (Fig. 15.1)). In addition we relate these concepts to the existing empirical literature and to the institutional differences among EU member states as to explain the heterogeneity in effectiveness of these channels among these countries. In the section "International Bank Lending Channels" we define the notion of an international bank lending channel of monetary policy more formally and summarize the recent empirical literature on this topic. The section, "Decomposition of Credit: The Bank Risk-Taking Channel" outlines research and findings on the bank risk-taking channel of monetary policy. The section "Conclusion and Future Research" draws the chapter to a close and provides some suggestions for future research.

The Local Bank Lending Channel of Monetary Policy

Various scholars have indicated the existence of a local *bank lending channel* of monetary policy in the USA (see, among others, the seminal work set out by Bernanke and Blinder (1988; 1992), Bernanke and Gertler (1995), Kashyap and Stein (1995) and Kashyap and Stein (2000)). Such a channel indicates that a change in the stance of monetary policy, often measured by a change in the local risk-free interest rate, can change a banks' loan supply. The rationale behind this particular transmission channel relies upon the following. When contractionary monetary policy reduces the total money supply this affects the *liabilities* side of the balance sheets of financial institutions, that is, it will reduce the amount of loanable funds (deposits). For this channel then to exist, banks must not be able to insulate their loan supply from such a shock to their reserves by simply reshuffling their portfolio of other assets and liabilities

(Oliner and Rudebusch (1995)). In addition, some firms must be *incapable* of substituting their bank loans for other types of financing without incurring extra costs, leading to a cut in investments. Given these two requirements, a bank will cut down on its lending during times of contractionary monetary policy thereby affecting output. The *bank lending channel* can hence be seen as a channel of supply: the bank cuts back on lending following contractionary monetary policy. However, contractionary monetary policy not only affects the supply of credit; it can, at the same time, affect the *demand* for credit. On this demand side, borrowers' interest expenses are increased and the value of their collateral is reduced, which makes bank financing more costly (Goddard et al. 2007). This demand effect is typically indicated in the existing literature as the *balance sheet channel* of monetary policy. The bank lending channel and the balance sheet channel are together known as the *credit channel* of monetary policy (see (Fig. 15.1) for a schematic representation). As changes in the monetary policy stance can, at the same time, affect both the demand and the supply of credit, it is difficult to find evidence in favour of one of these channels without first disentangling supply and demand. Various studies, however, have exploited econometric techniques in order to be able to provide evidence of the existence of a possible bank lending channel while trying to filter out a possible balance sheet channel effect, something that will be discussed in the

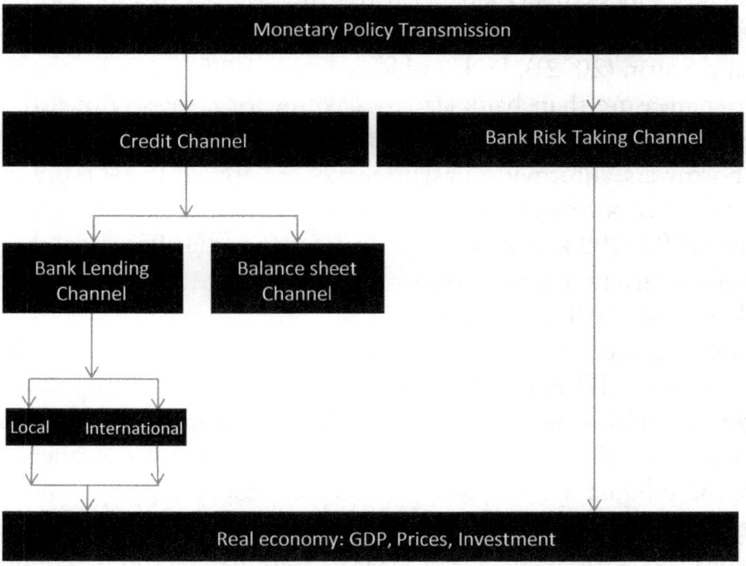

Fig. 15.1 Monetary policy transmission. Based upon Ciccarelli et al. (2015)

next section 'Identifying the Bank Lending Channel'. Many of these studies either rely on detailed bank (balance sheet) level data or belong to another stream of research that exploits micro data at the loan level. This section will first outline the literature that relies on bank (balance sheet) level data, and will then continue by presenting studies that rely on micro loan-level data. In addition it will draw further upon the differences found between countries, with, as a main focus, the heterogeneity in institutional factors and thereby financial market characteristics that may serve as an explanation for differences in the potency of the bank lending channel among European countries.

Identifying the Bank Lending Channel: Bank Balance Sheet Data

A vast number of studies have relied upon the methodological approach set out by Kashyap and Stein (1995) and Kashyap and Stein (2000) to identify a bank lending channel of monetary policy. This strand of literature exploits the heterogeneity among different types of banks and the differential effect monetary policy transmission can have on these banks (for evidence on the effect of monetary policy on the *aggregate* amount of bank lending volume see Bernanke and Blinder (1992)). For instance, smaller banks face more information problems compared to large ones and find it more difficult to neutralize monetary shocks; hence smaller banks should react in a more pronounced manner to changes in monetary policy in terms of their lending (see also Kakes and Sturm (2002)). Peek and Rosengren (1995) argue that bank capital is a better measure than bank size to account for cross-sectional differences between banks and their reactions to changes in monetary policy. On the side of the borrowers, information asymmetries are argued to be more predominant for smaller borrowers compared to larger ones. For instance Gertler and Gilchrist (1993; 1994) and Gilchrist and Zakrajsek (1995) show that for US firms, following a monetary contraction, bank credit to small firms is reduced more than bank credit to large firms.

The existing literature has identified various other bank characteristics that could explain the differential response to monetary policy changes among various types of banks besides banks' size—*liquidity* and *capital* among others. De Santis and Surico (2013) indicate that following a monetary contraction banks that are more liquid are less likely to contract money supply as they can utilize their liquidity to satisfy loan demand (see also Kashyap and Stein (2000); Chatelain et al. (2003); de Haan (2003); Kaufmann (2003); Loupias et al.

(2003)). Additionally, banks that have more capital can rely on more equity securities to absorb future losses (Kishan and Opiela 2000; Van den Heuvel 2002).

Kishan and Opiela (2000) indicate that small *and* under-capitalized US banks react more to monetary shocks than banks that are larger and well capitalized. The results of studies on the presence and magnitude of the bank lending channel within Europe are far from conclusive. Altunbaş et al. (2002) apply the same method as Kishan and Opiela (2000) to the balance sheets of European banks to estimate the response of bank lending to changes in the monetary policy stance between 1991 and 1999. Their results indicate that under-capitalized banks, of any size, react more strongly to policy changes. In a similar vein, De Bondt (2000) finds mixed evidence for the bank lending channel while studying bank-level panel data for six EU member states: Germany, France, Italy, the UK, the Netherlands and Belgium, for the period 1990–5. On the one hand he documents strong support for a bank lending channel in Germany, Belgium and the Netherlands, and particularly for small banks with illiquid balance sheets. On the other hand, some weak evidence is found for France and Italy, but not for the UK. Angeloni et al. (2003) have bundled several studies from various scholars on the transmission of monetary policy for pre-1999 Europe. Again the results here on the presence of a bank lending channel are not fully homogeneous among countries. Studying bank-level data for the period 1999–2011, De Santis and Surico (2013) reinforce this statement of heterogeneity further, as they document significant and heterogeneous effects of monetary policy on bank lending for Germany and Italy, but these are weaker and more homogeneous for Spain and France. Gambacorta (2005) finds evidence in support of a bank lending channel for Italy. Bank capital and liquidity can account for cross-sectional differences in the effectiveness of the bank lending channel; however, bank size is never relevant.

Loan-Level Data

A common identification issue when studying banks' balance sheets in order to detect a possible bank lending channel of monetary policy is to disentangle credit supply from credit demand. Tighter monetary conditions may reduce supply through increased agency costs of banks, but on the other hand may influence demand because of reductions in net worth (the value of collateral) and expected investment (De Santis and Surico 2013). In order to disentangle the two effects, several studies have focused on more micro loan level data, which makes it possible to control for credit demand. Valuable sources of data are national credit registers. Jiménez et al. (2012) exploit the Spanish credit register, maintained by Banco de España for such identification purposes. The availability of data on the borrower's (firm) side through the credit register makes it possible for them to study loan applications for loans made in the *same month* by the *same borrower* (firm) or for the same loan to *different* banks. Hence, including firm-month or, alternatively, loan-fixed effects to absorb unobserved firm heterogeneity and observed time-varying heterogeneity allows one to filter out the demand effect for credit and isolates the effect of monetary policy on the supply of credit. An additional challenge within this literature is the *endogeneity* of monetary policy. Monetary policy is often related to a country's business cycle which in turn could also directly affect credit extension as well as demand. Jiménez et al. (2012) rely upon the observation that monetary policy in Spain has been fairly exogenous during the sample period; as a peripheral country its business cycle did not converge with those of the core countries of the Eurozone (Giannone et al. 2010). The findings confirm the existence of a bank lending channel of monetary policy: higher short-term interest rates (or lower gross domestic product (GDP) growth) reduce the probability that a loan application is granted. This negative effect of short-term interest rates on loan granting is statistically stronger for banks with low capital or liquidity, whereas the negative effect of lower GDP growth is statistically stronger for banks with low capital.

In another study Garcia-Posada and Marchetti (2015) look at the effect of non-standard policy measures, in particular the introduction of two *very long-term refinancing operations* (VLTROs) in 2011 and 2012, respectively, on bank credit extended by Spanish banks. Within their framework of research they disentangle credit supply from credit demand by relying on the methodology first implemented by Gan (2007) and Khwaja and Mian (2008). They identify shifts in credit supply (here caused by the introduction of the VLTROs) by controlling for credit demand, exploiting micro-level data on bank loans for Spanish firms. As Garcia-Posada and Marchetti (2015) rely on data of Spanish firms and the levels of credit they have at multiple banks, they can exploit the fact that "many firms simultaneously borrow from several banks". This allows them to "compare credit growth across *different* lenders for the *same* firm in the *same* period. This *within-firm* comparison controls for all observable and unobservable, time-invariant and time-varying firm characteristics, including firm-specific changes in credit demand and risk (p.8)." They find that VLTROs had a positive, moderately sized effect on the supply of bank credit to firms, providing evidence of a bank lending channel in the context of unconventional monetary policy. This effect was greater for *illiquid* banks and was driven by credit to small and medium enterprises (SMEs), as there was no impact on loans to large firms. Other studies that investigate the transmission effect of non-standard monetary policy tools include Ciccarelli et al. (2015). They document that, while relying on country-level data, the bank lending channel has been (to a large extent) neutralized by the European Central Bank (ECB) non-standard monetary policy tools interventions. However, the policy implemented by the ECB until the end of 2011 was not sufficient to fully address credit availability problems that stemmed from deteriorated firm net worth and risk conditions, particularly for small firms in countries under stress.

In a related strand of research, Ciccarelli et al. (2015) exploit survey data from the Bank Lending Survey (BLS) for the Eurozone and from the Senior Loan Officer Survey for the USA, to conclude among others that a tightening of monetary policy also tightens the lending conditions related to bank lending for the Eurozone, but that the bank lending channel is not significantly present for the USA. The authors indicate that relying on survey data makes it possible to tackle the problem of unobserved credit channels (bank lending and balance sheet), which is not fully possible with micro-level data. They state that a micro approach is not able to fully identify the credit channel "as micro identification cannot analyze the total effect of a monetary policy shock on real activity, but only a difference-in-difference effect by comparing banks (see e.g., Kashyap and Stein (2000)) or non-financial borrowers (e.g., Gertler and Gilchrist (1994)) with different sensitivity to monetary policy".

Institutions and Potency of the Bank Lending Channel

The magnitude through which changes in monetary policy can affect the economy via the bank lending channel is dependent on a number of factors as discussed in the existing literature. Cross sectional differences between various types of banks in terms of *size*, *liquidity* and *capital* have been previously outlined as factors that can account for the potency of the bank lending channel. However, various studies (among others Cecchetti 1999; Guiso et al. 1999; Sander and Kleimeier 2004) have also indicated that on a country-level *institutional* factors can matter for the importance of such a channel as well. Cecchetti

Table 15.1 Legal origin as a determinant of the potency of the bank lending channel

Legal Family	Potency of the bank lending channel of monetary policy
English	Weakest
Scandinavian	Weak
French	Strong
German	Strongest

Source: Cecchetti (1999)

(1999) shows that differences in financial systems can account for the cross-sectional variation in the transmission mechanism of monetary policy among countries. Relating this to La Porta et al. (1997) and La Porta et al. (1998) who document a relationship between the legal system of a country and its financial system, Cecchetti (1999) argues that the root of the differences in financial systems and hence of the potency of the monetary policy transmission mechanism lies within the dissimilar legal origins of a country, that is, whether a country belongs to the legal class of the English, French, German or Scandinavian family (La Porta et al. 1998). The findings indicate that the legal structure, financial structure and the monetary transmission mechanism are interconnected. The bank lending channel of monetary transmission is likely to be less pronounced for countries belonging to the English (common law) legal family (see Table 15.1 for an overview of the expected strength of the bank lending channel of monetary policy and a country's legal family based upon Cecchetti 1999), as they are characterized by better legal protection for shareholders and debtors and have more developed financial markets to offset monetary shocks. This is in contrast to countries belonging to the French and German legal family, of

Table 15.2 Bank and financial market characteristics as determinants of the potency of the bank lending channel

Bank characteristics	Potency of the bank lending channel of monetary policy	Proxies
Bank size	–	Log of total assets
Bank capital	–	Capital and reserves over total assets
Bank liquidity	–	Liquid assets over total assets
Financial market characteristics		
Concentration and size	–	Number of credit institutions, banks per million people, HHI, concentration ratio: Top 5 banks For size: Number of publicly traded firms, publicly traded firms per capita, market cap/GDP, corporate debt/GDP, total bank loans/all other financing
Health of the financial sector	–	Return on assets, Loan loss provisions, Net interest margin, Operating costs, Avg. Thomson rating
Relationship Lending	–	Number of universal banks/total banks, number of bank-firm relations
Bank networks	–	Bank type: Savings/Cooperation networks

Source: Cecchetti (1999) and Ehrmann et al. (2003) and authors' own contribution

which the French are characterized by much smaller capital markets, thereby less able to absorb monetary shocks.

In line with this, Ehrmann et al. (2003) indicate that the structure of the banking sectors and financial markets matters for the role of banks in monetary policy transmission. Table 15.2 outlines some important bank and financial market factors that contribute to the potency of the transmission of monetary policy via bank lending as well as their measures as used by Cecchetti (1999). These factors will be discussed in more detail in the sections 'Bank Characteristics' and 'Financial Market Characteristics'.

Bank Characteristics:

Bank Size, Bank Capital and Bank Liquidity

Several studies have indicated that bank characteristics such as bank size, capital and liquidity are important factors in contributing to the importance of the transmission channel of monetary policy (Ehrmann et al. 2003). Bank size is often relied upon as a proxy for information asymmetries. Larger banks suffer less from these informational asymmetry problems compared to small banks and hence are better able to raise uninsured funds in times of a monetary tightening. Hence large banks can be expected to reduce their bank lending relatively *less* compared to small banks in times of a monetary tightening (Kashyap and Stein 1995). Within the empirical literature proxies of bank size often rely on measures based upon total assets.

In line with this, better capitalized banks are argued to have better access to non-deposit financing compared to poorly capitalized banks, and hence should be better able to absorb a monetary shock, thereby not having to reduce their loan supply as much as poorly capitalized banks (Peek and Rosengren 1995).

When categorizing liquid and less liquid banks, it is often indicated that liquid banks, as they can shield their loan portfolio from a monetary tightening by drawing upon their liquid assets, are less affected by such a monetary shock compared to less liquid banks that are not able to draw upon liquid assets (Kashyap and Stein 2000).

Financial Market Characteristics:

Bank Sector Concentration and Size

The concentration of and competition within the banking sector as well as its size have been highlighted as important factors that can be of importance for the strength of a possible bank lending channel of monetary policy within an economy. Monetary tightening may induce banks to cut their loan supply; however, the effect of such a monetary policy shock may be different for various types of banks and levels of market competition. If bank competition is mild, banks should have relatively easy access to alternative sources of funding such as certificates of deposit and interbank loans compared to higher levels of concentration. Hence a positive relationship between ease of access to alternative funding and bank competition following a monetary tightening can be expected. Investigating this hypothesis, Fungáčová, Solanko and Weill (2014) conclude that for 12 Eurozone countries the transmission of monetary policy via the bank lending channel is less pronounced for banks with extensive market power (for evidence on the USA see Adams and Amel (2005); for Latin America see Olivero et al. (2011a) and Olivero et al. (2011b); for a cross-country sample see Gunji et al. (2009)). Brissimis et al. (2014) find for a mixed sample of European and US banks that bank competition amplifies the bank lending channel. Leroy (2014) finds that, using banking micro-data from Eurozone countries in the period 1999–2011, banks with market power, as measured by the Lerner index, have a credit supply that is less sensitive to a monetary policy shock.

Health of the Banking Sector

The health of the banking sector can also play a role in monetary transmission via bank lending. Cecchetti (1999) indicates that according to the bank lending view, overall, the transmission mechanism will be stronger in those countries where the banking system is less healthy and less concentrated. The reasoning would be that as banks themselves have restricted access to non-reservable deposits when the banking sector is less healthy, they are forced to contract their balance sheets following a monetary tightening. To capture the health of the banking sector he relies on various measures: return on assets of banks and loan loss provisions, among others (see Table 15.2).

Other Factors: Relationship Lending and Bank Networks

Another factor that has been acknowledged to account for the potency of the bank lending channel is relationship lending. Relationship lending had been proven to be an important factor for the availability of bank credit (Bharath et al. 2007) and loan conditions (see Ongena and Smith (2000) and Degryse et al. (2009) for a review of bank relationships). Various scholars have identified that in countries where relationship lending is much more prevalent, monetary transmission is less pronounced compared to other countries (see Ehrmann (2005) for evidence on the quantity and Borio and Fritz (1995) for evidence on the interest rate pass through for bank loans). Hachem (2011) provides theoretical evidence as to why relationship lending should matter for monetary transmission. Kakes and Sturm (2002) argue that the bank lending channel of monetary policy on the one hand should be very pronounced for Germany as banks play an important role within the German financial sector; however, on the other hand, as relationship lending is also an important feature banks may try to shield their lending (loan portfolios) from monetary policy shocks. Their results find some evidence in line with the existence of a bank lending channel in Germany; however, the results are heterogeneous for the various banking groups active in the German financial sector (for more on the credit channel in Germany, see, e.g., Barran et al. (1997), De Bondt (2000), Küppers (2001), Kakes and Sturm (2002), Holtemöller (2003), von Kalckreuth (2003), Ehrmann and Worms (2004), Hülsewig et al. (2004), Ehrmann (2005)). Massa and Zhang (2013) show that debt inflexibility, the borrowing inflexibility to substitute between bond and bank financing, shifts US firms' capital structures towards equity and reduces investment. This effect is stronger during times of tight monetary policy and for smaller firms and firms without banking relationships. Ferri et al. (2014) indicate that a bank's business model, which is closely related to the types of bank ownership, can account for differences in bank lending following a monetary shock. They hypothesize and test, based upon Berger and Udell (2002), whether banks that rely on a relationship-based approach to lending are less willing to cut back on their loan provision to customers with whom they have long-term relationships. In order to do so they look at differences in lending behaviour of two types of banks after a monetary shock: shareholder banks, which exclusively focus on profit maximization, and stakeholder banks, which seek to maximize the consumer surplus of their customers. The results indicate that the loan supply of stakeholder banks (more relationship oriented) reacted less to changes in the short-term interest rate compared to that of shareholder banks. In addition Gambacorta and Marques-Ibanez (2011) also indicate that changes in a bank's business model matter for the strength of the transmission of monetary policy.

Ehrmann et al. (2003) indicate that banking networks also matter for the strength of the bank lending channel. They indicate that a network arrangement between banks can also have important consequences for the reaction of bank loan supply to monetary policy. In networks with strong links between the head institutions and the lower tier, the large banks in the upper tier can serve as liquidity providers in times of a monetary tightening, such that the system would experience a net flow of funds from the head institutions to the small member banks. This is confirmed by Ehrmann and Worms (2004) for Germany as there small banks receive a net inflow of funds from their head institutions after a monetary contraction (see also Ashcraft (2006) for evidence on bank holding companies versus stand-alone banks in the USA). Holod and Peek (2010) indicate that subsidiaries within a holding company can "insure" each other, particularly when active in distinctive geographic markets, as the holding company can move loanable funds from subsidiaries with an excess of funds to those short of liquidity.

Zaheer et al. (2013) investigate another factor that can account for the potency of the bank lending channel as they look at the potency of the bank lending channel for Islamic banks versus conventional banks. They argue that Islamic banks may be, on the one hand, unable or unwilling to substitute their Islamic loans for any other securities (from a social point of view) following a monetary contraction, which should make the bank lending channel more potent. On the other hand, however, they indicate that, as Islamic banks deal with arrangements entered into for religious reasons (see Khan and Khanna 2012; Baele et al. 2014) and as they attract singularly deposits and lend interest-free, Islamic banks may shield themselves from monetary policy shocks, making the transmission channel less potent. The results indicate that Islamic banks shield themselves from monetary policy shocks, which is in line with the latter prediction. This behaviour is typical for large conventional banks, as documented by other studies (e.g., Kashyap and Stein 2000). The authors hence conclude that if in many countries the Islamic segment of the banking sector grows in size, this may lead to a weakening in the potency of the credit channel of monetary policy.

Cecchetti (1999) and Ehrmann et al. (2001) provide an overview of other financial market factors that can account for heterogeneity in the transmission of monetary policy via the bank lending channel.

International Bank Lending Channels

As opposed to just one *local* bank lending channel research suggests that there may be several international channels present in a country at the same time (see, e.g., Temesvary et al. 2015). In this section we review the upcoming recent empirical literature that highlights the existence of such global bank lending channels, with a particular focus on Europe.

Not only may the appropriate domestic monetary policy (for instance, the short-term interest rates set by the ECB for the Eurozone countries) affect banks' lending behavior, but foreign monetary policies also can affect, when banks domestically lend in those foreign currencies, the local supply of loans through their own *international* bank lending channels. Interestingly, Ongena et al. (2015) find empirical evidence in favour of the existence of such an international bank lending channel in Europe. Using a novel, micro-level dataset from Hungary, involving the vast majority of bank lending to firms as well as information on the currency in which each loan is extended, they uncover the existence of such a channel. Local monetary policy has a differential impact on the supply of bank credit that is denominated in the local currency compared to the supply of credit denominated in other currencies. Accounting for time varying firm-specific changes in loan demand by including firm-time fixed effects, Ongena et al. (2015) find that a lower domestic monetary rate only increases the supply of credit in the domestic currency (Hungarian Forint) and not the supply of credit in foreign currencies. On the other hand, however, a decrease in the monetary rate induced by foreign central banks increases local lending in these foreign currencies by low versus high capitalized banks more than lending in the domestic currency. Hence, the *composition* of bank credit, in terms of currencies, may affect whether and to what extent international lending channels are present. Studying the effect of domestic monetary shocks, Beņkovskis (2008) finds that the supply of loans that are issued in foreign currencies is not affected by these shocks in Latvia.

Suggestive evidence of international transmissions of liquidity shocks through international banks is well documented. Schnabl (2012) shows that a negative liquidity shock originated in Russia affected international banks' bank-to-bank lending to Peruvian banks, and subsequently Peruvian banks' lending to Peruvian firms was also adversely affected. Focusing on multiple countries, the results in Cetorelli and Goldberg (2011) point out that adverse liquidity shocks to banking systems in developed countries have a negative effect on the loan supply in emerging countries. This spillover effect can be explained by three channels that are at work: foreign banks directly contract their cross-border lending; foreign banks' affiliates contract their local lending in emerging countries; and domestic banks decrease their loan supply due to the contraction in interbank cross-border lending. The results in Chava and Purnanandam (2011) indicate that adverse shocks to US banks' capital, caused by the Russian financial crisis in the autumn of 1998, led to a larger decline in firm value for those firms primarily dependent upon banks compared to firms that had previously had access to bond financing. Additionally, those banks affected by the crisis contracted their lending more and increased loan interest rates more substantially compared to non-affected banks, suggesting the transmission of financial shocks through the banking channel.

In an important study, building on the notion of an international transmission channel of financial shocks via banks as set forward in Peek and Rosengren (1997) and Peek and Rosengren (2000), Cetorelli and Goldberg (2012) document that global US banks are less affected by local monetary policy in terms of bank lending compared to local US banks. Hence, global banks may also alleviate the impact of a local bank lending channel through the use of internal capital markets—a finding that is in line with other studies, which find evidence suggestive of a reduced effect of monetary policy because of specific developments, such as securitization, in the banking sector (Loutskina and Strahan 2009). At the same time, however, Cetorelli and Goldberg (2012) find that domestic liquidity shocks also affect the cross-border lending conducted by US global banks' foreign affiliates. Instead of investigating internal capital markets, Temesvary et al. (2015) focus on external capital markets and study how changes in US monetary policy affect US banks' cross-border lending. The results indicate the presence of a global bank lending channel: in reaction to changes in US monetary policy US banks adjust their lending; subsequently, monetary policy easing, for example, increases cross-border lending significantly.

Recent literature also points out that European monetary policy can have spillover effects itself as well. Morais et al. (2015) examine the effect of, for instance, European monetary policy on the supply of credit to Mexican firms as well as the associated real effects and its effect on bank risk-taking. They observe that there is an international spillover of Eurozone and UK monetary policy to the supply of credit to Mexican banks provided by European banks. A contractionary monetary policy in the Eurozone or the UK decreases the supply of credit to Mexican firms from Eurozone/ UK banks, respectively. Additionally, expansionary monetary policy and quantitative easing foster banks to search for yields as credit supply to more risky borrowers, those with higher ex-ante loan rates but also significantly higher ex-post default rates, increases. Several other studies have investigated this spillover effect of monetary policies abroad, often with a particular focus on emerging market economies. The results in Ioannidou et al. (2015) show how changes in US monetary policy affect the supply of credit denominated in US dollars in Bolivia and indicate that low short-term rates spur the probability of granting new loans to riskier borrowers. For identification purposes, they exploit the fact that Bolivia was fully dollarized and that its currency followed a crawling peg with the US dollar, and there were hardly any restrictions in its capital account. Since its small economy was not synchronized with the US economy, changes in the US federal funds rate, which from the USA are transmitted into the Bolivian liquidity markets, provide exogenous variation in the relevant monetary policy rate. A more detailed discussion of Ioannidou et al. (2015) is given in the section "Decomposition of Credit: The Bank Risk-Taking Channel". In related research Mora (2013) finds that Mexican banks, especially smaller banks, which have a larger share of foreign currency deposits, are less responsive to local monetary rate changes. On the other hand, they are more sensitive to shocks in foreign monetary policy.

Given the interconnectedness and globalization of banking systems, both within Europe and around the world, all in all these findings suggest that more research is needed into the effects of local monetary policies abroad and vice versa.

Decomposition of Credit: The Bank Risk-Taking Channel

More recently, many scholars have argued that there is an additional channel of monetary transmission: the bank risk-taking channel of monetary policy. The *bank risk-taking channel* of monetary policy argues that not only the quantity—that is, the supply—of funds increases, following a period of low interest rates, but that also the quality of these funds is affected in the sense that banks tend to extend this extra available money in the form of loans to borrowers by softening lending standards and taking on extra risk in the search for yields (Rajan 2006; Stein 2013). Many scholars have indicated that (long) periods of low short-term interest rates may result in increased, or even excessive, risk-taking by banks (see, e.g., Taylor (2008); Blanchard (2009); Adrian and Shin (2009); Brunnermeier (2009); Calomiris (2009); Borio and Zhu (2012)).

Empirically testing for the presence of a bank risk-taking channel of monetary policy is a challenging task for several reasons. Ioannidou et al. (2015) list three main identification challenges. Firstly, monetary policy is endogenous to economic conditions (the business cycle), or, to put it differently, is low when risks are high. When regressing measures of bank risk-taking on measures of monetary policy (often short-term interest rates), if this is not addressed, it will yield biased results. Secondly, they indicate that, just as with the bank lending channel of monetary policy, changes in credit demand need to be disentangled from changes in credit supply following a change in the short-term interest rate. Thirdly, banks have the ability to adjust various loan terms (collateral and loan interest rates, among others) to incorporate the risk of loans that have a higher default probability. Hence, to make a correct statement on the possible presence of a bank risk-taking channel of monetary policy, a setting where monetary policy is exogenous needs to be identified and detailed and exhaustive data on lender, borrower and loan characteristics is needed.

Ioannidou et al. (2015) rely on the Bolivian credit register, which contains such detailed information to empirically test for such a channel. As Bolivia was fully dollarized, the US interest rate was the appropriate interest rate, and as the business cycle of Bolivia was not synchronized with that of the USA, the monetary policy interest rate was exogenous. Exploiting this setting and the detailed dataset on bank lending, the authors find that banks indeed take on extra risk without adjusting key loan conditions such as collateral and loan prices, when monetary policy rates decrease and indicate: "Lower monetary policy rates are found to increase the likelihood that loans to lower quality borrowers are granted, particularly by banks with more acute agency problems (p.97)." Thereby they confirm the existence of a bank risk-taking channel of monetary policy for Bolivia. For the Eurozone the bank risk-taking channel has also been studied widely.

In a related paper, Jiménez et al. (2014) find similar results for Spain to those Ioannidou et al. (2015) document for Bolivia. Relying on the credit register accommodated by the Banco de España that contains loan applications (and hence a two-stage estimation procedure) they arrive at very similar estimates to Ioannidou et al. (2015).

Other studies focusing on European countries, while relying on less detailed information, and hence less able to make fully causal statements on the effect of monetary policy on bank risk, are Gaggl and Valderrama (2010) for Austria, Geršl et al. (2015) for the Czech Republic, Bonfim and Soares (2014) for Portugal, and Apel and Claussen (2012) for Sweden, whom all find support for the existence of a bank risk-taking channel in one or more dimensions. For the USA various scholars, too, have indicated the existence of a risk-taking channel: Altunbas et al. (2014) document that for listed banks operating in the EU and the USA relatively low levels of interest rates over an extended period of time contributed to an increase in bank risk. In addition Delis et al. (2011), Paligorova and Santos (2013), Dell'Ariccia et al. (2013), Buch et al. (2014a) and Buch et al. (2014b) find evidence that supports the existence of a bank risk-taking channel of monetary policy in the USA. Maddaloni and Peydró (2011) show, using data on Eurozone and US lending standards from bank lending surveys, that lending standards to firms and households are softened when short-term interest rates are low, evidence that is in line with a risk-taking channel of monetary policy.

Dwarkasing (2014) shows that the bank risk-taking channel is not a new phenomenon. Relying on nineteenth-century loan-level data for a British bank, she shows that after loosening interest rates, more risk is taken by the bank, as less collateral-to-loan values are required for borrowers and loan interest rates go down. To address the endogeneity issue of monetary policy she exploits the fact that Britain was on the gold standard at the time, and hence uses gold rushes as an exogenous shock to the money supply and the interest rate set by the Bank of England, the British central bank.

Another stream of research shows that a monetary contraction can also have other effects on the economy rather than only through the previously discussed lending and risk-taking channel. Nelson, Gabor and Konstantinos (2015) indicate that monetary policy can affect the shadow banking system. They document that, in line with existing theory, commercial banks' asset growth declined after a monetary contraction; however, for shadow banks, it was the opposite: shadow banks' asset growth expanded after monetary contractions. "These findings highlight potential challenges associated with using monetary policy to lean against financial sector activity in pursuit of financial stability goals". (p. ii)

Conclusion and Future Research

Two widely discussed channels through which monetary policy can influence banks' lending behaviour are the bank lending and bank balance sheet channels of monetary policy. This chapter discusses and summarizes the extant empirical literature that assesses the existence and potency of these channels, with a specific emphasis on Europe.

Several factors seem to influence the potency with which monetary policy affects banks' lending behaviour, both at the individual bank level and at the more aggregate national level. Firstly, at the individual bank level, bank size and capitalization matter for the extent of the pass-through of monetary policy on bank lending. Smaller and less capitalized banks react more severely to monetary shocks. Secondly, more liquid banks are less responsive to changing monetary policy in their lending behaviour, as they can use their excess liquidity to extend loans following a monetary contraction.

At the national level several other factors influence the potency of the bank lending channel as well. Differences in legal origins and the accompanying heterogeneity in financial systems between countries matter for the potency of monetary policy transmission as well as banking sector concentration, size and health. For example, in countries where the banking sector is less healthy, the transmission of monetary shocks should be more pronounced. Cultural factors may mediate the effect of monetary policy transmission on bank lending. Islamic banks, for instance, are able to better shield themselves from monetary shocks by attracting singularly deposits and lending interest rate free.

Empirical evidence also points to the presence of a bank risk-taking channel of monetary policy and global bank lending channels. Foreign monetary rate changes affect domestic lending in the foreign currency and, in periods of decreasing monetary rates, banks not only increase their lending but also relax their lending standards in search for yields.

On the existence and potency of the bank lending channel in Europe the empirical findings are less conclusive. Several studies find a potent bank lending channel in certain European countries such as Germany and Belgium, whereas for other countries such as the UK there is only weak or no evidence of the existence of such a channel.

We suggest three suggestions or avenues for further research. Firstly, conducting effective monetary policy in Europe and within the European Monetary Union countries is a challenging task, especially given the considerable heterogeneity of institutional characteristics between countries and the corresponding mediating effects these differences may have on the ultimate effectiveness of this tool in a given country. Acknowledging these institutional differences and their interplay with monetary policy is therefore key when using monetary policy as an effective tool to control the money supply and when quantifying the effect this tool will have on banks' lending.

Secondly, recent advances in the empirical literature have shifted the focus from using aggregate bank balance sheet data to the use of micro-level data in order to disentangle the bank lending and balance sheet channels more precisely. Yet micro-level bank data from European countries is still quite scarcely available. Hence, a widening availability of micro-level bank data from more European countries to scholars enables to better quantify the potency of the bank lending channel of monetary policy for countries that have different institutional characteristics.

Finally, history may offer many interesting opportunities to study the effect of monetary policy transmission, taking care of possible endogeneity issues.

In addition we would like to conclude by highlighting the importance of studying the interaction between monetary and macro-prudential policy. Macro-prudential policies have as their main aim the induction of financial stability, and recent research has pointed out that there is an important interaction between monetary and macro-prudential policy. For instance, Maddaloni and Peydró (2013) indicate that, "monetary policy rates affect bank stability, and their impact depends both on bank balance sheet strength and on banking prudential policy. Therefore, monetary policy and prudential policy are connected and influence each other. Monetary policy decisions should pay more attention to financial stability issues, while banking prudential supervision and regulation should take into account the effects induced by a low monetary policy rate environment". (p.157). Institutional designs matter here, as the conduct of macro-prudential policies can interfere with the primary objective of various agencies involved. If a central bank is in charge of macro-prudential policy, it might have more difficulty communicating its monetary policy stance, compared to a setting where both policies are set and executed by different agencies (Claessens 2014). Hence studying the interaction between monetary and macro-prudential policies is of great importance for both scholars and practitioners.

References

Adams, R. M., & Amel, D. F. (2005). *The effects of local banking market structure on the bank-lending channel of monetary policy*. Washington DC: Federal Reserve Board.

Adrian, T., & Shin, H. S. (2009). Money, liquidity and monetary policy. *American Economic Review Papers and Proceedings, 99*(2), 600–605.

Altunbaş, Y., Fazylov, O., & Molyneux, P. (2002). Evidence on the bank lending channel in europe. *Journal of Banking and Finance, 26*, 2093–2110.

Altunbas, Y., Gambacorta, L., & Marquez-Ibañez, D. (2014). Does monetary policy affect bank risk-taking? *International Journal of Central Banking, 10*, 95–135.

Angeloni, I., Kashyap, A. K., & Mojon, B. (2003). *Monetary policy transmission in the euro area*. Cambridge: Cambridge University Press.

Apel, M., & Claussen, C. A. (2012). Monetary policy, interest rates and risk-taking. *Sveriges Riksbank Economic Review*, 68–83.

Ashcraft, A. (2006). New evidence on the lending channel. *Journal of Money, Credit and Banking, 38*, 751–775.

Baele, L., Farooq, M., & Ongena, S. (2014). Of religion and redemption: Evidence from default on Islamic loans. *Journal of Banking and Finance, 44*, 141–159.

Barran, F., Coudert, V., & Mojon, B. (1997). Interest rates, banking spreads and credit supply: The real effects. *European Journal of Finance, 3*, 107–136.

Beņkovskis, K. (2008). *Is there a bank lending channel of monetary policy in Latvia? Evidence from bank level data*. Riga: Bank of Latvia.

Berger, A. N., DeYoung, R., Genay, H., & Udell, G. (2000). Globalization of financial institutions: Evidence from cross-border banking performance. *Brookings-Wharton Papers on Financial Services, 3*, 23–120.

Berger, A. N., & Udell, G. F. (2002). Small business credit availability and relationship lending: The importance of bank organisational structure. *Economic Journal, 112*, 32–53.

Bernanke, B. S., & Blinder, A. S. (1988). Money, credit and aggregate demand. *American Economic Review, 82*, 901–921.

Bernanke, B. S., & Blinder, A. S. (1992). The federal funds rate and the channels of monetary transmission. *American Economic Review, 82*, 901–921.

Bernanke, B. S., & Gertler, M. (1995). Inside the black box: The credit channel of monetary policy transmission. *Journal of Economic Perspectives, 9*, 27–48.

Bharath, S. T., Dahiya, S., Saunders, A., & Srinivasan, A. (2007). So what do I get: A bank's view of lending relationships. *Journal of Financial Economics, 85*, 368–419.

Blanchard, O. (2009). *The crisis: Basic mechanisms, and appropriate policies*. Washington DC: International Monetary Fund.

Bonfim, D., & Soares, C. (2014). *The risk-taking channel of monetary policy—exploring all avenues*. Lisbon: Banco de Portugal.

Borio, C., & Zhu, H. (2012). Capital regulation, risk-taking and monetary policy: A missing link in the transmission mechanism. *Journal of Financial Stability, 8*, 236–251.

Borio, C. E. V., & Fritz, W. (1995). *The response of short-term bank lending rates to policy rates: A cross-country perspective*. Basle: Bank for International Settlements.

Brissimis, S., Delis, M., & Iosifidi, M. (2014). Bank market power and monetary policy transmission. *International Journal of Central Banking, 10*, 173–214.

Brunnermeier, M. K. (2009). Deciphering the liquidity and credit crunch 2007–2008. *Journal of Economic Perspectives, 23*, 77–100.

Buch, C. M., Eickmeier, S., & Prieto, E. (2014a). Search for yield? Survey-based evidence on bank risk taking. *Journal of Economic Dynamics and Control, 43*, 12–30.

Buch, C. M., Eickmeier, S., & Prieto, E. (2014b). Macroeconomic factors and microlevel bank behavior. *Journal of Money, Credit and Banking, 46*, 715–751.

Calomiris, C. W. (2009). The subprime turmoil: What's old, what's new and what's next? *Journal of Structured Finance, 15*, 6–52.

Cecchetti, S. (1999). Legal structure, financial structure, and the monetary policy transmission mechanism. *Economic Policy Review of the Federal Reserve Bank of New York, 5*, 9–28.

Cetorelli, N., & Goldberg, L. S. (2011). Global banks and international shock transmission: Evidence from the crisis. *IMF Economic Review, 59*, 41–76.

Cetorelli, N., & Goldberg, L. S. (2012). Banking globalization and monetary transmission. *Journal of Finance, 67*, 1811–1843.

Chatelain, J.-B., Ehrmann, M., Generale, A., Martínez-Pagés, J., Vermeulen, P., & Worms, A. (2003). Monetary policy transmission in the euro area: New evidence from micro data on firms and banks. *Journal of the European Economic Association, 1*, 731–742.

Chava, S., & Purnanandam, A. (2011). The effect of banking crisis on bank-dependent borrowers. *Journal of Financial Economics, 99*, 116–135.

Ciccarelli, M., Maddaloni, A., & Peydró, J.-L. (2015). *Trusting the bankers: A new look at the credit channel of monetary policy. Review of Economic Dynamics*: Forthcoming.

Claessens, S. (2014). *An overview of macroprudential policy tools*. Washington DC: International Monetary Fund.

De Bondt, G. J. (2000). *Financial structure and monetary transmission in Europe: A cross-country study*. Cheltenham: Edward Elgar.

de Haan, L. (2003). The impact of monetary policy on bank lending in the Netherlands. In I. Angeloni, A. K. Kashyap, & B. Mojon (Eds.), *Monetary policy transmission in the euro area*. Cambridge: Cambridge University Press.

De Santis, R. A., & Surico, P. (2013). Bank lending and monetary transmission in the euro area. *Economic Policy, 28*, 423–457.

Degryse, H., Kim, M., & Ongena, S. (2009). *Microeconometrics of banking: Methods, applications and results*. Oxford: Oxford University Press.

Delis, M. D., Hasan, I., & Mylonidis, N. (2011). *The risk-taking channel of monetary policy in the USA: Evidence from micro-level data*. London: Cass Business School.

Dell'Ariccia, G., Laeven, L., & Suarez, G. A. (2013). *Bank leverage and monetary policy's risk-taking channel: Evidence from the United States*. Washington DC: International Monetary Fund.

Dwarkasing, N. (2014). *Monetary conditions and bank loan risk taking: Evidence from the North and South Wales bank, 1881–1894*. Bonn: University of Bonn.

Ehrmann, M. (2005). Firm size and monetary policy transmission—evidence from German business survey data. In J.-E. Sturm & T. Wollmershäuser (Eds.), *IFO survey data in business cycle and monetary policy analysis*. Heidelberg: Physica Verlag HD.

Ehrmann, M., Gambacorta, L., Martinez-Pagés, J., Sevestre, P., & Worms, A. (2001). *Financial systems and the role of banks in monetary policy transmission in the euro area*. Frankfurt: European Central Bank.

Ehrmann, M., Gambacorta, L., Martinez-Pagés, J., Sevestre, P., & Worms, A. (2003). The effects of monetary policy in the euro area. *Oxford Review of Economic Policy, 19*, 58–72.

Ehrmann, M., & Worms, A. (2004). Bank networks and monetary policy transmission. *Journal of the European Economic Association, 2*, 1148–1171.

Ferri, G., Kalmi, P., & Kerola, E. (2014). Does bank ownership affect lending behavior? Evidence from the euro area. *Journal of Banking and Finance, 48*, 194–209.

Fungáčová, Z., Solanko, L., & Weill, L. (2014). Does competition influence the bank lending channel in the euro area? *Journal of Banking and Finance, 49*, 356–366.

Gaggl, P., & Valderrama, M. T. (2010). Does a low interest rate environment affect risk taking in Austria? *Monetary Policy and the Economy of the Oesterreichische Nationalbank, 32–48.*

Gambacorta, L. (2005). Inside the bank lending channel. *European Economic Review, 49*, 1737–1759.

Gambacorta, L., & Marques-Ibanez, D. (2011). The bank lending channel: Lessons from the crisis. *Economic Policy, 26*, 135–182.

Gan, J. (2007). The real effects of asset market bubbles: Loan- and firm-level evidence of a lending channel. *Review of Financial Studies, 20*, 1941–1973.

Garcia-Posada, M., & Marchetti, M. (2015). *The bank lending channel of unconventional monetary policy: The impact of the VlLTROs on credit supply in Spain*. Madrid: Banco de Espana.

Geršl, A., Jakubík, P., Kowalczyk, D., Ongena, S., & Peydró, J.-L. (2015). Monetary conditions and banks' behaviour in the Czech Republic. *Open Economies Review*, 1–39.

Gertler, M., & Gilchrist, S. (1993). The role of credit market imperfections in the monetary transmission mechanism: Arguments and evidence. *Scandinavian Journal of Economics, 95*, 43–64.

Gertler, M., & Gilchrist, S. (1994). Monetary policy, business cycles, and the behavior of small manufacturing firms. *Quarterly Journal of Economics, 109*, 309–340.

Giannone, D., Lenza, M., & Reichlin, L. (2010). Business cycles in the euro area. In A. Alesina & F. Giavazzi (Eds.), *Europe and the euro*. Cambridge MA: National Bureau of Economic Research.

Gilchrist, S. G., & E. Zakrajsek. (1995). The importance of credit for macroeconomic activity: Identification through heterogenity. In Joe Peek, and Erik S. Rosengren (Eds.), *Is bank lending important for the transmission of monetary policy?*(pp. 129–158). Boston: Federal Reserve Bank of Boston.

Goddard, J., Molyneux, P., Wilson, J. O. S., & Tavakoli, M. (2007). European banking: An overview. *Journal of Banking and Finance, 31*, 1911–1935.

Guiso, L., Kashyap, A. K., Panetta, F., & Terlizzese, D. (1999). Will a common European monetary policy have asymmetric effects? *FRB Chicago Economic Perspectives*, 56–75.

Gunji, H., Miura, K., & Yuan, Y. (2009). Bank competition and monetary policy. *Japan and the World Economy, 21*, 105–115.

Hachem, K. (2011). Relationship lending and the transmission of monetary policy. *Journal of Monetary Economics, 58*, 590–600.

Holod, D., & Peek, J. (2010). Capital constraints, asymmetric information, and internal capital markets in banking: New evidence. *Journal of Money, Credit and Banking, 42*, 879–906.

Holtemöller, O. (2003). Further VAR evidence for the effectiveness of a credit channel in Germany. *Applied Economics Quarterly, 49*, 359–381.

Hülsewig, O., Winker, P., & Worms, A. (2004). Bank lending in the transmission of monetary policy: A VECM analysis for Germany. *Jahrbuecher fuer Nationaloekonomie und Statistik, 224*, 511–529.

Ioannidou, V. P., Ongena, S., & Peydró, J.-L. (2015). Monetary policy, risk-taking and pricing: Evidence from a quasi-natural experiment. *Review of Finance, 19*, 95–144.

Jiménez, G., Ongena, S., Peydró, J.-L., & Saurina, J. (2012). Credit supply and monetary policy: Identifying the bank balance-sheet channel with loan applications. *American Economic Review, 102*, 2301–2326.

Jiménez, G., Ongena, S., Peydró, J.-L., & Saurina, J. (2014). Hazardous times for monetary policy: What do twenty-three million bank loans say about the effects of monetary policy on credit risk-taking? *Econometrica, 82*, 463–505.

Kakes, J., & Sturm, J.-E. (2002). Monetary policy and bank lending: Evidence from German banking groups. *Journal of Banking and Finance, 26*, 2077–2092.

Kashyap, A. K., & Stein, J. C. (1995). The impact of monetary policy on bank balance sheets. *Carnegie-Rochester Conference Series on Public Policy, 42*, 197–202.

Kashyap, A. K., & Stein, J. C. (2000). What do a million observations on banks say about the transmission of monetary policy? *American Economic Review, 90*, 407–428.

Kaufmann, S. (2003). The cross-sectional and the time dimension of the bank-lending channel: The Austrian Case. In I. Angeloni, A. K. Kashyap, & B. Mojon (Eds.), *Monetary policy transmission in the euro area*. Cambridge: Cambridge University Press.

Khan, A. K., & Khanna, T. (2012). Is faith a luxury for the rich? Examining the influence of religious beliefs on individual financial choices. In S. Nazim Ali (Ed.), *Building bridges across financial communities: The global financial crisis, social responsibility, and faith-based finance*. Cambridge MA: Harvard Law School.

Khwaja, A. I., & Mian, A. (2008). Tracing the impact of bank liquidity shocks: Evidence from an emerging market. *American Economic Review, 98*, 1413–1442.

Kishan, R. P., & Opiela, T. P. (2000). Bank size, bank capital, and the bank lending channel. *Journal of Money, Credit and Banking, 32*, 121–141.

Küppers, M. (2001). Curtailing the black box: German banking groups in the transmission of monetary policy. *European Economic Review, 45*, 1907–1930.

La Porta, R., Lopez-de-Silanes, F., Shleifer, A., & Vishny, R. W. (1997). Legal determinants of external finance. *Journal of Finance, 22*, 1131–1150.

La Porta, R., Lopez-de-Silanes, F., Shleifer, A., & Vishny, R. W. (1998). Law and finance. *Journal of Political Economy, 106*, 1113–1155.

Leroy, A. (2014). Competition and the bank lending channel in eurozone. *Journal of International Financial Markets, Institutions and Money, 31*, 296–314.

Loupias, C., Savignac, F., & Sevestre, P. (2003). Is there a bank lending channel in france? Evidence from bank panel data. In I. Angeloni, A. K. Kashyap, & B. Mojon (Eds.), *Monetary policy transmission in the euro area*. Cambridge: Cambridge University Press.

Loutskina, E., & Strahan, P. E. (2009). Securitization and the declining impact of bank finance on loan supply: Evidence from mortgage acceptance rates. *Journal of Finance, 64*, 861–889.

Maddaloni, A., & Peydró, J.-L. (2011). Bank risk-taking, securitization, supervision, and low interest rates: Evidence from euro-area and U.S. lending standards. *Review of Financial Studies, 24*, 2121–2165.

Maddaloni, A., & Peydró, J.-L. (2013). Monetary policy, macroprudential policy, and banking stability: Evidence from the euro area. *International Journal of Central Banking, 9*, 121–169.

Massa, M., & Zhang, L. (2013). Monetary policy and regional availability of debt financing. *Journal of Monetary Economics, 60*, 439–458.

Mora, N. (2013). The bank lending channel in a partially dollarized economy. *Journal of Applied Economics, 16*, 121–151.

Morais, B., Peydró, J.-L., & Ruiz, C. (2015). *The international bank lending channel of monetary policy rates and quantitative easing: Credit supply, reach-for-yield, and real effects*. Washington DC: World Bank.

Nelson, B., Gabor, P., & Konstantinos, T. (2015). *Do contractionary monetary policy shocks expand shadow banking?* London: Bank of England.

Oliner, S. D., & Rudebusch, G. D. (1995). Is there a bank credit channel for monetary policy. *Federal Reserve Bank of San Francisco Economic Review, 95*, 3–20.

Olivero, M. P., Li, Y., & Jeon, B. N. (2011a). Competition in banking and the lending channel: Evidence from bank-level data in Asia and Latin America. *Journal of Banking and Finance, 35*, 560–571.

Olivero, M. P., Li, Y., & Jeon, B. N. (2011b). Consolidation in banking and the lending channel of monetary transmission: Evidence from Asia and Latin America. *Journal of International Money and Finance, 30*, 1034–1054.

Ongena, S., Schindele, I., & Vonnák, D. (2015). *In lands of foreign currency credit, bank lending channels run through? The effects of monetary policy at home and abroad on the currency denomination of the supply of credit*. Zurich: University of Zurich.

Ongena, S., & Smith, D. C. (2000). Bank relationships: A review. In P. Harker & S. A. Zenios (Eds.), *The performance of financial institutions*. London: Cambridge University Press.

Paligorova, T., & Santos, J. A. C. (2013). *Monetary policy and bank risk-taking: Evidence from the corporate loan market.* Ottawa: Bank of Canada.

Peek, J., & Rosengren, E. S. (1995). Bank lending and the transmission of monetary policy. In Peek J. and E.S. Rosengren (eds.), *Is Bank Lending Important for the Transmission of Monetary Policy?, Federal Reserve Bank of Boston Conference Series, 39*, 47–68.

Peek, J., & Rosengren, E. S. (1997). The international transmission of financial shocks: The case of Japan. *American Economic Review, 87*, 495–505.

Peek, J., & Rosengren, E. S. (2000). Collateral damage: Effects of the Japanese bank crisis on real activity in the United States. *American Economic Review, 90*, 30–45.

Rajan, R. G. (2006). Has finance made the world riskier? *European Financial Management, 12*, 499–533.

Sander, H., & Kleimeier, S. (2004). Convergence in euro-zone retail banking? What interest rate pass-through tells us about monetary policy transmission, competition and integration. *Journal of International Money and Finance, 23*, 461–492.

Schnabl, P. (2012). The international transmission of bank liquidity shocks: Evidence from an emerging market. *Journal of Finance, 67*, 897–932.

Stein, J. C. (2013). *Overheating in credit markets: Origins, measurement, and policy responses.* St. Louis: Federal Reserve Bank of St. Louis.

Taylor, J. B. (2008). *The financial crisis and the policy responses: An empirical analysis of what went wrong.* Ottawa: Bank of Canada.

Temesvary, J., Ongena, S., & Owen, A. L. (2015). *A global lending channel unplugged? Does U.S. monetary policy affect cross-border and affiliate lending by global U.S. banks?* Clinton NY: Hamilton College.

Van den Heuvel, S. J. (2002). Does bank capital matter for monetary transmission? *FRB NY Economic Policy Review, 8*, 259–265.

von Kalckreuth, U. (2003). Investment and monetary transmission in Germany: A microeconometric approach. In I. Angeloni, A. K. Kashyap, & B. Mojon (Eds.), *Monetary policy transmission in the euro area.* Cambridge: Cambridge University Press.

Zaheer, S., Ongena, S., & van Wijnbergen, S. J. G. (2013). The transmission of monetary policy through conventional and Islamic banks. *International Journal of Central Banking, 8*, 175–224.

16

The Interplay Between Banks and Markets: Supervisory Stress Test Results and Investor Reactions

Giovanni Petrella and Andrea Resti

Introduction

Relative to non-financial companies, banks have a higher share of assets that suffer from a strong degree of opaqueness: loans are informationally sensitive and hard to evaluate for outsiders, while liquid assets can easily be sold, and this makes the information in the financial statements rapidly obsolete. As a result, banks may be harder to assess, for outsiders, than firms from other industries.

A proof of bank opacity is the fact that market prices react to supervisory announcements and inspections (Berger and Davies 1998; Flannery and Houston 1999; Jordan 2000), meaning that investors are not able to anticipate all relevant information. Also, split ratings tend to occur more often for banks than for non-bank companies (Morgan 2002; Iannotta 2006), suggesting that the former are harder to assess, due to stronger opaqueness. Regressions of bank stock returns on market indices show higher R-squares (Haggard and

Helpful suggestions by Thorsten Beck, Barbara Casu, Andrea Enria and Mario Quagliariello are gratefully acknowledged. All errors remain our own.

G. Petrella (✉)
Faculty of Banking, Finance and Insurance, Catholic University, Milan, Italy
e-mail: giovanni.petrella@unicatt.it

A. Resti
Department of Finance, Bocconi University, Milan, Italy
e-mail: andrea.resti@unibocconi.it

T. Beck, B. Casu (eds.), *The Palgrave Handbook of European Banking*,
DOI 10.1057/978-1-137-52144-6_16

Howe 2007); this means that firm-specific information plays a less significant role for bank stock prices because it is harder to extract than for non-banks.

Several supervisory tools are put in place, including deposit insurance and risk-based capital requirements, to prevent lenders and depositors from being scared off by bank opacity. As opacity tends to increase in times of crisis (Flannery et al. 2010), additional mechanisms are needed to reassure the market during a financial turmoil.

This was possibly the main motivation behind the supervisory stress tests carried out in the European Union (EU) (2009, 2010, 2011 and 2014),[1] and in the USA (2009, 2012, 2013, 2014 and 2015).[2] By disclosing information on each bank's strengths and vulnerabilities, the supervisors aimed at reducing market uncertainty, stabilizing stock prices and preventing panic.[3] The idea was that investors, when presented with a signal of each bank's reliability (based on an exercise that is comparable across banks and somewhat "certified" by the supervisors' intervention), would consider banks less opaque, and therefore better differentiate among them when setting individual risk premiums.

When bank supervisors run a stress test exercise, they may hope to be able to convince investors that the stability of the covered institutions is better than expected, thereby restoring market confidence and putting back stock prices onto an ascending trend. Still, even a stress test round leading to worse-than-expected results may prove beneficial for long-run financial stability. This is due to several reasons.

Firstly, transparency reduces the costs associated to uncertainty. In fact, the value assigned by investors to a bank depends on two key variables: expected future cash flows associated with net earnings and the discount rate at which the present value of those earnings is computed. Worse-than-expected results may induce investors to cut their forecasts for future cash flows, but the certification provided by supervisors, by dissipating uncertainty, may lead to a drop in the discount rate which more than offsets the lower expected earnings. This will send a positive signal to investors and calm down panic.

Secondly, as shown by Spargoli (2012), there may be cases where releasing results for weaker banks is socially optimal, either because supervisors can

---

[1] Committee of European Banking Supervisors (2009, 2010), European Banking Authority (2011, 2014).

[2] Federal Reserve (2009b, 2011, 2012, 2013a, 2014a, 2015a). As mentioned in the section "Institutional Framework", a stress test exercise was carried out by the Federal Reserve (Fed) also in 2011, but results were not publicly disclosed.

[3] To quote the Federal Reserve report whereby the 2009 stress test results were released, "the decision to depart from the standard practice of keeping examination information confidential stemmed from the belief that greater clarity [...] will make the exercise more effective at reducing uncertainty and restoring confidence in our financial institutions" (Federal Reserve 2009a, page 1).

force them to raise new capital (Shapiro and Skeie 2012) or because the social costs of a downsizing are lower than those of a default.

Thirdly, the disclosure of worse-than-expected results may also be used by supervisors as a reputation-building tool (Kreps and Wilson 1982) to signal their independence, although in the short term they may choose to withhold such information to prevent contagion (Shapiro and Skeie 2012; White and Morrison 2010). By showing that they are ready to disclose "bad" results, supervisors will forestall regulatory capture and induce banks to define their risk-taking approach accordingly.[4, 5]

This chapter provides an overview of European bank stress tests, one of the supervisory tools used to provide investors with in-depth information on the risks and profit drivers of big lenders. We review previous evidence on stress test exercises run by the Federal Reserve and by European supervisors (including the European Banking Authority (EBA) and the European Central Bank (ECB)), discussing the key differences in stress test programmes across the two areas, in terms of institutional designs, scenario assumptions and disclosure procedures. The interplay between banks and markets is analysed by looking at investor reactions upon the announcement of stress test results. The chapter also includes a comparison between stress tests in Europe and in the USA, and some brief concluding remarks.

Stress Test Exercises in Europe

Institutional Framework

Table 16.1 shows the main characteristics of the supervisory stress test exercises performed at a pan-European level and highlights the amount of information disclosed to investors.[6] While the first European stress test in 2010 only released a few key figures for each bank, the 2011 and 2014 tests were significantly more comprehensive, as they provided several thousand data items for each bank; these included a breakdown of sovereign bonds and other

[4] By regulatory capture (Laffont and Tirole 1991) we mean the risk that the special interest of a regulated entity (here, the bank) might influence the regulation or the supervision in any of its form.

[5] Additionally, as argued by (D'Cruz and Crippa 2012), releasing bad results helps focus industry attention on the need for better stress testing tools and principles, thereby improving the quality of future bank management.

[6] Stress testing exercises have also been carried out, with different scope and depth, by most national authorities in the European Union (EU). See Quagliariello (2009) for a complete picture of macro and micro stress testing approaches in many European countries.

Table 16.1 Stress test exercises in the EU

Exercise	Announcement date	Results release date	Banks covered	Number of released data items per bank	Minimum capital target(s)	Capital shortfalls found
2009 EU Stress Testing Exercise by the Committee of European Banking Supervisors	12 May 2009	1 October 2009	22 cross border banks, covering 60% of the assets in the EU banking system	N/A	No explicit capital target	No explicit shortfall measure
2010 EU Stress Testing Exercise by the Committee of European Banking Supervisors	2 December 2009	23 July 2010	91 banks, covering 65% of the assets in the EU banking system and at least 50% for each country	27	Tier 1 at 6%	7 banks (+17 "near fail"), €3.5 billion
2011 EU Stress Test by the European Banking Authority	12 January 2011	15 July 2011	90 banks, covering 65% of the assets in the EU banking system and at least 50% for each country	3456	Core Tier 1 at 5%	8 banks (+20 "near fail"), €2.5 billion
2014 EU Stress Test by the European Banking Authority	October 2013	26 October 2014	123 banks, covering 70% of the assets in the EU banking system and at least 50% for each country	About 12,000	Core Tier 1 at 5.5%	14 banks (+24 "near fail"), €9.5 billion
2016 EU Stress Test by the European Banking Authority		Early third quarter 2016	53 banking groups, covering approximately 70% of the assets in the EU banking system	Not available	None	No pass/ fail outcome

credit exposures by country and duration bands.[7] A similar level of detail is expected from the 2016 exercise, whose results will be disclosed after this book has gone to press.

Before discussing the peculiarities of the various exercises, we provide a short introduction to the different authorities that cooperate in carrying out stress tests in Europe, including their institutional mandates and interactions.

The Evolution of the Supervisory Framework

For the sake of clarity, we identify three different time windows to describe the evolution of the European institutional architecture on bank supervision when the various stress tests took place. These are:

- Before 2011, when national authorities were fully in charge and only a mild pan-European coordination mechanism was present.
- Between 2011 and November 2014, when pan-European coordination was based solely on the EBA, an agency of the European Commission endowed with some specific binding powers.
- After November 2014, when large banks in the Eurozone started to be directly supervised by a specialized division of the ECB.

Each of those three stages is briefly discussed below.

Before 2011, bank supervision was carried out exclusively at the national level. Member states in the EU had different authorities in place (National Competent Authorities (NCAs)), leading to different local implementations of the common rules on bank prudential requirements that were set by the EU's Capital Requirements Directives (CRDs)—including the original Capital Adequacy Directive and several subsequent amendments.[8] Since 2004, a forum for discussion and benchmarking across NCAs was provided by the Committee

[7] As most banks did not have an exposure to all countries and duration bands, many data points in the 2011 European stress test exercise were filled with zeroes (about 73% of the total); note, however, that those were meaningful zeroes, informing that a given bank was not exposed to that specific combination of duration and nationality. Another 5.3% of the data points included missing values; most of them were, again, "meaningful missings", for example, to indicate that banks did not expect any state aid in the following months.

[8] The 1999 Basel I capital requirements were regulated by the EU through the so-called Capital Adequacy Directive (Directive 93/6/EEC) issued in 1993. The first single Banking Directive (2000/12/EC), unifying previous regulatory texts, was passed in 2000 to improve the clarity and consistency of the EU banking legislation. The 2004 "Basel II" Accord was implemented in 2006 by two directives recasting the Capital Adequacy Directive (Directive 2006/49/EC) and the Banking Directive (Directive 2006/48/EC). Following the global financial crisis, prudential rules on banks were further tightened through Directive 2009/111/EC (CRD2) and Directive 2010/76/EU (CRD3) (focusing on capital requirements for the trading book and remuneration policies). The 2010 Basel III reform was transposed into European law

of European Banking Supervisors (CEBS), an independent advisory group including senior representatives of supervisory authorities and central banks. CEBS advised the European Commission on draft measures related to bank supervision and contributed to the consistent implementation of EU banking regulations (e.g., by promoting benchmarking exercises or information exchanges), although it had no binding powers vis-à-vis the national authorities.

On 1 January 2011, CEBS was replaced by the EBA, a regulatory agency tasked with the drafting of Binding Technical Standards (BTS) and Guidelines and the creation of a level playing field across national jurisdiction by means of a "Single Rulebook" of harmonized prudential rules. EBA also promotes supervisory convergence across NCAs, ensuring that rules are not only written, but also applied in a homogeneous way. The EBA Founding Regulation (1093/2010 EU) assigns some specific powers to the Authority, including consumer protection, the ability to issue decisions in emergency situations, and promoting and coordinating stress test exercises. Accordingly, since 2011, bank supervision in the EU became a two-layer architecture, with EBA coordinating national authorities, although with virtually no direct powers towards supervised institutions. Under its first chairperson, Andrea Enria, EBA has promoted an impressive list of initiatives aimed at tightening supervisory consistency across countries, including a common supervisory reporting framework (COREP), supervisory colleges to facilitate dialogue among NCAs for multinational banks, issuing recommendations aimed at achieving a fast and homogeneous repair, and deleveraging of bank balance sheets after the Eurozone sovereign crisis. However, the Eurozone crisis prompted calls for tighter integration among bank supervisors in the European Monetary Union; this led the European Council to an agreement, in June 2012, on entrusting the ECB with some direct oversight powers for large institutions in the Eurozone (the so-called Single Supervisory Mechanism (SSM), which became fully operational in November 2014).

Since November 2014, European bank supervision can be thought of as a three-layer architecture (see Fig. 16.1), with the EBA retaining its role to issue BTS and promote supervisory convergence, and Competent Authorities (now including NCAs and the SSM) supervising banks and other financial institutions. In turn, the SSM is a two-layer mechanism were an ad hoc division of the ECB is tasked with the direct supervision of the Eurozone's most significant banking groups (approximately 120) and the coordination of the operating practices followed by NCAs in the supervision of less significant

---

in 2013 through the so-called CRD4 package (including the Capital Requirements Regulation 575/2013 EU (CRR) and the Capital Requirements Directive 2013/36/EU (CRD4)).

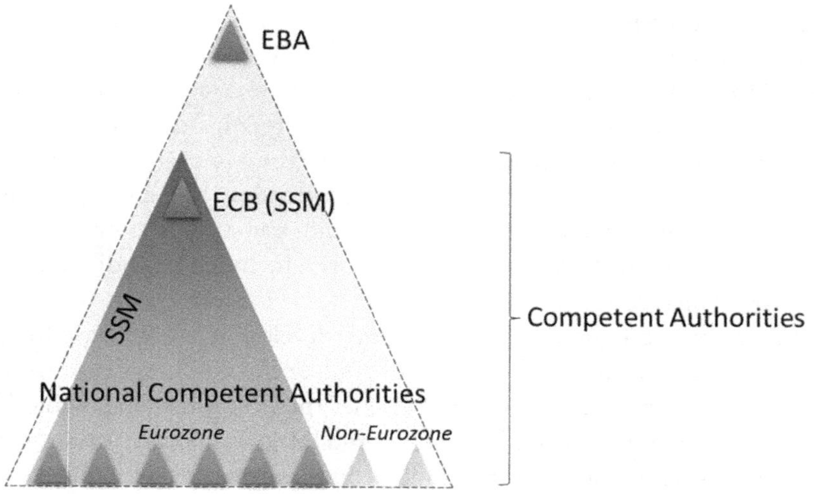

Fig. 16.1 Bank supervision in the European Union after November 2014: a three-layer architecture

institutions (Wiggins et al. 2014). In the supervision of large banks, the SSM operates through Joint Supervisory Teams (JSTs), staffed with experts provided by both the ECB and the national authorities. Concerning the figure it could be argued that, although the EBA certainly represents the top layer from a geographical point of view, its coordination powers are limited compared to those granted to the ECB (which, unlike EBA, may operate directly with supervised entities, as well as coordinate national authorities participating in the SSM), although they are crucial to preserve the consistency of supervisory practices across the whole of the EU.

The 2014 stress test exercise—completed in October 2014—was essential in facilitating the transition towards the new SSM-based supervisory mechanism; while it was performed for all EU countries, it was also used as a "due diligence" tool for the ECB, to carry out a comprehensive assessment of all large Eurozone groups that it was about to supervise directly.

The CEBS Stress Tests (2009 and 2010)

Although stress-testing experiments had already been conducted internally by large banks (and some coordinated exercises had been promoted by some national authorities) the first pan-European stress tests were coordinated by the CEBS in 2009 and 2010.

The 2009 exercise was embryonic in nature, with only 22 covered banks, no explicit capital target and no official list of "failing" banks (since the assessment of individual results and remediation plans was left entirely to national supervisors). The whole process took place very quickly, taking less than five months (including August) to complete. The main goal of the exercise was to reassure investors that large European lenders had enough capital in place to withstand an adverse macro-economic scenario. The final statement released by CEBS on 1 October 2009, however, included no individual assessments and failed to restore market confidence. Furthermore, it proved over-optimistic, in the light of the subsequent developments, at least for some large lenders that would suffer large losses due to the looming Eurozone crisis. The exercise was carried out by NCAs under their responsibility, while CEBS subsequently aggregated results across national jurisdictions. In an attempt to increase cross-country comparability, common macro-economic scenarios were agreed upon, as well as shared process guidelines.

The second exercise was announced on 2 December 2009 by the Committee for Economic and Financial Affairs of the European Council, asking CEBS to provide "insights as to the strength of banking systems' balance sheets, particularly the quality of assets and the adequacy of capital" (ECOFIN 2009, page 2). The new exercise, based on a set of commonly agreed macro-economic scenarios developed by CEBS, NCAs, the ECB and the European Commission, started in March 2010 and was finalized on 23 July. The focus of the simulation exercise (involving 91 participating banks, 65% of the assets in the EU banking system and at least 50% for each country) was on credit and market risk. It was conceived as a "bottom-up" exercise, where each bank would use its own internal risk parameters and portfolios to assess the impact of the commonly agreed scenarios. On 27 June, the European Council decided that results for individual banks would be publicly disclosed, increasing transparency in an attempt to prompt market scrutiny and restore credibility.

Under the adverse scenario, seven banks failed the 6% Tier 1 capital threshold set by CEBS, with an overall shortfall of 3.5 billion—this included five Spanish institutions (Unnim, Diada, Espiga, Banca Cívica and Cajasur), one in Germany (Hypo Real Estate) and one in Greece (ATEBank). As noted by the media,[9] the results were hailed as positive by national supervisors in Spain ("The exercise confirms that the Spanish banking system is sound, and in turn substantiates the savings bank restructuring and recapitalization process pursued over the past twelve months by the Bank of Spain"), Germany ("The

[9] See BBC News (2010), reporting statements by the Bank of Spain, Bafin, the Greek Finance Ministry and others.

German banking system has shown itself to be robust and proved its resilience even under very pessimistic assumptions") and Greece ("the Greek banking system can cope even in the extreme conditions of a stress test"). Yet market analysts were sceptical and argued that the downturn scenario was too mild to provide an adequate benchmark; furthermore, as individual results included less than 30 data points for each surveyed bank, it was impossible for outsiders to assess the impact of different macro-economic assumptions.

The EBA Stress Tests (2011, 2014 and 2016)

The 2011 stress test was the first exercise carried out by the newly established EBA and covered 90 banks accounting for more than 65% of the total assets in the EU banking system.[10] The underlying macro-economic assumptions included a baseline and an adverse scenario designed by the ECB, the European Commission and the European Systemic Risk Board. The adverse scenario featured a 15% drop in equity prices, a moderate gross domestic product (GDP) contraction, a generalized increase in risk-free rates and credit spreads for private and sovereign borrowers. Following the bottom-up approach, banks were requested to use their internal models to generate values for balance-sheet items and profit and loss (P&L) results. In doing so, however, they had to follow a detailed methodology dictated by EBA. Firm-specific assumptions, as well as results generated by individual banks, were subsequently cross-checked by national supervisors and by EBA, and further calibrated when necessary.

The stress test was based on a "static balance sheet" assumption, meaning that banks were supposed to remain unchanged in size and assets/liabilities mix (and were not allowed to deploy any actions to react to the adverse scenario).

On 15 July 2011, individual bank results were disclosed to the public through a Microsoft Excel template including data on risk-weighted assets (RWAs) and own funds, key P&L figures, details on provisions, loss rates and coverage ratios, and a breakdown of credit exposures by geographic area and counterparty type (with sovereign exposures sorted by duration bucket). Banks were deemed to have failed the test if high-quality capital ("Core Tier 1 capital") fell below 5% of RWAs under the adverse scenario. This was the case for 20 banks (with a combined capital shortfall of 26.8 billion euros);

---

[10] A variable number of banks were included for each country, starting from the largest one and stopping when at least 50% of the total assets were covered. National supervisors could add further banks to the sample (e.g., Spain included several other minor banks).

however, once capital actions already implemented in the first four months of 2011 were taken into account, the number of failing banks would fall to eight, with an overall shortfall of 2.5 billion euros.

On the disclosure date, more than 3000 detailed data items were provided for each institution; furthermore, Excel templates were distributed one week ahead of the final results, to allow market participants enough time to design proprietary computations and formulas. This enabled bank analysts to "perform their own stress tests" in case they wanted to simulate the impact of more conservative macro-economic scenarios than the ones designed by the supervisors. With remedial actions still in the hands of national authorities, the EBA chose to leverage on transparency to increase the credibility of the stress test exercise.

Before performing the next round of stress tests, in 2014, the EBA worked extensively with NCAs to establish a common set of definitions for capital-related securities and non-performing exposures, to ensure that results could be meaningfully compared across jurisdictions. The 2014 exercise covered 123 banking groups (including the EU and Norway), accounting for more than 70% of total banking assets (Crisan 2014). The EBA developed the common methodology, while the ESRB and the European Commission provided the underlying macro-economic scenarios. Compared to the 2011 exercise, a number of improvements were made to the stress testing methodology: firstly, the simulation window was extended from two to three years, making it possible to fully appreciate the impact of a negative macro-economic background; secondly, while the banks' internal models remained the core of the bottom-up methodology, their results were constrained with a set of caps and floors to improve comparability; and thirdly, the end-2013 data used as a starting point for the stress test was subjected to asset quality reviews by NCAs. This was also the case for the SSM, which—ahead of its formal start in November 2014—performed a combined exercise known as the "comprehensive assessment", including a supervisory analysis of the banks' strengths and weaknesses, an asset quality review focusing on securities and loans (drilling down to individual files on a sample basis) and the EBA stress test.

Competent Authorities were also in charge with quality assurance for stress test data and remedial actions following from capital shortfalls. Banks falling below a 5.5% threshold for Common Equity Tier 1 ("CET1") capital under the adverse scenario (8% in the baseline scenario) were deemed to have failed the test.

As results were announced on 26 October 2014, 24 banks were found to be below the defined thresholds, leading to an aggregate capital shortfall of 24.6 billion euros. However, once the additional capital raised in 2014 was taken into account, the number fell to 14 (with a 9.5 billion euros shortfall). In addition to a press release reporting capital ratios on a bank-by-bank basis, the EBA published granular data—including up to 12,000 items for each participating institution—on its website, where interactive tools were made available to replicate results for individual banks and countries. As in the 2011 stress test, special emphasis was given to sovereign debt holdings, including derivatives exposures and hedges, with detailed figures for duration bands and individual countries.

A new round of stress tests is planned by EBA for 2016, with results to be disclosed by the beginning of the third quarter. Notwithstanding a reduction in the number of institutions participating in the exercise (53 banks, 39 of which falling under the SSM), the coverage is still expected to be close to 70% of the EU banking sector. As for the previous round, a baseline and an adverse scenario will be used to perform a three-year simulation starting from year-end 2015 data; as in the past, supervisors will follow a "constrained bottom-up" approach, where banks will be required to project the impact of the proposed scenarios, subject to strict quantitative constraints and a common methodology. Remarkably, however, the EBA has decided that no minimum capital threshold will be set, leading to a binary pass/fail signal. Instead, stress test results will be used by NCAs as part of the so-called Supervisory Review and Evaluation Processes (SREP), an assessment of the individual banks' strengths and weaknesses in terms of capital resources, liquidity, funding sources, internal governance and business models. This will mark a break with the past, when "losers" could be easily identified as results were announced. Similarly, no bank will be "certified" to have passed the test; while reducing reputational risk for supervisors, this will motivate market participants to scrutinize individual bank data to elaborate an informed opinion on each institution's stability and soundness. Two innovations of the 2016 exercise will be the inclusion of foreign currency-denominated lending and conduct risk among the risks to be tested in the exercise. Regarding the latter, however, the lack of commonly agreed definitions and models may make it hard for EBA to ensure homogeneity across the assessments produced by different banks using their proprietary data and models.

Market Reaction

The market impact of stress tests has been investigated by several research papers; while many refer to the US context (see the section "Market Reaction"), several studies assess the European case with a view to analysing how stress test exercises were received by market participants and whether they succeeded in "reassuring" investors.

Blundell-Wignall and Slovik (2010) look at the 2010 EU stress test with a special focus on the treatment of sovereign debt. In the 2010 simulation, government bonds were subject to a haircut only when held in the trading portfolio, while no credit-related losses were imposed on sovereign exposures in the banking book.[11] They show that 83% of the sovereign debt held by EU banks at the end of 2009 was instead held in the banking book, and conclude that this could explain why the encouraging results of the 2010 stress test failed to reassure the market.[12]

Beltratti (2011) looks at the 2011 EU stress tests and argues that they provided relevant information to the market since their main outcome (i.e., the capital shortfall associated with individual banks) could not be forecast by combining variables that were already known to investors.

Cardinali and Nordmark (2011) study the stock market reaction to the 2010 and 2011 EU stress tests by looking at cumulative abnormal returns for tested and untested banks.[13] Their main findings are the following. Firstly, the 2010 results were relatively uninformative to investors. Secondly, the announcement of the methodology to be used in 2011 triggered negative CARs for stress-tested banks while non-tested institutions were roughly unaffected.[14] Thirdly, no major difference occurred between Portugal, Ireland, Italy, Greece and Spain (PIIGS) and non-PIIGS banks.

Bischof and Daske (2012) look at the 2011 EU stress test focusing on information on sovereign credit exposures. They find that banks participating in the stress test increased their subsequent voluntary disclosure on credit risk towards Eurozone peripheral countries, while experiencing a decrease in the equity bid-ask spread and an increase in liquidity. Furthermore, banks with

[11] The trading portfolio, or trading book, consists of financial assets held at fair value and includes the bank's own position in financial instruments for trading purposes (i.e., aimed at generating profits in the short run by buying and selling securities) as well as derivatives held to hedge that position. The banking book includes all other exposures (often long term) which are not held in the trading book.

[12] To some extent, their critique also applies to the 2011 exercise, as again no proper haircut was imposed on sovereign bonds outside the trading book; however, the credibility of the results was improved by the fact that losses were imposed also on sovereign exposures held in the banking book, although indirectly (through a floor on the "expected loss rate" applied to exposures towards banks and sovereigns located in different countries).

[13] The paper was written prior to the release of the 2011 results. Accordingly, it only focuses on the market reaction occurring when the stress test was announced and on days when clarifications were issued by EBA.

[14] This included the decision to focus on a "core Tier 1" target of 5% which was considerably more conservative than the one used in the past. Core Tier 1 refers to high-quality capital, such as common equity and government-sponsored hybrid securities, net of a number of deductions to make the final result robust and comparable across different banks and countries.

the most significant capital shortfalls were more active in reducing sovereign risk exposure between December 2010 and September 2011.

Ellahie (2012) also investigates the 2011 EU stress test to examine whether the disclosure of results lead to a change in information asymmetry (with the latter proxied by the bid-ask spread for stocks and bonds, as well as by the implied volatility of equity options). The paper finds no decline in information asymmetry. However, sovereign exposures disclosed in the stress test prove informative in predicting the direction of changes in bid-ask spreads, Credit Default Swaps (CDS) spreads and future stock returns for tested banks.

It should be noticed that—when evaluating market reactions to stress tests—equity prices, bond prices and CDS spreads provide different insights, as they capture different components of a bank's profit distribution.

On the one hand, stock-market reactions are usually dominated by dilution concerns, meaning that incumbent shareholders fear that supervisors may impose a capital increase, leading to lower equity values. This leads to a price drop for banks that emerge as a candidate for rights issues. In fact, investors anticipate that, due to regulatory pressure, such banks will not be able to optimize market timing and may be forced to press ahead with recapitalization plans even in an unfavourable market environment.

On the other hand, CDS spreads and bond prices may react favourably (with the former getting thinner and the latter increasing) as investors are reassured either by the clean bill of health provided by supervisors to banks passing the test, or by the prospect that equity will soon be restored to safer levels for failing institutions. Concerning the latter, however, new rules on bail-in (since 2016) may lead to different outcomes, over time, if investors believe that senior bonds may be devalued or forcedly converted into equity by resolution authorities.

While neither Bischof and Daske nor Ellahie run a proper event study on the 2011 European stress test exercise, two further studies use that technique to assess whether and how it affected bank stock prices: Candelon and Sy (2015) and Petrella and Resti (2013).

In the first study the authors note that stress tests have been investigated by two strands of literature: one strand examines the role of macro-prudential stress tests in curbing bank opaqueness, while another strand of literature uses case studies to take a closer look at the governance of stress tests. Building on this observation, the authors put together these two strands of literature and use event study methods to compare all the macro-prudential US- and EU-wide stress tests from 2009 to 2013. They first compare the market impact of the stress tests in the EU and the USA over time and across different exercises, and then use the results of the event studies to compare the governance of the stress tests. They look at the overall sign of the market reaction when the results of the 2011 stress test were released and find a statistically significant negative impact on bank stocks, also for banks that were not part of the stress test exercise. In comparison with other stress tests, the authors also note that the 2011 EU exercise is the only EU-wide stress test that resulted in a significantly negative market reaction. They conclude that, based on the comparison of past stress test exercises, the qualitative aspects of the governance of stress tests can matter more for stock market participants than technical elements, such as the level of the minimum capital adequacy threshold or the extent of data disclosure.

Petrella and Resti (2013) look instead at bank-by-bank reactions. Their analysis shows that the test's results were considered relevant by investors. The market did not simply look at the detailed historical data which was released after the tests, but also attached considerable importance to variables measuring each bank's vulnerability to the simulated downturn scenario (see Table 16.2). The latter include information on sovereign debt holdings. The study also finds that the market is not able to anticipate the test results and this is consistent with the idea of greater bank opaqueness prior to the disclosure of the stress test results. Overall, the empirical analysis shows that stress tests produce valuable information for market participants and can play a role in mitigating bank opacity.

Several studies have examined the 2014 SSM-led comprehensive assessment, some of which were openly critical of the process adopted and the underlying assumptions.

This is the case, for example, of Arnould and Dehmej (2015), who focus on several aspects, which in their opinion undermine the credibility of the (mostly positive) outcome announced by the EBA and the ECB. First, they argue that the stress test was based on mild scenarios, which were not conservative enough to ensure that the banks' resilience had been adequately verified. Second, they complain that the threshold between "passing" and "failing" banks had been set in terms of the risk-weighted capital ratio, a measure disregarded by many market analysts as it is biased by the differences among the average risk weights reported by individual banks. The authors argue that one should instead look at the banks' unweighted leverage ratio, which is not affected by internal risk measures and therefore leads to more homogeneous results for banks using internal models vis-à-vis institutions relying on the standardized approach. After setting the minimum threshold at 3% and 4%, respectively, the stressed leverage ratio would lead to a greater capital shortfall than its weighted counterpart—namely, the shortfall would increase from about 6% to approximately 11.5% for banks using Basel's standardized

Table 16.2 Cumulative abnormal returns on the results' announcement date for the 2011 stress test and the following two trading days

	Average cumulative abnormal return	*P*-value associated with CAR = 0 or difference between CARs = 0
(a) CARs for stress-tested banks and a control sample of non-tested banks		
Non-Tested Banks	0.1%	0.97
Tested Banks	1.1%	0.13
Non-Tested–Tested	−1.0%	0.06
(b) Results stratified by several financial indicators based on the stress test results		
Core Tier 1 ratio at the end of the simulation period in the downturn scenario		
Bottom 20%	−0.2%	0.89
Top 20%	2.5%	0.09
Bottom 20%–Top 20%	−2.7%	0.02
Decrease in core Tier 1 ratio at the end of the simulation period in the downturn scenario		
Bottom 20%	2.2%	0.08
Top 20%	0.2%	1.00
Bottom 20%–Top 20%	2.0%	0.04
Increase in risk-weighted assets at the end of the simulation period in the downturn scenario		
Bottom 20%	2.5%	0.02
Top 20%	0.7%	0.59
Bottom 20%–Top 20%	1.8%	0.04
Increase in coverage ratio for credit exposures (due to write-downs and provisions) at the end of the simulation period in the downturn scenario		
Bottom 20%	3.1%	0.01
Top 20%	0.0%	0.90
Bottom 20%–Top 20%	3.2%	0.01
Estimated loss on sovereign bonds issued by PIIGS* (set to 25% of current value) over Core Tier 1 at end 2010		
Bottom 20%	3.0%	0.01
Top 20%	−0.2%	0.98
Bottom 20%–Top 20%	3.2%	0.00
Coverage ratio for defaulted exposures at the end of the simulation period in the downturn scenario		
Bottom 20%	0.5%	0.61
Top 20%	2.4%	0.01
Bottom 20%–Top 20%	−2.0%	0.11

Source: (Petrella and Resti 2013)

* PIIGS refers to Portugal, Ireland, Greece, Italy and Spain.

approach, and from 5% to 12.5% for institutions using internal models for regulatory purposes.

Furthermore, the risk-weighted capital ratios used in the exercise were "transitional" ones, and did not account for the full implementation of the Basel III accord, which is bound to put further pressure onto the banks' capital adequacy measures. Additionally, notwithstanding the progress made by the SSM and EBA towards a common set of definitions for key balance sheet items, the exercise suffered from a lack of comparability across banks and jurisdictions. This is due to different risk measurement models, as well as to supervisory discretions applied by national regulators (including in the key area of provisions and non-performing loans). Finally, as the EU implementation of the Basel accords involves a zero-risk weight coefficient for most European Treasury bonds, the stress test under-estimated the actual risks owing to sovereign exposures by several tens of billions.

According to the Centre for European Policy Studies (De Groen 2014), a Brussels-based think-tank, the comprehensive assessment results were reported in a deliberately optimistic way. Using the detailed results of the stress test, CEPS estimates that approximately 23 banks (instead of 14, as indicated by the SSM after accounting for capital measures that were fully implemented before October 2014) fail to meet the minimum capital ratio under the adverse stress test scenario. The number would further increase to 47 if one were to look at the CET1 capital ratio assuming full implementation of the Basel III standards and of the unweighted leverage ratio.

Barucci et al. (2014) argue that the comprehensive assessment was mainly concentrated on the traditional loan book and somewhat overlooked other bank financial assets (including e.g., structured securities). They are also sceptical of the way RWAs were computed by individual banks leveraging on internal rating-based models.

Steffen (2014) criticizes the outcome of the SSM comprehensive assessment by benchmarking it against alternative models based entirely on public domain data. This includes the so-called "MES" ("marginal expected shortfall") approach by Acharya and Steffen (2013) and the "SRISK" measure by Acharya et al. (2014). Using the latter methodology and making reference to the results in Acharya and Steffen (2014), they conclude that large capital shortfalls exist, not only in countries such as Belgium, Cyprus and Greece, but also in "core Europe" jurisdictions such as France and Germany (above all if one looks at market-based measures of equity, as opposed to book measures). Consistent with Arnould and Dehmej (2015), the study also highlights three intrinsic weaknesses of the stress test exercise. Firstly, credible fiscal backstops were unclear, and this may have induced supervisors to "water down" the adverse scenario. Secondly, the use of RWAs in the target capital ratios may have left banks with too much leverage in terms of unweighted assets. Thirdly, the zero-risk weights attached to sovereign bonds may have induced banks to increase such exposures, exacerbating systemic risk.

In line with such criticisms, Sahin and de Haan (2015) find that financial markets apparently did not react to the publication of the comprehensive assessment results. Using a standard event study methodology, they find that stock prices and CDS spreads generally did not show any significant reaction; this is also the case for banks that were found to suffer from a capital shortfall.

Stress Test Exercises in the USA

Institutional Framework

In the USA the first supervisory stress tests were conducted in 2009 when the banking industry was heavily hit by the financial crisis. The exercise, named the Supervisory Capital Assessment Program (SCAP), was intended to assess whether the largest US banks had sufficient capital to withstand a worse-than-anticipated macro-economic scenario. In early 2011 the SCAP evolved into the Comprehensive Capital Analysis and Review (CCAR), a supervisory programme to assess capital positions and capital planning processes of the largest US banks. The CCAR was meant to integrate the stress testing activity into the ongoing supervision of large banks (Hirtle and Lehnert 2014). In 2013, the implementation of the Dodd-Frank Act provisions required both large bank holding companies (BHCs) and the Federal Reserve to conduct annual stress tests (the Dodd-Frank Act Stress Test (DFAST)) under macro-economic scenarios provided by the Fed. The DFAST results must be publicly disclosed annually by the BHCs and the Fed (Deng et al. 2015). The CCAR and DFAST programmes are closely linked but distinct,[15] as they pursue different objectives.

Table 16.3 summarizes the main features of the supervisory stress test exercises performed in the USA. Like Table 16.1, it highlights the amount of information disclosed to investors. While the first DFAST exercise in 2013 concerned only the major US banks, the scope of the 2014 DFAST was sig-

[15] The section of the Fed website devoted to “Stress Tests and Capital Planning” has two different subsections, one for the CCAR (http://www.federalreserve.gov/bankinforeg/ccar.htm) and a second for the DFAST programme run by the Fed (http://www.federalreserve.gov/bankinforeg/dfa-stress-tests.htm).

Table 16.3 Stress test exercises in the USA

Exercise	Announcement date	Results release date	Banks covered	Number of released data items per bank	Minimum capital target(s)	Capital shortfalls found
2009 Supervisory Capital Assessment Program (SCAP) by Federal Reserve, FDIC, OCC, OTS	10 February 2009	7 May 2009	19 domestic bank holding companies (BHCs)	17	Common Tier 1 at 4%, Tier 1 at 6%	10 banks, USD 75 billion
2011 Comprehensive Capital Analysis and Review (CCAR) by Federal Reserve	17 November 2010	18 March 2011	19 domestic BHCs participating in the 2009 SCAP	0		
2012 CCAR by Federal Reserve	22 November 2011	13 March 2012	19 domestic BHCs participating in the 2009 SCAP	41	Common Tier 1 at 5%, leverage at 3–4%	4 banks (shortfall not disclosed)
2013 DFAST by Federal Reserve	9 November 2012	14 March 2013	18 domestic BHCs	37	Common Tier 1 at 5%, leverage at 3–4%	1 bank (disclosed Tier 1 gap)
2014 DFAST by Federal Reserve	1 November 2013	20 March 2014	30 domestic BHCs	43	Common Tier 1 at 5%, leverage at 3–4%	1 bank (disclosed Tier 1 gap)
2015 DFAST by Federal Reserve	23 October 2014	5 March 2015	31 domestic BHCs	43	Common Tier 1 at 5%, leverage at 3–4%	None

nificantly larger than the previous one, as the total assets threshold for participating banks decreased from US$100 billion to US$50 billion.

In the rest of this section, we first describe the SCAP, and then turn to the DFAST and CCAR programmes.[16]

The Supervisory Capital Assessment Program (SCAP)

The SCAP consisted in the stress testing of the 19 largest US-owned BHCs, representing about two-thirds of the assets of the US banking system. It was launched in February 2009, a period of significant turmoil for the US banking industry, following the bankruptcy of Lehman Brothers in September 2008. The SCAP was designed to measure what additional capital buffer, if any, each bank would need to stand an unexpected economic slowdown. Banks needing to increase their capital as a result of the SCAP had one month to design a plan to raise additional equity, which had to be implemented by early November 2009. The ultimate goal of the programme was to reduce uncertainty and promote confidence in individual banks and in the banking system as a whole.

The SCAP stress tests assessed the impact of two hypothetical macroeconomic scenarios on each bank's net income and capital over a two-year horizon (until the end of 2010) based on data as of 31 December 2008. The "baseline scenario" reflected consensus expectations for the economy, while the "more adverse" one assumed a deeper and longer recession.

Capital ratios had to stay above minimum target levels defined for the more adverse scenario: 4% for the Common Equity Tier 1 ratio and 6% for the Tier 1 Capital ratio. Banks falling below such targets were required to raise enough capital to eliminate the shortfall. It is worth noting that the shortfalls were expressed in dollar terms. This means that banks with a capital shortfall in the SCAP had to raise a given dollar amount of capital, and could not meet the required target capital ratios by reducing lending or otherwise shrinking their balance sheets (Hirtle and Lehnert 2014).

The results for each BHC were publicly disclosed, along with a description of the methods used to generate its projections. The SCAP identified a capital shortfall for 10 out of 19 participating banks, totalling US$185 billion. After taking into account asset sales and capital restructurings (e.g., conversions of preferred shares into common equity) that had taken place during the stress test exercise, the total fell to US$75 billion.

[16] The material presented in this section is based on Federal Reserve (2009b, c, 2011, 2013a, b, 2014a, b, 2015a, b).

The SCAP was part of the Capital Assistance Program (CAP) designed by the US Treasury (US Treasury Department 2009), whereby the latter provided a capital backstop to all Qualifying Financial Institutions (QFIs, i.e., banks with RWAs above US$100 billion). This meant that QFIs that were unable to raise capital from market investors could issue common equity to the US government, under a bridge deal that was to be replaced by private capital in the future. Only one bank out of ten with a capital shortfall, Ally Financial, used the backstop. The other nine, as well as lenders without a SCAP shortfall, raised US$100 billion in common equity in the months following the stress test results. Although most banks did not use the CAP, the availability of government backstop proved a key factor in improving market sentiment about the future prospects of the US banking industry.

The SCAP was an innovation in the supervisory practice along several dimensions (Hirtle and Lehnert 2014). Firstly, static capital ratios were complemented by forward-looking simulations; this provided the Federal Reserve with a tool to address the shortcomings of standard regulatory capital measures. Secondly, the disclosure of firm-specific results (which the Federal Reserve saw as critical to achieving the programme's goal of reducing uncertainty and enhancing confidence in US financial institutions) marked a significant change with the past, when individual supervisory assessments were treated as confidential. Thirdly, the US Treasury capital backstop proved crucial in restoring investors' confidence.

The Supervision of Large US Banks After the SCAP

Following the SCAP in 2009, capital planning and stress testing became two key components of the US Federal Reserve's supervisory framework for large banks. The SCAP evolved first into the 2011 CCAR and then into the 2013 DFAST. The CCAR evaluates the adequacy of a BHC's capital levels and capital planning process (including distributions, such as dividend payments and common stock repurchases) and applies to all "large banks" (i.e., BHCs with US$50 billion or more in total consolidated assets). The DFAST requires the Fed and the individual banks to perform stress testing exercises in a forward-looking manner. Both are briefly discussed below; for the sake of clarity we start with the DFAST (in reverse chronological order), since some parts of it are used as an input in the CCAR process.

The Dodd-Frank Act Stress Testing (DFAST) Program

Under the Dodd-Frank Act (DFA), the Federal Reserve is required to conduct an annual stress test of large banks (i.e., BHCs with total assets above US$50 billion, also known as "covered banks"). Next to this "supervisory stress test", the DFA also requires covered banks to perform their own "company-run stress tests"[17] and report the results to the Fed twice a year.

In the supervisory stress tests, the Federal Reserve projects balance sheet, RWAs, net income and capital over a nine-quarter "planning horizon", on the basis of three underlying macro-economic scenarios (baseline, adverse and severely adverse). As concerns capital actions, the Fed uses a standard set of assumptions dictated by the DFA. Dividends are assumed to equal each bank's average dividend (in dollars) over the last four historical quarters, and new stock issuance and repurchases are assumed to be zero. This assumption is intended to be neutral across banks in the sense that it reflects the historical behaviour of the bank, rather than imposing supervisory assumptions about how the bank might behave under different scenarios (Hirtle and Lehnert 2014).[18]

Supervisory stress test adopt a common framework for all banks participating to the exercise. This implies the following trade-off: the results are comparable across banks but they suffer from a "one-size-fits-all" bias, as they do not take into account bank-specific conditions in the modelling assumptions that lead to the stress test results.

Bank-specific features may be accounted for in the company-run stress tests, which, however, use the same planning horizon, scenario and capital action assumptions as the supervisory ones, to enhance comparability. Both tests are intended to inform the supervisors, the bank's management and the general public about the potential effects on the bank's capital adequacy of a hypothetical set of adverse economic conditions. To ensure that this information is readily available, the DFA requires each bank and the Fed to disclose a summary of their stress test results. The disclosure covers both current and

---

[17] Under the Dodd-Frank Act, all financial companies with more than US$10 billion in total assets are required to conduct a company-run stress test on an annual basis. Additionally, covered companies are subject to a second company-run stress test each year, and to the supervisory stress test.

[18] For bank holding companies with more than US$10 billion but less than US$50 billion in total consolidated assets, a new rule adopted by the Fed on 25 November 2015—effective on 1 January 1 2016—eliminates the assumption of fixed dividends in company-run stress tests and requires to incorporate reasonable assumptions regarding payments of dividends consistent with internal capital needs and projections. This change does not apply to large banks as they are subject to the capital plan rule, and are required to incorporate their planned capital actions in their post-stress capital analysis. Thus, large banks can already incorporate more realistic dividend assumptions into their capital plans (see the section "The Comprehensive Capital Analysis and Review (CCAR) Program").

projected items, including capital ratios, RWAs, future loan losses by loan type, revenues, net income and other comprehensive income for a total of 43 data items for each bank (see Table 16.3).

Banks are required to take the results of the DFAST into account in their capital planning decisions. No specific supervisory actions are associated to the results of the stress tests (Hirtle and Lehnert 2014). The key contribution of the DFAST relies on disclosure, as it conveys to the public information about the capital strength of individual banks and the banking systems as a whole.

The Comprehensive Capital Analysis and Review (CCAR) Program

The Federal Reserve conducted the first CCAR in early 2011. In November 2011, it adopted the capital plan rule, which requires large banks to submit annual capital plans to the Fed for review, as well as company-run stress test results.

Capital plans describe the bank's internal processes for assessing capital adequacy, the policies governing capital actions (such as common stock issuance, dividends and share repurchases) and all planned capital actions over a nine-quarter horizon.

Company-run stress tests are based on the three supervisory scenarios used in the DFAST, as well as on company-specific scenarios.[19] The Fed projects post-stress capital ratios for each bank over the nine-quarter planning horizon based on the bank's planned capital actions. Using the loss and revenue estimates from the bank's stress tests, the Federal Reserve assesses whether the bank has enough capital to continue operations in times of economic and financial distress, and whether it has robust, forward-looking capital-planning processes.

As a result of this analysis, the Federal Reserve may choose to object to the bank's capital plans. If it does so, the bank may not make any capital distribution. Such objection may be made on quantitative and/or qualitative grounds (Hirtle and Lehnert 2014). The former relate to the bank's current capital position, relative to its business focus, portfolio, and risk exposure; in particular, the bank should be able to demonstrate that its Tier 1 common ratio would remain above 5% under all scenarios.[20] The latter involve a negative assessment of the

[19] Each bank participating to the CCAR is also required to use at least one stress scenario and a baseline scenario developed by itself.

[20] For bank holding companies that have total consolidated assets of US$50 billion or more, a new rule adopted by the Fed on 25 November 2015—effective on 1 January 1 2016—removes the Tier 1 common capital ratio requirement. According to this requirement, a large bank should demonstrate its ability to maintain a Tier 1 common capital ratio of 5% under expected and stressed scenarios. The Fed introduced the Tier 1 common capital ratio requirement in 2009 as part of the SCAP. At that time, the it had not yet

bank's internal capital planning processes, including stress testing models, data and assumptions, as well as the governance schemes supporting the bank's decisions about dividend payments, share repurchases and share issuance.

The results of the CCAR are publicly disclosed. The disclosure includes each bank's capital ratios under the adverse and severely adverse scenarios, as defined by the Federal Reserve, and whether its capital plan was objected (in which case, a brief motivation is also disclosed). The provides each bank with an opportunity to adjust its planned capital distributions after receiving its preliminary estimates of the bank's post-stress capital ratios. For banks submitting adjusted capital actions, the Federal Reserve also discloses the post-stress results incorporating the original capital actions in addition to the adjusted ones.

A Comparison of DFAST and CCAR

Both DFAST and CCAR programmes involve the projection of a bank's capital ratios in a stressed scenario; furthermore, pre-tax net income simulated in the DFA supervisory stress tests is a direct input to the CCAR post-stress capital analysis. Still, important differences exist between the two programmes, which mainly relate to the *capital action assumptions* used to estimate post-stress capital levels and ratios.

In the DFAST, the Federal Reserve uses a standardized set of capital action assumptions that are set by the DFA: dividend payments are unchanged from the previous year; stock repurchases and capital increases are set to zero. Conversely, the CCAR uses the individual bank's planned capital actions.[21] As a result, the post-stress capital ratios of the DFA supervisory stress tests can differ significantly from those of the CCAR. For example, the latter could be higher if a BHC plans a dividend cut.

To sum up, the CCAR is a broad supervisory exercise who leads to an evaluation of the bank's capital plans. It includes a stress test, but is a comprehensive assessment of the overall bank's capital adequacy. By contrast, the main outcome of the Dodd-Frank stress tests programmes—both company-run and Fed-generated—are the stress test results themselves.

---

adopted a minimum *common equity* capital requirement. In 2013, it revised its regulatory capital rules and introduced—effective on 1 January 2015—a minimum *common equity* Tier 1 capital requirement of 4.5% of risk-weighted assets (RWAs).

[21] This means that the CCAR post-stress capital analysis assumes that the bank continues to pay dividends according to the original capital plans, as in a baseline scenario, even if market conditions severely deteriorate. Hirtle and Lehnert (2014) refer to this feature as a "stringent test of capital actions".

Market Reaction

In this section, we review the evidence reported by recent papers that investigate the market impact of US stress tests. We include studies that look at DFAST, SCAP and CCAR.

(Hirtle et al. 2009) provide a *qualitative* assessment of how the 2009 SCAP exercise was received by US investors; they find that the process was perceived as rigorous and thorough, transparency was appreciated, the aggregate estimated capital shortfall was seen as reasonable and consistent with other analysts' forecasts, and the variation across firms was in line with market expectations. In short, the SCAP was appreciated by investors because it did not add any major unforeseen element to the market's information set; the main piece of news was that the supervisors agreed with market perceptions.[22]

A *quantitative* assessment of the SCAP's market impact is provided by Peristiani et al. (2010) using a standard event study methodology. Several dates are investigated, including the SCAP's initial announcement, the release of some important clarifications regarding its methodology and policy implications (in terms of mandatory capital injections and possible government interventions), and of course the final disclosure of bank-by-bank figures. Results show that the market only reacted to policy-related clarifications and to the publication of stress test results. Investors were able to anticipate what banks would be required to raise extra capital; accordingly, when actual results were released, the impact on stock prices was not driven by the "gross" capital shortfall for each bank, but rather by its "unanticipated" component (i.e., net of market expectations). Overall, the stress test exercise was informative to investors in the sense that it produced information about the size of the capital gap.

Neretina et al. (2014) investigate the effects of the announcement and the disclosure of several events related to the US banking stress tests. Specifically, they examine the effects of the disclosure of clarification, methodology, and results of the US stress tests on banks' equity prices, credit risk, systematic risk, and systemic risk in 2009–13. They consider both DFAST and CCAR programmes and find only weak evidence that stress tests after 2009 affected the stock price of large US banks. In contrast, CDS spreads declined in response to the disclosure of stress test results. They also find that bank systematic risk, as measured by betas, declined in some years after the publication of stress test

[22] However, Hirtle, Schuermann, and Stiroh also note that "whether the reception would have been positive if [...] there had been a negative "surprise" about a firm or a group of firms, remains open to debate" (page 11).

results. They find evidence that the decline in betas is partly driven by a reduction in the correlation of the banks' stocks with the market, and interpret these findings as a decrease in systemic risk. Overall, the evidence provided by Neretina et al. (2014) suggests that stress tests mainly affect systemic risk.

Flannery et al. (2015) claim that previous studies that investigate the market reaction to the disclosure of stress tests results found mixed evidence because of inappropriate assumptions embedded in standard event study methodology. In particular, the standard approach assumes that all treated firms react in the same direction, so a zero mean abnormal return implies no effect on treated firms. However, the authors point out that the average return for stress-tested banks could be zero for two quite different reasons: either the abnormal return is very small for all firms, or the returns are large in absolute value, but positive for some banks and negative for others. For this reason they consider the absolute value of the cumulative abnormal returns (|CAR|), instead of the simple CAR, and find that the |CAR| of stress-tested banks averages almost 3% around stress test announcement dates. The authors also study the behaviour of the trading volume and find that cumulative abnormal trading volumes are more than one percentage point higher than a market model would predict. Absolute value abnormal returns and volumes are higher for more levered and riskier firms. This paper also explores several theoretical hypotheses outlined in Goldstein and Sapra (2013) with respect to the possibility that the disclosure of stress test results might drive out private information producers (such as stock analysts), but find no evidence of negative welfare costs associated with the disclosure of stress test results. In short, the authors find evidence that the CCAR and DFAST produce information about the stress-tested firms as well as other, non-stress-tested banks.

Flannery et al. (2015) report evidence on the behaviour of the absolute cumulative abnormal return (|CAR|), cumulative abnormal volume (|CAV|) and the absolute value cumulative abnormal CDS spread change (|CACDS|) for stressed banks in the three-day window $[t-1, t+1]$ around the disclosure date of the results of nine stress test exercises. An interesting finding is that the size of the impact of the publication of stress tests results in the USA decreased over time.[23] This pattern can be attributed to the highly deteriorated market conditions at the time the 2009 SCAP results were released, coupled with the news about the availability of government backstop.

[23] Consistently with the evidence reported by Flannery et al. (2015), Candelon and Sy (2015) find that the 2009 US stress test had a large positive outcome, whereas subsequent US stress test exercises had lower impact on the market valuation of stressed banks as time went by.

Bird et al. (2015) study the disclosure of stress tests results to investigate the possibility that the Fed might bias the reported results of the stress tests in order to promote desirable market outcomes. They examine this hypothesis by looking at the effects of the disclosure of the CCAR results from 2012 to 2015. The authors first develop a structural model to estimate the 'quality' of the bank and then look at the capital market responses to CCAR reports to uncover the regulator's propensity to bias reports for each bank individually. When the Fed makes an announcement, the market updates its beliefs about bank quality; if the market reaction is weak relative to what the CCAR report would suggest, then they infer that the market perceives a Fed's bias on in the direction of the report (e.g., the report is very positive on the bank prospects but the market reaction is not as positive). Summing up, the authors find that the Fed biased upwards reported capital ratios to prop up large banks, but downwards to discipline poorly capitalized banks. Such biases have real effects on bank behaviour: propped-up banks are less likely to subsequently improve their capital ratios by raising equity or cutting dividends. This evidence shows that regulators face a trade-off between disciplining banks and promoting short-term stability.

The Key Differences Between Stress Tests in Europe and in the USA

As noted by Haben et al. (2013), several differences exist between the European stress tests and their US counterparts.

To begin with, the former were developed within a quickly developing and largely untested institutional framework, where increasing shares of sovereignty were being transferred to European bodies but national authorities remained in charge of the key supervisory functions (e.g., concerning the capital actions that were to be implemented by failing banks). Conversely, the US stress tests benefited from an institutional framework already in place, including a common national jurisdiction, a single supervisory decision-making body, a common backstop and a single communication channel.

Secondly, a higher degree of market concentration exists in the USA, making it easier for supervisors to focus their resources on a relatively small set of institutions, while covering a reasonably high share of the US banking industry. On the contrary, most European banks are still "national champions" with a large presence in their domestic market and a limited activity in other EU countries; this means that a comparatively higher number of lenders have to be tested in order to achieve an adequate coverage in terms of bank assets.

Thirdly, while the CAP provided the Federal Reserve with a credible way out, in case the 2009 stress tests had seen a large number of failing institutions, European supervisors could not rely on a common backstop or on clearly defined burden sharing mechanism. The lack of such a credible and uniform safety net undermined the ability of the European stress tests to restore market confidence, much more than "technical" aspects like the complexity or (insufficient) conservativism of the underlying macro-economic scenarios.

Finally, the European stress tests were different from the US ones in that they involved the disclosure of an extremely rich information flow concerning participating banks. While the data items released by the Federal Reserve came in tens, the EBA kept disclosing several thousands of detailed figures for each covered bank, using web-based tools to enable investors to quickly gain control of the data and use them for their own analyses.

The four aspects outlined above (institutional framework, market concentration, public backstops and data flows) are briefly discussed in the remainder of this section.

The Institutional Architecture

The US stress test exercises were mostly aimed at large BHCs.[24] Accordingly, they were consistently managed by the Fed throughout the whole process—from experiment design to scenario development; from the validation of data to the disclosure of results. In doing so, the Federal Reserve was adequately staffed and could rely on a stable supervisory framework, in terms of both rules and competent institutions.

By contrast, the institutional architecture underlying stress tests in the EU was a patchwork of different bodies and supervisory cultures. Supra-national authorities were charged with several key aspects of the exercise (with the EBA setting up the overall methodology and releasing the final outcome, and the European Commission, Central Bank and Systemic Risk Board designing the macro-economic scenarios). Nevertheless, NCAs were in charge of several key tasks (such as supervising the models used by banks to run simulations) and national governments were responsible for providing extraordinary financial support to failing banks.

EBA's ability to effectively coordinate Europe-wide stress tests was constrained not only by its legal mandate (which does not entrust it with direct bank supervision, and accordingly requires it to act via NCAs), but also by

[24] Starting in 2014 mid-sized banks (with US$10–50 billion in assets) were also required to conduct DFA stress tests. See also the section "The Dodd-Frank Act Stress Testing (DFAST) Program".

its size and staff levels. When the 2011 test was launched, the EBA—with a headcount of approximately 60—was bound to rely heavily on resources provided by national supervisors, including seconded experts who kept reporting to their original employers. This represented a significant weakness of the European stress tests, given that each participating country had local rules in place (including accounting standards and national discretions in the implementation of the Basel accords), which would have called for a strong coordination mechanism to ensure that the tests be run on a level playing field. In 2014 the advent of the SSM, while providing additional resources devoted to the coordination of national supervisory practices, also introduced an additional layer of complexity in the design and management of the European stress tests.

A significant aspect of the institutional landscape relates to accounting and fiscal rules; such legal provisions are partly national in nature, and may significantly affect the way loans and other risky assets are reported in a bank's financial statement used as the starting point for supervisory stress tests. In fact, one big difference between Europe and the USA is the higher consistency in accounting standards and practices enjoyed by the latter, relative to the limited integration observed in the EU. Loan loss provisions provide a good example: although in principle all large banks in the EU are bound to abide by the same set of accounting standards (namely, IAS39 on credit loss impairment, to be replaced by IFRS 9 since 2018), national implementations differ markedly. This could be due, for instance, to fiscal reasons: write-downs on non-performing loans are not fully deductible in some European countries, providing a further incentive towards forbearance and limited recognition of expected losses. Due to this situation, prior to the 2014 stress tests, the SSM engaged in the above-mentioned asset quality review and imposed some quality assurance rules, aiming—inter alia—at narrowing the gap across accounting practices followed by individual banks and countries. In this sense, the latest European stress test, although it remained a bottom-up exercise in line with previous rounds,[25] also had some top-down flavour, in that it allowed supervisors to discipline the banks' impairment policies by imposing a set of simplified common standards.

Market Concentration and Coverage

The US and the European banking industry differ in size and concentration levels. In the case of the former, bank total assets amount to approximately 80% of GDP, as opposed to about 350% for Europe. While being larger, the

[25] European Central Bank (2014).

EU's banking system is also more fragmented, with the top-ten institutions accounting for slightly more than one-third of the total, as opposed to 55% in the USA (Liikanen et al. 2012). This reflects the fact that European banks are still, to a large extent, "national champions", competing with a handful of fully integrated cross-border groups.[26] While the banking union could set an appropriate landscape for closer integration to happen, the increased segmentation in wholesale funding along national borders may slow down the process, making the benefits of multinational development harder to achieve.

Accordingly, when designing stress test exercises, European supervisors have been forced to include a significantly higher number of institutions, ranging from 91 in 2010 (when individual results were released for the first time by CEBS) to 123 in 2014. This follows from the fact that the sample used in the stress test had to be meaningful not only for the EU as a whole, but also for individual countries; accordingly, in the exercises carried out by EBA, at least 50% *of each national banking system* had to be covered by the participating banks. This wider coverage (compared with 20–30 institutions tested by US supervisors) has meant several consequences for the design and implementation of the stress tests.

On the one hand, European supervisors had to rely on a "bottom-up" exercise, where company-run stress tests are the only source of information on how the adverse scenarios would affect each bank's risks, profitability and capital. No top-down, supervisory stress tests can be deployed to serve as a benchmark for the banks' estimates, as the high number of participating institutions makes it virtually impossible to develop an adequate knowledge of each lender's portfolios, risk parameters, IT systems and business models.

On the other hand, company-run stress tests are harder to discipline, since they entail a huge variety of assumptions, market environments, econometric models and stress testing techniques. Supervisors can benchmark results submitted by different banks, isolate outliers and ask for additional clarifications when necessary. They can also impose caps and floors whenever they feel that too much discretion is being used by individual banks. But it is intrinsically hard for them to "do the math" behind each and every model, and override the findings reported by participating institutions.

This is not to say that bank-generated results represent a black box for European supervisors. The latter's ability to cross-check the figures submitted by individual banks has certainly increased over time, also thanks to the work done by the EBA to promote a common set of definitions for key bank balance

[26] On a purely national level, most European financial systems would be more concentrated than the US. Stress tests, however, are a pan-European phenomenon and require a Europe-wide perspective.

sheet items. Additional progress will soon be made, as the ECB promotes closer convergence among national discretions in the Eurozone. Still, stress tests are a moving target and new risks keep surfacing over time, for which there exists no agreed methodology—for example, while the focus in 2011 was on sovereign exposures, conduct risk is likely to play a pivotal role in the 2016 European exercise. As banks develop new models to deal with previously overlooked types of risk, having to deal with a high number of participating institutions makes it harder for supervisors to check how those models are built and used for stress testing purposes.

It is hard to tell whether regulators—as methodologies and involved institutions keep changing over time—will insist on ensuring consistency across subsequent exercises, or rather give priority to the refinement of the stress tests' design, in order to include new risks as they emerge. While investors may wish the structure of the tests to remain stable over time, to ensure they can readily decode new information as it becomes available, supervisors may opt for a more flexible layout, to capture relevant areas of concerns as they emerge and improve accountability towards governments, consumers and other relevant stakeholders.

The Credibility of the Fiscal Backstop

As discussed earlier in this chapter, ahead of the 2009 SCAP the US Treasury had made it clear that it would wholeheartedly stay behind the stress-test results, mandating under-capitalized banks to quickly raise extra funds and providing those funds when needed (that is, assuring investors that state money would be available in case of need).

Conversely, as noted by (Onado and Resti 2011), European governments did not reach an agreement on how to provide additional capital to failing banks, and could not provide investors with any precise commitment. Such a lack of coordination was especially unfortunate in 2011, when investors were shying away from banks because of the sovereign debt crisis, which had spread to large Eurozone countries such as Italy and Spain. In fact, if those countries had chosen to recapitalize weak banks, bailout costs would have increased government deficits and further dented confidence in those' countries creditworthiness.

Even for nations with stronger government budgets, however, the European rules on state aid may make it harder to convince investors that failing banks will be bailed out. In fact, any public rescue plan for ailing companies (including banks) has to be approved by DG COMP (the European Commission's

Directorate General for Competition), to ensure that state aids do not unduly distort competition. In order to give its consent to public backstops, DG COMP requires that an adequate "burden sharing" exist between the government and private investors. This means that equity and subordinated debt instruments may have to be written off before new capital can be provided by the Treasury. This is hardly the type of governmental support that can reassure financial markets.

The Different Degree of Detail in the Disclosed Results

As noted by Schuermann (2012), there are very large differences in disclosure between the USA and Europe. The former, while adjusting disclosure levels over time (with the 2011 CCAR representing the most "opaque" example, where only the macro-scenario was published, with no bank-level results), have consistently adopted a level of detail that is considerably lower than the one chosen by European authorities. The announcement of the US stress test results typically involves bank-level loss rates and dollar losses by major regulatory asset categories, including the main loan types and securities portfolios. On the other hand, European stress tests involved the delivery of thousands of data items of each bank, and the use of data in electronic, downloadable form.

The effect of stress tests on bank opaqueness and risk premiums clearly depends on the type of data that is conveyed to the market when results are released. Indeed, several authors have discussed what information can, or should, be disclosed. Goldstein and Sapra (2013) suggest that the disclosure of detailed information (e.g., on portfolio holdings) is preferable to that of aggregate information (like the overall capital shortfall) because the former not only provides market participants with the outcome of the stress test ("pass or fail"), but also allows them to assess its causes. Additionally, detailed information reduces the incentive and scope for individual banks to window-dress results.

Gick and Pausch (2012) use a theoretical model to show that a banking authority can optimally supervise the banking sector by committing to disclose both the stress test results and the underlying methodology. This result is derived through a disclosure game where supervisors deliver superior information to investors by sequentially disclosing the two types of information:[27] the methodology (i.e., the signal-generating process) and the stress test results

[27] "Superior information" here means information that persuades investors toward a socially optimal trade-off between individual risk-bearing and the provision of liquidity to the economy. See Gick and Pausch (2012) for details.

(i.e., the signal). This is consistent with the actual behaviour of supervisors both in the USA and in Europe, where the announcement of a new stress test round usually contains a commitment to disclose both the methodology and the results.

Spargoli (2012) argues that the socially optimal level of disclosure chosen by supervisors depends on their ability to force a recapitalization on weaker ("bad") banks. His argument goes like this: when a negative outcome is released, investors force bad banks either to downsize (that is, to shed assets) or to raise new capital. During a banking crisis the cost of new bank capital is very high, so downsizing may prove the only viable alternative. However, downsizing usually involves shedding assets with a positive net present value, so its social costs may exceed those of a default. If the supervisor can credibly threaten a "forced" recapitalization at a dilution cost higher than the market's, then the bad banks will recapitalize and thus avoid the value destruction implied by downsizing. If, instead, the supervisor cannot credibly commit to forced recapitalization (and if downsizing costs are greater than default costs), then it may be optimal not to disclose bad results (or to calibrate the stress test's adverse scenario mildly enough to ensure that only major weaknesses emerge for bad banks).

Schuermann (2012, 2014) suggests that the type of information disclosed with stress tests should depend on the current state of the banking industry. If investors are panicking and do not trust bank balance sheets because they are overly opaque, then stress tests should provide clarity by disclosing bank-specific details, allowing trust to be regained. Once trust is re-established, however, the cost-benefit of stress testing disclosures may tip away from bank-specific towards more aggregated information. This would leave adequate incentives for market participants to produce private information and trading on it, with all the downstream benefits of fully informative prices and market discipline.

Schuermann's dichotomy may help explain the difference between the more "secretive" US stress tests and the information-rich exercises carried out in Europe. When the US CCAR was carried out in 2011, large banks had already successfully tapped the market for more than US$300 billion in new equity, and the stock prices of listed lenders had risen considerably since the end of the global financial crisis of 2007–8. Accordingly, there was no reason to flood investors with details on individual banks. On the other hand, EBA had to pursue an increased level of disclosure in 2011 and 2014 to contrast a long-lasting crisis that prevented market prices from embedding all relevant information, helping markets overcome a phase of acute bank opaqueness.

Another explanation for the different degree of detail pursued by US and European supervisors may follow from the fact that the latter had to use transparency as a substitute for capital. Mandatory recapitalization measures were still in the hands of national supervisors and several cash-constrained governments were unwilling, or unable, to guarantee an unconditional public support to ailing banks ahead of the stress test exercise. This reduced the scope for the ECB (and the EBA) to impose a conservative, potentially disruptive adverse scenario, as the stress test results could not contemplate a large-scale capital shortfall that the European authorities could not handle in an ordered and coordinated way. Accordingly, transparency was the only way to shore up the credibility of what could be seen as a "weak" exercise (or, to put it more gently, a "mildly conservative" one). European supervisors strived to produce a full set of detailed results, as a way to compensate the hesitations of European politicians.

Concluding Remarks

This chapter presents an overview of stress tests, an oversight tool used to provide supervisors and investors with in-depth information on bank's strengths and vulnerabilities. By disclosing bank-specific data on balance sheet items and capital ratios under different macro-economic scenarios, including a stressed one, stress tests aim at reducing market uncertainty, as investors receive a "certified" signal about capital adequacy, based on a forward-looking approach.

The disclosure of bank-specific stress test results marks a significant change, with respect to previous supervisory practice, both in Europe and in the USA, where supervisory assessments of individual banks were traditionally treated as confidential. By contrast, supervisors increased transparency is an attempt to reassure investors, but also to prompt *market scrutiny* on the lenders risks, capitalization and liquidity. If such assumptions are well-grounded, then the financial markets (including markets for equity, bonds and/or credit default swaps) will appropriately react when stress test results are released. In fact, the use of forward-looking measures is in line with the standard discounted cash flow approach to firm valuation: by disclosing new information on a bank's income potential and vulnerability, the supervisors will help market participants to update their beliefs on future cash flows and risk-adjusted discount factors, triggering—if needed—a price adjustment process. That said, the actual price reaction will of course depend on the outcome of the stress test, the market's degree of informational efficiency and the credibility and transparency of the stress test exercise.

Four factors play a crucial role in the design of supervisory stress tests (see also Breuer 2014):

1. The definition of the macro-economic scenarios is particularly significant—namely, the degree of conservativism of the adverse scenario obviously affects the market reaction upon the stress test disclosure. The exercises carried out by CEBS in 2009 and 2010, which failed to reassure investors as the macro-economic assumptions were deemed too mild by banking experts, are instructive in this respect. Another key issue is whether or not the adverse scenario should be homogeneous across institutions: while making reference to a single scenario may (in principle) increase the consistency of the results, it could also be that, for some lenders, the adverse scenario represents, in fact, a favourable one. This could be the case, for instance, for banks headquartered in countries characterized by a high credit rating, which would benefit from increased funding opportunities due to the "flight to quality" of investors located in less reliable jurisdictions.

2. The results of the stress test depend crucially on the assumption used to simulate the evolution of the banks' balance sheets over time. The so-called "static balance sheet" approach (whereby the size and asset mix of a lender have to stay unchanged throughout the simulation period) may increase the comparability across firms; however, it unrealistically assumes that banks would not react to the stressed scenario, which may prove detrimental for the stress test's credibility.

3. When stress tests are run at a time of financial turmoil, the market reaction to the results is strongly affected by the availability of a strong, credible, unconditional public backstop.

4. The information set disclosed by supervisors may differ considerably. By comparing US- and EU-wide stress tests, one can see that it may range from less than 20 data points to more than 10,000. Such a difference is striking. It is unclear whether a richer information flow is worth its costs. Indeed, some empirical studies have shown that, when more details are disclosed, market participants do use the information provided to assess risk dimensions that would otherwise remain obscure.

In addition to being a prerequisite for market discipline, stress tests also represent a direct input to the supervisory process. However, no mechanical implications can be drawn, in terms of supervisory actions, from stress test results. Indeed, the latter are to be complemented by other relevant qualitative and quantitative information, to gain a comprehensive insight of each bank's soundness, financial viability, profitability and business model. Supervisors seem to have become increasingly aware about this on both sides of the Atlantic. In the USA, stress test results have become part of a more ambitious review process, which extends to the banks' internal capital planning processes and capital governance schemes. In the EU, stress tests have now abandoned the traditional pass/fail paradigm and are being conceived as part of a Supervisory Review and Evaluation Process (SREP), whereby NCAs (including the SSM) assess bank capital alongside liquidity, risk governance and long-term profitability.

Overall, stress tests seem to have come of age. They are no more an "emergency weapon" to be quickly deployed under exceptional circumstances, but rather have become a standard oversight tool that must be effectively coordinated with other supervisory actions and processes. They are no miracle cure that can offset the shortcomings of risk-weighted capital ratios, but can help in enhancing market discipline and promoting a stronger awareness about bank weaknesses and vulnerabilities that cannot be captured by standard, backward-looking supervisory tools.

References

Acharya, V. V., & Steffen, S. (2013). Analyzing systemic risk of the european banking sector. In J.-P. Fouque & J. A. Langsam (Eds.), *Handbook on systemic risk* (pp. 247–282). Cambridge: Cambridge University Press http://ebooks.cambridge.org/ref/id/CBO9781139151184A080.

Acharya, Viral V., & Sascha Steffen. (2014). *Falling short of expectations? stress-testing the european banking system* (CEPS papers). Centre for European Policy Studies. http://EconPapers.repec.org/RePEc:eps:cepswp:8803

Acharya, V., Engle, R., & Pierret, D. (2014). Testing macroprudential stress tests: The risk of regulatory risk weights. *Journal of Monetary Economics, 65*, 36–53. doi:10.1016/j.jmoneco.2014.04.014.

Arnould, G., & Dehmej, S. (2015). *Is the European banking system more Robust? An evaluation through the lens of the ECB's comprehensive assessment.* Documents de travail du Centre d'Economie de la Sorbonne. Université Panthéon-Sorbonne (Paris 1). Centre d'Economie de la Sorbonne. http://EconPapers.repec.org/RePEc:mse:cesdoc:15061

Barucci, Emilio, Roberto Baviera, & Carlo Milani. (2014). *Is the comprehensive assessment really comprehensive?* http://ssrn.com/abstract=2541043

BBC News. (2010, 23 July). Seven EU banks fail stress tests. *BBC News*. http://www.bbc.com/news/business-10732597.

Beltratti, Andrea. (2011). *Do stress tests carry useful information? Evidence from Europe.* mimeo, Bocconi University.

Berger, A. N., & Davies, S. M. (1998). The information content of bank examinations. *Journal of Financial Services Research, 14*(2), 117–144. doi:10.1023/A:1008011312729.

Bird, Andrew, Stephen A. Karolyi, Thomas G. Ruchti, and Austin Sudbury. (2015). *Bank regulator bias and the efficacy of stress test disclosures*. Available at SSRN 2626058. https://server1.tepper.cmu.edu/seminars/docs/BKRS-BankRegulation.pdf

Bischof, Jannis, and Holger Daske. (2012). *Can super*. JAR/NY FED conference.

Blundell-Wignall, A., & Slovik, P. (2010). *The EU stress test and sovereign debt exposures*. Paris: OECD.

Breuer, Thomas. (2014). Robustness, validity and significance of the ECB's asset quality review and stress test exercise. doi:10.13140/2.1.2004.9606.

Candelon, Bertrand, & Amadou N. R. Sy. (2015). *How do markets react to stress tests?* (IMF working papers 15/75). International Monetary Fund. https://ideas.repec.org/p/imf/imfwpa/15-75.html

Cardinali, A., & Nordmark, J. (2011). *How informative are bank stress tests? Bank opacity in the European Union*. Lund: Lund University.

Committee of European Banking Supervisors. (2009). *CEBS's press release on the results of the EU-wide stress testing exercise*. http://www.eba.europa.eu/documents/10180/15977/CEBS-2009-180-Annex-2-%28Press-release-from-CEBS%29.pdf

Committee of European Banking Supervisors. (2010). Aggregate Outcome of the 2010 EU wide stress test exercise coordinated by CEBS in cooperation with the ECB. Committee of European Banking Supervisors.

Crisan, L. C. (2014). *The stress test—A new challenge for the Banking Union*. Proceedings of international academic conferences 0702690. International Institute of Social and Economic Sciences. https://ideas.repec.org/p/sek/iacpro/0702690.html

D'Cruz, N., & Crippa, D. (2012). Stress testing. *Global Credit Review, 02*(01), 39–52. doi:10.1142/S2010493612500031.

De Groen W. P. (2014). *Was the ECB's comprehensive assessment up to standard?* (CEPS papers). Centre for European Policy Studies. http://EconPapers.repec.org/RePEc:eps:cepswp:9795

Deng, A., Hirtle, B., & Anna Kovner. (2015, 21 September). Are BHCs mimicking the Fed's stress test results? *Liberty Street Economics*.

ECOFIN. (2009). Press release of the 2981st council meeting. Council of the European Union.

Ellahie, A. (2012). *Bank stress tests and information asymmetry*. JAR/NY FED conference.

European Banking Authority. (2011). *EU-wide stress test: Methodological note*. European Banking Authority.

European Banking Authority. (2014). *Main features of the 2014 EU-wide stress test*. https://www.eba.europa.eu/documents/10180/563711/Communication+on+the+2014+EU-wide+stress+test.pdf

European Central Bank. (2014). *Comprehensive Assessment Stress Test Manual*. Frankfurt am Main: European Central Bank. http://bookshop.europa.eu/uri?target=EUB:NOTICE:QB0414734:EN:HTML.

Federal Reserve. (2009a). *The supervisory capital assessment program: Overview of results*. Washington, DC: Federal Reserve.

Federal Reserve. (2009b). *The supervisory capital assessment program: Design and implementation*. Washington, DC: Federal Reserve http://www.federalreserve.gov/newsevents/press/bcreg/bcreg20090424a1.pdf.

Federal Reserve. (2009c). *The supervisory capital assessment program: overview of results*. Washington, DC: Federal Reserve http://www.federalreserve.gov/newsevents/press/bcreg/bcreg20090507a1.pdf.

Federal Reserve. (2011). *Comprehensive capital analysis and review: Objectives and overview*. Washington, DC: Federal Reserve http://www.federalreserve.gov/newsevents/press/bcreg/bcreg20110318a1.pdf.

Federal Reserve. (2012). *Comprehensive capital analysis and review 2012: Methodology and results for stress scenario projections*. Washington, DC: Board of Governors of the Federal Reserve System.

Federal Reserve. (2013a). *Comprehensive capital analysis and review 2013: Assessment framework and results*. Washington, DC: Federal Reserve http://www.federalreserve.gov/newsevents/press/bcreg/ccar-2013-results-20130314.pdf.

Federal Reserve. (2013b). *Dodd-Frank act stress test 2013: Supervisory stress test methodology and results*. Washington, DC: Federal Reserve http://www.federalreserve.gov/newsevents/press/bcreg/dfast_2013_results_20130314.pdf.

Federal Reserve. (2014a). *Comprehensive capital analysis and review 2014: Assessment framework and results*. Washington, DC: Federal Reserve http://www.federalreserve.gov/newsevents/press/bcreg/ccar_20140326.pdf.

Federal Reserve. (2014b). *Dodd-Frank act stress test 2014: Supervisory stress test methodology and results*. Washington, DC: Federal Reserve http://www.federalreserve.gov/newsevents/press/bcreg/bcreg20140320a1.pdf.

Federal Reserve. (2015a). *Dodd-Frank act stress test 2015: Supervisory stress test methodology and results*. Washington, DC: Federal Reserve http://www.federalreserve.gov/newsevents/press/bcreg/bcreg20150305a1.pdf.

Federal Reserve. (2015b). *Comprehensive capital analysis and review 2015: Assessment framework and results*. Washington, DC: Federal Reserve http://www.federalreserve.gov/newsevents/press/bcreg/bcreg20150311a1.pdf.

Flannery, M. J., & Houston, J. F. (1999). The value of a government monitor for U. S. banking firms. *Journal of Money, Credit and Banking, 31*(1), 14–34. doi:10.2307/2601137.

Flannery, M. J., Kwan, S. H., & Nimalendran, M. (2010). *The 2007–09 financial crisis and bank opaqueness, Working paper series*. Washington, DC: *Federal Reserve Bank of San Francisco*.

Flannery, M. J., Hirtle, B., & Kovner, A. (2015). *Evaluating the information in the Federal Reserve stress tests*. http://www.ny.frb.org/research/staff_reports/sr744.pdf

Gick, W., & T. Pausch. (2012). *Optimal disclosure of supervisory information in the banking sector*. Available at SSRN 2006852. http://papers.ssrn.com/sol3/papers.cfm?abstract_id=2006852

Goldstein, I., & Sapra, H. (2013). *Should banks' stress test results be disclosed? An analysis of the costs and benefits*. Foundations and Trends in Finance Vol. 8, No. 1, 1–54.

Haben, P., Liesegang, C., & Quagliariello, M. (2013). EU-wide stress test versus SCAP and CCAR: Region-wide and global perspectives. In J. Zhang (Ed.), *Comprehensive capital analysis review (CCAR) and beyond—Capital assessment, stress testing and applications*. London: RiskBooks.

Haggard, K.S., & J.S. Howe. (2007). *Are banks opaque*. Unpublished working paper, University of Missouri, Columbia.

Hirtle, B., and Lehnert, A. (2014). *Supervisory stress tests*. (FRB of New York staff report, no. 696). http://papers.ssrn.com/sol3/papers.cfm?abstract_id=2521612

Hirtle, Beverly, Til Schuermann, & Kevin J. Stiroh. (2009). *Macroprudential supervision of financial institutions: Lessons from the SCAP. SSRN eLibrary*. http://papers.ssrn.com/sol3/papers.cfm?abstract_id=1515800

Iannotta, G. (2006). Testing for opaqueness in the european banking industry: Evidence from bond credit ratings. *Journal of Financial Services Research, 30*(3), 287–309.

Jordan, J. (2000). The market reaction to the disclosure of supervisory actions: Implications for bank transparency. *Journal of Financial Intermediation, 9*, 298–319. doi:10.1006/jfin.2000.0292.

Kreps, D. M., & Wilson, R. (1982). Reputation and imperfect information. *Journal of Economic Theory, 27*(2), 253–279. doi:10.1016/0022-0531(82)90030-8.

Laffont, J. J., & Tirole, J. (1991). The politics of government decision-making: A theory of regulatory capture. *The Quarterly Journal of Economics, 106*(4), 1089–1127.

Liikanen, E., H. Bänziger, J. M. Campa, L. Gallois, M. Goyens, J. P. Krahnen, M. Mazzucchelli, et al. (2012). *Report of the high-level expert group on reforming the structure of the EU banking sector*, Brussels.

Morgan, D. P. (2002). Rating banks: Risk and uncertainty in an opaque industry. *American Economic Review, 92*, 874–888.

Neretina, E., Sahin, C., & de Haan, J. (2014). *Banking stress test effects on returns and risks, DNB working papers 419*. Amsterdam: The Netherlands Central Bank, Research Department https://ideas.repec.org/p/dnb/dnbwpp/419.html.

Onado, M., and Resti, A. (2011). *European banking authority and the capital of European Banks: Don't shoot the messenger*. VoxEU.org., December 7. http://www.voxeu.org/article/defence-european-banking-authority

Peristiani, S., Morgan, D. P., & Savino, V. (2010). *The information value of the stress test and bank opacity, FRB of New York staff report no 460*. New York: Federal Reserve Bank of New York.

Petrella, Giovanni, and Andrea Resti. 2013. Supervisors as information producers: Do stress tests reduce bank opaqueness? *Journal of Banking & Finance* 37 (12): 5406–5420. doi:http://dx.doi.org/10.1016/j.jbankfin.2013.01.005

Quagliariello, M. (2009). *Stress-testing the banking system: Methodologies and applications*. Cambridge: Cambridge University Press.

Sahin, C., & de Haan, J. (2015). *Market reactions to the ECB's comprehensive assessment, DNB working papers 463*. Amsterdam: The Netherlands Central Bank, Research Department https://ideas.repec.org/p/dnb/dnbwpp/463.html.

Schuermann, T. (2012). *Stress testing banks*. Report prepared for the Committee on Capital Markets Regulation, New York.

Schuermann, T. (2014). Stress testing banks. *International Journal of Forecasting, 30*(3), 717–728. doi:10.1016/j.ijforecast.2013.10.003.

Shapiro, J., & D. Skeie. (2012). *Information management in banking crises*. Mimeo. http://www.qc-econ-bba.org/seminarpapers/IM_Shapiro.pdf

Spargoli, F. (2012). *Banks' recapitalization and the information value of a stress test in a crisis*. Mimeo. http://www.econ.upf.edu/eng/graduates/gpem/jm/pdf/paper/JMP%20Spargoli.pdf

Steffen, S. (2014). *Robustness, validity, and significance of the ECB'S asset quality review and stress test exercise, SAFE white paper series 23*. Research Center SAFE—Sustainable Architectue for Finance in Europe, Goethe University Frankfurt .https://ideas.repec.org/p/zbw/safewh/23.html

US Treasury Department. (2009). *The capital assistance program and its role in the financial stability plan*. https://www.treasury.gov/press-center/press-releases/Documents/tg40_capwhitepaper.pdf

White, L., & A. Morrison. (2010). *Reputational contagion and optimal regulatory forbearance*. http://papers.ssrn.com/sol3/papers.cfm?abstract_id=1603860

Wiggins, R. Z., Wedow, M., & Metrick, A. (2014). *European Banking Union A: The single supervisory mechanism* (Yale School of Management YPFS cases 56743). New Haven: Yale School of Management. https://www.ideas.repec.org/p/ysm/ypfswp/56743.html

Part IV

Cross-Border Banking

17

The Banking Union: An Overview and Open Issues

Dirk Schoenmaker

Introduction

The Banking Union is a milestone in European banking integration. While supervision of European banks by national supervisors was loosely coordinated through the European Banking Authority (EBA), the European Banking Union has positioned the European Central Bank (ECB) as centralized supervisor of the European banks, initially in the Eurozone. The European Banking Union creates a paradigm shift for the various stakeholders. French and Dutch banks become Eurozone banks. National supervisors work together with the ECB in the Single Supervisory Mechanism (SSM), with the ECB ultimately in charge. Customers may at some point choose a bank from another Eurozone country as their "home" bank.

While academics have argued for a long time that the increasing intensity of cross-border banking would need European banking supervision and resolution (e.g. Folkerts-Landau and Garber 1992; Schoenmaker 1997; Vives 2001; Goodhart and Schoenmaker 2009), the immediate reason for the sudden move to banking union was the intensifying euro sovereign crisis (Véron

The author is grateful to Sander Oosterloo and Nicolas Véron as well as the editors for useful discussions and comments.

D. Schoenmaker (✉)
Rotterdam School of Management, Erasmus University Rotterdam,
Rotterdam, The Netherlands
e-mail: schoenmaker@rsm.nl

T. Beck, B. Casu (eds.), *The Palgrave Handbook of European Banking*,
DOI 10.1057/978-1-137-52144-6_17

2011; Pisani-Ferry et al. 2012). The stated aim is to break the sovereign bank loop, whereby the credit standing of nation-states and banks are interlinked, and by implication, to organize bank risk-sharing at the Eurozone level.

This chapter indicates that bank risk-sharing is only partly achieved in the current set-up of the Banking Union. Some work remains to be done, notably in the field of deposit insurance (Gros and Schoenmaker 2014; Véron 2015). Moreover, the mix of national agencies (for deposit insurance) and European agencies (for supervision and resolution) makes the Banking Union arrangement potentially instable. There is no governmental mechanism to settle disputes between agencies operating at different levels.

Now that the euro sovereign crisis seems to be tamed, it is interesting to look at the long-term rationale for banking union. The chapter therefore documents cross-border banking trends in the European Union (EU). Importantly, we find that cross-border banking is not only pervasive in the Eurozone, but also in the non-Eurozone member states of the EU. The latter may wish to join the Banking Union at a later stage.

This chapter is organized as follows. The section "The Rationale for Banking Union" is followed by "Cross-border Banking". The next section, "An Integrated Framework", analyses what the new governance framework of the Banking Union is about. We stress that the Banking Union should be seen as an integrated framework. The section "How Does the Banking Union Work?" explains the completed building blocks of Banking Union, in particular single supervision and single resolution. Next, the section "Completing the Banking Union" discusses which building blocks are not yet completed, notably European Deposit Insurance. The final section concludes.

The Rationale for Banking Union

The decision to move to banking union was taken suddenly at the height of the euro sovereign crisis in 2012. The vicious circle between the solvency of nation-states in the Eurozone and the solvency of these nation-states' banks contributed to the crisis. The sovereign bank loop works two-way. First, banks carry large amounts of bonds of their own government on their balance sheet (Battistini et al. 2014). So, a deterioration of a government's credit standing would automatically worsen the solvency of that country's banks. Second, a worsening of a country's banking system could worsen the government's budget because of a potential government financed bank bailout. Alter and Schüler (2012) and Erce (2015) provide evidence of interdependence between government and bank credit risk during the crisis.

The sovereign bank loop argument relates to the Eurozone, where national central banks cannot issue money and buy government bonds without limit as the ECB is in charge. To break the loop, the European Council decided to move the responsibility for banking rescues at the Eurozone level. If ex post rescues are organized at this level, ex ante supervision should also be moved in tandem to minimize the need for such rescues (Goodhart and Schoenmaker 2009). So, the essence of Banking Union is supervision and resolution of banks at the Eurozone level. Nevertheless, we argue in "Completing the Banking Union" that the risk-sharing arrangements are not yet complete, as witnessed in the Greek (banking) crisis in June 2015.

The long-term reason for banking union is cross-border banking. The financial trilemma states that the three objectives of financial stability, cross-border banking and national financial policies cannot be achieved at the same time; one has to give (Schoenmaker 2011). The combination of cross-border banking and national supervision and resolution leads to coordination failure between national authorities, which put national interests first (see, for example, the abortive rescue of Fortis). This in turn puts financial stability at risk. The advance to banking union solves this coordination failure by adopting supranational policies. The coordination failure argument is related to the Single Market (which allows unfettered cross-border banking), and thus to the European Union as a whole.

The Banking Union has struck a compromise between these two goals. Participation is mandatory for Eurozone member states, and optional for non-Eurozone members (Hertig et al. 2010). In that way, the door is kept open to address the coordination failure in cross-border banking also for non-Eurozone members at a later stage. While the need for supranational supervision in the Economic and Monetary Union (EMU) as well as in an integrated Single Market was already argued in the 1990s (e.g. Folkerts-Landau and Garber 1992; Schoenmaker 1997; Vives 2001), a banking crisis was needed to get politicians into action. However, we are halfway with building the Banking Union. The political economy suggests that we might need another banking crisis to complete the Banking Union. It is clear how banking union should be completed, as set in the Five Presidents Report (2015) and discussed later in this chapter. But there is a strong reluctance in northern Europe, led by Germany, to rescue banks at the supranational level, because of moral hazard concerns.

The current policy agenda is therefore built on risk-sharing and risk reduction. Such risk or burden sharing is crucial to complete Banking Union (Goodhart and Schoenmaker 2009). The potential moral hazard can be addressed through two mechanisms. First, banks should diversify their government bond holdings on their balance sheet. While such holdings are useful for liquidity purposes, there is no need to keep an undiversified portfolio of own government bonds. Diversification requirements, such as a large exposures rule for government bonds, would help to reduce the riskiness of banks and address the first leg of the sovereign bank loop. Second, there is a need for strong supranational banking supervision, as currently done by the ECB. The irony is that Germany asked for supranational supervision before embarking on supranational banking rescues. Now we have such supranational supervision, it is dragging its feet on accepting European deposit insurance and using the European Stability Mechanism (ESM) as a fiscal backstop to the European banking system (see Schoenmaker (2015) for more detail on the role of the fiscal backstop in a fractional reserve banking system).

Cross-Border Banking

What is the intensity of cross-border banking in the European Union? The first sub-section "Inward Banking Flows" provides evidence on the level of inward banking at the country level. A high level of inward banking limits the capacity of national authorities to manage the stability of their financial system. Next, the second sub-section "Outward Banking Flows" documents the outward banking flows of the largest banks. The home country authorities only take the domestic share of a bank's business into account when considering a bank rescue, while they may have to pay the full cost of the rescue. A high cross-border share may therefore lead to coordination failure as witnessed with the Fortis rescue efforts in 2008 (Schoenmaker 2013).

Inward Banking Flows

The global financial crisis has led to a retrenchment of international banking. Troubled banks typically first cut back on their foreign business. Moreover, banks that received state aid were often pressured by national authorities to maintain domestic lending. Figure 17.1 illustrates the decline in cross-border penetration since 2007. Cross-border penetration is defined as the percentage of a country's banking system assets from other European Union or third countries. Third countries are non-EU countries. New figures for 2014 suggest that the decline has been halted.

The aggregate figures for the European Union can be split according to Banking Union countries (the 19 Eurozone members) and non-Banking

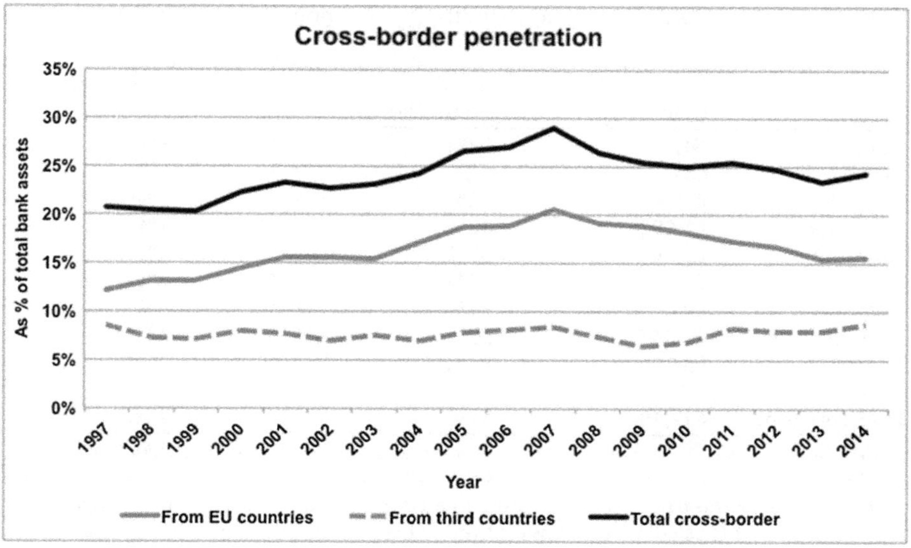

Fig. 17.1 Cross-border penetration of European banking (EU; in % of total banking assets) (*Source:* Author calculations based on EU Structural Financial Indicators, ECB)

Table 17.1 Banking systems across three regions: BU, EU and USA; end-2014

	Number of banks	Total assets in billion	Of which: home	Other EU	Third country
Banking Union	5,516	€30,772	83%	14%	3%
Non-Banking Union	1,752	€12,196	57%	19%	24%
European Union	7,268	€42,968	76%	16%	9%
United States	5,643	€12,360	84%		16%

Note: Total banking assets come from the home country, other EU countries, and third countries (i.e. outside the EU or the USA). The three components add up to 100 %
Source: Author calculations based on ECB for European banks and Federal Reserve and FDIC for US commercial banks

Union countries (the 9 outs). Table 17.1 shows that the Banking Union covers over 70 % of total European Union banking assets. Next, Table 17.1 shows that the intensity of cross-border banking in the non-Banking Union is higher than in the Banking Union countries, which suggests that the supranational approach may also be useful for the outs. Zooming in on the outs, Table 17.2 shows that the large share from third countries comes from the United Kingdom, where London acts as international financial centre. But also the share from other EU countries is larger in the out countries than in

Table 17.2 Cross-border banking penetration in non-Eurozone member states; end-2014

	Total assets (€billion)	Of which: home (%)	other EU (%)	Third country (%)
Bulgaria	€47	23%	74%	3%
Croatia	€57	n.a.	n.a.	n.a.
Czech Republic	€196	12%	88%	0%
Denmark	€1,082	82%	17%	1%
Hungary	€110	55%	42%	4%
Poland	€380	34%	59%	7%
Romania	€91	31%	69%	0%
Sweden	€1,245	90%	9%	1%
United Kingdom	€8,990	52%	17%	32%
Non-Eurozone	€12,196	57%	19%	24%

Notes: Share of business from domestic banks, share of business of banks from other EU countries, and share of business of banks from third countries are measured as a percentage of the total banking assets in a country. Figures are for end 2014. Non-Eurozone is calculated as a weighted average (weighted according to assets). The new division of Eurozone (19 member countries) and non-Eurozone (9 members) as of 1 January 2015 is taken

Source: Author calculations based on ECB Structural Financial Indicators

the Banking Union countries. In particular, the Eastern European countries, including Poland, have a large cross-border share from Western Europe. These data indicate that the outs may consider Banking Union membership, which is optional. Such membership depends, of course, on wider political economy considerations. But if and when Banking Union becomes a success, we should not be surprised to see voluntary members knocking on the door (Hüttl and Schoenmaker 2015).

Outward Banking Flows

The next step is to investigate the outward banking flows of the largest banks. The international orientation of most of these large banks can lead to the earlier mentioned coordination failure, whereby the home authorities concentrate on the domestic activities in crisis resolution. Foreign activities, either in the rest of the EU or in the rest of the world, are thus ignored. To gauge the potential for coordination failure, we split the assets of these banks into assets in the home country, in other EU countries and in third countries. Financial stability concerns are related to a bank's assets in several ways. The benefits of a potential bailout can be thought of as preventing a temporary reduction of credit availability (credit crunch) through shortening of balance sheets by a forced liquidation of the loan book in a particular country. Another source of benefits is the safeguarding of financial stability of the total banking system, which might be jeopardized by a fire sale of assets or other externalities impacting negatively on aggregate investment in a country (Acharya 2009).

When information on the geographical segmentation of assets is not available, we use the segmentation of credit exposures of the loan book, the most important asset class, as a proxy. The basis source for our data is banks' annual reports. Further information on credit exposure is available in the published stress test results for 2014 of the European Banking Authority. The full methodology for measuring geographic segmentation is described in Schoenmaker (2013). Under the new Capital Requirements Directive (CRD IV), financial institutions must disclose, by country in which it operates through a subsidiary or a branch, information about turnover, number of employees, and profit before tax. This extra information allows us to refine the geographical split at country level.

Table 17.3 shows the top 25 banks in the banking union have 24 % of their assets in other EU countries and 17 % in third countries. The potential improvement of banking union is the 24 % share in other EU countries, as the supranational resolution agency takes all banking union assets into account when considering a bailout (Schoenmaker and Siegmann 2014). Moving to the non-banking union, Table 17.4 indicates that the top ten banks in the non-banking union countries have 18 % of their assets in other EU countries and 32 % in third countries. The European share is slightly less, while the global share is far larger for the UK banks. The similarity in the European share confirms that banking union can have the same benefits for the outs (see also Darvas and Wolff 2013, who provide detailed case studies). In particular, the Scandinavian banks, Nordea, Danske, Svenska, SEB Group and Swedbank, would benefit from the risk-sharing in a banking union. But that is also valid for Barclays, which is inter alia active in France, Germany, Italy and Spain (Hüttl and Schoenmaker 2015).

The actual improvement in resolution has to be calculated on the basis of the Banking Union Area (BUA), which is confined to the Eurozone countries at the time of writing but may expand to non-Eurozone ones on a voluntary basis. The new home base is the entire Banking Union Area. To assess the improvement, we split banks' assets in other EU countries into other BUA countries and non-BUA countries. Table 17.5 shows that the new home share in the Banking Union amounts to 74 % ($BU = 0.74$), an improvement of 15 percentage points compared to the home share in the pre-Banking Union era ($h = 0.59$).

The improvement is visualized in Fig. 17.2. In terms of costs C (x-axis) and benefits B (y-axis), the efficient benchmark is that a bailout takes place when the aggregate (world-wide) benefits exceed the total costs, so that the line is

Table 17.3 Top 25 banks in banking union in 2014 (based on pre-BUA segmentation)

	Banking groups	Total assets (in billion)	Of which: home	other EU	Third country
1	BNP Paribas (FR)	€2,077	34%	44%	22%
2	Crédit Agricole (FR)	€1,762	80%	10%	10%
3	Deutsche Bank (DE)	€1,708	29%	28%	43%
4	Société Générale (FR)	€1,308	72%	14%	14%
5	Banco Santander (ES)	€1,266	26%	40%	34%
6	Groupe BPCE (FR)	€1,223	90%	2%	8%
7	UniCredit (IT)	€844	43%	51%	6%
8	ING Bank (NL)	€828	36%	50%	14%
9	Crédit Mutuel (FR)	€706	89%	8%	3%
10	Rabobank (NL)	€681	75%	6%	19%
11	Intesa Sanpaolo (IT)	€646	87%	10%	3%
12	BBVA (ES)	€632	43%	16%	42%
13	Commerzbank (DE)	€557	50%	34%	16%
14	DZ Bank (DE)	€402	76%	16%	8%
15	ABN AMRO (NL)	€387	75%	15%	9%
16	La Caixa Group (ES)	€339	89%	10%	2%
17	Landesbank Baden-Württemb. (DE)	€266	76%	16%	8%
18	KBC Group (BE)	€245	52%	43%	5%
19	Bankia (ES)	€242	86%	13%	1%
20	Bayerische Landesbank (DE)	€232	77%	15%	8%
21	Banque Postale (FR)	€213	93%	7%	0%
22	Nord LB (DE)	€198	84%	12%	4%
23	Erste Group (AT)	€196	46%	52%	2%
24	Belfius (BE)	€194	71%	24%	5%
25	Banca Monte dei Paschi (IT)	€183	94%	6%	1%
	Top 25 Banking Union	€17,335	59%	24%	17%

Notes: Top 25 banks are selected on the basis of total assets (as published in *The Banker*). Assets are divided over the home country, the rest of Europe and the rest of the world. Top 25 banks is calculated as a weighted average (weighted according to assets)

Source: Author calculations based on annual reports

characterized by $B = C$, i.e., a slope of 1. Thus, in the cost–benefits space, the line that separates bailout from no-bailouts has a slope of one. The solution pre-Banking Union (home country resolution) is to have a bailout only when the home country (h) benefits exceed the total costs, i.e., $h \cdot B \geq C$, which leads to the line $B = C/h$ above which a bailout takes place. Under a Banking Union supranational authority, bailouts take place when BU-specific (BU) benefits exceed total costs, i.e $BU \cdot B \geq C$. The supranational approach thus improves to the line $B = C/BU$. The grey area in Fig. 17.2 identifies the area of improvement, where the burden sharing in Banking Union can improve on the outcome under home country resolution.

Table 17.4 Top 10 banks in non-banking union in 2014

	Banking groups	Total assets (in billion)	Of which: home	Other EU	Third country
1	HSBC (UK)	€2,170	33%	9%	58%
2	Barclays (UK)	€1,745	37%	24%	38%
3	Royal Bank of Scotland (UK)	€1,350	74%	5%	21%
4	Lloyds Banking Group (UK)	€1,099	96%	2%	1%
5	Nordea (SE)	€669	24%	74%	1%
6	Standard Chartered (UK)	€598	12%	4%	84%
7	Danske Bank (DK)	€465	62%	38%	0%
8	Svenska Handelsbanken (SE)	€300	59%	27%	14%
9	SEB Group (SE)	€281	60%	32%	8%
10	Swedbank (SE)	€226	76%	19%	5%
	Top 10 non-banking union	8,902	50%	18%	32%

Notes: Top 10 banks are selected on the basis of total assets (as published in *The Banker*). Assets are divided over the home country, the rest of Europe and the rest of the world. Top 10 banks is calculated as a weighted average (weighted according to assets)

Source: Author calculations based on annual reports

An Integrated Framework

Before turning to the working of the Banking Union, we first define the overall governance framework for supervision and resolution. The mandate and role of the various agencies should be assessed in an integrated framework to ensure a comprehensive coverage of supervisory and stability concerns and to align incentives of the agencies.[1]

The framework for governance starts with the rule-making authority. For the financial sector, the ministry of finance (in the European context) typically prepares proposals for financial legislation, which is subsequently amended and approved by parliament. The ministry of finance thus drives the policymaking agenda and has ultimate responsibility for the overall design of the regulatory and supervisory framework. The precise division of powers between the executive (government) and the legislative (parliament) differs across countries. In Europe, the executive is more firmly in the driving seat.[2] For example, HM Treasury initiated the creation of the former UK FSA, after

[1] This section draws on Chapter 7 in Schoenmaker (2013).

[2] There are a few exceptions. The Finnish parliament has broad constitutional powers. A case in point is the Parliamentary Oversight Council overseeing Suomen Pankki, the Finnish central bank.

Table 17.5 Top 25 banks in Banking Union in 2014 (based on BUA segmentation)

	Banking groups	Total assets (in billion)	Of which: BUA	Non-BUA	Third country
1	BNP Paribas (FR)	€2,077	68%	10%	22%
2	Crédit Agricole (FR)	€1,762	87%	3%	10%
3	Deutsche Bank (DE)	€1,708	48%	8%	43%
4	Société Générale (FR)	€1,308	77%	9%	14%
5	Banco Santander (ES)	€1,266	34%	32%	34%
6	Groupe BPCE (FR)	€1,223	91%	1%	8%
7	UniCredit (IT)	€844	71%	23%	6%
8	ING Bank (NL)	€828	74%	12%	14%
9	Crédit Mutuel (FR)	€706	96%	1%	3%
10	Rabobank (NL)	€681	78%	3%	19%
11	Intesa Sanpaolo (IT)	€646	92%	5%	3%
12	BBVA (ES)	€632	54%	5%	42%
13	Commerzbank (DE)	€557	68%	16%	16%
14	DZ Bank (DE)	€402	85%	6%	8%
15	ABN AMRO (NL)	€387	88%	3%	9%
16	La Caixa Group (ES)	€339	94%	4%	2%
17	Landesbank Baden-Württemb. (DE)	€266	89%	3%	8%
18	KBC Group (BE)	€245	71%	24%	5%
19	Bankia (ES)	€242	95%	4%	1%
20	Bayerische Landesbank (DE)	€232	87%	5%	8%
21	Banque Postale (FR)	€213	98%	2%	0%
22	Nord LB (DE)	€198	93%	3%	4%
23	Erste Group (AT)	€196	60%	37%	2%
24	Belfius (BE)	€194	87%	8%	5%
25	Banca Monte dei Paschi (IT)	€183	98%	1%	1%
	Top 25 Banking Union	€17,335	74%	9%	17%

Notes: Top 25 banks are selected on the basis of total assets (as published in *The Banker*). Assets are divided over the home country (which is the Banking Union Area), the non-Banking Union Area in Europe and the rest of the world. Top 25 banks are calculated as a weighted average (weighted according to assets)
Source: Author calculations based on annual reports

the landslide victory of Labour in 1997. Europe follows the standard pattern with the executive (either the president/prime minister's office or the finance ministry) proposing new rules and the parliament amending and approving these new rules. At the EU level, the European Commission (EC) has the right of initiative for new legislation.

The next stage in the framework is supervision. The supervisory agency aims to prevent a financial crisis occurring. Regulation and supervision can be seen as a form of *preventive* crisis management. By contrast, the other financial agencies—lender of last resort, resolution, and deposit insurance—have to deal with a financial crisis once it occurs. That is the *resolution* stage. The two stages are interrelated. In a game-theoretical framework, the endgame of

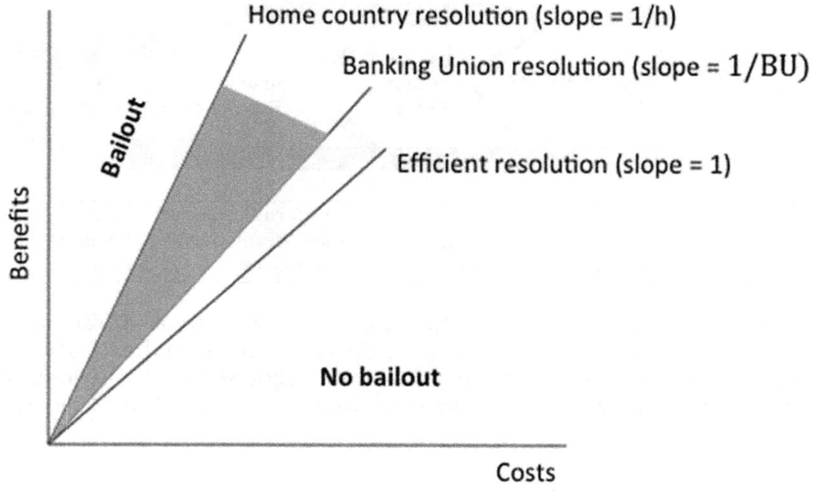

Fig. 17.2 Outcomes for the different resolution mechanisms (*Source:* Adapted from Schoenmaker and Siegmann (2014))

resolution also determines the actions of the supervisory agency (Schoenmaker 2013). We therefore apply a backward-solving approach, starting from the fiscal backstop in Fig. 17.3.

The guiding principle for decision-making on crisis management is "he who pays the piper calls the tune" (Goodhart and Schoenmaker 2009). So long as recapitalizations are organized and paid on a national basis, the national governments will normally want to oversee and undertake the function of supervision. When recapitalizations would be done at the European level, then supervision should also be moved to the same level.

Figure 17.3 illustrates the various functions involved in the governance framework for financial supervision and stability. The framework starts with the rule-making and supervisory functions. So far, we have used the broad term of resolution for crisis management. In the initial stage, the central bank may provide lender of last resort assistance to help one or more banks. If that does not work, the deposit insurance and resolution authority comes in to decide on the appropriate line of action. The global financial crisis showed (again) that deposit insurance is not only meant for depositor protection -originally initiated for protection of "widows and orphans"—in the case of an idiosyncratic failure, but also for maintaining financial stability. The level of deposit insurance was increased across the world during the global financial crisis to prevent bank runs that would further destabilize the financial system (Engineer et al. 2013).

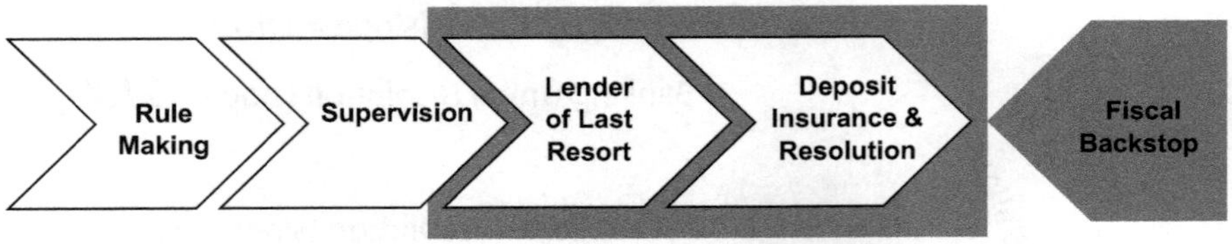

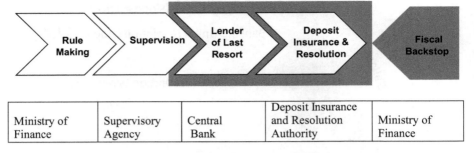

Ministry of Finance	Supervisory Agency	Central Bank	Deposit Insurance and Resolution Authority	Ministry of Finance

Fig. 17.3. Governance framework for financial supervision and stability (*Note*: The framework illustrates the five stages from rule-making to the fiscal backstop. The top line illustrates each function. The bottom line shows the generic agency for each function in the national setting; *Source*: Adapted from Schoenmaker (2013))

Deposit insurance and resolution can thus be regarded as an integrated function (Gros and Schoenmaker 2014). The least cost principle requires the resolution authority to choose the resolution method in which the total amount of the expenditures and (contingent) liabilities incurred has the lowest cost to the deposit insurance and resolution fund. The basic resolution methods include a (assisted) take-over by a healthy bank, a public assistance programme, and a liquidation with payouts to retail depositors under the deposit insurance scheme. The only exception to the least cost principle is if there are systemic risks affecting the financial system.

The final stage in the governance framework is the fiscal backstop. Crises affecting banks are commonly macro-economic and general in nature, following asset market collapses and economic downturns. The deposit insurance and resolution fund can thus run out of funds. The ultimate backup of government support is needed to give the fund credibility. Legislation may contain an explicit provision for a loan from the Treasury or ministry of finance to the fund. Alternatively, there is an implicit backstop.

Similarly, the government is the ultimate backstop for the central bank. While a central bank can provide unlimited liquidity (by expanding its balance sheet), its capacity to bear losses is limited to its capital (Goodhart and Schoenmaker 1995). In the case of large losses on lender of last resort loans, the government may need to replenish the capital of the central bank. Because of the risk to public funds, the Memorandum of Understanding on Crisis Management between HM Treasury and the Bank of England requires Treasury approval for any emergency liquidity assistance (lender of last resort) provided by the Bank. The arrow for the fiscal backstop is backward in Fig. 17.3, illustrating our backward-solving approach towards governance.

How Does the Banking Union work?

The governance framework can be applied to the new Banking Union. Figure 17.4 provides an overview of the agencies in the current Banking Union framework. The European Commission (EC) is the rule-maker and the key policy-maker initiating new policies and rules for the financial system. In parallel, the European Banking Authority (EBA) drafts technical standards and develops the single rulebook for the EU internal market. It is important to note that this rule-making has a EU-wide reach, while the Banking Union Area only includes the Eurozone and opting-in countries. The second function, supervision, has now been delegated to the ECB under the SSM.

The shaded areas then deal with crisis management. The first leg of crisis management is lender of last resort support (also called emergency liquidity assistance) for illiquid, but solvent, banks. This should also become the responsibility of the ECB. However, at the time of writing, the responsibility still rests with the national central banks (NCBs), although NCBs needs approval from the ECB to provide emergency liquidity assistance. Nevertheless, such assistance is currently for the risk and account of NCBs. The end game of any crisis is reached when banks are insolvent and have to be restructured or dissolved, which requires deposit insurance and/or resolution. Accordingly, we would argue for a Single Deposit Insurance and Resolution Board (SDIRB) (Gros and Schoenmaker 2014).

Nevertheless, the legislation provides only for a Single Resolution Mechanism (SRM) with a Single Resolution Board (SRB) and a Single Resolution Fund (SRF). Deposit insurance remains at the national level, though based on a

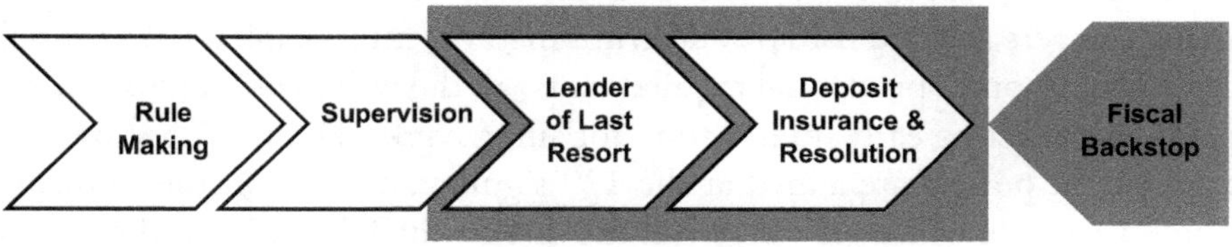

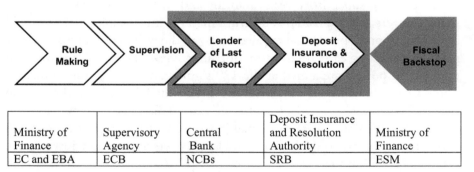

Ministry of Finance	Supervisory Agency	Central Bank	Deposit Insurance and Resolution Authority	Ministry of Finance
EC and EBA	ECB	NCBs	SRB	ESM

Fig. 17.4. Agencies in the current Banking Union framework (*Note*: The framework illustrates the five stages from rule-making to the fiscal backstop. The top line illustrates each function. The middle line shows the generic agency for each function in a national setting. The bottom line shows the (European) body for each function; *Source*: Adapted from Schoenmaker (2013))

common framework. This halfway house is not viable in the medium term. The political reality in the direct aftermath of two financial crises is that politicians and citizens are currently wary of underwriting all insured deposits at the Eurozone level. When the banking system is more stable (inter alia better capitalized) and the economy has resumed its growth path, it may be a more suitable time to shift deposit insurance from the national to the Eurozone level.

The European Stability Mechanism (ESM) has been created to provide the fiscal backstop to member countries and possibly the banking systems of member countries in financial distress. We argue that the ESM should also be able to provide a credit line to the SRM as well as to provide direct recapitalization of troubled banks (see Section "Completing the Banking Union").

The Single Supervisory Mechanism (SSM)

The ECB started its supervisory role, in conjunction with the national supervisors (officially called national competent authorities) in November 2014. Within the SSM, the ECB has the central role. Just like the ECB Governing Council for monetary policy, the SSM is governed by a Supervisory Board of 25 members, of which six designated by the ECB and 19 from national supervisors. An important feature is that decisions are made by a single authority, by simple non-weighted majority rule, which enhances its European orientation. Day-to-day supervision of individual banks is conducted by groups of ECB and national supervisors, called Joint Supervisory Teams, acting under the coordination of the ECB. A team is in place for each supervised bank (see Angeloni 2015).

The ECB has extensive powers over the banks under its direct responsibility, covering all supervisory tasks: granting and withdrawing licenses, authorizing mergers and acquisitions, determining how much capital banks should hold, setting other prudential requirements, all the way to asking for recovery plans and enacting early intervention for ailing banks. Figure 17.5 shows that these direct powers are aimed at the 129 significant banks in the Eurozone. These are not only the very large banks discussed in Table 17.3 in the Section "Cross-Border Banking". Mody and Wolff (2015) differentiate between banks that fall into three size categories: small (assets below €100bn), medium (assets between €100bn and €500 billion), and large (assets more than €500 billion). Of the €22 trillion in assets, the 'small' group has about 80 banks with €3.1 trillion, the 'medium' group has about 30 banks with €6.3 trillion, and the 'large' group has only 13 banks with aggregate assets of €12.5 trillion.[3]

[3] Checking the vulnerability of the SSM banks, Mody and Wolff (2015) find that the largest banks, with their scale economies and internationally diversified assets, appear to be out of the woods. But many of

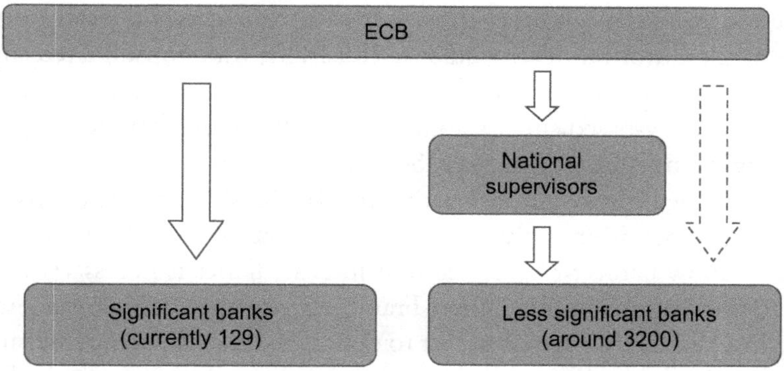

Fig. 17.5. The Single Supervisory Mechanism (*Note*: This diagram depicts the working of the Single Supervisory Mechanism)

The ECB has indirect powers over the around 3,200 less significant banks. The national supervisors are the first point of call for these smaller banks. Nevertheless, the ECB has the power to overrule the national supervisors and give directions to less significant banks if the national supervisors are not complying with the agreed single regulatory framework. Moreover, the ECB has some direct powers, such as granting and withdrawing licenses, and authorizing mergers and acquisitions, over the smaller banks. These direct powers relate to important milestones in a bank's life (birth, marriage and death). Using game theory, this latent power gives national supervisors a strong incentive to play the cooperative game with the ECB. Otherwise, it may lose its powers over the less significant banks. The SSM system is thus incentive compatible and makes a single integrated approach towards the supervision of significant and less significant banks possible. For all practical purposes, we can thus truly speak of a single supervisory mechanism.

Going forward, an interesting question is at which level the ECB should enforce the regulatory requirements, such as capital and liquidity requirements (Angeloni 2015). Should that be at the consolidated level or at the regulated entity level? In the former case, an integrated Banking Union market may emerge, where cross-border banking groups can transfer excess capital and liquidity across the group (while, of course, meeting the minimum requirements at entity level). In the latter case, enforcement at the level of individual subsidiaries, which are often organized at country level, would reinforce the segmentation between national banking markets. This enforcement question

the small and medium-sized banks remain under considerable stress. The weakest of these banks are burdened by non-performing corporate loans and may need to be downsized or closed, where the SRM can play a useful role.

is related to the organization of deposit insurance. A single deposit insurance scheme at the European level would be consistent with consolidated supervision, while the current system of national deposit insurance schemes is consistent with entity-based supervision. It should be noted that most banks run their business in an integrated way (Schoenmaker 2013).

Another issue is the regulatory perimeter. The SSM is currently constrained to banking supervision only, which means that the ECB cannot extend towards shadow banks or other relevant intermediaries if necessary. It might be interesting to note that the Dodd-Frank Act gave the US Financial Stability Oversight Council the express power to designate other financial intermediaries as systemically significant, and subsequently turn them over to the Federal Reserve for supervision. The SSM Regulation is based on Article 127(6) of the Treaty on the Functioning of the EU (TFEU),[4] which was included in the Maastricht Treaty to enable the conferral of supervisory responsibilities to the ECB (Véron 2015). This legal basis allows expansion to supervision of other intermediaries, with the exception of insurers. So, there is the legal flexibility to broaden the regulatory perimeter of the SSM Regulation.

Finally, the SSM allocates micro- and macroprudential powers to the ECB. A full discussion of the macroprudential instrument is beyond the scope of this chapter. Nevertheless, we note the asymmetry between the instruments. While the ECB is the first mover on microprudential instruments, the national authorities have first mover powers in the macroprudential field. The ECB may, if deemed necessary, apply more stringent measures (e.g. higher countercyclical capital buffers) with some procedural safeguards (see Article 5 of the SSM Regulation). In a separate paper, we argue that the ECB should have a more central role in macroprudential supervision. While the application of macroprudential instruments should differ across the Eurozone due to differences in the financial cycle of member countries, the ECB would be able to address cross-border effects and safeguard a consistent and timely application across the Eurozone (Schoenmaker and Wierts 2016).

The Single Resolution Mechanism (SRM)

The Single Resolution Board (SRB) started its resolution role, in conjunction with the national resolution authorities, in January 2016. The SRM will

[4] The text of Article 127(6) is as follows: 'The Council, acting by means of regulations in accordance with a special legislative procedure, may unanimously, and after consulting the European Parliament and the European Central Bank, confer specific tasks upon the European Central Bank concerning policies relating to *the prudential supervision of credit institutions and other financial institutions with the exception of insurance undertakings*' (italics added by author).

inter alia apply the new bail-in rules of the Banking Recovery and Resolution Directive (BRRD), which requires that at least 8 % of total liabilities is bailed-in from shareholders and creditors before resolution is undertaken. Within the SRM, the SRB has a central role, but it has to work closely with the national resolution authorities, which are close to the banks and thus speak the language and know the local conditions. The SRB has an executive board with a chair, a (generally non-voting) vice-chair, and four other members. The division of labour is largely similar to that of the SSM. The SRB decides on the significant banks (as in the SSM) as well as cross-border banks. The national resolution authorities are responsible for resolution of the smaller national banks, unless there is funding from the Single Resolution Fund, and for the execution of large banks' resolution schemes after these have been decided by the SRB. For the smaller banks, the SRB thus gets involved when resolution funding is needed in order to minimize the use of such funding. It should be stressed that the SRM is applicable to all banks in the participating countries (initially the Eurozone countries). The task of the SRB is twofold: preparing ex ante resolution plans and deciding on ex post resolution actions.

The SRB meets in two settings: an executive and a plenary session. In the executive session, the SRB consists of the executive board (i.e. the chair and the four executive directors) and the member(s) from the relevant national resolution authorities of the countries in which the (troubled) bank is operating. The executive session decides on the resolution plans and schemes for individual banks (with one exception, as explained below). The executive session decides by consensus. If there is no consensus, the chair and four executive members vote by simple majority. This voting procedure ensures that the European public interest is taken into account, while avoiding national interests.

In its plenary session, the SRB comprises the executive board and all national members. The plenary session is responsible for general resolution policies and for resolution schemes whereby the funding from the Single Resolution Fund exceeds €5 billion. So the large cases in need of substantial funding are dealt with in the plenary session.

The ECB and the European Commission have permanent observers, without voting power, in the SRB. Before taking a resolution action, three conditions need to be met: 1) the bank is failing or likely to fail; 2) there are no alternative private sector solutions; 3) resolution is necessary in the public interest. The ECB, as supervisor, decides on the first condition, after consultation of the SRB. But the SRB can also decide on the first condition, after informing the ECB. This ensures that the SRB has the power to act in case of forbearance by the ECB (see ASC (2012) on forbearance). Next, the SRB decides on meeting the second and third condition.

After that the SRB decides on the draft resolution scheme, in particular which liabilities to exclude from bail-in. The decision on the resolution scheme is reviewed by the European Commission (within 24 hours) to safeguard that the internal market principles are not violated (State Aid control). The European Commission can object to the amount of funding from the Single Resolution Fund or judge that there is no threat to the public interest. In these cases, the Economic and Financial Affairs Council (ECOFIN) gets involved. ECOFIN can approve or object (with motivation) to the Commission proposal when the European Commission concludes an absence of public interest or when the European Commission changes 5 % or more in the proposed amount of funding from the Single Resolution Fund. After the decision is final, the SRB instructs the relevant national resolution authorities to take the necessary measures to implement the resolution scheme.

It should be stressed that the aim of the new legislation (BRRD and SRM) is to minimize resolution funding. As discussed above, a resolution scheme for a failed bank starts with the bail-in of shareholders and creditors for at least 8% of this bank's total liabilities. Next, funding from the Single Resolution Fund is restricted to a maximum of 5 % of total liabilities. The Single Resolution Fund aims to accumulate 1 % of covered deposits of the Eurozone banks, which amounts to €55 bn. Importantly, the Single Resolution Fund represents private funding, collected through annual contributions levied on the Eurozone banks. For the building-up of the Single Resolution Fund, there is an eight-year transition period, which is covered by an Intergovernmental Agreement (IGA) between the Eurozone countries. In the first year, 40 % of the national funds will be mutualized in the Single Resolution Fund; in the second year, a further 20 %. In the next 6 years, 6.67 % is added each year. This adds up to a 100 % mutualization of national compartments, which will then disappear.

For the use of the Single Resolution Fund, there are separate voting procedures. During the transition period, a two third majority of the voting Board members representing 50 % of contributions is needed. After the transition, again a two third majority of votes representing 30 % of contributions is needed. Note that each Board member has one vote. Figure 17.6 summarizes the working of the SRM.

The complicated decision-making structure is a shortcoming of the new SRM regime. Because of involvement of the European Commission and the ECOFIN, the decision-making can easily become prolonged while time is of the essence in crisis management. Moreover, the process might become politicized, in particular when 'national champions' are the subject of potential resolution measures. To close, or restructure, troubled banks with a firm

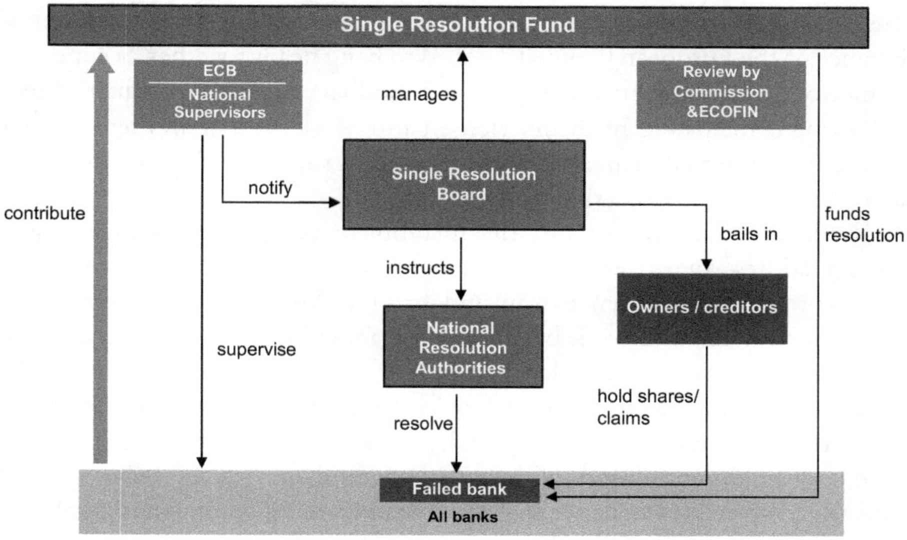

Fig. 17.6. Single Resolution: Players and decision-making structures (*Note*: This diagram depicts the working of the Single Resolution Mechanism; *Source*: Adapted from Petersen (2014))

hand, some distance from the political process is necessary. The FDIC is an example of a well-functioning agency with resolution powers in the US. On a positive note, it is good that the chair and executive members of the Single Resolution Board at the centre can press ahead in the case that national resolution authorities vote against.

Completing the Banking Union

The original rationale for Banking Union is to organize bank risk-sharing (crisis management) at the Eurozone level. By inclination, the prevention (regulation and supervision) should also be organized at the Eurozone level. While the latter has been largely achieved, the risk-sharing is still very incomplete. That makes the Banking Union arrangement potentially instable. First, there may be fights between the agencies operating at different levels, which go beyond the usual bureaucratic clatter of weapons. For example, if a bank would fail and the guaranteed deposits need to be repaid, the national deposit insurance authority may complain about the lack of supervision by the ECB and start a quarrel about the appropriate timing of closure (and hence deposit insurance pay-outs). As these agencies do not operate at the same level, there is no governmental mechanism (being the Prime Minister/Minister of Finance or the European Council/Ecofin) to bang heads together. Second, the framework is not incentive compatible (Goodhart and Schoenmaker 2009). Following principal-agent theory (Jensen and Meckling 1976), there is a risk of under-provision of supervisory effort, when a supervisor is not confronted with the costs of its (in)actions.

Third, and most important, the incomplete risk-sharing does not adequately address the sovereign bank loop. While there is uncertainty about the future divide between bail-in and bailout (Véron 2015), nation-states may still have to fund bank bailouts, with potential ESM support given to the state. This instrument is labelled indirect recapitalization (Art 15, ESM Treaty). Only when a state cannot provide support without triggering a fiscal crisis, the ESM may directly recapitalize a bank. Moreover, banks can still keep large holdings of bonds of their own government on their balance sheet. Erce (2015) provides evidence that the transmission of sovereign to bank risk works through the size of banks' exposures to the sovereign.

A case in point of incomplete risk-sharing is the resurgence of the Greek crisis in June 2015, which led to a standstill of the Greek banking system, with a closure of banks to stem the deposit flight (to abroad and into cash). A large of part of the subsequent rescue package for Greece was reserved for strengthening the Greek banking sector. If the ESM would have been able to recapitalize the Greek banks directly, the impact on Greece's government budget would have been far smaller and dampened the crisis dynamics.

Need for European Deposit Insurance

How to complete the Banking Union? Figure 17.7 shows the agencies in a completed Banking Union. On the top of the list is moving the lender of last resort and deposit insurance functions to the Eurozone level. That makes the overall governance system incentive compatible. Moreover, it causes that the fiscal backstop of these functions is no longer at the national level. That breaks the transmission from bank to sovereign risk in the bank-sovereign loop. A final element would be to enable direct bank recapitalization from the ESM, without first waiting for the country to go bankrupt before enacting such direct recapitalization. In risk-sharing terms, the ESM is behind the bank risk-sharing, both indirectly by providing a credit line to the Single Deposit Insurance and Resolution Board, and directly by providing direct bank recapitalization. The European arrangements would then match US arrangements for bank risk-sharing (Gros 2012a).

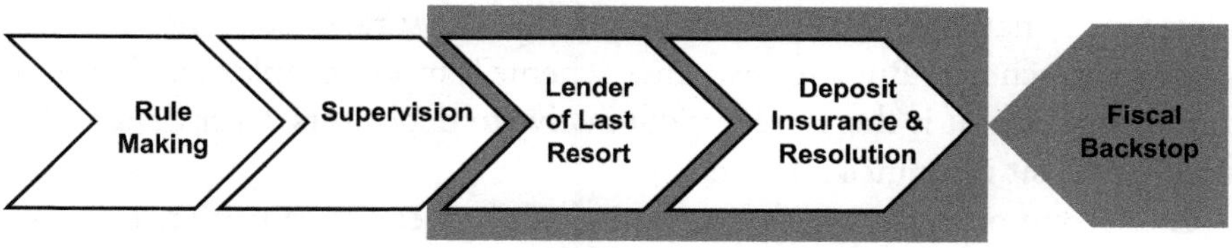

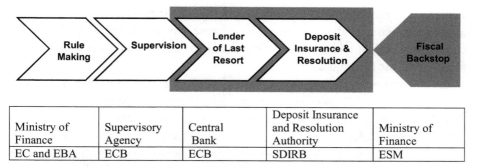

Ministry of Finance	Supervisory Agency	Central Bank	Deposit Insurance and Resolution Authority	Ministry of Finance
EC and EBA	ECB	ECB	SDIRB	ESM

Fig. 17.7. Agencies in a 'completed' Banking Union framework (*Note*: The framework illustrates the five stages from rule-making to the fiscal backstop. The top line illustrates each function. The middle line shows the generic agency for each function in a national setting. The bottom line shows the (prospective) European body for each function; *Source*: Adapted from Schoenmaker (2013))

A Single Deposit Insurance and Resolution Board would also send an important signal to bank depositors. Depositors do not have to check the solvency of the local deposit insurance fund before depositing their money with a bank from a Banking Union Area country. In that way, depositors are then in a position to consider any bank from the Banking Union as their "home" bank. The history in the United States of deposit insurance is revealing (Gros and Schoenmaker 2014). Before the introduction of the FDIC as part of the New Deal legislation in the 1930s by Franklin Roosevelt, many of the state-level deposit guarantee schemes went bankrupt because of a lack of geographic diversification and size (Golembe 1960). The vicious circle between the national governments and banks is a reflection of a similar problem in Europe today. A final argument for a broad fund is that it keeps up the notion of an integrated banking market, at least in the Banking Union Area.

Note that we argue for a fully fledged Single Deposit Insurance (and Resolution) Fund. There are proposals to create a re-insurance scheme (Gros 2012b). The national deposit insurance schemes remain in place, but they reinsure themselves in a larger European fund in case the deposit insurance payouts exceed the national fund. As usual with re-insurance, the national schemes pay a premium for this cover of extreme risks. Although this helps insuring against tail risk of multiple small national banks or a mid-sized/large bank failing, the national fund need to be refinanced by extra (future) premiums on the remaining national banks. If the national parts are relatively large in comparison to the re-insurance part, the drag on the economy remains because national banks have to refund the national fund through future deposit insurance premiums (Schoenmaker and Wolff 2015). If, by contrast, the national parts are small, then the re-insurance scheme is basically a European scheme. But a re-insurance scheme is more complex and has more operational risk. It is therefore less conducive to depositors' trust than a plain federal deposit insurance scheme.

The second open issue is the transmission of sovereign to bank risk, caused by banks' large holdings of government debt (European Systemic Risk Board 2015). These sovereign exposures carry a zero risk weight and are exempt from large exposure rules in micro-prudential supervision. A large exposure limit on such holdings would be very powerful to break the sovereign-bank loop by forcing banks to diversify their government bond holdings. Such large exposure limits on companies work very well to prevent banks going bankrupt when a large company defaults on its bank loans.

Political economy considerations suggest that the policy actions are interrelated. It is possible that before northern Europe agrees to "European" deposit insurance they may want at the minimum to ensure that the banks covered by this European deposit insurance scheme are not overly exposed to the southern European governments.

Conclusions

The idea of Banking Union is very powerful. It neatly complements the Economic and Monetary Union and has been instrumental in arresting the euro sovereign crisis. But after the immediate crisis was over, governments have started to shop selectively on the Banking Union list. The main message of this chapter is that the government framework for banking supervision and crisis management should be considered as an integrated package. Selective shopping creates new instabilities by non-aligned national and European agencies. We therefore advocate transferring the lender of last resort and deposit insurance functions to the European level to join the European supervisory and resolution functions. A final recommendation is a fiscal backstop to the "European" banking system by the European Stability Mechanism.

Another tenet of this chapter is that the long-term rationale behind Banking Union is related to cross-border banking in the Single Market. We therefore suggest that non-Eurozone members may also wish to join Banking Union at a later stage. Fortunately, the Banking Union legislation allows for such voluntary membership of the outs. That would also help to reduce the increasing tension between the "ins" and the "outs" within the European Union.

References

Acharya, V. (2009). A theory of systemic risk and design of prudential bank regulation. *Journal of Financial Stability, 5*, 224–255.

Advisory Scientific Committee. (2012). *Forbearance, resolution and deposit insurance*. Reports of the Advisory Scientific Committee No. 1, European Systemic Risk Board, Frankfurt.

Alter, A., & Schüler, Y. (2012). Credit spread interdependencies of European states and banks during the financial crisis. *Journal of Banking and Finance, 36*, 3444–3468.

Angeloni, I. (2015). *Banking supervision and the SSM: five questions on which research can help*. Speech at the CEPR's Financial Regulation Initiative Conference organized by Imperial College Business School/CEPR, 30 September, London.

Battistini, N., Pagano, M., & Simonelli, S. (2014). Systemic risk, sovereign yields and bank exposures in the euro. *Economic Policy, 29*, 203–251.

Darvas, Z., & Wolff, G. (2013). Should non-Euro area countries join the single supervisory mechanism? *DANUBE: Law and Economics Review, 4*(2), 141–163.

Engineer, M. H., Schure, P., & Gillis, M. (2013). A positive analysis of deposit insurance provision: Regulatory competition among European Union countries. *Journal of Financial Stability, 9*, 530–544.

Erce, A. (2015). *Bank and Sovereign Risk Feedback Loops* (ESM working paper series No. 1, European Stability Mechanism, Luxembourg).

European Systemic Risk Board. (2015). *ESRB report on the regulatory treatment of sovereign exposures*. European Systemic Risk Board, Frankfurt.

Folkerts-Landau, D., & Garber, P. (1992). *The European Central Bank: A bank or a monetary policy rule* (NBER working papers No. 4016).

Golembe, C. (1960). The deposit insurance legislation of 1933. *Political Science Quarterly, 76*, 181–200.

Goodhart, C., & Schoenmaker, D. (1995). Should the functions of monetary policy and banking supervision be separated? *Oxford Economic Papers, 47*, 539–560.

Goodhart, C., & Schoenmaker, D. (2009). Fiscal burden sharing in cross-border banking crises. *International Journal of Central Banking, 5*, 141–165.

Gros, D. (2012a). *Banking Union: Ireland vs Nevada – An illustration of the importance of an integrated banking system*. CEPS Commentary, 18 October, CEPS, Brussels.

Gros, D. (2012b). Principles of a Two-Tier European Deposit (Re-)Insurance System. *Kredit und Kapital, 45*, 489–499.

Gros, D., & Schoenmaker, D. (2014). European deposit insurance and resolution in the banking union. *Journal of Common Market Studies, 52*, 529–546.

Hertig, G., Lee, R., & McCahery, J. (2010). Empowering the ECB to supervise banks: A choice-based approach. *European Company and Financial Law Review, 7*, 171–215.

Hüttl, P., & Schoenmaker, D. (2015). Should the 'outs' join the banking union? *European Economy, 3*, 89–112.

Jensen, M., & Meckling, W. (1976). Theory of the firm: Managerial behavior, agency costs and ownership structure. *Journal of Financial Economics, 3*, 305–360.

Mody, A., & Wolff, G. (2015). *The vulnerability of Europe's small and medium-sized banks* (Bruegel working paper 2015/07).

Petersen, A. (2014). Banking Union in a Nutshell. Focus, Allianz Global Investors, Frankfurt.

Pisani-Ferry, J., Sapir, A., Véron, N., & Wolff, G. (2012). What kind of European Banking Union? Policy Contribution 2012/12, Bruegel.

Schoenmaker, D. (1997). Banking Supervision and Lender of Last Resort in EMU. In M. Andenas, L. Gormley, C. Hadjiemmanuil, & I. Harden (Eds.), *European economic and monetary union: The institutional framework*. London: Kluwer International.

Schoenmaker, D. (2011). The financial trilemma. *Economics Letters, 111*, 57–59.

Schoenmaker, D. (2013). *Governance of international banking: The financial trilemma*. New York: Oxford University Press.

Schoenmaker, D. (2015). On the need for a fiscal backstop to the banking system. In M. Haentjes & B. Wessels (Eds.), *Research handbook on crisis management in the banking sector* (pp. 42–54). Cheltenham: Edward Elgar.

Schoenmaker, D., & Siegmann, A. (2014). Can European bank ailouts work? *Journal of Banking & Finance, 48*, 334–349.

Schoenmaker, D., & Wierts, P. (2016). Macroprudential supervision: From theory to policy. *National Institute Economic Review, 235*, 50–62.

Schoenmaker, D., & Wolff, G. (2015). What options for European deposit insurance? Blogpost, 9 October, Bruegel, Brussels.

The Five Presidents' Report. (2015). *The Five Presidents' Report: Completing Europe's Economic and Monetary Union*, Brussels.

Véron, N. (2011). Europe must change course on banks. VoxEU column, 22 December.

Véron, N. (2015). *Europe's radical Banking Union*. Bruegel Essay and Lecture Series.

Vives, X. (2001). Restructuring financial regulation in the European monetary union. *Journal of Financial Services Research, 19*, 57–82.

18

Recent Trends in Cross-Border Banking

Ralph De Haas and Neeltje van Horen

Introduction

The European banking landscape, and cross-border banking in particular, has gone through a process of deep transformation since the mid-2000s. Two episodes of financial turmoil—the global financial crisis and the European sovereign debt crisis—occurred in rapid succession and put the model of European banking integration to the test. These crises have resulted in a more fragmented banking landscape that is characterized by new players, ongoing adjustments in banks' funding structures and a growing role for corporate bond markets.

This chapter identifies and describes a number of recent trends in European cross-border banking. To do so, we take a geographical perspective and divide Europe into three parts. We define Europe's *Core* as Austria, Belgium, Denmark, Finland, France, Germany, the Netherlands, Norway, Sweden and the United Kingdom. The European *Periphery* is made up of Cyprus, Greece,

R. De Haas (✉)
European Bank for Reconstruction and Development, London, UK

Tilburg University, Tilburg, The Netherlands
e-mail: dehaasr@ebrd.com

N. van Horen
Bank of England, London, UK
CEPR
e-mail: Neeltje.Vanhoren@bankofengland.co.uk

T. Beck, B. Casu (eds.), *The Palgrave Handbook of European Banking*,
DOI 10.1057/978-1-137-52144-6_18

Ireland, Italy, Portugal and Spain. Finally, Europe's *East* comprises Eurozone countries (Estonia, Latvia, Lithuania, the Slovak Republic and Slovenia), other EU countries (Bulgaria, Croatia, the Czech Republic, Hungary, Poland and Romania) and Eastern neighbourhood countries (Armenia, Azerbaijan, Belarus, Georgia, Moldova and Ukraine).[1]

In most of our analysis, we contrast two points in time: 2007 and 2014. In 2007, a decade-long credit boom ended when French bank BNP Paribas on 9 August suspended three funds that invested in subprime mortgage debt, citing a "complete evaporation of liquidity". The year 2014 is the most recent point in time for which comprehensive data is available.

The chapter is structured as follows. We first distinguish between two main modes of international banking: cross-border versus multinational banking. Cross-border banking occurs when a bank in country A lends directly to a borrower in country B. Multinational banking, on the other hand, takes place when a bank in country A lends to a borrower in country B via a local bank affiliate (a branch or a subsidiary) in country B. We describe which countries rely more on cross-border banking and which ones on multinational banking and assess how both forms of banking integration fared during the recent crises. The remainder of the chapter then focuses on trends in European banks' funding structures, the source countries of cross-border and multinational banking, and the recent growth of corporate bond markets in Europe as an alternative to bank credit.

International Banking in Europe

Cross-Border Versus Multinational Banking

Countries that want to benefit from access to foreign financial services can either facilitate the cross-border trade in such services (cross-border banking) or allow foreign direct investment in their banking sector (multinational banking).[2] Different countries have taken different approaches in this regard,

---

[1] While various other ways to group countries are of course possible, we follow a geographical approach for two reasons. First, geography is constant over time whereas institutional arrangements (such as EU membership) and currency regimes (euro versus a national currency) fluctuated during our sample period. Such time variance would have shifted country samples, impairing our ability to compare the same country groups over time. Second, international banks themselves consider our *East* region as one geographical region, largely ignoring institutional differences (see, for instance, http://www.bankaustria.at/en/about-us-our-cee-banking-network.jsp).

[2] Lending by brick-and-mortar multinational bank affiliates tends to be less volatile than cross-border lending flows (Peek and Rosengren 2000; García Herrero and Martinez Peria 2007).

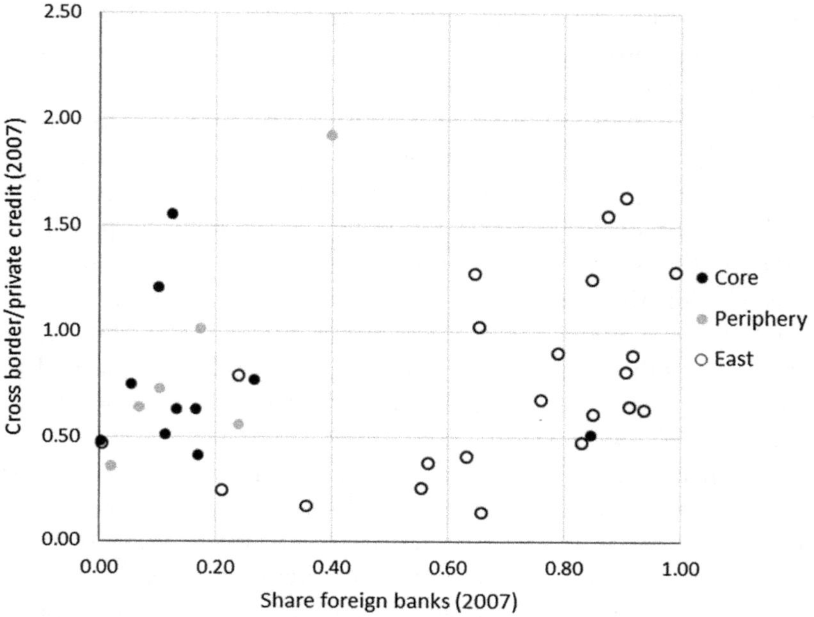

Fig. 18.1 Models of banking integration: Cross-country heterogeneity (*Note*: This figure shows the share of banking assets owned by foreign banks in 2007 (*horizontal axis*) and the amount of cross-border lending to a country (as a share of total credit to the private sector) in 2007 (*vertical axis*). Numbers reflect end-year data. Data on cross-border lending refer to total international claims (cross-border lending plus local claims in foreign currency) as taken from the Bank for International Settlements (BIS) consolidated banking statistics on an immediate borrower basis. Data on total lending to the private sector (*Private credit*) are from the World Bank. *Share foreign banks (assets)* is based on BankScope and ownership data from Claessens and Van Horen (2015))

both with respect to their overall reliance on international bank credit and the relative importance of the two modalities.

Figure 18.1 shows the models of international banking integration that European countries had established before the crisis (2007). We contrast the share of banking assets owned by foreign banks (horizontal axis) with cross-border lending to the country as a share of total credit to the private sector (vertical axis).[3] The horizontal axis hence measures the importance of multinational banking whereas the vertical axis indicates the level of cross-border

[3] Cross-border lending refers to total international claims (cross-border lending plus local claims in foreign currency) as taken from the BIS consolidated banking statistics on an immediate borrower basis. The share of foreign-bank assets is based on the bank-ownership database of Claessens and Van Horen (2015). This database does not include foreign branches as balance-sheet data are not available for most countries. The foreign-assets share therefore reflects a lower bound.

banking. The figure reveals wide cross-country variation, both between and within the three European sub-regions, in the importance of both modalities of international banking integration.

Three patterns stand out. First, there is little correlation between the level of cross-border integration and the level of multinational bank integration of a country. Some countries rely heavily on cross-border credit while local foreign-bank activity is very low. Examples are Belgium, Cyprus and the Netherlands. Other countries have a banking system that is majority foreign owned while their reliance on cross-border credit is marginal. Examples include Armenia, Georgia, FYR Macedonia and Ukraine. A third group of countries have both very high shares of foreign-owned bank assets and a high reliance on cross-border credit. Countries like Croatia, Estonia, Romania and Serbia are part of this group.

Second, there exists a clear East–West divide in the degree of multinational banking (measured on the horizontal axis). All but one country in the European *Periphery* and *Core* have relatively low foreign-bank shares (well below 25 % in most cases).[4] Among other things, this reflects that many Western European countries have taken a cautious and sometimes protectionist attitude towards foreign take-overs in the financial sector.

Countries in *East* on the other hand tend to have very high shares of foreign-owned bank assets. In countries such as Albania, Bosnia and Herzegovina, Croatia, Estonia, Lithuania and the Slovak Republic even over 90 % of all bank assets are in foreign hands. Clear outliers are Belarus (only 21 % of banking assets are foreign owned), Moldova (36 %) and Slovenia (24 %). These three countries kept their banking systems relatively closed to foreign investors.

The strong presence of foreign banks in most of the *East* region reflects that these countries were in dire need of both bank capital and banking expertise after the collapse of communism. On the "sell side", many local politicians therefore took a liberal stance towards foreign strategic investors that wanted to invest in banks. On the "buy side", numerous Western European banks with saturated home markets were attracted to the region because of its scope for financial deepening at high margins. These foreign banks either bought former state banks or opened new branches and subsidiaries across the region.[5]

Third, while there is a clear east-west divide in the degree of multinational banking, the data show more within-region variation in countries' reliance on

[4] The exception is Finland where 85 % of assets are foreign owned. Two of the largest banks in Finland are Danish Danske bank and Nordea. While Nordea regards itself as a "Nordic" financial-services group, its headquarters is in Sweden. We therefore consider it a foreign bank from a Finnish perspective.

[5] See also Haselmann et al. in this volume.

Table 18.1 Cross-border and multinational banking across Europe

	Multinational banking (share of all banking assets)		Cross-border banking (share of private credit)		Cross-border banking (share > 2 years)	
	2007	2013	2007	2014	2007	2014
	[1]	[2]	[3]	[4]	[5]	[6]
Core	0.11	0.12	0.67	0.47	0.25	0.36
Periphery	0.10	0.07	0.62	0.32	0.42	0.48
East	0.76	0.68	0.87	0.47	0.54	0.57
Europe (total)	*0.12*	*0.12*	*0.66*	*0.43*	*0.30*	*0.34*

Note: This table shows the share of bank assets in Europe's *Core, Periphery* and *East* owned by foreign-owned banks (columns 1–2), total cross-border lending to borrowers as a share of total private credit in those regions (columns 3–4) and the share of long-term lending (>2 years) in total cross-border lending (columns 5–6). Numbers reflect end-year data. Cross-border data refer to total international claims (cross-border lending plus local claims in foreign currency) as taken from the BIS consolidated banking statistics on an immediate borrower basis. Data on total lending to the private sector (*Private credit*) are from the World Bank. *Multinational banking (share of all banking assets)* is based on Bankscope and ownership data from Claessens and Van Horen (2015)

cross-border borrowing (measured on the vertical axis). For instance, within the European *Periphery*, Spain displayed a ratio of cross-border borrowing to domestic credit of just 36 % in 2007. This contrasts with another peripheral country, Ireland, where cross-border inflows were almost double the amount of domestic private sector credit.[6] Other countries with high pre-crisis cross-border borrowing include Belgium (*Core*), Croatia and Romania (both *East*). This again shows that trends in cross-border banking tend to be quite different from those in multinational banking.

Recent Adjustments in International Banking Models

Not surprisingly, many European countries had to adjust their banking models as a result of the global financial and European sovereign debt crises. Table 18.1 summarizes how the three different regions adjusted their reliance on international bank credit. A comparison of the years 2007 and 2013 shows, first of all, some downward adjustment in the amount of foreign direct investment in the banking sectors of the European *Periphery* and *East* (columns 1

[6] Because cross-border lending (numerator) includes international claims on the public sector and on banks while the denominator only includes bank credit to the private non-financial sector, this ratio can exceed one.

and 2).[7] Yet, by and large, divestitures of foreign subsidiaries have been limited and in many cases involved sales from one foreign bank to another one (thus keeping the total involvement of foreign banks constant). For instance, Irish bank AIB sold its Polish subsidiary Bank Zachodni WBK SA to Spanish group Santander in 2011.

The strongest decline in foreign ownership took place in the *East*, the region where foreign-bank penetration had been the highest to begin with. Here foreign ownership declined from 76 % to 68 % of all banking assets. Ukraine, where a number of foreign banks left the country, experienced the sharpest decline. Many Western European parent banks had to strengthen their balance sheets and needed to comply with stricter capital requirements in the wake of the crisis. One way of doing so was to reduce their international operations. Crisis-affected parent banks typically consolidated their foreign operations by selling smaller, more recent and more distant acquisitions (Claessens and Van Horen 2015). Nevertheless, as many parent banks continued to see countries in the *East* region as strategic growth markets, most multinational banks decided to stay put. The successful implementation of the Vienna Initiative also helped ensure that foreign banks continued (though scaled back) their operations in those *East* countries that participated.[8]

The adjustment in cross-border banking activity has been much more severe, with cross-border lending declining on average from 66 % to 43 % of all domestic credit to the private sector (columns 3 and 4). The decline was particularly strong in the *Periphery* (62–32 %) and the *East* (from 87 % to 47 %) and somewhat less steep in the European *Core* (67–47 %). As many European banks were hit by unexpected losses, including on US subprime investments, their capital base eroded. Refinancing opportunities quickly dwindled as well. Banks consequently started to reduce their lending at home but in particular abroad (De Haas and Van Horen 2012; Giannetti and Laeven 2012). This increase in 'home bias' was especially pronounced when protectionist regulators and politicians pressured banks to reduce foreign exposures (Rose and Wieladek 2014).

---

[7] Calculation based on the bank ownership data of Claessens and Van Horen (2015) and Bankscope. As 2013 is the last year for which ownership data are available, we compare 2007 with 2013 rather than 2014.

[8] The Vienna Initiative was launched in January 2009 as a coordination platform for multinational banks, home and host country supervisors, fiscal authorities, the IMF and development institutions. The goal was to safeguard a continued commitment of parent banks to their subsidiaries. International financial institutions provided a €33 billion package in support of this objective while various multinational banks signed country-specific commitment letters in which they pledged to maintain exposures and to provide subsidiaries with funding. De Haas et al. (2015) show that foreign banks that took part in the Vienna Initiative were relatively stable lenders. See also Haselmann et al. in this volume.

Interestingly, the last two columns of Table 18.1 show that the sharp reduction in cross-border bank lending to the three European regions was not accompanied by a general shortening of loan maturities. If anything, maturities *increased*. This partly reflects that when short-term debt matured it was often not renewed, so that the remaining stock of outstanding debt saw a gradual increase in average maturity (World Bank 2015).

Figure 18.2 visualizes in more detail how international banking adjusted very differently along the cross-border lending margin and the foreign direct investment (FDI) margin (i.e. foreign-bank ownership). The top panel shows how countries with a higher reliance on cross-border borrowing in 2007 saw a much sharper decline in cross-border borrowing over the subsequent 2007–14 period. This negative relationship is particularly pronounced for countries in Europe's *East* and *Periphery* (indicated by the white and grey dots, respectively).

In sharp contrast, the panel at the bottom shows no obvious relationship between foreign-bank penetration in 2007 and the change in banking FDI over 2007–13. Foreign bank penetration increased or decreased pretty much independent of countries' initial level of foreign-bank presence. Note, however, that a few countries with very low initial foreign-bank penetration showed relatively sharp declines as (some of) the foreign banks that were present left the country. Examples include the departure of French Crédit Agricole from Greece and the demise of Belgian Fortis which had a substantial presence in the Netherlands.

Figure 18.3 shows that in all three sub-regions, lending by BIS-reporting banks to local banks came down much more than lending to non-financial corporates.[9] As a result of the Eurozone debt crisis, the cross-border adjustment was particularly strong for bank-to-bank lending to the European *Periphery*. Lending to peripheral banks peaked in 2007 at USD 2.6 trillion and then declined to just 1 trillion in 2014 (−61 %). In contrast, cross-border lending to corporates in peripheral Europe peaked only in 2009 and then declined from a high of USD 1.5 trillion to just over USD 1 trillion in 2014 (i.e. a decline of 'only' 31 %).

A somewhat different pattern can be observed in the *East*. Cross-border lending to banks peaked in 2008 at USD 329 billion and then declined to USD 186 billion in 2014 (−43 %). Lending to corporates in this region peaked a year later, in 2009, and declined from USD 253 billion to USD 151

[9] Figure 18.3 is based on BIS locational statistics which capture outstanding claims and liabilities of banks located in BIS reporting countries. These claims include intra-group positions between offices of the same banking group (i.e. lending by parent banks to foreign affiliates through an internal capital market).

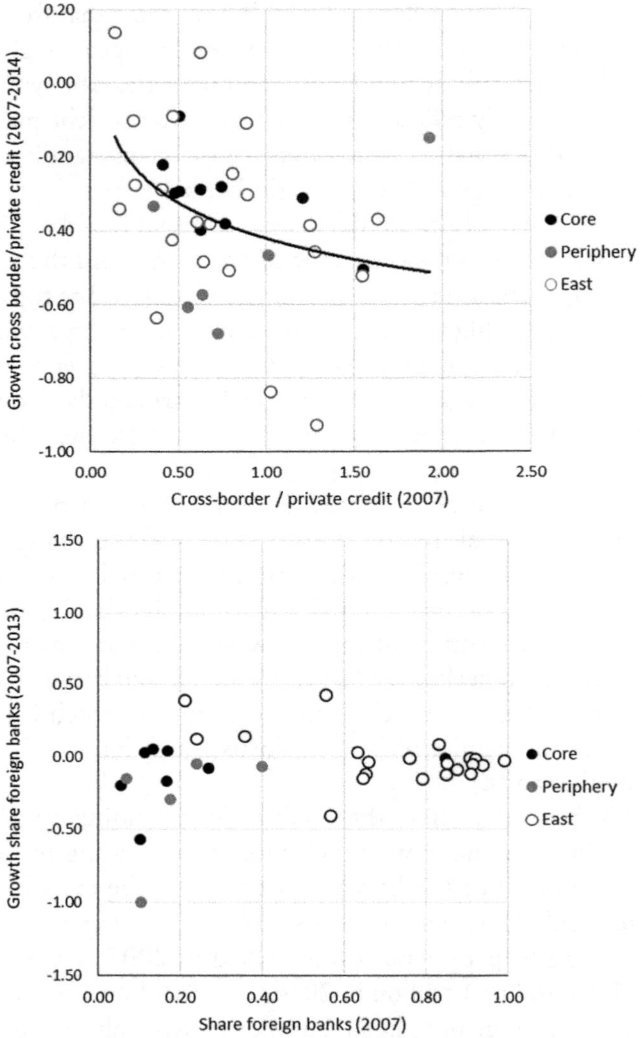

Fig. 18.2 Adjustments in cross-border and multinational banking across Europe (*Sources*: BIS, World Bank, BankScope and Claessens and Van Horen (2015). Cross-border data refer to total international claims (cross-border lending plus local claims in foreign currency) as taken from the BIS consolidated banking statistics on an immediate borrower basis. (*Note*: This figure shows the relationship between countries' reliance on cross-border bank lending before the crisis (2007) and the change in their reliance on cross-border lending over the period 2007–14 (*top pane*) and the relationship between the share of banking assets owned by foreign-bank subsidiaries before the crisis (2007) and the change in foreign ownership of bank assets over the period 2007–13 (*bottom pane*, includes all countries with foreign-bank ownership >5 % in 2007))

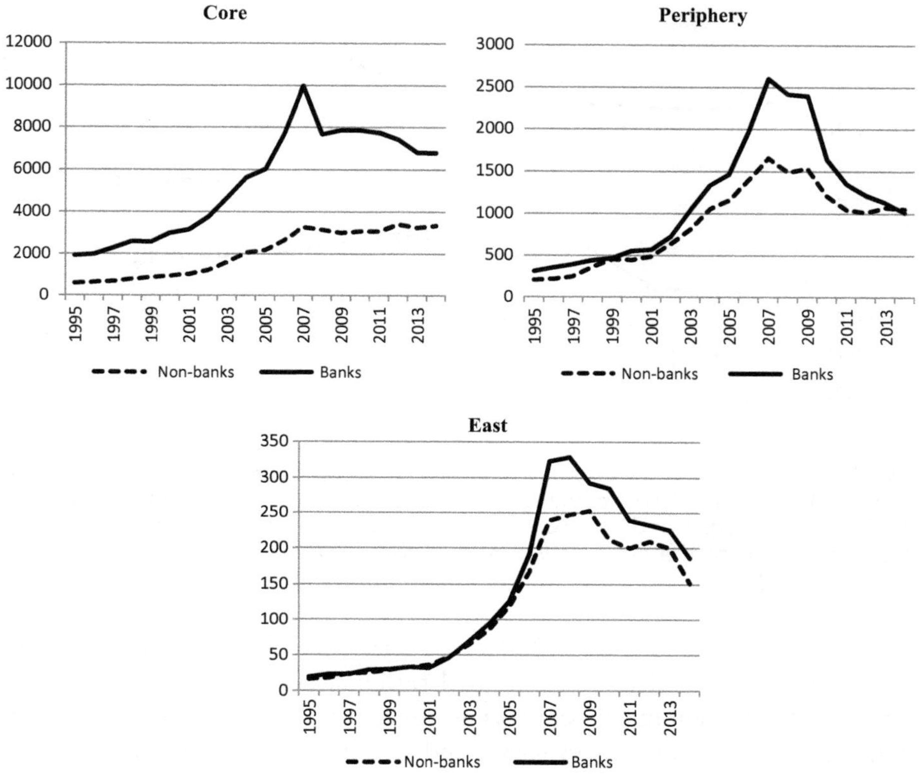

Fig. 18.3 Cross-border deleveraging: Banks versus non-banks (*Source*: BIS locational statistics; *Note*: This figure shows the development over time of the external positions of reporting banks vis-à-vis banks and non-banks in all currencies (US$ billion; adjusted))

billion in 2014 (−40 %). In relative terms lending to the bank and non-bank sector where therefore hit similarly in the *East*.

In *Core* Europe, cross-border lending to banks peaked in 2007 at nearly USD 10 trillion, ending a long credit boom in the wake of the introduction of the euro. Lending to *Core* banks then declined to almost 7 trillion in 2014 (−32 %). In contrast, lending to *Core* European corporates peaked at USD 3.3 trillion in 2007 and then stayed pretty much stable at that level until 2014. This relative and absolute stability in lending to European *Core* companies partly reflects that US banks significantly increased their activities in *Core* Europe, by 58 %, over this period.

Overall, these figures indicate a rapid decline in the share of cross-border lending absorbed by banks. In *Core* Europe this share declined from 65 % in 2007 to 60 % in 2014. In peripheral Europe this share declined from 62 %

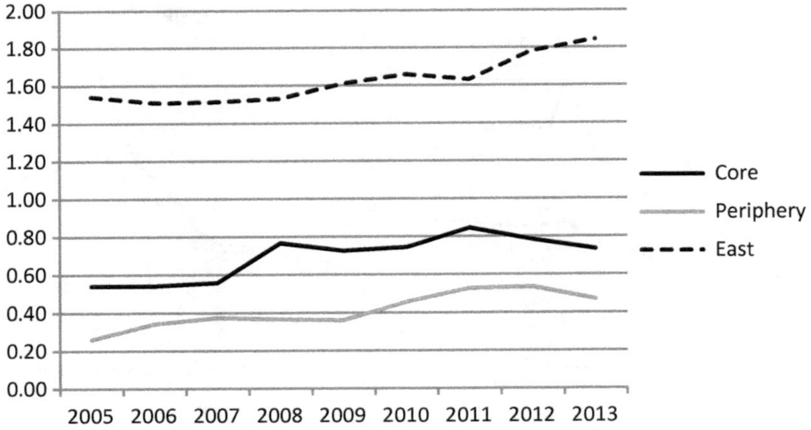

Fig. 18.4 Banking integration: from international to multinational banking (*Source*: BIS (consolidated banking statistics on an immediate borrower basis), Bankscope, Claessens and Van Horen (2015); *Note*: This figure shows the development over time of the ratio between total foreign bank assets and total cross-border claims)

to 48 % and in the *East* from 25 % to 15 %.[10] The fact that bank-to-bank lending shrank considerably more (and earlier) than bank-to-firm lending, reflects that the banking system was at the core of the crisis and that banks find it particularly difficult to screen and monitor other lenders in times of uncertainty.[11]

The combination of substantial negative adjustments in cross-border lending to the three European regions and limited reductions in bank FDI, implies a gradual shift from cross-border towards multinational banking. Figure 18.4 illustrates this trend by showing the ratio between foreign-bank assets and cross-border claims. This ratio is not only considerably higher in the *East* but it has also increased further over the last couple of years (to 1.84) as cross-border inflows dwindled rapidly. In the European *Core* and *Periphery* the ratio is much lower, indicating a stronger use of cross-border credit and less reliance on foreign-bank affiliates. Over time this ratio has nevertheless increased in both these regions as well, albeit less dramatically: to 0.73 in the *Core* and 0.47 in the *Periphery*

[10] The relatively low bank-to-bank lending into the *East* reflects that many Western parent banks use their subsidiaries in this region to fund local companies. While parent banks provide these subsidiaries with cross-border intragroup funding (De Haas and Van Lelyveld 2010), and these flows are included in the BIS locational statistics, these subsidiaries also attract significant local funding.

[11] See De Haas and Van Horen (2013) for empirical evidence from the cross-border syndicated loan market.

Trends in the Structure and Sources of European Bank Funding

Adjustments in Bank-Funding Structures

The global financial crisis has underlined the importance of bank-funding structures as a determinant of lending stability as it became clear that short-term wholesale funding in particular exposes banks to bouts of illiquidity. A prominent example is the failed UK bank Northern Rock, which saw its wholesale lenders run before retail depositors did.

Banks that are deeply integrated across national borders can access foreign wholesale funding by either financing themselves in international wholesale markets or by receiving funding from parent banks through their internal capital markets. It is therefore interesting to see how banks in the European regions adjusted their funding structures when access to both these funding sources became heavily curtailed.

Figure 18.5 compares the European regions in terms of their (weighted) loan-to-deposit ratios, an often-used proxy for banks' dependence on wholesale funding. The data show a rapidly increasing reliance on non-deposit funding in the run up to the crisis, in particular in the *East* where the ratio increased from 0.80 in 2005 to 1.16 in 2008. At the same time this ratio stood at 1.39 in Europe's *Core* and even at 1.51 in the *Periphery*. In the UK, many

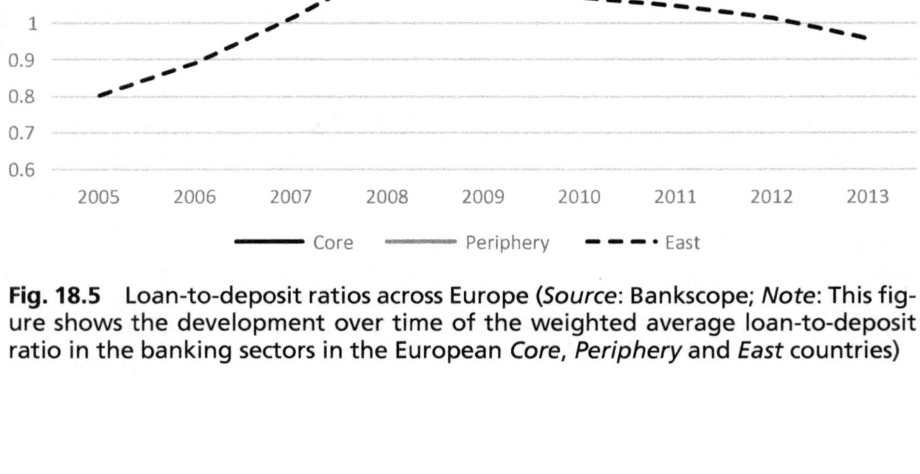

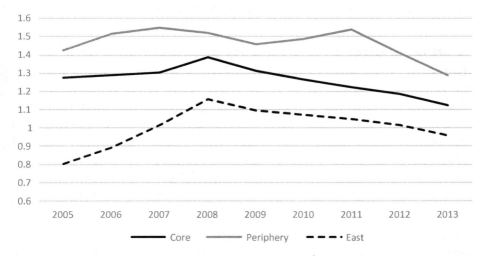

Fig. 18.5 Loan-to-deposit ratios across Europe (*Source*: Bankscope; *Note*: This figure shows the development over time of the weighted average loan-to-deposit ratio in the banking sectors in the European *Core*, *Periphery* and *East* countries)

banks relied on secured funding, especially mortgage-backed securities and covered bonds, whereas in the rest of Europe many banks also relied on unsecured wholesale funding.

Against the background of deteriorating US liquidity due to the subprime meltdown, a sharp reversal of this trend takes place in 2007–08, which has since then continued. All regions have much lower loan-to-deposit ratios in 2013 compared to their peak levels.[12] Several factors can explain this reduction in banks' reliance on wholesale funding. First, a number of European banks, especially those that relied heavily on short-term wholesale funding, had to reduce new lending and dispose of non-core assets.[13] Second, partly due to regulatory pressure, some domestic and foreign-owned banks made efforts to increase their deposit base, thus further reducing the ratio between loans and deposits. Third, weaker demand for loans due to recessions in many European countries also contributed to the downward trend in loan-to-deposit ratios. Finally, exposure to impaired sovereign debt made some banks reduce their (cross-border) lending (Popov and Van Horen 2015) while a higher demand for sovereign debt—due to risk-shifting and carry trading—resulted in some crowding out of lending to the real sector (Acharya et al. 2014).

Banks not only adjusted their loan-to-deposit ratios, and therefore the quantity of wholesale funding, many of them also changed the quality and type of the (remaining) wholesale funding they used. European banks started to shift towards covered bonds and official (ECB) funding sources. Especially banks in the *Periphery* have by now replaced much of their wholesale funding with central bank funding (Babihuga and Spaltro 2014).

Shifting Sources of Cross-Border and Multinational Banking

The global financial crisis and the European sovereign debt crisis did not affect all banks equally. Internationally operating banks that were more exposed to the crisis faced a stronger need to reduce cross-border credit (Cetorelli and Goldberg 2011; De Haas and Van Horen 2012). Furthermore, the academic literature suggests that—contrary to a general "run for the exit"—there are clear patterns as to how banks readjusted their cross-border loan portfolio

[12] Notwithstanding these adjustments, European banks remain relatively reliant on wholesale funding when compared to for instance the USA and other regions where loan-to-deposit ratios are typically far below 100 %. In the USA this ratio stands at about 62 % and in Japan at 78 % (Le Leslé 2012).

[13] See Yorulmazer and Goldsmith-Pinkham (2010) for the United Kingdom; Rocholl et al. (2011) for Germany; De Haas and Van Lelyveld (2014) for Emerging Europe; and Iyer et al. (2014) for Portugal.

during and after a crisis. De Haas and Van Horen (2013) show that cross-border (syndicated) lending declined in particular to more distant countries, countries where banks were less experienced, and countries where banks were less integrated into a network of domestic co-lenders. How did these dynamics play out in Europe?

Figure 18.6 uses confidential bilateral consolidated data on international claims at the immediate borrower level from the BIS to assess to what extent the composition of total bank lending to the three European regions has changed in the wake of the global financial crisis.[14] The figure shows that in *Core* Europe, there has been a shift in source countries away from *Peripheral* Europe and other *Core* European countries towards more inflows from other Organisation for Economic Co-operation and Development (OECD) countries. Before the crisis, many European banks were heavily involved in cross-border dollar intermediation as they extended (relatively cheap) dollar credit to non-US borrowers (Shin 2012; McCauley et al. 2015). This role was quickly reduced during the crisis. In relative terms there was a particularly sharp decline in cross-border lending by Belgian and Dutch banks and by Spanish and Italian to (other) *Core* countries.[15]

At the same time, there was an increase (both in relative terms and in absolute volumes) in cross-border lending by American and Swedish banks. While US banks ranked number 8 in 2007 in terms of total cross-border lending volume into Europe's *Core*, they had become the second largest lender to *Core* Europe in 2014 (with German banks remaining in the top spot and French banks in the third position). Low US interest rates and an international search for yield by American banks partly explain their increased role as European financiers. In addition, US banks also rebalanced their portfolios towards relatively risky European companies as these borrowers were most affected by the retrenchment of European banks. As US banks were effectively still operating under the Basel I regime, this shift in risk did not affect their capital requirements (Bacchetta and Merrouche 2015).

In peripheral Europe, lending by *Core* and other peripheral European countries more than halved in absolute terms, again highlighting the strong fragmentation in European cross-border lending. Belgian, Dutch and especially Irish banks were among the lenders that most rapidly deleveraged. Here as well, US banks stepped in and quickly became the number 3 aggregate lender (from 9th position in 2007).

[14] International claims include both cross-border claims and local lending by foreign subsidiaries and branches in foreign currency. As the data are on a consolidated basis, intra-office positions are netted out.

[15] Part of the decline in cross-border lending by Dutch banks is due to the sale and subsequent split of ABN Amro into RBS, Santander and Fortis.

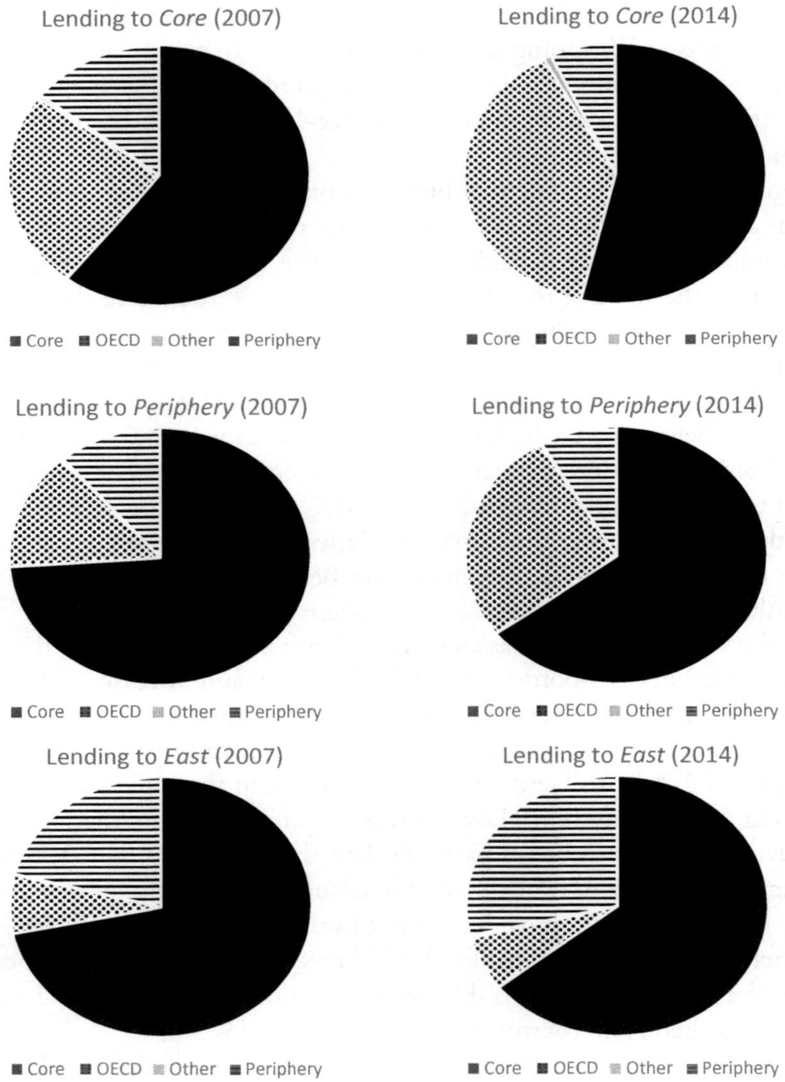

Fig. 18.6 Cross-border bank lending to Europe: Shifting source regions (*Source*: BIS bilateral bank lending statistics; *Note*: This figure shows shifts in the relative importance of various source regions of cross-border lending into the European *Core*, *Periphery* and *East* in 2007 (*left*) and 2014 (*right*))

In the *East*, there has been a relative increase in lending by peripheral countries while the share of *Core* European lenders declined. Cross-border lending by Belgian, Swedish and Irish banks declined in particular and the literature has shown that this reduction in cross-border lending was an important channel through which the global financial crisis was propagated eastwards (Ongena et al. 2015). American banks also expanded their activities in this region (both in absolute as in relative terms) as did Portuguese and Spanish banks (albeit in all three cases from a relatively low base level).[16]

Figure 18.7 provides a similar analysis but now with a focus on shifts in the ownership structure of banking systems in the three European regions. It is immediately apparent that the composition of FDI has proven remarkable stable over the 2007–13 period, in particular in *Core* and *Peripheral* Europe. In *Core* Europe, most foreign-owned bank assets remained in the hands of banks that are based in other *Core* and/or OECD countries. In the *Periphery*, the local presence of foreign banks declined overall as banks from *Core* countries reduced their activities. This increased the relative market power of subsidiaries owned by banks headquartered in other peripheral countries.

Finally, in the *East*, there was a limited reduction in the assets owned by foreign banks from the *Core* and other OCED countries, with an increase in asset ownership by banks from the *Periphery*, the *East* and—in particular—other emerging markets (which includes Russia). A good example of this trend is the purchase of the Central and Eastern European subsidiary network of Austria's Volksbank by Russia's Sberbank. Other examples include the sale of Denizbank in Turkey to, again, Sberbank and Optima Bank (formerly ATF Bank) in Kyrgyzstan which was Italian owned but became Kazakh owned. Finally, Chinese banks have also gradually become more active in Eastern Europe as they follow Chinese firms into this region. Major (state-owned) Chinese banks, such as Bank of China, ICBC and China Construction Bank have opened representative offices, subsidiaries or branches in countries like Hungary and Poland.

This trend of increased banking regionalization is by no means unique to the *East* region, but is prevalent in other parts of the world as well (Claessens and Van Horen 2015). For instance, Chile's Corpbanca recently bought the Colombian operations of Santander while British HSBC sold its operations in Costa Rica, El Salvador and Honduras to Banco Davivienda of Colombia.

[16] Note that the data compare the stock in outstanding claims between 2007 and 2014. Even though Spanish and Portuguese banks were heavily affected by the European sovereign debt crisis, which made them curtail new cross-border lending flows, the 2014 stock of cross-border loans also reflects pre-crisis commitments.

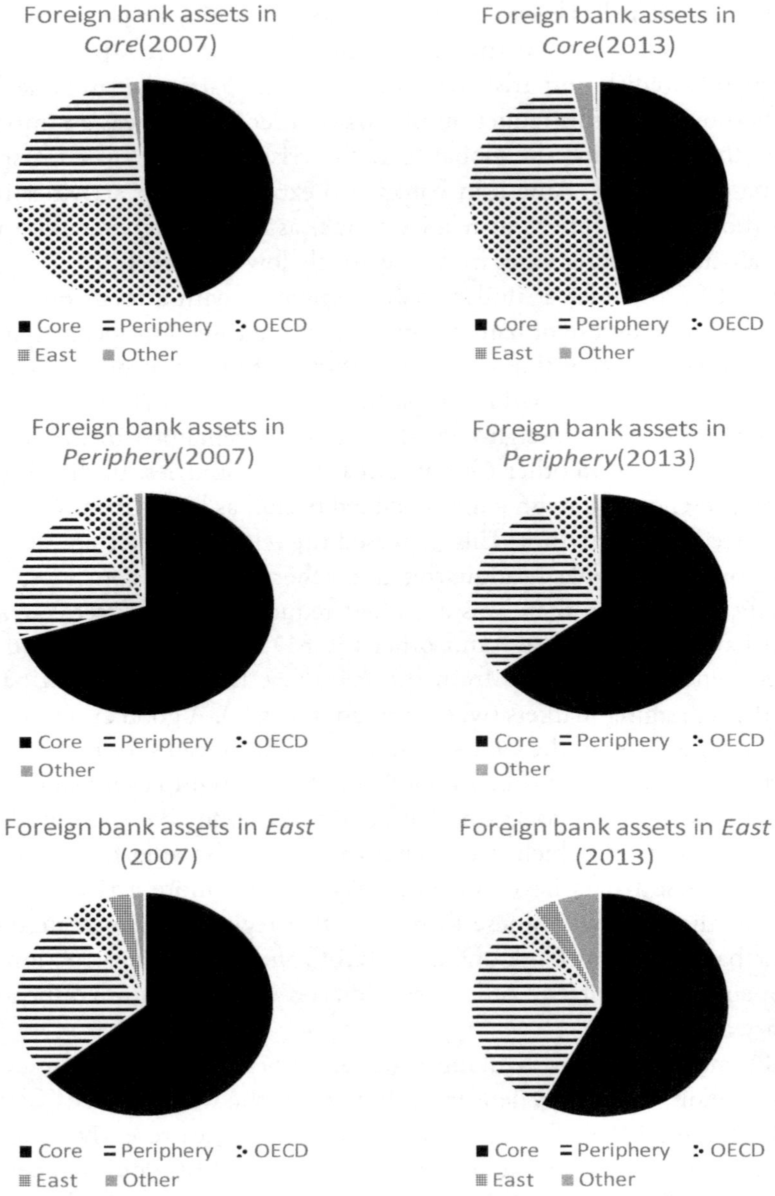

Fig. 18.7 Foreign bank presence in Europe: Source regions (*Source*: Bankscope and Claessens and Van Horen 2015; *Note*: This figure shows the home regions of foreign investors in European banking assets in 2007 (*left*) and 2013 (*right*). Each pie chart shows the distribution of foreign-owned bank assets in that destination region split by source region)

What are the possible consequences of this change in ownership patterns? The academic literature suggests that the benefits and risks posed by foreign banks can differ substantially depending on where the parent bank is based and what business model it employs. On the one hand, strategic investors from nearby countries may introduce technologies that are better adapted to the specific needs of the countries in which they invest. They may also be better placed to collect and process 'soft' information and hence to lend to more opaque borrowers. On the other hand, there may be less scope for the transfer of state-of-the art lending and risk-management technologies and know-how. How these effects will play out on aggregate remains unclear. What is evident, however, is that the increased prominence of "east-east" banking is likely here to stay as it reflects the growing role of emerging markets in the global financial markets and economy more widely.

Disintermediation: The Increasing Role of Corporate Bond Markets

Before the global financial crisis, European banks with easy access to wholesale funding played an important role in intermediating abundant dollar liquidity to corporate borrowers in Europe and other non-US destinations (Rey 2013). The previous section has shown how the subsequent rapid decline in cross-border lending by European banks has been partially counterbalanced by an expansion of cross-border lending by American banks into Europe.

A second 'safety valve' has been the fast expansion of bond issuance by large companies. An increasing number of firms outside the USA have started to issue dollar bonds as demand from investors searching for yield was high. This demand was in turn boosted by the compressed bond term premiums as a consequence of the Federal Reserve's bond-buying programs (Ayala et al. 2015). As a result, the stock of dollar bonds issued by corporate borrowers outside of the US has been growing faster and more steadily in recent years than the bank debt of these borrowers (Shin 2013; McCauley et al. 2015). Corporate bond funding has turned out to be a less procyclical source of finance than bank lending.

Also in Europe, corporate bond issuance has been growing in the wake of the global financial crisis. Figure 18.8 shows the increase in corporate bond funding for Europe's three regions. As a percentage of gross domestic product (GDP), corporate bond issuance in the *Core* has increased from just below 1 per cent of GDP in 2007 to almost 4 % in 2014. In the European *Periphery*,

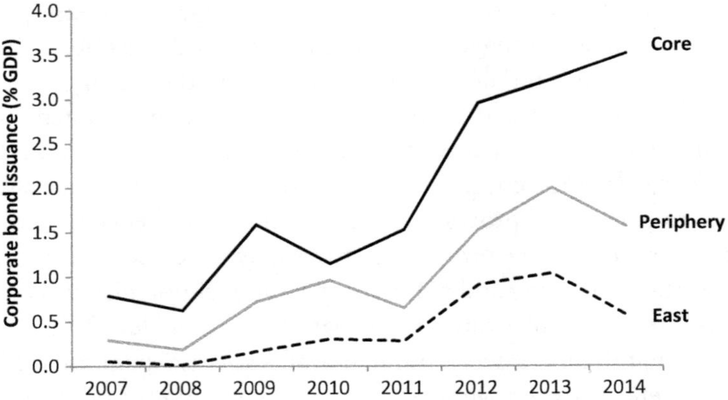

Fig. 18.8 New corporate bond issuance (% GDP) (*Source*: Bloomberg and IMF; *Note*: This figure shows the development over time of bond issuance by non-financial companies in the European *Core*, *Periphery* and *East* (as a percentage of GDP))

these numbers were 0.3 % in 2007 and 1.6 % in 2014. In the *East*, corporate bond issuance was virtually absent in 2007 and amounted to 0.6 % of GDP in 2014.[17] Many of these bond issuances are international in nature and involve the raising of funds abroad (World Bank 2015; Gozzi et al. 2015). The resulting bonds are typically not held by banks but by other financial players, including mutual funds and pension funds. This means that the associated credit risk is now less concentrated in—relatively well-regulated—banks but has spread through other parts of the financial system.

Figure 18.9 shows that over this period corporate bond issuance has increased from 15 % to 21 % of all corporate debt of the non-financial private sector in Europe's *Core*. In the *Periphery* and *East* the relative importance of corporate bonds has increased as well—from 7.1 % to 10.3 % in the *Periphery* and from 4.4 % to 9.1 % in the *East*. While (the largest) European corporates seem to have become less dependent on bank credit, the figure also suggests that there is still ample room for a further expansion of corporate bond funding in Europe, especially for smaller companies. In the USA, bonds make up 68 % of all debt to the non-financial corporate sector whereas this percentage is 42 % in Latin America.

Building the Capital Markets Union, aimed at a deeper and more integrated European capital market, can be expected to help accelerate this

[17] The recent (2014) declines in the *Periphery* and the *East* are driven mostly by Italy and Ireland in the former region and Ukraine in the latter.

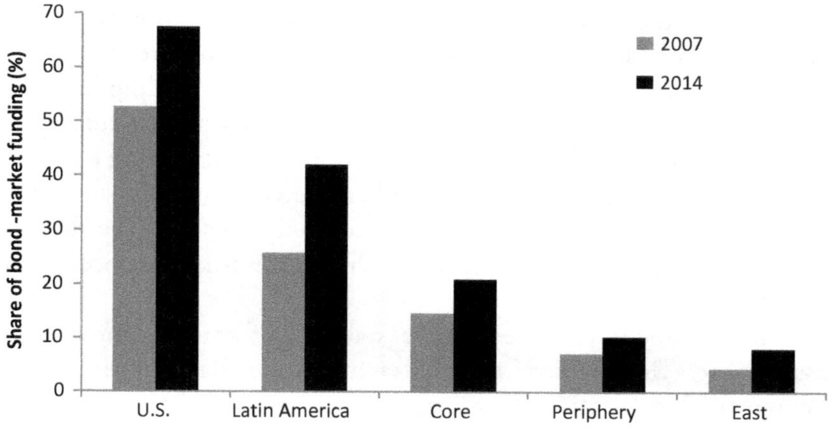

Fig. 18.9 Outstanding corporate bonds (% total non-financial corporate debt) (*Source*: Fed; Eurostat, BIS, national sources and IIF; *Note*: This figure shows for selected regions the GDP-weighted share of outstanding corporate bonds within the total non-financial corporate debt. *East* here includes Bulgaria, Croatia, Czech Republic, Estonia, Latvia, Lithuania, Hungary, Poland, Romania, Slovak Republic and Slovenia. *Latin America* includes Argentina, Brazil and Mexico)

trend.[18] It may ensure the availability of more diversified sources of finance available to corporates, including SMEs, by improving access to non-bank funding. Furthermore, the deepening integration of bond and equity markets will strengthen cross-border risk sharing and provide a buffer against shocks to the financial sector. The Capital Markets Union will also help to create a level playing field as insolvency regimes are harmonized and the overall quality of rules and regulation converges towards international best practices.

Conclusions

This chapter has provided a succinct overview of European banking trends during and in the immediate aftermath of the global financial and Eurozone debt crises. We first document a sharp retrenchment in cross-border bank lending. The growth losses due to this increased fragmentation of European banking markets are likely to be substantial (Schnabel and Seckinger 2015). Cross-border bank deleveraging may undo some of the tangible benefits that banking integration has had in terms of speeding up the economic converge of Europe's *Periphery* and *East* with its *Core* (Friedrich et al. 2013).

[18] See the Green Paper "Building a Capital Markets Union", European Commission, 18 February 2015.

Second, the crisis-related reduction in cross-border lending was strongest in countries that had built up the largest cross-border exposures before the crisis. Moreover, reductions in bank-to-bank cross-border lending have turned out to be much more volatile than those in bank-to-corporate lending.

Third, we show that the decline in cross-border bank lending has partially been replaced by bank lending from other source countries—in particular the USA—and by an increase in corporate bond issuance. The funding of the European corporate sector has slowly shifted towards more bond and less bank funding.

Fourth, we document the relative stability of multinational banking across Europe. That is, little overall fragmentation has occurred in terms of foreign-bank ownership. In Europe's *East*, there has been a gradual but notable expansion of the ownership of bank assets by banks headquartered in Eastern European or other emerging countries. At the same time, the role of Western European (*Core*) banks as strategic owners of Eastern European subsidiaries has been somewhat reduced. It is possible that also in cross-border banking a shift has taken place towards more funding by banks from Europe's *East* and other emerging markets. However, as only a very small number of emerging markets report to the BIS it is currently not possible to capture these trends.

Fifth, we show that banks across all three European regions continue to adjust their funding structures. There has been a sharp reduction in banks' loan-to-deposit ratios since the start of the global financial crisis as banks were cut off from wholesale funding and had to rely more on customer deposits to finance their loan portfolios.

For now, it remains an open question to what extent the abovementioned trends will continue in the future. With liquidity gradually restored in wholesale markets, European banks may regain some of their business in intermediating dollar liquidity. Furthermore, part of the reduction in cross-border lending is demand driven and cross-border credit flows are hence likely to pick up when growth in Europe accelerates. Finally, a continued divergence of interest rates between the US and the Eurozone may shift the attention of US banks and investors back to their home country as their search for foreign yield becomes less pressing. This may in turn slow down the growth of European corporate bond markets.

Going forward, two other issues are likely to affect European cross-border banking. First, we expect that emerging-market banks continue to expand their role as cross-border lenders in Europe, reflecting their growing role in the global economy. This trend will probably involve banks from a variety of emerging markets, but Chinese banks may play a special role. Confronted with slowing economic and credit growth at home, Chinese banks have become more outward oriented. The Chinese government's Belt and Road Initiative—a huge drive to increase Chinese foreign direct investment along the former Silk Road from Central Asia to Europe—has the potential to deepen Sino-European trade and investment links. This will present an opportunity for Chinese banks to follow their clients abroad and in the process they may also start servicing local companies. We therefore expect increased cross-border lending from China into Europe as well as an expansion of Chinese banks' presence on the ground. The recent acquisition of Turkey's Tekstilbank by the Industrial and Commercial Bank of China (ICBC) can be seen as a precursor to this trend.[19]

Second, future cross-border lending in Europe will also depend on how large European banks will deal with new total loss-absorption capacity (TLAC) regulations. This regulation aims to ensure that banks have sufficient access to loss-absorbing liabilities so that shareholders and creditors (and not the taxpayer) bear the brunt of any bank resolution. Subsidiaries of European G-SIBs—globally systemically important banks such as BNP Paribas, Nordea and Unicredit—as well as banks that are domestically systemically relevant (D-SIBs) may therefore be required to issue more liabilities with high loss-absorbing capacity. This will in particular be the case for subsidiaries of banks that decide to follow a so-called multiple point of entry approach. Such subsidiaries need to take care of their own external TLAC rather than get internal TLAC allocated to them by their parent banks (as would happen in a single point of entry approach where the parent is part of a global resolution plan). To the extent that European G-SIB subsidiaries will be part of multiple point of entry regimes, they will thus face their own TLAC requirements as independent resolution entities. In particular in Europe's *East*, this could once more increase subsidiaries' dependence on (FX denominated) cross-border wholesale funding (Santiago Fernández de Lis 2015). Such a development could then offset some of the gains these banks have made in recent years in terms of bringing down their loan-to-deposit ratios to more sustainable levels.

[19] The African experience suggests that increased ownership stakes of Chinese banks in Europe and rising cross-border lending flows from China to Europe may go hand-in-hand. For instance, in October 2007 ICBC acquired a 20 % stake in South Africa's Standard Bank. About two years later, ICBC—together with Bank of China, China Development Bank, and China CITIC Bank—provided Standard Bank with a US$ 1 billion cross-border loan.

References

Acharya, V., Eisert, T., Eufinger, C., & Hirsch, C. (2014). *Real effects of the sovereign debt crisis in Europe: Evidence from syndicated loans* (CEPR discussion paper no. 10108).

Ayala, D., Nedeljkovic, M., & Saborowski, C. (2015). *What slice of the pie? The corporate bond market boom in emerging markets* (IMF working paper no. 148). Washington, DC: International Monetary Fund.

Babihuga, R., & Spaltro, M. (2014). *Bank funding costs for international banks* (IMW working paper no. 71). Washington, DC: International Monetary Fund.

Bacchetta, P., & Merrouche, O. (2015). *Countercyclical foreign currency borrowing: Eurozone firms in 2007–2009* (CEPR discussion paper no. 10927).

Cetorelli, N., & Goldberg, L.S. (2011). Global banks and international shock transmission: Evidence from the crisis. *IMF Economic Review, 59*(1), 41–76.

Claessens, S., & van Horen, N. (2015). The impact of the global financial crisis on banking globalization. *IMF Economic Review, 63*(4), 868–918.

De Haas, R., & Van Horen, N. (2012). International shock transmission after the Lehman Brothers collapse. Evidence from syndicated lending. *American Economic Review Papers & Proceedings, 102*(3), 231–237.

De Haas, R., & Van Horen, N. (2013). Running for the exit? International Bank lending during a financial crisis. *Review of Financial Studies, 26*(1), 244–285.

De Haas, R., & Van Lelyveld, I. (2010). Internal capital markets and lending by multinational bank subsidiaries. *Journal of Financial Intermediation, 19*(1), 1–25.

De Haas, R., & Van Lelyveld, I. (2014). Multinational banks and the global financial crisis: Weathering the perfect storm? *Journal of Money, Credit, and Banking, 46*(1), 333–364.

De Haas, R., Korniyenko, Y., Pivovarsky, A., & Tsankova, T. (2015). Taming the herd? Foreign banks, the vienna initiative and crisis transmission. *Journal of Financial Intermediation, 24*(3), 325–355.

Fernández de Lis, S. (2015). TLAC implementation in retail banks in emerging markets: The multiple point of entry model, European economy. *Banks, Regulation, and the Real Sector, 2015*, 2.

Friedrich, C., Schnabel, I., & Zettelmeyer, J. (2013). Financial integration and growth—Why is emerging europe different? *Journal of International Economics, 89*(2), 522–538.

García Herrero, A., & Martínez Pería, M. S. (2007). The mix of international banks' foreign claims: Determinants and implications. *Journal of Banking & Finance, 31*(6), 1613–1631.

Giannetti, M., & Laeven, L. (2012). The flight home effect: Evidence from the syndicated loan market during financial crises. *Journal of Financial Economics, 104*(1), 23–43.

Gozzi, J., Martinez Peria, M. S., Levine, R., & Schmukler, S. L. (2015). How firms use corporate bond markets under financial globalization. *Journal of Banking and Finance, 58*, 532–51.

Haselmann, R., Wachtel, P., Sobott, J. (2016). Creditor rights and bank lending in Central and Eastern Europe. In T. Beck & B. Casu (Eds.), Handbook of European banking. Chapter 20. NewYork: Palgrave Macmillan.

Iyer, R., Peydró, J. L., da-Rocha-Lopes, S., & Schoar, A. (2014). Interbank liquidity crunch and the firm credit crunch: Evidence from the 2007–2009 crisis. *Review of Financial Studies, 27*(1), 347–372.

Le Leslé, V. (2012). *Bank debt in Europe: Are funding models broken?* (IMF working paper no. 299). Washington, DC: International Monetary Fund.

McCauley, R., McGuire, P., & Sushko, V. (2015). Global dollar credit. *Economic Policy, 30*(82), 187–229.

Ongena, S., Peydro, J. L., & van Horen, N. (2015). Shocks abroad, pain at home? Bank-firm level evidence on the international transmission of financial shocks. *IMF Economic Review*, forthcoming.

Peek, J., & Rosengren, E. S. (2000). Implications of the globalization of the banking sector: The Latin American experience. *New England Economic Review*, (September/October): 45–63.

Popov, A., & van Horen, N. (2015). Exporting sovereign stress: Evidence from Syndicated Bank lending during the euro area sovereign debt crisis. *Review of Finance, 19*, 1825–1866.

Rey, H. (2013). *Dilemma not Trilemma: The global financial cycle and monetary policy independence.* Proceedings of the Federal Reserve Bank of Kansas City Jackson Hole economic symposium, Federal Reserve Bank of Kansas City, 285–333.

Rocholl, J., Puri, M., & Steffen, S. (2011). Global retail lending in the aftermath of the US financial crisis: Distinguishing between supply and demand effects. *Journal of Financial Economics, 100*, 556–578.

Rose, A. K., & Wieladek, T. (2014). Financial protectionism? First evidence. *Journal of Finance, 69*(5), 2127–2149.

Schnabel, I., & Seckinger, C. (2015). *Financial fragmentation and economic growth in Europe* (CEPR discussion paper series no. 10805). London.

Shin, H. S. (2012). Global banking glut and loan risk premium. *Mundell-Fleming lecture IMF Economic Review, 60*(2), 155–192.

Shin, H. S. (2013). *The second phase of global liquidity and its impact on emerging economies.* Keynote address at the Federal Reserve Bank of San Francisco Asia economic policy conference, Federal Reserve Bank of San Francisco, 3–5 November.

World Bank. (2015). *Long-term finance, global financial development report 2015–2016.* World Bank Group Washington, DC.

Yorulmazer, T., & Goldsmith-Pinkham, P. (2010). Liquidity, bank runs, and bailouts: Spillover effects during the northern rock episode. *Journal of Financial Services Research, 37*(2), 83–98.

Part V

European Banking Systems

19

Banking in the UK

Philip Molyneux

Introduction

UK banking has been impacted by major shocks, including the turmoil of the 2007–8 global financial crises, the 2011 euro sovereign debt crisis, the mis-selling of payment protection insurance (PPI), LIBOR, FX and other rate-fixing scandals. As a consequence of these 'shocks' UK banking has suffered big losses, forced significant government intervention and led to major regulatory reform. The scale of government intervention has been unprecedented and has included three main types of intervention: guarantees for bank liabilities; recapitalisations; and various asset support measures. According to EU (2015) total state support to UK banks between 2008 and 2013 amounted to 19 % of the country's (2013) gross domestic product (GDP). Around €191 billion was for guarantees and other liquidity measures and the remainder went to recapitalizations and asset relief (€140 billion). The significant injection of state funds, coupled with subsequent regulatory reforms (including moves to adhere to Basel III capital and liquidity requirements, see Farag et al. 2013) have aimed to boost banking system soundness, limit excessive risk-taking, and improve banking sector conduct. A new bank resolution regime has also been put in place (Gracie et al. 2014). The authorities have also been active in promoting new bank entrants—known as "challenger" banks

P. Molyneux (✉)
Bangor Business School, Bangor University, Bangor, UK
e-mail: p.molyneux@bangor.ac.uk

T. Beck, B. Casu (eds.), *The Palgrave Handbook of European Banking*,
DOI 10.1057/978-1-137-52144-6_19

to compete with the big four—Barclays, HSBC, Lloyds and Royal Bank of Scotland (NatWest). There has also been ongoing investigation into the competitive nature of UK banking, most recently highlighted by the findings of the Competition and Markets Authority (CMA) (2016) report on retail banking. This highlights the authorities desire to increase competition in the system, especially in the light of the high degree of market concentration (see Haldane 2011) in certain sectors of the banking business—especially personal and small and medium- size enterprise (SME) areas. It also illustrates concerns over "too-big-to-fail" or "too systemically-important-to-fail" issues that surround the largest banks—Liikanen (2012) noted that HSBC, Barclays and RBS (NatWest) all had consolidated assets greater than national GDP. While the aforementioned CMA review ruled out the possibility of the break-up of the major banks they did suggest that impediments to competition remained and they recommend a variety of measures aimed at facilitating customer switching (with potential benefits at £70 per customer over a year).

It is against this backdrop, that this chapter outlines these developments. The chapter is structured as follows: the "Trends and Challenges" section outlines recent trends and challenges faced by the UK banking system, followed by "UK Regulatory Developments". The next section, "Structural Reforms", provides a brief comparison of UK, EU and US reforms and the "UK and European Banking Union" section outlines views on the European Banking Union. "Structure and Performance Features of UK Banking" follows, and the penultimate section covers "Challenger Banks". The final section concludes.

Trends and Challenges

UK banking continues to face a challenging operating environment despite signs that the economy is recovering. Since the global financial crisis banks have had to significantly boost their capital and liquidity positions in line with increased domestic as well as international (Basel III) requirements. Typically, banks have boosted their capital strength by issuing more capital and at the same time reduced their risk-weighted assets (RWA). Investment banking / trading activities have been scaled back, as have other riskier areas of lending. Another interesting feature of the aforementioned developments relates to the downsizing of the international operations of both HSBC and Barclays. Furthermore, all the major banks have made substantial provisions for potential future litigation concerning LIBOR and other rate fixing cases as well as for the mis-selling of various retail financial products (especially payment protection insurance). By the start of 2016 the major UK banks were all close to becoming (or were) Basel III compliant.

The ongoing structural reform process encapsulated in the Vickers (2011) recommendations (and incorporated into the Financial Services (Banking Reform) Act of 2013) are also gradually being implemented (with a deadline of 2019)—this includes the "ring-fencing" of low-risk retail banking from high risk trading activities as well as other limitations to bank's proprietary trading activity.

Tougher regulations reducing bank's ability to take on higher risk and therefore higher margin/fee activities is helping to make banks' safer but also reducing their revenue generating capability. Moreover, increased compliance and other operating costs are also squeezing profitability, returns have suffered—since 2013 none of the top five UK banks have posted return-on-equity (ROE) greater than 10 %, and given the fragile macroeconomic environment and weak future growth forecasts its seems likely that this level of returns will be made in the years up to the end of the decade.

The domestic banking market remains highly concentrated and there are concerns about competition in the retail and SME banking areas. It is probable that the major players will continue to introduce new services that facilitate low-cost customer switching. There have also been moves by the authorities to set up new (so-called) challenger banks (the first established in 2010) aimed at offering niche retail and SME business through a range of different operational models and distribution networks—typically with a heavy reliance on new technology. It is too early to tell whether these new banks will pose a big threat to the long-established operators.

UK Regulatory Developments

The UK authorities have introduced extensive reforms aimed at making the banking sector more resilient to shocks, easier to fix when faced with problems and also reducing the likelihood and severity of future financial crises. As in the case of US and EU reforms, the aim is to make sure that taxpayers do not have to bail out troubled banks and that retail customers are least affected (minimizing the likelihood of bank runs) by banking crises. The main structural reform has been the Financial Services (Banking Reform) Act of December 2013 where the legislation aims to improve bank loss-absorbing capacity and also to ring-fence retail and wholesale banking activities. Increased loss absorbency relates to UK banks having to comply with regulatory capital requirements that are higher than the measures proposed by Basel III (the new global regulatory standard on bank capital adequacy and liquidity). Ring-fenced banks will be required to have a ratio of equity to risk-weighted assets of at least 10 %, compared with an EU-wide requirement of 7 %.

In addition, the legislation seeks to impose higher standards of conduct on UK banks. The legislation enacts the recommendations of the Independent Commission on Banking (the Vickers Commission, named after Sir John Vickers) set up by the government in 2010 to consider structural reform of the banking sector. It also introduces key recommendations of the Parliamentary Commission on Banking Standards, which was asked by the government to review banking conduct—namely, professional standards and culture—in the banking industry.

The Act impacts on all UK banks that have more than £25 billion of deposits (just the largest five banks—Barclays, Lloyds, HSBC, RBS and Santander UK). By mid-2016 all these major banks were in the process of finalizing how their activities should be separated, with much legal discussion as to what parts of the bank should be inside or outside the fence. Ultimately, they have to shift their retail operations into separate subsidiaries legally apart from investment banking activity, with 2019 as the deadline date. The main objective of the ring-fencing is that in the event of extreme stress an institution can be recovered or, in the event of failure, rapidly resolved and so reduce the likelihood of contagion through parts of the same banking group. The new legislation imposes higher standards of conduct on UK banks by introducing criminal sanctions on bank employees if their actions lead to bank failure. The legislation also gives depositors, protected under the Financial Services Compensation Scheme, preference if a bank enters insolvency. Depositor protection stands at £75K (£150k for joint accounts) in line with the €100k in the EUs Deposit Guarantee Schemes Directive. (In July 2015 the UK also introduced a £1mn limit for 'temporary high balances'—typically these are proceeds from specific life events like house sales, insurance policy payouts, compensation payments and so on.). The Act also provides government with more (legal) power to ensure that banks are able to absorb losses and it also introduced various restrictions on payday lenders.

Another important feature of recent legislation has aimed to change banker behaviour and industry culture. It is widely believed that behaviour and culture played a major role in the global financial crisis as well as other UK banking scandals such as LIBOR rate fixing and Payment Protection Insurance (PPI) mis-selling. However, the legal and regulatory framework was unclear about how inappropriate cultures and individual behaviour should be dealt with. As such a Parliamentary Commission on Banking Standards (PCBS) was established in July 2012 to evaluate professional standards and culture in the banking sector, (while also taking into account regulatory and competition investigations into the LIBOR rate-setting process). The Commission investigated issues surrounding corporate governance, transparency and actual and potential conflicts of interest and the implications they had for UK regulation and government policy. In June 2013, the Commission released its (fifth) final report, "Changing Banking for Good" that focused on individual accountability, corporate governance, competition and long term financial stability. The recommendations of the Commission proposed:

- A new Senior Managers Regime (SMR) for individuals who are subject to regulatory approval, which will require banks to allocate a range of responsibilities to these individuals and to regularly vet their fitness and propriety;
- A Certification Regime requiring relevant firms to assess the fitness and propriety of certain employees who could pose a risk of significant harm to the firm or any of its customers;
- A new set of Conduct Rules. These cover individual and senior manager conduct rules. The former cover such things as: acting with integrity, due skill, care and diligence, and being cooperative with the regulators. The latter relate to responsible management, taking care that the business is controlled effectively, complying with regulatory requirements, making sure appropriate staff discharge their delegation responsibilities effectively, and dealing in an honest and open manner with regulators.

In July 2014 the Prudential Regulatory Authority took on board the Commission's recommendations and consulted on a new framework aimed at encouraging individuals to take on more responsibility for their actions, making it easier for both firms and regulators to hold individuals to account. The consultation sought to take industry views on enhancing individual accountability through a range of measures, mainly via clarifying the specific responsibilities of senior managers and expanding the population in relevant firms subject to standards of conduct. Details of how these conduct rules have to be implemented have yet to be finally agreed.

Recall that the Financial Services (Banking Reform) Act came into force in December 2013 proceeding and updating the Financial Services Act of April 2013. This made fundamental changes to the way that banks and other financial services firms are regulated. The latter gave the Bank of England primary responsibility for ensuring economic stability by overseeing three new bodies: the Financial Policy Committee (FPC), the Financial Conduct Authority (FCA) and the Prudential Regulatory Authority (PRA). The FPC operates as a committee of the Bank of England and is responsible for assisting the Bank of England in achieving its objectives and macro prudential regulation (Tucker et al. 2013). The PRA and FCA have been formed from the previous main regulatory body, the Financial Services Authority (FSA). The PRA is responsible for the prudential regulation of deposit takers, insurers and significant investment firms. The FCA is responsible for conduct and compliance, with its main operational objectives being consumer protection, integrity and effective competition.

One can observe that the above mentioned legislation highlights the dramatic changes to the way in which banks have to adjust their activities, change their behaviour and deal with a new regulatory architecture to respond to challenges in a new operating environment. Another ongoing regulatory theme has been concern over the competitive features of the industry, particularly retail banking services. The industry has been subject to a range of competition investigations, including Sir Donald Cruickshank's review of retail banking in 2000 and the Independent Commission on Banking in 2011. The Cruickshank review recommended a Competition Commission investigation into current account services and SME business and the establishment of what became the Payment Systems Regulator. The Independent Commission on Banking made broad recommendations including the introduction of a switching service (the seven-day Current Account Switch Service (CASS) launched in 2013). The Parliamentary Commission on Banking Standards in 2013 also made a range of recommendations including a review of account number portability and a voluntary code to provide free basic bank accounts (BBAs) and free use of automated teller machine (ATMs). Both Independent and Parliamentary Commissions recommended that the Competition and Markets Authority should undertake an investigation into the retail banking market and this reported in mid-2016 highlighting obstacles to account switching (among other things).

A challenge in keeping abreast of all these developments is that they take substantial time to feed through into legislation. Take the Financial Services (Banking Reform) Act passed in December 2013, the legislation will not be converted into regulation until the first half of 2016 and will not have to be implemented until 2019 (when Basel III comes into force). Also the cost of compliance is by no means insignificant. The UK Treasury estimates that the annual cost of implementation will be in the range of £1.7 billion–£4.4 billion - the majority of which is the cost associated with ring-fencing.

In addition to these compliance costs, other regulations are put in place to 'make banks pay'! UK banks have to contribute to government finances by paying a bank levy on UK bank debts (introduced in 2011) and a surcharge on banking profits (from summer 2015). The levy is seen as a mechanism for banks to contribute more to the UK economy but also as a measure to discourage them from risky borrowing. When first introduced the levy rate was set at 0.05 %—it was increased to 0.21 % by mid-2015 (in 2014 the levy raised £2.2 billion for the UK Treasury). The levy is not paid on deposits that are covered by deposit insurance; borrowing backed by the UK government; and on the first £20 billion of the bank's taxable debts. Banks also pay only half the tax rate on long-term debts. It is this levy that has led some banks, such as HSBC, to say that it penalizes UK banks that have global operations as they are taxed on global debt, as opposed to other international operators headquartered elsewhere that have sizeable UK operations (and are only taxed on their UK debts). These criticisms (it appears) have been noted as the UK Government's 2015 summer budget stated that the bank levy rate was to be reduced from 0.21 % progressively down to 0.10 % by January 2021. Also of that date the levy will only be calculated on bank's UK based balance sheets (as opposed to their global balance sheets). However, there was a "sting in the tail" in the summer 2015 Budget as the government announced that it was introducing an ongoing 8 % surcharge on bank corporate tax rates (above profits of £25mn) to offset losses from the bank levy, and even though the corporate tax rate is falling from 20 % to 18 % by 2021, banks will then face a marginal tax rate of 26 % on their UK banking profits in 2021 (compared with 20 % nowadays).

From the above one can see that UK banks operate in a new and challenging regulatory environment. Their operations are being reconfigured, de-risked and behaviourally altered. The aim is to improve economic and financial stability, reduce the likelihood of future crises and to enhance the way in which banking business is conducted—enhancing ethical and responsible managerial behaviour. Reforms are being put in place so that by 2019 (a deadline for many regulatory initiatives in the banking arena) UK taxpayers are best protected from any future banking sector meltdowns.

Structural Reforms

Given the consensus that large banks focused too heavily on high risk non-interest revenue generation—particularly through securities trading and investment banking activity—in the run-up to the global financial crisis, this led the USA, UK and Europe to introduce a series of major structural reforms aimed at reducing bank risk and eliminating / minimizsing the likelihood of taxpayer bailouts.

The UK and USA

The structural reforms in the UK stem from the September 2011 Independent Commission on Banking (incorporated in the Financial Services (Banking Reform) Act of 2013) and in the USA in the Dodd-Frank Wall Street Reform and Consumer Protection Act of July 2010. These reforms are similar but they vary in detail. In the UK, the reform ring-fences retail and various investment banking activities whereas the Dodd-Frank Act of 2010 does not allow banks to undertake proprietary trading and limits their hedge fund and private equity activity.

Implementation of these reforms is ongoing. US banks are ahead with implementation of Dodd-Frank and the largest banks are moving rapidly towards full compliance, and, as mentioned earlier, the UK banks are targeting 2019 as the deadline date (the same as Basel III). Clearly, the legislation is at different stages of development and has various features. The US rules outlined in Dodd-Frank are unlikely to be amended. In contrast, the UK law still needs to be converted into regulation, something the UK authorities plan to be in place during 2016.

A comparison of UK and US reforms reveals that both recommend either legal separation or ring-fencing the deposit bank from the investment bank or trading arm, with slight variations. All insured banks have to separate deposit and investment banking activity in the USA whereas in the UK the new rules say that ring-fencing should occur only for banks with retail deposits greater than £25 billion. In the UK trading and investment banking activity can be undertaken by a company in the same corporate group as the deposit bank—so long as it does not pose resolution problems although the US legislation prohibits propriety trading in any group that contains a deposit bank (and the parent of the bank must be a financial holding company if it is to conduct any investment banking / trading). Deposit banks are also prohibited from an array of securities activities—in the USA, for instance, deposit-taking banks are precluded from investing in most securities and entirely from securities dealing (including market-making) and underwriting. Under Dodd-Frank they will also have to move out of some derivatives and credit default swap (CDS) activities that are currently done in the deposit-taking bank. In the UK reforms there is a long list of proposed prohibited securities activities (including propriety trading, securities lending, trading, origination, securitization originated outside the ring-fence and so on)—but these can be conducted if they are regarded as ancillary to the main business. The legislation appears tougher and more restrictive in the USA in regard to the (legal) relationships between deposit banks and investment banks in the same corporate entity, and goes far beyond large intragroup exposure rules (this is because of big US corporate finance interest in conflicts and problems that can be caused by activities such as tunnelling). In contrast, UK rules appear somewhat less clear on these issues. The UK proposes a detailed bank resolution regime whereas Dodd-Frank asks banks themselves to develop their own resolution plans (living wills). Moreover, the UK legislation proposes the use of bail-in debt whereas this is not the case in the USA (although Dodd-Frank may encourage the Fed to ask the biggest banks—systemically important financial institutions, SIFIs—to hold more contingent capital). Systemically important banks have to hold more tier 1 capital than non-systemic banks in both the UK and USA.

The problem for banks is that although the broad features of the US and UK reforms are similar, they differ in detail and in the latter case still need to be fully transposed into regulations. Legal clarity is emerging, but some large international banks fear that dealing with different rules may force them to have a variety of structures in different jurisdictions, which will add significantly to compliance costs.

Europe

Structural banking sector reforms in Europe stem from recommendations made in October 2012 by the EU High-level Expert Group on Reforming the Structure of the EU Banking Sector chaired by Erkki Liikanen (otherwise known as the Liikanen Report). These are to be implemented into EU law by 2017 following a European Council agreement in June 2015. The European reform proposals are similar to those of the UK and USA but have some differences. For instance, the EU plans to legally separate proprietary trading and related trading activities (for only the biggest banks—those with assets over €30 billion and trading activities of at least €70 billion or 10 % of their total assets).

It is interesting to compare the main differences between the UK and EU recommendations. The former proposals stem from a brief to consider structural and related non-structural reforms to the UK banking sector to promote financial stability and competition. The main UK proposals state that:

- Retail banking is to be ring-fenced from wholesale and investment banking;
- Different parts of the same bank should have separate legal entities;
- Systemically important banks and large UK retail banking operations should have a minimum 10 % equity to assets ratio;

- Contingent capital and debt should be available to improve loss absorbency;
- Risk management should become self-contained and less complex for retail banking, but remain complex for wholesale/investment banking;

Key recommendations of the EU's Liikanen Report are:

- Proprietary trading and other significant trading activities should be assigned to a separate legal entity if the activities to be separated are a significant part of a bank's business;
- Banks need to draw up and maintain effective and realistic recovery and resolution plans as proposed by the Recovery and Resolution Directive;
- Banks should build up bail-inable debt and such debt should be held outside the banking system;
- There should be application of more robust risk weights in the determination of minimum capital standards and more consistent treatment of risk in internal models;
- Corporate governance reforms should be enhanced via specific measures that: strengthen boards and management; promote the risk management function; rein in compensation for bank management and staff; improve risk disclosure and strengthen sanctioning powers.

A comparison of UK and EU reforms (as with the US comparison) shows that both recommend either legal separation or ring-fencing the retail from the investment bank The Liikanen proposals also refer to the prohibition of deposit bank's credit exposure to hedge funds and investments in private equity. In terms of intra group exposures and deposit bank / non-bank relationships both EU and UK rules appear somewhat less clear-cut than in the USA. Liikanen asked the Bank for International Settlements (BIS) and the European Commission (EC) to look at these issues in more detail. As we have noted, the EC proposals (linked to other legislation), like those for the UK, outline a detailed resolution plan (in the USA Dodd-Frank asks banks themselves to develop their own living wills). On capital requirements the EC (and therefore UK) banks are subject to the Capital Requirements Directive 4 (CRD IV) and Capital Requirements Regulation (of 2011) that are broadly in line with Basel III. Liikanen also recommended that more capital should be held against trading book exposures and real estate lending and also (as in the UK) systemic institutions should hold more capital than previously.

UK and European Banking Union

Following the turmoil created by the euro sovereign debt crisis in 2011 in June 2012 the European Council outlined proposals to create a European Banking Union as part of a programme aimed at resolving problems in Europe's financial system as well as to create a more robust financial system (European Council 2012; also see Chap.17 in this volume). The proposals had three key elements. First, the responsibility for bank supervision should be at the European level, and common mechanisms should be put in place to second, resolve banks and, thirdly to insure customer deposits.

The first step involved establishing a Single Supervisory System (SSM) with both a European and national dimension—this was established in November 2014 at the European Central Bank. The European level would be given supervisory authority and pre-emptive intervention powers that apply to banks. Part of the process of moving towards a SSM involves implementing regulatory reform of the European Banking Authority (EBA) to adapt its role to the new situation, plus the adoption of new rules on capital regulation (the EUs Capital Requirements Regulation) as well as the fourth Capital Requirements Directive (CRD4). The objective here is to implement a single harmonized supervisory rulebook based on Basel III, rather than on divergent national arrangements.

A major concern of the UK authorities who (along with Sweden) have said they will not participate in the SSM relates to the potential for differential treatment for Eurozone and non-Eurozone member countries. The arrangements are being established to protect 19 euro members banking systems, and the remaining nine non-euro members are being asked whether they will enter into "close cooperation arrangements" to participate. In addition, there are worries that the new arrangements will undermine the position of the European Banking Authority (EBA), an independent EU Authority, established to "ensure effective and consistent prudential regulation and supervision across the European banking sector … The main task of the EBA is to contribute to the creation of the European Single Rulebook in banking whose objective is to provide a single set of harmonised prudential rules for financial institutions throughout the EU" (EBA 2016 http://www.eba.europa.eu). The UK's House of Lords (2012) argues that the SSM is seeking to establish a set of supervisory rules for euro member banks at the expense of efforts by the EBA to create a single rulebook across all EU members. Differential treatment for euro member and non-members also raises concerns about the role of the European Systemic Risk Board as well as the BIS based Financial Stability

Board (chaired by the Governor of the Bank of England) in its role in harmonising regulatory standards across countries.[1]

The second pillar, a European resolution scheme, is to be mainly funded by banks and could provide assistance or support in the application of measures to banks overseen by European supervision. The key objective is to have a mechanism for the orderly shutdown of non-viable banks, so protecting taxpayers in the likelihood of bank failure. Features of the proposed resolution scheme are incorporated in the 2012 Recovery and Resolution Directive that (among other things): applies to all credit institutions and most investment firms, including financial groups; requires firms to have "living wills"; provides for supervisory early intervention powers; specifies minimum harmonized resolution tools (including the power to sell businesses to third parties, to transfer a business to a state-owned bridge institution or bad assets to a publicly owned asset management firm); bail-in debt where debt converts to equity (institutions are required to hold a minimum amount of "bail-inable" liabilities by January 2018); national member states would have to set-up pre-funded resolution funds; national deposit guarantee schemes would be configured for resolution funding purposes.

UK policy makers are sceptical as to whether the EU can establish a credible and effective bank resolution regime. Notwithstanding concerns about different treatment for Eurozone and non-Eurozone members, it is argued that European policy makers and investors have little experience of orderly bank resolution as most bank failures in the past have been dealt with via nationalization or taxpayer capital injections. The bailout of the Fortis bank (a Belgium, Dutch and Luxembourg firm), was regarded an exception and not a resounding success. Moreover, in Europe, insolvency law follows national lines, which suggests the need for a major reform of such laws if a single resolution scheme is to be introduced. In principle, an effective resolution regime should reduce banking sector stability and the cost to taxpayers associated with bank rescues; in practice, however, there is little historical evidence that coordinated orderly resolution can be undertaken to deal with major bank failure.

Finally, the third pillar of the Union is to set up a European deposit insurance scheme, along with the resolution fund, under a common resolution authority. The argument goes that bank deposits must be seen as just as safe in every EU or euro member country, because if capital is mobile, in the event of banking problems deposits will flee to safe havens. This proposal, however, is also controversial as it implies a form of debt mutualization within the EU or Eurozone whereby deposit

[1] Mark Carney (Governor of the Bank of England) chairs the Financial Stability Board in a personal (non-ex officio) capacity.

protection, say, funded by a member with an orderly banking system, would be used to protect depositors in a country with a failing banking system. Schoenmaker (2016) discusses these issues in detail, highlighting that ongoing political objections mean that a common Eurozone deposit insurance scheme seems a long way off. UK policy makers are also generally sceptical regarding the effectiveness of such a scheme. There are doubts as to whether it could be funded appropriately and work effectively in the event of a major European banking crisis. As such, it seems that bank reform and resolution will follow a unilateral path in the UK.

Structure and Performance Features of UK Banking

UK banking has altered markedly following the 2007–8 financial crises. Trends such as deregulation, technological change, as well as further integration through the creation of a European single market have all impacted on the economics of the sector (Goddard et al. 2010). Figure 19.1 highlights the decline in the number of UK banks between 1985 and 2013, as well as in the mutual building society sector. The fall in number of banks, however, has not limited the growth of the industry: "it has grown from around 100 % of nominal GDP in 1975 to around 450 % of GDP in 2013" (Bush et al. 2014, p. 387). In terms of a proportion of nominal GDP the UK banking system is larger than those in the ten biggest EU countries, as well as Japan and the

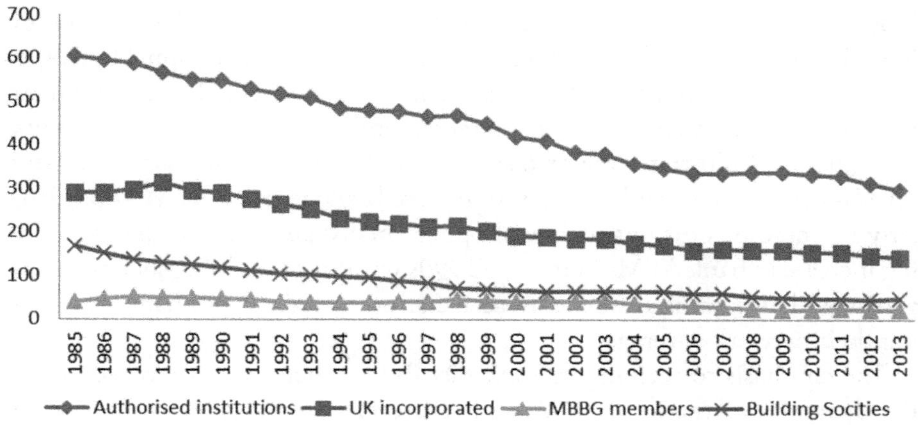

Fig. 19.1 Number of UK banks and building societies (1985–2013) (*Source*: Casu et al. (2015); *Note*: MBBG are major British banking groups comprising the largest UK banks)

USA. Some have also questioned whether European banking overall (including the UK) is overbanked (European Systemic Risk Board 2014).

The reasons for the UK banking sectors relatively large size relates mainly to the international nature of banking business reflecting London's role as a major financial centre. In particular, the aforementioned authors note that the large size stems from four key elements: benefits from clustering in financial hubs; comparative advantage; and various historical factors—all these factors relate to the role of London as a major financial centre. The fourth reason links to bank size and implicit subsidies (lowering funding costs, better credit ratings) associated with "too big to fail" (TBTF) (Noss and Sowerbutts 2012). The International Monetary Fund (IMF) (2014) estimates that in 2011–12 these subsidies amounted to US$20 billion to US$110 billion for major UK banks, US$15 billion to US$70 billion for major US banks, and US$90 billion to US$300 billion for major euro-area banks. As noted already, the largest UK banks dominate certain sectors of the banking market, four (Lloyds, HSBC, RBS and Barclays) currently control nearly 50 % of the mortgage market, 77 % of the personal current account market and 85 % of small business banking. The latter areas have been scrutinized by the competition authorities on a number of occasions (as discussed earlier) and still remain an area of regulatory concern.

It should be also noted also that two of the largest banks—Lloyds and RBS—continue to have a significant government ownership since their rescues in 2008. The authorities have already been successful in offloading other holdings including Bradford and Bingley and Northern Rock Holdings. As at 31 March 2015, the government held 21.8 % of the total share capital of Lloyds and 62 % of voting share capital and 79 % of total share capital of RBS. In August 2015 the government reduced its total share capital by 5.4 % (see http://www.ukfi.co.uk/about-us/market-investments). The government continues to seek ways and means to return both banks to private ownership.

Figure 19.2 illustrates major distribution channels, namely branches and ATMs—clearly the trend has been to replace branches with ATMs—particularly in 'remote' locations such as shopping malls, airports and the like. The big increase in bank ATMs in the late 1990s was due to building societies converting to bank status as well as an acceleration of mainstream banks expanding their network coverage.

The emphasis to reconfigure their distribution networks is a reflection of the dynamics of the industry as well as pressure to reduce costs in a more challenging operating environment. In the run-up to the 2007–8 crises all the main UK banks benefited from a buoyant domestic economy fuelled by loose monetary policy, a booming stock and housing market. Bank's lending books

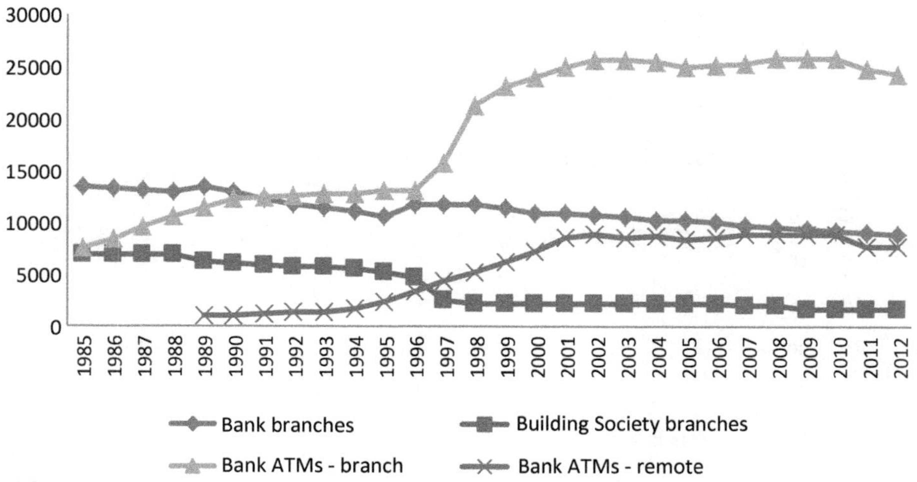

Fig. 19.2 Number of UK branches and ATMs (*Source*: Casu et al. (2015))

became increasingly dominated by mortgage finance at the expense of other forms of lending (consumer lending had been cut back from 2005 to 2006 due to growing impairments) and trading assets also grew relative to other long-term assets. Interest margins remained healthy—in the 3–4 % range—and all the major banks consistently posted ROE in excess of 15 %—easily exceeding cost of capital (generally around 10–11 %). These were the good times of course and all changed after the crisis. Growth and property prices became stagnant, trading income collapsed, regulatory calls for more capital and liquidity forced industry wide de-risking and margins plummeted. The heady days of earning returns in excess of 15 % reverted to a much more conservative environment with banks (by 2015) lucky if they achieved return in double digits (this has led some bank analysts to comment that 10 % is the new 15 %!). See Fig. 19.3.

Since 2010, major UK banks have consistently had to lower earnings forecasts due to a variety of ongoing pressures (Goldman Sachs 2015). Revenues are down due to tighter margins, lower loan growth and trading income. Tougher trading conditions combined with demands to boost regulatory capital have forced all the large banks to reduce their risk-adjusted assets mainly via a contraction of their investment banking activities. Cost reductions have not matched the decline in revenues so this has further put pressure on profitability, although there are at least some positive outcomes on solvency positions. By 2015 all the major banks had capital positions well in excess of the regulatory minimum (Citi Research 2015). According to their

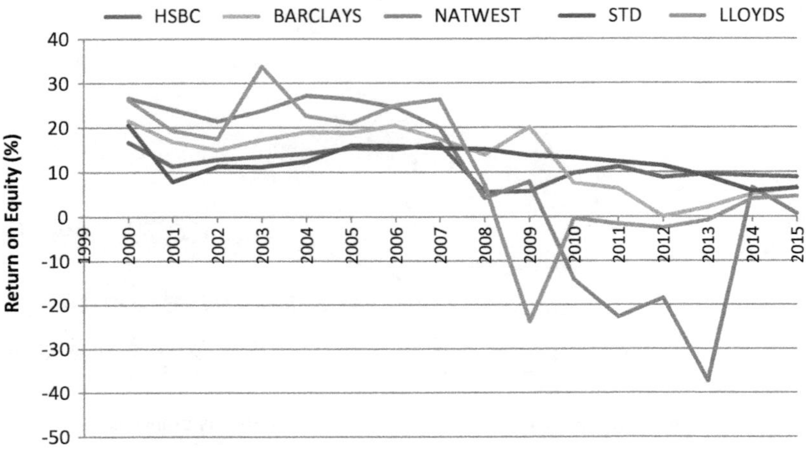

Fig. 19.3 Return-on-equity of major UK banks (*Source*: Bankscope; *Note*: *STD* Standard Chartered Bank)

annual reports, Barclays targets a Basel III core Tier ratio of 11.75 %; Lloyds 12 %, HSBC 12.5 % and RBS 13 %. They are all close to these targets and all now meet leverage (equity to assets) requirements. The liquidity position of the big banks is also improving and all are also close to achieving the new liquidity requirements of Basel III. Returns for 2014 hovered around the 6–8 % level. However, there remain various cost pressures that could still feed through to dampen future profitability (UBS 2015). Conduct and litigation provisions continue to mount. Since 2011 Barclays has dedicated provisions of £3 billion, and NatWest £5.4 billion to deal with settlements in PPI mis-selling, LIBOR and other pending legal actions. Also, margins continue to be squeezed as a result of the narrowing in yield curves brought about by Bank of England Quantitative Easing (QE). Evidence suggests that when QE ends margins will increase and this is also what will happen when official interest rates move up—something most commentators expect from 2017 onwards—so larger margins will feed through into greater revenues and therefore boost net income.

One area that offers growth potential (relative to other parts of the banking business) is in retail banking. Deutsche Bank (2012) analysed key products and returns for the top 23 operators in the market and found that these were earning average returns ranging between 10 % and 17 % between 2009 and 2011—the highest in Europe. Despite low growth and margins, UK retail banking customers have low switching rates, and cost containment is more achievable with the move to greater use of technology and automation. The report provides some interesting insights into product profitability, and it shows that returns are primarily driven by mortgage and deposit business. Deutsche (2012) estimate a mortgage ROE of 28 %, with personal loans and credit cards less attractive at 9 % and 12 %. They forecast that that modest GDP growth would feed through into deposit growth and improvements in the property market boosting mortgage business—both factors that came to fruition by 2015. (In fact the mortgage market has become so buoyant, particularly in the south-east / London region, that the Bank of England has had to introduce Loan-to-Value (LTV) and Loan-to-Income (LTI) restrictions on bank lending books to try and dampen mortgage lending). Buoyancy in the UK retail market is also reflected by the entry of new so-called challenger banks—these are discussed in the following section.

Challenger Banks

Attractive growth prospects, coupled with both regulatory and political efforts to inject competition into the retail banking sector, have encouraged the start-up of a range of new entrants into the UK market (see British Bankers Association 2014). Metro Bank was the first to obtain a full banking licence in 2010 in over a century and six new banks have been authorized by regulators since April 2013. These new entrants—referred to as challenger banks because they compete in a market dominated by long-established operators—Barclays, Lloyds, HSBC, Royal Bank of Scotland (NatWest) as well as the UK subsidiary of Santander. KPMG (2015) identify two main groups of challengers:

(1) *Large Challengers* (Virgin Money, First Direct, William and Glyns, TSB, National Australia Bank NAB, Nationwide)—these are longer established, although Virgin Money and Williams and Glyn are relatively new—both acquired / inherited large portfolios of loans and other business from other bank divestments / sales.
(2) *Smaller Challengers* (Aldemore, Handelsbanken, OneSavings, Metro, Shawbrook and STB)—these have all been established since 2010, were private equity financed initially, and all are now publicly listed.

The challenger bank sector in the UK is one of the major developments and the smallest have been growing their loan books rapidly—some 32 % over 2012–14, compared with 3.2 % for the larger challengers and 2.9 % for the big banks (KPMG 2015). The smaller challengers have also been remarkably profitable generating returns of over 18 % in 2014, compared with 2.1 % for the larger challengers and 2.8 % for the big five. This is mainly a function of their lower cost bases (cost–income ratios around 55 % compared with 63 %+ for other competitors) and slightly higher margins boosted by lower funding costs. Their operations tend to be niche, transparent and simple. Distribution models also tend to vary, Virgin Money (see Goldman Sachs 2014) take deposits via phone banking, post, online and branch/store transactions (and the latter two modes account for 66 % of deposits). In contrast Aldermore deals with its retail and SME customers almost entirely online. Areas which these banks tend to have focused on are consumer credits, buy-to-let mortgages, and some SME lending. The new operators attract clients via other new offerings such as providing loyalty points, store discount cards, free coffee in branches and even free dog biscuits! (Metro Bank). Although it's an early start the challengers are making some inroad into the UK retail banking market. The *Financial Times* (2015) reports that 26 firms have enquired about applying for a banking licence lured by potential opportunities—a 4 % decline in the market share of the big banks up to 2020 translates into a £100 billion lending opportunity with a £5 billion revenue potential. One such bank that aims to start is Atom Bank that plans to use technology and online services to operate at a cost to income ratio of 30 %.

In addition to the success of the small challengers some larger challengers are making inroads into the current account market. TSB (spun out of Lloyds Group in 2014) reported that it was attracting 10 % of new current accounts and Santander UK has become a major beneficiary of a new service making it easier for customers to switch accounts. Also the major retailers, Marks & Spencer's (M&S), Asda Money, Tesco and Sainsbury's all are developing their retail banking services via online and store offerings.

So the retail market is becoming more vibrant offering consumers a broader array of banking services. It remains to be seen whether these challengers, however, can make major inroads into the market share of the big operators (UBS 2015). Some argue that niche specialist offerings can only take the business so far and the industry will need to advance more low cost innovative solutions if it is to have a major impact on the competitive features of the industry.

Conclusions

UK banks continue to operate in a challenging environment with continuing regulatory and operational burdens, although the economic situation is gradually improving. On a positive note, they have embraced a host of reforms and been successful in strengthening their capital positions well in excess of the regulatory requirements. They are already virtually Basel III compliant, have made significant provisions for potential litigation and reduced impairments. So financially they are stronger now than at any time since the global financial crisis of 2007–8. On the negative side, they have significantly de-risked, reducing exposure to investment banking and trading activities, and shrinking the riskier parts of their loan books. Loan growth for the largest banks has been negative so that credit supply has suffered. Major banks still continue to wrestle with their costs and are making gradual improvements, but returns are muted—none of the big banks earn double digit returns on equity. Prior to the global financial crisis returns in excess of 15 % were commonplace, nowadays 10 % is the new target return benchmark.

With increased concentration, particularly in the retail and SME banking areas, there remains regulatory concern that competition is being stifled. Major banks are being encouraged to facilitate more rapid account switching to improve customer dynamics. This is also being bolstered by the start-up of a range of new challenger banks—the first bank to obtain a new retail banking licence in over a century was granted in 2010 and now a range of other operators are entering the market offering niche services through a variety of operational models and distribution networks. The recent growth and financial performance of these small challengers has been impressive but it remains to be seen whether they will make major inroads into the market share of the major banks.

Overall, the capacity for the UK banking system to withstand major shocks has improved, the regulatory framework has been overhauled and there are continuing initiatives to enhance both the governance of banks as well as the conduct of bankers. These and other factors all suggest that the UK banking landscape is heading in the right direction—quite an achievement given the "slings and arrows of misfortune" it has suffered in the recent past.

References

British Bankers Association (BBA). (2014). *Promoting competition in the UK banking industry*. London: BBA.

Bush, O., Knott, S., & Peacock, C. (2014). Why is the UK banking system so big and is that a problem? *Bank of England Quarterly Bulletin, 54*(4), 385–394.

Casu, B., Girardone, C., & Molyneux, P. (2015). *Introduction to banking*. London: Financial Times Prentice Hall, Pearson Education.

Citi Research. (2015). *UK banks in 2015. Earnings, restructuring, capital and dividends*. London: Citi Research.

Competition and Markets Authority. (2015, October 22). *Retail banking market investigation* (Summary of provisional findings report). London: CMA.

Deutsche Bank. (2012). *UK banks. Retail banking 2012: Past, present and future*. London: Deutsche Bank.

European Council. (2012). *Report by the president of the European Council, Herman Van Rompuy, towards a genuine economic and Monetary Union*, June 2012. Available at http://www.ec.europa.eu/economy_finance/focuson/crisis/documents/131201_en.pdf

European Systemic Risk Board. (2014). *Is Europe overbanked?* (Reports of the Advisory Scientific Committee No. 4). Frankfurt: ECB.

European Union. (2015). *State aid scoreboard 2014. Aid in the context of the financial and economic crisis.* Available at:http://www.ec.europa.eu/competition/state_aid/scoreboard/financial_economic_crisis_aid:en.html

Farag, M., Harland, D., & Nixon, D. (2013). Bank capital and liquidity. *Bank of England Quarterly Bulletin, 53*(3), 201–215.

Financial Times. (2015, January 4). Challenger banks try to shake up big four. *Financial Times.*

Gracie, A., Chennells, L., & Menary, M. (2014). The bank of England's approach to resolving failed institutions. *Bank of England Quarterly Bulletin, 54*(4), 409–418.

Goddard, J., Molyneux, P., & Wilson, J. O. S. (2010). Chapter 32: Banking in the European Union. In A. N. Berger, P. Molyneux, & J. O. S. Wilson (Eds.), *The Oxford handbook of banking* (pp. 777–806). Oxford: Oxford University Press.

Goldman Sachs. (2014). *Virgin money holdings. An uncomplicated domestic growth story.* London: Goldman Sachs.

Goldman Sachs. (2015). *United Kingdom banks. 2Q15 preview. Focus on sdtrategy, execution and impact of tax changes.* London: Goldman Sachs.

Haldane, A (2011). *The big fish small pond problem.* Available at http://www.bankofengland.co.uk/publications/Documents/speeches/2011/speech489.pdf

House of Lords. (2012). *European Banking Union: Key issues and challenges: Report, House of Lords (HL) paper 88.* London: HMSO.

IMF. (2014). *How big is the implicit subsidy for banks considered too important to fail?' Chapter 3 in global financial stability report: Moving from liquidity to growth-driven markets.* Washington, DC: IMF.

KPMG. (2015). *The game changers. challenger banking results.* London: KPMG.

Liikanen, E. (2012). *High-level expert group on reforming the structure of the EU banking sector.* Brussels: EU.

Noss, J and Sowerbutts, R. (2012). *The implicit subsidy of banks* (Bank of England financial stability paper no. 15). Available at http://www.bankofengland.co.uk/research/Documents/fspapers/fs_paper15.pdf

Schoenmaker, D. (2016). Chapter 17: The banking union. In B. Casu & T. Beck (Eds.), *The handbook of European Banking.* London: Palgrave Macmillan.

Tucker, P., Hall, S. and Pattani, A. (2013). Macroprudential policy at the Bank of England. *Bank of England Quarterly Bulletin, 53*(3): 192–200. Available at http://www.bankofengland.co.uk/publications/Documents/quarterlybulletin/2013/qb130301.pdf

UBS. (2015). *UK banking monitor, (not quite) a balancing act.* London: UBS Global Research.

Vickers, J. (2011). *Independent commission on banking, final report.* London: HMSO.

20

Banking in Italy

Elena Beccalli and Claudia Girardone

Introduction

This chapter provides an overview of the evolution of the banking industry in Italy and examines the current structural features, strategic challenges and concerns in the aftermath of the financial crisis of 2007–8. In essence, the Italian banking industry appears to be dominated by polyfunctional groups oriented to relationship lending, and from the 1990s operates according to a banking law allowing banks to act as firms. Such a framework raises new issues such as the large amount of non-performing loans (NPL) affecting Italian banks and the need for further reforms, especially for cooperative banks.

The starting point for our discussion is the 1936 Banking Act, which was in force for over 50 years and officially recognized deposit-taking institutions and credit activities as public services. The process of liberalization started in Italy in the mid-1980s and was substantially influenced by the wide deregulation and harmonization efforts at EU level. It culminated with the enactment

E. Beccalli (✉)
School of Banking, Finance and Insurance, Università Cattolica del Sacro Cuore, Largo Gemelli 1, 20123 Milano, Italy
e-mail: elena.beccalli@unicatt.it

C. Girardone
Essex Business School, University of Essex,
North Towers Road, CO4 3SQ Colchester, United Kingdom
e-mail: cgirard@essex.ac.uk

T. Beck, B. Casu (eds.), *The Palgrave Handbook of European Banking*,
DOI 10.1057/978-1-137-52144-6_20

of a new banking law in 1993 that is still in force today and which essentially allowed banks to operate as firms, subject to prudential supervision. In addition, advances in information technology have proved fundamental driving forces behind the modernization and rationalization of the industry, changing banks' strategic focus towards greater efficiency, cost-effectiveness and innovation (Girardone et al. 2004). The process has been unprecedented and to a large extent it is still ongoing as distribution channels that employ new technologies—such as the remote and mobile banking—are increasingly being used (Bank of Italy 2015). Financial innovation has transformed the dynamics of banking globally; in Italy one of the consequences of the merger waves of the 1990s and early 2000s was the creation of large conglomerates or polyfunctional groups.

Until 2007 the Italian banking sector closely followed a path towards the creation of a European single market in financial services. The process of integration was significantly affected by the global financial crisis and the Eurozone sovereign debt crisis. Currently several challenges have emerged in Italy, as the number of bank branches and employees has dropped (by 5.6 % and 9 % respectively over 2008–14), margins shrunk and NPLs increased steadily. In addition, recent controversial reforms have affected the legal and governance status of the largest cooperative banks (*banche popolari*). Another reform that is also being discussed at the time of writing concerns mutual banks (*banche di credito cooperativo*), which aims to improve the efficiency of their lending process and strengthen their governance and resilience (Barbagallo 2015).

This chapter provides an overview of selected issues that are important to understand the present state of the Italian banking sector and is organized as follows. The section "The Evolution of the Italian Banking Sector" gives a bird's eye view of the evolution and key reforms of the Italian banking sector. Next, "The Structure and Performance Features of the Italian Banking Industry" examines the most fundamental changes in the structure and performance of Italian banks over the past 20 years or so. The section "Current Issues In Italian Banking In the Aftermath of the Crisis" focuses on the current challenges affecting the industry. The final section offers some concluding remarks.

The Evolution of the Italian Banking Sector

The level of transformation experienced by the banking industry in Italy since the 1930s has been remarkable. Banking in the period before the Second World War was essentially an activity undertaken in the public interest, and even in the post-war years of reconstruction and development helped the government to pursue stability and growth. Among its fundamental principles were structural controls, conduct rules—including branch restrictions and credit quotas—public ownership dominance and the separation between banks and industry. In addition, banking institutions were classified according to their institutional specialization (ordinary and special credit institutions) and maturity (short- and long-term credit). Most of them were state-owned either directly or indirectly via non-profit-making foundations (*fondazioni*) that were themselves government-supervised (Jassaud 2014).

The policies carried out over those years addressed issues that Italy historically has had to tackle: namely, the marked north–south economic gap and the dense fabric of small and medium-sized businesses (SMEs) that characterizes the backbone of the country's industrial structure. In fact, these policies had a substantial role in shaping the structural features of the banking sector. This is because the Italian authorities focused, on one hand, on the need to redistribute savings across regions; and on the other, on creating a sector with small and medium-sized banking institutions that could serve effectively the financial needs of the many local SMEs. Italian banks became a major conduit for the expansion of credit to the economy, although government intervention and controls were extensive. Restrictions on competition in particular affected the efficient allocation of financial resources and banks' ability to grow (Fratianni and Spinelli 1997; Albareto and Trapanese 1999; Guiso et al. 2006). As a result, until the 1970s the Italian banking industry developed as a highly fragmented, overbanked and overspecialized sector.

From the mid-1980s the process of deregulation gradually reduced authorities' discretional powers: credit controls, lending restrictions and bank branches limitations were abolished and entry liberalized. In addition, Italy implemented several European banking directives that were enacted to accelerate the transition towards the creation of a single market for financial services. This programme was part of a larger objective aimed at integrating goods and markets in the European Union. One of its most fundamental aims was to harmonize rules and regulations to create uniform safety and soundness standards; another was to "level the playing field" by creating a comparable competitive environment across member states (see Casu et al. 2015 for more detail).

In this context, public sector banks were allowed to convert into joint-stock companies; bank mergers were encouraged; and the structural separations between short and long-term lending institutions were abolished in favour of a "universal banking" model. However, in Italy the organizational model that prevailed was the so-called polyfunctional group structure that was preferred to the classical universal bank model that was common, for example, in Germany (see Casu and Girardone 2002 and Chap. 23 in this Handbook). Typically, polyfunctional groups are controlled by a commercial bank (the parent company) and are allowed to offer a wide range of financial services—such as leasing and factoring—that are offered by separate institutions within the same banking group. The main advantages of this model are the greater opportunity of exploiting economies of scale and scope; the capacity of the group to isolate risk from its different activities; organizational flexibility; and facilitation of alliances with other businesses. However, these groups also posed greater concerns for supervisors because of their size and complexities in terms of governance, interconnectedness and too-big-to-fail status.

The Structure and Performance Features of the Italian Banking Industry

The Italian banking industry was highly specialized for many years. The reforms that started in the mid-1980s aimed at providing banks with the structural and organizational models that would allow them to thrive in a more contestable and dynamic market. In 2014 the Italian banking sector included 663 banks, of which 150 belonged to 75 banking groups. As shown in Table 20.1, the segmentation into different types of banks reveals 171 commercial banks (limited company banks accepting short-term funds), 37 cooperative banks (named *banche popolari*), and 376 cooperative mutual banks (named *banche di credito cooperativo*). The cooperative structure is the most common in Italy and comprises over 60 % of all banks.[1]

Focusing on the largest banking sectors in the Eurozone, the Italian banking industry is similar to the French in terms of number of banks although the consolidation trend has been more extensive in France than Italy, as shown in Fig. 20.1. Compared with the years following the implementation of the Second Banking Co-ordination Directive in 1993, the industry has restructured considerably and the total number of banking institutions decreased by over a third. The crisis had a significant impact on the proportion of active banks as the number fell by around 17 % between 2008 and 2015.

[1] It should be noted, however, that while operationally there is no difference between a bank in the form of a company limited by shares and co-operative *popolari* banks, for mutual banks (*banche di credito cooperativo*) there are specific regulations and local and mutual assignments that apply.

Table 20.1 Number of banking institutions, Italy 2014

		Members of banking groups	Not members of banking groups	All banks (No.)	All banks %
Banking groups				75	
Banks	Description	150	513	663	
of which:					
Commercial	*Banche SpA* (limited company banks accepting short-term funds)	120	51	171	*25.8%*
Cooperative *of which:*					
	Banche popolari (cooperative banks)	18	19	37	*5.6%*
	Banche di credito cooperativo (cooperative mutual banks)	11	365	376	*56.7%*
Branches of foreign banks	Foreign-owned banks	1	78	79	*11.9%*

Source: Authors' elaboration on Bank of Italy's data.
[a]Includes former public law banks, banks of national interest, savings and *popolari* banks that changed their legal status since 1990
[b]Includes former rural and artisans' banks

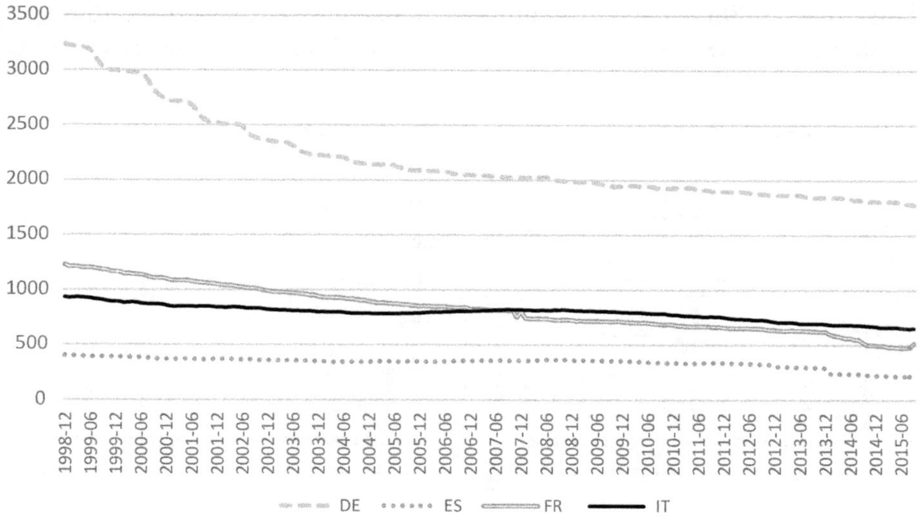

Fig. 20.1 Total number of banks in the four largest banking sectors in the Eurozone (1998q4–2015q2)
Note: *DE* Germany; *FR* France; *IT* Italy; *ES* Spain
Source: Authors' elaboration on ECB Data

Panel (a) of Fig. 20.2 clearly illustrates that in Italy the mutual sector (BCC banks) has experienced the largest decline. The banking industry also underwent wide reorganizations through the rationalization of distribution channels. Over the past 20 years mutual banks have strategically chosen to steadily increase their presence in the country by building up an extensive branch network (panel b). In contrast, the trend in the number of branches of commercial banks follows an inverted u-shape curve thus suggesting a rapid drop post-2007, possibly reflecting a change in strategic focus and cost cutting. Between 2008 and 2014 the number of bank employees was also reduced by 17,900 (5.6 %) (Bank of Italy 2015).

The importance of the Italian banking sector relative to gross domestic product (GDP) has increased significantly since the mid-1980s (Fig. 20.3). From that time the size of the Italian banking industry was slightly above the average of the Eurozone; however, the trend reversed in 2009. In 2014 the Bank of Italy reported that total financial assets were 2.6 times GDP, as against 3.1 in the Eurozone and Germany and 4.0 in France. When compared with its European peers the Italian banking market appears moderately concentrated (Fig. 20.4, panel a). Although concentration has progressively increased over the 1990–2014 period, the consolidation process has not been as prominent as in Germany, Spain and the UK (panel b).

The size of the "typical" Italian bank has also increased over time, particularly during the 2007–8 financial crisis (Fig. 20.5). The number of large (assets>€860m) and medium-sized banks (assets between €250m and €860m), has grown substantially as they acquired many smaller banks (assets

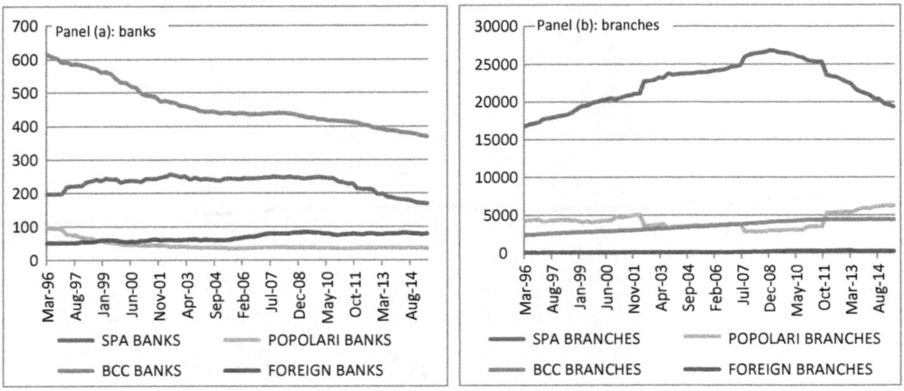

Fig. 20.2 Number of banks and branches in Italy by ownership type (1996–2014)
Note: Commercial banks are referred to as SPA; cooperative banks are the *popolari* banks, and cooperative mutual banks are *banche di credito cooperativo (BCC)*
Source: Authors' elaboration on Bank of Italy's data

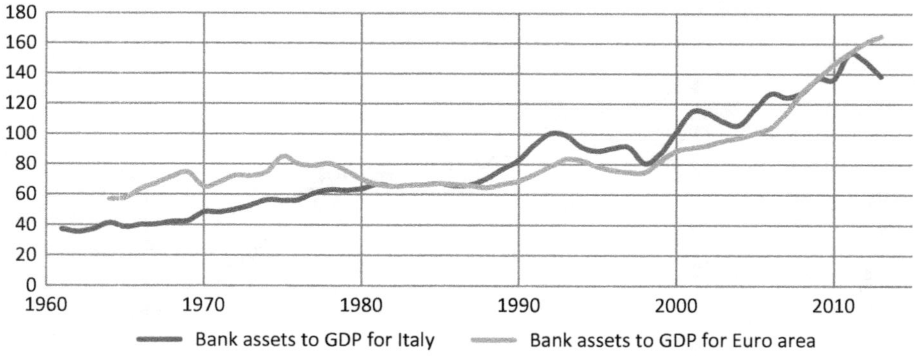

Fig. 20.3 Deposit money to bank assets to GDP: Italy v Euro area
Source: Authors' elaboration on World Bank data

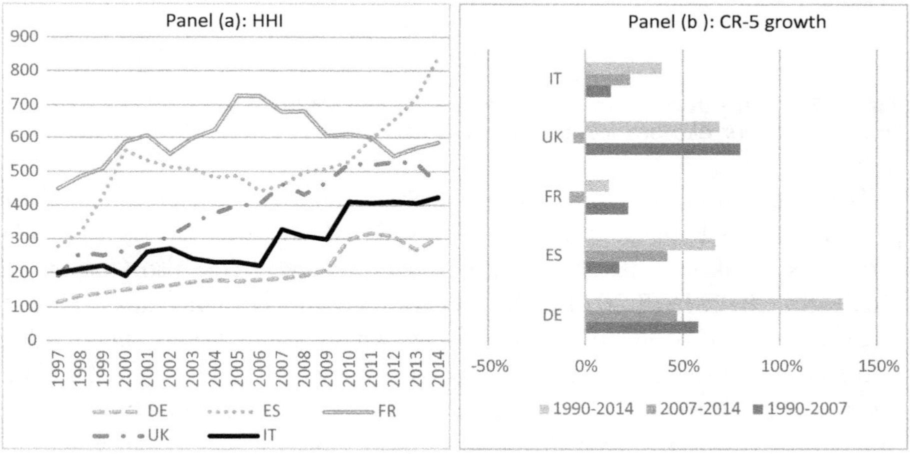

Fig. 20.4 Herfindahl–Hirshmann Index and CR-5 growth in five selected EU countries
Note: *HHI* Herfindahl–Hirshman Index of concentration; *CR-5* = Concentration ratio calculated on the first five banks. *DE* Germany; *FR* France; *IT* Italy; *ES* Spain; *UK* United Kingdom
Source: Authors' elaboration on ECB data.

<€250m), as further explained later in this chapter. Interestingly, in 2010 the number of small and medium banks was equal to the number of medium banks, although over time they show opposite time trends (i.e. increasing trend for medium banks, decreasing trend for small banks). Interpreting these three time series, one could infer that medium and large Italian banks are looking for scale economies deriving from the increase in their size.

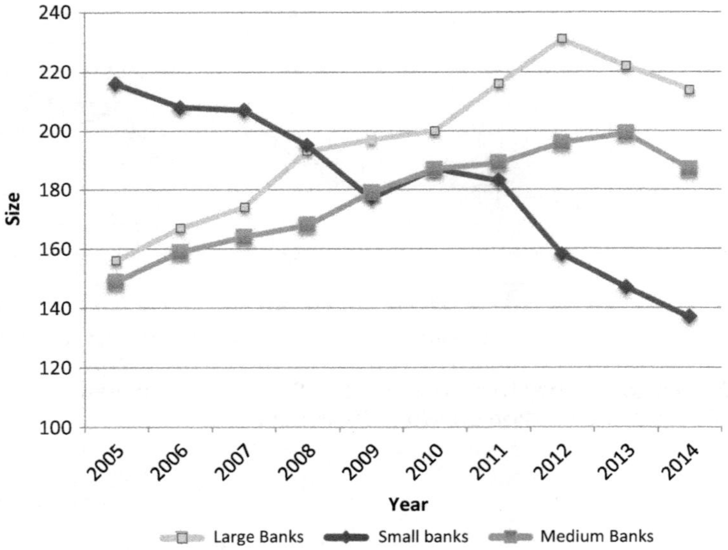

Fig. 20.5 Distribution of Italian banks by size (2002–2014)
Source: Authors' elaboration on Bankscope data

The global financial and sovereign debt crises have severely affected the performance of Italian banks, that have suffered low margins, rising regulatory costs, weak loan demand and high cost of credit (see also Cosma and Gualandri 2012; IMF 2014). The relatively low performance after the outbreak of the 2007–08 crisis is clearly shown in Fig. 20.6 by the trend in Return on Assets (ROA) and the rising cost-to-income ratios. From Fig. 20.7 it is also possible to note how dramatically the income sources of Italian banks have changed over the past 25 years, with non-interest income growing rapidly particularly in the period 1990–2006.

Current Issues in Italian Banking in the Aftermath of the Crisis

The global financial and sovereign debt crises have caused and exacerbated several aspects of the Italian banking system. First, the crises have led to a sharp rise in NPLs, whose incidence has increased to record levels compared with European counterparts. A second result has been the dominance of relationship banking over transaction banking, and its implications for firm financing. Third, the downsizing of the market for bank mergers and acquisitions, nowadays mainly motivated by the need to restructure the target or by reasons

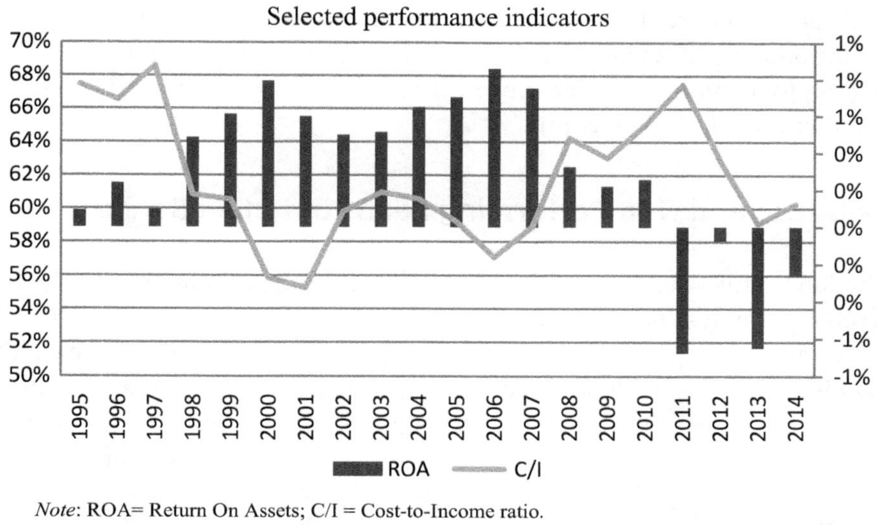

Fig. 20.6 Selected performance indicators
Note: *ROA* Return On Assets; *C/I* Cost-to-Income ratio
Source: Authors' elaboration on Bank of Italy's data

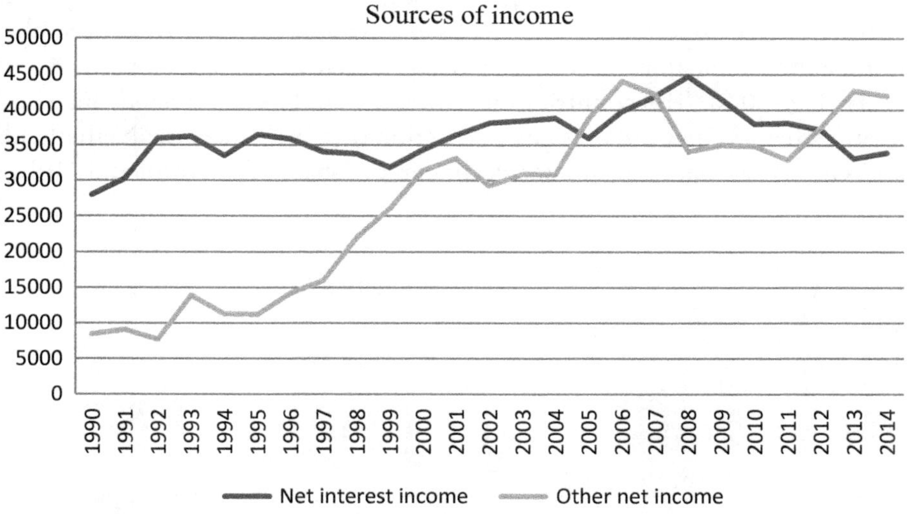

Fig. 20.7 Sources of income
Source: Authors' elaboration on Bank of Italy's data

of defensive nature. Fourth, the need to enhance competition in the system, by introducing a new legal and governance framework for *banche popolari*, leading to a considerable ferment in the sector. These issues are discussed in detail in the following sections.

Doubtful and Non-Performing Loans of Italian Banks

The long crisis which since 2007 has affected financial systems and the real economy has resulted in, among other things, a large amount of NPLs in the balance sheets of European banks, and particularly of Italian banks. The banking system as a whole meets the capital requirements, but at the end of 2014, the stock of NPLs amounts to €350 billion, a level that is four times the European average. The issue concerns primarily the extent of the exposure and the related flows, and especially the presence of such a large amount "freezing" bank balance sheets. The primary challenge connected to the large amount of NPLs in banks' balance sheet lies in greater difficulties to have the necessary flows for lending to customers (that turn into the so-called credit crunch).

The evolution of the phenomenon is very diverse across European countries (Beccalli et al. 2015). A clear segmentation exists between banking systems that have suffered a sharp rise in NPLs and banking systems where the phenomenon has remained very low, showing no particular tightening in recent years (Fig. 20.8). The countries most affected are Greece, Ireland, Italy and Spain, whereas there are no signs of deterioration in France, the Netherlands and Germany (that even shows a decline in the share of doubtful and NPLs).

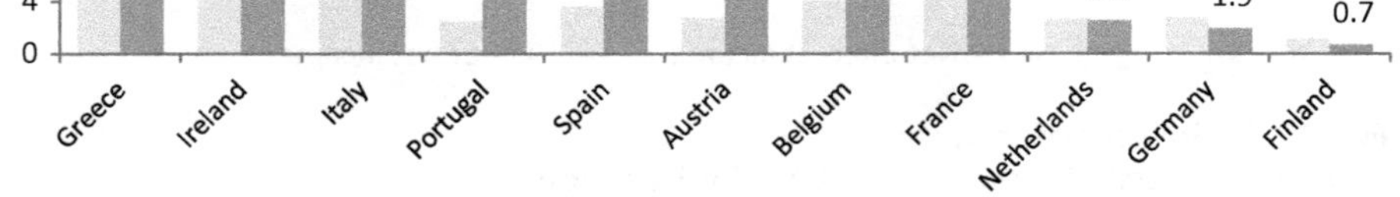

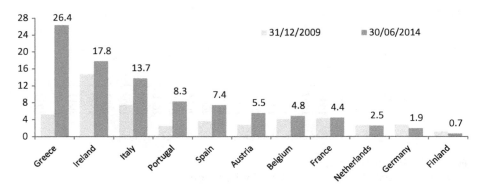

Fig. 20.8 Gross total doubtful and NPLs as a percentage of total debt instruments and total loans and advances (2009 and 2014)
Source: Authors' elaboration on ECB data

Note, however, that in the absence of harmonized statistics on the phenomenon, the European comparison should be conducted with caution, being distorted by differences existing between various countries: the main differences being in terms of definition (Barisitz 2013) as discussed later in this section.

In addition, we observe different behaviours even within the countries most affected by the decline in credit quality. In particular, in Spain and Ireland, the phenomenon has emerged with the private debt crisis and the real estate market crisis and has significantly affected residential mortgages to families and to the construction sector (Bank of Italy 2013). In Italy, on the other hand, the continuous and sustained emergence of NPLs slightly affected families and mostly interested business loans. Changes in the rate of new NPLs of households showed no particular problems, despite the very unfavourable employment context. The relative resilience of Italian households was favoured by their limited level of debt and the very low level of interest rates, as well as initiatives by the banking industry in favour of debt sustainability.

In Italy, as a result of the 2007 financial crisis, the default rate has risen to nearly the highs reached following the 1992–3 recession. However, the current phase is longer than the past one, with the quarterly decay rate of non-financial companies consistently higher than the threshold of 1 % for nine consecutive quarters from the end of 2012 to the end of 2014.[2] With the recession 1992–3, this threshold was exceeded for six consecutive quarters. In the current crisis, the peak of the phenomenon seems to have been reached in 2013 and also in 2014, driven by the outcome of the ECB Asset Quality Review and an unsatisfactory performance of the economy.

The continuous and sustained increase in the default rate has fuelled the growth of the stock of doubtful and NPL (known as *sofferenze*), that has reached 10 % of the total gross loans for the entire Italian banking industry. Such a value is four times higher than that registered at end 2008/early 2009 and is the highest since mid-1998. The average figure comes in a value close to 17 % for non-financial firms and to 7 % for households, with respectively, an increase of nearly 14 percentage points and 4.7 percentage points from the end of 2008, when the incidence of doubtful and NPLs of the two segments was about the same (3 % for non-financial firms and 2.5 % for households). Interestingly within non-financial firms, doubtful and NPLs of the construction industry exceeded a quarter of all loans.

As discussed in Beccalli et al. (2015), there are several factors which influence the level and trend of doubtful and NPLs, primarily the economic cycle,

[2] The decay rate is computed as the flow of doubtful and non-performing loans in a given quarter divided by the stock of loans.

the characteristics of borrowers, the lending policies of banks and other bank-specific characteristics. Then there are factors concerning bank regulation and supervision, standards and accounting practices, taxation, the legal system and the efficiency of the judicial system. While the last two categories of factors have typically a national dimension, what concerns the bank regulation and accounting rules strictly speaking should have a high degree of harmonization at European level. However, at least until the start of the single supervision and adoption of standards on non-performing exposures and forbearance issued by the EBA, there remained significant national differences in terms of regulatory and accounting practices with respect to: (i) classification of loans between performing and the various categories of NPLs; (ii) value adjustments; (iii) disclosure on NPLs. As a consequence, with the increasing deterioration of the loans observed in recent years, it is difficult to compare the credit quality of different European banking systems and, in some jurisdictions, even among banks in the same country. Specifically, the Italian case was distinguished in comparison to the European framework as for: (i) the high degree of disclosure on doubtful and NPLs and the harmonization of the definitions among banks; (ii) the consistency between accounting and supervisory definitions; (iii) the segmentation into distinct categories for increasing abnormality of the credit including, among other things, the class of restructured loans (often considered to be performing in other jurisdictions); (iv) the extensive approach to the borrower rather than for individual positions in default; (v) the reporting including guaranteed non-performing exposures, differently from other jurisdictions considering NPLs net of those secured by collateral. Nevertheless, as said, the latest developments (i.e. the Single Supervisory Mechanism and the adoption of EBA technical standards) go in the direction of overcoming national peculiarities and improve the comparability of data. However, the timing of the adoption of the EBA reporting standards does not yet enables us to have harmonized data on NPLs at European level.[3]

The high level of Italian NPLs, as explained in Beccalli et al. (2015), is also determined by factors external to the banking sector, linked to the characteristics of the tax system, the procedures for settlement of corporate crises, and the functioning of the judiciary system. In particular, in Italy, the stock of bad loans is a result also of the slow procedures for debt recovery, that force banks to keep NPLs in their financial statements longer than in other countries. The relationship between the stock of bad debts to total loans depends not only on

[3] The Asset Quality Review (AQR) conducted by ECB in 2014 saw the implementation of a simplified version of the EBA standard.

the rate of entry in distress, but also on the rate of extinction (defined as the ratio of doubtful and NPLs extinction and the overall total). Between 2007 and 2011 such rate of extinction was reduced by 11 %, from 27 % to 16 %, corresponding to a lengthening of extinction from four to six years (Bank of Italy 2013). Due to the longer timing of debt recovery and insolvency procedures than the EU average, other conditions being equal, the ratio of bad debts is higher in Italy than in jurisdictions where debt recovery is quicker (Bank of Italy 2013). Recently, the International Monetary Fund (IMF) has focused on the slow pace of derecognition of loans in Italy, highlighting the determinants and the negative implications and suggesting a strategy for the development of a market for NPLs in Italy (Jassaud and Kang 2015).

Relationship vs. Transaction-Based Lending

The Italian banking system, like other bank-oriented systems, is typically based on relationship lending (see Angelini et al. 1998). This feature is especially relevant in Italy because SMEs, which are highly bank-dependent for their funding, account for a larger share of output than in most comparable countries.

Several advantages characterize relationship banking: lower financial constraints and better credit terms and conditions are documented for firms that borrow from a small number of banks, or concentrate the bulk of their funding in one relation with a bank, and preserve their relation for a relatively long period (Elsas 2005). Nevertheless, the stability and the efficiency of relationship lending appear vulnerable to several factors: higher switching costs due to the relevance of soft information; the risk that competition in credit markets might limit the incentives for banks to engage in close relationships; and the fact that the efficiency in collecting and processing soft information depends on the internal organization of banks, with small banks usually having a comparative advantage over larger ones.

Recent studies devote attention to the impact of the crisis in Italy with regard to relationship vs. transaction lending. Gambacorta and Mistrulli (2014) investigate how the bank–firm relationship has influenced interest rate setting since the 2008 collapse of Lehman Brothers. Their evidence shows that interest rate spreads increased by less for those borrowers having closer lending relationships. Bolton et al. (2013), using detailed information for Italian banks before and again after the Lehman Brothers' collapse, study how relationship vs. transaction banks responded to the crisis. Their empirical analysis shows that relationship banks charged a higher spread before the crisis, offered more favourable continuation-lending terms in response to the crisis, and suffered fewer defaults, thus confirming the informational advantage of relationship banking. De Mitri et al. (2010) investigate whether relationship lending has had a significant effect in mitigating the credit contraction that followed Lehman's default. Their empirical findings document that firms borrowing from a higher number of banks (or firms diversifying their borrowing, and concentrating a smaller proportion with the main bank) suffered on average a larger contraction in bank credit and a higher probability of experiencing a reduction in outstanding bank debt. The duration of the bank–firm relationship also contributed to mitigate the credit restriction. Finally, if there was a contraction in credit, the decrease was mitigated by the intensity of the relationship (i.e. a lower number of financial institutions from which the firm borrows), the concentration of lending and the duration of the relationship.

Mergers and Acquisitions

There were many mergers and acquisitions (M&As) in the Italian banking system before the global financial crisis. A sharp turnaround was recorded during the financial crisis, however, when M&As slowed down considerably, especially when cross-border (Fig. 20.9).

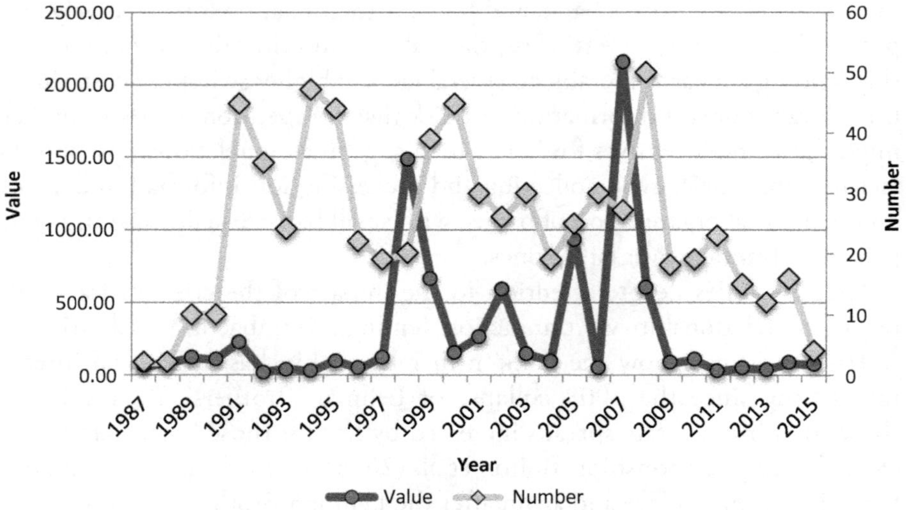

Fig. 20.9 M&A deals (number and value by Italian banks (1987–2015))
Source: Authors' elaboration on Thomson One Banker data

By classifying deals on the basis of the location of the target, cross-border deals have become less frequent since 2007, to the point that there has been no operation with foreign targets in the years 2009–2014. The value of these cross-border deals increased between 2005 and 2008 compared with the 2002–4 period. This indicates that, in the years before the crisis, Italian banks planned fewer cross-border transactions but of greater size. Moreover, during the period 1987–2015, cross-border deals include more frequently targets located in Germany, France and Spain than in other European countries. It is also interesting to note that Serbia, Russia and Hungary were typical countries involved in cross-border deals with Italian banks. Moreover, some 76.4 % of the targets were located in Eastern Europe.

Domestic deals, in contrast to cross-border operations, have been relatively constant over the entire period with a peak in 2008, as well as a higher average size from that same year (when the average value per transaction equals €108 million, i.e. 4,113 billion in total). This indicates that, although Italian banks contined the process of aggregation even during the crisis, the process is mainly focused on domestic deals rather than cross-border deals.

Evidence of the ability of M&As to create value ex post remains uncertain (DeYoung et al. 2008). Recently more attention is devoted to the investigation of the determinants of M&A deals (Beccalli and Frantz 2013). The management of banks is interested in the characteristics that make a business combination more likely in order to identify both potential targets in relation to the strategic choices of expansion and potential acquirer with regard either to integration strategies or defence. Moreover, institutional investors are interested to know the characteristics that can predict the target banks, with reference to choices of composition of their portfolio. Finally, regulators and supervision authorities are interested in the determinants of business combinations, especially among larger banks, for any consequences that they may determine in terms of creating banks too-big-to-fail rather than in terms of supervision in the context of the Banking Union.

As documented in Beccalli and Lenoci (2014), the characteristics of Italian banks that make them more likely to become an acquirer in a cross-border deal are their larger size, lower specialization in traditional lending activity, higher capitalization and the better quality of loan portfolio. Foreign banks that are most likely to become targets are smaller banks, with higher liquidity, better quality of loan portfolio and a history of low growth. The determinants of domestic deals are very different. Only the larger banks are likely to become acquirers along with those banks with a better quality of loan portfolio, whereas banks with lower operating efficiency and a worst funding gap are likely to become targets. Whilst domestic deals appear to be primarily motivated by the need to restructure the target or by reasons of defensive nature such as maximizing the size, cross-border deals seem to be strategic operations motivated by expansion into new markets (i.e. expansion of the client base into new markets and support to Italian companies in their international business needs).

During the crisis, however, given the sharp downsizing in cross-border deals and the strong differences in the determinants of the operations, the main motivation for cross-border transactions appears to have been size maximization pursued via M&As. Consequently, Italian acquirers favoured larger foreign targets, perhaps also seeking the status of too-big-to-fail. This change in the motivation for M&As welcomes the transfer of banking supervision within the Banking Union: the presence of large banks, which tend to become bigger and bigger through cross-border deals, shows that it is appropriate that these banks have a single supervisory authority rather than a plurality of national supervisors.

The Reform of *Banche Popolari*

The reform of *banche popolari* has modified several provisions included in the 1993 Banking Act,[4] that is, the pillar of the regulation of the modern Italian banking system, as discussed in the section "The Evolution of the Italian Banking Sector". This reform aims at strengthening the ability of *popolari* to thrive in a fast-changing banking market, by introducing a new framework of regulation and supervision based on high capital requirements, severe periodic stress tests and the early involvement of shareholders and creditors in any losses.

The reform, as implemented by primary legislation mentioned above, gives the Bank of Italy the task of issuing the secondary legislation. The secondary legislation is intended to complete the arrangements applicable to the *popolari* allowing these banks to adapt to the new reform within18 months (that is by July 2016).[5] Interestingly, the framework in which the Bank of Italy is operating follows the entry into force of the single supervisory mechanism

[4] Decree (*Decreto legge*) issued on 24 January 2015 (no. 3 published in the *Gazzetta Ufficiale*), and approved into law on 24 March 2015.

[5] In view of the urgency of implementing the reform, the Bank of Italy issued the document in a very short time after the entry into force of the law converting the Decree. The outcome of the consultation takes on the guise of an update of the "Supervisory Provisions for Banks" contained in the Circular of the Bank of Italy No. 285 of 17 December 2013 (Bank of Italy 2015) and enters into force on the day following its publication on the website of the Bank of Italy, although a transitional regime has been provided.

(SSM) and of the legal transposition in Italy of Directive 2013/36/EU (the "CRD IV"). At the same time, the regulatory intervention of the Bank of Italy fits into the legal framework defined by the banking crisis on the European Directive on the recovery and resolution of banks. In this context, if capital needs are not met in a short time, they may come to set the conditions for the "resolution" of the bank and shareholders and creditors (other than depositors) would be called to participate in the losses (the so-called "bail-in").

As for the recipients of this reform and how they are identified, the banks under the new framework are the ten *popolari* banks with assets exceeding €8 billion, including seven listed banks and three banks with shares widely distributed among the public (excluding those *popolari* banks whose parent company is itself a *popolari* bank).[6] These entities account for over 90 % of total assets of *popolari* banks. The reform is clearly across-the-board in that it takes as a reference the level of bank assets regardless of how it is distributed among investors and regardless of whether listed or not.

The reform introduces primarily the obligation for banks with assets of over €8 billion to transform into joint-stock company (*Società per Azioni*, SpA) or approve the voluntary liquidation, unless the bank opts for the reduction of capital within twelve months after the threshold is exceeded. The choice is left to the assembly and the lack of a decision of the latter would result in the application of surveillance measures by the Bank of Italy. Moreover, the criteria for calculating the threshold of €8 billion are delegated to the secondary regulations.

Banks that fall within the parameter of assets exceeding €8 billion will have to abandon the principle of the "vote" system (so that in the assembly of shareholders every member can express a single vote regardless of the number of shares he owns or represents). This determines a change of great importance for the governance structure of *banche popolari* because they have always been marked by the importance of per capita voting for the equal participation of members in decisions; in fact, it means that an individual or a bank, Italian or foreign, might come to have an absolute majority in their company. And that *popolari* banks, some of which are in crisis and are looking for new capital, could also be included in the process of merger or acquisition exactly like other lenders. Institutions, in the same meeting that launched the transformation in a joint-stock company, could introduce in the statute a limit of 5

[6] The system of *popolari* banks comprises 70 institutions, but only the top ten are involved (from the largest to smallest: Banco Popolare, UBI Banca, Banca Popolare dell'Emilia Romagna, Banca Popolare Milano, Banca Popolare di Vicenza, Veneto Banca, Banca Popolare di Sondrio, Credito Valtellinese, Banca Popolare Etruria and Lazio, Banca Popolare di Bari). The reform does not apply to credit cooperative banks or small *popolari* banks (that is, those with assets less than €8 billion).

% to the exercise of voting rights. This is a clause that allows defensive protection from the risk of climbing. The cap will be introduced with this majority; however, it is limited to a maximum of 24 months.

The new regime that substantially affects the legal and governance aspects of *popolari* banks has created a considerable ferment in the sector, given that aggregation among the recipients of the new discipline is seen as the only possibility of avoiding possible hostile takeovers and given that it may result in a more competitive banking system after the application of the reform. In fact, one of the consequences of the new rules may be to make easier rising the competition in the system and the attractiveness of Italian banks. Moreover, many observers have seen the risk that the new regime could endanger the lending policies of popolari, because of the concern of exceeding the threshold imposed for maintaining the popolari status. Others have called for a rethinking of the reform to avoid, with the transformation into "joint-stock company", the loss of the participatory democracy principle and relatedly the link with local communities (Barbanti 2015).

Conclusions

From many decades banking in Italy was essentially an activity undertaken in the public interest. A process of liberalization began in the mid- 1980s and culminated in the enactment of a new banking law in 1993 that is still in force today and which allowed banks to operate as firms, subject to prudential supervision. This chapter has offered a synopsis of the recent evolution of the Italian banking sector and has focused on its structural and performance features and current strategic challenges and concerns.

There is no doubt that the performance of domestic banks has been affected significantly by the recent financial crises. Because of the international nature of these events, many of the difficulties that have arisen for Italian banks in recent years are common to other developed countries in the Western world. However, in Italy, as illustrated in this chapter, the crises have caused a sharp rise in bad loans, whose incidence has risen to record levels. Although the deterioration in credit quality affected European countries with different intensity, the Italian banking system appears among those most affected, with a ratio of NPLs among the highest.

One of the most controversial reforms in recent years is that relating to the *banche popolari* that will transform them into joint-stock companies in an effort to make them more competitive and more likely to survive in the fast-changing banking and financial marketplace. Another reform that is currently ongoing and causing considerable ferment in the sector is that relating to cooperative mutual banks (*banche di credito coooperativo*). Stability and efficiency motives are behind these reforms and will no doubt trigger many mergers and acquisitions. As discussed in this chapter, empirical evidence for the ability of bank M&As to create value is not unambiguous. Nonetheless, the organizational structures that are likely to result from these reforms are expected to be better equipped to withstand the pressures of the markets and the increasingly demanding regulatory requirements at the European level.

References

Albareto, G., & Trapanese, M. (1999). La politica bancaria negli anni cinquanta. In F. Cotula (Ed.), *Stabilità e sviluppo negli anni cinquanta*. Laterza: Roma-Bari.

Angelini, P., Di Salvo, R., & Ferri, G. (1998). Availability and cost of credit for small business: Customer relationships and credit cooperatives. *Journal of Banking and Finance, 22*, 925–954.

Bank of Italy. (2013). *Rapporto sulla stabilità finanziaria*, No. 5.

Bank of Italy. (2015). *Annual report for 2014*, Rome.

Barbagallo C. (2015). *Seminario istituzionale sulle tematiche relative alla riforma del settore delle banche di credito cooperativo*. Rome: Senato della Repubblica, 15 October.

Barbanti V. (2015). Riforma delle banche popolari: la finalizzazione dell'impianto normativo nella consultazione Banca d'Italia. *Allen & Overy*.

Barisitz S. (2013). Non-performing loans in Western Europe—A selective comparison of countries and national definitions. In *Focus on European Economic Integration Q1/13*, OENB.

Beccalli, E., & Frantz, P. (2013). The determinants of mergers and acquisitions in banking. *Journal of Financial Services Research, 43*(3), 265–291.

Beccalli E., & Lenoci, F. (2014). *Le determinanti delle operazioni di aggregazione delle banche italiane*. Bancaria 7/8, pp. 27–51.

Beccalli, E., Coletti, E., & Simone, C. (2015). NPLs delle banche europee: Determinanti macroeconomiche e di impresa. *Osservatorio monetario, 2*, 3–24.

Bolton, P., Freixas, X., Gambacorta, L., & Mistrulli, P. E. (2013). Relationship and transaction lending in a crisis. *Temi di discussione Banca d'Italia, n., 917*.

Casu, B., & Girardone, C. (2002). Comparative study of the cost efficiency of Italian Bank conglomerates. *Managerial Finance, 28*(9), 3–23.

Casu, B., Girardone, C., & Molyneux, P. (2015). *Introduction to banking* (2nd ed.). London: Person Education.

Cosma, S., & Gualandri, E. (Eds.). (2012). *The Italian banking system: Impact of the crisis and future perspectives*. New York: Palgrave Macmillan Studies in Banking and Financial Institutions.

De Mitri S., Gobbi G. and Sette, E. (2010). Relationship lending in a financial turmoil. *Temi di discussione Banca d'Italia*, n. 772.

DeYoung, R., Evanoff, D., & Molyneux, P. (2008). Mergers and acquisitions of financial institutions: A review of the post-2000 literature. *Journal of Financial Services Research, 36*(3), 87–110.

Elsas, R. (2005). Empirical determinants of relationship lending. *Journal of Financial Intermediation, 14*, 32–57.

Fratianni, M., & Spinelli, G. (1997). *The monetary history of Italy*. New York: Cambridge University Press.

Gambacorta, L., & Mistrulli, P. E. (2014). Bank heterogeneity and interest rate setting: What lessons have we learned since Lehman Brothers? *Journal of Money Credit and Banking, 46*(4), 753–778.

Girardone, C., Molyneux, P., & Gardener, E. P. M. (2004). Analysing the determinants of bank efficiency: The case of Italian banks. *Applied Economics, 36*(3), 215–227.

Guiso, L., Sapienza, P., & Zingales, L. (2006). *The cost of banking regulation.* NBER working paper No. 12501.

IMF. (2014). *Italy: Selected issues.* IMF country report No. 14/284, Washington, DC.

Jassaud, N. (2014). *Reforming the corporate governance of Italian banks*. IMF working paper, WP/14/181.

Jassaud, N., & Kang, K. (2015). *A strategy for developing a market for non-performing loans in Italy*. IMF working paper, WP/15/24.

21

The German Banking System

Patrick Behr and Reinhard H. Schmidt

Introduction

Germany has a banking system in which privately owned banks have coexisted for more than 200 years with banks marked by direct government involvement. The privately owned banks comprise large commercial banks active on a national and international level such as Deutsche Bank and Commerzbank and a number of other, more specialized private banks as well as the regionally focused, relatively small credit cooperatives. The banks with government involvement are the large, mostly nationally active *Landesbanken* and the smaller, regionally focused savings banks. The savings banks and the cooperative banks follow similar, relatively simple business models focusing on deposit-taking and lending, even though they also offer investment banking activities such as buying and selling securities and, mainly through their networks, also managing investment funds and the like. Hence, these banks can be characterized as universal banks,

P. Behr (✉)
Getulio Vargas Foundation (FGV), Brazilian School of Public and Business Administration (EBAPE), Rio de Janeiro, Brazil
e-mail: patrick.behr@fgv.br

R.H. Schmidt
Faculty of Economics and Business Administration, Goethe-University, Frankfurt, Germany
e-mail: schmidt@finance.uni-frankfurt.de

T. Beck, B. Casu (eds.), *The Palgrave Handbook of European Banking*,
DOI 10.1057/978-1-137-52144-6_21

although the extent to which the local units engage in investment banking activities is rather limited. Both savings and cooperative banks are geographically constrained as their by-laws allow them to provide loans only to borrowers from the same administrative district. On the other hand, the large commercial banks and, to a lesser degree, the *Landesbanken*, offer the full range of products from loans, through investment banking services to insurance products. In particular the large private commercial banks can therefore be characterized as typical universal banks.

The private commercial banks, the small credit cooperatives and the savings banks and *Landesbanken* make up what is often referred to as the "Three-Pillar-Banking-System". This structure makes the German banking system unique, with only the Austrian banking system showing a somewhat similar structure in Europe. In sections "Structural Features of the German Banking System" and "The Structure of the German Banking System", we will give a detailed description of the current structure of the German banking system and its recent developments.

The financial crisis of 2007–8 affected the German banking system and threatened the existence of some large banks from the private sector as well as banks with government involvement. The consequences of the financial crisis of 2007–8 for the German banking system and other challenges facing German banks are discussed in the section "Challenges Facing German Banks".

In the "German Banking in an International Comparison" section we provide a brief comparison of the German banking system with other European banking systems to point out the uniqueness of the German system. Interestingly, contrary to the banking systems of many other European countries, the German system did not undergo major structural changes in the last decades until 2015.

The strong role and involvement of the government in German banking is subject to ongoing debate. The general view on government involvement in banking is that government banks are inefficient because of agency problems, corruption and fraud (e.g. La Porta et al. 2002; Carvalho 2014). However, recent research on the German banking system draws a somewhat different picture. Some authors argue that the existence of small, regionally focused banks has positive effects for local economic development. Others argue that banks with government involvement can help reduce financial constraints for small and medium-sized companies and stabilize the economy and the banking system by displaying less cyclical lending behaviour. We will elaborate more on this and discuss the findings of recent empirical research on the German banking system in the section "Results of Recent Research on the German Banking System". "Concluding Remarks" offers a conclusion and an outlook for the future.

Structural Features of the German Banking System

The Long-Term Development of the German Banking System

The basic structure of the present German banking system already emerged as early as the nineteenth century. While private banks, closely held and often owned by individual families, dominated German banking in the early nineteenth century, they had soon lost ground to what is now known as the "Three-Pillar-System". This system is composed of three groups of banks: private banks including the so-called big banks, banks with government involvement and cooperative banks. The latter group consists of the large *Landesbanken* and the smaller savings banks with a local focus. This group comprises the banks with the longest tradition, dating back to the turn from the eighteenth to the nineteenth century. Then, around 1850, the cooperative banking group emerged as another important group of financial institutions. The "big banks"' were founded at the time of the creation of the Second German Empire after the Franco-Prussian war of 1870–1.

The Great Depression of 1930 led in 1934 to the issuance of the first German banking law. This created a general regulatory and supervisory regime through which savings banks and cooperative banks were on the same regulatory basis as the private commercial banks. Mainly for political reasons, the economic importance of the savings and cooperative banks rose considerably in the period after the Second World War. This is partly due to the fact that these banks had been less involved in the crimes of the Nazi regime than the big private banks. Then, after German reunification in 1990 and under the joint influence of European integration, a general policy of economic liberalization and the acceleration of globalization, the private banks gained economic importance and market share until the global financial crises started in 2007–8. This crisis affected the large private banks more than other banking groups because they were more involved in investment banking activities.

The German Banking System as Part of the German Financial System

For a very long time, the German banks have been the most important part of the German financial sector and even of the entire German financial system.[1] Financial systems are often classified as being either bank-based or capital-

[1] While the term "financial sector" refers to the totality of the financial institutions of a country, we use the term "financial system" in the sense of the interplay between the financial sector as the supplier of financial services and the "real economy" as its customer. Of course, the financial sector is a central ele-

market-based. Together with Japan, Germany is considered as the prototype of a country with a bank-based financial system (e.g. Allen and Gale 2001). This classification is still largely appropriate for Germany today, even though the extent to which the German financial system as a whole is bank-dominated is less evident now than only around the year 2000.

Bank dominance is reflected in the fact that banks are more important in their roles as a source of investible funds for non-financial firms and as an outlet for household savings than other financial intermediaries such as pension funds and life insurance companies as well as in comparison to organized capital markets. Moreover, in a bank-based financial system the relationships between banks and their corporate clients tend to be close according to the so-called house-bank model. Banks often also have a strong influence on many other institutions within the financial sector such as, for instance, investment funds, which tend to be part of large banking groups. Finally, banks also play an important role in the corporate governance of non-financial firms. In all of these respects, bank dominance was evident in Germany at least around the turn of the last century (Schmidt and Tyrell 2004).

Well-functioning financial systems are composed of elements which complement each other and are consistent in the sense of "fitting together well". For many years, the German bank-based financial system was consistent, as is the case for the capital market-based financial systems of Great Britain and the United States. In Germany, the dominant role of banks in the financial sector used to complement the strong role of bank financing for non-financial firms, the prevalence of block-holdings of listed firms, the liberal approach to banking regulation and the Pay-As-You-Go pension system, which does not rely on accumulated funds.

An additional element of the traditional German financial system was the strong role of the three largest private banks in the corporate governance of large German corporations. In contrast to the previously mentioned features, this aspect has by now virtually disappeared. This change poses a true challenge to the former consistency of the German financial system and raises the question of whether there is a tendency of the entire financial system to converge towards a stronger capital-market orientation. However, as we will argue below, even if this should be the case, it would not be due to a change in the structure of the banking system but rather be a consequence of changes in the business model of the largest banks and, as a parallel development, in the corporate governance regime of Germany's large corporations.

---

ment of the financial system. See Schmidt and Tyrell (2004) on the importance of this terminological distinction.

The Structure of the German Banking System

Overview

By international standards, the most important and most remarkable feature of the German banking system is that it is still today a three-pillar system. There are three parts of the banking system and correspondingly three important groups—or types—of banks that differ considerably in terms of their institutional structures and that also compete fiercely for market share.

Pillar one is made up of private credit institutions, classified as such according to both their legal forms and their ownership structures. Since they mainly have private owners, it can be assumed that they are also clearly more profit oriented than banks belonging to the two other groups. The group of private credit institutions is quite heterogeneous. It comprises several subgroups. One of them are the so-called big banks, which maintain large branch networks and offer all kinds of banking services to a wide spectrum of clients in Germany and worldwide. [2] Then there are a considerable number of smaller banks called "regional banks and other commercial banks"in official statistics. In terms of total assets, pillar one makes up about 40 % of the entire German banking system; of which two-thirds are contributed by the big private banks and one-third is contributed by the other, smaller credit institutions.

Pillar two is the savings bank group. It also consists of two parts: that of the local savings banks and that of the regional banks or *Landesbanken*. In terms of aggregate total assets, the entire savings bank group is about as large as that of the private credit institutions, and the respective total assets of the local savings banks and the *Landesbanken* are of almost equal size.

Pillar three is the cooperative banking group. This comprises a larger number of independent institutions than the other two groups, whereas in terms of total assets it is only about half the size of the two other pillars. The cooperative banking group can also be subdivided into two parts, one of them are the local cooperative banks, and the other are its central financial and non-financial institutions.

Strictly speaking, the German banking system extends beyond the three pillars as there is also a fourth group, called "other banks". Among them are mortgage banks, building and loan associations and the so-called special

[2] Big banks (*Grossbanken)* is also the term used in the statistics and publications of the Bundesbank, Germany's central bank, designating banks with a large network of branches.

purpose banks, which include promotional banks (*Förderbanken*) such as the government-owned KfW (Kreditanstalt für Wiederaufbau) Banking Group, currently Germany's second largest bank. Since this fourth group is so heterogeneous, it is not referred to as the fourth pillar. In what follows, we do not take this group into account.

An overview of the development of the three pillars of the German banking system from 2000 to 2014 is provided in Tables 21.1 and 21.2. Table 21.1 shows the numbers of institutions and branches.

Table 21.2 contains information on the groups' market shares with respect to total assets, loans to non-banks and deposits and borrowing from non-banks for the years 2000 and 2014.

Table 21.1 Number of banks and branches by banking groups in 2002 and 2014

	Institutions				Branches			
	2000		2014		2000		2014	
	number	(%)	number	(%)	number	(%)	number	(%)
Private commercial banks	294	(10.7)	296	(16.2)	6,520	(15.1)	9,955	(28.2)
Big banks	4	(0.1)	4	(0.2)	2,873	(6.6)	7,443	(21.1)
Regional banks and others	200	(7.3)	177	(9.7)	3,567	(8.2)	2,364	(6.7)
Branches of foreign banks	90	(3.3)	115	(6.3)	80	(0.2)	148	(0.4)
Savings banks group	575	(21.0)	425	(23.2)	17,530	(40.5)	12,368	(35.0)
Savings banks	562	(20.5)	416	(22.7)	16,892	(39.0)	11,951	(33.9)
Landesbanken and DekaBank	13	(0.5)	9	(0.5)	638	(1.5)	417	(1.2)
Cooperative banks group	1,796	(65.5)	1,052	(57.5)	15,357	(35.5)	11,280	(32.0)
Cooperative banks	1,792	(65.4)	1,050	(57.4)	15,332	(35.4)	11,269	(31.9)
Central institutions	4	(0.1)	2	(0.1)	25	(0.1)	11	(0.0)
Other banks	75	(2.7)	57	(3.1)	3,887	(9.0)	1,691	(4.8)
Realkreditinstitute	31	(1.1)	17	(0.9)	192	(0.4)	48	(0.1)
Bausparkassen	31	(1.1)	21	(1.1)	3,677	(8.5)	1,619	(4.6)
Banks with special tasks	13	(0.5)	19	(1.0)	18	(0.0)	24	(0.1)
All banks	2,740	(100.0)	1,830	(100.0)	43,294	(100.0)	35,294	(100.0)

Source: Based on Deutsche Bundesbank 2015

Table 21.2 Market share by banking groups in 2000 and 2014

	Total assets		Loans to non-banks		Deposits and borrowing from non-banks	
	2000	2014	2000	2014	2000	2014
Private commercial banks	28%	39%	26%	28%	26%	36%
Big banks	16%	25%	15%	12%	14%	15%
Regional banks and others	10%	11%	10%	15%	12%	17%
Branches of foreign banks	2%	3%	1%	2%	0%	4%
Savings banks group	35%	28%	35%	36%	39%	34%
Savings banks	16%	14%	19%	22%	26%	25%
Landesbanken and DekaBank	20%	14%	16%	14%	13%	9%
Cooperative banks group	12%	14%	12%	16%	18%	18%
Cooperative banks	9%	10%	11%	15%	17%	17%
Central institutions	4%	4%	2%	2%	1%	1%
Other banks	24%	20%	26%	20%	17%	12%
All banks (in billion Euros)	6,148	7,853	3,479	3,901	2,261	3,339

Source: Based on Deutsche Bundesbank 2015

Private Commercial Banks

The most important private commercial banks are those with large branch networks. For many years this group had consisted of three banks, Deutsche Bank (founded in Berlin in 1870), Dresdner Bank (founded in Dresden in 1872) and Commerzbank (founded in Hamburg in 1870). In their early years, these banks, as well as other similar banks of that time which have since then disappeared for various reasons, were almost exclusively focused on serving the financial needs of corporate clients. They played an important role in the creation and growth of Germany's large corporations, helping them to expand, get access to the stock market, build up international operations and acquire other firms through mergers and acquisitions.[3] Therefore, the big banks were crucial in the process of Germany's "belated industrialization" (Gerschenkron 1962).

Out of their original role emerged the close relationship of the big banks with the German industry. The big banks became the house-banks of large firms and they maintained this role until the turn from the twentieth to the

[3] A famous example for the latter function is the merger between the two formerly competing car makers Daimler and Benz, which was engineered by Deutsche Bank in 1926.

twenty-first century. Being the house-bank means first of all being the main provider of credit, which had for a very long time been the dominant form of external finance for German corporations, and of other financial services including those now called investment banking services. In most cases the house-banks also played an important part in the governance of the corporations. This governance role was supported by the banks' own substantial shareholdings, seats on the supervisory boards of corporations and depository voting rights in the general shareholder meetings based on the shares which they held in custody for their private clients.

Only in the 1960s did the big banks open up to the general population as clients and expanded their branch networks substantially. However, their business focus was still almost exclusively on Germany. Due to two world wars they had lost their foreign subsidiaries twice and therefore had for a very long time after the Second World War kept their international ambitions at bay.

Another structural transformation began in the 1990s, when the three big banks started to reach out to international markets and attempted to become important players in the area of investment banking. Deutsche Bank was the leader in this process and was very successful with its new strategy. Though with less determination and evidently with less success, Dresdner Bank and Commerzbank imitated Deutsche Bank's new strategy. One consequence of this reorientation was that Deutsche Bank, and to a certain extent the others too, discontinued their role as house-banks, sold most of their substantial blockholdings in German corporations, and ceased taking seats on supervisory boards.

In 2000, an attempted merger between Deutsche Bank and Dresdner Bank failed, and in the following years the situation for Dresdner Bank deteriorated consistently. Just before the outbreak of the global financial crisis in 2007, Commerzbank, traditionally number three among the big banks, acquired Dresdner Bank, traditionally number two. As it turned out, this acquisition was a (too) heavy burden for Commerzbank, which had to be rescued by the German government in the course of the global financial crisis. Nevertheless, at end-2015, the German government held around three-quarters of the shares of Commerzbank.

Almost in parallel with the demise of Dresdner Bank and the quasi-nationalization of Commerzbank, the composition of the group of banks which the German central bank, the Bundesbank, classifies as big banks, changed substantially. In addition to Deutsche Bank and Commerzbank this group now comprises HypoVereinsbank (HVB) and Postbank. HVB has grown out of the merger in 1998 of two former regional banks, Hypobank and Bayerische Vereinsbank, operating almost exclusively in the southern state of Bavaria. After the merger, HVB expanded into Central and Eastern Europe, and in 2005 it was acquired by the Italian banking group UniCredito. Postbank had formerly been a part of the government-owned postal service. It was spun off in 1990 and made public in 2004. In 2010, Deutsche Bank bought up the majority of its shares, but in the second quarter of 2015 decided to sell Postbank AG again in a way that is yet to be specified. HVB, and even more so Postbank, have large branch networks but, unlike Dresdner and Commerzbank, have never been involved in a substantial way in the financing and the governance of large German corporations. As Commerzbank has largely withdrawn from its former role and now focuses on serving small and mid-sized corporate clients and the general population, and Deutsche Bank has reoriented itself to being an international investment bank, the old triad of Germany's big banks and their close relations to the top layer of German corporations is a thing of the past.

The large private banks all have the legal form of a joint-stock corporation, and therefore their governance structure conforms to the corporate law for this type of corporation. This implies that there is a strict separation between the supervisory board and the management board and that they are subject to the legally imposed codetermination regime. As far as ownership is concerned, the situation has greatly changed over the years. The old group of the three large banks had only widely distributed shareholdings, which corresponded to a very limited role of shareholders in their governance. The present set of four "Grossbanken" is more heterogeneous in terms of ownership. Deutsche Bank's shares are still mainly held by small private and some institutional shareholders. In the case of Commerzbank, the German government is still today the largest shareholder, due to a crisis-induced rescue operation, and HVB and Postbank are currently owned by other big banks, UniCredit and Deutsche Bank, respectively.

In addition to the big banks, there are some 200 small private banks. Most of them are specialized in some respect. Some are truly regional banks, others focus on certain industries as their main clientele, and others offer only a narrow range of services. Finally, the group of private banks also comprises the (small) subsidiaries of foreign banks.

The Savings Bank Group

The most important banks with government involvement in Germany are those of the so-called savings bank group. This group comprises some 415 local savings banks, seven *Landesbanken* as regional financial institutions, the

Deka Bank AG as a central financial institution and a considerable number of specialized financial and non-financial organizations such as building societies and data processing centers. In addition, there is a system of associations that represent the group vis-à-vis policy-makers and the general public. All in all, at end-2014, the group comprised more than 500 institutions and employed 341,000 staff members.

The traditional core of the group are the local savings banks. They are legally independent small and mid-sized banks. They have many branches and mainly serve their local clients. For decades, saving banks have been the market leaders in lending to small and medium sized firms, in mobilizing local deposits and in granting loans to private households, especially mortgage loans.

Almost all local savings banks operate under a public law regime. They are closely affiliated with the public bodies dominating the local area in which they operate and to which they are by law also largely confined in their operations. The respective municipality or the county[4] are not owners in a legal sense but rather owner-like "supporting institutions",[5] which have certain property rights and obligations. But these rights are weaker than those of the owners of a private bank. In most cases, the mayor or the political head of a county is the chairperson of a savings bank's administrative council.[6] But the extent to which a city or a county can claim a share of the profits of a savings bank is limited. The overwhelming part of a savings bank's profit is retained to strengthen its equity or used for various public welfare projects. This is in line with the fact that, according to the relevant savings banks laws, the purpose of a savings bank is to support the local economy and the local population and not to make as much profit as possible. However, despite their promotional mandate, savings banks are, by law, required to operate in an efficiency oriented and profitable way.[7]

---

[4] In an increasing number of cases, the supporting political entities responsible for a local savings bank are by now not merely one municipality or county (*Landkreis*) but groups of municipalities or counties.

[5] The German term is *Träger*, a term for which there is no adequate English translation.

[6] Formerly, a supporting entity had the formal responsibility to assure the functioning of 'its' savings bank (the so-called maintenance obligation) and also to guarantee all obligations of a savings bank (the so-called guarantee obligation). These public guarantees were abolished in 2005, based on an agreement between the German Government and the EU Commission. This agreement was reached in 2001 after the Association of Private Banks had filed a complaint against the public banks, arguing that these forms of public support were incompatible with the EU rules concerning state aid and EU competition laws; for details see Schmidt (2009). However, as far as savings banks are concerned, these guarantees were never invoked after World War II.

[7] The legal and economic aspects of the promotional mandate are discussed in detail in Brämer et al. (2010).

While all local savings banks are formally independent legal entities, they are at the same time also parts of a dense integrated network of affiliated institutions.[8] In addition to the local savings banks, this network comprises the *Landesbanken*, the Deka Bank and other central financial institutions, a host of non-financial support institutions, such as data processing centres, and associations of savings banks at the regional and the federal level, as well as a complex common guarantee system managed by the associations. Being part of this network enables the local savings banks to combine flexibility, autonomy and proximity to their local clientele with the economies of scale and scope which outsourcing certain functions to central institutions belonging to the network may make possible.

This network structure, which already emerged more than 100 years ago, can be considered as the basis for the enduring success of the savings banks as a group. Its functioning relies heavily on the so-called regional principle, that is, the rule that the operations of a savings bank are, in principle, confined to the catchment area of the political entity that supports it. Because of the regional principle, the individual savings banks and their managers tend to regard their peers as partners and not as competitors, a fact that is a prerequisite for a close and fruitful cooperation.

The second main part of the savings bank group is comprised of the *Landesbanken*, a term which can literally be translated as "state banks". However, the term "regional banks" would represent their traditional nature more accurately. Some of them have the legal form of a corporation and some are public law institutions. Owners and shareholders or, as the case may be, sponsoring institutions are one or several federal states in which a state bank is domiciled and the local savings banks of the region.

The traditional functions of a *Landesbank* have been to serve as the main relationship bank of the respective state or states (hence their name), to act as the clearing bank for the local savings banks in their region and to provide those services to clients for which a local savings bank would be too small. This includes co-financing larger loans to local clients, various investment banking services and most international operations. However, over the years the scope of their operations has increased considerably. During the 1980s and 1990s, several *Landesbanken* started to operate on a national and even international scale and to compete vigorously with the large private banks. In some cases, they also began to compete with the savings banks which they were formerly

[8] The German term, for which there is also simply no English translation, is *Verbund*. The fact that there is no English term that corresponds to *Verbund* is that in English speaking countries such networks do not exist.

only supposed to support. Following several episodes of financial crises over the past decades, several *Landesbanken* had to be rescued by merging them with stronger ones such that at the end of 2015 only seven remain.

Cooperative Banks

In many respects, the cooperative banking group is similar to the savings bank group. At its core are local, small to mid-sized cooperative banks. They are locally rooted and they have a rather simple business model, which mainly consists of mobilizing local deposits and lending them out to local small and medium-sized enterprises (SMEs) and households. Originally created in the middle of the nineteenth century to fight financial exclusion, their objective, to this day, is to support the business activities of their members, and not necessarily to maximize profit.

Like the local savings banks, local cooperative banks are independent legal entities, which are at the same time embedded in a dense network of affiliated institutions. This network also comprises two central financial institutions,[9] a considerable number of other centralized financial institutions that perform special functions for the local banks and their clients,[10] many non-financial support institutions and two layers of association, which also run a deposit insurance system. The regional principle applies also for the cooperative banks and provides the economic basis for the close cooperation within the network. At year-end 2014, the German cooperative banking group comprised around 1,050 institutions, out of which some 1,000 are local cooperatives. The total staff amount to almost 200,000.

The specific feature of any cooperative—and thus also a criterion for distinguishing cooperative banks from other banks—is its institutional structure. Cooperatives are organized like clubs, which is why the owners and providers of equity are called members. Three principles shape their institutional structure. The 'principle of self-help' implies that they are self-governed private organizations. According to the "principle of identity", members are their main clients and conversely many of their clients are also members. Then there is the "democratic principle", which manifests itself in the rule that one

[9] A central financial institution, which serves the cooperative banks in almost all parts of Germany and their clients, is DZ-Bank AG. WGZ-Bank AG is the central hub for the cooperative banks in the German federal state of North-Rhine-Westphalia. It is the only regional central bank that remained after a process of consolidation starting in the 1960s. In the second half of 2015, it was decided that DZ Bank AG and WGZ Bank AG will merge in 2016.

[10] Among them are the Bausparkasse (Building Society) Schwäbisch-Hall and the asset management company Union Investment. Both are among the largest institutions of their kind in Germany.

member has only one vote in the annual general meetings, irrespective of how many shares he or she may hold. Moreover, members cannot sell their shares if they want to exit. They can only hand them back and in return retrieve what they initially invested, plus their part of accumulated profits. This feature has both negative and positive implications. On the negative side, it implies that the members' incentives to monitor managers' performance are weak since they hardly benefit from policies that would increase the value of their shares as long as a default is avoided, and they cannot exert pressure on management since it is impossible to accumulate voting rights. As a consequence, managers' incentives to perform well and to increase the going-concern value of cooperative banks are also weak. Evidently, this constitutes a handicap for cooperative banks in their competition with other banks. This deficiency of cooperative governance is, however, compensated by the fact that the regional associations perform an audit function which not only refers to the accounting side of a cooperative bank but also oversees whether the management of a cooperative bank is doing its job carefully, efficiently and in the spirit of the mandate to support the members.[11]

On the positive side, the "democratic principle" and the limited incentives for management to achieve high profits imply that potentially powerful members cannot dominate a cooperative and make its management exploit weaker members, for instance by paying low interest rates on deposits. For the same reason, the incentives to incur high risks as a means of achieving high profits are weak. This incentive structure has allowed the cooperative banks to survive many challenges over the past 150 years.

The Special Features of the German Banking System

The foregoing characterization of the three main banking groups serves as a basis for briefly summarizing what might be the most important features of the German banking system and what makes it special in comparison to those of other countries. Most of these features are intrinsically related to the three-pillar system.

1. Only a minority of all German banks, representing not even half of total bank assets, is private and at the same time exclusively profit oriented. Banks with government involvement have a mandate to support the local or regional or, as in the case of the KfW-Banking Group, the national

[11] On the effectiveness of this monitoring role of the associations see Ayadi et al. (2010), p 38.

economy. In the case of cooperative banks, the dominant objective is also not to maximize bank profitability, but rather to support the business of their members. Naturally, these mandates limit their profit orientation, but whether they also affect their profitability in a negative way is an open issue (see below).

2. One positive consequence of this limited profit orientation is the stability of the German banking system. Before the global financial crisis started in 2007, Germany was almost unique among the industrialized countries in that it had not experienced a major banking crisis after the Second World War.
3. Still today, the local savings and cooperative banks adhere to the so-called regional principle. This principle means that the local banks that belong to the same network are not expected to compete with each other. While intra-pillar competition is still limited, the level of inter-pillar competition is very high.[12]
4. Not least because of the high level of competition between the banks that belong to the different "pillars" the level of bank profitability appears to be generally low by international standards. Another reason for German banks' relatively low profitability may also be that because of their legal form the majority of German banks, especially the public banks and the cooperative banks, do not strictly aspire to maximize profit, as explained above.
5. The level of bank concentration is also low by international standards, at least if one counts the individual savings and cooperative banks as individual institutions. However, if one considers all savings and cooperative banks, respectively, as being merely parts of one highly decentralized group, the level of bank concentration in Germany is in line with that of other countries.
6. Almost all German banks are universal banks. They offer at least some services that one can classify as commercial and investment banking services. The predominance of the universal banking model is based on the German banking law and it conforms to the tradition of the German banks and to the expectation of their clients to obtain all banking services from one institution.
7. Close relationships between banks and their clients also used to prevail in the market for corporate banking services. This is why, at least until the beginning of the 2000's, so-called house-bank relationships used to exist between large banks and their large exchange listed corporate clients (Elsas and Krahnen 2004). Most of these traditional house-bank relations have by now

[12] See Fischer (2005) and Fischer and Pfeil (2004).

disappeared. However, house-bank relationships still exist and are important. Today, many large and medium-sized firms that belong to the so-called *Mittelstand* have a main bank or a house-bank, which is, however, now more often a savings or a cooperative bank rather than a large private bank.

8. Traditionally, the level of foreign bank presence in Germany has been quite limited. In view of the peculiarities of German banking described above, it is not surprising that foreign banks are reluctant to enter the German market in any other way than by buying a German bank.

A Comparison of the Three Banking Groups

Figure 21.1 provides performance indicators of German branch banking and allows for an assessment of the financial situation of those banks in the three pillars that have extended branch networks and are therefore comparable. The first panel shows that the cost–income ratio is lower for savings banks and cooperative banks than for the large commercial banks. As shown in the middle panel, return on equity is on average higher and clearly more stable for savings banks and cooperative banks. The last panel shows that the interest margins for all banks have been steadily declining, but throughout the years the interest margins are higher for those banks that mainly rely on local deposits as their main funding source.[13]

It is not only standard performance indicators that show that local banks performed about as well and, in general, even better than the private big banks. A more elaborate ways of analysing and comparing performance confirm this result for the years before the financial crisis began in 2007.[14]

Challenges Facing German Banks

German Banks and the Global Financial Crisis of 2007–8

Some German banks were severely hit by the global financial crisis of 2007–8. Two specialized private banks, Hypo Real Estate (HRE) and Industrie-Kreditbank (IKB) and the two big banks, Deutsche Bank and Commerzbank,

---

[13] The performance indicators of the central financial institutions of the savings bank group and the cooperative bank group, which are not shown in Fig. 21.1., are largely similar to those of the big banks.

[14] See for example, Altunbas et al. (2001) and Ayadi et al. (2009 and 2010). Their empirical findings may appear surprising given that these banks pursue the dual objective of profit and benefit for their customers. Probably less surprising, but equally relevant, is the empirical evidence that savings banks and cooperative banks are on average less risky than privately owned commercial banks (Beck et al. 2009).

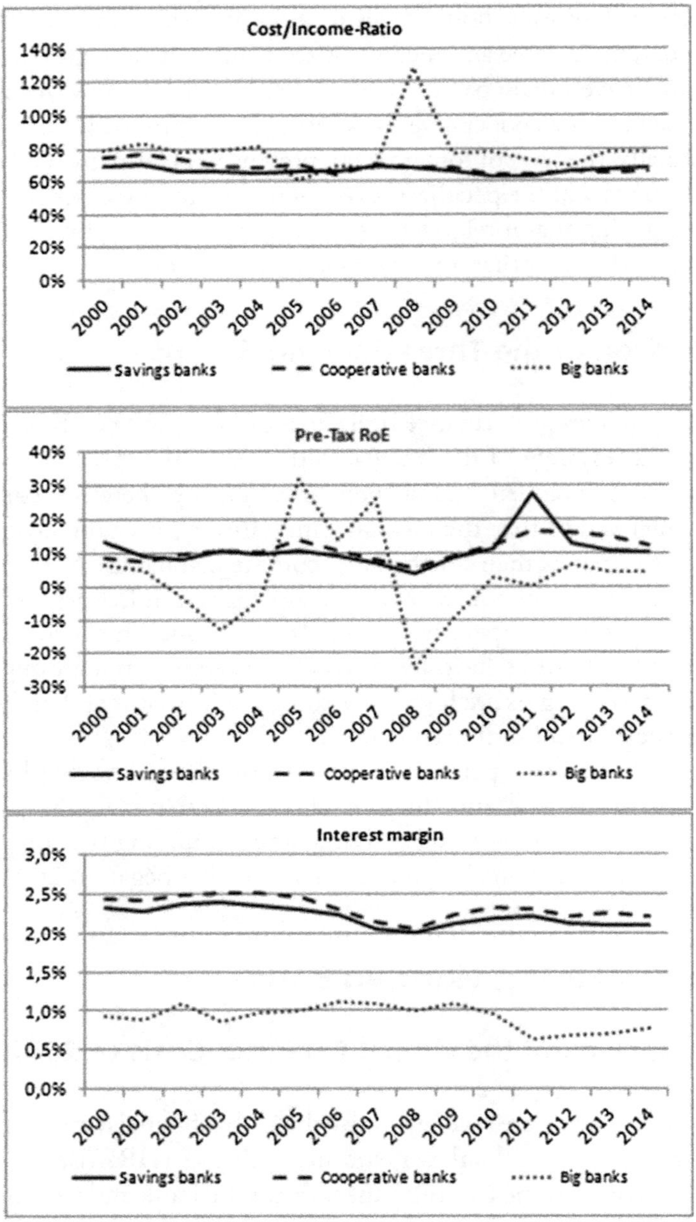

Fig. 21.1 Performance indicators of German branch banking (*Source*: Deutsche Bundesbank, several monthly reports)

experienced large losses due to overly risky investments and off-balance sheet activities of a precarious nature in the years preceding the crisis. HRE, IKB and Commerzbank had to be rescued with substantial government interventions, which went as far as a full nationalization in the case of HRE. Only Deutsche Bank prided itself for surviving the crisis without government help.

In contrast, the local savings and cooperative banks weathered the storm largely unharmed. Almost all of them managed to remain stable and even profitable during the crisis years.[15] This is largely due to their traditional business model and corresponds to their mission and tradition. They benefitted from their strong customer deposit-gathering ability and their close client relationships and the fact that their by-laws prevent them from being involved in many of the more risky activities.

Nevertheless, the savings banks group as a whole was affected by the financial crisis. Four *Landesbanken* (HSH Nordbank, BayernLB, SachsenLB and WestLB) suffered greatly, indirectly also causing losses to other institutions in the group, due to their roles as co-owners and business partners. This is one reason why some *Landesbanken* were merged with stronger ones, were largely liquidated, or are currently re-aligning their business models.

Being even less involved in structured finance and capital markets products than the savings banks, the cooperative banks survived the financial crisis better than any other banking group.

Challenges Resulting from the New Regulatory Regime

Large German private and public banks have not only been negatively affected by the global financial crisis, they, as well as all other banks, now also have to face the challenges posed by the new regulatory regime that was put in place after the crisis. Some parts of the new regime have already been implemented, and others are in the process of being put in place.

Higher capital requirements and strict liquidity rules, based on Basel III and transformed into EU law trough CRD IV, are likely to be the most important challenge that German banks face. The requirements are equally severe for banks that do not have access to the public equity market as for those that have suffered from crisis induced losses and find it difficult to issue new shares—in other words, it affects all types of German bank.

[15] One cooperative bank, Apo Bank, also reported a loss in 2008. Interestingly, it is an atypical cooperative bank since it is not regionally focused and instead serves two professions, those of doctors and pharmacists, as its clientele.

The Single Supervisory Mechanism (SSM) creates additional challenges as it requires banks to deal with new supervisors who may not be fully familiar with the peculiarities of the German banking system and the legal and institutional forms of a large number of German banks, even though savings and cooperative banks are not subject to direct EU supervision in the framework of the SSM. Current discussions to introduce a single deposit insurance scheme for all banks as a part of the EU Banking Union project might add to these difficulties, in particular for the small banks and their networks. The way and the extent to which the Single Resolution Regime and the concomitant bail-in requirements will ultimately affect the German banks can at present not be assessed.

Apart from Basel III/CRD IV and SSM, there are many new regulatory rules and reporting requirements with which all banks have to comply, forcing them to increase the relevant staff substantially, thereby significantly raising the costs of banking. This factor is particularly burdensome for the numerous small German banks and may induce a merger wave among them.[16]

Finally, a new German law already in force and additional plans at the EU level which will require a certain degree of separation between commercial and investment banking activities is a threat to the established business models of many large banks and forces them to adjust these models accordingly.[17]

The adjustment process induced by the hard lessons of the global financial crisis and the ensuing new regulatory regime started some time ago. Most German banks have already redesigned processes, products and, among other things, compensation systems. How far these changes will ultimately go is impossible to assess in the present situation. However, there are reasons to believe that they are not likely to affect the traditional German banking structure, since the networks ('*Verbünde*') tend to shield the local savings and cooperative banks from the most serious negative consequences (Hönig 2014).

German Banking in an International Comparison

Today, banking structures differ significantly between European countries. This is related both to historical reasons and to developments over the last decades. In every country, we find a small number of large banks, which typically are

[16] The list of new regulations and reporting requirements increases continuously. A nearly complete list as of the time of writing and an assessment of their cost implications for German banks is provided in Hönig (2014).

[17] Germany has already implemented core elements of the separation concept in a national law, informally called Trennbankengesetz. The plans of the EU Commission, which are based on the recommendations of the High Level Expert Group (HLEG 2012), go even further than the German law (KPMG 2014).

the most important banks in terms of total assets and numbers of branches. In some countries, such as Great Britain, the big banks are by far the dominant players in the banking market, while in others they share the market with savings banks and/or cooperative banks. To date, savings banks play an important role in Germany, Austria and Spain, but no longer in several other countries. In France and Austria cooperative banks are powerful market participants, while their role is very limited in some other countries.

Formerly, these national differences were much less pronounced. Until about 20 years ago, almost all European countries had a three-pillar banking system. However, since then many countries have implemented far-reaching reforms, which have mainly affected the two pillars of the savings and cooperative banks. In a nutshell the changes are as follows:

- In Austria the three networks of formerly independent local savings and cooperative banks have been transformed in such a way that their respective central institutions have gained far reaching power over the now de facto subordinated local and regional institutions.
- In France savings banks have been converted into yet another group of cooperative banks and have been phased out as a special type of financial institution.
- In Italy, savings banks were partially privatized and several of them were integrated into large commercial banks such as UniCredit and INTESA, and the regional principle was abolished.
- In Spain, the savings banks have been privatized and the regional principle was abolished.

In some countries the changes have gone even further. For instance in Belgium savings and cooperative banks have essentially disappeared, and in Great Britain the former public savings bank (TSB) was sold to Lloyds Banking Group, and several cooperative banks, the so-called building societies, were converted into corporations and some of them were sold to large private banks.[18] Only Germany stands out as the special case in which there was no substantial change in the banking structure during the last decades.[19] As far as their legal and institutional structures and their economic roles

[18] Most of the converted building societies or the private banks that had bought them ran into problems during the financial crisis. The best-known examples are Northern Rock, a converted former building society, and HBOS which was formed by the merger of Bank of Scotland with the former converted building society Halifax in 2001. HBOS was eventually taken over by Lloyds TSB in the midst of the financial crisis.

[19] An exception is the phasing out of public guarantees for *Landesbanken* and local savings banks since 2005.

are concerned, the German savings and cooperative banks are today almost exactly as they had been 50 and even 80 years ago.

Several factors drove the changes in Europe. Certainly, the political climate of the time and EU-wide harmonization were important. However, there was also the presumption that in their former set-up, small local banks, whose legal form differs from that of a corporation owned by private shareholders, were not competitive. To a certain extent, this may have been true, and it may have been due to the fact that in most countries savings and cooperative banks had long been subject to different and more restrictive regulation than "normal" banks. Furthermore, their small size and/or their "unconventional" institutional and governance features may have reduced their competitiveness.

As one of the motives for initiating far reaching reforms was the belief that the efficiency of local savings and cooperative banks is lower than that of other banks with comparably large branch networks, it is instructive to take a closer look at the situation in Germany, since the German experience does not support this belief. Comparative studies show that this is in fact almost the same in many other countries. The presumption that there are differences in efficiency resulting from the legal form and the ownership structure could not be supported empirically until the start of the global financial crisis in 2007.

In the financial crisis, most national savings and cooperative bank systems even fared better than most of their competitors from the ranks of large private banks. However, there are exceptions. The most important one is that of the Spanish savings banks. The Spanish *cajas* were very seriously affected by the crises. Most probably their current problems are related to the fact that they had been transformed in an unbalanced way a few years before the crisis[20] and that the regional principle was abolished.[21] As a consequence, the *cajas* started to compete vigorously among one another, putting pressure on their profitability. By now, there is hardly any cooperation between them left, nor a network that may strengthen them, provide support and impose discipline on the individual *caja*.

[20] A critical assessment of the governance of Spanish savings banks after the reforms—and thus of the half-hearted privatization—can be found in Mai (2004).

[21] The causes and consequences of the problems of the Spanish *cajas* are investigated in Ilueca et al. (2014).

Results of Recent Research on the German Banking System

As we pointed out above, by international standards, the role of the state is relatively strong in German banking. There is an ongoing debate as to the question of whether government involvement in banking is desirable or not and to what extent the government should play an active ownership role in the banking sector.

On the one hand, a large part of the existing research on public banks uses international data from a broad range of countries and argues that government-owned banks are not performing well, are allocating credit in an inefficient way. This literature further argues that agency problems, political influence, fraud and corruption are a fundamental characteristic of all public banks (e.g., La Porta et al. 2002; Sapienza 2004; Dinç 2005; Illueca et al. 2014; Carvalho 2014). On the other hand, some authors emphasize and document positive effects of government ownership in banking on economic development and social welfare (e.g., Stiglitz 1993; Burgess and Pande 2005; Butzbach and von Mettenheim 2014).

The empirical banking literature that uses data from Germany focuses mostly on the comparison of banks with government involvement with privately owned banks. Since government involvement in the banking industry is more extensive in Germany than in most other comparable countries, we believe that it is instructive to provide an overview of the results of some recent empirical banking research that uses data from Germany.

For instance, Engel and Middendorf (2009) analyse differences in the investment and financing behaviour of firms that are clients of either German savings or cooperative banks and find that there does not seem to be a strong link between firms' financial constraints and whether the role of the government in the bank is important or not. On the other hand, Behr et al. (2013) find evidence that the lending of German savings banks helps reduce financial constraints of SMEs. These authors also show that the savings banks do not underperform nor that they take more risks than the privately owned cooperative and commercial banks. In a related study, Behr et al. (2015) compare the lending cyclicality of German savings banks to that of German cooperative banks and find that the lending behaviour of the savings banks is significantly less cyclical.[22] This implies that banks with some government involvement might help to smooth business cycles because they do not purely focus on

[22] The mentioned study also includes a comparison of the lending cyclicality between savings and privately owned commercial banks, but this is not the central point of the study.

profit maximization, but also pursue other goals such as supporting local economies. In line with this idea, Hakenes et al. (2015) show that German savings banks play an effective role in enhancing local economic development, in particular in underdeveloped regions.[23]

But there also seem to be negative aspects of government involvement in German banking. Puri et al. (2011) analyse the effect of the global financial crisis 2007–8 on retail lending using data from German savings banks. They find that in the years after 2008 savings banks with substantial (indirect[24]) equity holdings in *Landesbanken* reduced retail lending more than the savings banks from areas in which the savings banks are not co-owners of a *Landesbank* that experienced severe problems in the course of the financial crisis. The authors further show that this effect was particularly pronounced for smaller and more liquidity-constrained savings banks. Another negative effect of the role the state and its representatives play in German banks is documented by Gropp et al. (2014) who argue that government involvement in the form of public guarantees may be associated with moral hazard: German savings banks took more risks at the time when public guarantees still existed compared with the time when such guarantees had been abolished. Interestingly, Fischer et al. (2014) show the opposite effect: the removal of public guarantees for *Landesbanken* induced these banks to lend to riskier customers and this effect was most pronounced for the *Landesbanken* with the highest expected decrease in franchise value in the event of a removal of the guarantees. Behn et al. (2014) show that politicians' interests and ideologies impact their bailout decisions using a sample of distressed German savings banks. They further show that taxpayers' money is injected more often in distressed savings banks in a year after an election, but it is injected less often if the relevant politicians are associated with the conservative party. Moreover, the performance of distressed savings banks is shown to be lower if they are bailed out by politicians rather than by the savings bank group. Finally, Gropp et al. (2015) argue that public bank guarantees, which existed for the savings bank group in Germany until 2005, reduced allocative efficiency in the economy.

As some of the studies we have mentioned argue that government involvement in the German banking sector may indeed be desirable while others suggest the opposite, we think that it is impossible to come to a final conclusion

[23] For comparisons between different banking groups along other performance dimensions and with different methodologies in various European countries and an overview of the relevant literature, see Ayadi et al. (2009) and Ayadi et al. (2010).

[24] "Indirect" because in those cases where savings banks hold equity participations in a *Landesbank* this typically takes the form of a participation of the respective regional associations of local savings banks and not of the savings banks themselves.

regarding this important structural feature of the German banking system. The reason is that none of the existing studies provides a full-fledged welfare analysis that would allow such a conclusion. Hence, whether the German banking system would be better off with or without a strong role of the state, remains an open question in our view. This is not only so because very much depends on how exactly the state's role is implemented and used and on how state agents behave and are controlled, but also for methodological reasons. Any attempt to provide a final answer would have to be based on an empirical setup that compares all relevant dimensions (such as efficiency of the banking sector, credit supply, social costs, etc.) in a world with the existence of banks with government involvement to a world without those banks with all the other elements of the economy being optimally adjusted to the fact that state interventions exist or, as the case may be, do not exist. Such a general equilibrium analysis poses theoretical and empirical challenges that appear extremely hard to meet. Nevertheless, we can at least argue that having the state playing a prominent role in the banking sector can indeed yield positive effects. Therefore, the German banking system is not only interesting because of its distinct and unique structure, but it also seems to be a system that is functioning quite well—despite the strong role of the government or perhaps, rather, because of it. More research is definitely needed to understand better whether a strong role of banks with government involvement is harmful or rather beneficial.

However, even if at the present state of knowledge one were to firmly conclude, in the spirit of La Porta et al. (2002), that a strong role for public banks is not desirable from a public policy standpoint, one would have to acknowledge that having a banking system with a diversified legal and ownership structure has the important advantage that diversification provides risk protection. In the context discussed here, it protects against the danger that the "current state of knowledge" would at some future time turn out to be erroneous and that it would then prove desirable to have government involvement in banks and the knowledge of how to manage and use this feature in a sound and efficient manner. In this sense, one can plead for maintaining banks with government involvement—and also cooperative banks—and thus for maintaining diversity in the banking system with the same argument with which ecologists plead for biodiversity and for safeguarding endangered species: they help us to retain a kind of social capital whose value we might overlook because we do not see it today.[25]

[25] For this argument, see Schmidt et al. (2014).

Concluding Remarks

The German banking system is unique as it comprises three pillars of high importance: privately owned commercial banks, including large banks with extensive branch networks; smaller, privately owned and regionally focused credit cooperatives; and public banks (or banks with government involvement) comprising the small, regionally oriented savings banks and the larger *Landesbanken*. The banks in these three pillars have coexisted for more than 150 years with relatively little structural change over time.

The German banking system has been a relatively stable banking system, with no major banking crisis in recent history, although some of the commercial banks—in particular Commerzbank and Hypo Real Estate, and some of the *Landesbanken*—were massively affected by the global financial crisis in 2007–8 and needed strong government support or were forced to merge. Some observers and recent empirical research attribute the overall stability of the German banking system to its unique structure and the stabilizing role that the savings and cooperative banks play for local economic development due to their lower lending cyclicality.

We have no final verdict on the question whether the strong role state-related entities play in the German banking system is for better or for worse. Nevertheless, we believe that having banks with some government involvement as an integral part of the banking system has at least some important advantages. A substantial part of the recent research on the German banking system seems to support this view, but more research in this area is needed.

Moreover, we believe that the structure of the German banking system will not change in a fundamental way in the short- and medium-term future, because this mixed system has functioned well in the past and there are no strong indications that this will change or convincing reasons why it should change. However, it will be interesting to observe how German banks cope with the challenges that are waiting ahead, in particular with the ongoing fundamental changes in the regulatory environment.

References

Allen, F., & Gale, D. (2001). *Comparing financial systems*. Cambridge: Cambridge University Press.

Altunbas, Y., Evans, L., & Molyneux, P. (2001). Bank ownership and efficiency. *Journal of Money, Credit and Banking, 33*, 926–954.

Ayadi, R., Carbo-Valverde, S., & Schmidt, R. H. (2009). *Investigating diversity in the banking sector in Europe: The performance and role of savings banks*. Brussels: Centre for European Policy Studies.
Ayadi, R., Llewellyn, D., & Schmidt, R. H. (2010). *Investigating diversity in the banking sector in Europe: Key developments, performance and role of cooperative banks*. Brussels: Centre for European Policy Studies.
Beck, T., Hesse, H., Kick, T., & von Westernhagen, N. (2009). *Bank ownership and stability: Evidence from Germany*. Working paper.
Behn, M., Kick, T., Vig, V., & Haselmann, R. (2014). *The political economy of bank bail-outs*. Working paper.
Behr, P., Norden, L., & Noth, F. (2013). Financial constraints of private firms and bank lending behavior. *Journal of Banking and Finance, 37*, 3472–3485.
Behr, P., Foos, D., & Norden, L. (2015). *Cyclicality of SME lending and government involvement in banks*. Working paper.
Brämer, P., Gischer, H., Pfingsten, A., & Richter, T. (2010). Der öffentliche Auftrag der deutschen Sparkassen aus der Sicht des Stakeholder-Managements. *Zeitschrift für öffentliche Unternehmen, 33*, 311–332.
Burgess, R., & Pande, R. (2005). Do rural banks matter? Evidence from the Indian social bank-ing experiment. *American Economic Review, 95*, 780–795.
Butzbach, O., von Mettenheim, K. (Eds.). (2014). *Alternative banks and financial crisis*. London: Chatto and Pickering eds.
Carvalho, D. (2014). The real effects of government-owned banks: Evidence from an emerging market. *Journal of Finance, 69*, 577–608.
Dinç, S. (2005). Politicians and banks: Political influences on government-owned banks in emerging markets. *Journal of Financial Economics, 75*, 453–479.
Elsas, R., & Krahnen, J. P. (2004). Universal banks and relationships with firms. In J. P. Krahnen & R. H. Schmidt (Eds.), *The German financial system* (pp. 197–232). Oxford: Oxford University Press.
Engel, D., & Middendorf, T. (2009). Investment, internal funds and public banking in Germany. *Journal of Banking and Finance, 33*, 2132–2139.
Fischer, K.-H. (2005). *Banken und unvollkommener Wettbewerb. Empirische Beiträge zu einer Industrieökonomik der Finanzmärkte*. Gabler: Wiesbaden.
Fischer, K.-H., & Pfeil, C. (2004). Regulation and competition in German banking: An assessment. In J. P. Krahnen & R. H. Schmidt (Eds.), *The German financial system* (pp. 291–349). Oxford: Oxford University Press.
Fischer, M., Hainz, C., Rocholl, J., & Steffen, S. (2014). *Government guarantees and bank risk taking incentives*. Working paper.
Gerschenkron, A. (1962). *Economic backwardness in a historical perspective*. Boston: Harvard University Press.
Gropp, R., Gründl, C., & Güttler, A. (2014). The impact of public guarantee on bank risk-taking: Evidence from a natural experiment. *Review of Finance, 18*, 457–488.
Gropp, R., Güttler, A., & Saadi, V. (2015). *Public bank guarantees and allocative efficiency*. Working paper.

Hakenes, H., Hasan, I., Molyneux, P., & Xie, R. (2015). Small banks and local economic development. *Review of Finance, 19*, 653–683.

HLEG. (2012). *Report of the European commission's high-level expert group on bank structural reform*. Brussels: EU Commission.

Hönig, M. (2014). Regulatory impacts of the financial crisis on German banks. *Revista de Economia Politica, 24*, 149–183.

Illueca, M., Norden, L., & Udell, G. (2014). Liberalization and risk taking: Evidence from government-controlled banks. *Review of Finance, 18*, 1217–1257.

KPMG. (2014, February). Strukturreform des Bankensektors. *KMPG Newsletter*. Strukturreform Financial Services.

La Porta, R., Lopez-de-Silanes, F., & Shleifer, A. (2002). Government ownership of banks. *Journal of Finance, 57*, 265–301.

Mai, H. (2004). Spain's cajas: Deregulated, but not depoliticized. Deutsche Bank Research, EU Monitor No. 20.

Puri, M., Rocholl, J., & Steffen, S. (2011). Global retail lending in the aftermath of the US financial crisis: Distinguishing between supply and demand effects. *Journal of Financial Economics, 100*, 556–578.

Sapienza, P. (2004). The effects of government ownership on bank lending. *Journal of Financial Economics, 72*, 357–384.

Schmidt, R. H. (2009). The political debate about savings banks. *Schmalenbach Business Review, 61*, 366–392.

Schmidt, R. H., & Tyrell, M. (2004). What constitutes a financial system in general and the German financial system in particular? In J. P. Krahnen & R. H. Schmidt (Eds.), *The German financial system* (pp. 19–67). Oxford: Oxford University Press.

Schmidt, R. H., Bülbül, D., & Schüwer, U. (2014). The persistence of the three pillar system in German banking. In O. Butzbach & K. v. Mettenheim (Eds.), *Alternative banks and financial crisis* (pp. 101–121; 256–259). London: Chatto and Pickering.

Stiglitz, J. E. (1993). *The role of the state in financial markets*. Proceedings of the World Bank annual conference on economic development, Washington DC, International Bank for Reconstruction and Development/World Bank, 19–56.

22

Banking in Spain

Joaquin Maudos and Xavier Vives

Introduction

Before the global financial crisis of 2007–8 the Spanish banking sector was comprised of three types of deposit institutions: commercial banks, saving banks (*cajas de ahorros*), and cooperative banks. However, savings banks were restructured after the crisis, reducing in number from 45 to 12 groups, and most of them have become banking foundations that own a commercial bank. The result is a more concentrated banking system.

The Spanish banking sector's evolution in recent years has paralleled the economic cycle.[1] Focusing on the period since the start of the twenty-first

[1] See Caminal et al. (1990) for an appraisal of competition in Spanish banking before 1990 and Vives (2012) for an overview of the banking sector in Spain up to 2010.

University of Valencia and IVIE. J. Maudos acknowledges financial support from the Spanish Ministry of Science and Innovation (ECO2013-43959-R) and Valencian Government (PROMETEOII/2014/046).
IESE Business School. X. Vives acknowledges financial support from the Generalitat de Catalunya, AGAUR grant 2014 SGR 1496, and from the Spanish Ministry of Economy and Competitiveness, grant ECO2015-63711-P.

J. Maudos (✉)
Faculty of Economics, University of Valencia and IVIE, Valencia, Spain
e-mail: joaquin.maudos@ivie.es

X. Vives
IESE Business School, University of Navarra, Pamplona, Spain
e-mail: XVives@iese.edu

T. Beck, B. Casu (eds.), *The Palgrave Handbook of European Banking*,
DOI 10.1057/978-1-137-52144-6_22

century, an initial phase of strong growth lasting up until the onset of the international financial crisis in mid-2007 gave way to a period of crisis in Spain, accompanied by the bursting of the property bubble. The imbalances that built up in the banking sector during the period of expansion (among them, excessive credit growth, a high concentration of risk in the property sector, rapid growth of the branch network and number of employees, excessive reliance on wholesale financing, and weaknesses in the savings banks' governance structures) took their toll in terms of a loss in the value of bank assets, creating the need for a restructuring so intense that it forced the Spanish government to ask for financial assistance from the European rescue funds. The Memorandum of Understanding (MoU) of 2012 that accompanied the banking system bailout set out the roadmap Spain's banks have followed in the last few years to lead them out of the crisis. The deep restructuring that took place to correct the imbalances of the past explains why Spain's banks went from being bailed out in June 2012 to successfully passing the European Central Banks (ECB's stress tests in November 2014. Reduction of overcapacity, write-offs, improved solvency, narrowed liquidity gap, the comprehensive reform of the savings banks and the sector's consolidation through mergers explain why Spanish banks have returned to (very moderate) profitability and are coming back to perform their role as intermediaries and in financing the economy.

This chapter aims to explore recent developments in the Spanish banking industry and the measures adopted in recent years to correct the imbalances that built up during the expansion, in order to give an up-to-date picture of the sector in the international context. To this end, the chapter is divided into four sections. The section following the Introduction examines the importance of the banking sector in the Spanish economy using various indicators of banking penetration. The next section, "Characteristics of the Spanish Banking Sector: Recent Trends", looks at key features of the banking sector and its evolution in terms of a range of measures, including margins, profitability, efficiency, solvency, specialization and market concentration. The section "Crisis and Restructuring: From the 2012 Bailout to Passing the Stress Tests in 2014" describes the imbalances that built up during the expansion, which lasted until 2008, and which provided the rationale for the subsequent restructuring, analysing the main measures taken and the restructuring's outcome. Finally, to conclude, the section "Lessons of the Banking Crisis and Future Challenges" sets out the lessons of the banking crisis and the challenges the Spanish banking sector faces going forward.

The Importance of the Banking Sector in the Spanish Economy

As Fig. 22.1 shows, the banks account for a large portion of Spain's financial system. Thus, monetary financial institutions (among which the banks predominate) accounted in 2013 for almost three quarters of the total assets of the Spanish financial system, i.e. 17 percentage points (pp) more than the Eurozone average. Although a process of disintermediation was under way during the expansion, with the crisis the weight of monetary financial institutions (MFIs) again increased, to the detriment of other intermediaries and financial auxiliaries. This contrasts with the situation elsewhere in the Eurozone, where MFIs have been losing market share in the financial system almost continuously.

The growth phase enjoyed by the Spanish economy was accompanied by even more intense growth in banking activity, such that bank assets grew as a share of gross domestic product (GDP). Thus, bank assets rose from 178 % of GDP in 2000 to a record high of 339 % in 2012, implying a virtual doubling of the bank-assets-to-GDP ratio (Fig. 22.2). This strong growth in banking activity explains how bank assets rose to a share of GDP close to the European average in 2012 from a level 67 percentage points below it in 2000.

In contrast to this strong growth in bank penetration, the contraction in banks' balance sheets is explained by the Spanish economy's deleveraging in recent years, with the bank-assets-to-GDP ratio dropping by 58 percentage

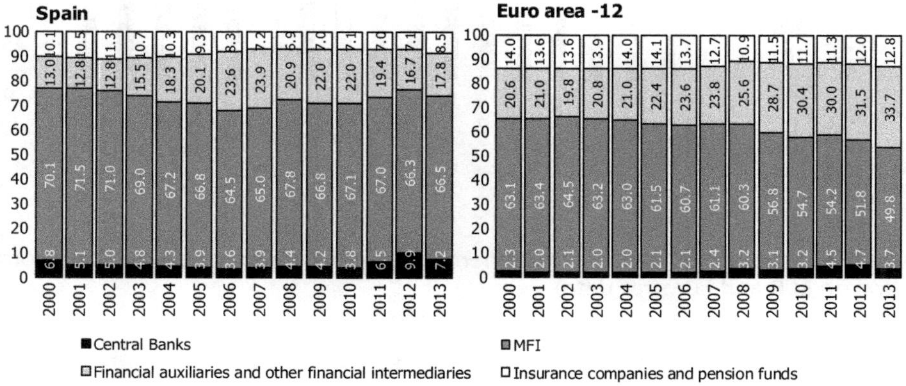

Fig. 22.1 Distribution of financial assets by type of intermediary. Percentage (*Source*: Authors' elaboration on Eurostat data; *Note*: MFI includes Money Market Funds)

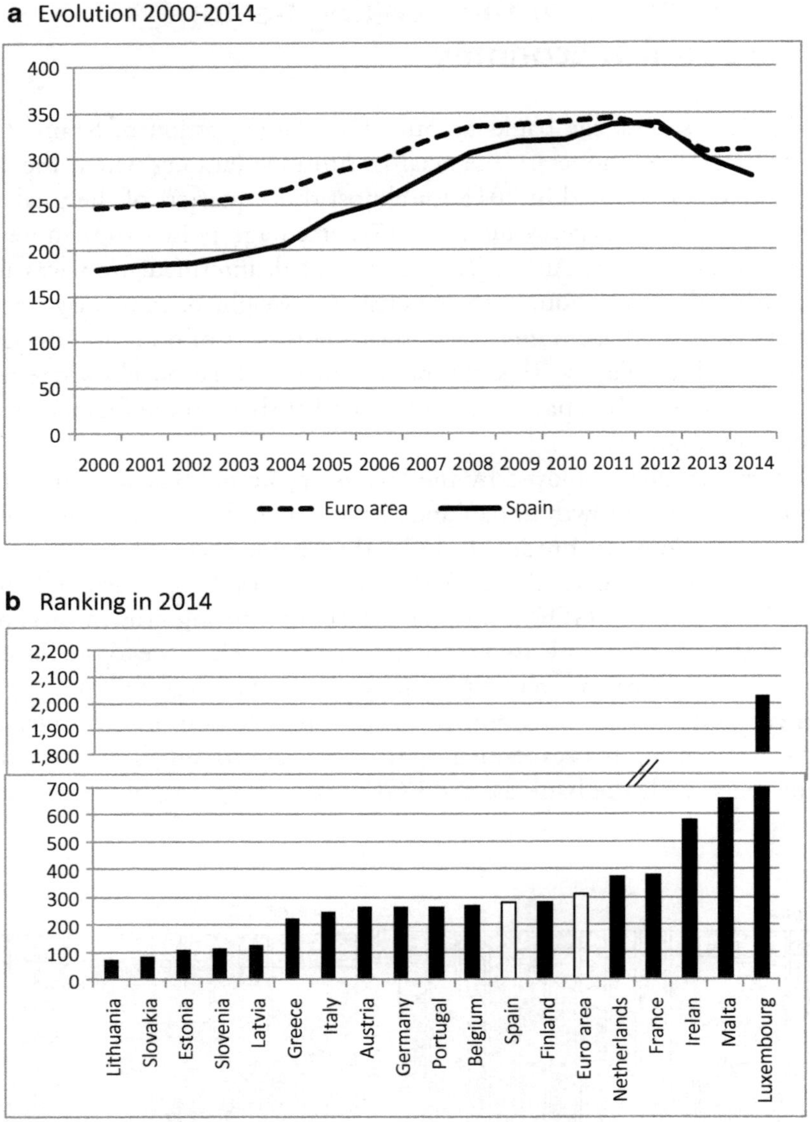

Fig. 22.2. Banking (MFI) assets as a percentage of GDP (*Source*: Authors' elaboration on ECB and Eurostat data)

points between 2012 and 2014, ending the period at 29 percentage points below the European average. Compared with the major European economies, Spain's ratio of banks assets to GDP is above Germany's and Italy's, but below that of France.

The rapid pace of growth in credit to the private sector was the main factor underlying the expansion of the Spanish banking sector's balance sheet, and it also explained the subsequent deleveraging process in the recent crisis years. Between 2000 and 2008 credit grew at an average annual rate of 16 %. This was the fastest growth anywhere in the Eurozone, and a rate more than twice the European average (7 %). Credit continued to grow until mid-2010, since when the growth rate has been negative. In particular, between mid-2010 and end-2014 the stock of credit to the non-financial private sector in Spain fell by 27 %. Nevertheless, despite the sharp decline in credit, it remains the Spanish economy's most important source of financing by far, standing at 130 % of GDP in 2014, 25 % above the European average and only exceeded by three countries (Fig. 22.3). It is worth pointing out that banks tend to provide credit to larger firms in relation to savings banks which may have had some advantages to provide credit to small to medium-size enterprises (SMEs) because of their local and relational knowledge (Carbó and Rodríguez 2012; Maudos 2013).

An additional indicator of the degree of bank penetration in the economy is the banks' share of the economy's total added value and employment.[2] In the case of value added, as Fig. 22.4 shows, the weight of the Spanish banking sector generally remained above the European average until 2010, peaking at 4.3 % in 2010. The thorough clean-up of the banking system in the following years explains the sector's losses, which reduced its added value and share of the economy to 2.7 % in 2012, thus dropping below the European average. In terms of employment (Fig. 22.5), the Spanish banking sector's contribution has always been below the European average, accounting for 1.4 % of jobs in 2012, compared with a European average of 1.6 %. Consequently, the overall picture is that the contribution of banking to employment in Spain is below the European average while in terms of GDP it has fluctuated around the Eurozone average.

Spain has a dense network of branch offices. As Fig. 22.6 shows, Spain ranks second in the EU in terms of network density, behind only Cyprus. Specifically, in Spain there was a branch for every 1,454 inhabitants in 2014, compared with one branch per 2,109 inhabitants in the Eurozone, or one per 2,295 inhabitants in the EU-28.[3] Spanish branches tend to be small, having

---

[2] See in Beck et al. (2014) different measures of the size of the financial sector and the degree of intermediation and their effects of growth and volatility.

[3] Note, however, that Spain has a population density of 92 inhabitants per square km while the Eurozone average stands at 128 (2014 data).

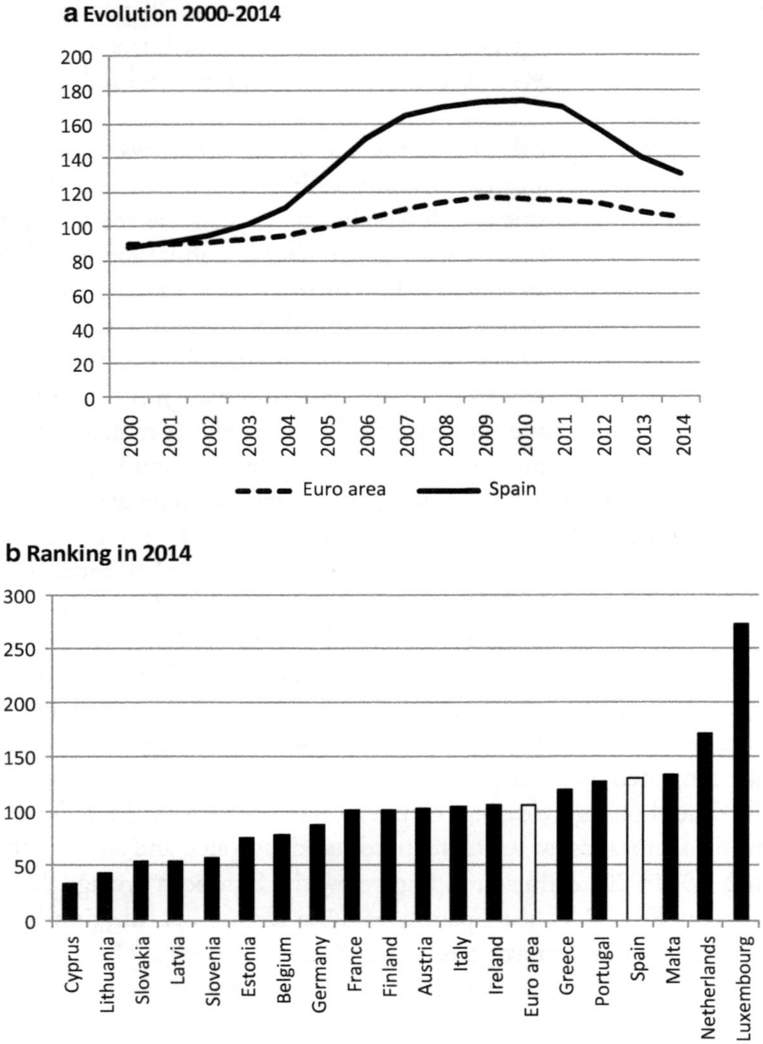

Fig. 22.3 Credit to the non-financial private sector as a percentage of GDP (*Source*: Authors' elaboration on ECB and Eurostat data)

assets of 109 million euros and 6.3 employees, compared with averages of 168 million euros and 12.5 employees in the Eurozone and 206 million euros and 15 employees in the EU-28 (Fig. 22.7). Consequently, as will be noted below when discussing the outstanding challenges, despite the sharp reduction in the number of branches resulting from the crisis, there is still leeway for further closures in view of the small average size of Spain's bank branches.

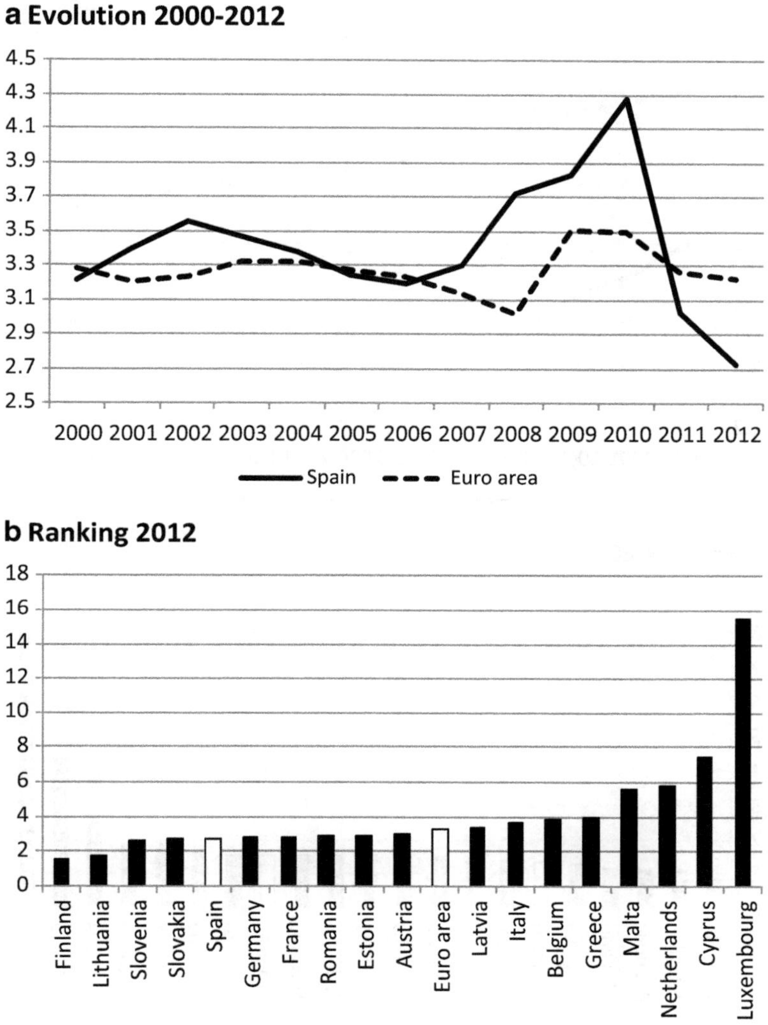

Fig. 22.4 Percentage of banking value added over total economy (*Source*: Authors' elaboration on Eurostat data)

To round off this section analysing the significance of the banks in the Spanish economy, it is worth describing the relative size of the three types of deposit-taking institution that make up the Spanish banking sector. At the end of 2014, the Spanish banking sector comprised 223 deposit-taking institutions (113 of which were Spanish institutions, the rest being subsidiaries of foreign banks), compared with 286 in 2008. The sector includes

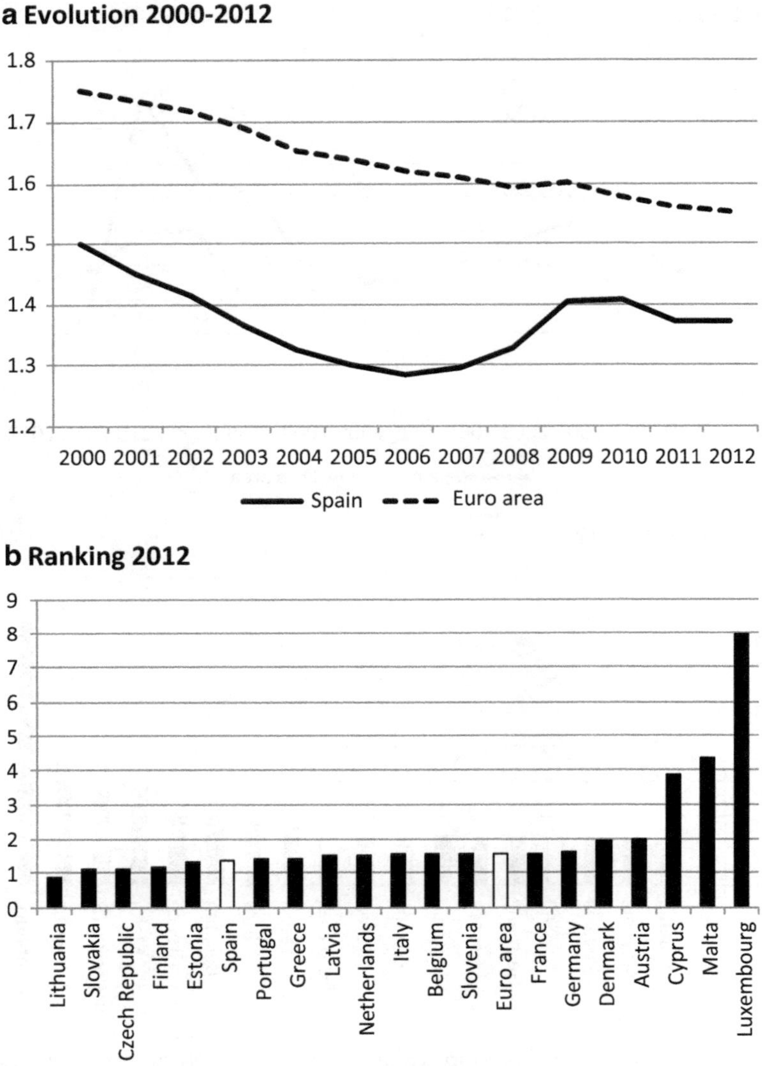

Fig. 22.5 Percentage of employment in the banking sector over total employment (*Source*: Authors' elaboration on Eurostat data)

35 consolidated groups: 19 non-FROB banks and savings banks;[4] 2 FROB banks and savings banks; and 14 cooperative banks. The consolidation of the banking sector taking place in the last few years is primarily explained by

[4] The FROB (Fund for Orderly Bank Restructuring) manages the restructuring and resolution processes of credit institutions.

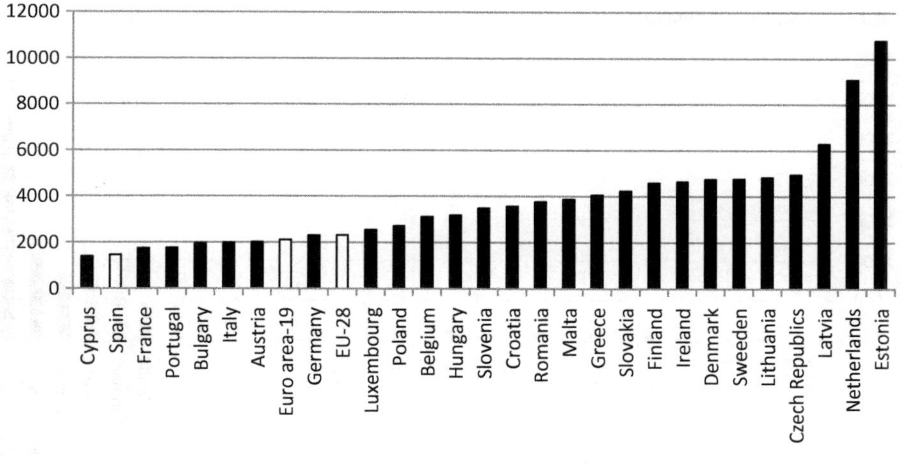

Fig. 22.6 Population per bank branch. Ranking in 2014 (*Source*: Authors' elaboration on ECB data)

the reduction in the number of *cajas de ahorro* or savings banks, which have dropped from 45 in 2008 to 12 groups in 2014: with ten groups operating as banks owned by banking foundations (Caixabank and BFA-Bankia are the biggest ones), and two very small ones being still savings banks (Caixa Ontinyent and Caixa de Pollença).

Focusing on domestic business,[5] as Fig. 22.8 shows, in 2000 the commercial banks held 58 % of total assets, while savings banks and cooperative banks had market shares of 38.4 % and 3.6 %, respectively. At the start of the financial crisis in 2008 the savings banks increased their market share by 6.6 percentage points at the expense of the banks,[6] as a consequence of the rapid rate of growth in credit granted by the savings banks, particularly for property-related business. However, the crisis consequently hit the savings banks particularly hard due to their greater exposure to the sector worst affected by the crisis, losing 7 % of their share of business to the commercial and cooperative banks. Nevertheless, the savings banks and the new banks created by the savings banks that have converted into banking foundations

[5] At the end of 2014, total assets of consolidated groups (including business abroad) were around €3,579 bn while total assets of individual institutions (domestic business) were around €2.653 bn. The business abroad of Santander and BBVA is the main reason that explains the difference between the size of the Spanish banking sector including the business of Spanish banks abroad and not including it.

[6] The start of the crisis of the Spanish economy is dated in the third quarter of 2008 when the GDP growth rate was negative and remained negative until the end of 2009. While the GDP grew in 2010, in 2011 the economy went back into recession. In the third quarter of 2013 the economy left the recession.

a Assets per branch (millions of euros)

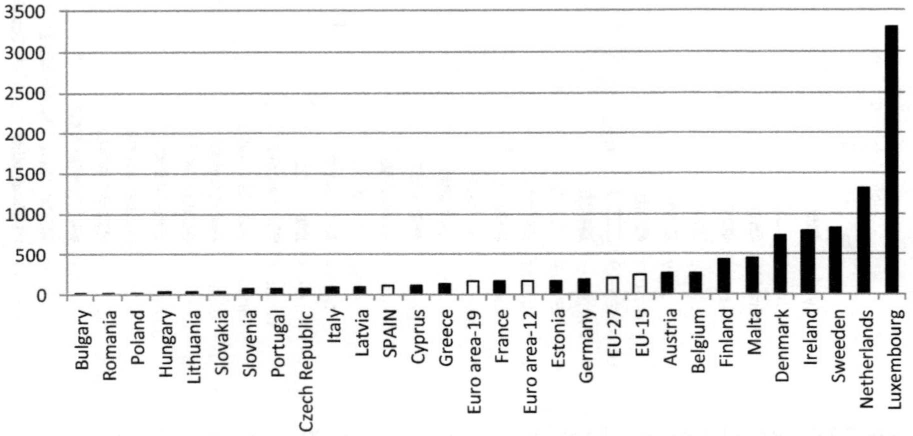

b Number of employees per branch

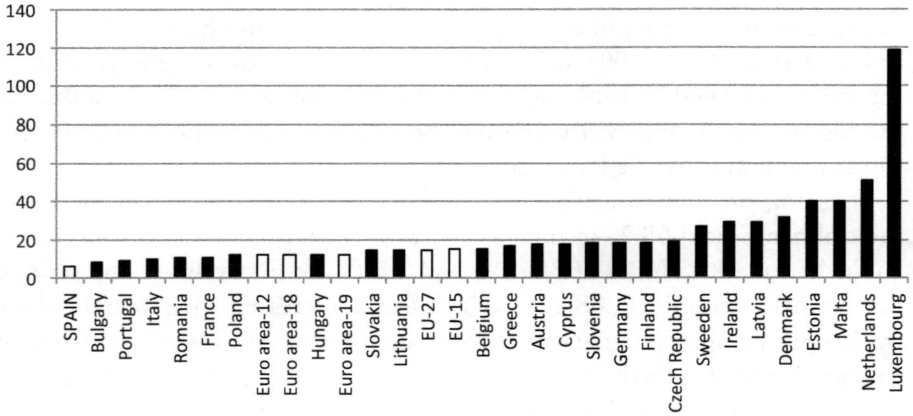

Fig. 22.7 Average size of a bank branch in Europe 2014 (*Source*: Authors' elaboration on ECB data)

remain a very important part of the Spanish banking sector, with a market share by assets in 2014 of 38 % compared with the banks' 57 % and cooperative banks' 5 %. The latter have a very small average size (only €2 billion, compared with €81 billion of a savings bank/new banks created by savings banks, and €26 billion of a commercial bank)[7] and have a strong retail focus, mainly providing credit to the primary sector of the economy (farming and fishing).

[7] Note that many small banks remain in the market.

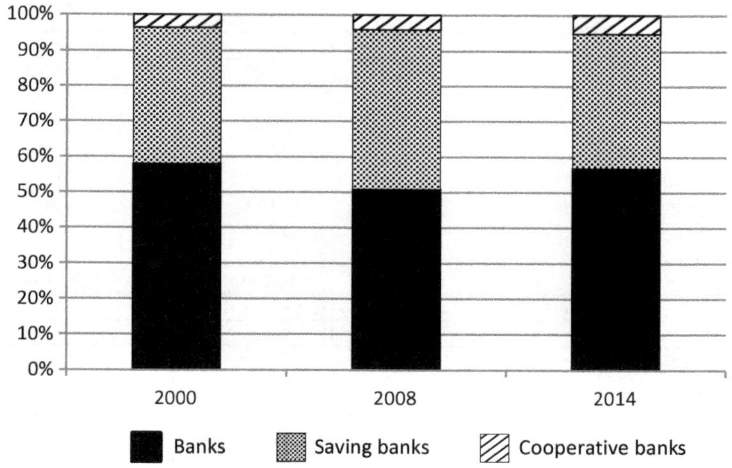

Fig. 22.8 Market share of credit institutions in Spain (percentage) (*Source*: Authors' elaboration on AEB, CECA and UNNAC data; *Note*: *Savings banks in 2014 includes banks owned by banking foundations)

Characteristics of the Spanish Banking Sector: Recent Trends

Of the various types of bank business model, the model predominating in Spain is traditional financial intermediation, with loans and deposits accounting for a large share of the balance sheet, and a large portion of income coming from interest charges. These features can be seen clearly when comparing the percentage distribution of the Spanish banking sector's balance sheet with the Eurozone average (Table 22.1). The latest data, referring to December 2014, show that loans to the non-financial private sector account for 46.4 % of Spanish banks' total assets, 12 percentage points more than the European average. Similarly, deposits taken by the private sector account for 51.3 % of the balance sheet in Spain, which is 15 percentage points more than is the case for Europe's banks as a whole. By contrast, there is less interbank activity in Spain, on both the asset and liability sides. The predominance of deposits as the main source of financing for Spanish banks explains why market finance is more limited than in other European countries.

This financial-intermediation-based business model is also reflected in the greater relative weight of interest income in total income. As Maudos (2014) shows (using 2012 data), Spain is 11 percentage points above the Eurozone average for the net interest income to total income ratio, making it one of the countries in which net interest income is most important. For Spanish banks,

ASSETS	2000 Euro area	2000 Spain	2014 Euro area	2014 Spain
Loans to MFI	21.08	17.29	16.47	8.21
Loans to the Goverment	4.91	2.73	3.58	3.41
Loans to the private sector	36.56	49.06	34.08	46.41
Holdings of debt securities	13.87	11.63	14.60	19.82
Money market funds	0.14	0.00	0.13	0.00
Shares/other equity	4.51	4.72	3.76	4.38
External assets	12.13	7.21	13.70	6.14
Fixed assets and others	6.81	7.35	13.67	11.63
Total	100.00	100.00	100.00	100.00
LIABILITIES	**Euro area**	**Spain**	**Euro area**	**Spain**
Deposits of non-financial sector	32.28	44.66	36.47	51.29
Deposits of MFI	22.08	19.68	17.42	16.03
Money Market funds	1.94	2.87	1.46	0.25
Debt	16.28	4.50	13.03	8.74
External liabilities	13.80	13.73	10.79	3.89
Capital and reserves	5.62	8.19	7.70	11.33
Other liabilities	8.00	6.37	13.13	8.48
Total	100.00	100.00	100.00	100.00

Table 22.1 Percentage distribution of MFIs' balance sheets. Spain and Eurozone*Source*: Authors' elaboration on ECB data

fees and charges are the most important component of non-interest income. Most of these fees are for collection/payment services, which are related to lending and deposit-taking activities.

The comparison of the balance sheet in 2014 with that in 2000 reveals a number of interesting features: (a) lending to the non-financial private sector has become less significant, as a result of the intensive deleveraging that has taken place; (b) interbank business has declined sharply on the asset side, and to a lesser extent on the liabilities side; (c) investments in fixed-income securities have increased; (d) the share of own funds has increased; (e) the relative importance of financing through debt issues has grown.

Proximity to the customer, supported by a network of branches, is important when specializing in the retail banking business. This specialization is usually associated with higher income and lower financial costs, hence the financial margin is greater. This is true in the Spanish case, where the net interest income (as a percentage of assets) is above that of European banks (Fig. 22.9), despite its decline in recent years. As of June 2014, Spanish banks' financial margin was 1.78 % (compared with an average for the European banking system of 1.2 %), i.e. above that of the banking sector in the main European countries.

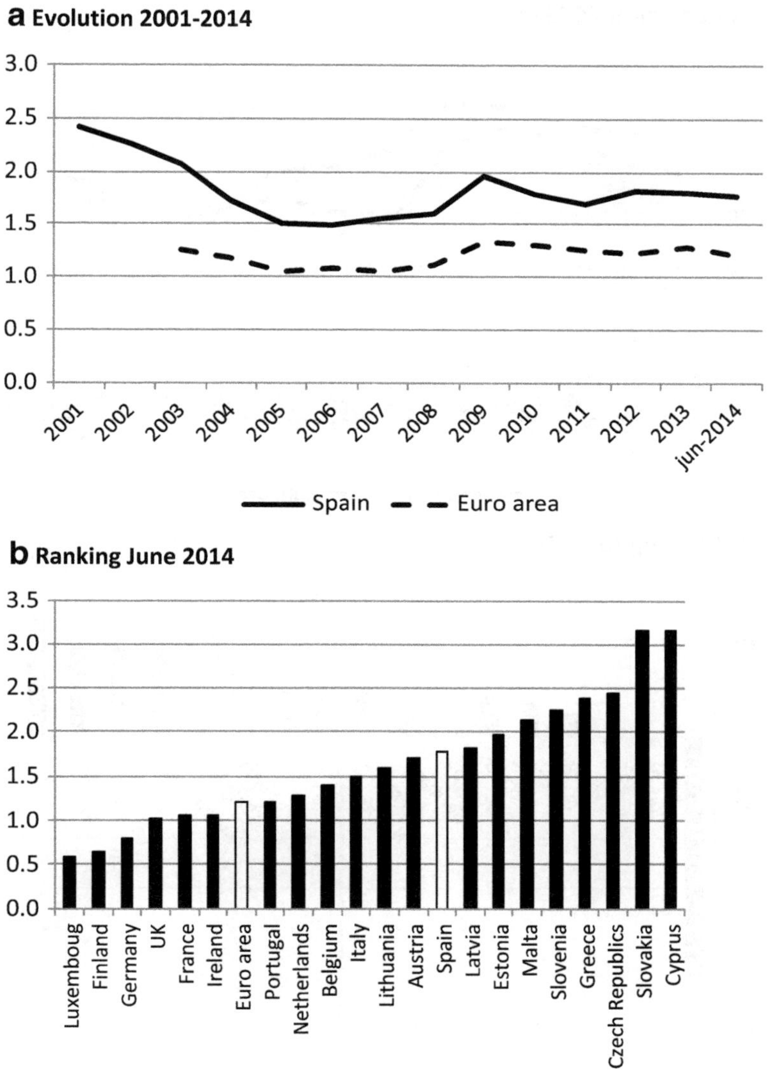

Fig. 22.9 Interest margin. Percentage of total assets (*Source*: Authors' elaboration on ECB data)

Another feature of the Spanish banking system that stands out in the European context is its high level of profitability. Except during the period 2012–2103, when it was affected by the clean-up imposed by Royal-Decree Laws 2/2012 and 18/2012, which obliged banks to recognize the losses deriving from their exposure to the property market, this has always been above the European average. As Fig. 22.10 shows, return on equity (ROE) stood at

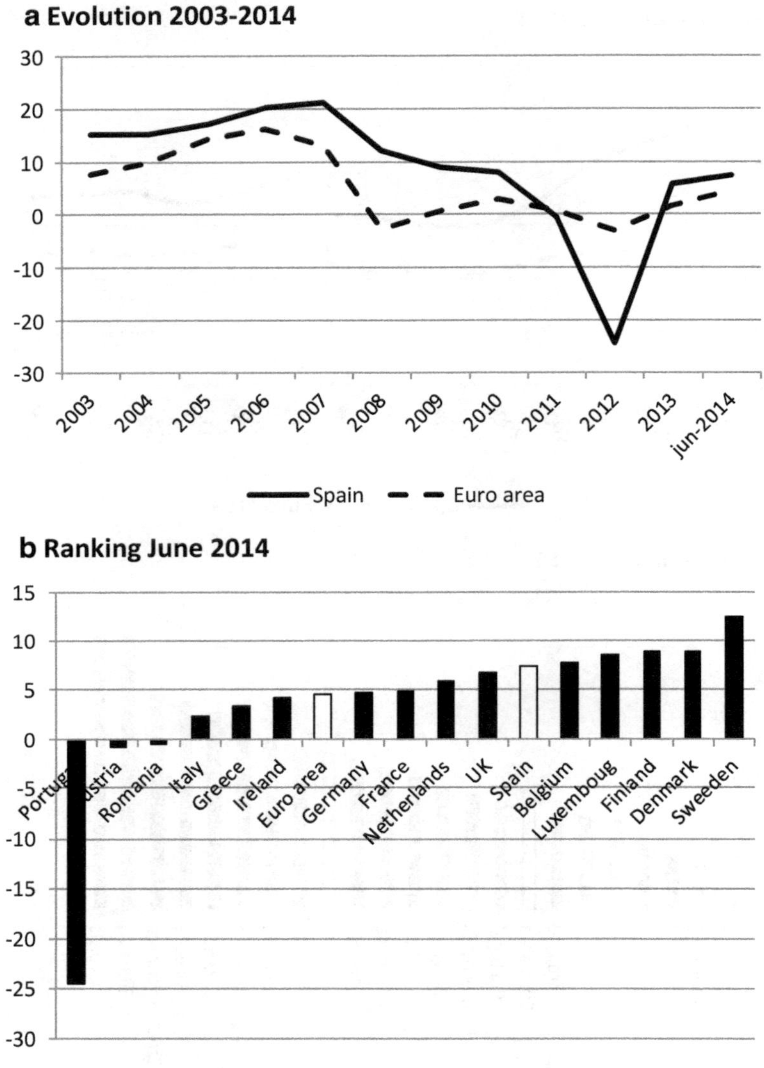

Fig. 22.10 Bank profitability: Return on equity (ROE). Percentage (*Source*: Authors' elaboration on ECB data)

over 20 % before the property-market bubble burst. The subsequent crisis obviously resulted in a drop in profitability, which is being recouped since the Spanish economy emerged from recession in the second half of 2013. The latest information available, referring to June 2014, places Spanish banks' ROE at 7 %, which is above the 5 % for European banks, and higher than in major European countries such as Germany, France and Italy.

As well as profitability, Spanish banks stand out for their high level of operational efficiency (in terms of cost to income ratio), which has always been well above that of other European banks (Fig. 22.11). The drastic cuts in operating expenses made prior to 2008 took place in a context of narrowing gross profit margins,[8] although costs fell faster, such that the operational efficiency ratio improved, reaching 43 % compared with 53 % in the Eurozone. In the following years, the collapse in gross margin explained the loss of efficiency, although Spanish banks remained more efficient than their European counterparts. The recovery in margin in 2014 and the reduction in operating costs has enabled further efficiency gains, situating Spain's ratio at 47 % compared with 55.3 % in the Eurozone[9].

The information published by the ECB allows the solvency of the Spanish banking sector to be compared with the Eurozone average over the period since 2008. The picture that emerges from Fig. 22.12 is that the total solvency ratio of the Spanish banking system is below the average in recent post-crisis years, reaching a maximum difference of 2.8 pp in June 2014, when the Spanish ratio was 13.4 % compared with 16.2 % for the Eurozone. Spanish banks are second from bottom of the ranking of Eurozone countries by solvency, trailed only by Portugal's banks.

However, the data in Fig. 22.12 need to be interpreted with caution as a result of the differences in how countries treat the ratio's denominator. Thus, although the numerator is harmonized internationally thanks to the Basel Accords, the denominator (risk-weighted assets, RWA) is not, and the evidence suggests that Spanish banks weight risks more strictly. Indeed, the ranking changes substantially if it is drawn up in terms of the equity-to-asset ratio, without risk weightings. This ratio for Spain is above the major European banking sectors: 7.06 % compared with 4.94 % in Germany, 5.43 % in France and 5.74 % in the United Kingdom. [10]

To complete this comparison of the Spanish banking sector with its counterparts elsewhere in Europe, it is worth analysing the market structure concentration,[11] given the possible implications its level and evolution can have on the intensity of competition[12]. As Fig. 22.13 shows, although

[8] See Maudos (2012) for a detailed analysis.

[9] Although several papers have been published analyzing the efficiency of the Spanish banking sector in the international context, the results are very sensitive to techniques used, the selection of variables and time period.

[10] See Bank of Spain (2012).

[11] The indicator used, reported by the ECB, is calculated on a non-consolidated basis, meaning that banking subsidiaries and foreign branches are considered to be separate credit institutions.

[12] However, it is important to point out that concentration measures might not be the best measure of competition (see Carbó et al. 2009).

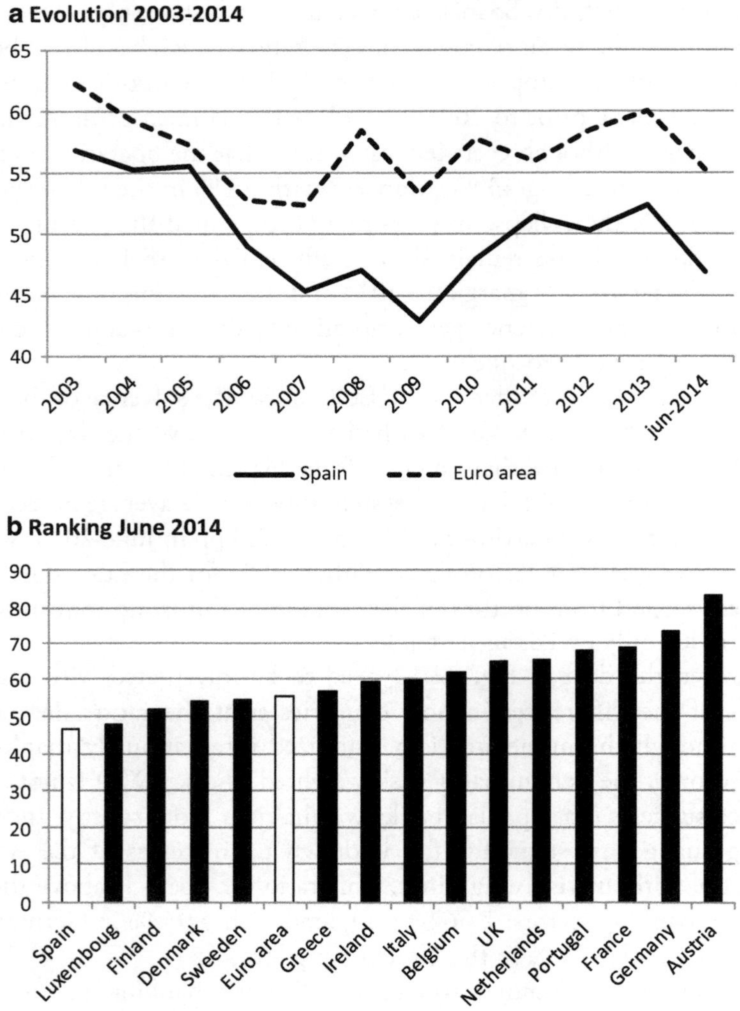

Fig. 22.11 Cost to income ratio. Percentage (*Source*: Authors' elaboration on ECB data)

the Herfindahl index (which is defined as the sum of the square of the market shares of the firms in the industry) is below the (weighted) average for European banks in the period up to 2011, the intense growth in recent years as a result of restructuring and mergers raised the index to 839 in 2014, which is above all the European averages (703 in the case of the EU-15). In this latter year, the market concentration in the Spanish banking sector exceeded that of the sectors in major European countries such as Germany, France, Italy and

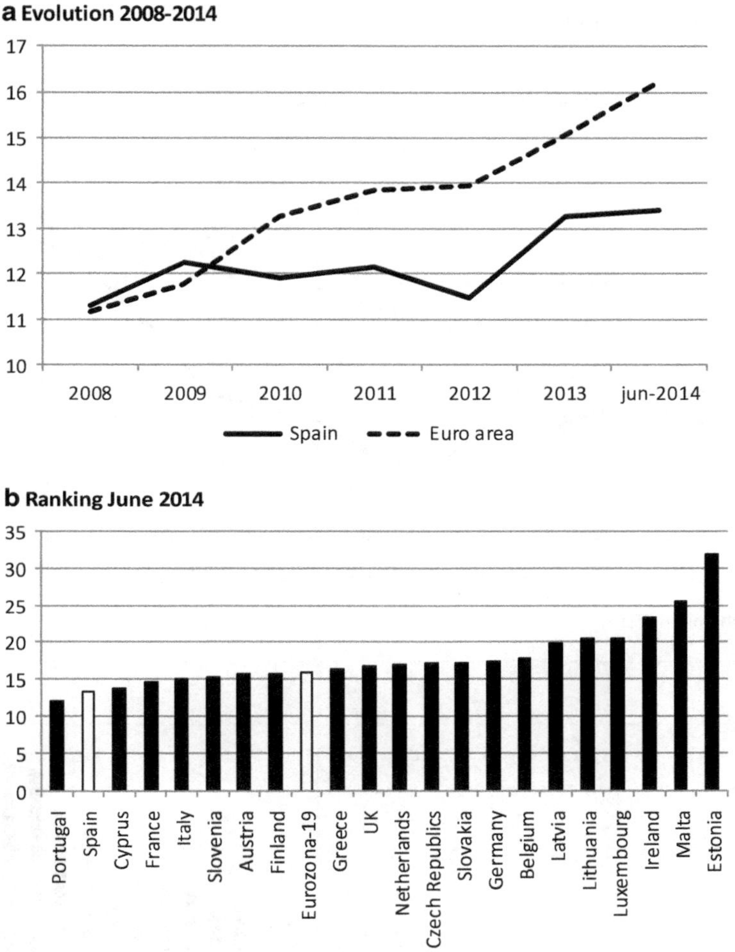

Fig. 22.12 Overall solvency ratio (as percentage of RWA) (*Source*: Authors' elaboration on ECB data)

the United Kingdom. Although it is not shown in Fig. 22.13, Spain's CR5 index (market share of the five largest banks in terms of assets) is 58 %, which above the EU-15's 47.6 % (weighted) and the levels in the largest European economies. The question that therefore arises is the possible impact of this sharp rise in concentration on competition. We have to note, however, that what matters for competition is concentration in relevant product and geographical markets and not at the aggregate level. Carbó et al. (2009) in a study of a large sample of European banks for 1995–2001 in 14 countries find that different measures of competition (including the Herfindahl index, the

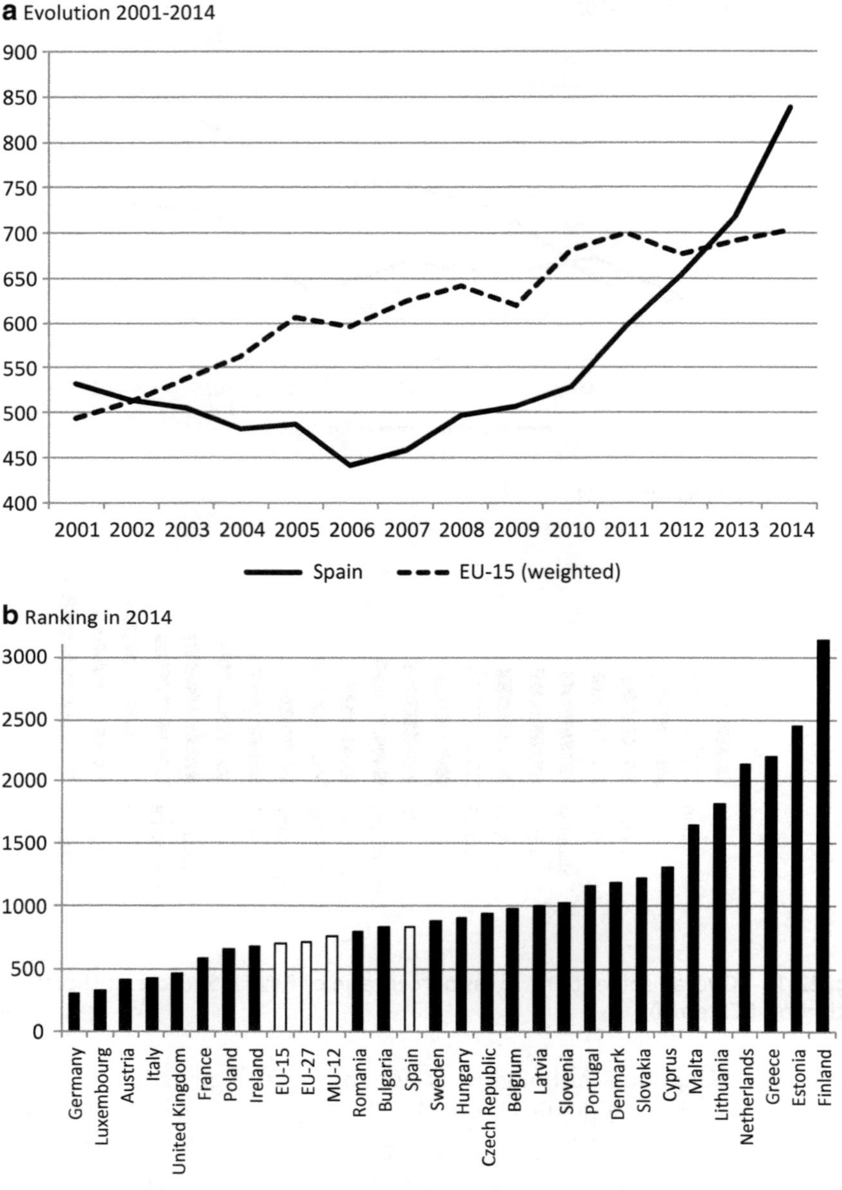

Fig. 22.13 Bank concentration in Europe: The Herfindahl index in terms of assets (*Source*: Authors' elaboration on ECB data)

Panzar-Rosse H-statistic, and the Lerner index, or the return on assets (ROA)) identify in a consistent way the most and least competitive banking markets. Spain scores overall relatively low on competition. Using the Lerner index and the Boone indicator as measures of competition, Fernandez de Guevara and Maudos (2016) analyse the impact of the crisis on competition in the banking sector in Europe's largest economies over the period 2002–12. In the specific case of the lending market, the results show market power to have increased in many countries, including Spain. The effects on stability, however, may be beneficial. Jiménez et al. (2013) found that nonperforming loans in Spanish banks fell as the loan market's Lerner index increased.[13]

Crisis and Restructuring: From the 2012 Bail-Out to Passing the Stress Tests in 2014

The Origins of the Spanish Banking Sector's Problems

Apart from the direct impact of the outbreak of the Great Recession in mid-2007, the Spanish banking sector has suffered the consequences of the bursting of the property-market bubble resulting from the imbalances that built up in the preceding years of expansion. These imbalances can be summarized as: (a) excessive rate of credit growth; (b) a high concentration of risks in the construction and property sector; (c) excess installed capacity in terms of branches and employees; (d) a high degree of reliance on funding from wholesale markets as a result of the liquidity gap; and (e) weak governance structures at many savings banks.

As we saw in Fig. 22.3, credit grew strongly in Spain during the years of expansion leading up to 2008, with Spain being the Eurozone's leader in terms of average credit growth rates between 2000 and 2008. This growth relied heavily on lending to the construction industry and property business, which grew by as much as 40 % in 2006. However, lending for other purposes also grew strongly, with growth rates of up to 30 % some years in credit to both businesses and households (Fig. 22.14). The subsequent crisis and excess private-sector debt made intense deleveraging unavoidable, which explains why the stock of credit to the non-financial private sector has been posting negative growth rates since 2009.

[13] The authors also find that an intermediate level of competition may maximize financial stability. See Vives (2016) for thorough exploration of the relationship between competition and stability in banking.

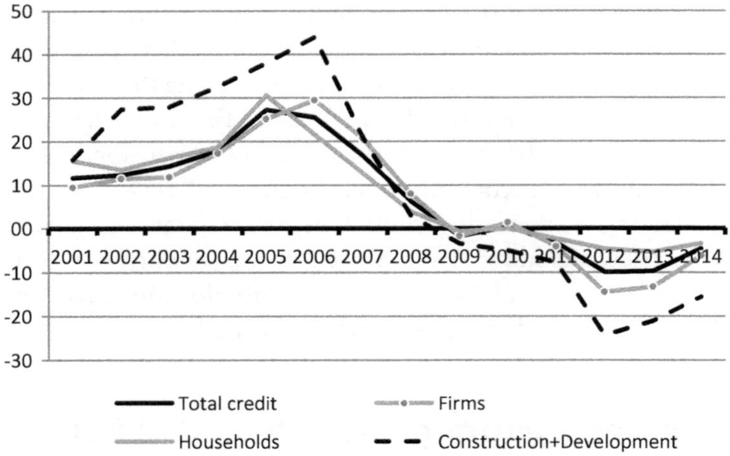

Fig. 22.14 Annual growth rate of the credit to the non-financial private sector in Spain. Percentage (*Source*: Authors' elaboration on Bank of Spain data)

Growth in lending to activities related to the property sector (construction, property development, and home purchases) rose from 45 % of total lending to the private sector in 2000 to a peak of 61.5 % in 2006. The subsequent crisis affecting these activities reduced their share to 56 % in 2014, partly due to the transfer of the property exposures of bailed out banks to the "bad bank" (SAREB). The strongest growth was in lending for property development, which along with construction, suffered the highest default rates. In late 2014 the default rate on construction and property development loans (Fig. 22.15 and Fig. 22.16) reached 34.7 %, while defaults on mortgages remained modest (6 %). As a result, the Spanish banking sector's problems have been concentrated in the construction and property development sector, on account of the provisions they have had to set aside for losses.

A rate of bank lending growth this rapid demanded an expansion in installed capacity, particularly in the case of the savings banks, which scaled up their business most and had the biggest concentration of risk in the property sector. As Fig. 22.17 shows, between 2000 and 2008 the network of bank branches expanded by 18 % in Spain, compared with a Eurozone average of 5 %. Over the same period, employment in the sector grew by 13 % in Spain, while banks in other European countries were trimming their headcount somewhat. During the crisis, it was necessary to severely cut back the overcapacity that had built up, with the result that in between 2008 and 2013, 31 % of branches closed and staffing levels were cut by 27 %. Indeed, those banks receiving public financial aid were obliged to

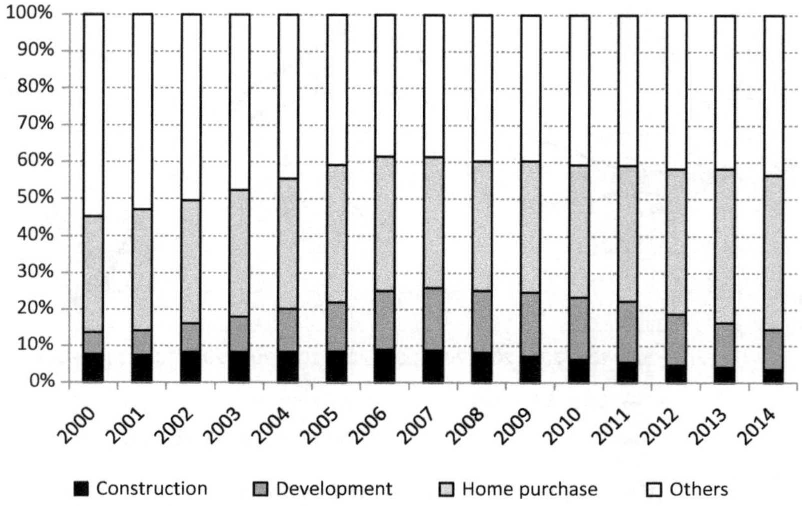

Fig. 22.15 Percentage distribution of credit to the non-financial private sector in Spain (*Source*: Authors' elaboration on Bank of Spain data)

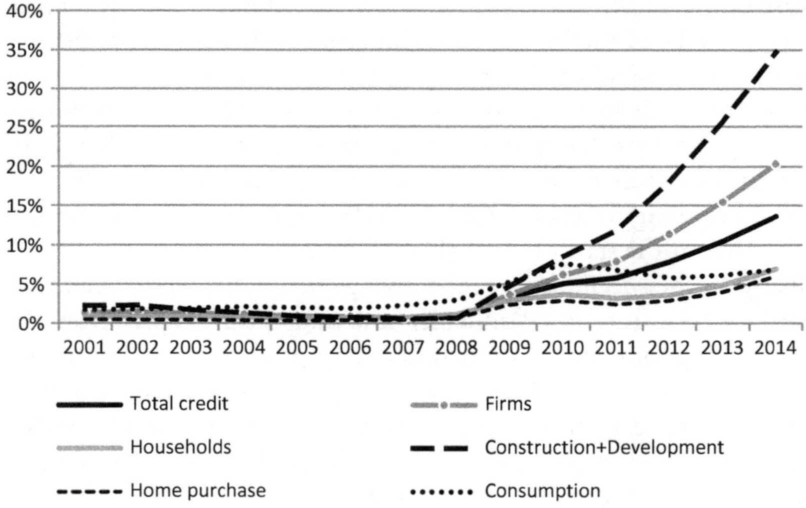

Fig. 22.16 Percentage of doubtful loans as a share of total loans in each sector (*Source*: Authors' elaboration on Bank of Spain data)

reduce their capacity, and this was one of the conditions in the MoU for the banking-sector bailout in June 2012.

During the years of credit expansion, domestic savings and deposits were insufficient to finance this lending. Spanish banks therefore tapped the wholesale markets for funding, and were able to issue debt with ease. The credit/

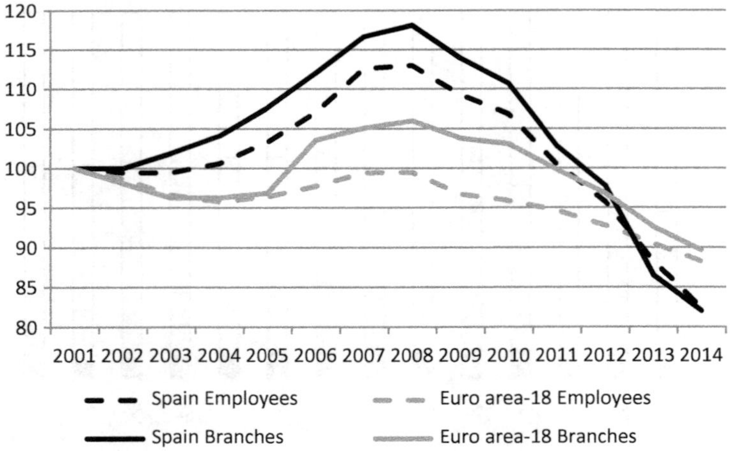

Fig. 22.17 Evolution of the number of branches and employees in the Euro area and Spanish banks. 2001 = 100 (*Source*: Authors' elaboration on ECB data)

deposits liquidity gap therefore widened, reaching a value of close to 1.3 in the case of the non-financial private sector. The closure of the wholesale markets in the wake of the international financial crisis left the Spanish banking system in an extremely vulnerable position when it came to rolling over its existing debt. This forced it to turn to deposits (with a war breaking out to attract deposits by offering interest rates that damaged some banks' bottom line to the extent that the Bank of Spain had to step in to penalize excessive rates) and funding from the ECB.[14] This brought the liquidity gap to a ratio of below one at the start of 2014 (Fig. 22.18).

Finally, in the specific case of the savings banks, on top of the imbalances referred to above, they faced difficulty obtaining quality capital from the market. Not being joint-stock companies (being private non-profit foundations conducting financial activities), they could not issue shares to raise equity when they needed to shore up their solvency. The only way in which they could improve their capitalization was by allocating profits to reserves, which was impossible in a scenario in which they were making losses. Although they could issue non-voting primary capital certificates, these were not attractive to investors, as they lacked voting rights. In fact, only one savings bank (Caja de Ahorros del Mediterráneo) managed to issue primary capital certificates.

[14] In August 2012 Spanish banks absorbed as much as 34% of the ECB's gross lending, three times its weight in the Eurosystem. In early 2015 the percentage had dropped to 26%, and gross lending was less than a third.

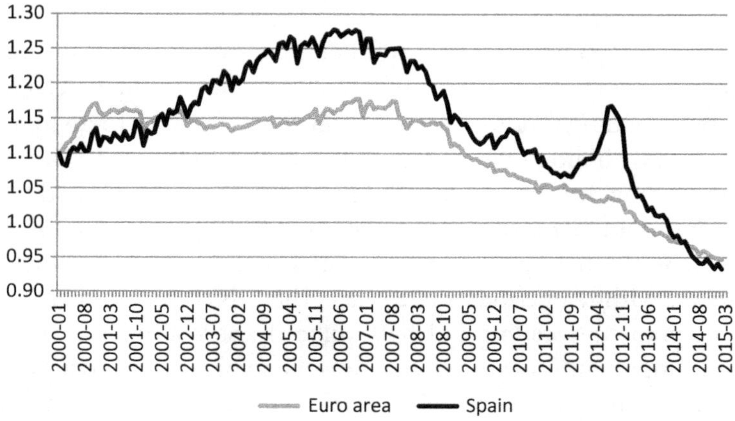

Fig. 22.18 Liquidity gap. Credit/deposits to the non-financial private sector (*Source*: Authors' elaboration on Bank of Spain data)

Measures Taken in Response to the Crisis

The specific features of the banking crisis in Spain made it necessary to adopt a wide range of measures to correct the imbalances that had built up, on top of the measures taken at the international level to prevent similar crisis in the future (such as the new Basel III Accords, which demand more and higher quality capital, liquidity ratios, leverage ratios).

To understand the rationale and time sequence of the measures adopted in 2008, the prevailing perception when the crisis erupted needs to be taken into account. The official view at the time was that the problem was not one of solvency but liquidity, so the first measures put in place were intended to facilitate access to liquidity. Thus, in 2008 the Financial Assets Acquisition Fund (FAAF) was created, with initial funding of €30 billion, later expanded to €50 billion, to be used to buy top quality assets from the banks. This measure was justified as a means of stimulating credit to businesses and households.

Along the same lines, as a further liquidity measure, later that year the European Commission authorized the Spanish government to grant guarantees backing issues of bank debt. This authorization was extended over several years until 2012, with the total volume of guaranteed debt reaching €110,895 million.

As time went by, given the severity of the economic crisis, it became necessary to adopt measures to restructure the banking sector. The first such measure was the creation of the Fund for Orderly Restructuring of the Banking Sector (FROB) in June 2009. This had two goals: strengthening intervention mechanisms in distressed entities whose difficulties affected their future viability;

and restructuring the sector in order to shed the excess installed capacity and achieve efficiency gains through consolidation, so as to increase the size of institutions and improve their access to market finance. The FROB bolstered solvency by providing funding to support mergers. In order to do so it had initial funding of €9 billion (with potential for up to a tenfold increase), a quarter of which was provided by the Deposit Guarantee Fund (FGD) and the rest by the state. It should be noted that initially the FROB provided aid in the form of capital (conditional upon submission of a feasibility plan), which entities were to repay within a period of five years. The FROB financed eight mergers and the aid granted (totalling €11,559 million) was lost in its entirety.

The next important measure adopted was the reform of the savings banks law in July 2010 in order to allow savings banks to access quality capital, raise the professional standards of their management, and depoliticize their governing bodies (reducing the presence of representatives of public administrations on their governing bodies from 50 % to 40 %). The reform therefore allowed the savings banks to create banks to which to transfer their business, and so access quality capital from the markets through them. This reform kicked off the process of turning the sector's entities into banks, as of the 45 savings banks that existed at the time, only two have retained their original status. The remainder of the former savings banks have been converted into banking foundations, which conduct their financial activity indirectly through banks that have been set up for the purpose.

Against the backdrop of a climate of widespread financial instability right across Europe in the wake of the sovereign-debt crisis in April 2010, triggered by the first Greek bailout, Royal Decree-Law 2/2011 was passed in February 2011, aiming to strengthen the Spanish financial system in an effort to dispel the uncertainties surrounding the banks' solvency, given the large volume of property assets on their balance sheets. The law raised the solvency ratio required in Spain considerably, reaching 10 % of core capital as a percentage of risk-weighted assets (RWA) in those entities that did not have at least 20 % of private capital and were more than 20 % dependent on wholesale market funding. These latter entities were the most vulnerable, due to their high degree of market dependence, and their difficulties accessing private capital. Although the law does not explicitly say so, the institutions it has in mind are obviously the savings banks. As the law required a lower solvency ratio (8 %) for other entities, it represented an incentive for the savings banks to create banks, as if they were able to place at least 20 % of their capital on the market the lower solvency ratio would apply to them, and they would consequently save capital.[15] Entities that were unable to obtain the capital necessary to

[15] This was the reason for Bankia's stock market flotation.

comply with the law by their own means were financed by the FROB, which injected capital (to the tune of 7,551 million euros) and consequently nationalized part of the savings bank sector.

It would be necessary to wait until February 2012, following a change of government, for the serious solvency problem arising from the unprovisioned losses caused by the bursting of the property-market bubble to be recognized. Thus, on 3 February 2012, Royal Decree-Law 2/2012 on the reorganization of the financial sector was passed, requiring new provisions to be set aside to address the impairment of loans and foreclosed assets from property developments held on 31 December 2011. The provisions necessary to meet the new requirements were estimated at €54 billion, of which €15 billion would be in the form of a capital buffer (charged to undistributed profits, obtained from capital increases, or by converting hybrid instruments such as preferred shares, convertible bonds or subordinate debt) and the remainder in the form of specific and general provisions. The latter, which are exclusive to the Spanish banking sector, are associated with assets classed as standard exposures, implying tacit recognition that property risk may in fact not be entirely "standard". It is important to note that in August 2012, following the bank bailout, there was a further reform as a consequence of the obligations under the MoU. This demanded a transitory increase in the solvency ratio for all entities and the repeal of the €15 billion capital buffer requirement laid down by the Royal-Decree Law of February 2012 on the cleaning-up of the financial sector.

In May that year, a further Royal Decree-Law (RDL 18/2012) was passed on the write-down and sale of banking sector real-estate assets. This required fresh general provisions of 30 billion euros for standard exposures to the property sector, which was somewhat surprising given that this again concerned provisions for assets classed as standard exposures after having required similar provisions (although of a smaller amount) just three months earlier. The reason for this new requirement was that in March 2012 the International Monetary Fund (IMF) published its preliminary Financial Sector Assessment Programme (FSAP) conclusions for Spain. In its conclusions the IMF mentioned that it had performed a stress test that found capital shortfalls at certain institutions and that "Lender forbearance—which the supervisory authorities have indicated they are monitoring closely—could not be fully incorporated into the stress tests due to lack of data, and this may have masked the extent of credit risk in some institutions." In other words, the IMF suspected that there were troubled assets that were being classed as standard exposures. The government's response to this suspicion was to demand additional provisions for this property exposure classed as "standard".

The Banking-Sector Bail-Out and the MoU

Given the scale of the write-downs required by these two royal decree-laws, compounded by the capital shortfall detected by the IMF in its report,[16] in June 2012, against the backdrop of a soaring risk premium on sovereign debt, the Spanish government found itself obliged to apply for a banking-sector bailout from the European funds. This request for financial assistance marked a turning point for the Spanish banking sector, as it brought the solvency problems part of the sector was facing to the fore. Given its systemic nature, Bankia (the biggest bank owned by a banking foundation) was the main focus of concern. Its size was equivalent to 30 % of Spain's GDP, similar to that of Fannie Mae and Freddie Mac relative to US GDP. The Bankia's capital shortfall detected by the stress test undertaken in 2012 by Oliver Wyman represents 46 % of total capital shortfalls.

The MoU that accompanied the bailout shaped the reforms undertaken from then on. The measures included, among others, running further bank-by-bank stress tests, additional reform of the savings banks, enhanced information transparency, the creation of a "bad bank" (SAREB), a new bank resolution framework, higher solvency requirements, reforms to supervision methods, and promoting non-bank intermediation.[17]

Of the set of reforms imposed by the MoU, two stand out in particular for their importance: Law 28/2013 on savings banks and banking foundations; and the SAREB.

The new savings bank reform laid down a series of conditions for the savings banks to continue being classed as such, requiring them to return to their traditional role. These conditions include having assets of less than €10 billion or a share of deposits of more than 35 % of the total in the autonomous region in which they operate. They are also required to focus on retail customers and SMEs, and operate within geographical limits that may not exceed one autonomous region or ten contiguous provinces. The reform reduced the weight of the public sector in their governing bodies from 40 % to 25 %[18]. As well as depoliticizing the savings banks, the reform aims to avoid a repetition the errors of the past, when excessive growth in scale and reach beyond their home regions led some of them to bankruptcy. For the larger savings banks, the reform requires them to create a bank to which to transfer their banking

[16] See International Monetary Fund (2012).

[17] For details, see Spain, MoU on Financial Sector Policy Conditionality, 20 July 2012.

[18] Illueca et al. (2014) find that the governance of the Spanish savings banks significantly affected the way in which they expanded their lending activities. Savings banks subject to political influence by regional governments exhibited higher ex ante risk-taking and higher ex post loan defaults. This is confirmed by Akin et al. (2014).

business, and to convert into a banking foundation if the savings banks keeps in the bank more than 10 % shareholding.

The new law establishes that banking foundations holding more than 30 % of the shares in a credit institution must submit a management protocol regarding this shareholding for approval by the Bank of Spain; the latter, as the supervisory authority, will have the power to establish the criteria for the management of the foundation's shareholding in the bank, the relationship between the bank and the foundation, the rules on related-party transactions, and the financial plan to meet the capital requirements. Banking foundations that have a shareholding of over 50 % or which hold positions of control in a credit institution will be obliged to submit an investment diversification and risk-management strategy together with their financial plan to avoid the concentration of assets. Importantly, the foundation also needs to have a reserve fund to meet possible equity needs and guarantee liquidity. Basically, given how difficult it is for a banking foundation to possess such a reserve fund, the aim is for foundations to have shareholdings in banks of less than 50 % so as to avoid their holding a controlling stake.

The SAREB, or "bad bank", is an important factor in reducing the uncertainty over the viability of bailed-out entities, as they are obliged to transfer their property exposure to it. The SAREB (the Spanish acronym for the Company for the Management of Assets proceeding from the Restructuring of the Banking System) was initially given a period of 15 years over which to conduct the orderly divestment of the €51 billion of assets under management (loans, foreclosed assets, and shareholdings in property developers acquired by the SAREB by paying for these assets with government-backed bonds). The SAREB is a private entity in which the FROB holds 45 % of the capital. The remaining 55 % is held by private investors (banks and insurance companies). It was important that the FROB not hold more than 50 % of SAREB's shares as that would have made a public law institution, and its debt would consequently have been considered government debt and its losses included in the public deficit.

The Spanish Banking System After the Restructuring

The fact that the Spanish banking sector has gone from having to request financial assistance from European funds to successfully passing the ECB's stress tests in November 2014 in just two years is a sign of the success of the restructuring carried out. Thus, overcapacity has been reduced, balance sheets cleaned up (equivalent to 29 % of GDP between 2008 and 2014), solvency improved, the liquidity gap has narrowed, and there has been a consolidation of the sector.[19]

[19] The average size of banking institutions has quadrupled as a result of the restructuring.

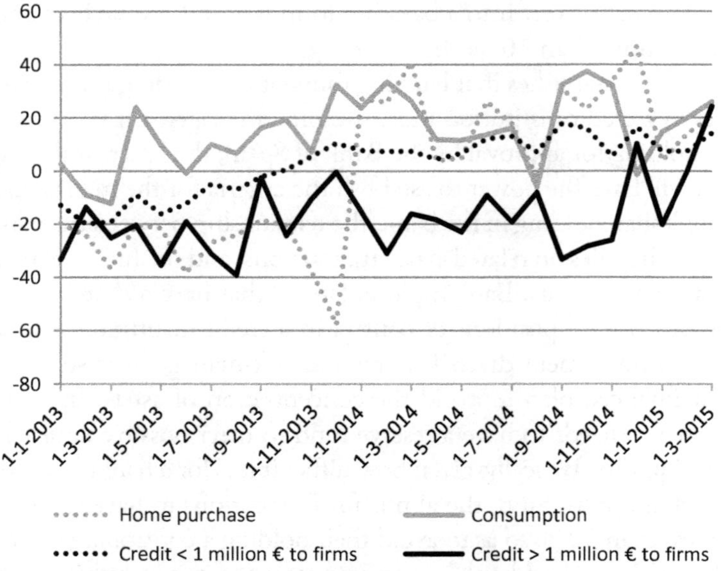

Fig. 22.19 Annual growth rate of credit (new business) to the non-financial private sector. Percentage (*Source*: Authors' elaboration on Bank of Spain data)

The latest information available, referring to June 2014, shows (Figure 22.10) profit levels above the European average, and better than those of banks in the main European economies. Nevertheless, they still face higher default rates, albeit with a level of coverage similar to the European average.

Following the restructuring and write-downs, Spanish banks are in a better position from which to perform their role as intermediaries and to finance the real economy. Although the stock of credit continues to fall (albeit at ever slower rates), new lending transactions (necessary to finance new investment projects) are growing. This includes lending both to SMEs (using loans of less than a million euros as a proxy) and households, both for consumption and home purchases (Fig. 22.19). Competition has also picked up, as is revealed by the narrowing of the spreads over the Euribor banks are able to charge on the loans they grant.

Lessons of the Banking Crisis and Future Challenges

Lessons of the Crisis

The initial diagnosis of the crisis that it was only a problem of liquidity, and not of solvency, had consequences for the effectiveness of the measures enacted. This diagnosis was left unchanged for too long, and it was even claimed at some point that Spain's banking sector was the world's most solvent. This view was the result of an underestimation of both the severity and duration of the crisis, leading to the belief that the counter-cyclical provisions set aside (around €30 billion), and for which the Bank of Spain was a pioneer, would be sufficient to meet the losses. Indeed, Spain was one of the few countries in Europe that used macro-prudential tools before the crisis.[20] Alberola et al. (2011) show that, during the recent financial crisis, dynamic provisions proved useful to mitigate —to a limited extent— the build-up of risks and, above all, to provide substantial loss absorbency capacity to the financial institutions. Their effectiveness in smoothing the credit supply cycle has been tested by Jiménez et al. (2015) who find that a policy-induced one percentage point increase in capital buffers extends credit to firms by 9 points.

Spain provides an example of softer lending standards in the boom than in the bust, in particular in real state. Akin et al. (2014) claim that the mechanism by which banks were able to increase mortgage supply bypassing loan-to-value restrictions is through upward biases in real state appraisals. The build-up for risk in the banking system was compounded by loose monetary policy. Lower overnight interest rates led undercapitalized banks to relax their credit policy by extending and expanding credit to riskier firms with larger loan volumes and lower collateral requirements in the period 2002–8 (Jiménez et al. 2014).

This initial misdiagnosis meant public capital was not injected early enough, when it would still have been possible given the treasury's ability to issue public debt at reasonable rates and start the cleanup of damaged balance sheets. Between 2008 and 2010 public aid to the banking system in the form of capital came to 1.2 % of GDP in Spain, which was tiny compared with the sums involved in the EU-27 (3.3 %), Germany (4.5 %), the Netherlands (4 %) or the United Kingdom (7.3 %).

Another lesson from the banking crisis is that mergers are not the solution when all the entities involved are in difficulties. To put it bluntly, the merger of several weak entities delivered an even weaker large entity. It is clear that the *Sistema Institucional de Protección* (SIP) mechanism (which stands for institutional protection system in Spanish, also referred to as "cold fusion", and consists of a group of institutions creating a bank to which to transfer their

[20] Currently, there are two types of provision: (a) specific provisions which depend on observed non-performing loans; and (b) generic provisions, which depend on the stock of performing loans. Until 2004, there was a third type of provision, the so-called statistical provisions, designed to offset specific provisions along the cycle. With the 2004 reform, generic provisions absorbed the old statistical provision. Although generic provisions smoothed the impact of the crisis, the anti-cyclical impact was smaller than expected.

banking business) was sometimes a failure, resulting in the new groups created by the savings banks being taken over and bailed out by the FROB. Some of the mergers that took place were defensive moves by savings banks based in the same region, as regional governments did not want to lose control over them. All the intraregional mergers that took place resulted in entities that had to be taken over, bailed out, and later sold off, with the state suffering huge losses.

Another lesson of the crisis is that injecting public capital will not solve the problems unless there is a change of management. This was seen in the case of the first aid given by the FROB, where there was barely any change in the composition of the management bodies of the new institutions created by mergers.

Finally, a lesson of the crises is the importance of geographical diversification. Santander and BBVA, the two biggest Spanish banks, have suffered less from the consequences of the crisis in the Spanish economy, partly due to the high weight of business that is outside Spain and that has offset the decline in activity in Spain with other areas of rapid credit growth and low banking penetration.[21]

Future Challenges

Spain's banking sector has made major progress thanks to the restructuring, as the most recent reports from the authorities involved in rescuing the Spanish banking system (IMF 2014; European Commission 2015) highlight. Those authorities, however, point also to certain vulnerabilities and challenges going forward. A major concern, which is shared by the banking systems of major developed economies, is to regain the trust lost by customers and investors because of misbehaviour in the run-up to the crisis. In our view, there are six challenges:

(a) Low interest rate scenario

Following the ECB's various non-conventional measures to tackle the problems of deflation and stagnation in the Eurozone, a scenario of very low interest rates has become established, holding back the recovering in bank profitability. Although the initial effect of low interest rates was positive, as costs fell faster than interest income (as shown by Spanish banks' widening net interest margins in 2014) and the capital gains obtained

[21] BBVA Group offers financial services in 31 countries. It has a strong leadership position in the Spanish market; is the largest financial institution in Mexico and it has leading franchises in South America and in the US "Sunbelt"; it also has a significant presence in Turkey (through investments in Garanti Bank), and operates an extensive network of offices around the world. Santander group has a balanced diversification in its main 10 markets. Spain (14 % of its business), United Kingdom (19 %), Brazil (19 %), USA (10 %), Mexico (8 %), Chile (6 %), Poland (6%), Germany (5 %), Argentina (4 %) and Portugal (2 %).

from the sale of assets (such as public debt, largely acquired with finance from the ECB in carry trade transactions), going forward the margin for further lending rate cuts is slender, while assets will continue to decline, with the consequent drop in net interest income. It will also be difficult to obtain capital gains similar to those in the past from the sale of assets. In this scenario banks will seek to increase the share of income from sources other than interest charges (such as fees), which requires changes in the banking business.

(b) Large volume of non-performing assets

Although the non-performing loan rate has been falling since 2014, the volume remains considerable. But as well as these bad loans (equivalent to 17 % of GDP at end-2014), foreclosed assets, valued at a total of €82.5 billion in late 2014, are also considered troubled assets. The non-performing loan rate, including both types of troubled asset, therefore stands at close to 18 %, with a large volume of assets generating financial and operational costs but no income. Managing this huge volume of non-performing assets is therefore a challenge for the Spanish banks, and a constraint on their returning to profitability. Indeed, the digestion of the explosion of the real-state bubble is very heavy and slow.

(c) Regulatory requirements

A third element of vulnerability is the so-called regulatory tsunami that demands that banks hold more and higher quality capital in the new regulatory environment of Basel III. Spanish banks have increased their capital by over €100 billion, but even so, they do not stand out on the international solvency rankings. They therefore need to continue strengthening their own funds, and it is not easy to attract capital when the profitability of the business is still recovering. With a return on equity of 5 % (ROE of banking business in Spain, and 7 % when considering subsidiaries abroad) and estimated cost of attracting capital of 8 %, it is difficult to tap the markets for capital. Moreover, what is important is not only the level of solvency required by the regulations, but also that of market competitors.

Against the backdrop of the need to bolster own funds, the legislation on corporate tax was reformed, first in 2013 and again in 2015, such that a portion of the sector's deferred tax assets (DTAs) converted into deferred tax credits by government guarantee, deriving from expenses that cannot be offset against current profits, and so represent a future claim against the public treasury, continue to be considered Tier 1 capital, without their being classed as state aid. The reform, which involves a cost to the banks for the government guarantee and that eliminates the possibility in the future of generating guaranteed DTAs when no taxes are paid on a given fiscal year, was negotiated with the European Commission and the Bank of Spain.

(d) New capacity adjustments

In a context of low interest rates and high volumes of non-performing assets, banks need to continue making efficiency gains in order to boost their profitability. These efficiency gains will require further adjustments to capacity, although there is now less room for manoeuvre, given that the branch network had already been cut by 31 % by 2014. Online and mobile banking will become more important in the future, leading to branch closures. A problem faced by Spanish banks is that although all the banks are aware of the need to close branches, it is difficult to take the first step given the risk of losing market share.

(e) The new context of banking union

Banking union was designed to complete the institutions necessary for monetary union. The Single Supervisory Mechanism came into force in November 2014, the Single Resolution Mechanism in 2015, and the new bail-in rules will come into effect in 2016. A common Eurozone deposit insurance fund will have to wait for the moment. Progress towards a single banking market in Europe will lead to a more competitive scenario given the growth in cross-border activity.

In this new, integrated market, Spanish banks that have grown rapidly in recent years through mergers will need to consider new, cross-border mergers, as geographical diversification of the business is one strategy for reducing future risks. Experience has shown that the two largest Spanish banks (Santander and BBVA) have been in a better position to confront the crisis partly because a large part of their business is diversified across multiple countries. However, banks with concentrated banking business in Spain may seek also to expand internationally to higher margin countries, but perhaps outside the Eurozone, in order to restore profitability.

(f) The impact of increased concentration on competition

Increased international competition is compatible with niches of market power in sub-national markets. Some of the mergers taking place in Spain in recent years have led to important increases in market concentration in some provinces/regions, with levels of concentration that would attract the attention of competition authorities in some other countries. As an illustration, using 2013 data, the Herfindahl index (constructed in terms of branches) is over 1,800 points in 17 of Spain's 52 provinces, and in 47 it rose by more than 200 points during the crisis (coinciding in 13 provinces). Therefore, based on the 1,800/200 rule,[22] the level of concentration out of mergers in 13 Spanish provinces would require an analysis of the impact on competition. It is worth noting the classical tension between the role of mergers to reduce excess capacity and save fixed costs and their potential impact on competition.

(g) Increase in non-bank competition

The spread of shadow banking and the expansion of finance offers from new, non-bank competitors (from the digital world, such as Google or Apple) could change the landscape of banking competition. This factor is a concern from the regulatory perspective, which seeks to avoid hidden build-up of risk. Furthermore, it is a factor that will induce competition and demand a response from traditional banks. One possible response that is taking shape in some of the main Spanish banking groups is to develop online and mobile banking, as a future channel for access to banking services as well as trying to integrate some of the new competitors.

(h) The volume of public debt on bank balance sheets

During the crisis, Spanish banks scaled up their investments in public debt substantially. This was for several reasons: the advantages in terms of reduced capital consumption in the calculation of RWA; the lack of solvent demand for credit; and the low cost of borrowing from the ECB, enabling high returns to be obtained by buying higher yield debt via the carry trade. Over the period 2007–14 the share of public debt in total assets rose by 7.2 percentage points to 9.9 %.

These large holdings of public debt have made a positive contribution to profits in two ways: financial income, particularly when the risk premium was high; and capital gains from their sale. The problem is that going forward it will not be possible to generate so much revenue this way (firstly because of the drop in the risk premium and secondly because of the loss of potential for the carry trade), which will have a negative impact on the bottom line. Moreover, it would not be surprising to see a change in international regulations tending to limit the concentration of public debt on bank balance sheets, given the negative consequences the sovereign-debt crisis had on the vicious cycle of public and bank debt in the recent past.

---

[22] According to this rule, which is used by the U.S. Department of Justice, a merger's raising the Herfindahl index by more than 200 points, when post-merger the Herfindahl goes above 1,800, requires a close examination of the intended merger, given the potential effects on the degree of competition. This rule is met in 13 of Spain's 52 provinces. Note, however, that relevant markets in loan and deposits should be defined and that the use of branches in provinces is only an imperfect substitute of a proper analysis.

References

Akin, O., García Montalvo, J., Garcia Villar, J., & Raya, J. M. (2014). The real estate and credit bubble: Evidence from Spain. *SERIEs, the Journal of the Spanish Economic Association, 5*, 223–243.

Alberola, E., Trucharte, C., & Vega, J. L. (2011). *Central banks and macroprudential policy: Some reflections from the Spanish experience* (Occasional paper 1105). Madrid: Bank of Spain.

Bank of Spain. (2012, November). *Financial stability report.*

Beck, T., Degryse, H., & Kneer, C. (2014). Is more finance better? disentangling intermediation and size effects of financial systems. *Journal of Financial Stability, 10*, 50–64.

Caminal, R., Gual, J., & Vives, X. (1990). Competition in Spanish Banking. In J. Dermine (Ed.), *European Banking in the 1990's*. London: Basil Blackwell.

Carbó, S., & Rodriguez, F. (2012). Nuevas Perspectivas para el Crédito Relacional a las Pymes en España. In *Pequeña y Media Empresa: Impacto y Retos de la Crisis en su Financiación, Papeles de la Fundación* 45 (pp. 163–178). Madrid: Fundación de Estudios Financieros.

Carbó, S., Humphrey, D., Maudos, J., & Molyneux, P. (2009). Cross-country comparisons of competition and pricing power in European banking. *Journal of International Money and Finance, 28*, 115–134.

European Commission. (2015). *Post-programme surveillance report Spain, Spring 2015* (Occasional papers 211). Luxembourg: Publications Office.

Fernandez de Guevara, J., & Maudos, J. (2016). Competition in the European banking markets in the aftermath of the financial crisis. In J. A. Bikker & L. Spierdijk (Eds.), *Handbook on competition in banking and finance*, forthcoming.

Illueca, M., Norden, L., & Udell, G. F. (2014). Liberalization and risk-taking: Evidence from government-controlled banks. *Review of Finance, 18*, 1217–1257.

International Monetary Fund. (2012). *Spain: Financial stability assessment*, June 2012 (IMF Country Report No. 12/137). Washington, DC: IMF.

International Monetary Fund. (2014). *Spain: Financial sector reform—final progress report* (IMF Country Report No. 14/59). Washington, DC: IMF.

Jiménez, G., López, J. A., & Saurina, J. (2013). How does competition affect bank risk-taking? *Journal of Financial Stability, 9*(2), 185–195.

Jiménez, G., Ongena, S., Peydró, J. L., & Saurina, J. (2014). Hazardous times for monetary policy: What do 23 million loans say about the impact of monetary policy on credit risk taking? *Econometrica, 82*(2), 463–505.

Jiménez, G., Ongena, S., Peydró, J. L., & Saurina, J. (2015). *Macroprudential policy, countercyclical bank capital buffers and credit supply: Evidence from the Spanish dynamic provisioning experiments* (European Banking Center discussion paper 2012-011). Tilburg, The Netherlands.

Maudos, J. (2012). *El Sector Bancario Español en el Contexto Internacional: el Impacto de la Crisis, Fundación de las Cajas de Ahorro*. Madrid, Spain.

Maudos, J. (2013). *Las Relaciones Bancarias de las Empresas Españolas* (*Fundación de las Cajas de Ahorro*). Madrid, Spain.

Maudos, J. (2014, September). Cambios de Especialización y Estructura de Ingresos de la Banca Española: el Impacto de la Crisis. *Papeles de Economía Española*, pp. 59–74.

Vives, X. (2012). The spanish financial industry at the start of 21st century: Current situation and future challenges. In J. L. M. de Molina & P. Martín-Aceña (Eds.), *The Spanish financial system. Growth and development since 1900*. New York: Palgrave Macmillan.

Vives, X. (2016). *Competition and stability in banking: The role of regulation and competition policy*. Princeton University Press.

23

Banking in France

Laetitia Lepetit, Céline Meslier, and Amine Tarazi

The French banking system has experienced major changes since the mid-1980s, with the deregulation process triggered by the Banking Act of 1984 and the broader reform of capital markets in 1985. The aim of these actions was to improve the performance and the efficiency of the entire banking industry and enhance competition between financial institutions and markets by allowing various types of agent, and specifically non-financial firms, to directly borrow from the market by issuing short-term debt. The money market became accessible to non-banks both to issue debt (various types of security such as certificates of deposits issued by banks or commercial papers issued by non-financial firms) and acquire securities and hence, in 1985, banks and other financial institutions lost the monopoly position they had had for long regarding short- and medium-term funding. Before 1985, any lending operation with less than seven years of duration was channeled by the banking system. Banks and markets not only started competing on the loan market but also on the savings market which gradually lead to a sharp decrease in their interest margins. As in other countries, banks in France started diversifying their activities to maintain their profitability which was probably made easier because the French Banking Act of 1984 promoted the concept of universal banking by allowing any chartered institution to conduct any intermediation activity provided by credit organizations.

L. Lepetit • C. Meslier • A. Tarazi (✉)
Laboratoire d'Analyse et de Prospective Economiques (LAPE),
Université de Limoges, Limoges, France
e-mail: laetitia.lepetit@unilim.fr; celine.meslier@unilim.fr; amine.tarazi@unilim.fr

T. Beck, B. Casu (eds.), *The Palgrave Handbook of European Banking*,
DOI 10.1057/978-1-137-52144-6_23

The Architecture of the French Banking System

Although various categories of financial institutions were still maintained in the system, with the Banking Act of 1984 they all became credit institutions (Etablissements de crédit) which initially comprised French Banking Federation (Fédération Bancaire Française) banks (the so-called Banques) such as Banque Nationale de Paris (which later became BNP Paribas) or Société Générale, the cooperative and mutual banks (Banques mutualistes ou coopératives) such as Crédit Agricole, Banque Populaire or Crédit Mutuel, the savings banks (Caisse d'épargne), the municipal credit institutions (Caisses de crédit municipal), the so-called specialized financial institutions (Institutions financières spécialisées, IFS) which were mandated to achieve a general interest goal (reconstruction after the war, housing, etc.), and the so-called financial societies (Sociétés financières, SF) essentially focused on consumer loans.

The Different Types of Credit Institution in 2014

Since January 2014, to comply with European regulation and standards, the former Institutions financières spécialisées (IFS) and Sociétés financières (SF) no longer exist and have been replaced by Etablissements de crédit spécialisés (ECS). Hence, according to the figures provided by the French bank supervision authority (Autorité de contrôle prudentiel et de résolution 2014a, ACPR), in December 2014 the number of Credit Institutions (Etablissements de crédit) was (see Table 23.1):

- 253 banks (*Banques*), including 67 branches and 10 subsidiaries of banks from the European Economic Area (EEA), and 21 branches and 14 subsidiaries of banks headquartered outside the EEA;
- Banks are allowed to conduct any bank operations: receiving deposits, granting loans, providing all services involving means of payments. They are also allowed to deal with foreign currencies, gold and other precious metals. They can trade securities and any financial assets (buy, hold, manage, custody activities, and so on). They can provide assistance and advice in portfolio and wealth management and conduct fiduciary activities in general.
- 91 cooperative and mutual banks (*Banques mutualistes ou coopératives*);[1]

[1] In 1999, savings banks (*Caisses d'Epargne*) were transformed by law into mutual banks.

- Cooperative and Mutual banks are also allowed to conduct all such operations but with compliance with their specific status. As a whole, however, there are almost no operations provided by ordinary banks that cannot be provided by cooperative banks. Each mutual or cooperative group has a similar structure: (i) a network of regional banks which are fully-fledged banks and (ii) a central institution serving the regional entities and coordinating the internal liquidity market within the group. The regional banks have a majority stake in the central institution which in turn partly owns the regional entities. A specific case is the organization of the Crédit Agricole Group whose central body (Crédit Agricole SA) has been listed on the stock market since 2001.
- 18 municipal credit institutions (*Caisses de crédit municipal*);
- Municipal credit institutions have a monopoly position in pawn brokerage activities.
- 106 Specialized credit institutions (*Etablissements de crédit spécialisés, ECS*);
- Specialized credit institutions are not authorized to conduct all banking operations. Specifically, they are generally not allowed to collect deposits. The operations they are allowed to carry out depend on the approval they obtain from regulators. Most commonly, such institutions focus on either consumer loans, property leasing, equipment leasing, factoring, guarantees, and so on.

Table 23.1 provides information on the number of banks and other lending institutions in France for the years 2013 and 2014 by recalling the number of institutions that were in place in 2003. As most banking systems in Western countries, France experienced a consolidation of its banking industry that kept running through the years 2000s and particularly in the mid-2000s. The number of institutions fell from 887 in 2003 to 468 in 2014 with the sharpest decline affecting the specialized credit institutions but also traditional banks, while the number of branches of foreign banks headquartered in the EEA has risen from 52 in 2003 to 66 in 2014.

Figures for 2014 (Table 23.2) show that most credit institutions (more than 70 %) are controlled by banking groups, of which around half to French mutual banking groups and around 20 % to large private groups. The remainder (almost 30 % of credit institutions) are controlled by non-banking entities. Around 5 % of these institutions are controlled by the public sector and around 2 % by individuals or families. A notable characteristic of the French banking sector is the significant presence of non-financial firms (industrial groups) in banks' ownership.

Table 23.1 Number of credit institutions (*Etablissements de crédit*)

Number of credit institutions	Was in 2003	2013	2014	Change 2014/2013
Institutions allowed to conduct all bank operations	**452**	**366**	**362**	**– 4**
Banks	*304*	*256*	*253*	*– 3*
o/w Branches of banks headquartered from the EEA	*(52)*	*(66)*	*(66)*	–
o/w Subsidiaries of banks headquartered from the EEA	*(47)*	*(10)*	*(10)*	–
o/w Branches of banks headquartered outside the EEA	*(28)*	*(21)*	*(21)*	–
o/w Subsidiaries of banks headquartered outside the EEA	*(16)*	*(14)*	*(14)*	–
Cooperative and Mutual Banks	*128*	*92*	*91*	*– 1*
Municipal Credit Institutions	*20*	*18*	*18*	–
Specialized credit insitutions	**435**	**250**	**106**	**–144**
Total number of credit institutions	**887**	**616**	**468**	**–148**

Source: ACPR (French Prudential Supervision Authority), Authors' translation

Table 23.2 French-owned credit institutions, by type of ownership at end-2014

Ownership	Banks	Mutual banks	Financial corporations	Other[a]	Total	Number of shareholding groups in 2014
Large private-sector banking groups	31		53		84	2
Public-sector banking insitutions	2		4	20	26	4
Mutual banking groups	57	90	85		232	4
Insurance companies	3	1	5		9	7
Industrial, commercial, services, construction and public works, professional groups	15		18		33	20
o/w public sector	2		3		5	1
Institutions with mixed ownership (credit institutions, investors, institutional investors)	4		21		25	24
Diversified financial groups	1		2		3	2
Natural persons	9		8		17	15
Total	**122**	**91**	**196**	**20**	**434**	**79**

Source: ACPR (French Prudential Supervision Authority)

[a]Municipal credit institutions and specialized financial institutions

Any financial institution established in France is required to be affiliated to a professional association or an institution which is itself affiliated to the Association Française des Etablissements de Crédit et des Entreprises d'investissement (AFECEI). As of July 2015, AFECI comprises 13 affiliates, among them the Fédération Bancaire Française (FBF) which has 383 banks of various types (commercial, cooperative or mutual as members in 2015, The Association Française des marchés financiers (AMAFI), The Association Française des Sociétés Financières (ASF), and so on).

Deposit Insurance and Regulatory Authorities

All these institutions (Etablissements de crédit) have to subscribe to a deposit insurance system managed by the Fonds de Garantie des Dépôts et de Résolution (FGDR). This principle applies to all deposit institutions and investment companies established in France but also to French branches of institutions outside the EEA. Deposits are insured up to a level of 100,000 euros and custody accounts (stocks, bonds, mutual funds, and so on) to a limit of 70,000 euros. As of July 2015, there are 605 members insured with regards to deposits, 378 with regards to securities.

Regardless of their type, all these institutions have to comply with the rules implemented by the same three authorities which are linked to the Banque de France. Initially the Banking Act introduced the Banking Regulation Committee (Comité de régmentation des banques, CRB), the Credit Organizations Committee (Comité des établissements de crédit, CEC) and the Banking Commission (Commission Bancaire, CB). After the global financial crisis of 2008, the Banking Commission later became in 2010 a prudential control and supervision authority with enlarged responsibilities (Autorité de contrôle prudentiel, ACP) and later further gained in power in 2013 by being mandated to deal not only with the prevention but also the resolution of bank failures and banking crises (Autorité de contrôle prudentiel et de résolution 2014b, ACPR). This authority is an independent administrative authority linked to the Banque de France in charge of ensuring the stability of the financial system but also of protecting bank and insurance companies' customers.

As of July 2015, financial institutions (*Etablissements de crédit*) are under the authority of:

(i) The Autorité de contrôle prudentiel et de résolution (ACPR)

This body provides approvals at the individual level to all kinds of financial institutions after receiving in certain cases approval by the financial market authority. It is also in charge of controlling operations and taking sanctions.

Organization of ACPR (French Prudential Supervision Authority)

(Source: ACPR Website, http://acpr.banque-france.fr/en/acpr/organisation.html)

The Supervisory College: The responsibilities entrusted to the ACPR are exercised by the Supervisory College, which has several configurations depending on the issues being addressed. It has 19 members and is chaired by the Governor of the Banque de France.

The plenary session of the College deals with general supervisory issues concerning the banking and insurance sectors. It analyses risks in both sectors with regard to the economic situation. It also makes decisions on the authority's organizational, operating and budget principles and sets the ACPR's Rules of Procedure. Each year, it sets the supervisory priorities.

The Sub-Colleges, one for banking, the other for insurance, each of which has eight members, have jurisdiction over specific matters and general issues relating to their respective sectors. The Supervisory College meets in **restricted session** (also consisting of eight members) to deal with individual issues having a material impact on the two sectors or on financial stability as a whole, as well as matters relating to the supervision of financial conglomerates.

The Resolution College: The Resolution College was established by Banking Separation and Regulation Act 2013-672 of 26 July 2013. It is chaired by the Governor of the Banque de France, Christian Noyer, and has six members. The Resolution College is tasked with supervising the preparation and implementation of measures to prevent and resolve banking crises.

The Sanctions Committee: The Sanctions Committee is responsible for punishing violations of the laws and regulations applicable to reporting institutions.

The Audit Committee: The Audit Committee is tasked with ensuring that the ACPR's resources are used appropriately.

The consultative committees and the Scientific Consultative Committee: The ACPR's Supervisory College relies on several consultative committees to provide guidance on specific topics: The Consultative Committee on Prudential Affairs; The Consultative Committee on Anti-Money Laundering and Counter-Terrorist Financing; The Consultative Committee on Business Practices; The duties of the Scientific Consultative Committee are to promote synergies between financial research and prudential supervision and to keep abreast of developments liable to affect the banking an insurance sectors.

(ii) The French financial market authority (*Autorité des marché financiers, AMF*)

This authority regulates and controls all operations performed by firms listed on the stock market and all market activities performed by financial institutions. It also grants approvals to all portfolio management firms and is in charge of protecting customers and supervising financial markets as a whole.

(iii) The French Ministry of the Economy.

Aside of its legislative power, the Ministry of the Economy has a regulatory power which allows the introduction of new rules after consulting two main committees which are the Comité consultatif de la législation et de la réglementation financières (CCLRF) which is in charge of reviewing all the proposed changes in law and the Comité consultatif du secteur financier (CCSF) which is in charge of all matters related to bank/customer relationships.

Consolidation and the Changing Nature of Bank Activities

Mergers, Acquisitions and Internationalization

From 1990 to the mid-2000s, the consolidation process mostly occurred on a domestic basis and consisted of mergers and acquisitions within and between domestic banking groups. Within each of the four mutual/cooperative and saving national groups (Crédit Agricole, Caisse d'Epargne, Crédit Mutuel, Banque Populaire), mergers of regional entities occurred and led to a sharp reduction in the number of these local entities. Between 1984 and 2014, the number of cooperative and mutual banks has been reduced from 661 to 92, with the sharpest reduction occurring over the 1984–91 period (from 661 to 204).[2] Studies on the impact of these intra-group operations on the post-merger efficiency and economies of scale of the merged groups lead to mixed results. Dietsch and Oung (2001) find contrasting effects regarding post-merger cost and profit efficiency, which are found to be dependent on the efficiency of the bidder before the operation. While the most efficient banks benefit from a significant improvement in their cost efficiency, they fail to improve their profit efficiency following the acquisition. On the contrary, when the acquirers were among the less efficient banks, these operations do not lead to an increase in post-merger cost efficiency but to an improvement in their profit efficiency. However, on the whole, these intra-group operations lead to a reduction in post-merger overcapacity and allow the merged group to benefit from economies of scale. Mergers and acquisitions also occurred

[2] This sharp reduction is the consequence of the consolidation of the French saving group over this period.

Table 23.3 Main characteristics of the French banking system and comparison with Eurozone countries in 2013

	Total assets of domestic groups[a]	Total assets of foreign-controlled subsidiaries and branches[a]	Density[b]	Concentration[c]
France	91	9	1,736	46
Netherlands	92	8	7,760	84
Italy	88	12	1,992	40
Germany	89	11	2,271	31
Ireland	51	49	4,325	48
Spain	92	8	1,362	56
Euro area	–	–	2,039	47

Source: European Central Bank (2014b)
[a]In percentage of the total assets of the whole banking sector
[b]Population per local branch
[c]Share of total assets of the five largest institutions in percentage

between mutual and cooperative groups.[3] Moreover, the largest two private banking groups (Société Générale and Banque Nationale de Paris) have acquired small-locally owned banks and regional banking groups[4] in order to increase their presence in local markets. As in other developed countries, this consolidation process has led to a significant decline in the number of banks, mostly small locally-owned banks and to an increase in the concentration of the French banking industry both at the local and at the national level (Meslier et al. 2016). The density of the French banking system is among the highest in Europe (see Table 23.3). Dietsch (2003) finds that this consolidation process improved bank credit availability for French firms, especially for small and medium-size enterprises (SMEs). Bertrand et al. (2007) also highlight a significant improvement in allocative efficiency across non-financial firms after the deregulation process, with a sharp decrease in bank debt for the least performing firms and an increase in the interest rate spread between poorly and better performing firms.

The French banking system is dominated by six major French banking groups (BNPP,[5] Groupe BPCE, Groupe Crédit Agricole, Groupe Crédit Mutuel, La Banque Postale and Société Générale). Among them, the cooperative and mutual banking groups (Groupe BPCE, Groupe Crédit Agricole, Groupe Crédit Mutuel) account for a large share of banking operations.

[3] On 31 July 2009, two of these national groups (*Caisse d'Epargne* and *Banque Populaire*) merged their central institutions, giving birth to the second largest French banking group (*BPCE*).

[4] For example, acquisition of the group *Crédit du Nord* by *Société Générale* in October 2009.

[5] Creation of *BNP Paribas* (*BNPP*) through the acquisition of the *Banque Paribas* by *Banque Nationale de Paris in March 1997.*

According to the figures provided by the European Association of Cooperative Banks, the three cooperative and mutual banking groups represent in 2013 more than half of the French banking system in terms of total assets and they provide 60 % of the total amount of loans granted to the French economy. While the number of branches of foreign banks has increased during the 2000s, the presence of foreign banks in the French banking system remains relatively small.

Moreover, French banks were also involved in mergers and acquisition with insurance companies and wealth management companies. These operations led to the creation of large integrated groups which allow French banks to provide a large range of banking and non-banking activities. Among these new activities, selling of insurance products by banks have created a new business model, the *bancassurance*. While the French law has allowed banks to sell some insurance products since the 70s, the Banking Act of 1984 has accelerated this process. French banks have created subsidiaries dedicated to insurance activities (for example Pacifica for Credit Agricole) or have developed strategic partnerships with existing insurance companies (AGF for Société Générale or UAP for BNPP). The largest part of products consists of life insurance policies which generate substantial amount of fees for banks. The selling of life insurance products by banking groups represents in 2014 more than half of the total amount collected on the French market.

Like banks in other countries, French banks have also diversified their activities at the international level and they have been involved in cross-border mergers and acquisitions. While French banks had started to expand their international activities a long time ago, the internationalization of their activities remained relatively low until the beginning of the 2000s. The internationalization of French banks' activities, which started in the end of the 1990s, was boosted in the 2000s by the European integration process. The foreign claims of the main French groups[6] as a share of their total balance-sheet rose from 25 % in 2006 to 35 % in 2013.[7] A substantial part of French banks' foreign expansion was towards Eurozone countries (Belgium, Germany, Greece, Italy and Spain). During the last ten years, French banks have also expanded their activities in emerging markets, with a stronger presence in Russia, China and Turkey.

---

[6] The term "main French groups" refers to the five following banking groups: *BNP Paribas* (BNPP), *Groupe BPCE*, *Groupe Crédit Agricole*, *Groupe Crédit Mutuel* and *Société Générale*.

[7] All foreign exposure statistics provided in this section are from the Bank of International Settlement consolidated banking statistics.

The 2007–8 global financial crisis and the subsequent sovereign debt crisis have led to significant changes in the level and the distribution of foreign exposures. Since 2010, French banks have reduced their involvement in euro-zone countries and they have increased their expansion in other Organisation for Economic Co-operation and Development (OECD) countries (United States and Japan). After the collapse of Lehman brothers and the freeze in the interbank market in 2008, French banks have sharply reduced their international interbank exposures (from €633 billion in 2007 to €383 billion in 2013). Moreover, following the first Greek bailout and the subsequent spread to Ireland, Italy and Portugal, French banks significantly reduced their exposure to foreign public sector in these countries (from €80 billion in 2006 to €60 billion in 2013) but increased their exposure to public sector and central bank in the United States. In 2013, the largest two exposures of French banks to public sector debt were in the United States and in Italy.

Despite these recent evolutions, French banks are still strongly involved in Europe (52 %), mostly in Eurozone countries (Italy, Belgium and Germany). The second largest area of exposure consists of other OECD countries, such as the United States (10 %) and Japan (11 %). The breakdown by type of counterparty highlights a strong exposure to large companies (39.4 %), government and central banks (20.25 %) and to a lesser extent to retail consumers (15.5 %) and credit institutions (15 %). 80 % of the total exposure of French banks are denominated in euros (45.6 %) or in dollar (20.3 %). While the upward expansion of international activities has slowed down since the global financial crisis, the internationalization of French banks' activities remains relatively high. The foreign claims reported by French banks account for 10 % of the total amount of cross-border claims for all reporting banks. The international presence of French banks is the second largest in Europe after UK banks which hold 12 % of the total amount of cross-border claims.

Moreover, three of the major French banking groups (BNP Paribas, Société Générale and Crédit Agricole) are among the Top 20 European banks in terms of market capitalization (Table 23.4) and four of the six major French banking groups (BNPP, Groupe BPCE, Groupe Crédit Agricole and Société Générale) are on the list of the 30 Global Systematically Important Banks (G-SIBs) identified by the Financial Stability Board. The relatively large presence of G-SIBs in the French banking system raises the issue of the resilience or persistence of banks' solvency to macroeconomic or financial shocks. Results of the Asset Quality Review (AQR) and stress tests undertaken in 2014 by the European Central Bank (ECB) highlight

Table 23.4 Market capitalization of major international banks

Top 20 European banks by market capitalization

Ranking					Market cap as of 06/30/14	Change from (%)	
06/30/14	12/31/13	06/30/13	Company (trading symbol)	Country	(€M)	12/31/13	06/30/13
1	1	1	HSBC Holdings Plc (HSBA-LON)	United Kingdom	141,309	-5.72	-4.71
2	2	3	Banco Santander SA (SAN-MAD)	Spain	89,575	21.50	70.68
3	4	2	Lloyds Banking Group Plc (LLOY-LON)	United Kingdom	66,305	-2.10	25.93
4	3	4	BNP Paribas SA (BNP-PAR)	France	61,643	-12.41	18.30
5	8	10	Banco Bilbao Vizcaya Argentaria SA (BBVA-MAD)	Spain	54,730	5.86	54.37
6	7	5	UBS AG (UBSN-SWX)	Switzerland	50,290	-3.42	2.34
7	10	9	Royal Bank of Scotland Group Plc (RBS-LON)	United Kingdom	46,786	1.88	30.60
8	5	13	Allied Irish Banks Plc (AIB-DUB)	Ireland	46,586	-20.20	46.51
9	6	7	Barclays Plc (BARC-LON)	United Kingdom	43,652	-17.08	4.38
10	12	11	Nordea Bank AB (NDA-OME)	Sweden	41,463	5.67	20.73
11	9	6	OAO Sberbank of Russia (SBER-ME)	Russia	39,047	-18.64	-17.41
12	17	17	Intesa Sanpaolo SpA (ISP-MIL)	Italy	36,775	26.12	83.64
13	11	8	Standard Chartered Plc (STAN-LON)	United Kingdom	36,774	-7.08	-8.89
14	16	15	UniCredit SpA (UCG-MIL)	Italy	35,874	15.11	72.08
15	14	12	Deutsche Bank AG (DBK-ETR)	Germany	35,435	0.28	8.11
16	13	14	Credit Suisse Group AG (CSGN-SWX)	Switzerland	33,163	-6.50	5.00
17	15	16	Société Générale SA (GLE-PAR)	France	29,746	-9.23	46.81
18	18	21	Crédit Agricole SA (ACA-PAR)	France	26,473	14.00	60.97
19	23	28	CaixaBank SA (CABK-MAD)	Spain	25,206	32.41	126.85
20	19	18	Svenska Handelsbanken AB (SHB.A-OME)	Sweden	22,692	0.37	16.46

Rankings finalized July 21, 2014.
Market capitalization is inclusive of capital infusion by the government.
Source: SNL Financial

SNL

an estimated total capital shortfall of €24.6 billion, mainly concentrated on banks from Cyprus, Greece, Portugal and Italy (ECB 2014a). Regarding the outcomes of both AQR and adverse stress-tests, French banks display an aggregate Common Equity Tier1 ratio of 9 % as at the end of 2016, well above the 5.5 % threshold at which recapitalization plans are required. However, alternative assessments of capital shortfall developed by Acharya et al. (2014) lead to significant differences compared to this regulatory assessment. Building on the capital shortfall measure implemented by Acharya et al. (2012) and Brownlees and Engle (2016), the SRISK measure,[8] Acharya et al. (2014) obtain the largest expected shortfall in a systemic crisis for French banks (€189 billion). Moreover, according to the findings of Engle et al. (2015), systemic risk is at the highest in the French and UK banking systems. In their assessment BNP Paribas, Crédit Agricole and Société Générale turn out to be among the five riskiest institutions in Europe. Nevertheless, as argued by Colliard et al. (2016) the metrics used in such studies provide global measures of systemic risk based on market risk and are model-dependent. Further work is needed for an integrated approach to measure systemic risk.

[8] "This measure (SRISK) represents the expected amount of capital an institution would need to raise during an economic crisis to restore a target capital ratio. The crisis or stress scenario is defined by a 40% drop in the market equity index over six months." Acharya et al. (2014).

Business Mix and Main Drivers of French Banks' Profitability

After a decade of sharp reduction in their profitability between 1985 and 1994, French banks experienced a significant improvement in their profitability after 1995, even if they did not benefit from lower market interest rates (Goyeau et al. 1998, 2002). In a context of increased competition in both loan and savings markets, intermediation margins have indeed been cut and the relative share of non-traditional activities such as insurance, asset management or investment banking in their total income has sharply increased. Through the 2000s and until the beginning of the global financial crisis, these non-traditional banking activities have continued to boost their profitability. Indeed, while retail banking remained the main source of bank profitability, the contribution of this line of business to the growth of the net banking income was relatively low. Between 2000 and 2007, asset management as well as corporate and investment banking were the main drivers of the growth of banks' profitability.

This shift towards non-traditional activities has led to a structural change of the composition of banks' operating income. From 20 % of the net banking income in 1993, the share of fees and commissions accounted for 36 % in 2006. Moreover, net income from trading activities have also sharply increased and represented 36 % of the net banking income before the financial crisis. While this functional diversification process is not specific to the French banking system, French banks earn relatively less of their income from traditional intermediation activities than other European banks, and more from fees and commissions.

During the 2007–8 financial crisis, their universal model allowed French banks to maintain their net profit despite a sharp reduction in their return on assets (from 0.51 % in 2006 to 0.14 % in 2008). Losses in international corporate and investment banking activities were indeed mostly covered by strong margins from domestic retail banking and asset management activities. French banks have therefore rebalanced their activities following the crisis and increased their involvement in retail banking. From 58 % in 2006, the contribution of retail banking to net banking income rose to 69.4 % in 2014 (see Table 23.5). The contribution of corporate and investment banking sharply fell from 27 % before the crisis to 16.7 % in 2014. Globally, French banks appeared to be more resilient than other European banks. Laeven and Valencia (2010), using several criteria to identify countries that experienced a systemic banking

Table 23.5 Contribution of major business lines to net income before and after the financial crisis for the major French banking groups (in %)

	2006	2010	2011	2012	2013	2014
Retail banking	58	64.8	66.5	70.8	71.2	69.4
Corporate and investment banking	27	20.2	17.3	17.4	16.9	16.7
Asset management and insurance	15	12.2	12.6	14.1	14.2	14.9
Others	–	2.8	3.6	−2.3	−2.3	−1.0

Source: Financial disclosures of the top six major French banking groups and ACPR (French Prudential Supervision Authority)
"Others" refers to activities that have not been assigned to a specific business line

crisis in 2007–9, consider France as a borderline case while Germany and the United Kingdom meet their definition of a systemic banking crisis. They estimate direct fiscal costs associated with financial sector restructuring at around 1 % of gross domestic product (GDP) for France, against around 9 % and more than 12 % of GDP for the United Kingdom and the Netherlands, respectively. Coffinet and Lin (2013), who investigate the sensitivity of French banks' profitability to adverse economic shocks over the 1993–2009 by using the supervisory data (BAFi dataset), confirm that overall the French banking system was quite resilient to the set of tested scenarios. Chaffai and Dietsch (2015) further find that banks focused on retail banking businesses were less affected by the crisis than financial institutions running other business models.

Between 2009 and 2013, loans to large companies (€68 billion) and loans to the government, credit institutions and other financial corporations (€125 billion) substantially fell,[9] while retail loans (which include loans to households and to SMEs) increased (€153 billion). While new loans to households and to small companies slowed down in 2009 and in 2011, their growth remained higher than in Europe on average. Investigating the underlying factors of the evolution of loans to French SMEs, Kremp and Sevestre (2013) do not find evidence of credit rationing following the 2007–8 financial crisis. This result is in line with the survey undertaken by the ECB on firms' access to finance (ECB 2011). Moreover, estimations of structural breaks in the evolution of credit to French firms highlight significant differences across local markets. Higher market share and lower geographic diversification of local banks are associated with a weaker reduction of credit to firms during the 2007–8 financial crisis (Meslier et al. 2016).

[9] This reduction is partly explained by a shift from bank loans to market funding (commercial paper, bonds....).

Specific Nature of French Savings Products and Loans: Risk Implications

While the deregulation of the financial system has allowed French banks to enter in new markets, and to develop new activities during the last three decades, French banks still face some constraints which significantly impact their balance sheet structure. A first constraint is related to the structure of households' financial savings which mainly consist of life insurance products and regulated saving accounts. Whereas a significant part of households' financial savings is channelled by banks (in 2013, this share represented 63 % of the financial assets held by households), only part of these resources remain on the banks' balance sheet. Indeed, more than 50 % of life insurance funds are sold by French banks but are managed by separate entities (subsidiaries or insurance companies). While this activity accounts for an increased share of banks' net income (around 6 % in 2014), the collected funds are not fueling banks' balance sheets. Moreover, the funds of the regulated savings accounts collected by banks have to be transferred to the Caisse des Dépôts et Consignations. This public institution, created in 1896, is in charge of the management of these funds to finance social housing.[10] These two characteristics, which are specific to the French financial system organization, lead to a structural liquidity mismatch and to a strong reliance on wholesale funding. As a consequence, in comparison with their European counterparts, French banks faced a relatively high ratio of loans-to-deposits, with a downward trend since 2000 (Fig. 23.1). Since the global financial crisis, French banks have restructured their balance sheets. In order to reduce their reliance on wholesale funding, especially on short term and US dollar wholesale funding, they have strongly increased their retail deposits with a substantial rise in customer deposits. The loan-to-deposit ratio has therefore further fallen since 2009 but still remains relatively high in the upper range among European banks.

On the asset side, another characteristic of French banks' balance sheets is the predominance of fixed-rate loans in the total amount of mortgage loans granted to households (more than 80 %) in comparison to Spain or to the UK where more than 90 % and 70 % of mortgage loans are variable-rate loans, respectively. Given this preponderance, French banks are relatively more exposed to interest rate risk. However, their exposure to mortgage risk is likely to be lower than some of their European counterparts in UK or Spain.

[10] While, before 2009, only savings banks (*Caisse d'Epargne*), one cooperative bank (*Crédit Mutuel*) and one bank (*La Banque Postale*) were allowed to collect savings through these instruments, the reform of regulated savings in 2009 has allowed all French banks to do it.

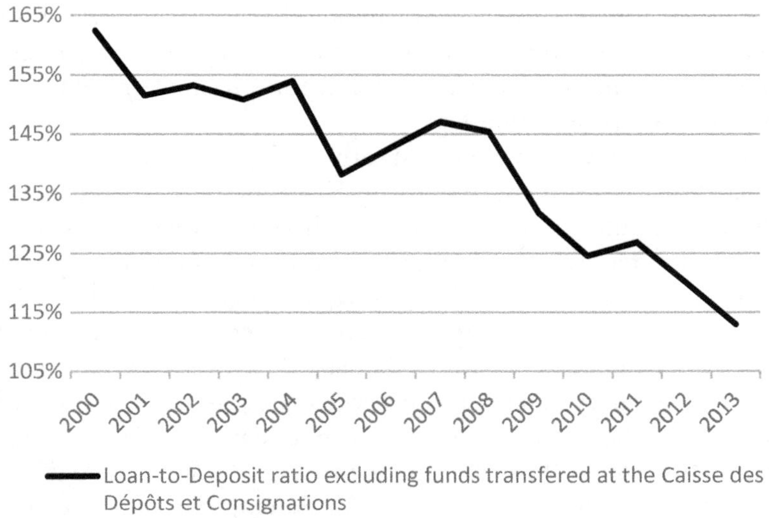

Fig. 23.1 Loan-to-deposit ratio, French banking system (2000–2013) (*Source*: ACPR (French Prudential Supervisory Authority))

Indeed, in order to prevent excessive risk-taking on mortgage loans, French banks use an implicit rule whereby debt repayments must not exceed a third of the borrower's disposable income.

Post-crisis Regulatory Pressure and Banks' Business Model Adjustments

French banks have begun to adapt their business models in response to the strengthening of legal and regulatory constraints since the global financial crisis of 2007–8.

Firstly, French banks have made significant balance sheet adjustments to improve their liquidity and solvency to comply with the Basel Committee on Banking Supervision recommendations, formally applied in Europe on 1 January 2014 by the Capital Requirements Regulation and Directive (Capital Requirements Regulation, CRR/Capital Requirements Directive, CRD IV). To reduce their reliance on wholesale funding, they pursued strategies aimed at raising retail deposits by, for instance, rechanneling funds that used to fuel the life insurance market and by lengthening funding maturities. They also, to some extent, deleveraged investment banking activities. French banks manage to have a reliance on wholesale funding close to those of their international peers in 2015, although they remain among the largest wholesale borrowers. They have also increased their solvency ratios, mainly through retained earnings and by limiting capital intensive and less profitable activities that are dependent on short-term funding.

Secondly, the TLAC (Total Loss Absorbing Capacity) rules designed by the Financial Stability Board and adopted in November 2015 by the G20 require globally systemically important banks (G-SIBs) to further increase their capital and leverage ratios to ensure that they will not require the support of the taxpayers in the future. Under the new requirements banks will need to hold loss absorbing liabilities and capital of 16 % in terms of risk-weighted assets (TLAC RWA Minimum) as from 1 January 2019. In addition, the amount of a bank's regulatory capital and unsecured long-term debt cannot be less than 6 % of the Basel III leverage ratio denominator (TLAC Leverage Ratio Exposure Minimum). This will increase to 18 % of RWAs and 6.75 % of the leverage ratio exposure by 1 January 2022. Among the four French G-SIBs, BNP Paribas and Société Générale have the biggest shortfall in TLAC-eligible debt, requiring an additional amount of €34 billion and €20 billion, respectively. The French government announced in December 2015 its plan to create a new class of senior bank debt (non-preferred senior debt) that will be subordinated to existing senior debt (preferred senior debt) and that can be used to absorb losses in the event of failure. If this proposition is confirmed by legislation in 2016, it will provide French banks the possibility to build multiple layers of loss absorption by protecting their most senior debt holders.

Thirdly, the French law n° 2013/672 on the Separation and Regulation of Banking Activities (Loi de Séparation et de Régulation des Activités Bancaires (SRAB)) was passed on 27 July 2013, in line with the Volcker rules (2013) and the recommendations of the Liikanen report (2012). The first part of the bill implements a structural reform to separate risky speculative activities from traditional bank operations while taking into account the assets of the universal banking model. Trading activities or unsecured financing to hedge funds have to be carried out within separate trading entities; these are not allowed to raise retail deposits and cannot engage in high frequency trading and speculative derivatives trading on agricultural commodities. The goals of this are: (i) limiting the risk taken by banks by banning given trading activities; (ii) to protect customer deposits from risks taken by banks on proprietary trading activities. French banks were required to identify prohibited activities to be transferred by 1 July 2014, and then to transfer these activities to a trading subsidiary by 1 July 2015. Ten banks were identified by the French supervisor (ACPR) as being prone to potentially set up a trading subsidiary; only two actually did so, i.e. BNP Paribas with Opera Trading Capital, and Société

Générale with Descartes Trading. These two trading subsidiaries represent only 1 % of the corporate and investment business of the parent companies; the eight other banks stopped engaging in prohibited activities.

The second part of the bill strengthens the powers of supervisory authorities and introduces a new recovery and resolution framework. SRAB was amended to reflect the Bank Recovery and Resolution Directive (BRRD) formally adopted by the European Commission on May 2014 and effective since 1 January 2015. The French supervisor has now the power to assess the suitability of board members, block the appointment of a board member, and restrict the remuneration of managers and traders such that the variable part of salary does not exceed the fixed component. The ACPR also requires banks to define a recovery plan (*plan préventif de rétablissement*) outlining preventive actions that will be triggered in case of significant deterioration of their financial situation. In addition, the ACPR has to adopt a resolution plan (*plan préventif de résolution*) that will organize and facilitate its intervention in case of crisis.

Finally, the new regime for the prudential regulation of European insurance companies, Solvency II, which came into force on 1 January 2016, will also have an impact on *bancassurance* activity. As we mentioned above, French banks distribute insurance products to their customers, especially life insurance products which generate high fees. Solvency II will significantly tighten requirements for how much capital will have to be held for life insurance products. This might encourage portfolio reallocation out of equities towards both government and corporate bonds or any inflows invested exclusively in bonds. The present low interest rate environment might, however, make it difficult to offer attractive life insurance products.

Future Prospects and Major Challenges

Like their European and international peers, French banks will face major challenges in the near future. They will need to adjust to more stringent capital requirements, higher loss absorbing capacities and they will also be affected by regulators' aim to implement clearer and more credible failure resolution processes. However, a notable difference with French banks is that they will also have to adjust their business model in a specific manner due to new Basel Committee guidelines on the management of interest rate risk and because of the impact of new innovation on the banking industry.

The Basel Committee on Banking Supervision has issued a consultative document entitled "The risk management, capital treatment and supervision of interest rate risk in the banking book", in June 2015, to ensure that banks have appropriate capital to cover potential losses from exposures to changes in interest rates. As mentioned above, given their strong reliance on short-term wholesale funding and the predominance of long-term fixed-rate or quasi-fixed rate mortgages, French banks are highly exposed to interest rate risk. The Basel Committee views such an exposure as too high, especially in the current environment with strong expectations of rising interest rates. One of the principles advocated by the Committee is to generalize variable-rate mortgages in order to transfer the interest risk exposure to households. The new guidelines have not yet been incorporated in the EU regulation, but they have been extensively discussed to evaluate how institutions should improve their current practices in order to comply with new regulations. If similar principles are adopted, the challenge for French banks will be to convince their clients to accept variable-rate mortgages as they are deeply attached to fixed-rate mortgages. Moreover, variable-rate mortgages might increase default rates in case of a substantial increase in interest rates, which is a common concern in other countries that rely more heavily on variable-rate mortgages.

The development of mobile banking is another challenge that will force French banks to change their traditional retail banking business model. According to the figures provided by the Fédération Bancaire Française (2014), around 78 % of bank customers in France used their mobile phones to consult their bank accounts in 2014 and 58 % to make a transfer. At the same time, bank customers have reduced their visits to their bank branches, with only 21 % going at least once a month to a branch, compared with 67 % in 2007. French banks have begun to reduce their number of branches in France from 44.5 branches per adult in 2008 to 38.7 in 2013 (The World Bank, Global Financial Development database). However this number is still relatively high compared with the other European countries where the downward trend is stronger. Moreover, retail banks have digitized only 20 to 40 % of their process and invest less than 0.5 % of their total spending on mobile banking; French banks are therefore just able to offer basic functions. But bank customers are now expecting more advanced services such as mobile check deposits, real-time updates on account activity, notifications about possible fraud or irregular activity on their account, low balance notifications and reminders about upcoming bill payments. The challenge for French banks is to make the necessary investment to innovate and become more responsive to their customers' needs before competitors do, particularly as they are behind their international peers in this process.

Moreover, French banks face the competition of financial technology companies (FinTech), which are contributing to change the way financial services are accessed and delivered, by offering innovative solutions using the Internet, mobile, social technologies and cloud computing. They operate in a diverse set of domains and offer many financial services, including: (i) money transfer services, especially foreign exchange services (e.g. TransferWise); (ii) peer to peer lending and crowdfunding (e.g. Prêt d'Union, Unilend, Credit.fr, Lendix and Finsquare in France); (iii) payments and transactions such as mobile payments, opening of a banking account in convenience stores (Financière des Paiements Electroniques (FPE) through Compte-Nickel in France); (iv) mobile trading on commodities exchanges and digital wallets (e.g. AAPL by Apple and GOOG by Google), and (v) financial advisory services and robo-advisor sites (e.g. LearnVest and Betterment). FinTech companies build and implement technologies to make systems more efficient and hence to offer either lower fees or lower loan interest rates than traditional banks. Many FinTech companies are bypassing banks to directly offer their solutions/products to customers over the Internet, reducing the banking sector's profitability.

Technology, social and business digital innovations are therefore taking customers and potential customers out of banks' networks. They are also changing customers' expectations about personalization and convenience. While it appears that many French banks have not yet made the necessary investments, they need to fast track their development to compete with fast-growing FinTech companies. One way to do this might be to use predictive data analytics to analyse large sets of internal and external data on customers. Relationship managers in charge of either households, firms or corporate clients are likely to be better suited than FinTech companies leverage big data and better skilled to anticipate customers' particular requirements.

References

Acharya, V., Engle, R., & Richardson, M. (2012). Capital shortfall: A new approach to ranking and regulating systemic risks. *American Economic Review, Papers & Proceedings, 102*(3), 59–64.

Acharya, V., Engle, R., & Perret, D. (2014). *Testing macroprudential stress tests: The risk of regulatory risk weights.* Journal of Monetary Economics, 65, 36–53.

Bertrand, M., Thesmar, D., & Schoar, A. (2007). Banking deregulation and industry structure: Evidence from the French banking reforms of 1985. *The Journal of Finance, 53*(2), 597–628.

Brownlees, C. T., & Engle, R. F. (2016). SRISK: A Conditional Capital Shortfall Measure of Systemic Risk. *The Review of Financial Studies,* forthcoming.

Chaffai, M., & Dietsch, M. (2015). Modelling and measuring business risk and the resiliency of retail banks. *Journal of Financial Stability, 16*, 173–182.

Coffinet, J., & Lin, S. (2013). Stress-testing banks' profitability: The case of French banks. *Journal of Financial Perspectives, 1*(2), 67–80.

Colliard, J. E., Benoit, S., Hurlin, C., & Pérignon, C. (2016). Where the risks lie: A survey on systemic risk. *Review of Finance*, forthcoming.

Dietsch, M. (2003). Financing small business in France. *European Investment Bank paper, 8*(2), 92–119.

Dietsch, M., & Oung, V. (2001). L'efficacité économique des restructurations bancaires en France au cours des années 1990. *Bulletin de la Commission bancaire*, n° 24, avril.

Engle, R., Jondeau, E., & Rockinger, M. (2015). Systemic risk in Europe. *Review of Finance, 19*(1), 145–190.

European Central Bank. (2011). *Survey on the access to finance of small and medium-sized enterprises in the Euro-Area.*

European Central Bank. (2014a, October). *Aggregate report on the comprehensive assessment.*

European Central Bank. (2014b, October). *Banking structures report.*

Fédération Bancaire Française. (2014). *Chiffres clés.*

Goyeau, D., Sauviat, A., & Tarazi, A. (1998). Sensibilité des résultats bancaires au taux d'intérêt. *Revue Française d'Économie, 13*(2), 169–200.

Goyeau, D., Sauviat, A., & Tarazi, A. (2002). Rentabilité bancaire et taux d'intérêt de marché. Une application aux principaux systèmes bancaires européens sur la période 1988–1995. *Revue d'économie politique, 112*(2), 275–291.

Kremp, E., & Sevestre, P. (2013). Did the crisis reduce credit rationing for French SMEs? *Journal of Banking and Finance, 37*, 3757–3772.

Laeven, L., & Valencia, F. (2010). *Resolution of banking crises: The good, the bad, and the ugly* (IMF working paper WP/10/146). Washington, DC: International Monetary Fund.

Meslier, C., Rous, P., Torre, P., & Sauvait, A. (2016). Structure bancaire locale et évolution du crédit à l'échelle des départements français : l'expérience de la crise financière de 2007–2008. *Revue Economique, 67*(2), 279–314.

24

Credit Institutions, Ownership and Bank Lending in Transition Economies

Rainer Haselmann, Paul Wachtel, and Jonas Sobott

Introduction

The transition of banking sectors in Central and Eastern Europe in the first 15 years of transition was nothing short of remarkable. When the communist regimes fell, none of the transition countries had a functioning financial system that could provide intermediary services. Most observers at the time assumed that the development of market-based banking systems would take many years. However, by the early years of the twenty-first century, the transition of banking sectors in Central and Eastern Europe (though not in many countries of the former Soviet Union) was largely complete. For the most part, the countries in the region have market-oriented banks that utilize modern banking technologies and are largely independent of direct government influence.

R. Haselmann (✉)
Faculty of Finance, Goethe University Frankfurt, Frankfurt, Germany
e-mail: haselmann@safe.uni-frankfurt.de

P. Wachtel
Stern School of Business, New York University, NewYork, NY, USA
e-mail: pwachtel@stern.nyu.edu

J. Sobott
Bonn Graduate School of Economics, University of Bonn, Bonn, Germany
e-mail: sobott@uni-bonn.de

T. Beck, B. Casu (eds.), *The Palgrave Handbook of European Banking*,
DOI 10.1057/978-1-137-52144-6_24

Why and how did this remarkable success story take place? Early in the transition period, observers attributed the improvements to banking reforms—recapitalizations and privatization—and, importantly, the early entry of foreign banking (Bonin et. al. 1998 and 2005; Bonin and Wachtel 1999). Foreign bank entry, though resisted at first, began in the mid-1990s and was a catalyst for change. In this view, the rapid transition of the banking sector can be attributed to foreign owners who brought modern technology, market-oriented decision-making, independence from vested interests and competition.

By 2000, foreign banks owned a majority of bank assets in virtually every transition country and almost all assets in several countries. Credit expanded very rapidly in the region in the years prior to the global financial crisis. There are many reasons for this but, importantly, the foreign ownership of banks facilitated and spurred these credit booms. If the domestic deposit base was small or growing slowly, foreign owned banks were able to fund their expansion with cross-border flows (see De Haas and van Horen 2016). Foreign banks could shift liabilities to their foreign subsidiaries with loans or deposits, make equity investments and facilitate flows from other home country entities. Moreover, the expansion of credit in the transition countries had one particular characteristic, lending to households expanded much more rapidly than lending to any other sector.

The global financial crisis challenged the idea that foreign banks were in every respect a positive influence. All of a sudden, the parent banks from large countries were under intense pressure to deleverage and increase liquidity. They could reduce or even pull back financing to their transition country subsidiaries. In this view foreign bank ownership could magnify the impact of the global real sector shock on the transition countries. Foreign ownership, which had been a catalyst for financial sector development for a decade, was now, perhaps, the source of fragility. Financial systems in transition countries were particularly vulnerable to the crisis shock. Surprisingly, there were only two transition countries with systemic bank crises in 2009—Latvia and the Ukraine—and two more with near systemic problems—Hungary and Russia.

The experience since 2000—a credit boom that created financial fragilities which amplified the crisis shock—indicates that foreign bank ownership might be a mixed blessing. The question is essentially an empirical one and we will see below that the evidence in the literature, though mixed, tends to absolve the foreign banks. Foreign banks may have amplified the transmission of the crisis shock to transition countries but in most instances they retained their commitment to these secondary home markets and foreign subsidiaries. More importantly, we argue that the banking sectors in transition economies withstood the crisis shock because they had developed their own solid institutions—an effective supervisory structure and legal framework.

There is more to the story behind the success of banking in transition countries than foreign ownership. The quality of institutions in the financial sector plays a major role in fostering the development of the banking sector. The significance of legal institutions, regulatory structures and the institutional infrastructure for financial relationships was overlooked in the early transition years. This is not surprising because until the late 1990s economists did not pay much attention to the role of institutions in economic growth. For example, La Porta et al. (1997) argued that better creditor rights are associated with better developed credit markets in a large cross-section of countries. This law and finance literature developed quickly to show how improved legal structures are associated with better financial development (Djankov et al. (2007)), fewer loan covenants (Qian and Strahan (2007)) and better corporate investment decisions (Giannetti (2003)).

The story of banking in transition countries is as much the story of institution building as it is a story of foreign ownership. Our view of transition banking is that institutions are key. Modern market oriented banking systems emerged when institutional structures were in place. This included a reliable legal framework for the conduct of banking business, a framework for regulation and the conduct of monetary policy and the end of direct or implicit government influence on banking activity. Foreign banks were interested in entering the markets when these conditions were in place.

To summarize, most transition countries experienced credit booms which were followed by the shock of the global financial crisis. The presence of foreign banks, which was pervasive by this time, might have exacerbated credit booms and the impact of the crisis. Nevertheless, the banking sectors in transition countries were very resilient. Our hypothesis is that the degree of resilience to the boom and crisis shocks related primarily to the quality of domestic institutions and policy decisions.

The transition in Central and European from a command to a market economy has been an important laboratory for the so-called law and finance literature which was emerging towards the end of the 1990s. Literature on the region examined specific legal arrangements relevant to financial development. For example, Dahan (2000), Pistor (2004) and Pistor et al. (2000) described how creditor rights have been introduced in these countries. Haselmann et al. (2010) documented the changes in creditor rights that occurred in the transition countries as the World Bank and the European Bank for Reconstruction and Development (EBRD) advised countries to adopt legislation. They construct indicators of the strength of collateral law and bankruptcy law and relate them to the growth of lending. Their results indicate that better creditor rights are associated with more lending and the existence of good collateral law has a stronger impact on lending than the strength of bankruptcy protections, probably because collateral law is a prerequisite for introducing protections to creditors in bankruptcy proceedings. In related work, Haselmann and Wachtel (2010) showed that legal differences are associated with differences in loan composition. Good collateral law results in more private credit formation and more lending to small and medium-size enterprises (SMEs) as opposed to large firms. Finally, good creditor rights seem to be especially important for foreign banks and therefore more of them will enter if creditor rights are good.

In addition to the legal framework for lending, banks rely on credit information in order to make credit judgements. Credit information effects lending for several reasons (see Japelli and Pagano 1993). First, if banks have more information on borrowers, they are better able to assess their credit worthiness and price loans accordingly. Second, information-sharing reduces the market power of banks over borrowers as information is "stored" outside the bank. Information sharing might have a more pronounced effect in countries with weak creditor protection since enforcement of the contract is costly.

The empirical literature lends support to the hypothesis that information-sharing increases lending, and decreases credit spreads and default rates. Jappelli and Pagano (2002) and Djankov et al. (2007) find a positive correlation between information-sharing and lending to the private sector and a negative correlation with default rates. Brown et al. (2009) confirm this finding with firm-level data for Eastern Europe: firms in countries with more information-sharing have easier access to credit and pay lower interest rates. The effect is larger for countries with weak creditor protection suggesting that credit registers can serve as a substitute for underdeveloped legal systems.

In this chapter we begin with a brief survey of banking in the transition economics. The discussion takes us through the first decade—the 1990s—when commercial banks emerged, and the 2000s, the era of foreign bank ownership. Our emphasis in on the structure of banking—the emergence of foreign banking—and the role of institutions.

It is difficult to distinguish the influence of good institutions from the influence of foreign bank ownership because they emerged at the same time and clearly influenced each other. However, the crisis provides a quasi-experimental context for evaluating the role of ownership and institutions. We present some suggestive econometric results that test whether foreign ownership and good institutions enable banking systems to withstand the crisis shock. Specifically, we will show that well-functioning credit information systems can help dampen the impact of financial crisis on the financial sector.

The crisis originated in the American mortgage markets so it can be viewed as an external or exogenous shock for the transition countries. The shock resulted in an increase in uncertainty about the future of the real economy and a general increase in credit risks. If credit information systems help overcome such uncertainties by providing idiosyncratic information on individual borrowers we would expect that markets that have a better creditor information system would be more resilient to the shock.[1]

Our empirical investigation examines the volume of lending and its composition among the major sectors: households, non-financial corporations and government. The extent of information asymmetry and uncertainty around the crisis event varies for different types of borrowers. It should be larger for SME borrowers as compared with large borrowers and for corporate borrowers compared to the government. We use data on credit institutions from the World Bank and find that the quality of institutions, especially the coverage of credit information systems affects post-crisis loan volume.

Transition Banking: The First Decade

In the early years of transition, banking sectors consisted of state-owned banks that were competing with newly privatized banks and new entrants in a system largely devoid of effective regulation. The state-owned banks, at the behest of the government, continued to lend to loss-making state-owned enterprises (SOEs) and even privatized banks continued lending to their old customers, which led to the rapid growth of bad loan portfolios. New entrants, so-called Greenfield banks, took advantage of loose oversight to take on risky and too often shady deals. The collapse of trading relationships with the Soviet Union and the absence of any other markets led to large transition recessions while at the same time the liberalization of prices and large government deficits resulted in episodes of hyperinflation.

The first transition development was the creation of banking institutions where none had existed before (see Bonin et al. 2015). Some centrally planned economies had advanced industrial enterprises which were in some instances internationally competitive but none had banks that resembled those in developed countries. The planning framework had no place for banks or financial intermediaries. Capital was allocated by plan and the role of the banks, usually a national mono-bank, was just to provide a payments system and accounting mechanism for transactions among enterprises. Thus, a first

[1] As already noted, many transition countries were experiencing a credit boom prior to the crisis so the crisis might to have some extent been endogenous to the region. We would still expect countries with better credit institutions to bounce back from the shock more rapidly.

step in transition was to create banks by separating the mono-bank into a central bank and one or more state-owned commercial banking entities.[2]

Commercial banks were created before functioning regulatory structures were in place and before the relationship between SOEs and banks were restructured. As a result, every one of the transition countries experienced at least one banking crisis in the early 1990s that required the re-nationalization of banks that had been privatized, widespread losses to depositors and the recapitalization of state-owned banks by the government. These experiences point to the importance of institution building, in this case both the structure of banks and the regulatory framework.

At the start of transition, governments were reluctant to allow foreign ownership of banks as a matter of national pride. The banking system—the overseer of the nation's money—was an important symbol of sovereignty; the monetary system was viewed as a national treasure that should not be subject to foreign control. By the mid-1990s attitudes began to change with the realization that foreign strategic investors in banks were, like any other foreign direct investment (FDI), a fixed investment (in this instance bank capital) and a source of technology transfers (see Claessens et al. (2001)). The first such deal was the sale of Budapest Bank, a state-owned bank with a serious bad loan problem, to GE Capital in 1995. That opened the floodgates and by 2000, a majority of bank assets were in foreign owned institutions in Czech Republic, Hungary, Poland, Bulgaria, Croatia, and the three Baltic countries. The only exceptions in central and Eastern Europe were Slovakia, Romania, Serbia and Slovenia; by 2005, Slovenia was the lone exception where government policy limited foreign participation in banking.[3] Small countries such as Estonia, Lithuania, Slovakia and Croatia seem to maintain their sovereignty even as over 90 % of bank assets are in entities controlled by foreigners.

Foreign banks brought modern banking technology and products and introduced arm's length relationships between banks and their loan customers.[4] Further, improved banking practices spilled over from the foreign owned institutions to the domestic banks including state-owned institutions. However, the emphasis on the catalytic effect of foreign bank ownership overlooks the role of institutions. Foreign entry would not have occurred with-

[2] This simplification abstracts from the differences among transition countries. Yugoslavia, for example, established somewhat independent commercial banks in the 1950s; Hungary always had a foreign trade bank and savings bank. Similarly, there were differences in the way commercial banks were created. Bulgaria granted every office of the central bank a universal banking license in 1990 while neighbouring Romania created one state-owned commercial bank.

[3] Slovenia suffered a serious banking crisis in 2013 and then began to relax ownership restrictions.

[4] For example, the banking systems skipped the use of paper checks and were early adopters of electronic payments systems. On the asset side, banks imported credit scoring models from their parents.

out improvements in the institutional structure. The introduction of banking laws and regulatory structures were often due to foreign influences starting in the 1990s. USAID, the World Bank, EBRD, EU Phare all provided support and expertise for writing legislation (see Pistor et al. 2000). Foreign influence increased when six transition countries began accession talks with the European Union (EU) in 1998.

Basic institutions such as a banking law, accounting standards and regulatory authorities were introduced in the 1990s. However, it often took some time before an arm's length relationship developed between regulators and the banks. Further, it took additional time for the legal structures used in banking to emerge, including reliably functioning court systems for commercial disputes, credit information systems and laws regarding the use and taking of collateral.

In Hungary, the first country to welcome foreign bank ownership, legislation in 1992 introduced modern banking law, international accounting standards and a new bankruptcy law.[5] The sale of Budapest Bank took place in late 1995, after the legal reforms.[6] In the Czech Republic, an ambitious programme of voucher privatisation of enterprises started in 1991, before corporate governance reforms and capital market regulations were in place. The program was soon enveloped in scandals involving bank sponsored privatization funds and lending to bank controlled enterprises. By 1998 bad loans were about one-quarter the size of Czech gross domestic product (GDP). Enterprise and legal reforms started around 1999 as the Czech Republic entered serious negotiations with the EU on accession. Bank restructuring and reprivatisation began soon thereafter. In 1999 foreign banks owned about one-quarter of Czech bank assets and two-thirds in Hungary. By 2005, foreign ownership was about 90 % in both countries. Foreign ownership in both instances followed institutional reforms.

Transition Banking After 2000

In the decade prior to the financial crisis, GDP growth in the transition economies was faster than growth in developing Asia (with the exception of India and China) and credit markets deepened substantially. The credit expansion was largely driven by capital inflows, particularly bank flows from Western Europe and external debts (borrowing by banks and by sovereigns). There

[5] Foreign entry developed much more slowly in the former Soviet Union (other than the Baltics) where legal and regulatory institutional developments lagged those in Central and Eastern Europe.

[6] The sale was controversial because the government agreed to take back bad loans that might be uncovered after the sale.

were a number of reasons why the flows were large including the global savings glut, confidence in the transition economies generate by EU accession and the expectation that euro adoption would follow, as well as demand generated by structural reforms.

The credit boom and the shift in the composition of lending from non-financial business to households in the 12 transition countries in our sample are shown in Figure 24.1.[7] In all the countries shown the share of lending going to households has increased over the last decade and in many instances the share is as large at the share going to non-financial businesses. The foreign banks brought credit scoring models which were easily applied to household lending but not readily adopted for lending to enterprises. Further the banks had only recently cleaned up loan losses and reduced lending to large unprofitable SOEs. Lending to enterprises, particularly newer or smaller enterprises, is often relationship based. Household lending took off before bank–enterprise–client relationships had time to develop. Commenting on developments in Polish banking, Wiesiolek and Tymoczko (2015, p. 315) conclude that:

> The model of banking which involved promoting loans for households (mostly housing loans) on a large scale was imported from headquarters before a culture of cooperation with enterprises had sufficient time to emerge. As a consequence, households rather than enterprises have become the most important clients of banks (…)

Another feature of lending was that by 2008 lending denominated in foreign currencies exceeded 50 % of all loans in some countries (e.g. Hungary, Bulgaria, Croatia, Romania; see Bonin (2010).

By the time of the crisis, foreign banks were a pervasive presence in all the countries in our sample except Slovenia and the Ukraine.[8] The differential impact of the crisis does not seem to be related to the foreign bank share of assets or loans, which are in most instances little changed after the crisis. There are small declines which might reflect tighter lending standards in the post-crisis period by foreign banks.

GDP dropped sharply in almost every country when the crisis started and in most instances it rebounded after a year. Movements in private credit after the crisis differed from place to place. For example, in Poland, there was a short sharp decline in credit that was quickly reversed and credit was back on trend by 2010. In Slovakia the impact of the crisis on GDP was small and

---

[7] The 12 transition countries in our sample are Bulgaria, Croatia, Czech Republic, Estonia, Hungary, Latvia, Lithuania, Poland, Romania, Slovakia, Slovenia and the Ukraine.

[8] The foreign share of bank assets in each country in 2008 is shown in Table 24.1.

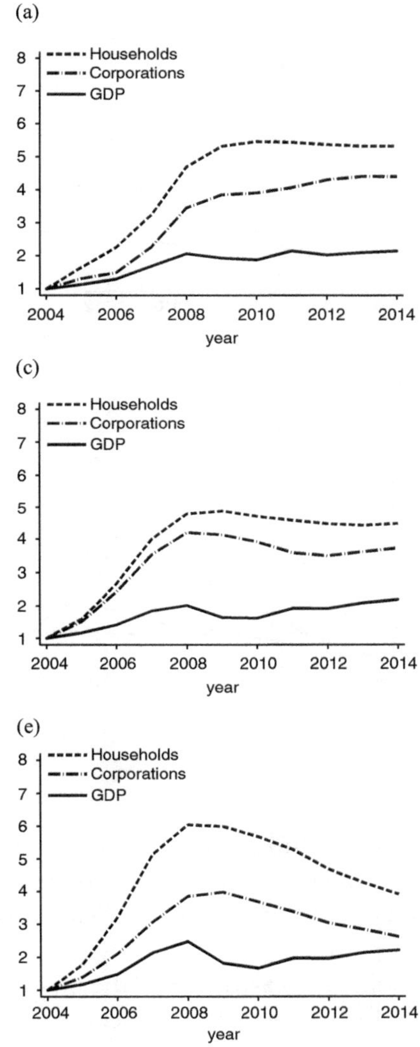

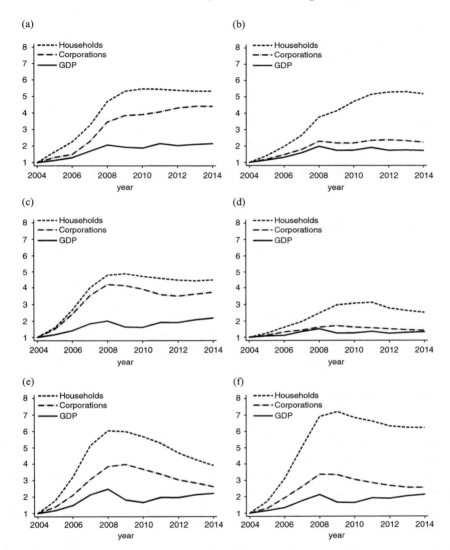

Fig. 24.1 Household and business lending and GDP, 2004–2014 **(a)** Bulgaria **(b)** Czech Republic **(c)** Estonia **(d)** Hungary **(e)** Latvia **(f)** Lithuania **(g)** Poland **(h)** Romania **(i)** Slovenia **(j)** Ukraine (*Note*: The figure depicts the development of loans to households, non-financial corporations and nominal GDP normalized to 1 in 2004. The data are from the European Central Bank (ECB) and, if not available from the ECB, from the national central banks. For non-euro currencies, the loan volume is converted into EUR using the average exchange rate in that month. The development for Slovakia and Croatia are not shown due to limited data availability in 2004.)

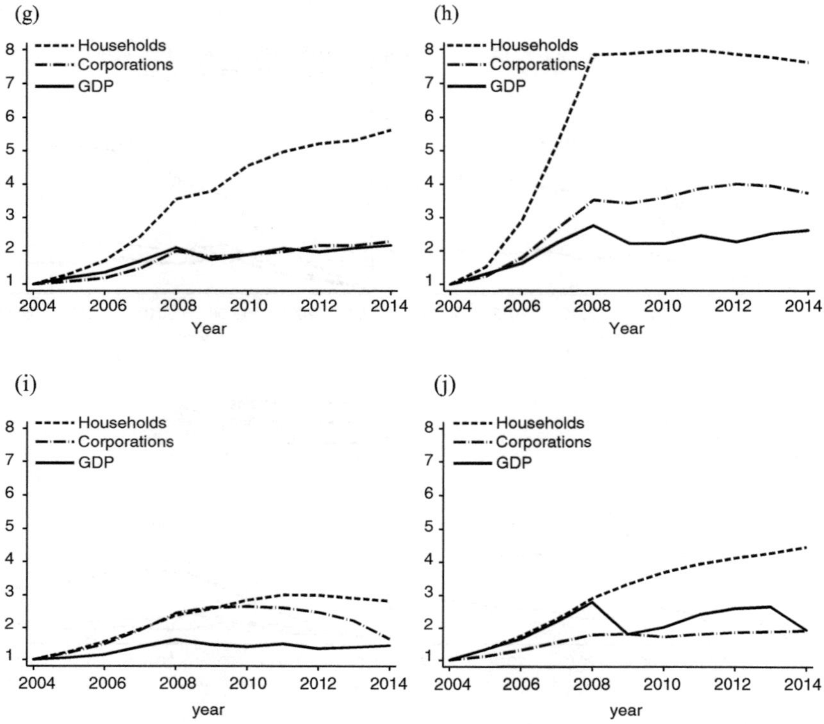

Fig. 24.1 (continued)

credit continued to grow. However, in Romania and Hungary the credit slowdown was long lasting and five years after the crisis, credit had not reached it prior peak. In Hungary, Slovenia, the Ukraine and the Baltic States credit growth in the post-crisis years has been negative.

The share of lending going to households increased before the crisis and then tended to level off at about 40 % of all lending in most countries. In most countries, the share of lending going to government and to financial corporations together was below 20 % so any increase in the household share was at the expense of lending to non-financial business. Lending to households was concentrated in mortgage lending in Poland and Hungary in particular. In Hungary, the largest type of lending was mortgages dominated in foreign currency which led to both maturity and currency mismatch on bank balance sheets and a banking system that was particularly vulnerable during the crisis. The only counties where the share of lending to the non-financial business sector has increased since the crisis are Romania, Slovakia and Hungary all of which experienced declines in total lending.

The impact of the financial crisis on the transition countries was severe as demand for their exports dropped quickly after the crisis shock. Further, there was immediate concern that financial crises would ensue as capital inflows halted suddenly. From the very start of the crisis there was concern that banking customers in the transition economies where most financial services were provided by foreign banks would suffer. Popov and Udell (2012) use survey data on small and medium-sized enterprises (SMEs) in the region to investigate the transmission of the crisis shock through credit supply to SMEs. They find that SMEs report larger credit constraints in areas where the local banks' parents were more severely affected by the crisis. According to De Haas et al. (2015), the contraction in credit by foreign bank subsidiaries in transition countries occurred earlier and was deeper than that of domestic banks during the crisis years of 2008 and 2009. These studies indicate that the developed country financial crisis was quickly transmitted to the transition countries through a foreign bank ownership channel.

The fear of transmission of the financial crisis to the transition economies led immediately to a broad international policy response known as the Vienna Initiative. The Vienna Initiative was an unusual private-public, multilateral response to the crisis. As the global crisis was deepening in January 2009, the international financial institutions (including the EBRD, the International Monetary Fund [IMF] and the European Investment Bank [EIB]) and the private foreign parent banks in the region reached an agreement to cushion the effects of the shock. The banks agreed to maintain their exposures to the transition countries and recapitalize banks as necessary while the IFIs offered support of 33 billion euros to maintain bank stability. Among the larger transition countries, Hungary, the Ukraine, Poland and Romania all opened lending arrangement with the IMF. These efforts contributed to the post-crisis recovery of banking and credit creation in the region.

The discussions that led to the Vienna Initiative began in November 2008.[9] There was good reason for concern that the global crisis would be transmitted to and magnified in the region because of the extensive foreign ownership. Thinking about foreign bank ownership which had been widely supportive since the late 1990s was quickly reversed. In the IMF's retrospective view:

> Many western banks in emerging Europe operate their subsidiaries as if they are branches, with risk management centralized at the group level and local supervisors relying on parent banks' home supervisors to monitor the changes in the

[9] The large foreign banks originated the idea of a coordinated approach, which resulted in the Vienna Initiative, in a letter expressing concern for the financial stability of the region sent to the European Commission in November 2008.

> risk profile of their foreign affiliates. Foreign-owned banks can often evade regulatory measures, including by switching from domestic to cross-border lending or by switching lending from banks to non-banks, such as leasing institutions (owned by foreign-owned banks). Foreign-owned banks are also less likely to be influenced by domestic monetary policy measures, such as the raising of domestic interest rates. Often, these banks are systemically important in the host country although only a small part of the overall bank group. (Bakker and Klingen 2012, pp. 21–22).

The evidence is that the Vienna Initiative was successful; De Haas et al. (2015) found that banks that participated in the Vienna Initiative were less likely to contract credit in the region than banks that did not participate. This is particularly important because De Haas and Van Lelyveld (2014) found that around the world multinational bank subsidiaries curtailed credit growth during the crisis much more than domestic banks.

Nonetheless, Epstein (2014) argues that it was the business models of the banks themselves rather than the Vienna Initiative intervention that mitigated the effects of the crisis. The foreign parent banks in the regions were committed to their longer-term objectives of maintaining market share and reputation in their "second-home" markets. Further, Bonin and Louie (2015) show that the six large multinational banking groups with transition subsidiaries maintained their commitment to the region during both the global financial crisis and the Eurozone crisis.

For more than a decade, differences in banking performance among transition countries was often attributed to the beneficial presence of foreign banks. The crisis experience dispelled that notion; there was evidence that foreign ownership transmitted or magnified the crisis shock. Nevertheless, most countries in the region demonstrated a great deal of resilience in face of the crisis shock albeit with the help of the Vienna Initiative. Bonin (2010) notes that countries with and without extensive foreign ownership were affected by the crisis and argues that other factors were at work. For example, Slovenia, with little foreign ownership but serious macro-economic imbalances, suffered a banking crisis. Hungary on the other hand, with extensive foreign ownership, was severely affected by the crisis. In order to stem capital outflow and maintain financial sector stability, the Hungarian central bank had to raise its base lending rate by 300 basis points at the end of 2008. However, the problem in Hungary was the extent of lending in foreign currency and bank portfolios with both maturity and currency mismatch. Bank regulators probably and mistakenly assumed that foreign bank parents would absorb all risks. There was both a failure of domestic bank supervision and poor risk management by banks. In the post-crisis period, Hungarian authorities have tried to develop macro-prudential policy tools to prevent a recurrence. A few South Eastern European countries, particularly Croatia, used macro-prudential tools prior to the crisis to rein in a credit boom with some limited success.[10] Poland performed well during the crisis despite extensive foreign ownership. Poland's banking system was less concentrated than elsewhere and more competitive with diverse foreign ownership and little foreign currency lending. Lending in the Ukraine declined and more recently some Russian banks have replaced risk-adverse owners from the West. Banking experience after the crisis was diverse and seems to have more to do with domestic policy and the quality of regulation than the extent of foreign ownership.

In the next section we discuss how institutional characteristics effect the banking system's ability to withstand a crisis shock. Our hypothesis is that the crisis shock increased uncertainty about lending; it should have a lesser effect when good institutional structures provide a shock absorber.

Credit Information Systems in Transition Countries

The literature on law and finance cited earlier emphasizes the importance of legal institutions. Clearly defined property rights, contract law, a commercial code and a court system that can adjudicate disputes fairly, quickly and without corruption are essential for a modern business economy. There are many nations around the world where many of these things are missing but they are in place in most of the transition countries, partly as a result of reforms that were required to secure EU membership. The World Bank's Doing Business surveys introduced in 2003 have become a standard source for measures of the general context for business activity (see Besley (2015)). Generally, the transition countries score well on the Doing Business indicators. The average overall doing business distance to the frontier (a value of 100 representing best practices) for the 12 countries in our empirical analysis was 74.5 in 2014, only a few points below the average for Organisation for Economic Co-operation and Development (OECD) countries.

The two principal roles of banks are the provision of deposits used as the transactions medium and financial intermediation by providing credit to deficit units. The ability to provide credit efficiently relies on the existence of

[10] A variety of interventions were used to curb types of lending or reduce capital inflows. See Dimova et al. (2016).

Table 24.1 Institutional and bank data in 2008

	Bulgaria	Croatia	Czech Republic	Estonia	Hungary	Latvia	Lithuania	Poland	Romania	Slovakia	Slovenia	Ukraine
Credit information												
Depth of credit information index	6	3	5	5	5	0	6	5	4	4	0	0
Credit bureaus	5 %	72 %	65 %	21 %	10 %	0 %	7 %	50 %	25 %	40 %	0 %	3 %
Credit registers	31 %	0 %	5 %	0 %	0 %	4 %	9 %	0 %	5 %	1 %	3 %	0 %
Strength of legal rights index	9	7	6	6	7	10	5	8	9	8	4	9
Bankruptcy & insolvency law												
Enforcement length (days)	564	561	653	425	335	279	210	830	537	565	–	387
Enforcement costs (% of Claim)	24 %	14 %	33 %	17 %	15 %	16 %	24 %	19 %	20 %	26 %	19 %	44 %
Recovery rate	32 %	30 %	21 %	39 %	38 %	35 %	49 %	34 %	29 %	45 %	47 %	9 %
Insolvency costs (% of estate)	9 %	15 %	15 %	9 %	15 %	13 %	7 %	15 %	9 %	18 %	8 %	42 %
Foreign banks												
Share of foreign banks	84 %	91 %	85 %	98 %	84 %	66 %	92 %	76 %	88 %	99 %	31 %	51 %
Share Vienna	41 %	54 %	45 %	89 %	40 %	48 %	64 %	15 %	56 %	20 %	43 %	6%

The 2008 value is displayed. *Depth of Credit information*, *Coverage private bureau*, *Coverage public register*, and *Strength of Legal Rights Index* are taken from the annual Worldbank "Doing-Business" Survey. *Depth of Credit Information* is an index ranging from 0 to 8. Likewise, the *Strength of Legal Rights Index* from 0 to 12. Larger index values indicate more and deeper information on borrower in the credit register or better protection of lenders and borrowers. *Enforcement Length (Days)* is the time to resolve a dispute, counted from the moment the plaintiff files the lawsuit in court until payment. This includes both the days when actions take place and the waiting periods between. *Enforcement Costs (% of Claim)* are the cost in court fees and attorney fees, where the use of attorneys is mandatory or common, expressed as a percentage of the debt value. *Recovery Rate* calculates how many cents on the dollar secured creditors recover from an insolvent firm at the end of insolvency proceedings. *Insolvency Costs (% of Estate)* are the average cost of insolvency proceedings. *Share of Foreign Banks* is the asset-weighted market share of foreign banks. *Share Vienna* is the fraction of banks whose parents participated in the Vienna Initiative. Description of the credit information, and bankruptcy and insolvency law partly taken from the Worldbank "Doing Business" report

institutions that support lending operations. For our empirical investigation, we are particularly interested in the data on credit institutions from the Doing Business Surveys.[11] There are data on the existence and functioning of both public credit registries and private credit bureaus that maintain data bases on payment history and credit outstanding for both enterprises and individuals. All of the 12 transition countries in our empirical analysis have one or the other and five have both. The existence of credit information is just the first step; it has also to be available and usable to lenders.

The World Bank Doing Business reports also provide an summary index, the "Depth of Credit Information", which is based on responses to questions regarding the availability of credit information and another summary index, the "Strength of Legal Rights" which measures legal rights of lenders in regard to collateral and bankruptcy.[12] Table 24.1 shows the 2008, pre-crisis, value of the indicators and also the asset-weighted market share of foreign banks for the 12 countries in our empirical analysis below.

The quality of credit information systems differs among countries. Some countries, such as Lithuania and Bulgaria, scored well on the "Depth of Credit Information" index while Latvia, Slovenia and the Ukraine have scores of zero indicating the absence of any formal credit information systems. Cross-country variation in the "Strength of Legal Rights" index, though substantial, is less pronounced. In 2008, index values range from 4 out of 10 in Slovakia to 10 out of 10 in Latvia and an overall average of approximately 7. Interestingly, the indicators are uncorrelated. The correlation between the 2008 values of two indices is 0.15. Most notably, Latvia has a weak credit registry with very little coverage and a maximal score on the "Strength of Legal Rights" index. In addition, both indices have only a weak correlation with the foreign bank share.[13] The correlation of the foreign bank asset share in 2008 with the depth of credit index is 0.21 and with the strength of legal rights index it is 0.01.

Coverage by registers and bureaus varies among those countries which have such an institution in place. Coverage is measured as the number of entities in the database plus the number of credit inquiries for which there was no entry, all as a ratio to the adult population. For private credit bureaus in 2008, the

[11] For a description of the World Bank's methodology regarding data on getting credit see: http://www.doingbusiness.org/methodology/getting-credit

[12] The questions in each index are found under the aforementioned link.

[13] The foreign bank lending shares were calculated by combining the "Bank Ownership Database" (see Claessens and Van Horen (2015) with Bankscope data. The highest consolidation level in Bankscope and the ownership data base were merged by index number or by name. Unmatched banks were dropped if their loans was below 1 % in every year. Ownership of the others was determined from annual reports, press articles and self-descriptions on the homepages.

coverage ranges from 3 % in the Ukraine to 72 % in Croatia with an overall mean of 28 %. Coverage by public registers ranges 1 % in Slovakia to 31 % in Bulgaria with an overall mean of 4 %.[14]

The credit information systems are not the only potentially relevant institutional structures in which the countries differ. We also find variation regarding the enforcement of contracts (measured by length in days required and the costs of enforcement as a percentage of the claim) and the insolvency system (measured by the recovery rate and the costs of the procedure as a percentage of the estate).

We turn next to an empirical examination of the influence of these indicators on bank lending and the resilience of lending to the crisis shock.

Empirical Analysis

We use a panel data for our 12 transition countries for the period 2004–14 to examine the effects of institutional quality and the extent of foreign ownership on the volume of bank lending. The global financial crisis presents an opportunity to examine how good institutions cushion the effects of the shock. We treat the global financial crisis as an exogenous shock and examine how lending is affected during the crisis.[15] Specifically, we relate the pre-crisis characteristics of the financial sector to the strength of lending after the crisis shock. The regression framework for the analysis is shown by:

$$\log(\mathit{Loan\ Volume})_{i,t} = \alpha_i + \alpha_t + \delta\ \mathit{Institution}_{i,2008}{}^{*}\mathit{Crisis}_t + \theta\ \mathit{Controls}_{i,t} + \varepsilon_{i,t} \quad (24.1)$$

The dependent variable is the log of the volume of loans to a particular sector in current euros in country i in year t. The coefficient of particular interest is δ, the coefficient on the interaction of the crisis indicator, Crisis_t which has a value of onepost-2008, and a measure of institutional quality, $\mathit{Institution}_{i,2008}$, in the pre-crisis year (2008). A positive δ indicates that institutional quality cushioned the effect of the financial crisis on loan volume.

Other variables on the right-hand side are fixed effects for both countries and years and macro and banking sector controls. To control for economic development, we include real GDP growth and inflation from the IMF *World Economic Outlook*. We control for possible effects the Vienna Initiative with a variable that reflects the influence of the policy initiative in each country. We identify the banks in each country that participated in the Vienna Initiative or are owned by

[14] Some of the large differences can be attributed to the scope of the register or bureau. In some countries with low values coverage is restricted to firms.

[15] The crisis originated in the USA and was quickly transmitted around the world. See also Behn et al. (2016).

Table 24.2 The effect of credit information and foreign bank ownership on lending

	Total	Households	Loans to Business	Government
	Panel A: Bureau coverage			
	(1)	(2)	(3)	(4)
Crisis Bureau*	0.002	0.007***	0.002	0.000
	(0.003)	(0.002)	(0.002)	(0.011)
Observations	121	121	121	121
R-squared	0.81	0.94	0.86	0.31
	Panel B: Register coverage			
	Total	Households	Loans to Business	Government
	(1′)	(2′)	(3′)	(4′)
Crisis Register*	0.012***	0.001	0.013***	0.044***
	(0.003)	(0.003)	(0.002)	(0.008)
Observations	121	121	121	121
R-squared	0.83	0.92	0.88	0.42
	Panel C: Foreign banks			
	Total	Households	Loans to Business	Government
	(1″)	(2″)	(3″)	(4″)
Crisis Foreign*	−0.003***	−0.003***	−0.007**	−0.007**
	(0.001)	(0.001)	(0.003)	(0.003)
Observations	121	121	121	121
R-squared	0.81	0.92	0.87	0.33

The table reports δ of equation 24.1: $\log(\textit{Loan Volume})_{i,t} = \alpha_i + \alpha_t + \delta\ \textit{Institution}_{i,2008} * \textit{Crisis}_t + \theta\ \textit{Controls}_{i,t} + \varepsilon_{i,t}$. Each specification includes country and year fixed effects and macro control variables (as described in the text). Loans to Businesses exclude loans to financial corporations. *Bureau* is the number of individuals and firms listed in the largest credit bureau as percentage of adult population. *Register* is the number of individuals and firms listed in the credit register as percentage of adult population. *Foreign* is the asset-weighted market share of foreign banks. *Crisis* is a post-crisis dummy which is equal to one post 2008. Standard errors are adjusted for clustering at the country level and reported in parenthesis

Note: *indicates statistical significance at the 10 % level, **at the 5 % level and ***at the 1 % level.

a bank that participated in the Vienna Initiative. The control variable is the asset-weighted share of these "Vienna-Parent"-banks in each country.[16]

Estimates of equation 24.1 are in Table 24.2. Since the existence of asymmetric information might vary considerably between different sectors, institutions may play a very different role for different borrowers. In order to learn about this, we present separate regressions for lending to households, non-financial businesses and the government sector, as well as total lending. We present results for the coverage of credit institutions and for the foreign bank

[16] The bank asset data are from Bankscope.

share. Other measures of institutional quality did not have any significant impact. Estimates use ordinary least squares (OLS) and the standard errors are clustered by country.

To identify the effect of the institutional variables on lending, we use the crisis shock as a quasi-experiment. That is, we examine whether there is a differential reaction in lending in response to the shock depending on the quality of institutions, e.g. the extent of coverage of the credit register. As noted earlier, the failure of Lehman brothers in September 2008 and the subsequent strain on the global financial system did not originate in Eastern Europe and can therefore be considered exogenous. The coefficient δ in equation 24.1 describes how much of the shock was absorbed bythe institutional variable. Intuitively, δ describes how lending in countries with good pre-crisis institutions fared compared to countries with poor institutions.

In order to measure the effectiveness of credit institutions we apply the coverage of private credit bureaus as explanatory variable in panel A and the coverage of public credit registers in panel B. With regards to aggregate lending, we find that well-functioning credit information institutions measured by public registers are able to cushion the effects of the crisis. More specifically, once the crisis shock hit the Eastern European economies, aggregate lending decreased by 12 % less as a response to the shock in a country where the coverage of the public credit register is by 10 percentage points higher relative to another country. When we measure the quality of credit institutions by the coverage of private credit bureaus we do not find a significant impact on aggregate lending.

Looking at the different sectors reveals a more distinct pattern. High bureau coverage increases lending to households post crisis whereas high register coverage increases lending to non-financial corporations. Reason for this asymmetric effect is possibly the different scope of bureaus and registers: bureaus tend to focus on individuals whereas registers primarily collect information on firms. We conclude that the availability of creditor information mitigated the effects of the financial crisis.

In Panel C, we look at the effect of foreign banks on the post crisis reaction. We find that the presence of foreign banks did not shield countries from the effect of the crisis. On the contrary, the negative interaction coefficients suggest that countries with a high presence of foreign banks recovered more slowly after the crisis shock.

We also test a series of other institutional measures—for example the duration of the insolvency procedure or the costs of contract enforcement—but none of these variables has a systematic influence on the post-crisis reaction of lending.

Conclusion

Early studies of transition banking starting in the late 1990s tended to emphasize the importance of foreign bank entry. The literature on the law and finance nexus was just emerging at that time and the importance of institutional development in transition banking was not at first appreciated. In addition, measurement of institutional quality is difficult and the World Bank data on specific institutional characteristics was not collected until after 2003. Economics tends to emphasize things that can be measured. Changes in ownership provided concrete data while institutional change is harder to measure. With the limited data available, our regression framework gives some broad indication of the role of institutions on lending in transition countries and shows that institutions—particularly credit institutions—can mitigate the effects of the crisis. During the global financial crisis, foreign ownership was a burden mitigated by Vienna Initiative, while good credit institutions were a cushion.

Acknowledgments Research assistance from Nate Katz, Isabel Schaad and Daniel Seeto is appreciated.

Bibliography

Bakker, B., & Klingen, C. (2012). *How emerging Europe came through the 2008/09 crisis: An account by the staff of the IMF's European Department*. Washington, DC: International Monetary Fund.

Behn, M., Haselmann, R., & Wachtel, P. (2016). Pro-cyclical capital regulation and lending. *Journal of Finance, 71*(2), 919–955.

Besley, T. (2015). Law, regulation, and the business climate: The nature and influence of the world bank doing business project. *Journal of Economic Perspectives, 29*(3), 99–120.

Bonin, J. (2010). From reputation amidst uncertainty to commitment under stress: More than a decade of foreign-owned banking in transition economies. *Comparative Economic Studies, 52*(4), 465–494.

Bonin, J., Hasan, I., & Wachtel, P. (2015). Banking in transition economies. In A. Berger, P. Molyneux, & J. Wilson (Eds.), *The Oxford handbook of banking* (Chapter 39, 2nd ed., pp. 746–768). Oxford: Oxford University Press.

Bonin, J., & Louie, D. (2015). *Did foreign banks cut and run or stay committed to emerging Europe during the crises?* (BOFIT discussion papers, (31/2015)). Helsinki: Bank of Finland.

Bonin, J., Mizsei, K., Szekley, I., & Wachtel, P. (1998). *Banking in transition economies: Developing market oriented banking sectors in Eastern Europe*. Cheltenham/Northampton: Edward Elgar Publishers.

Bonin, J., & Wachtel, P. (1999). Toward market-oriented banking in the economies in transition. In M. Blejer & M. Skreb (Eds.), *Financial sector transformation: Lessons for the economies in transition*. Cambridge/New York: Cambridge University Press.

Bonin, J. P., Hasan, I., & Wachtel, P. (2005). Privatization matters: Bank efficiency in transition countries. *Journal of Banking and Finance, 29*(8–9), 2155–2178.

Brown, M., Jappelli, T., & Pagano, M. (2009). Information sharing and credit: Firm-level evidence from transition countries. *Journal of Financial Intermediation, 18*(2), 151–172.

Claessens, S., Demirguc-Kunt, A., & Huizinga, H. (2001). How does foreign entry affect domestic banking markets? *Journal of Banking and Finance, 25*(5), 891–911.

Claessens, S., & van Horen, N. (2015). The impact of the global financial crisis on banking globalization. *IMF Economic Review, 63*(4), 830–867.

Dahan, F. (2000). Law reform in Central and Eastern Europe: The transplantation of secured transaction laws. *European Law Journal, 2*(3), 69–84.

De Haas, R., Korniyenko, Y., Pivovarsky, A., & Tsankova, T. (2015). Taming the herd? Foreign banks, the Vienna initiative and crisis transmission. *Journal of Financial Intermediation, 24*(3), 325–355.

De Haas, R. & van Horen, N. (2016). Chapter 16, Recent trends in cross-border banking in Europe. In *The handbook of European banking*. Palgrave Macmillan.

De Haas, R., & Van Lelyveld, I. (2014). Multinational banks and the global financial crisis: Weathering the perfect storm? *Journal of Money, Credit and Banking, 46*(1), 333–364.

Dimova, D., Kongsamut, P., and Vandenbussche, J. (2016). *Macroprudential policies in Southeastern Europe* (IMF Working Paper 16/29). Washington, DC: International Monetary Fund.

Djankov, S., McLiesh, C., & Shleifer, A. (2007). Private credit in 129 countries. *Journal of Financial Economics, 12*(2), 77–99.

Epstein, R. A. (2014). When do foreign banks cut and run? Evidence from West European bailouts and east European markets. *Review of International Political Economy, 21*(4), 847–877.

Giannetti, M. (2003). Do better institutions mitigate agency problems? Evidence from corporate finance choices. *Journal of Financial and Quantitative Analysis, 38*(1), 185–212.

Haselmann, R., Pistor, K., & Vig, V. (2010). How law affects lending. *Review of Financial Studies, 23*(2), 549–580.

Haselmann, R., & Wachtel, P. (2010). Institutions and bank behavior: Legal environment, legal perception, and the composition of bank lending. *Journal of Money, Credit and Banking, 42*(5), 965–984.

Japelli, T., & Pagano, M. (1993). Information sharing in credit markets. *Journal of Finance, 48*(5), 1693–1718.

Japelli, T., & Pagano, M. (2002). Information sharing, lending and defaults: Cross-country evidence. *Journal of Banking and Finance, 26*(10), 2017–2045.

La Porta, R., Lopez-de Silanes, F., Shleifer, A., & Vishny, R. (1997). Legal determinants of external finance. *The Journal of Finance, 52*(3), 1131–1150.
Pistor, K. (2004). Patterns of legal change: shareholder and creditor rights in transition economies. *European Business Organization Law Review, 1*(1), 59–110.
Pistor, K., Raiser, M., & Gelfer, S. (2000). Law and finance in transition economies. *The Economics of Transition, 8*(2), 325–368.
Popov, A., & Udell, G. (2012). Cross-border banking, credit access, and the financial crisis. *Journal of International Economics, 87*(1), 141–161.
Qian, J., & Strahan, P. (2007). How laws and institutions shape financial contracts: The case of bank loans. *The Journal of Finance, 62*(6), 2803–2834.
Wiesiolek, P., & Tymoczko, D. (2015). The evolution of banking sectors in Central and Eastern Europe the case of Poland. In *What do new forms of finance mean for EM central banks?* (Number 83 in BIS papers, pp. 313–323). Basel: Bank for International Settlement.

Index

Note: Page numbers followed by 'n' refer to foot notes.

T. Beck, B. Casu (eds.), *The Palgrave Handbook of European Banking*,
DOI 10.1057/978-1-137-52144-6

C

D

E

O

Q

R

CPI Antony Rowe
Chippenham, UK
2018-06-28 09:41